pauline frommer's

SPAIN

spend less see more

1st

GW00686174

by Patricia Harris, David Lyon & Peter Stone

Series Editor: Pauline Frommer

WILEY
Wiley Publishing, Inc.

Published by:

Wiley Publishing, Inc.

111 River St.
Hoboken, NJ 07030-5774

ISBN 978-0-470-28774-3

Editor: Ian Skinnari
Production Editor: M. Faunette Johnston
Cartographer: Andrew Dolan
Photo Editor: Richard Fox
Interior Design: Lissa Auciello-Brogan
Production by Wiley Indianapolis Composition Services
Front and back cover photo ©Grant Faint/Getty Images
Cover photo of Pauline Frommer by Janette Beckmann

For information on our other products and services or to obtain technical support,
please contact our Customer Care Department within the U.S. at 800/762-2974,
outside the U.S. at 317/572-3993 or fax 317/572-4002.

Wiley also publishes its books in a variety of electronic formats. Some content that
appears in print may not be available in electronic formats.

Manufactured in the United States of America

5   4   3   2   1

Contents

1 The Best of Spain..........................2
Best of the Best...............................3
Best Churches.................................4
Best Non-Ecclesiastical Sights................5
Best Museums 6
Best Travel Experiences 6
Best of the "Other" Spain 7

2 Madrid..................................9
Don't Leave Madrid Without 9
A Brief History of Madrid 10
Lay of the Land 12
Getting to & Around Madrid 12
Accommodations, Both Standard & Not 16
Dining for All Tastes 29
Why You're Here: The Top Sights & Attractions.........45
The Other Madrid.............................64
Attention, Shoppers! 68
Nightlife in Madrid 72
Get Out of Town 76

3 Central Spain..........................79
Don't Leave Central Spain Without 79
A Brief History of Central Spain.............80
Lay of the Land 81
Toledo.......................................83
Cuenca 98

Segovia 104

Avila 113

Salamanca 117

4 Andalusia 127

Don't Leave Andalusia Without 127

A Brief History of Andalusia 128

Lay of the Land. 129

Seville (Sevilla). 131

Córdoba 145

Granada 154

Málaga. 167

Costa del Sol. 177

Ronda 185

Jerez de la Frontera 191

Cádiz. 201

5 València, City & Region 210

València (the City). 211

Alicante. 229

6 Barcelona 242

Don't Leave Barcelona Without 243

A Brief History of Barcelona 243

Lay of the Land. 245

Getting to & Around Barcelona 246

Accommodations, Both Standard & Not. 250

Dining for All Tastes 262

Why You're Here: The Top Sights & Attractions. 271

The Other Barcelona. 296

Active Barcelona 298

Attention, Shoppers! 299

Nightlife in Barcelona 303

Get Out of Town 305

7 Catalonia...311

Don't Leave Catalonia Without 311

Tarragona 311

Girona 320

The Costa Brava 328

Lleida 334

8 The Basque Country.....................342

Don't Leave the Basque Country Without 343

Lay of the Land. 343

A Brief History of the Basque Country 343

Bilbao (Bilbo). 344

San Sebastián (Donostia) 357

Vitoria-Gasteiz 366

Navarre (Navarra) 373

9 Galicia, Asturias & Cantabria 383

Don't Leave Galicia, Asturias & Cantabria Without 383

Galicia. 384

Asturias 398

Cantabria 413

10 Majorca, Minorca & Ibiza 425

Don't Leave the Balearic Islands Without 425

Majorca (Mallorca). 426

Minorca (Menorca). 450

Ibiza (Eivissa). 464

11 The Essentials of Planning. 474

When to Visit 474

Entry Requirements 479

Getting to Spain 480

Getting Around Spain. 485

Saving on Accommodations. 487

Money Matters 489
Health & Safety. 491
What to Pack 493
Specialized Travel Resources 494
Staying Wired While You're Away 496
Recommended Books & Films 496

12 The Art & Culture of Spain 501
Cuisine & Dining in Spain. 501
A Primer of Spanish Arts & Culture. 504

13 Useful Terms & Phrases 509

Index 516
Accommodations 529

List of Maps

Madrid Metro 14

Madrid Accommodations. 18

Madrid Dining. 30

Madrid Attractions. 46

Madrid Environs 77

Central Spain 82

Toledo. 84

Cuenca 99

Segovia 105

Avila 115

Salamanca 119

Andalusia (Andalucía) 130

Seville (Sevilla). 133

Córdoba. 147

Granada & the Alhambra. 155

Granada. 157

Málaga 169

Costa del Sol 179

Ronda 187

Jerez de la Frontera. 193

Cádiz. 203

València. 213

Alicante. 231

Costa Blanca. 239

Barcelona Accommodations &
 Dining 252

Barcelona Attractions. 272

Barri Gòtic 275

Catalonia 313

Tarragona. 314

Girona 321

Costa Brava 329

The Basque Country. 345

Bilbao 347

San Sebastian. 359

Vitoria. 367

Pamplona. 375

Galicia. 385

Santiago de Compostela 393

Asturias & Cantabria 399

Oviedo. 401

Santander 415

The Balearic Islands. 427

Majorca (Mallorca). 429

Palma de Majorca 431

Minorca (Menorca). 451

Mahòn (Maò) 453

Ciutadella (Ciudadela) 455

Ibiza (Eivissa) 465

Ciudad de Ibiza. 467

An Invitation to the Reader

In researching this book, we discovered many wonderful places—hotels, restaurants, shops, and more. We're sure you'll find others. Please tell us about them, so we can share the information with your fellow travelers in upcoming editions. If you were disappointed with a recommendation, we'd love to know that, too. Please write to:

Pauline Frommer's Spain, 1st Edition

Wiley Publishing, Inc. • 111 River St. • Hoboken, NJ 07030-5774

An Additional Note

Please be advised that travel information is subject to change at any time—and this is especially true of prices. We therefore suggest that you write or call ahead for confirmation when making your travel plans. The authors, editors, and publisher cannot be held responsible for the experiences of readers while traveling. Your safety is important to us, however, so we encourage you to stay alert and be aware of your surroundings. Keep a close eye on cameras, purses, and wallets, all favorite targets of thieves and pickpockets.

About the Authors

Patricia Harris and **David Lyon** have journeyed the world for American, British, Swiss, and Asian publishers to write about food, culture, art, and design. They have covered subjects as diverse as elk migrations in western Canada, the street markets of Shanghai, winter hiking on the Jungfrau, and the origins of Mesoamerican civilization in the Mexican tropics. In the name of research they have eaten hot-pepper-toasted grasshoppers, English beef, and roasted armadillo in banana sauce. When good wine or craft beer is unavailable, they drink Diet Coke. Wherever they go, they are continually drawn back to Spain for the flamenco nightlife, the Moorish architecture of Andalucía, the world-weary and lust-ridden saints of Zurbarán and the phantasmagoric visions of El Greco—and the sheer joy of conversing with the regulars in a thousand little bars while drinking the house wine and eating tapas of Manchego and chorizo.

Peter Stone was born in London England and started his working life in the Foriegn Office in Downing Street before moving on to journalism and translating. He's lived nearly three decades in different parts of Spain including Málaga, Barcelona, Alicante, Palma de Mallorca, and Las Palmas de Gran Canaria and also resided in Greece and Tunisia. A lifelong lover of Spanish culture, history, and language, he made his home in Madrid in 1998, and his publications on the Spanish capital include *Madrid Escapes* and *Frommer's Madrid*. He has contributed to wide variety of international magazines and guidebooks including *Time Out, Insight*, and *Spain Gourmetours,* and is also author of *Frommer's Barcelona.*

Acknowledgments

Pat and David want to thank Pilar Vico and Estefanía Gómez for their unflagging help and advice. Pat also wishes to thank Señor Sibursky, her Polish-Argentine-American teacher who opened the Spanish-speaking world to a headstrong teenager who didn't want to study French like everyone else.

Star Ratings, Icons & Abbreviations

Every restaurant, hotel, and attraction is rated with stars ✦, indicating our opinion of that facility's desirability; this relates not to price, but to the value you receive for the price you pay. The stars mean:

No stars: Good
✦ Very good
✦✦ Great
✦✦✦ Outstanding! A must!

Accommodations within each neighborhood are listed in ascending order of cost, starting with the cheapest and increasing to the occasional "splurge." Each hotel review is preceded by one, two, three, or four dollar signs, indicating the price range per double room. Restaurants work on a similar system, with dollar signs indicating the price range per three-course meal.

Accommodations
€ 60€ or less per night
€€ 61€–100€
€€€ 101€–130€
€€€€ 131€ and up

Dining
€ Meals for 7€ or less
€€ 8€–12€
€€€ 13€–20€
€€€€ 21€ and up

In addition, we've included a kids icon 🧒 to denote attractions, restaurants, and lodgings that are particularly child friendly.

Frommers.com

Now that you have this guidebook to help you plan a great trip, visit our website at **www.frommers.com** for additional travel information on more than 4,000 destinations. We update features regularly to give you instant access to the most current trip-planning information available. At Frommers.com, you'll find scoops on the best airfares, lodging rates, and car rental bargains. You can even book your travel online through our reliable travel booking partners. Other popular features include:

- ◆ Online updates of our most popular guidebooks
- ◆ Vacation sweepstakes and contest giveaways
- ◆ Newsletters highlighting the hottest travel trends
- ◆ Podcasts, interactive maps, and up-to-the-minute events listings
- ◆ Opinionated blog entries by Arthur Frommer himself
- ◆ Online travel message boards with featured travel discussions

I started traveling with my guidebook-writing parents, Arthur Frommer and Hope Arthur, when I was just 4 months old. To avoid lugging around a crib, they would simply swaddle me and stick me in an open drawer for the night. For half of my childhood, my home was a succession of hotels and B&Bs throughout Europe, as we dashed around every year to update *Europe on $5 a Day* (and then $10 a day, and then $20 . . .).

We always traveled on a budget, staying at the mom-and-pop joints Dad featured in the guide, getting around by public transportation, eating where the locals ate. And that's still the way I travel today, because I learned—from the master—that these types of vacations not only save money but offer a richer, deeper experience of the culture. You spend time in local neighborhoods, meeting and talking with the people who live there. For me, making friends and having meaningful exchanges is always the highlight of my journeys— and the main reason I decided to become a travel writer and editor as well.

I've conceived these books as budget guides for a new generation. They have all the outspoken commentary and detailed pricing information of the Frommer's guides, but they take bargain hunting into the 21st century, with more information on using the Internet and air/hotel packages to save money. Most important, we stress "alternative accommodations"—apartment rentals, private B&Bs, religious retreat houses, and more—not simply to save you money, but to give you a more authentic experience in the places you visit.

A highlight of each guide is the chapter that deals with the "other" side of the destinations, the one visitors rarely see. These sections will actively immerse you in the life that residents enjoy. The result, I hope, is a valuable new addition to the world of guidebooks. Please let us know how we've done! E-mail me at editor@frommers.com.

Happy traveling!

Pauline Frommer

Pauline Frommer

1 The Best of Spain

by Peter Stone

AS YOU FLY INTO SPAIN, YOU CAN SEE, WAY BELOW YOU, A PARCHED, RUGGED, ochre-mauve landscape that matches to perfection the "rumpled lion's skin" described long ago by the classical historian Strabo. There's a timeless grandeur about it. You could almost imagine that nothing has changed in the 2,000 or so years since the Greek sage penned those words.

Yet, over the course of that time, a hell of a lot of water has flowed under the many bridges that dot that landscape, and changes aplenty have surely taken place. The Moors, with their 800-year rule, were the first to bequeath a genuine, lasting legacy, constructing ornate mansions, forts, and mosques, and embellishing their exotic southern cities of Córdoba and Granada with those magical, flower-lined patios and cool, twinkling fountains so beloved by today's visitors. The Catholic monarchs who ousted them went one better, presiding over the almost superhuman construction of some of the finest religious monuments the world had ever seen—highlighted by giant cathedrals such as those in Seville and Toledo, which took centuries to finish and leave you speechless with wonder as you enter their portals. The Bourbon kings were next to try their hand, creating elegant, wide, tree-lined boulevards and sumptuous neoclassical palaces in an attempt to "Europeanize" major cities like the capital city, Madrid, while later avant-garde innovators, like Antoni Gaudí in Barcelona, turned the whole concept of architecture upside down with controversial moderniste creations like the Sagrada Familia—a must for fans of the surreal. Today, amid all that multifaceted grandeur, we also have a brave new world of 50-story concrete and glass tower blocks; futuristic, cutting-edge cultural centers such as Bilbao's Guggenheim Museum and Valencia's City of Science; and 300kmph (186-mph) trains that can glide across that "rumpled lion's skin" in a twinkling of an eye—a heady mixture of centuries straddling sights, almost daunting in the richness of their scope.

But some of the most memorable images—those that linger on long after you've returned home—are the smaller, more personal ones. The white villages that cling impossibly to steep Andalusian hillsides; the squat windmills on the flat central plains of La Mancha, which Cervantes's scholar knight vainly attacked thinking they were giants; the tiny Romanesque chapels nestling peacefully amid Pyrenean woodlands—attractions large and small in a country (perhaps mini-continent is a more accurate term) that would take a small eternity to really know. The problem is where to start, which is why we've picked out the very best places for you to see during your stay, to save you the hassle and make your visit a bit easier.

BEST OF THE BEST

THE PRADO   You gotta hand it to the Spanish royalty: They knew what they were doing when it came to art. The royal collection forms the basis for the Prado Museum (p. 48), an institution that is on a par with the Hermitage, the Louvre, the British Museum, and the Metropolitan Museum of Art in New York thanks to the remarkable breadth and richness of its collection. At any one time, some 1,300 pieces will be on view, though the strengths of the museum are, not surprisingly, its Spanish Masters (particularly Velázquez). Beyond that are works of unparalleled genius from Hieronymus Bosch, Fra Angelico, and other world-renowned artists. Though there are many reasons to come to Madrid, if you leave without touring the Prado, you haven't done the city (or country) justice.

THE ALHAMBRA   This fairy-tale pleasure dome, with its serene courtyards, intricate filigree decor, archways, and scented gardens overlooked by the snow-capped Sierra Nevada, was the apogee of Moorish luxury and beauty. At its center is the small dreamlike Patio de los Leones, whose slender columns surround a central fountain with 12 small lions at its base, while, high above it, the orange tree–scented Generalife Gardens are a real fantasy Arabian Nights setting come true—especially when floodlit after dark.

SEGOVIA'S ALCAZAR   Majestically perched on a high bluff above Segovia's twin rivers Eresma and Clamores, this is the most picturesque and most photographed castle in all Spain. Its turrets and spires are said to have inspired Walt. It's in this formidable fortress that Isabella of Castilla (of Ferdinand and Isabella fame) took refuge when her brother died and, with the support of the army, marched from the fortress to the Plaza Mayor to be proclaimed queen.

SEVILLE'S CATHEDRAL   When its planners ambitiously proclaimed "Let us built a church so big they will think us mad," they weren't kidding! Seville's Gothic masterpiece is the greatest cathedral in Spain and third largest in all Europe after London's St. Paul's and Rome's St. Peter's—a true marvel of a monument that took nearly 3 centuries to complete and whose height positively overwhelms you as you pass through its portals. The top attraction here is the main chapel's exquisite retable (altarpiece) said to be—no surprise here—the biggest in the world. It was the work of the accomplished Flemish artist Pieter Dancart and depicts the life of Christ in a blend of intricate oak and walnut carvings and lavishly applied gold leaf whose details you could study for hours.

THE SAGRADA FAMILIA   Barcelona's intricate and idiosyncratic **Sagrada Familia,** originally intended as an expiatory temple before assuming the mantle of a (still unfinished) cathedral, was designed by 19th-century architect Antoni Gaudí and is the supreme example of Catalán moderniste religious work. Its eight knobby towers (four by Gaudí, four by architects who picked up the torch after his death in 1926) rise above the Eixample cityscape like huge, calloused fingers cocking a snoot at convention.

Sun, Sand & Sea

It doesn't all have to be culture in Spain, though, as around 95% of its visitors will happily tell you. They've come for just three basic things: sun, sea, and sangria. For five decades, Spain has been only too willing to feed visitors' hedonistic dreams, with the result that tourist numbers have mushroomed from 8 million a year in the late 1950s to six times that figure today.

The golden egg here (as laid by the golden goose) is the country's magnificent choice of beaches, which range from the Atlantic-washed strands of the Basque country's Costa Verde and Cádiz's Costa de la Luz, to the more popular coves and bays of the sun-soaked Mediterranean coasts, which extend from Andalusia's Costa del Sol and Alicante's Costa Blanca to Catalunya's Costa Brava and—greatest Lotus Eater's haven of them all—the Balearic Islands. Between them, this latter quartet has turned Spain into the most successful mass-market summer destination in all of Europe. And the eye boggling overabundance of buildings and amenities that extend along those southern coasts is there to prove it.

So far, the Mediterranean goose has avoided the fate of the hapless one in the famed fable, for among the aforementioned excesses, a few (relatively unspoiled) gems still stand out. Our short list of favorite sun-blessed beach resorts—in alphabetical order—is, accordingly, Cadaqués (Costa Brava), Estepona (Málaga), Mitjorn (Formentera), and Puerto Pollensa (Mallorca). Up in the cooler, cloudier, but more sophisticated north, in addition to our top choice San Sebastián (Basque Country), we recommend Baiona (Galicia), Llanés (Asturias), and Santander (Cantabria).

BILBAO'S GUGGENHEIM Frank Gehry's seductively curvaceous **Guggenheim Museum,** set in the once-grimy heart of old Bilbao port, is a paradigm shifting landmark. Its shimmering titanium outline somehow manages not only to slot in smoothly with its dour city surroundings but also to interact fluidly with its neighboring River Nervión.

BEST CHURCHES

Montserrat Monastery.   The shrine of Catalán regionalism, this awesome 9th-century Benedictine monastery stands 4,000 feet high atop a phantasmagorical formation that's said to have inspired Wagner when he was writing *Parsifal.*

Real Monasterio de San Lorenzo de El Escorial.   Stunningly located in the foothills of the Guadarrama Mountains north of Madrid, this chillingly austere "Castilian Colditz" boasts a dazzling library, with its unique collection of scientific books, and the long battle room lined with frescoes of Lepanto and other notable military engagements.

Toledo Cathedral.   Spain's greatest Gothic pile, built between the 13th and 15th centuries and located in the heart of a magnificent walled city that was formerly the Visigothic capital of Spain, contains some truly marvelous artifacts including a massive silver gilt monstrance, some beautifully carved choir stalls, and an elaborate Baroque section behind the main altar known as the *transparente*, as its exotic rococo figures of saints and marble cherubs on fluffy clouds are gloriously flooded with natural light when the sun shines through a hole pierced in the dome high above.

Santiago de Compostela Cathedral.   For over 800 years, pilgrims have been trekking to this Christian mecca from all corners of Europe, awed by its Baroque facade as well as the Botafumeiro incense burner inside that is swung to and from a high transept during important services. (Its trajectory is low and very quick, so don't get in its way.)

Córdoba's Mezquita.   In the 8th century, Córdoba, with a population of half a million, was the powerful capital of one of the Arab world's most wealthy caliphates (kingdoms). Today its huge *mezquita* (mosque), is a remarkable blend of Arabic and Christian features where red-and-white-striped Mudéjar archways, and lines of jasper and marble pillars shelter a central Catholic church erected by empire builder Charles V.

BEST NON-ECCLESIASTICAL SIGHTS

Madrid's Palacio Real.   Constructed by 18th-century Bourbon rulers, it's no longer the permanent royal residence. Instead, the public gets to enjoy its Tiepolo ceiling frescoes, lavish chandeliers, and priceless Flemish tapestries as they pass from one ornate salon to another.

Aranjuez's Palacio Real.   Half an hour's train ride south of the capital, Aranjuez's French-influenced neoclassical palace is less lavish inside than its Madrid counterpart but compensates by having a truly magnificent expanse of riverside gardens containing the delightful *Casita del Labrador,* a sort of Spanish Petit Trianon aimed at complementing the palace's would-be Versailles.

Barcelona's moderniste buildings.   With their innovative use of concrete (which they bent and twisted), wrought iron, and mosaics, the late 19th-century modernistas, led by Antonin Gaudí, reshaped the face of Barcelona and literally shifted the course of Western architecture. What once had been all about symmetry, in the tradition of the ancient Greeks and Romans, now took its inspiration from nature in all its glorious chaos. See all their ornate, exuberant work in the Eixample district of the city, in particular.

Valencia's City of Science.   A cutting-edge, 21st-century construction of steel, glass, and white granite, the City of Science is the most ambitious and stylish entertainment center in the land, offering every kind of diversion from concerts to a water world inhabited by Beluga whales and performing seals.

Salamanca's university.   The intellectual center of Spain for nearly 6 centuries, the Universidad de Salamanca trained a number of saints, a conquistador or two, and most of the great literary figures from Cervantes to Unamuno. Its golden sandstone buildings occupy roughly a quarter of the Old City of Salamanca, and the portions of the institution open to the public hint tantalizingly at other unseen treasures. Test your powers of observation by seeking out the tiny frog on the sculpted facade of the Escuelas Mayores, and don't miss the Cielo de Salamanca, the magical remnants of a 15th-century ceiling mural that blends astrology and astronomy.

BEST MUSEUMS

Seville's Bellas Artes.   The Andalusian capital's Bellas Artes Museum is to the city what the Prado is to Madrid, though on a more limited level. Here you'll find another repository of great Spanish art, located in a magnificent former 17th-century convent and concentrating mainly on religious works by artistic giants of the country's Golden Age.

Barcelona's Picasso Museum.   This fascinating overview of the Malagüeno artist's works is located in a quintet of converted mansions in the medieval Born district. It mainly covers paintings from his formative youth—in particular, his Blue period—and it's fascinating to compare the pure naturalism of his early creations with the later, mold breaking Cubist images, some of which—including his own controversial take on Velazquez's *Las Meninas*—are also on display.

Figueras's Teatro-Museu Dalí.   Undoubtedly the most eccentric museum on the peninsula, Dalí's extravaganza considerably livens up the otherwise nondescript northern Catalán town of Figueras (where the artist was born). Exhibits range from sculptures, gouaches, and paintings, including the bizarre mauve-purple *Happy Horse,* to a furniture assembly—including a sofa with large red cushions—arranged to look like Mae West's face.

BEST TRAVEL EXPERIENCES

Watching a bullfight.   The best places to see this visceral semi-pagan activity are at Las Ventas in Madrid or La Real Maestranza in Seville, where you'll find the largest two *plazas de toros* (bullrings) in Spain. Many find the sequence of the bloody ritual—the *banderilleros,* the *picadores,* the *torero* executing the final kill—cruel, brutal, and downright anachronistic. Others are moved by its timeless symbolism, vivid color, and artistic beauty.

Listening to flamenco in an Andalusian *tablao.*   More Spanish passion, but this time without physical pain and suffering (except perhaps that inflicted on the eardrums of the uninitiated by the high-pitched wails of the *cantaor*). Accompanied by hand clapping and the sultry strains of the guitar while a colorfully clad, raven-haired beauty stomps the floor, this mournful yet captivating blend of Arabic-Gypsy-Asian sounds and movements is the other great Hispanic draw, often, alas, commercialized beyond belief. Though Madrid has the most elegant *salas de fiestas,* Andalusia is its spiritual home.

Running with the bulls in Pamplona. During the packed-to-capacity fiestas known as the San Fermines, bulls run through the streets accompanied by either a brave or the wine-inebriated public in a wild ritual that's without equal for devil-may-care recklessness, excitement, and atmosphere anywhere else in Spain. Even the bullfight-haters love this one.

Exploring Gypsy Granada. Gypsies have made their homes in Sacromonte, the hillside *barrio* above Granada, for hundreds of years. A few still live in quite pleasant caves carved out of the rock—an experience you can have yourself by booking one of the apartments of Las Cuevas El Abanico (p. 154). The Museo Cuevas de Sacromonte (p. 165) serves as an educational and social center of newfound Roma (Gypsy) pride. The neighborhood also developed its own distinctive flamenco idiom, called *zambra*, still performed nightly in many *salas de fiestas* (nightclubs).

Following the Camino de Santiago de Compostela. Probably the oldest tourist itinerary in Europe, the foot slog from the easterly Pyrenees to westerly Galicia takes in some of the most fascinating architecture and scenery in Spain. It began in the Middle Ages when pilgrims headed for St. James's shrine in Santiago de Compostela's cathedral and—after a period of decline—is all the rage again with ecologically aware and religiously minded visitors who make their leisurely way along the same route, usually walking but sometimes on horseback or bicycle.

BEST OF THE "OTHER" SPAIN

Cooking your own meal with locals in a Guipuzcoan *txoko* or taking a Barcelona cooking class. Ever since Ferran Adrià shook things up on the culinary scene to such an extent that the *New York Times* referred to him as the best chef in the world, people have been looking at Catalán cuisine with different eyes. Better then the French? Why not? Barcelona offers you the chance to join this illustrious circle with sophisticated courses on creating Adrià-style dishes (p. 296). If you're a male foodie, head to San Sebastián where you might be able to wrangle an invitation to a *txoko*, basically a social event where guys gather in a clubhouse to cook together and share recipes (p. 363).

Visiting private courtyards in Córdoba. The citizens of Córdoba are so proud of their flower-strewn private patios that many of them admit visitors during the annual Córdoba Patio Festival during the first two weeks of May. It's as much a social occasion as a competition, and if you're friendly and respectful, you might find yourself being offered a glass of wine, given a cutting from a prized philodendron, or invited to join a songfest. Best of all, life as usual continues: Family members eat their meals, sweep the floor, greet their friends, or just sit in the shade of a lemon tree and read the newspaper.

Catching a match with fans of Real Madrid. A Madrid friend once told us that the only time she ever saw her grandfather cry was when Real Madrid lost a championship for the second year in a row. Few passions so seize Spaniards as their loyalty to local football (soccer) clubs. In Madrid, try to get tickets to Real Madrid's home field, Estadio Santiago Bernabéu. But if the scalpers want too many euros, take heart. You can have an equally great communal experience watching the match on cable in a smoky bar (p. 65).

Learning flamenco in Seville.   Learning to dance or play flamenco is a little like learning a language—nothing works like full immersion, and that's what you can get at the Taller Flamenco in Seville's Macarena barrio (p. 143). Classes embrace all the sub-disciplines of choreography, dance technique, flamenco guitar, flamenco singing, *compás* and *palmas* (clapping), and percussion. To fully live the flamenco life, share an apartment with other students in the Macarena district.

2 Madrid

The regal center of Spain

by Patricia Harris & David Lyon

OVER GLASSES OF THE HOUSE VERMOUTH ONE NIGHT AT ANTIGUA CASA Ángel Sierra, we started chatting with Juan Rafumann, a nattily dressed man of about 80 who said he'd been a regular at the *taberna* since he was 16—and that it hadn't changed an iota in all those years. We looked at the high walls covered in Andalusian tiles and the tobacco-stained ceiling, and we couldn't imagine it any other way. Bidding Juan *adios,* we walked 2 blocks down calle Libertad, only to discover hip, young Spaniards actually lined up on the street at 8:30pm to get into a restaurant. Generally speaking, only great-grandmothers and foreigners eat dinner before 10pm in Madrid. But Bazaar, a sleekly modern restaurant with an international take on *cocina creativa* (and low, low prices), was proving irresistible.

That's Madrid in a nutshell: a city that treasures its past and eagerly embraces the future. By Spanish standards, it's a young city. It's been the national capital for less than 350 years, and most of Madrid was built after 1850—a far cry from Spanish towns and cities that assert their history in millennia rather than centuries. As the national center of power, Madrid is studded with monumental architecture; is blessed with vast, green parks; and boasts an embarrassment of riches among its art museums. At the same time, Madrid's new hotels are unmistakably 21st century in their design, and its new restaurants rival the cutting-edge cuisine of Barcelona and Catalonia. In fact, the city is constantly *en obras* (under construction)—old rooming houses are becoming Wi-Fi-enabled mini-hotels, and it's hard to walk down any street without having to step around some scaffolding.

The biggest change in Madrid in recent years, however, is in the attitude of Madrileños. The sour and fearful rigidity of the Franco years is largely gone (although you'll still find the occasional older, mean-spirited hotel reception clerk), replaced by an optimistic openness and cocksure attitude that come with economic good times. Besides, it's hard to stay downbeat very long in the sunniest capital in Europe. The weather may be hot in summer and chill in winter, but the sky defines cerulean blue. As Madrileños say, *de Madrid al cielo:* from Madrid to heaven.

DON'T LEAVE MADRID WITHOUT . . .

Visiting with the great Spanish masters. Spanish painting has been an ongoing conversation among geniuses across the ages, and most of that dialogue is captured at the Prado (p. 48). Don't miss Velázquez's court portraits and Goya's moving "dark paintings." At the Reina Sofía (p. 51), Picasso's *Guernica* is still the defining image of the horrors of war.

Spending Sunday in the park with Jorge.   All of Madrid comes out for the Sunday promenade in Parque del Retiro, the lush, green flip side to Madrid's extensive stone and concrete pavements. See p. 50.

Tapas-hopping around Plaza Santa Ana.   Madrileños may not sit down to dinner until 10pm or later, but they stand to nibble from the time they get out of work. Join the parade of peripatetic snacking. You won't be an honorary Madrileño until you've tossed your crumpled paper napkins into the trough at the base of the bar. See p. 41.

Experiencing the flamenco revival.   Andalusia may be the birthplace of flamenco, but Madrid is the center of its artistic renaissance. Catch a full-fledged *tablao* or a more casual performance at a bar. Either way, you'll never clap or tap your feet the same again. See p. 72.

Having chocolate and *churros* in the *Madrugada* at San Ginés.   Spanish-style thick hot chocolate and *churros* dusted with powdered sugar are great snacks at any hour, but they definitely taste best after 2am. See p. 32.

A BRIEF HISTORY OF MADRID

Unusual among capital cities because it commands neither a strategic river nor the high ground of a plain, Madrid achieved its modern prominence almost by happenstance. There really wasn't even a community on the site until 863, when the Moorish ruler Muhammed I established a military outpost to protect his capital of Toledo from the Christian armies of northern Iberia. (A wall of his medina remains below the Almudena cathedral, looking for all the world like an unfinished handball court.) The fortress held until Alfonso VI, king of Castille and Léon, took Madrid and Toledo in 1083.

Madrid then made few ripples in Spanish history until the 16th century, when, in 1561 Felipe II moved the royal court from Toledo to Madrid—against the advice of his father, the Hapsburg Holy Roman Emperor Carlos V (a.k.a., Carlos I of Spain), who had suggested Lisbon. Felipe II apparently liked the good hunting in the nearby countryside, though the woods adjacent to Madrid were soon cut down for firewood as the city dramatically expanded with the presence of the royal court. Felipe was already at work on the monastery, palace, and tombs of El Escorial, and by placing the royal residence nearby, he could keep an eye on his pet project.

Over the next century, the "Madrid of the Asturias," or Hapsburg Madrid, sprang up. This is the Old City of La Latina and Lavapiés, of Puerta del Sol and Plaza Mayor, of the royal gardens at what is now Parque del Retiro. It is also the Madrid of Spain's "Golden Age"—when Miguel de Cervantes penned *Don Quixote;* Diego de Velázquez created his brilliant (and merciless) portraits of the chinless Hapsburg royals; and Jesuit-educated dramatists Lope de Vega, Tirso de Molina, Calderón de la Barca, and Quevedo electrified playgoers in the open-air theaters where Plaza Santa Ana now stands.

By 1700, the Spanish branch of the Hapsburg line had, to all intents and purposes, petered out and the monarchy had been passed to the Bourbon line that sits on the throne today. The new royals, whose cousins could boast of the glories of Versailles, sought to put their own stamp on the city. When the old fortress palace (the Alcázar) burned in 1734, Felipe V ordered the construction of the grand Palacio Real, built of stone with brick vaults so it would be impervious to fire. His son Carlos III remade the city during his 1759–88 reign, paving and lighting the streets, and creating the Jardín Botanico, among other projects—he is still affectionately known as the "mayor-king." His era marked the beginnings of what is now called "Bourbon Madrid."

His immediate heirs were rather less competent. (Francisco de Goya captured the stupefied air and thick ankles of Carlos IV perfectly in an 1801 portrait of the royal family.) When Carlos IV abdicated in 1808, his son foolishly asked Napoleon Bonaparte for help. As part of the push that would ultimately make him emperor of much of Europe, Napoleon sent troops—and his brother—to rule Spain. Madrid rose in spontaneous but unsuccessful rebellion against the French on May 2, 1808—an act of resistance still celebrated as a national holiday and captured in horrifying detail by Goya in paintings on view at the Prado.

Madrid was effectively a battlefield city for the next five years of French occupation, which ended only when a international coalition of forces finally defeated Napoleon. Spanish government, however, remained unstable until 1870, and Madrid's population began to swell as the dispossessed flocked in from the troubled, often war-torn countryside.

So crowded were the old quarters that new neighborhoods sprang up. Construction of open, airy, and orderly Salamanca began in 1870. The municipal population, which had stood at 170,000 in 1797, swelled to 1 million at the dawn of the 20th century and doubled again by 1930. When Alfonso XIII married in 1906, he was so embarrassed by Madrid's lack of modernity that he cajoled investors into building grand hotels—albeit too late for the nuptials. In 1910, he personally launched the demolition work to create Gran Vía on the model of a Parisian boulevard.

The high hopes for Madrid that Alfonso XIII represented stalled with the worldwide economic collapse in 1929, and improvement schemes were permanently shelved when the Spanish government spun into a downward political spiral. The Spanish Civil War (1936–39) turned Madrid into a garrison city, and the Franco dictatorship effectively isolated the whole country from modern Europe for 40 years. Once the 1978 constitution restored democracy, Madrid flowered with the "movida," an artistic ferment in film, literature, and music that introduced Pedro Almodóvar and Antonio Banderas to the world. Madrid reentered Europe with a bang, and was named European Cultural Capital in 1992. That same year high-speed train service to Andalusia began, marking the inauguration of a fast train network to unite the far-flung corners of the country. Civic construction has continued into the new millennium, with the 2005 opening of Jean Nouvel's new wing for the

> "Madrid is truly a moral triumph, heightening man's belief in his own virtue. And when I say 'virtue,' I mean tenacity and strength. That is why straight off, from the first moment, Madrid arouses sympathy, as a landmark of human triumph."
>
> —Nikos Kazantzakis, *Spain*

Reina Sofía and the 2007 opening of Moneo's extension to the Prado. In 2006, two new runways and the futuristic Terminal 4 opened at Barajas International Airport, making Madrid an air-traffic gateway to Europe on a par with Paris, Rome, and London.

LAY OF THE LAND

Everyone slices and dices Madrid a little differently. We think of almost everything in Madrid in relation to the **Puerta del Sol,** and there's some logic to back us up: The square is Kilometer Zero for Spain's road system, and street addresses are assigned in ascending order from Sol outward. Besides, you can always find Sol by looking for the Tío Pepe neon sign on the skyline. It's also the crossroads of lines 1, 2, and 3 on the Metro. (We also have a sentimental attachment to the Puerta del Sol: On our first flight from Boston to Madrid, our Madrileño seat mate warned us away from Sol as "dangerous, dirty, and cheap." We heard *cheap* and went there straight from the airport.)

Walking west-northwest out of Sol leads to the **Plaza de Oriente,** and more important for most visitors, **Palacio Real (Royal Palace).** Heading east from Sol, you'll get to the **Prado** and **Retiro Park.** These sites form the borders of Madrid's highly walkable historic district. We call the area around the Prado the "Museums District" later in the chapter. Also in this historic area (you walk west-southwest out of Sol on calle Mayor) are the **Plaza Mayor** and behind that, the neighborhood known as **La Latina** after the Metro stop of the same name (it, too, is part of the historic district).

Streets leading north out of Sol intersect **Gran Vía,** which is home to many theaters, both stage and screen, and the attendant subculture that goes with such districts. (Caveat emptor: The lady who hails you from a doorway may be no lady at all.) North of Gran Vía are the **Chueca** and **Malasaña** neighborhoods, though this area goes under many pseudonyms, including the Gay District and Universidad (even though the university has moved farther northwest).

South and east of La Latina is a web of hillside streets we've lumped together under the dominant Metro stop, **Lavapiés,** a somewhat rough-and-tumble immigrant neighborhood that's also a happening nightlife spot.

Finally, north of Parque del Retiro and mostly east of the Paseos is the posh neighborhood of **Salamanca.** Officially, this includes parts of Recoletos, Castellana, and Lista, but those are fine distinctions you'll mostly find if you peruse properties for sale here (at 600,000€ and up).

GETTING TO & AROUND MADRID

With its high-capacity airport, Madrid is the natural gateway for travelers coming from Europe or overseas. Once you've arrived, excellent public transit makes it easy to get around the city—or to make connections elsewhere in Spain.

GETTING TO & FROM THE AIRPORT

Handling more than 52 million passengers a year, Madrid Barajas International Airport (MAD) is the world's 10th busiest airport, served by more than 100 airlines. Terminals 1 through 3 are home to SkyTeam and Star Alliance airlines, while Iberia and its One World partners use Terminal 4, inaugurated in 2006.

Metro Line 8 (pink) runs 6am to 1:30am between central Madrid and terminals 4 and 2 (you can walk from terminal 2 to terminals 1 and 3). Metro service to and from the airport carries a 1€ surcharge. You have to change trains at Nuevas Ministerios, as the airport segment of the line uses different platforms, but the Metro is still the fastest and most convenient way to get to the city. There is also **bus service** on lines 200 and 204 between the airport and the avenida de America bus terminal. On a good day, either mode of transport takes 20 minutes. Keep your baggage to a minimum for Metro or bus travel, as you'll have to watch it and your wallet at the same time. If convenience trumps cost, the plentiful airport taxis cost 30€ to 35€ to get to central Madrid.

GETTING AROUND

You can **walk** almost anywhere in central Madrid, and if you have the time and the stamina for the hills, it's the best way to experience the city. You'll soon realize that Madrid was sited on the high ground to command the modest valley of the Manzanares River. In fact, the Palacio Real sits on a cliff overlooking the river. The rest of the city flows mostly downhill from this point, meaning that you'll be doing a fair bit of walking up and down.

TRANSPORTATION OPTIONS

Madrid has some of the most thorough and least-expensive public transit in Europe. For a full overview, check the website for **Consorcio Transportes Madrid** (www.ctm-madrid.es).

You'll find the Metro far and away the most convenient way to cover a lot of ground in little time. It operates 6am to 2am, while buses run 6am to 11pm. Twelve main Metro lines and three additional short lines to connect hub stations cover most of the city. Don't overlook using the **Circular** (which circles around the edges of Old Madrid) as a quick connector among the other lines. Be forewarned that Madrileños are very aggressive when entering and exiting the subway cars. He who hesitates is lost, so push right through. Ever wonder how they manage to stay out late at night and still put in a full day's work? Look for nappers among the lucky few who snag a seat.

The **public buses,** marked EMT, are most useful for moving around the circular roads, or *rondas,* such as getting from Atocha to Puerta de Toledo, or for moving quickly up and down the Paseos. Tickets for single rides on the Metro or bus are 1€, but few people buy just one.

If your stay is short and you have to move around the city quickly, then it can be worth your while to purchase an **Abono Transportes Turístico** for unlimited rides on Madrid's Metro and buses. The passes, which are available at Metro stations and tourist offices, are sold for one, two, three, five, and seven days (for 4€, 7.15€, 9.50€, 15€, and 21€, respectively). The Abono is valid only for the ticket holder. But most travelers are better off with the **Metrobus pass,** good for 10 subway or bus rides for 6.70€. Two or more people can share one Metrobus pass. They're sold at any Metro ticket window or ticket vending machine.

The **Cercanía** (www.renfe.es/cercanias/madrid) train network, which is designed as suburban commuter rail but is a convenient way to visit El Escorial (from Chamartín station), or Alcalá de Henares and Aranjuez (from Atocha station) for less than 3€ in each direction. Fares on the *Cercanías* run 1.15€ to

Madrid Metro

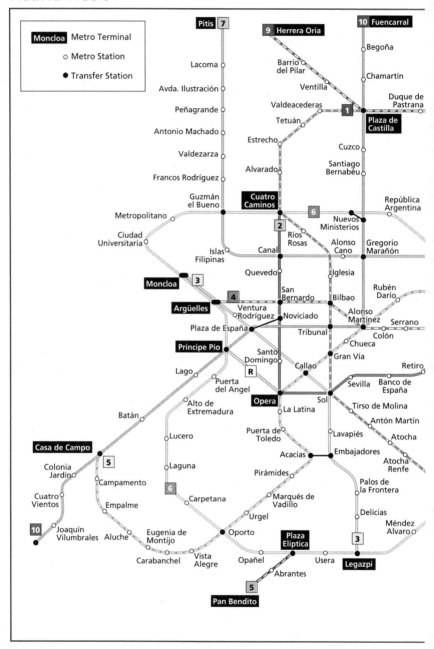

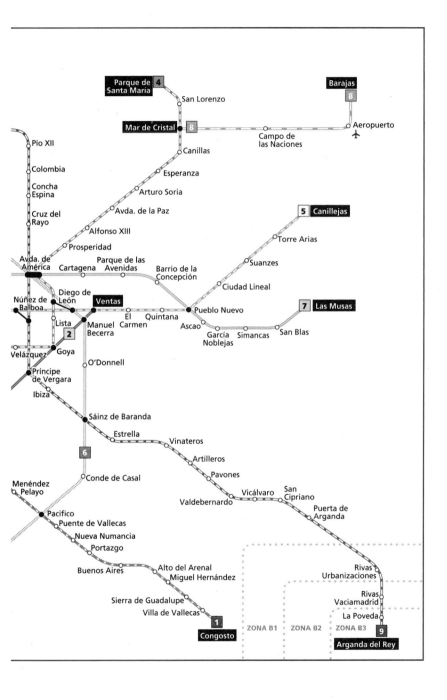

Parque de Santa Maria 4

San Lorenzo

Barajas 8

Mar de Cristal 8

Aeropuerto

Campo de las Naciones

Pío XII

Canillas

Colombia

Esperanza

Concha Espina

Arturo Soria

Cruz del Rayo

Avda. de la Paz

5 Canillejas

Alfonso XIII

Torre Arias

Prosperidad

Avda. de América

Parque de las Avenidas

Suanzes

Cartagena

Barrio de la Concepción

Núñez de Balboa

Diego de León

Ciudad Lineal

Ventas

Pueblo Nuevo

7 Las Musas

Lista

El Carmen

Quintana

Ascao

Manuel Becerra

García Noblejas

Simancas

San Blas

Velázquez

2

Goya

O'Donnell

Príncipe de Vergara

Ibiza

Sáinz de Baranda

Estrella

Vinateros

6

Artilleros

Pavones

Menéndez Pelayo

Conde de Casal

Vicálvaro

San Cipriano

Valdebernardo

Puerta de Arganda

Pacifico

Puente de Vallecas

Nueva Numancia

Portazgo

Rivas Urbanizaciones

Buenos Aires

Alto del Arenal

Miguel Hernández

Rivas Vaciamadrid

Sierra de Guadalupe

La Poveda

Villa de Vallecas

1

9

Congosto

ZONA B1   ZONA B2   ZONA B3

Arganda del Rey

15

3.80€, depending on zone. ***Note:*** *Cercanías* are not included in the Abono Turistico or the Metrobus pass.

Taxis

Taxis in Madrid are reasonably priced, especially for Europe. Official taxis in Madrid are white and have a diagonal red stripe on the door along with the city's coat of arms. While there are taxi stands all over the city, you can also flag one down on the street—a sure sign of civilization. Rates of roughly 1€ per kilometer plus a flag drop fee of 2€ to 3€ (the higher rate is at a taxi stand or public transport station) are about 20% higher between 10pm and 6am. Make sure the driver turns on the meter when you get in the cab or you could be overcharged a "flat rate" that he makes up on the spot. It's a rare taxi ride in the central city that exceeds 10€.

Driving

Let the Madrileños do the driving in Madrid. Even if you manage to reach your destination, you'll be hard-pressed to find parking. Renting a car for excursions is another matter, as pickup points are usually at train stations or the airport, where it's easy to reach outlying highways. Citizens of non-EU countries must obtain an **International Drivers Permit** before arriving in Spain. Without one, police can fine you up to 400€ and some agencies will refuse to rent you a car. Car rentals from at the airport include **Avis** (☎ 917-43-88-67; www.avis-europe.com), **Hertz** (☎ 917-46-60-04; www.hertz.es), **Europcar** (☎ 917-43-87-58; www.europcar.com), and **National Atesa** (☎ 917-46-60-60; www.atesa.es). You'll find that prices vary little among companies, so stick with whichever one dovetails with your frequent-flyer program. Most can also arrange downtown pickup.

ACCOMMODATIONS, BOTH STANDARD & NOT

Your choice of type and location of accommodations will depend in large part on how long you're staying in the city, how many people are in your party, and what sights and activities you want to take in. Apartments are often the best bet for longer-term stays or visits with a family group, but hotels usually offer slightly greater convenience.

APARTMENT RENTALS

Renting an apartment is a good way to share in the life of the city, as most apartments are located in residential neighborhoods where you'll meet your neighbors and get a taste of what it's like to inhabit Madrid, as opposed to merely passing through. An apartment also gives you more space than a hotel room, and provides a kitchen where you can keep snacks and cold wine. Moreover, it's usually less expensive. To avoid disappointment it's best to use an agency, such as those listed below. We've had mixed success renting apartments directly from individual owners. We once rented a one-bedroom spot in another Spanish city that had the contemporary furnishings depicted in online photos that the owner described. Alas, he failed to mention that the bedroom was directly above a bar featuring live rock music until 3am—and that the building was across a narrow street from a transvestite club where certain tourists trolled for dates. (Perhaps the final straw was that the "girls" in their evening finery were often better dressed than Pat in her practical travel garb.)

Live and learn. If we were going to rent a short-term apartment in Madrid, we'd go directly to Raquel Román, proprietor of **Homes for Travellers** ★★ (☎ 629-19-68-83; homesfortravellers.com; MC or V for reservation, balance of payment cash). Román curates the collection to a standard of middle-class good taste, and weeds out properties that don't meet her picky standards. "I won't represent a place where I wouldn't stay myself or send my friends and family," she says. She saw the need when she purchased a new apartment a few years ago and decided to rent out her old apartment in an historic building. Local law requires giving long-term leases to conventional renters, and she couldn't find anyone local who would represent properties for short-term rentals to transients. So began a career, and now Homes for Travellers is the exclusive representative for more than 60 apartments, usually furnished as private homes rather than rental properties.

The apartments are embedded in residential quarters in Chueca, Malasaña, near Opera and Plaza Mayor—even in tony Salamanca. Román requires owners to equip the units with TVs, DVD players, and washing machines. Most also have air-conditioning, dishwashers, and high-speed Internet access. For example, one apartment on calle Barco in Malasaña features a fireplace in the living room, a dining area off the fully equipped kitchen, a bedroom with double bed and small balcony, and a marble bathroom. It has stylish modern furniture, and we wouldn't mind the climb to the third floor. If stairs are an issue, be sure to ask for a unit with an elevator. The apartment rents for 120€ per night, while an adjoining tiny one-bedroom rents for 95€ per night either as a stand-alone or a suite extension.

Román also has new-construction flats like one on Victor Hugo off Gran Vía in a building that opened in mid-2007 (110€). The very contemporary studio has a small kitchen, and a dining/sleeping/sitting area with an entire wall of windows. But nothing tops the views of the Palacio Real from the living room of a giant flat on calle de Santiago near Teatro Real. Two large bedrooms look out on a quiet plaza, two tiny ones have no views. The furniture is older and less stylish than in some other apartments, but certainly comfortable. It's priced at 200€ per night for four (or fewer). In general, minimum rentals are for three nights, and prices drop 10% for 7 to 20 nights, 30% for a month or more. Román employs her own cleaning staff, and renters pay a 40€ cleaning fee for one-bedroom units and 60€ for two-bedroom units, so factor that into your calculations.

Students, bargain-hunters, and bohemian travelers should look for more basic apartments through **RoomMadrid** (Conde Duque 7; ☎ 915-48-03-35; www.room madrid.es; cash only), a locally based agency that handles everything from family stays to semester-long rentals to single overnights. Most properties are in Malasaña's student quarter, La Latina, or the immigrant barrio of Lavapiés. Decor and modernity run the gamut from a sparsely furnished tiny studio on calle Cristo in Malasaña (50€/night or 300€/week) to an arty loft in La Latina on Travesia de las Vistillas (100€/night or 600€/week). Pierre Vanham, who runs the agency, prides himself on matching clients with the right property, and actively dissuades would-be lodgers from units he thinks wouldn't please them. Ask about the cleaning fee and discounts for longer-term stays, as both vary.

Most Madrid **apartment hotels**—essentially furnished apartments that rent by the night—are located too far from the city's attractions to be practical for most short-term visitors, but there are a few exceptions. The modern concrete and

Madrid Accommodations

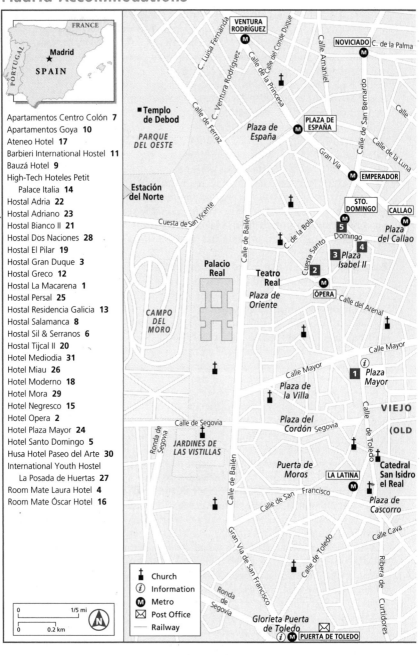

Apartamentos Centro Colón **7**
Apartamentos Goya **10**
Ateneo Hotel **17**
Barbieri International Hostel **11**
Bauzá Hotel **9**
High-Tech Hoteles Petit
  Palace Italia **14**
Hostal Adria **22**
Hostal Adriano **23**
Hostal Bianco II **21**
Hostal Dos Naciones **28**
Hostal El Pilar **19**
Hostal Gran Duque **3**
Hostal Greco **12**
Hostal La Macarena **1**
Hostal Persal **25**
Hostal Residencia Galicia **13**
Hostal Salamanca **8**
Hostal Sil & Serranos **6**
Hostal Tijcal II **20**
Hotel Mediodia **31**
Hotel Miau **26**
Hotel Moderno **18**
Hotel Mora **29**
Hotel Negresco **15**
Hotel Opera **2**
Hotel Plaza Mayor **24**
Hotel Santo Domingo **5**
Husa Hotel Paseo del Arte **30**
International Youth Hostel
  La Posada de Huertas **27**
Room Mate Laura Hotel **4**
Room Mate Óscar Hotel **16**

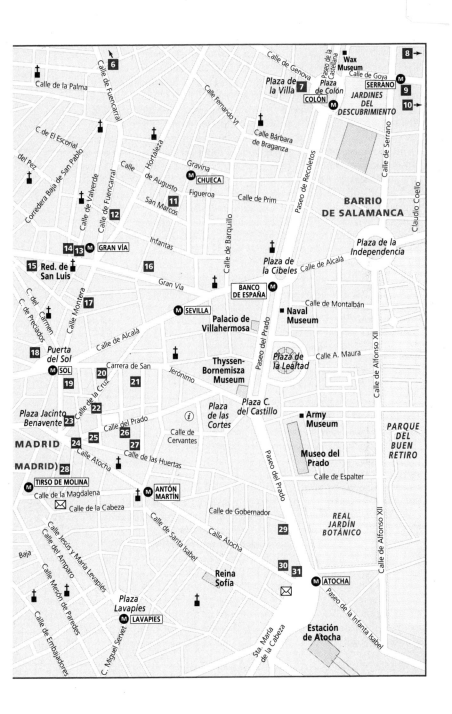

glass tower of **Apartamentos Centro Colón** 🧒 (Marques de la Ensenada 16; ☎ 913-49-00-02; www.apartamentos-centro-colon.com; AE, DC, MC, V; Metro: Colon), for example, is right off Plaza Colón near Spain's Supreme Court. The units are modest but have fully functional kitchens. Among the building's 90 units are 40 studio apartments, which are the most affordable at 100€ per night, 90€ per night for a week, or 60€ per night for a month. Just make sure you don't feel the need to spread out amid the IKEA-style furniture, as quarters are tight. An apartment with a separate bedroom is 150€ per night—about the same price as a modestly upscale hotel room, but you do get more room and a kitchen.

Apartamentos Goya 🧒 (General Pardiñas 13; ☎ 917-81-89-30; www.apartamentosgoya75.com; MC, V; Metro: Goya) occupies one corner of the intersection of calles Goya and General Pardiñas in Salamanca, yet the entrance is so obscure that it seems deliberately camouflaged to fit into the neighborhood. The small one-bedroom units (around 375 sq. ft.) feature inexpensive blond-wood furniture and cork floors, both of which show some wear. The combined sitting/dining area is compact, and the kitchen is so basic that it fits behind folding doors. But the combination of upscale neighborhood, front-desk security, good elevators, and privacy make the apartments an excellent choice for older travelers, while the fully functional kitchen makes it a good bet for those traveling with kids. The rates are fabulous for Salamanca, starting at 91€ per day and dropping the longer you stay—78€ per day for a week or more, 67€ per day if you stay 30 days or longer. You can even get parking on a similar sliding scale (17€/10€/8€). You're in the heart of Salamanca shopping, and close to the Goya Metro stop when you want to return to the real world.

HOTELS & HOSTALES

The first time we visited Madrid in the early 1980s, we stayed in a fourth-floor walkup *pensión* where all the units shared one bathroom. It was only $7 a night, and from our tiny balcony we watched the elderly woman across the alley water the geraniums on *her* tiny balcony. Since it was August and hot, we convinced ourselves that the icy-cold shower was refreshing. Our tolerance for spartan accommodations has changed, but so have Madrid accommodations. The lowest categories have almost vanished, as owners have rehabilitated their properties to make rooms larger where possible and added en suite bathrooms. We're truly impressed with the quality of beds in even modest places, and many lodgings have invested in new furniture, double-glazed windows, and fresh paint. You can still find the charm of geranium gardens across the way—along with hot water from your own tap, and probably Wi-Fi to boot. The rooms in all the hotels and *hostales* (a Spanish term for small, often family-run hotels that occupy one or more levels of a larger building) in this chapter have televisions, telephones, heat, air-conditioning, free Wi-Fi access, and private bathrooms unless otherwise indicated. And unless noted otherwise, neither breakfast nor the 7% tax is included. Most *hostales* ask for full payment when you check in.

Accommodations Around Puerta del Sol

We like Sol for its central location—you can easily walk to Plaza Mayor, the Palacio Real, the museums, Plaza Santa Ana, and the nightlife of bars in La Latina and Lavapiés. Metro lines 1, 2, and 3 will take you anyplace else you'll want to go.

Although many travelers (us included) have a horror story about an overpriced fleabag (especially near the Sevilla Metro), there are decent hotels at fair prices in the neighborhood.

€   For example, we often send friends on a budget to modest gems on the side streets heading uphill out of Puerta del Sol toward Plaza Ángel—like the 15-room **Hostal Bianco II** (Echegaray 5, 1st Floor; ☎ 913-69-13-32; www.hostalbianco. com; MC, V; Metro: Sevilla). You can tell the care that has been put into the place from the fresh paint on the walls and the new, if inexpensive, curtains and bedspreads. Structural issues have been harder for the owners to address, of course, so small shower stalls rather than tubs are the rule. "Madrid has to conserve water," the friendly desk clerk explained to us. Another oddity: There are no phones in the rooms, but there's a pay phone in the lobby. The strikingly good prices make up for these small lapses, with singles starting at 35€, doubles at 44€, and triples at 55€. It's always good to ask about a discount here, as they will cut rates for longer stays or for groups booking together.

€   A similar bargain lodging a few streets over, **Hostal El Pilar** 🧒 (Carretas 13; ☎ 915-31-26-26; www.hostalelpilar.net; MC, V; Metro: Sevilla) is a top pick for families, as several of its 38 rooms are large enough to sleep three or four people easily and affordably (just 88€ for a quad, 52€ double). And you'll sleep well: Double-glazed windows cut the noise, so there's no need to pick a view-free interior room. The light streaming in the windows also brightens the look—draperies and curtains reflect traditional Spanish taste for muted, subdued colors. The bathrooms are compact but gleamingly new, which is unusual in this price class. Management is adamant about never giving discounts, but, in truth, the discount's already built in; unlike most lodgings, the rate includes the 7% tax.

€€   It's half again more expensive to step up to **Hostal Tijcal II** ✦ (Cruz 6; ☎ 913-60-46-28; www.hostaltijcal.com; AE, MC, V; Metro: Sevilla) in the same general neighborhood, but you'll have more sophisticated fellow guests if you do. Featuring new furniture a la IKEA, and orange-and-yellow plaid draperies and bedspreads, it's a nice departure from the typically somber decor of older Sol hostales. Several rooms have balconies overlooking calle de la Cruz, the busy diagonal that cuts through a crosshatch of streets lined with tapas bars, but soundproof windows keep out the noise of the barflies. Lobby vending machines sell coffee, sodas, and candy. Continental breakfast is available for an extra 3.50€ per person, and the AC (when needed) is 5€. Rooms with one double bed are 79€; with two twin beds they're 84€. Repeat clientele here tends to be more adult and better-heeled than in other Sol *hostales*.

€€–€€€   Opened in 2003, **Ateneo Hotel** (Montera 22; ☎ 915-21-20-12; www.hotel-ateneo.com; AE, MC, V; Metro: Sol) embodies the new standard of Madrid hotel style with its pale furniture and walls, marble bathrooms (with tub-shower combination), and flat-screen TVs. Many rooms also have good-sized desks. Unfortunately, the Ateneo also subscribes to the increasingly common standard of wildly fluctuating room rates. The usual price for a double with breakfast buffet is 100€ but can drop as low as 70€ or surge as high as 130€. Hit it right and you can get a very good deal.

€€–€€€   Instead of playing the room-rate guessing game, you can view a graph of "normal" room rates by day for several months in advance at the website of **Hotel Moderno** ✦✦✦ (Arenal 2; ☎ 915-31-09-00; www.hotel-moderno.com; AE, DC, MC, V; Metro: Sol). Asking for an even lower rate may get you a discount, or at least an upgrade. This 97-room hotel right in Sol opened in 1939, and is now managed by Santiago Bello Gonzalez-Echenique, son of the founder. His sister decorates with a creative use of color, soft indirect lighting, and well-cushioned furniture. Rooms are small, as the support beams of the 1857 building limit expansions, but rooms on floors 5 through 7 (a 20th-century addition) are about 10% larger. Marble and tile bathrooms are especially nice for this price range, which generally runs around 100€ for a double, 130€ for one of the 17 doubles with outdoor patio. Exterior rooms have views of the pedestrian street of Arenal or of the main entrance of El Corte Inglés. The Moderno lays out a good 10€ per-person buffet breakfast. The second floor lounges get almost no use, which is too bad because they're large and comfortable, and one has a big-screen TV and bar service. One nice touch: Sheets and towels have a fresh scent because the hotel does its own laundry and dries them on the roof.

Accommodations Around Opera & Palacio Real

Of the two advantages of staying near the Opera Metro stop, the chief is the Metro itself. The other is that the neighborhood is simply more spacious—you don't feel the same human crush as in neighboring Sol or Gran Vía.

€   Just around the corner from the Teatro Real, **Hostal Gran Duque** (Campomanes 6; ☎ 915-40-04-13; www.hostalgranduque.com; MC, V; Metro: Opera) is a bargain in a pricey neighborhood. A double usually sells for 60€ but can drop as low as 49€. At these prices, there are some trade-offs. The 23 rooms occupy a single floor beneath a backpacker hostel whose clients clog the stairwell as they wait to check in (they're not exactly quiet at night, either), and the traditional somber Spanish furniture is merely serviceable. But maintenance is top-notch, air-conditioning is now available throughout, and the rate includes tax.

€€€   There's a kitchen in every room at **Room Mate Laura Hotel** ✦✦ 🧒 (Travesía de Trujillos 3; ☎ 917-01-16-70; www.room-matehotels.com; AE, DC, MC, V; Metro: Opera), but many of the kitchens are hidden in what seems to be a locked closet and you'll have to ask to have yours revealed. Such a utilitarian amenity is surprising in a hotel where over-the-top postmodern design means bold splashes of bright colors and enough mirrors to satisfy a narcissistic runway model. (The conceit of this Room Mate hotel is that your "roommate" for your stay is the spirit of Laura, a sexy PR agent with a taste for extreme sports.) The oddly narrow building results in some unusual room layouts. All the rooms on the first and second floors have ladder-like stairs to reach their upper lofts, where you'll find the sole bed in the standard duplex, or a second bed (the main one is downstairs) and half-bath in the deluxe duplex. If climbing to bed isn't doable for you, opt for a more conventional room on the third floor. Fourth-floor "penthouse" rooms sprawl beneath oddly angled ceilings, but have extra beds that are good for families. Rates are very fluid. Standard rooms usually cost 100€ to 120€, but you might get a duplex (usually 140€–160€) for that price. Book a month ahead at the website for a 10% discount. Rates include an excellent buffet breakfast served until noon—nice if you start going out to nightlife that starts after midnight.

€€€–€€€€   Given the gingerbread architecture of the Teatro Real and the surrounding streets, we always looked askance at the boxy brick building of **Hotel Opera** ✪✪ (Cuesta de Santo Domingo 2; ☎ 915-41-28-00; www.hotelopera.com; AE, DC, MC, V; Metro: Opera). But sweeping renovations completed in 2008 have transformed it into a boutique hotel with graceful designer furniture, lots of indirect lighting, and striking contemporary art on the walls. And, for the time being, the price is right. (The independent hotel is requesting a reclassification by the government, which could raise prices.) Booking in advance increases the chance of scoring one of five rooms on the eighth floor with outdoor terraces, which cost the same as other doubles and are great for honeymooners. If you're in a romantic mood, the glassed-in Jacuzzi tub in the bathroom of 801 looks out on the balcony. Under the current classification, doubles never exceed 140€ to 150€ and are often as low as 100€. Book it while you can.

€€€–€€€€   While a kind of Pop art minimalism seems to be the dominant decorating style in many Madrid hotels these days, **Hotel Santo Domingo** (Plaza de Santo Domingo; ☎ 915-47-98-00; hotelsantodomingo.com; AE, MC, V; Metro: Santo Domingo) turns back the clock to the gilded era of baroque. The owner's extensive art collection is displayed throughout, and the lobby decor borrows heavily from the Carlos III rooms at the Palacio Real. The Santo Domingo books through the Best Western network as a Best Western Premium hotel, meaning that it's geared for American travelers: It's one of the rare Madrid hotels with a nonsmoking floor. Equally American, its rates change almost hourly. Official rack rate for a double is 199€, but actual rates go as low as 77€ in slow season. Expect to pay 120€ to 140€ most of the time. Wi-Fi charges are exorbitant, but Internet cafes are nearby. Skip the airport shuttle, as two people can rent a cab for the same price. (Or you could just take the Metro for 2€.)

Accommodations on or near Gran Vía

Hotels with a Gran Vía address seem to inflate their rates accordingly. Though the street has an after-dark glamour appeal, walk a few steps away from the bright lights and traffic, and the hotel price-value ratio definitely improves.

€–€€   For example, many of the rooms at **Hostal Residencia Galicia** (Valverde 1, 4th Floor; ☎ 915-22-10-13; www.hostalgaliciamadrid.com; MC, V; Metro: Gran Vía) overlook Gran Vía, but because the entrance and, therefore, the address are on a less prestigious side street, rates remain reasonable. We're partial to Room 304, where a little balcony offers a sweeping panorama of Gran Vía that could have you saluting the adoring crowds below. The official rate for a double here is 79€, but the price rarely rises above 56€ and drops to 42€ during July and August, when the lack of air-conditioning can make some of the clean and simply furnished rooms very hot. Rate includes a basic continental breakfast. There's elevator service to the fourth-floor entrance, but the rooms are on four different levels and are connected only by narrow staircases.

€€–€€€€ With its smallish rooms furnished only with a double bed and a good work desk, it's easy to guess that **Hotel Negresco** (Mesonero Romanos 12; ☎ 915-23-86-10; www.partnernegresco.info; AE, MC, V; Metro: Callao) caters to the economy-minded business traveler. The 24-hour espresso machine in the lobby is another hint, and you'll often find other guests informally continuing their meetings there in the evenings. Its 20 rooms on two floors are well maintained but rather generic, which is fine for a short stay but could grow tiresome over time. (There's a flower shop nearby—a few posies would go a long way toward brightening the room.) The location about 150 meters off Gran Vía is far enough to cut down on noise. Rates fluctuate, generally in the 90€ to 100€ range, sometimes dropping to 70€. Like many small chains (this is a Partners hotel), rates are slightly cheaper when booked through the company website.

€€–€€€ We're generally underwhelmed by the High-Tech Hoteles chain, which gives old rooming houses a quick makeover with free Wi-Fi, and then makes computers and exercise bikes available for a 20€ surcharge. But occasionally we find one where the location and cheerful staff overcome the hype, like **High-Tech Hoteles Petit Palace Italia** (Gonzalo Jiménez de Quesada 2; ☎ 915-22-47-90; www.hthoteles.com; AE, DC, MC, V; Metro: Callao). The conversion of this 61-room former *hostal* just off Gran Vía left hallways wide and rooms often very small but furnished with brightly painted inexpensive furniture (think medium-density fiberboard pieces). Forget the "high-tech" amenities, and accept that the mild tackiness is a small tradeoff for the great Gran Vía location. Prices can drop to 85€ for a double but are usually closer to 100€. Breakfast is extra, and overpriced at 10€.

Accommodations in Chueca & Malasaña

Chueca and Malasaña are Madrid's quickly gentrifying neighborhoods, where very basic and old-fashioned hostales are often found on the same block with design-conscious (and, thus, more expensive) new hotels. These neighborhoods north of Gran Vía are great for dining but can be somewhat less convenient for seeing the sights. Plan on riding the Metro more if you stay here.

€ No one ever said youth hostels were luxurious, but **Barbieri International Hostel** ✪ (Barbieri 15, 2nd Floor; ☎ 915-31-02-58; www.barbierihostel.com; MC, V; Metro: Chueca) is scrupulously clean, cheerfully friendly, and perfectly located a block below Plaza de Chueca and a short stroll from Gran Vía. It can also be a super bargain, as per person rates apply (15€ weeknights in slow seasons to 20€ weekends in the summer) whether you're in a dorm room (sleeping 7) or manage to snag a double or triple room. These more private accommodations can be reserved in advance by telephone but not on the Internet; if you want one, call well in advance as they go fast. Bathrooms are gender specific, but they're literally the cleanest shared facilities we've ever encountered. There's a charge for Internet (0.50€ for 15 minutes) and for use of the washing machines (full load for 8€). No curfew and 24-hour reception befit the late-night reputation of Chueca. Alas, there's no air-conditioning. To get a 10% discount, book ahead by more than 7 days or show your IC card when you arrive.

€ The gregarious, late-night atmosphere of a backpacker hostel isn't for everyone, of course. So it's only a few euros more for a couple seeking some privacy and quiet to book into **Hostal Greco** (Infantas 3, 2nd Floor; ☎ 915-22-46-31; MC, V; Metro: Gran Vía) a few streets away. Here, Rosa Blanco and her husband have run their rooming house for 30 years. Blanco couldn't be friendlier, but speaks only Spanish and a little French—no English. The 16 doubles and 2 single rooms feel like spare bedrooms at your country grandma's house—welcoming but small and furnished with small floral print curtains, chenille bedspreads, and similarly old-fashioned wooden furniture. (Mattresses, however, are brand-new.) They lack air-conditioning, so ask for a cooler (and quieter) inner-courtyard room in summer. Room 1 overlooking calle Hortaleza has a delightful iron balcony—fully glassed in for the sunny view without the dust. The double rate of 54€ includes taxes.

€€ Other *hostal* owners pride themselves on modernizing. Ricardo Gonzalez told us that "you have to look to the future," so when he renovated **Hostal Sil & Serranos** ★ kids (Fuencarral 95, 2nd Floor; ☎ 914-48-89-72; www.silserranos.com; MC, V; Metro: Gran Vía), he made sure that the 29 rooms on two floors were large by Spanish standards, and that each had air-conditioning and Wi-Fi. Most have brand-new marble and tile baths, usually with tub showers rather than shower stalls, and sleek contemporary furniture. We like Room 203, where two balconies overlook different streets. Several rooms are set up for three or four people traveling together. A solo traveler should ask for Room 311 (57€), which is tiny but has a gloriously romantic view of Malasaña's red-tiled rooftops. Double rooms are 73€. Some units on the fourth floor have a second small bedroom, making them an excellent choice for traveling with children. Triples are 94€, quads 112€.

€€–€€€ The gimmick at all Room Mate properties is that the hotel is modeled on the personality of a specific person, your "room mate" for the course of your stay. At **Room Mate Óscar Hotel** ★★★ (Pl Vásquez de Mella 12; ☎ 917-01-11-73; www.room-matehotels.com; AE, DC, MC, V; Metro: Gran Vía), which opened in fall 2007 as the newest of the Room Mate hotels in Madrid, your "host" is a lover of the glamorous cocktail bars of the Gran Via, and the guestrooms aim for witty sophistication. One might have whimsical stenciling on the walls; another startles with its tangerine and white color scheme and curvaceous couches; still another is a spa white with photographs of women's bare backs as a headboard for the bed. Some showers are set in all-exposing glass stalls, so inquire if you're shy. But though it's all high design, prices aren't exorbitant: Interior rooms start at 90€ but usually sell for 110€ to 130€, while executive rooms with exterior views start at 100€ but usually sell for 120€ to 140€. Booking online a month in advance gets a 10% discount. All rates include taxes, free Wi-Fi, and an extensive breakfast buffet that's served until noon. On each level, Room 01 is next to the service closet and can be a little noisy if you want to sleep late. On the other hand, these are the largest rooms.

Accommodations in Plaza Mayor & La Latina

The neighborhood around Plaza Mayor is vital and vigorous, which is a good thing when you're out partying at a bar or restaurant and a not-so-good thing when you're trying to sleep. But most lodgings are set up to seal out the racket.

The bars start serving coffee on the plaza before the sun comes up, and the whole neighborhood is strong on cafes that serve inexpensive breakfasts.

€€   The strong suit at **Hostal La Macarena** ✦ (Cava de San Miguel 8, 2nd Floor; ☎ 913-65-92-21; www.silserranos.com; MC, V; Metro: Opera) are its good looks, which you shouldn't undervalue, as they can affect the mood of your whole trip. Crisply maintained balconies (with geraniums) on the exterior are matched inside by simple and elegant decor in soothing honey tones. Moreover, the rooms are spacious, especially at only 73€ for a double. Sound too good to be true at this rate? Well, you won't find air-conditioners here, though the rooms do have ceiling fans and excellent insulation. Even the balconies are encased in glass to keep out noise and summer heat. No Wi-Fi.

€€   Despite its name, **Hotel Plaza Mayor** ✦✦ (Atocha 2; ☎ 913-60-06-06; www.h-plazamayor.com; AE, DC, MC, V; Metro: Tirso de Molina) sits at one corner of Plaza de Santa Cruz and was carved out of the former Santa Cruz church in 1997. The mass of that old building makes it surprisingly quiet and cool, though interior rooms can be oddly shaped. However, we very much like the solid well-made furnishings, shiny wood floors, and the fact that every room comes with wall-mounted flat-screen TVs. As for prices, the 35 rooms run 85€ to 95€, except for the penthouse suite, which is a worthwhile splurge at 130€. (It has an outdoor patio with views across the tiled roofs of Hapsburg Madrid, and light floods into the unit through skylights in the slanting ceilings.) If the penthouse is booked, opt for one of the "superior" rooms on the corner to get views of Plaza Santa Cruz, one of our favorites in Madrid's old quarters. Multilingual, effervescent Fedra Martínez at the front desk is one of the hotel's key assets, and sets the breezy, young international vibe for this value lodging. The large buffet breakfast is an extra 7.50€ per person.

Accommodations in Lavapiés

€   We have only one hotel to recommend in this area, as it's not a hub of tourism. However, if you choose **Hostal Dos Naciones** (Conde de Romanones 8, 3rd Floor; ☎ 913-69-35-42; cash only; Metro: Lavapiés), you'll see what life is like in an authentic, working-class neighborhood, and you're likely to meet people from all over the world—the place is particularly popular with Eastern European and Portuguese visitors. We'd say they pick it because, though not plush, the staff here tries hard to please (owner Serafin Moran Rio will talk your ear off if you can converse in Spanish or French), and the facilities are lovingly maintained. When we last visited rooms had been treated to a fresh paint job, new floor coverings, and spanking-new bathrooms. You don't get breakfast, a TV, air-conditioning, or a phone in your room, nor do you get discounts off the 45€ rate for a double. But pick Room 1 and you'll have a tiny balcony and your own potted geraniums. The few singles (25€) are best as adjunct bedrooms for groups traveling together, as they have sinks and toilets but no showers.

Accommodations Around Plaza Santa Ana

Plaza Santa Ana is where the districts of Sol, Lavapiés, and La Latina all converge, placing lodgings conveniently near restaurants, tapas bars, and nightlife. It can get a little rowdy at night, but oozes Old Madrid charm.

€   If your kids were backpacking around Europe, you could only hope they would stay somewhere as earnest and clean-cut as **International Youth Hostel La Posada de Huertas** ✸✸ (Huertas 21; ☎ 914-29-55-26; www.posadadehuertas. com; MC, V; Metro: Antón Martín). Smoking and drinking aren't allowed in the rooms, and silent hours begin at 11pm. Rates start at 25€ per person for two people sharing a room and drop 1€ for each additional person. Dorm rooms hold up to eight, and a few double rooms are available. Bathroom facilities are shared, as are the free laundry, three computer work stations, and fully equipped kitchen.

€€   Call it one-stop shopping: One phone number reaches reception at the 22-room **Hostal Adriano** (Cruz 26; ☎ 915-21-13-39; www.hostaladriano.com; MC, V; Metro: Sevilla or Sol) and the brand-new 12-room **Hostal Adria** (Nuñez de Arce 15; same phone; MC, V; Metro: Sevilla or Sol) companion lodgings less than 50m away. The color schemes fairly vibrate with combinations like blue and orange or magenta and green, and the comfortable beds are as new and fresh as the paint job. The street can be a bit loud on weekends, so opt for an interior room unless you're an inveterate night owl. Large doubles are 65€ to 70€ including tax, and every room has a small refrigerator.

€€   The era of shared bathrooms has mostly vanished, even in budget *hostales,* but sometimes architecture doesn't allow a bathroom per bedroom. **Hostal Persal** 🏷️kids (Plaza del Angel 12; ☎ 913-69-46-43; www.hostalpersal.com; MC, V; Metro: Tirso de Molina) solved the problem neatly by linking some of the bedrooms into suites sharing a single bath (110€–140€). Rooms within the suite are small—well, honestly almost all the doubles are cramped here—but because you get two bedrooms, they're a sensible option for families (or very friendly groups). Bathrooms are also Lilliputian—some bathrooms are so tiny that you'll reach sideways once inside to close the door. Get claustrophobic? Slightly larger rooms with brand-new furniture, paint, and mattresses are on the fourth floor (not that furniture and decor on the other floors is shoddy), but here's the rub: The elevator only goes as far as the third. Doubles range 68€ to 98€, including breakfast, varying with season.

€€–€€€   The hipper choice in this same neighborhood is the **Hotel Miau** (Príncipe 26; ☎ 913-69-71-20; www.hotelmiau.com; AE, DC, MC, V; Metro: Tirso de Molina), a pioneer in contemporary styling among small hotels. Staying here is sure to impress your Madrileño friends, though the minimalist furniture and striking use of bold colors has become slightly dated (we think). Whatever your stylistic proclivities, the location remains fabulous. The 20 rooms rise above a bar-restaurant by the same name that does most of its business during tapas hours and turns quiet by dinner time. You'll find queen beds in some of the doubles (90€–105€ including breakfast and tax, sometimes as low as 80€); those with the more traditional pair of twin beds lack the sitting couch but may have a table and chair set. Singles are just big enough to walk around the bed. The elevator is tiny and the bedroom walls are *extremely* thin (or maybe something about the place inspires guests to have unusually passionate sex). No Wi-Fi.

Accommodations near the Museums

The grace and pomp of the museum district comes at a price. This is the neighborhood of the ultra-luxe Ritz and Palace hotels, after all, the high-society bookends that were created after King Alfonso XIII couldn't find suitable lodging for his 1906 wedding guests. (They face each other across the Neptuno fountain traffic circle.) Even if you expect to spend every day in the galleries, it's usually wisest to stay near Sol or Gran Vía and walk (or take a cab with the savings). That said, here are three good budget options within hailing distance of the art.

€€   One is right next to the Reina Sofía. The name of the **Hotel Mediodía** ✯ (Plaza del Emperador Carlos V, 8; ☎ 915-30-70-08; www.mediodiahotel.com; AE, MC, V; Metro: Atocha) reflects the fact that it's been around since the days when Atocha train station was called Mediodía. While *mediodía* is also slang for "nooner," this is a dignified old rail hotel that has kept up with the times. A stalwart of the package tour industry, it gives good value with doubles starting at 76€ (4€ extra per person for breakfast). The hotel can usually honor requests for interior rooms or a choice of views of the train station on one side or the Reina Sofía museum on the other. We prefer the Reina Sofía view from the balcony of Room 405. Mediodía is also good if you're in town on business, as the spacious first-floor lounge is excellent for entertaining colleagues.

€€   You're more likely to notice the busy cafe before you realize it's attached to a six-story hotel, but **Hotel Mora** (Paseo del Prado 32; ☎ 914-20-15-69; www.hotelmora.com; MC, V; Metro: Atocha) stands right across the Paseo del Prado from the Botanical Garden. Reserving a room that overlooks the Paseo is another matter, as the hotel refuses to guarantee a view even if you prepay. In typical old-Madrid fashion, most rooms have twin beds and rather small footprints. The solid-wood furniture affects a timeless unadorned style (though it's all new), and new bathrooms with low-flow toilets and contemporary sinks have been installed on the third and fourth floors. It's a pretty fancy address for only 78€.

€€€–€€€€   While the address is just as chichi at the **Husa Hotel Paseo del Arte** ✯✯ (Atocha 123; ☎ 912-98-48-00; www.husa.es; AE, DC, MC, V; Metro: Atocha), but the hotel is far more international in style and demeanor than others in the area. It's the first place we send friends visiting Madrid, assuming the logistics work out. In addition to the generic coddling of a good business hotel, the Paseo del Arte is within a 5-minute walk of all three big museums and convenient to the Atocha Metro. (That's a mixed blessing, since trains on line 2 are infrequent and crowded.) With 260 rooms and a lot of meeting space, it's no surprise that the hotel attracts small conferences and company gatherings. (Nor is it a surprise that the web connection fees are exorbitant.) But if you choose dates that the meeting planners have overlooked (like summer), you get a modern double room with marble bath, comfortable bed, and nice linens for around 120€. Pick the wrong date (a big conference or a festival week) and prices can double.

Accommodations in Salamanca

Although it's a little removed from attractions and nightlife, Salamanca remains one of the most desirable residential neighborhoods, and one of the most expensive. If you fall in love with the elegance and order of the barrio and plan to spend at least three days, look into an apartment from **Homes for Travellers** (p. 17). Owner Raquel Román says her Salamanca apartments rent for about the same rates as those elsewhere in the city.

€   Being able to get quickly to the rest of the city is important if you're staying in Salamanca, and **Hostal Salamanca** (José Ortega y Gasset 89, 3rd Floor; ☎ 914-02-40-06; www.hostalsalamanca.com; MC, V; Metro: Manuel Bercera) sits very near a stop on Metro line 2, six stops from Puerta del Sol. It's on the east edge of the neighborhood, where the streets are wide, quiet, and residential, and at 60€ for a double, represents a good value. (Doubles that share a bath are only 40€.) Private baths here are shoehorned into the rooms and can be hard to maneuver once you close the folding door for privacy. Rooms are spread over four floors, and each floor has a guest refrigerator in the common sitting area. Rates include tax but not breakfast, though a local cafeteria gives a breakfast discount to *hostal* guests. Groups of travelers might like the two-bedroom apartment with living room and one bathroom for 90€ to 100€ per night.

€€€€   More in the heart of Salamanca and boasting the room service and amenities you'd expect in a fancy neighborhood, **Bauzá Hotel** (Goya 79; ☎ 914-35-75-45; www.hotelbauza.com; AE, MC, V; Metro: Goya) was a pioneer among spare modern boutique hotels in Madrid. In contrast to traditional Spanish hotels, light floods in on all levels, making spaces seem larger and airier than they are. The Bauzá's spacious fitness center boasts separate men's and women's saunas. Standard doubles are usually around 175€ but drop to 149€ on weekends.

DINING FOR ALL TASTES

Dining practices in Spain confound foreigners, and nowhere more than in Madrid, where despite the posted hours, many restaurants don't expect you to order your evening meal before 10pm. In practice, Spaniards seem to eat constantly. Order a *café con leche* at a bar, and it is usually accompanied by a small biscuit or piece of chocolate. Order a *caña* (small draft beer), and you may get a free plate of potato chips or a few olives. These nibbles are tapas, and they serve the same purpose as nuts or pretzels in an American bar—they make you good and thirsty. Moreover, the distinctions among bars, cafes, and restaurants are blurry at best. It's not uncommon to see Madrileños take brandy or vermouth with their morning *cortado* (a short coffee with a little milk), and a bar that serves snacks at all hours may cover the tables with linens for the midday meal and again for dinner. Unlike many European capitals, Madrid has few vendors of street food—a hungry Madrileño simply pops into the nearest bar for a *pincho* (small serving) of potato omelet or a few anchovies on a slice of grilled bread.

    In general, you can count on meal service 2 to 4pm and again 9 to 11pm. To eat economically, take advantage of the fixed-price *menu del día* for a big midday meal, then dine lightly on tapas in the evening. And don't overlook the higher-priced restaurants, as many have bar areas where you can eat affordably from the tapas menu.

RESTAURANTS AROUND PUERTA DEL SOL

Since Sol is basically a transportation crossroads, a lot of the food available is unremarkable fast food for people on the go. Just head up any of the side streets, though, and the dining picture immediately brightens.

€–€€   Andalusia gave Spain bullfighting and sherry, and it also gave Madrid a certain style of tavern, of which **Taberna Alhambra** (Victoria 9; ☎ 915-21-07-08;

Madrid Dining

Alquezar **18**
Antigua Casa Ángel Sierra **32**
Asador Real **6**
Bazaar Restaurant **30**
Bocaito **29**
Café de Oriente **4**
Café Gijon **35**
Café-Restaurante
  Arola Madrid **19**
Casa Labra **24**
Casa Marta **7**
Casa Patas **21**
Cerveceria Plaza Mayor **11**
El Brillante **20**
El Inca **33**
El Ñeru **8**
Fast Good **38**
Galopín Sidreria **27**
Ginger **22**
José Luis **36**
La Bola Taberna **3**
La Camarilla Restaurante
  Taberna **12**
La Gloria de Montera **28**
La Muralla II **15**
La Tabernilla del Gato
  Amadeus **1**
La Viuda Blanca **2**
Maitetxu Asador **34**
Nebraska **25**
Restaurante Botín **10**
Restaurante Salvador **31**
Restaurante Vinoteca
  Maestro Villa **9**
Salon La Biblioteca **37**
Taberna Alhambra **26**
Taberna Almendro 13 **14**
Taberna de Antonio
  Sanchez **17**
Taberna del Alabardero **5**
Taberna Txakoli **13**
Tia Cebolla Taberna **23**
Toma que Toma **16**

Church
Information
Metro
Post Office
Railway

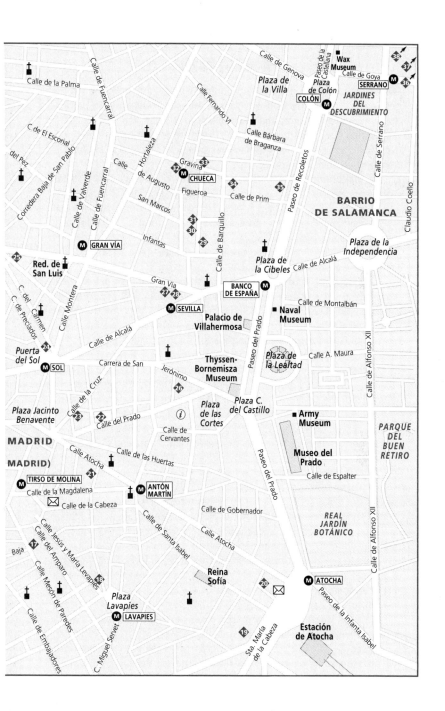

A Sweet Pause

Americans might call it the afternoon coffee break, but in Madrid it's the *merienda,* and the fare is usually sugary. All ages of shoppers, in particular, descend on the cafes and pastry shops for a snack and some socializing during the midafternoon break when restaurants are closed. By extension, any snack time that involves sweets and a place to sit down is sometimes called a *merienda.*

La Mallorquina ✪ (Puerta del Sol 8; ☎ 915-21-12-01; salon 9am–9pm; MC, V; Metro: Sol) pastry shop has been a classic hangout for the *merienda* since it opened its doors in 1894. If you can pull yourself away from the downstairs display cases, you'll find a little tearoom upstairs where you can order sandwiches (2.30€–6€), pastries (1.30€–2.80€), or ice-cream concoctions (3.50€–4€). A window seat gives you a great view of the hubbub in Puerta del Sol.

La Mallorquina makes a fine hot chocolate, but you can get a better chocolate fix at any hour at **Chocolateria San Ginés** ✪✪ (Pasadizo San Ginés 5; ☎ 913-65-65-46; daily 9am–6am; cash only; Metro: Sol or Opera), where chocolate is more than a drink—it's a ceremony. When you walk in you'll see cups lined up on the marble bar with all the handles facing the same way and a spoon on each saucer. Order a cup of the very thick, slightly bitter hot chocolate with a plate of *churros* (fried sticks of dough)—3.20€ by day, 3.50€ at night—and proceed to dust your hot *churros* with the sugar. Dip and enjoy. With its long hours, the *chocolatería* is also a favorite roost for night owls. We imagine that clubgoers from the Joy disco next door often stop in for a snack after a night of dancing.

Or how about chocolate with the postmodern treatment so typical of Madrid, a city where art and cuisine often overlap? Bonbons filled with black olives, black truffles, or anchovy and hazelnut are sold in the shop side of **Cacao Sampaka** ✪✪ (Orellana 4, ☎ 915-63-31-38; also Paseo de la Habana, 28, ☎ 915-63-31-38; www.cacaosampaka.com; store daily 10am–9:30pm, cafe until 9pm; MC, V; Metro: Bilbao). Because the fillings are so carefully matched to the subtle differences among chocolate from different sources, each bonbon is a precious delicacy. Too precious for us, maybe—we prefer our chocolate straight up in liquid form. Sampaka takes a gourmet stance on chocolate, championing the idea that where the cacao beans were grown has as much bearing on the taste as where wine grapes are grown. You can taste the differences by ordering hot chocolate in the cafe. The traditional is made with 58% cocoa butter, and the *Suizo* (Swiss) is diluted with gobs of whipped cream. The Azteca, at 64% cocoa butter, is wonderfully intense and not very sweet—much like hot chocolate from the cacao-growing southern highlands of Mexico. But then, that's the point. The best time to visit is between 10am and noon Monday through Saturday, when you can get *churros* (3€) with that cup of chocolate.

www.tabernaalhambra.es; noon–1am; cash only; Metro: Sevilla) is a prime example. Founded in 1929, it's retained the color of a Granada barroom down to the tiled walls designed by Alfonso Romero, who also created the tiles for Las Ventas bullring. Dishes are largely charcuterie—sausages, air-dried hams or beef, smoked and dried tuna. Most come in a choice of tapas, *raciones* (meal-size plates), or *media raciones* (half-size).

€€€ You have to push your way through a packed tapas scene in the bar at **El Ñeru** ★ (Bordadores 5; ☎ 915-41-11-40; Tues–Sun 1:30–4:30pm and 8:30–11pm; AE, MC, V; Metro: Sol or Opera) to get to the stairs in the back that lead to an underground warren of elegantly tiled rooms largely undiscovered by tourists. The cuisine of "The Nest" is Asturian, another regional favorite with Madrileños, and it's reflected in the fish-intensive menu, including the Asturian classic of hake braised in cider (20€). You don't have to be a fish-lover to eat Asturian, though. El Ñeru makes a hearty *fabada Asturiana* (14€) of large white beans stewed with ham and sausage, and, for the more adventurous, a stew of tripe and garbanzo beans (10€). A Madrid friend swears that the restaurant also makes the city's best *arroz con leche* (4.50€), a creamy rice pudding with a caramelized top. Bread service is expensive at 3€ but includes a great spread of butter blended with Cabrales blue cheese, and the meal ends with a complimentary thimble of a yellow-green digestive liqueur.

€€€ Neither the passage of time nor the enmity of the Franco government could kill one of Sol's classic eateries. Founded in 1860, **Casa Labra** (Tetuán 12; ☎ 915-31-00-81; meals 1:15–4pm and 8:45–10:15pm, bar service 10am–11pm; cash only; Mero: Sol) remains unrepentantly old-fashioned with its polished dark wood and blue-and-white tiles, looking just as it did when it was a popular gathering spot for Franco's Republican enemies during the Civil War. The specialty of the house, appropriately enough, is *bacalao,* the fish that's been the foundation of Spanish cuisine since true restaurants started popping up in Madrid in the 19th century. Stop in the bar for fried fresh cod (2.50€ per piece), or a small plate of bacalao croquettes for 1€ each. The dining menu runs the gamut of cod dishes, from a woodsy version with wild mushrooms, capers, and orange juice, to a more ethereal presentation with saffron and rice, both under 16€. Another historic footnote: The Spanish Socialist Workers' Party (PSOE) was founded here in 1879.

RESTAURANTS AROUND OPERA & PALACIO REAL

Old classics and new styles blend seamlessly in the streets radiating off Plaza Isabel II in front of the Teatro Royal. In this rather formal neighborhood, full-fledged restaurants actually outnumber bar-restaurants.

€€ A big smile goes a long way at **Casa Marta** ★ (Santa Clara 10; ☎ 915-48-28-25; www.restaurantecasamarta.com; daily 1:30–4pm and 9pm–midnight; MC, V; Metro: Opera), a friendly if generally non-English-speaking mom-and-pop restaurant on a side street off Vergara. Founded in 1925, it was recently honored by the city for its contributions to Madrid dining. While that suggests a stuffy temple of high cuisine, Casa Marta is a true home-cooking restaurant with old-fashioned favorites like roasted stuffed green peppers or a casserole of veal-and-almond meatballs—both around 10€. Don't miss the house croquettes (6€).

They're the perfect balance of béchamel and tuna with just a hint of onion, lightly fried so they explode with flavor on the first bite.

€€–€€€€   César Augusto is a star chef in the making who has worked with such seminal figures as Martín Berasategui and Ferran Adrià, founders of Spain's new cooking style. He runs the kitchen at **La Viuda Blanca** ★★★ (Campomanes 6; ☎ 915-25-52-14; www.laviudablanca.com; Tues–Sat 1:30–5pm and 9pm–midnight or later; AE, DC, MC, V; Metro: Opera), a surprisingly casual restaurant where even the 14€ *menu del día* shows real finesse. The midday menu includes short-cut plates like grilled vegetables, which are good but don't show Augusto's talents at their best. Opt instead for the menu's constructed dishes such as *pistou Manchego* (a ratatouille of typical La Mancha vegetables) with puff pastry and *bravas* sauce. The chef's style is even more pronounced in such evening entrees as lasagna composed of sheets of cured salmon, thin sheets of pasta, and tartar sauce of bittersweet and pickled cucumbers (12€).

€€€   It's a safe bet that the menu has barely changed since **La Bola Taberna** (Bola 5; ☎ 915-47-69-30; www.labola.es; 1–4pm and 8:30–11pm, closed Sun evening; cash only; Metro: Opera) opened for business in 1870. People make the pilgrimage here for *cocido madrileño*, a hearty stew of sausage and mixed cuts of meat (including tripe and other offal). It's a relatively expensive dish (18€), but you should try this Madrid classic at least once, preferably on a day when you're especially hungry . . . and not feeling squeamish.

€€€   Talk about culture clash! The same building on Plaza Isabel II houses a McDonald's at street level, and the elegant Basque **Asador Real** (Plaza Isabel II 1; ☎ 915-47-11-11; www.asadorreal.com; daily 1:30pm–midnight; AE, MC, V; Metro: Opera) downstairs with a door facing calle Escalinata. Given the proximity to the Teatro Real, the emphasis on substantial cuts of meat, and the formality of the restaurant, Asador Real has surprisingly reasonable prices. If you're so inclined, you can watch the grill masters prepare your food, though it seems gauche to stand there drooling as a baby pig or lamb sizzles in front of you. (One-quarter piglet or lamb serves 2 for under 35€.)

€€€€   Basque cuisine is also part of the draw at **Taberna del Alabardero** (Felipe V 6; ☎ 915-47-25-77; open for meals 1:30–4pm and 8–11pm, noon–midnight for drinks and tapas; MC, V; Metro: Opera), but so is the decor of tiled walls, wine skins on pegs, and hanging braids of garlic and dried peppers. It's more rustic-chic than true country, of course, as a glance at the menu will tell you. But it's probably the only place you'll find roast pheasant (22€) marinated in juniper berries and stuffed with the odd but tasty combination of mushrooms and pineapple. The full-fledged tasting menu is 49€, but it's just as much fun to hang out in the crowded bar for evening tapas or to enjoy afternoon nibbles at one of the tavern's tables on Plaza de Oriente.

€€€€   With its view of the Palacio Real, Plaza de Oriente is probably the most swank place in Madrid for outdoor dining, and the **Café de Oriente** (Plaza de Oriente 2; ☎ 915-41-39-74; cafe 10am–1am, dining rooms 1:30–4pm and

A Dining Revolution (Sort Of)

Once you've grown accustomed to the Spanish pace of dining late and slow, it can be a shock to the system to discover a group of popular, budget-priced restaurants that not only open for dinner at the unthinkable hour of 8:30pm, but also have a queue of Madrileños waiting to get it. They all operate on a formula of small portions and good prices for light international fare. Since similar urban bistros are found in most U.S. cities, the Madrid group hardly represents revolutionary dining, but each is a welcome and low-priced change from a steady diet of Spanish ham and cheese, and it's fun to see how Spaniards think it's all so novel.

The most popular of the group is Chueca's **Bazaar Restaurant** ★ (Libertad 21; ☎ 915-23-39-05; www.restaurantbazaar.com; daily 1:15–4pm and 8:30–11:45pm; AE, DC, MC, V; Metro: Chueca), where the kitchen is so fast that the restaurant turns the tables at least twice a night. Like other members in the group, its menu is a list of smaller dishes, so it's up to you to mix and match to make a meal. Salads are usually big enough to split, while main dishes (like whole roasted dorado for 8.90€ or chicken with sun-dried tomatoes, pine nuts, and fettuccine for 6.70€) are modest portions. As a general rule, the food's well-executed, offering very good value for the money and the atmosphere is trendy, with large windows on the main floor perfect for people-watching. The odd prices reflect the included taxes. Wine is available only by the bottle; to economize, order beer.

The more elegant venue of the group is **La Gloria de Montera** ★ (Caballero de Gracia 10; ☎ 915-23-44-07; www.lagloriademontera.com; 1:15–4pm and 8:30–11:45pm; AE, DC, MC, V: Metro: Gran Vía), just off Gran Vía. At lunchtime, you'll see folks in suits and ties (savvy economists from nearby banks, we imagine) tucking into such modern dishes (and anything in Spain that includes protein and vegetables on the same plate is modern) as grilled sea bass with green asparagus (10€) or risotto with asparagus and artichokes (6.65€). *Menu del día* is a good value at 8.95€.

Located amid the tapas bars of the Plaza Santa Ana district, **Ginger** ★ (Plaza San Angel 12; ☎ 913-69-10-59; 1:15–4pm and 8:30–11:45pm; AE, MC, V; Metro: Tirso de Molina) has an open feel similar to its siblings, with white tablecloths, cheerfully bright lighting, and the constant buzz of busy and excited diners. But the food is more Spanish, albeit in lightened form. For less than 8€, you can dine on black rice with black sausage and squid, or cod risotto with black olives. Even roasted monkfish with garlic, usually an expensive dish, is under 10€. They count on you running up the bar bill to make up the difference.

9pm–midnight; AE, DC, MC, V; Metro: Opera) is the fanciest place on the plaza. The complex's two indoor restaurants serve expensive French and Basque food, which is fine if you're getting engaged to royalty. (The lunchtime *menu del día* is 29€, and dinner easily runs 75€ each.) But if an outdoor cafe table is free, you can try this sniffy place for less, perhaps choosing a tiny but affordable sandwich of ham, cheese, and chicken (5.70€) or a tart of chicken with white and green asparagus (3.80€ a slice). Top it off with a *copa princessa* (6€) of scoops of vanilla and peach ice creams drenched in peach sauce. That's royal enough for us.

RESTAURANTS ON & NEAR GRAN VÍA

Before the Civil War, poets, painters, and bullfighters had their own cafe hangouts on Gran Vía. Alas, most of the luster is gone, and eating options now tend toward hotel dining and convenience food. There's even a Starbucks. But don't overlook the greatest slice of pop culture on the street, the vast cafeteria with the prominent neon signs, **Zahara** (p. 65).

€–€€   Or, for that matter, one of the original "American" cafeterias. Back in the 1950s, "American" food, especially burgers and ice cream, swept Madrid and chains sprang up with names like California and Nevada. One of the best is **Nebraska** 🧒 (Gran Vía 31, ☎ 915-22-63-08; Gran Vía 55, ☎ 915-42-53-19; also at Goya 39 in Salamanca, ☎ 914-35-46-39; Sun–Thurs 8am–12:45am, Fri–Sat 8am–1:15am; MC, V; Metro: Gran Vía). The Gran Vía 31 venue opened in 1955 and looks its age, with all that retro aluminum-trimmed Formica. There may be no food more American than a burger, but the Nebraska burger keeps its Spanish identity: The bacon cheeseburger with lettuce, tomato, and onion is topped with two fried eggs and a dollop of mustard (9€). More simple is a *mixto* sandwich of toasted ham and cheese (6€), the two main Spanish food groups.

€€–€€€   **Galopín Sidreria** (Caballero de Gracia 22; ☎ 915-21-46-27; 1–4pm and 8:30pm–midnight; AE, DC, MC, V; Metro: Gran Vía) upholds tradition as one of Madrid's best-loved Asturian cider houses—a style featuring hearty northern Spanish food appropriate for eating with the region's famous hard cider shipped from up north. (The huge barrel embedded in the wall is a dead giveaway.) The Asturians are legendary cod fishermen, so codfish figures prominently on the menu. But crab-stuffed red-pepper starters (2.50€ each) and roast duck breast main course (12€) are also perfect foils for the tangy house cider.

RESTAURANTS IN CHUECA & MALASAÑA

If all the restaurants in Madrid were up for roles in a Hollywood movie, they'd cast the character-actor parts from Chueca and Malasaña. Eateries here tend to have deep character lines and flaws that keep them from being the marquee names—but each does one thing better than anyone.

€   In some cases, that might be drink rather than food. In his tight jeans and delicate earring, Ramón Segersbol hardly looks the type to gush about an old-time working-man's bar—"the most ancient, the most beautiful!"—but Chueca is less rough-and-tumble than it used to be, and the handsome young barman at **Antigua Casa Ángel Sierra** (Gravina 11; ☎ 915-31-01-26; noon–2am; cash only;

Metro: Chueca) is justifiably proud of the Andalusian tiles and the cellar full of vermouth barrels. When the bar opened in 1917 as an outlet for a vermouth maker in Castille–La Mancha, people would bring their own bottles to have them filled. Now they stop by for a glass and a few tapas (1.50€–2.50€) such as tuna in *escabeche* (vinaigrette), sardines in oil, or smoked anchovies. The neighborhood may be in transition, but some things never change.

€–€€€ Also a classic neighborhood joint, **Bocaito** ★ (Libertad 4–6; ☎ 915-32-12-19; www.bocaito.com; Mon–Fri 1–4:30pm and 8:30pm–midnight, Sat 8:30pm–midnight; AE, DC, MC, V; Metro: Chueca) is packed nightly with an over-35 crowd that's eating, drinking, and talking boisterously. There are two bars (one side is ostensibly nonsmoking but shares the air with the smoking side), and many people order full meals to eat while standing up. A pork-chop plate with salad and fried potatoes is 9.90€, a plate of fried pork sweetbreads is 7.60€. But you can enjoy the scene just as well with an inexpensive *bocaito* (sandwich on a small bun) for 3€ or less.

€€ Since the mid-1970s, Peruvians have come to **El Inca** (Gravina 23; ☎ 915-32-77-45; daily 1–3pm, Mon–Sat 9pm–midnight; AE, MC, V; Metro: Chueca) for a taste of home. Best bet here is to elect one of two degustation menus (12€) to sample most of the kitchen's specialties, including a delectable lamb marinated in cilantro and dishes that use dried potatoes. Dessert? Split an order of the airy almond-lemon meringues called *suspiros* (6.50€).

€€ Patrons attending exhibits and concerts at the Centro Cultural Conde Duque often gravitate to **La Tabernilla del Gato Amadeus** (Cristo 2; ☎ 915-41-41-12; noon–4pm and 8pm–midnight, closed Mon midday; cash only; Metro: Plaza de España) for a bite and a sip. The bar is literally a hole in the wall. But chef-proprietor Monica Bardem, sister of Oscar-winning actor Javier, is known for ham (6.90€) and bacalao (7.25€) croquettes. House wine is sold by the bottle and priced by age: 12€ for the 2-year-old, 15€ for the smoother 4-year-old.

€€€–€€€€ We always cringe to watch the crowds eating at a place that serves Shang-Dong noodles, Yugoslav-style hamburgers, and Indonesian curry when right across the street, **Restaurante Salvador** ★ (Barbieri 12; ☎ 915-21-45-24; Mon–Sat 1:30–4pm and 9pm–midnight; MC, V; Metro: Chueca) oozes Andalusian color and flavor. Salvador is an immediate immersion in classic Spanish dining, from the walls covered with graphic bullfight photos to the close, ill-ventilated rooms that turn blue with cigarette smoke. In fact, a faded photo from the 1960s of matador El Cordobés with a cigarette drooping from his lips says everything about the attitude. It's a restaurant that Hemingway would have loved, had he ever visited the neighborhood. House specialties include a delicious soupy casserole of white beans and ham (8€). If the bull photos don't bother you, opt for a grilled veal chop (10€) or a gristly but flavorful sirloin steak (12€).

€€€–€€€€ Baker Jesus Tirado of Pastelería Gravina—a real Chueca character and a man who knows how to eat—first steered us to **Maitetxu Asador** ★★ (Alimirante 2; ☎ 915-31-01-09; open 1:30–4pm and 9–11:30pm, closed Sun and

Just a Bite

Jesus Tirado's father, from Granada, founded **Pastelería Gravina**, a.k.a. **La Casa de los Piononos** ✪✪ (Gravina 22; ☎ 915-21-57-16; Tues–Sun 9am–2:30pm and 5–8pm, Sun 9am–2:30pm; cash only; Metro: Chueca) back in 1954 with a recipe for Piononos that was given to him by the nuns of Santa Fé, near Granada. You can find this complex pastry all over Andalusia, but Tirado is one of the few artisans plying his trade in Madrid. The little treats consist of a sweet biscuit base filled with *crema Castellana,* topped with custard, and then soaked in sugar syrup. Each tray holds 55 *piononos* and Tirado makes four to five trays a day. "There's no fat except for the eggs and milk," he tells customers. They're so good that they inspired a poem—a copy of which hangs on the wall.

Mon–Wed evenings; MC, V; Metro: Chueca), a family-run grill in the southeast corner of Chueca. Thank you, Jesus! There are only a half-dozen tables and the wood-burning grill takes up a third of the room. Wherever you sit, you can watch the chef grill your *besugo* (sea bream), a splurge at 31€ per person and only made for two. Not everything is so pricey. The smaller sea bass is 15€, or delicious mountain baby lamb chops are 11€. The family's proud of their Basque heritage and promote the restaurant with the slogan *el norte en su plato* (the north on your plate).

RESTAURANTS IN PLAZA MAYOR & LA LATINA

There's no more public place to eat in Madrid than in sun-drenched Plaza Mayor, where establishments beneath the arcades all set out tables in the square. It's a kick to sit here and feel like you own the city. Expect to pay a premium for the privilege, but the pleasure is worth it, and if you don't take *all* your meals here, you'll hardly notice the dent in your wallet. Streets off the back of the plaza, especially Cava Baja and Cava San Miguel, are famed for their tapas bars.

€ And that bustling tapas scene on Cava Baja behind Plaza Mayor leads many bars to inflate prices to cash in on the tourist trade. That being said, it's hard to quibble with either quality or price at **Taberna Txakoli** (Cava Baja 26, ☎ 913-66-48-77; 1:30–4pm and 8pm–2am; cash only; Metro: La Latina), where the food and wine are *very* Basque (Basque food is generally considered the best in Spain) and very inexpensive. House wine is 1€ a glass, and brochettes of either squid, cod, or sirloin tips are 3€. The most expensive and most popular dish is the "Bomba"—a heap of mashed potatoes studded with meat and swimming in mushroom gravy (5€). You'll have to muscle your way to the bar to order, then back through the crowd to a place where you can eat standing up. The newer location at Cava Baja 42 is larger and brighter, but it's less of a scene.

€ Back on the Plaza Mayor itself, our first recommendation for frugal travelers who want to enjoy the plaza ambience is **Cervecería Plaza Mayor** (Plaza Mayor 2; ☎ 913-65-06-46; 7am–1am; cash only; Metro: Opera or La Latina). Because it's basically a beer hall with food rather than a restaurant with drinks, it's one of the best deals on the Square. Order a beer for 2.50€ (on tap) to 3.75€ (bottled) and add a few simple tapas like a slice of tortilla (3€), potatoes fried with garlic (3.50€), or fried slices of chorizo (7€) and sit as long as you like.

€–€€   Because it's located in a tangle of streets near Cava Baja and steps off Plaza San Andrés, visitors to Madrid usually find **Taberna Almendro 13** (Almendro 13; ☎ 913-65-42-52; 1:30–4:30pm and 8pm–1am; cash only; Metro: La Latina) only because it's touted by the city as one of Madrid's most historic taverns. A Hollywood set designer couldn't imagine a more "typical" Spanish bar, from the dark wood and ancient tiles right down to the barrel of manzanilla that you can order for 1.30€ per glass. In fact, when you go in, it will take a while for your eyes to adjust to the reduced illumination. The perfect complement to that mild sherry is a 3.60€ *ración* of *queso* and *membrillo* (cheese and quince paste). For a meal, it's hard to beat the *pisto* (ratatouille) with fried egg (8.40€ *racion*/5.70€ for a half portion). For authenticity's sake, do your eating and drinking while standing.

€–€€€   On a busy tapas-hopping night, Cava Baja begins to feel like a tunnel with the buildings on each side looming over you as you walk down the middle of the narrow street oblivious to traffic. But there is light at the end of the tunnel, where Cava Baja empties onto a broad square behind La Cebada market. Since it's not on the tourist maps (until now), **La Muralla II** (Plaza Puerta de Moros 7; ☎ 913-65-75-60; 8am–midnight; MC, V; Metro: La Latina) offers a beacon of relative calm. The plaza tables fill fast, but there's a warren of tiny rooms inside so tightly packed that you'll make instant friends with diners at surrounding tables. But there's far less yelling and smoking than in the tapas bars. People come here to eat. Most menu items are under 12€, and some much less, like the omelets with mushrooms, artichokes, or asparagus (5€–7€) or the fried calamari (9€). The *sopa castellana* (chicken broth with garlic, bread slices, and a poached egg) and a loaf of country bread will only set you back 5€, but it's only 4€ more for the *menu del día*.

€€   Chef Gary Morales of **La Camarilla Restaurante Taberna** (Cava Baja 21; ☎ 913-52-02-07; www.lacamarillarestaurante.com; Fri–Tues 1:30–5pm, Sun–Thurs 9pm–midnight, Fri–Sat 9pm–1am; DC, MC, V; Metro: La Latina) has figured out how a restaurant can thrive on a street where most diners go for tapas. In addition to his usual entrees, he offers a *menu tapeo*. For 17€, the diner gets a choice of two tapas dishes, soup, and pastry. Extremely popular with young Madrileños for its beautifully plated (and delicious) food and its roomy tables with comfortable chairs, Camarilla is a welcome sit-down alternative to the standing-room-only tapas scene of Cava Baja.

€€–€€€€   Hemingway did actually eat at **Restaurante Botín** (Cuchilleros 17; ☎ 913-66-42-17; www.botin.es; 1–4pm and 8pm–midnight; AE, DC, MC, V; Metro: Opera), later identified by the Guinness Book of World Records as the oldest restaurant in the world (1725). It's a charming tourist trap with tasty if expensive food. As you enter, peek into the kitchen to see racks of suckling pigs ready to go

Location, Location, Location

Once you've settled on a place for lunch or dinner, *where* you sit (or stand) will have some bearing on the final tally of your bill. Expect to pay a premium of up to 20% for outdoor dining. And even if you opt for eating indoors, sitting at a table will likely cost you 5% to 10% more than standing at the bar.

into the wood oven. The 37€ menu gets you garlic soup, said suckling pig, a drink, and ice cream. But you can enjoy the atmosphere and eat just as well on roast chicken for 10€.

€€€   Just across the street, it's always tempting to drink more than you eat at **Restaurante Vinoteca Maestro Villa** ✮ (Cava de San Miguel 8; ☎ 913-64-20-36; www.restaurantemaestrovilla.es; 1–4:30pm and 8pm–midnight; AE, DC, MC, V; Metro: Opera), where house wines are only 1.20€, and regional wines from the deep list only cost 1.40€ to 3€ per glass, including the cavas and well-aged reds from Ribera del Duero. Tostas (5€–6€) make the perfect complement—Cabrales cheese and jelly with a randy Rioja, salmon, and cream cheese with a tart Rueda. This elegant dining room stands out from the old-fashioned bars of the neighborhood, so it's not surprising that the menu is upscale Basque, the traditional gourmet cuisine of Madrid. It's a great spot to try stewed veal cheeks (18€).

RESTAURANTS IN LAVAPIÉS

Long one of Madrid's poorer working-class neighborhoods, Lavapiés has become a magnet for new immigrants. Two styles of eating predominate: old-fashioned bar food, and inexpensive sit-down dining on kebabs and other Near Eastern fare.

€   **Toma que Toma** ✮ (corner del Carnero and Ribera de los Curtidores; no phone; 1:30pm–midnight or later; cash only; Metro: Puerta de Toledo) is of the bar persuasion, and your introduction to the establishment may well be on a Sunday, when El Rastro flea market is in full swing and shoppers stream into this handsomely tiled watering hole to snack on cheap tostas (1€–3€) of shrimp or sliced sausage. But the place hops all week as neighbors come by to watch sports on TV while they hoist a pint. The food is tasty and cheap, and the company is convivial. What more could you ask from a bar?

€–€€   Try to visit **Alquezar** ✮✮ (Lavapiés 53; ☎ 915-27-72-61; 1:30–6pm and 8pm–midnight; cash only; Metro: Lavapiés) on the weekend, when the mother of this family-run Arabic restaurant hand-rolls her own couscous and simmers delicious chicken or lamb tagines to accompany it (8.50€). The rest of the week, settle for beef or chicken kebab plates accompanied by a pilaf of rice studded with vegetables, raisins, and almonds (8.50€ each or 9.50€ combo). By your second visit, the proprietors might hug you like family.

€€   Few establishments in Lavapiés have accreted more local color than **Taberna de Antonio Sanchez** ✮✮ (Méson de Paredes 13; ☎ 915-39-78-36; meals

1:30–4pm and 8–11pm, bar noon–midnight; cash only; Metro: Tirso de Molina). Founded in 1830, the walls are covered with faded (but signed) photos of matadors and a mounted bull's head. Although there is a tiny, smoky dining room far in the back (entrees 8.50€–14€), the *taberna* might offer the barrio's most varied tapas, including small 3€ casseroles of meatballs, white beans, or sausage in wine. A tapa-size serving of *cocido madrileño* (3€) or Madrid-style tripe (8€) will let you try these dishes without damaging your budget.

€€–€€€   Famed for some of the best live flamenco performances in Madrid (p. 72), **Casa Patas** (Cañizares 10; ☎ 914-29-64-71; www.casapatas.com; Mon-Sat 1–4:30pm, Mon–Thurs 8pm–midnight, Fri-Sat 7:30pm–1am; MC, V; Metro: Antón Martín or Tirso de Molina) is also a surprisingly good place to eat, whether or not you're planning to stay for the show (which is in a separate room in the back). The choices of hams, cheeses, and sausages at the bar rank among Madrid's best, while the dinner menu has pickled partridge (10€) and suckling lamb chops (16€).

RESTAURANTS IN & NEAR PLAZA SANTA ANA

Some people claim that the streets around Plaza Santa Ana gave birth to the tapas-hopping phenomenon, in part because it was a good way to get a light meal before or after the performances at one of the theaters, for which the area has been known for 400 years—and still is. Alas, some of the colorful seediness of the district has been cleaned up in recent years, but it's still a great area to eat cheaply and well.

€€   Also colorfully. Old bullfight photos, half a dozen hams hanging from the ceiling, pitchers of sangria on the bar, and Camarón de la Isla's mournful voice on the sound system—**Tia Cebolla Taberna** (Cruz 22; ☎ 915-22-90-50; 2pm–2am; cash only; Metro: Sevilla) has every Spanish restaurant cliché down pat. Give a pass to the midday menu (where spaghetti is a staple), and chow down on what might be the most generous free tapas in the barrio when you order drinks. (Tuna empanadas, a savory turnover, could make a light meal.) Or order a bottle of wine (11€–14€) and a plate of dried beef, Iberian ham, chorizo, and Manchego cheese to split for 15€.

Tapas Bars Around Plaza Santa Ana

So-called tapas restaurants in the U.S. usually encourage customers to settle in at a table and order lots and lots of small plates of food. But tapas are ideally eaten standing at a bar and should be a movable feast: Enjoy the specialty of the house, and then move on to the next stop. Plaza Santa Ana has one of the best concentrations of tapas bars, which start serving food between noon and 2pm and remain open until the last customer staggers out in the early morning. Peak hours for tapas are usually 6 to 9pm, and a place that was empty at 5pm will have people drinking in the street by 7pm. We find tapas-hopping ideal for eating an early dinner. It's also a great way to try food you're not sure you'll like (like tripe), or specialties that are too expensive for a full meal. Most tapas bars don't take credit cards, even if their attached restaurants do. Cash keeps the pace moving. You should do the same.

€   **Las Bravas** ✗ (Espoz y Mina 13; ☎ 915-21-35-07; 1pm–1am; cash only; Metro: Sevilla) claims to have invented the Spanish bar staple, *patatas bravas.* They hold a patent on the spicy red paprika sauce, which they also serve on pig's ear (3.90€), fried baby squid (9.35€), chicken wings (5.10€), and a whole 6-inch tortilla Española (3.45€). We always grab a ledge on the mirror-covered wall so we can keep track of how much sauce we've smeared on our faces and clothes.

€   "Cinco Jotas" (or "5J") refers to the highest possible score in a ham grading system employed in Jabugo in Andalusia. The 5J ham sells at a premium, but once you've tasted it, it's as hard go back to generic *jamón* serrano than to switch from single-malt Scotch to cheap beer. Try it at **Méson Cinco Jotas** (Plaza Santa Ana 1; ☎ 915-22-63-64; www.mesoncincojotas.com; noon–1am; AE, DC, MC, V; Metro: Antón Martín), where the 5J tapa (3.60€) consists of three paper-thin squares of ham to wrap around five conical crackers. If you like the gamy taste more than the gummy texture, order the *caña de lomo* 5J tapa (4€) for a larger helping of sausage made from the same grade of ham.

€   If you're among the fortunate, you'll score standing room at the bar or one of the seats on the elevated platform in the back at **La Venencia** (Echegaray 7; ☎ 914-29-62-61; noon–midnight; cash only; Metro: Sevilla). If so, you're in for about as Andalusian a drinking experience as you can find in Madrid. La Venencia serves *fino, oloroso,* and *amontillado* sherries straight from the cask—or famous marques from the bottle. (Cask sherry is common in Andalusia, but rare in Madrid.) Drinking is primary here, and eating secondary. We like to nibble some pickled sardines or roasted peppers (2€–4€) while savoring the taste of Spain's most famous wines.

€   On a Sunday afternoon, it seems like everybody *but* Hemingway is tossing back draft beer and munching on *montaditos* (tasty bits mounted on a diagonal slice of baguette) at **Cervecería La Fábrica** ✗ (Jesus 2; ☎ 913-69-30-67; 1:30pm–1am; MC, V; Metro: Antón Martín). The variety is jaw dropping, especially if you like fish. Most flavor for the euro are the smoked tuna and the combination of blue cheese with salt-packed anchovies. Prices range from 1.80€ to 2.20€.

€–€€   The quintessential fish tapas of Madrid, however, belong without question to **La Trucha** ✗ (Manuel Fernández y González 3; ☎ 914-29-58-33; noon–1am; AE, MC, V; Metro: Antón Martín), just off the northeast corner of Plaza Santa Ana. Go for the house specialty of smoked trout (one slice on toast for 2€, a whole plate for 11€), or the salad of mixed smoked fish (6.60€). Draft beer is only 1.25€. The dinner menu features a homemade special each day for 6.70€ to 11€.

€€   It's all shrimp all the time at "Grandpa's House," as **La Casa del Abuelo** ✗ (Victoria 12; ☎ 915-21-23-19; www.lacasadelabuelo.es; 1:30pm–1am; DC, MC, V; Metro: Sevilla) translates. There's another location nearby, but stick with the calle Victoria space, opened in 1906, for its patina of age. Fortunately, this bar accepts credit cards, as the *cuenta* counts up quickly when you indulge (as you should) in the house shrimp specialties. *Gambas* plainly grilled or sizzled with garlic run 7.20€ to 7.90€; a smaller serving breaded and fried in olive oil is 7.20€. If you like the house wine (1.90€ a glass), buy a bottle to go for 7.50€.

Top 10 Tapas

Traditional bars usually provide a free tapa such as potato chips or olives each time you order another beer or wine. You can buy more substantial tapas from a list either on a chalkboard or printed menu. At some bars, you're expected to look at selections under glass and simply choose. Here are the tapas dishes you're most likely to encounter:

Tortilla Española. Thick Spanish omelet with potato, usually served by the slice.

Pimientos rellenos. Skinless red peppers usually stuffed with tuna or cod.

Croquetas. Small fitters of thick béchamel sauce with ham, tuna, or cod.

Jamón serrano. Thin slices of air-cured mountain ham.

Jamón ibérico de bellota. Highly prized air-cured mountain ham from Iberian black pig fed entirely on acorns. Most expensive ham in the world.

Queso Manchego. Slices of the nutty sheep's-milk cheese of La Mancha.

Gambas a la plancha. Shrimp grilled in their shells.

Morcilla. Cooked slices of spicy blood sausage, served with bread.

Chorizo. Slices of smoked pork sausage seasoned heavily with Spanish paprika.

Boquerones/Anchoas. White anchovies in vinegar or anchovies in oil served with toast.

RESTAURANTS NEAR THE MUSEUMS

It's a cardinal rule of travel that eating spots near major attractions usually offer convenience over value or quality. (That's why you see the American fast food chains.) The rule holds true in Madrid—with a few great exceptions.

€   In fact, some of our favorite cheap eats in Madrid are found at **El Brillante** ★★ (Atocha 122; ☎ 914-68-05-48; 6:30am–midnight or later; cash only; Metro: Atocha), a place so large that one door faces the Atocha train station and another faces the Reina Sofía. Madrileños flock here for sandwiches on fresh rolls. The specialty of the house is the fried calamari sandwich, but the choices range from sliced pork with cheese or peppers to anchovies with tomatoes or the veggie delight of asparagus, lettuce, tomato, and mayonnaise. *Mini-bocadillos* are 2.50€ to 2.75€; 10-inch *super bocatas* are 4€ to 5.60€. Whatever you order, you'll probably have to eat it standing at one of the stainless-steel bars. Chairs are few and far between.

€€€   Dining at superchef Sergi Arola's Madrid flagship restaurant, Gastro, would set you back 140€ per person, but you can get a taste of his style at the **Café-Restaurante Arola Madrid** ★ (Museo Reina Sofía extension, Argumosa 43; ☎ 914-67-02-02; www.arola-madrid.com; cafe Mon and Wed–Sat 10am–9pm, Sun

Cool Stuff

In case you hadn't noticed, Madrileños are mad for ice cream, and **Giangrossi** ★★ (Velazquez 44; ☎ 917-81-30-73; www.giangrossi.es; Mon–Fri 8am–1am, Sat 9am–1am, Sun noon–1am; cash only; Metro: Goya) makes some of the best in town. Hard-core fans order the five-flavor sampler for 6.50€, maybe mixing scoops of lemon, mango, pineapple, and honey-macadamia. The shop also sells pastries and coffee, since not everyone eats ice cream for breakfast.

10am–5pm; restaurant Wed–Mon 1–4pm; AE, V; Metro: Atocha). The futuristic space is what Madrileños call "New York style" and what New Yorkers would probably call "L.A. style." Alternating walls of cool gray and hot red, low benches, molded white plastic tables, and an all stainless-steel bar produce a chic industrial look, while the food is traditional Spanish bar fare given Arola's own twist. His *patatas bravas* (14€–18€) are elegant stuffed rolls of potato, and he turns blood sausage into punchy little panini (6€).

€€€–€€€€   From the 1860s until the Spanish Civil War, Madrid boasted a lively cafe society where *tertulias*—discussion groups—met to air opinions about art, life, and politics. Franco's dictatorship put an end to public discussion, and hence to many of Madrid's grand cafes. Nowadays the people at the tables at **Café Gijon** (Paseo de Recoletos 21; ☎ 915-22-37-37; www.cafegijon.com; cafe daily 10am–midnight, dining salon 1–4pm and 8–11pm; Metro: Banco de España) are more likely to be savoring the plate of assorted canapes (16€) or shrimp sautéed in olive oil with garlic (28€) than discussing the next leader of the ruling party. But you can still savor the Belle Epoche ambience of the 1888 cafe over prof-iteroles (5.90€) and a *café con leche* (2.50€).

RESTAURANTS IN SALAMANCA

Salamanca is the moneyed quarter of central Madrid, and restaurants here tend to cater to the deep-pocketed residents. Choose carefully, though, and you can eat like a king on a plowman's budget.

€   In the last few years, the high priests of contemporary Spanish haute cuisine have tried to bring the quality and some of the imagination of their food to casual dining. Ferran Adriá, Spain's most celebrated chef, says simply, "Ours is a splendid cuisine, born out of the pleasure of eating. . . ." He has partnered with NH Hoteles on **Fast Good** (Juan Bravo 3; ☎ 915-77-41-51; www.fast-good.com; Mon–Fri 8am–midnight, Sat–Sun noon–midnight; MC, V; Metro: Nuñez de Balboa). The name says it all, keeping in mind that names in English have special cachet for Spaniards. Grab a metal shopping basket to select salads, drinks, desserts, and prepared sandwiches. When you reach the cashier, you're ready to go—or you can order a hot dish that's ready in minutes. Meal-size healthy salads (escarole and apple, or noodles with shredded chicken) are under 6€. Roast chicken with a choice of potatoes, couscous, or rice is also under 6€. You can also order lean, perfectly grilled burgers at 5.50€ to 6.50€.

€€–€€€   Chef Pedro Larumbe's **Salon La Biblioteca** (Serrano 61, 4th Floor; ☎ 915-75-11-12; www.larumbe.com; 1:30–4:30pm; AE, DC, MC, V; Metro: Serrano) is the budget alternative to his adjacent upscale dining room in the ABC shopping center. Alas, it's only open for the midday meal. Spring for the *menu del día* (18€) and you'll feast on the salad buffet, a main course of meat or fish, dessert, and a drink. You can eat more lightly on a ham and cheese sandwich and fries (3.20€) or skewers of fish and baby squid (9.80€). Prices are slightly higher on the rooftop terrace with great views of surrounding architecture.

€€€   Talk about efficiency: You can have a great meal and get your shoes shined at the same time at **José Luis** ★★★ (Serrano 89/91; ☎ 914-84-43-00; www. joseluis.es; daily 9am–1am; AE, MC, V; Metro: Gregorio Marañon), a local favorite since it opened in 1957. The dining room (noon–4pm and 8pm–midnight) has a genial elegance (entrees 12€–20€), but it's not uncommon for patrons to consume an entire meal of soup, salad, fish, and dessert while perched on a bar stool in the *cerveceria,* which also has some of the city's best pinchos at 1.90€ to 3.50€. Try the egg and shrimp salad montadita (3€) with a draft beer, followed by a slice of the heavenly *tarta de limón* (4€). The shoeshine man does a steady business with customers who stand at the bar near the door.

WHY YOU'RE HERE: THE TOP SIGHTS & ATTRACTIONS

Madrileños keep late hours, so you can pack a lot into even one day. But don't rush. It's better, we think, to experience a few things fully rather than to see everything in a blur. Remember that lingering in cafes, bars, and restaurants is a big part of the Madrid experience.

SUGGESTED ITINERARIES

If You Have Only 1 Day in Madrid

Begin at the **Museo Nacional del Prado** (p. 48) and concentrate on works by the great Spanish painters Velázquez and Goya. Then, from the broad *paseos* of Bourbon Madrid, head to the narrow streets surrounding **Plaza Santa Ana** (p. 41), where Spain's literary Golden Age bloomed in the 16th century. You'll have plenty of time to immerse yourself in the tapas scene around the plaza before you take in a late-night flamenco performance at **Casa Patas** (p. 72). And you'll still have time for hot chocolate and *churros* at **Chocolatería San Ginés** (p. 32) before it closes at 6am. (Repeat nightly if staying longer.)

If You Have Only 2 Days in Madrid

Stick with the one-day itinerary and begin your second day amid pomp and circumstance at the **Palacio Real** (p. 52). Stroll the palace gardens and linger in elegant **Plaza de Oriente.** Walking down calle Mayor from the new **Catedral Santa María de La Almudena** (p. 54), you'll pass the ancient Plaza de la Villa on your way to claim an outdoor table at **Plaza Mayor** (p. 60), perhaps the city's liveliest gathering spot. Plan to get an overview of Madrid history at nearby **Museo de San Isidro** (p. 61). For the evening, take your choice of bars and restaurants along the lively street **Cava Baja** (p. 38).

Madrid Attractions

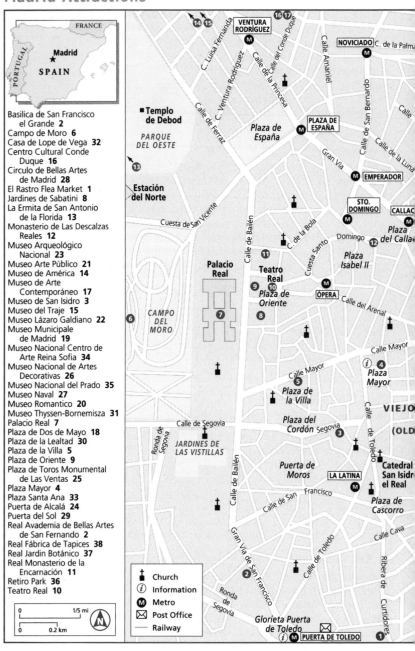

Basilica de San Francisco
  el Grande **2**
Campo de Moro **6**
Casa de Lope de Vega **32**
Centro Cultural Conde
  Duque **16**
Circulo de Bellas Artes
  de Madrid **28**
El Rastro Flea Market **1**
Jardines de Sabatini **8**
La Ermita de San Antonio
  de la Florida **13**
Monasterio de Las Descalzas
  Reales **12**
Museo Arqueológico
  Nacional **23**
Museo Arte Público **21**
Museo de América **14**
Museo de Arte
  Contemporáneo **17**
Museo de San Isidro **3**
Museo del Traje **15**
Museo Lázaro Galdiano **22**
Museo Municipale
  de Madrid **19**
Museo Nacional Centro de
  Arte Reina Sofia **34**
Museo Nacional de Artes
  Decorativas **26**
Museo Nacional del Prado **35**
Museo Naval **27**
Museo Romantico **20**
Museo Thyssen-Bornemisza **31**
Palacio Real **7**
Plaza de Dos de Mayo **18**
Plaza de la Lealtad **30**
Plaza de la Villa **5**
Plaza de Oriente **9**
Plaza de Toros Monumental
  de Las Ventas **25**
Plaza Mayor **4**
Plaza Santa Ana **33**
Puerta de Alcalá **24**
Puerta del Sol **29**
Real Avademia de Bellas Artes
  de San Fernando **2**
Real Fábrica de Tapices **38**
Real Jardin Botánico **37**
Real Monasterio de la
  Encarnación **11**
Retiro Park **36**
Teatro Real **10**

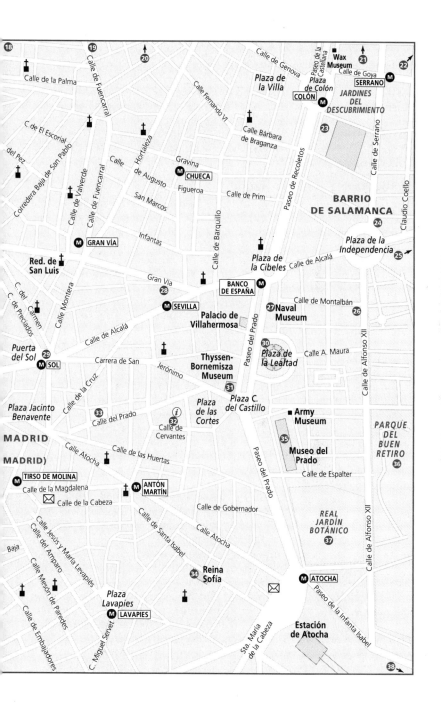

Calle de la Palma

Calle de la Palma

Calle de Fuencarral

C. de El Escorial

del Pez

Corredera Baja de San Pablo

Calle de Valverde

Calle de Fuencarral

Calle

Hortaleza

Calle de Augusto

San Marcos

Gravina

Figueroa

CHUECA

Infantas

GRAN VÍA

Red. de
San Luis

Gran Vía

C. del Carmen

C. de Precados

Calle Montera

Calle de la Cruz

Puerta
del Sol

SOL

Carrera de San

Jerónimo

Plaza Jacinto
Benavente

MADRID

MADRID)

Calle del Prado

Calle de Cervantes

Calle de las Huertas

Calle Atocha

TIRSO DE MOLINA

Calle de la Magdalena

Calle de la Cabeza

ANTÓN
MARTÍN

Calle de Santa Isabel

Calle Jesús y María

Calle del Amparo

Baja

Calle Mesón de Paredes

Levapiés

Plaza
Lavapies

LAVAPIES

Calle de Embajadores

C. Miguel Servet

Reina
Sofía

Sta. María
de la Cabeza

Estación
de Atocha

Calle de Genova

Plaza de
la Villa

Calle Fernando VI

Calle Bárbara
de Braganza

Paseo de la
Castellana

Wax
Museum

Calle de Goya

Plaza
de Colón

COLÓN

SERRANO

JARDINES
DEL
DESCUBRIMIENTO

Paseo de Recoletos

Calle de Prim

Calle de Barquillo

Plaza de
la Cibeles

Calle de Alcalá

BANCO
DE ESPAÑA

SEVILLA

Palacio de
Villahermosa

Thyssen-
Bornemisza
Museum

Plaza
de las
Cortes

Plaza C.
del Castillo

Calle de Gobernador

Calle Atocha

Paseo del Prado

Paseo del Prado

Naval
Museum

Calle de Montalbán

Plaza de
la Lealtad

Calle A. Maura

Army
Museum

Museo del
Prado

Calle de Espalter

REAL
JARDÍN
BOTÁNICO

ATOCHA

Paseo de la Infanta Isabel

Calle de Serrano

Claudio Coello

BARRIO
DE SALAMANCA

Plaza de la
Independencia

Calle Serrano

PARQUE
DEL
BUEN
RETIRO

Calle de Alfonso XII

Calle de Alfonso XII

If You Have Only 3 or 4 Days in Madrid

Add a visit to the **Centro de Arte Reina Sofía** (p. 51), where the collections pick up where the Prado leaves off. Don't miss Picasso's *Guernica* but leave some time for the whimsy of Miró. Time a window-shopping visit to the upscale **Salamanca** neighborhood to enjoy a leisurely lunch among Madrileños at **José Luis** (p. 45); then complete your excursion to the good life with a visit to the **Casa-Museo Sorolla** (p. 63). Even if you've passed through **Puerta del Sol** (p. 12) on foot or by Metro, allow yourself a couple of hours to get caught up in the scene and shop at **El Corte Inglés** (p. 71).

If You Have 1 Week in Madrid

Split your Sunday between family-friendly **Parque del Retiro** (p. 50) and the market frenzy at **El Rastro** (p. 62). Reserve an afternoon to shop and explore the up-and-coming neighborhoods of **Chueca** and **Malasaña** and linger into the evening for drinking and dining. To explore a Madrid neighborhood in depth, select one of the walking tours offered by the city tourist office. For more insight into Spanish history and character, visit the **Museo Naval, Museo de América** (p. 59), or tour **Las Ventas** (p. 66) bullring. Art lovers should visit **Museo Thyssen-Bornemisza** (p. 50), a major collection with less emphasis on Spanish art. Buy tickets for an opera at **Teatro Real** (p. 74) or a zarzuela performance at **Teatro Lírico Nacional de la Zarzuela** (p. 74).

ATTRACTIONS AROUND THE MUSEUMS

We think of the Paseo del Prado and the area around Madrid's top art museums as the city's other royal quarter, which developed from the 17th-century royal retreat known as Buen Retiro. Carlos III opened the district to the public in the late 18th century when he had architect Ventura Rodríguez create a boulevard on the west side of the property. The road became the elegant **Paseo del Prado,** which with the Paseo de Recoletos and Paseo de Castellana forms the north-south artery through the city. The fountains on mythological themes—**Cibeles** at the juncture with Alcalá and **Neptuno** at Plaza de Cortes—have been emblematic of regal Bourbon Madrid ever since.

Madrid's single biggest draw is the **Museo Nacional del Prado** ✯✯✯ (Paseo del Prado; ☎ 913-30-28-00; http://museoprado.mcu.es; Tues–Sun 9am–8pm; 6€ adults, 3€ students, seniors and 17 and under free, free Tues–Sat 6–8pm and Sun 5–8pm; Metro: Atocha or Banco de España). It was created by Fernando VI in 1819 to consolidate the royal art collections—hence, all those portraits of Spanish kings and their families—and to prove to the rest of Europe that Spanish art was equal to that of any other nation.

Felipe was right. The Prado exhibits a mind-numbing 1,300 works at a time, but when in Spain, concentrate on the Spaniards (the strength of the collection anyway), even if it takes a little gallery-hopping. You can begin at the beginning with the often overlooked but powerful Romanesque mural paintings from Santa Cruz de Maderuelo displayed in a re-created chapel in the basement.

The greatest works by El Greco (1541–1614) are found in Toledo (p. 83), as the Prado came late to an appreciation of this singular master, not even classifying him as a Spanish artist until after 1910. But other museums that have been absorbed into the Prado thought better of El Greco. Make a point of visiting **Sala**

> ## In Stitches
>
> Francisco de Goya got his first big break when Carlos III commissioned him and his brother-in-law to paint sylvan and pastoral idylls as cartoons for tapestries to decorate the Palacio Real de El Pardo. Most of Goya's cartoon paintings now hang in the Prado. To see where the tapestries were made, visit the **Real Fábrica de Tapices** (Fuenterrábia 2; ☎ 914-34-05-50; www.realfabricadetapices.com; Mon–Fri 10am–2pm; closed Aug; 3€ adults, 2€ children; Metro: Atocha). The factory was founded in 1721, and weavers still use the 18th-century looms.

10A to study the haunting aspect of *The Nobleman with his Hand on his Chest* and the swirling composition of *Adoration of the Shepherds.*

One charm of the Prado is that, while its collections are far from encyclopedic, they're often deep. The museum owns 50 paintings by Diego Velázquez—arguably the best 50 that survive. They occupy an entire suite of galleries (**Salas 12–16).** You've seen reproductions of the royal family portrait called *Las Meninas* a thousand times, but the large and masterful painting will captivate you in person. The focus of the painting is on the young infanta Margarita (daughter of Felipe IV) and her diminutive ladies in waiting. It is easily the most popular painting in the Prado with 3-foot-tall grade-school students.

For the last 37 years of his life, Velázquez was the court painter to Felipe IV, a king only a few years his junior. He painted the king as a vacuous-looking young man, as a thoughtful king in middle age, and as an aging ruler weary from grief and depression—a remarkable psychological progression that the painter witnessed firsthand, and perhaps shared.

Since most paintings by Velázquez were never seen by the public until they were deposited in the Prado, Francisco de Goya (1746–1828) found it an immense boon to gain access to the royal palaces when he began working for the crown in the late 1770s. For the rest of his life, he cited Velázquez as one of his most important influences.

Goya's mature work, especially after Carlos IV made him court painter in 1799, shows an understanding of character on a par with Velázquez. *The Family of Carlos IV* in **Sala 32,** painted in 1801, shows a burly king uncomfortable in his finery who would rather hunt than rule. In 1808, Carlos abdicated when the going got tough, and his foolish son invited Napoleon in to tidy up Spain.

Goya captured the horrors of the French occupation in *The Executions on Principe Pío Hill,* a *cri de coeur* that ranks with Picasso's *Guernica* and complements his heroic *Dos de Mayo* showing the popular uprising in Puerta del Sol. These late paintings that made his modern reputation are found in **Salas 38** and **39.** The especially somber Dark Paintings, such as *Saturn Devouring One of His Sons,* would inspire German Expressionists a century later.

Concentrating *entirely* on Spanish art in the Prado will cost you dearly, as the collections span a millennium of European painting. Some of the works are so famous, you'd expect them to be in their own national museums: Fra Angelico's sweet *Annunciation* (**Sala 49**) and the nightmarish *Garden of Earthly Delights* by Hieronymus Bosch (**Sala 56A**).

Temporary exhibitions, often highlighting new acquisitions, are mounted in the smoothly unassuming new wing of the Prado designed by Rafael Moneo and opened in November 2007. The subtle building, centerpiece of the 152€-million renovation, also holds a delightful surprise: the reassembled 16th-century cloister from the adjacent San Jerónimo church.

Walk north from the Prado along the Paseo, and you'll soon pass the **Plaza de la Lealtad,** where an eternal flame pays homage to the martyrs of the Dos de Mayo uprising, so vividly depicted by Goya.

Just past the plaza is a rare military museum worth a visit: **Museo Naval** ✪ (Paseo del Prado 5; ☎ 915-23-87-89; www.museonavalmadrid.com; free admission; Tues–Sun 10am–2pm; Metro: Atocha or Banco de España), which covers the greatest hits of Spanish naval preeminence, including the discovery and exploration of the Americas and Pacific, the Spanish Armada, and the feared Spanish galleons of the 17th and 18th centuries. A scale model of Columbus's flagship, the *Santa Maria,* shows what a fat little tub it was. By contrast, the large cutaway models of a circa-1700 galleon bristling with cannons can be seen as the birth of the modern battleship. Coverage of the Battle of Trafalgar is so grand that you could forget that the Spanish lost. We marvel over Juan de la Cosa's handwritten map of 1500, said to be the oldest map of Europe that shows the Americas—including such inhabitants as men with faces in their stomachs. *Important note:* Have your passport handy when you arrive at the museum as you must show official national identification and submit all bags for X-ray. Only 300 visitors at a time are allowed, so go early on weekends to avoid waiting.

Just north of the Museo Naval, is the city's most domesticated museum, **Museo Nacional de Artes Decorativas** (Montalbán 12; ☎ 915-32-64-99; http://mnartes decorativas.mcu.es; Mon–Sat 9am–3pm, Sun 10am–3pm; 2.40€, free Thurs 5–8pm; Metro: Banco de España). Displays can be encyclopedic (and between you and me, only a scholar could tell one blue-and-white glazed plate from another). The reconstructed 18th-century Valencian kitchen, however, with its exuberant tiles from Manises is truly memorable.

A short walk north of the museum is the grand **Puerta de Alcalá,** the city gate on Plaza de Independencia constructed for Carlos III. Originally a symbol of royal majesty, it has become a symbol of Spain—the Arc de Triomphe and the Statue of Liberty rolled into one.

As you look at the arch, you're standing at the "front gate" of **Parque del Retiro** ✪ (6am–10pm in winter, 6am–midnight in summer). Carlos III was the first king to open the grounds to the public, and Madrileños have been flocking here ever since, especially on weekends. Check at the entry for the list of free concerts on Saturday and Sunday evenings May through September. Even winter chills don't discourage Madrileños with their kids and their dogs. Any sunny weekend you'll see tarot readers, tai chi practitioners, and puppet shows playing to rapt audiences of children sitting on the ground. Street musicians provide the soundtrack, and for 4.40€ you can rent a rowboat for 45 minutes on the man-made lake constructed so Felipe IV could stage mock naval battles.

Back to art. The Baron Thyssen-Bornemisza compiled one of the 20th century's great private art collections and in 1993 sold it to Spain. Today called the **Museo Thyssen-Bornemisza** ✪✪ (Paseo del Prado 8; ☎ 913-65-01-91;

www.museothyssen.org; Tues–Sun 10am–7pm; 6€ adults, students and seniors 4€, free for children 11 and under; Metro: Banco de España), it's a perfect complement to the adjacent Prado, filling in some of that larger museum's gaps in European art. Spanning the 13th to 20th centuries, the Madrid portion of the collection (part of it, a smaller part, is in Barcelona), resides in the late 18th-century Villahermosa Palace (redesigned inside by Rafael Moneo to function as a museum). It's been supplemented recently by the collection of the Baron's wife, Carmen. In 2004, the museum opened a new 40€-million, 86,000-square-foot wing to display her purchases. The collections remain separate but equal, with the Baron's showing great strengths in Italian and German Gothic art and 20th-century German Expressionism. Carmen also scored some outstanding German Expressionist works and showed a real affinity for the Spanish Moderns (Picasso, Dalí, and Miró) as well as Abstract Expressionist works by Americans.

The museum is just coming to grips with marrying the two collections, so sometimes the walk-through on a given floor has some awkward transitions. On **Floor 1,** move quickly through the Dutch and Flemish masters—by the time the Baron started buying, the field was pretty picked over—to get to the Impressionist and later work. After galleries filled with brown-toned canvases, **Sala 32** brightens with paintings by Manet. When you enter **Sala 34,** the explosion of primary colors and bold pointillism of André Derain's *Waterloo Bridge* signals a modern sensibility. Keep moving, as it gets even better in the Expressionist galleries, where Ernst Ludwig Kirschner stars on the Baron's side, and Max Pechstein on Carmen's.

It's only a 6-block walk down the Paseo and around the Atocha roundabout to the **Museo Nacional Centro de Arte Reina Sofía** ✪✪✪ (Santa Isabel 52; ☎ 917-74-10-00; www.museoreinasofia.es; Mon and Wed–Sat 10am–9pm, Sun 10am–2:30pm; 6€ adults, free students and seniors, free for all Sat 2:30–9pm and Sun; Metro: Atocha). By providing an international context for 20th- and 21st-century Spanish art, the Reina Sofía picks up where the Thyssen-Bornemisza and Prado leave off. Until the museum reconfigures floors 1 and 3, exhibition galleries are limited to floors 2 and 4.

The **second floor** views the history of modern art through Spanish eyes, citing Pablo Picasso, Juan Gris, Joan Miró, and Salvador Dalí as the polestars of every pre–World War II art movement. Thus, the avant-garde galleries that show Picasso and Gris also display works by Braque, Léger, Jacques Lipchitz, and the Delaunays—all of whom had close ties to Spain.

The most powerful section of Floor 2 is dedicated to *Guernica,* Picasso's 1937 warning to the world of the barbarism overtaking Spain—and soon, Europe. Picasso would not allow the work to return to Spain as long as Franco lived; now it is the most venerated painting in Madrid. Surrounding galleries include many of the preliminary drawings. What gives the painting such resonance is the inclusion nearby of work by others who exhibited at the 1937 Spanish Pavilion in Paris: Alexander Calder, Joan Miró, and war photographer Robert Capa.

A comparable approach illuminates the surrealism galleries, where the divergent strains of Dalí's pseudorealism and Miró's spare abstraction are mediated by the surreal photos of Man Ray and Dora Maar, the humorous inventions of Tanguy, and the dynamic abstract clutter of Tapiés. Exhibition galleries on **Floor 4** are more fluid, since they represent art since about 1950. The museum puts a

Museums on the Cheap

With careful planning, you could have your fill of Madrid museums without spending a single euro on admission fees. Most of the museums in this chapter are always free or have free admission times every week. Even the Prado grants art lovers 2 to 3 free hours every evening when it's open and there's no better way to avoid museum fatigue than to spend a leisurely hour with the great Spanish masters on every day of your visit.

The trade-off is that museums are often more crowded when admission is free—and your touring style may be more free spirit than by the clock. So you may want to consider the discount pass options. The **Paseo del Arte pass** (14.40€) saves you almost 4€ off the combined entrance fees for the Prado, Reina Sofía, and Thyssen-Bornemisza museums. It can be a good deal, but note that the Reina Sofía also has generous free hours. The pass is sold at all the museums, is good for a year or more, and allows one visit per museum.

The **Madrid Card,** sold at tourist offices and travel agencies, is less of a good deal than it looks at first glance. It touts free entry to more than 50 museums, exhibition halls, and royal palaces. But about two-dozen of those sites are free anyway, or have free admission times. The card does give you the privilege of jumping the line at several of the more crowded attractions, but you must cram your museum-going into 24, 48, or 72 hours (for 42€, 55€, or 68€, respectively). Skip the card, unless you definitely want to ride the Madrid Vision bus (p. 57), which is included, and you're certain that you'll take adequate advantage of the modest discounts

strong emphasis on living Spanish artists, many young enough that they came of age after Franco's death.

The bold, abstract 2005 addition by Jean Nouvel gives the Reina Sofía room to grow. It also houses the extraordinary art library, bookstore, and hip cafe run by Michelin-starred chef Sergi Arola (p. 43).

ATTRACTIONS AROUND OPERA & PALACIO REAL

As you approach the regal quarter of Madrid, the dark and narrow streets of the Old City open into sun-splashed plazas. Comparisons to the Paris Opera and the palace of Versailles are inevitable: Everything you see was built under Bourbon kings with French taste. From the Metro, exit at Opera, where the stairs deliver you to Plaza Isabel II on the back of Teatro Real. The broad expanse between theater and palace is **Plaza de Oriente,** constructed in the first half of the 19th century and peopled with statues of Spanish kings and queens. If Plaza Mayor is where people sit at cafes in their shirtsleeves to catch some rays, Plaza de Oriente is where they sit at more expensive cafes in smart suits to be seen and admired.

In 863, Muhammed I, the Moorish ruler of Toledo, built the first fortress on the promontory where the **Palacio Real** ★★ (Bailén; ☎ 914-54-88-00;

at participating shops, restaurants, and theaters. Discounts on car rentals, by the way, are one of the better deals with the Madrid Card, as is the free tour of Berbabéu Stadium, usually 15€.

Always Free
Ermita de San Antonio de la Florida
Museo Arqueológico (until renovations are done)
Museo de Arte Contemporaneo (Conde Duque)
Museo de Arte Público
Museo de San Isidro
Museo Naval

Free Tuesday through Friday 6 to 8pm, Saturday 5 to 8pm
Museo Nacional del Prado

Free on Wednesday
Real Academia de Bellas Artes de San Fernando

Free after 2:30pm on Saturday & All Day Sunday
Museo del Traje
Museo Nacional Centro de Arte Reina Sofia

Free on Sunday
Museo de América
Museo Lázaro Galdiano
Museo Nacional de Artes Decorativas

www.patrimonionacional.es; Oct–Mar Mon–Sat 9:30am–5pm, Sun 9am–2pm; Apr–Sept Mon–Sat 9am–6pm, Sun 9am–3pm; 10€ guided visit, 8€ unguided, 3.50€ ages 5–16; extra 1€ for picture gallery; Metro: Opera) now stands as a barrier against a potential Christian invasion from the north. When the invasion finally came and Alfonso VI seized Madrid in 1083, the military outpost simply changed armies. Even when Madrid became the capital, the Spanish kings kept refurbishing the dark medieval fortress, using it as an official seat of power while they lived most of the year at other royal residences. A 1734 fire that ravaged the alcazar gave Felipe V a chance to build something more to his liking. From 1738 to 1755, much of the treasure from Spain's overseas colonies went into building the palace that you see today, which was first occupied by Carlos III in 1764.

Most visitors enter on the south side of the palace complex, where you can rent a useful but not essential audioguide for 2€. When you walk into the blinding sunlight of the Plaza de la Armería, everyone will run toward the palace. Ignore them and cross the plaza to start at the **Armory.** The collection of personal armor really allows you to take the measure of the Spanish royals since the plate and chain armor were individually tailored. Felipe I, the Austrian who married Juana la Loca in 1496, was a medium-slender man nearly 6 feet tall—a giant in his day.

Wednesday Blues

You're probably thinking that it won't do you a lot of good to know that the **Monasterio de Las Descalzas Reales, Monasterio de La Encarnación,** and **Palacio Real** are free on Wednesdays for citizens of European Union countries. But free admission swells visitation on those days and can create a real logjam at the two monasteries, both of which keep short hours and limit entry to a few people at a time. Plan accordingly. If you're thinking of doing some day trips, note that the same deal applies at the royal palaces at El Pardo, El Escorial, and Aranjuez (p. 76).

Many other royals were almost a foot shorter, and generally speaking, the shorter the noble, the bigger the metal codpiece on his armor.

Once you enter the palace, you're not allowed to backtrack on the rigidly delineated tour. Move quickly through the first few ceremonial rooms until you enter the **Throne Room** (or Hall of Ambassadors), which marks the start of the Carlos III era. Tiepolo takes political flattery to new heights in the vault fresco, *The Apotheosis of the Spanish Monarchy.*

It's easy to be overwhelmed by the next sequence of rooms, where the decor morphs from baroque into rococo, but you also get a sense how the royals lived amid such splendor. You see the **drawing room** where Carlos III usually had lunch, the over-the-top **Gasparini Room** where he dressed, and the **bedroom** where he died. The **Yellow Room,** which had been Carlos III's study, is rich with avian and floral tapestries woven at the Real Fabrica de Tapices. Finally, you'll reach the grand **dining hall,** which was first used by Alfonso XII in November 1879 to celebrate his marriage.

Some of the smaller, more intimate rooms on the tour are not always open, but they show Alfonso XIII as a more domestic king, screening movies with the family on Sunday afternoons. What remains of royal silver and china is also on display; Joseph Bonaparte sold much of it to finance French military adventures. Unless you have a lot of time, skip the **Farmacia Real's** numbing collection of apothecary jars and take a walk in the formal gardens.

The orderly and graceful **Jardines de Sabatini,** on the north side of the palace, were installed in the 1930s based on 19th-century plans. The **Campo de Moro** (named for the site where a Moorish army camped in 1109) below the palace is more a wooded park than a garden. The single public entrance is located opposite the palace on the busy Paseo de la Virgen del Puerto (Metro: Principe Pío).

Directly adjacent to the Palacio Real is the **Catedral de Santa María de la Almudena** (Bailen 10; ☎ 915-42-22-00; www.archimadrid.es; free admission; 10am–2pm and 5–9pm; Metro: Opera), finally finished in 1993. It sits on the site of the city's original mosque, and if you walk across the street on the south side, you can see the last remains on an Arabic wall on the embankment beneath the church.

Next, spend your time exploring the riches of a religious order known for its vows of poverty. (You can skip the tour of the nearby **Teatro Real,** though a show there [p. 74] is a treat.) While Felipe II was building palaces in the countryside, his sister, Juana de Austria, had a retreat of another kind in mind. In 1559, she founded a Franciscan convent, the **Monasterio de Las Descalzas Reales** ✪✪ (Plaza de las Descalzas; ☎ 915-47-53-50; www.patrimonionacional.es; Tues–Thurs and Sat 10:30am–12:30pm and 4–5:30pm, entrance for no more than 20 people at a time, roughly every 15 minutes; 5€ adults, 2.50€ students; Metro: Opera) in a palace originally built for the royal treasurer.

It's still a working convent, home to about 20 nuns. After visitors leave, it's easy to imagine the nuns gliding silently along the upper cloister, praying at the tiny chapels, and shivering against the chill of the tile floors and stone walls. Guided tours are in Spanish, but one glimpse of the massive staircase, covered with magnificent murals of saints, angels, and Spanish rulers immediately explains the conjunction of art, royalty, and faith that defines Spanish history. The nuns' former dormitory is hung with tapestries woven from cartoons by Rubens. (Take a moment to notice the floor tiles that delineate each nun's tiny sleeping area.)

If you have visited the Descalzas, you might find its sister institution, the **Real Monasterio de la Encarnación** (Plaza de la Encarnación 1; ☎ 914-54-88-00; www.patrimonionacional.es; Tues–Thurs and Sat 10:30am–12:45pm and 4–5:45pm, Fri 10:30am–12:45pm, Sun 11am–1:45pm; 3.60€ adults, 2€ students; Metro: Opera) a letdown. An Augustinian convent, founded in 1611 by Marguerite of Austria, wife of Felipe III, its main attraction is the harmonious architecture. But between the privacy needs of the cloistered nuns and the painfully slow restoration, you see little but religious paintings on the one-hour guided tour. The highlight is the reliquary room, packed floor to ceiling with vials of blood, cross splinters, personal objects of saints, and innumerable chalices and monstrances.

ATTRACTIONS AROUND PLAZA SANTA ANA

Santa Ana was Madrid's entertainment district for a good three centuries before Gran Vía was even a twinkle in a civil engineer's eye. **Plaza Santa Ana** ✪✪ replaced the Santa Ana convent destroyed by Joseph Bonaparte in 1810—but the theater scene is far older. The **Corral des Comedias de Principe,** one of Spain's first theaters, began packing in the crowds in 1583. **Teatro Español,** built in the mid-19th century, anchors the east side of the plaza and still serves as Madrid's premier classical stage (p. 74). Medallions on the facade depict the pantheon of Spanish playwrights, from Calderón de la Barca (1600–81) on the right to Federico García Lorca (1898–1936), appropriately enough on the far left.

Intellectual revolutionaries dominated the Plaza Santa Ana cafes in the 1830s and, a century later, Lorca electrified the neighborhood with a production of his radical play *Bodas de Sangre (Blood Wedding).* More recently, when filmmaker Pedro Almodóvar needed a fashionable late-night bar for *High Heels,* he trained his cameras on the tiled walls of Villa Rosa. Today the plaza and surrounding streets are best known for classical tapas bars (p. 41) and genial beer halls.

Beyond soaking up the atmosphere of the streets and looking for historic plaques (you'll see the home of Cervantes at calle Cervantes 2), this area's major sight is **Casa de Lope de Vega** ✪ (Cervantes 11; ☎ 914-29-92-16; free admission; Tues–Fri 9:30am–2pm, Sat 10am–2pm; Metro: Antón Martín). When we last visited the house, the guide referred to this towering figure from the Golden Age of Spanish literature as a "lover, writer, husband, and priest." In each instance she

The Birthplace of Spanish?

The city calls this area the **Barrio de las Letras,** or "neighborhood of letters," drawing boundaries at calles Atocha and Cruz, the Paseo del Prado, and Carrera de San Jerónimo. Those narrow streets and shady alleys, now paved instead of cobbled, are the same medieval paths walked by Tirso de Molina, Cervantes, and the brilliant scoundrel Lope de Vega.

It could be argued that the modern Spanish language was forged in this neighborhood, as playwright Lope de Vega put the vernacular into the mouths of his characters rather than the scholarly Latinate Castilian of the day. Theater was the leading popular art of the early 17th century, and the plays of Madrid came to define how Spanish was spoken, just as the Elizabethan stage of Shakespeare came to shape the English tongue.

was right, though Félix Lope de Vega y Carpio (1562–1635) carried everything to an extreme. Some 425 of his plays survive—less than a third of his work. He married three times and fathered a passel of children, in and out of wedlock. He was involved in multiple lawsuits resulting from his amorous activities. At age 50, he became a priest. But like a modern actor for whom rehab only serves to burnish his career, Lope de Vega flourished. In 1610, at the height of his powers, he purchased the house now preserved as a museum. Visiting is like being plunked down in the Madrid of the Hapsburgs. As a bonus, you'll also learn more about the story of this fascinating figure (though the restoration of the house, which was bombed during the Civil War, sometimes plays loose with historical accuracy).

ATTRACTIONS AROUND PUERTA DEL SOL

The origins of **Puerta del Sol** ✪✪✪ are lost in time, though many historians believe that the plaza sits at the eastern (sunrise) gate of 15th-century Madrid. Even before Madrid became the national capital, Sol was a hub where roads radiated out to other important communities of central Spain. Sol assumed its present form over the last 200 years, as church buildings along its edges were razed in favor of government and commercial edifices, reflecting a shift in Madrileños's preoccupations from saving their souls to spending their money.

But even with the shift from sacred to secular, Sol has retained its status as the center of things. The first streetcars departed from Sol, and the Metro line began here. When citizens were moved to protest—or even to outright rebellion, as they were on May 2, 1808, against Napoleon's soldiers—they generally chose Sol as their battleground. During the Civil War, Sol was among the last strongholds of the Republicans. When Franco won, he made full use of symbolism by installing his security police and their torture squads in the most imposing building on Sol, the **Casa de Correos,** the old post office (built 1766–68 under Carlos III).

Trying to spot the landmarks of Sol is a little like one of those children's games of finding the bunny in a complicated drawing. Two centuries of accreted detail make Puerta del Sol one of the most visually complex areas within Madrid. The post office, a far more benign presence these days as the headquarters of the

Madrid regional government, is the key landmark. A plaque on the building acknowledges the Dos de Mayo uprising. Embedded in the pavement out front is the **Zero Kilometer marker** from which all distances in Spain are calculated. The clock on the building tower displays Spain's official time.

Across the plaza, the bronze figure on horseback is **Carlos III,** the 18th-century "mayor king" responsible for many of the city's improvements. He may be the last ruler toward whom no faction feels strong antipathy. Nearby at the opening of calle del Carmen is Puerta del Sol's cutest statue, a bronze depiction of the Community of Madrid's official symbol, the **bear and the strawberry tree** (*arbutus* in botanical Latin, *madroña* in Spanish). The official statuary pales, however, beneath the sky-high neon Tío Pepe sign with its hat-wearing bottle.

All manner of humanity teems through Sol day and night, which is why at every corner you'll find a lottery ticket seller and a beggar, and in every nook a street musician. And there are lots of corners and nooks in Puerta del Sol, which is the knot where 10 streets are tied together. Walk north on **Preciados, Carmen,** and **Montera** to a thicket of shopping streets where some of Sol's best street musicians play tangos and *bulerías.* On the west, regal 19th-century buildings march down **Arenal** and **Mayor,** respectively, to the Teatro Real and past Plaza Mayor to La Almudena cathedral. North of Sol, **Correos, Carretas,** and **Espoz y Mina** ascend a hill into the city of Lope de Vega and Cervantes. On the east side of Sol, **Carrera de San Jerónimo** and **Alcalá** are lined with banks and other monumental buildings on their way to the Paseos.

Just out of Puerta del Sol on Alcalá you'll find the barrio's major attraction: **Real Academia de Bellas Artes de San Fernando** ✯ (Alcalá 13; ☎ 915-24-08-64; http://rabasf.insde.es; Sun–Mon 9am–2:30pm, Tues–Fri 9am–7pm, Sat 9am–2:30pm and 4–7pm; 3€ adults, free for seniors and children 17 and under, free Wed; Metro: Sevilla or Sol). We enjoy visiting the Academia, an art museum in a city with three huge ones, precisely because it's *not* encyclopedic and the art is displayed in an intimate setting. Founded in 1752, the academy has occupied its current palace since 1773. Young Francisco de Goya was twice rejected as a prospective student but became a member in 1780 and in 1795 was named director. His stamp remains firmly on the museum's first-floor collection, which he arranged according to his theory of the development of Spanish painting, in

---

Deal or No Deal?

Snapping photos of Madrid's glorious architecture from the open top deck of a double-decker tour bus always looks like fun, and **Madrid Vision** gives you ample opportunity as the red buses ply two sightseeing routes through the city. But there are much less expensive ways to get good pictures. Madrid Vision passes are 16€ for 1 day, 21€ for 2 days (8.50€ or 11€, respectively, for students and seniors) and allow you to hop on and off all day. (They're available at most travel agencies, at many hotels, or from the bus driver.) However, unless you're planning to hit *only* the standard tourist sites and do it all in one great burst, skip these sightseeing buses and take public transit.

which all roads lead to Goya. Follow the circuit counterclockwise to enjoy, among other works, a few excellent El Grecos and five masterful paintings of saints by Francisco de Zurbarán. The circuit ends at the Goya galleries, where 13 of his paintings—including an unflinchingly homely self-portrait—are on display. His final palette, circled by a gilded garland, rests beneath glass. The second- and third-floor galleries of 19th- and 20th-century art are sometimes closed due to staff shortages. But as a guard once told us, the first floor is the essence of the collection.

ATTRACTIONS ON & AROUND GRAN VÍA

Depending on your point of view, **Gran Vía** ✪ is either a triumph of will or failure of ego. The project to construct a grand diagonal street running from the northwest corner of Salamanca to the similarly planned neighborhood of Argüelles (bypassing messy Old Madrid) had been a subject of public discussion since the late 19th century. Early proponents sought to emulate the boulevards of Paris. King Alfonso XIII repackaged the old plan to modernize Madrid, and personally launched the project in 1910, obliterating whole neighborhoods to make way for a grand modern thoroughfare designed for automobiles.

That first stretch of Gran Vía from Alcalá to the junction with Fuencarral, built 1910 to 1917, remains the best. Striking Art Nouveau buildings, such as the **Metropolis** (at the junction with Alcalá), dot the street between block-long stretches of dignified neoclassical buildings. The second section, built in the 1920s, begins with the promising bang of Madrid's first skyscraper, the **Teléfonica** building (on the corner with Fuencarral at the Gran Vía Metro stop). The plain stepped form by American architect Louis S. Weeks anticipates Art Deco, but the formal decorations over the doors and at the peak are pure Spanish baroque.

From the Teléfonica building Gran Vía literally goes downhill all the way to Plaza Callao, where Madrid's modern theater district is located. Built in the 1920s and 1930s, much of this stretch features live theaters and cinemas in full-blown American Deco style. The most beautiful of the theaters is the ocean-liner-like **Cine Capital** (Gran Vía 41), which opened in 1933. The final segment of Gran Vía, connecting Plaza Callao to Plaza de España, was to have been Franco's legacy, and like the dictator, it is unsubtle and uninspired.

The most intriguing attraction of the neighborhood, **Circulo de Bellas Artes de Madrid** (Alcalá 42; ☎ 913-60-54-00; www.circulobellasartes.com; Metro: Banco de España), is right off Gran Vía across the street from the Metropolis. The art center was built in 1919 to 1920, and its interior architecture shows all the foment and contradiction of that age, with a grand marble staircase and classical statuary, the great domed rotunda of the Salon de Baile, and plentiful bas-relief decoration where classical motifs blend into Art Deco style. The center now dabbles in digital and electronic arts as well as still serving as a lecture hall and theater; you might recognize it from Pedro Almodóvar's 1993 film, *Kika.*

ATTRACTIONS IN CHUECA & MALASAÑA

North of Gran Vía, **Chueca and Malasaña** ✪✪ are divided by calle Fuencarral but otherwise united as a bohemian barrio on the way up. The residential areas underwent a sea change when Franco's death unleashed a pent-up spirit in

Three Museums Worth Going Out of Your Way For

Even using the Metro and then walking, it will take you an extra 15 to 30 minutes of travel time to reach any one of these three museums north and west of Chueca/Malasaña, but each repays the effort with a very specialized experience.

Although the focus is tightly on the New World regions colonized by Spain, the **Museo de América** ✪✪ (Reyes Católicos 6; ☎ 915-49-26-41; http://museode america.mcu.es; Tues–Sat 9:30am–3pm, Sun 10am–3pm; 3€, free Sun; Metro: Moncloa) is one of the best combined history and anthropology museums in the world. Its origins lie in the natural history "cabinet" created by Carlos III and the artifacts returned by Spain's concerted scientific expeditions in the 18th century. The museum maintains a judicious balance between the adventures of the conquistadors and the civilizations they destroyed. This museum truly demonstrates that the discovery and exploitation of the New World was the crucible for post-Reconquista Spanish identity. Do not miss the extraordinary collection of Inca textiles from A.D. 100 through 1450.

A great quotation from Dutch artist Gabriel Van der Leeuw (1645–88) in the opening exhibit of the **Museo del Traje** ✪ (Juan de Herrera 2; ☎ 915-49-71-50; http://museodeltraje.mcu.es; Tues–Sat 9:30am–7pm, Sun 10am–3pm; 3€; Metro: Moncloa or Ciudad Universitaria) sums up this clothing and fashion museum in a nutshell: "The study of clothing is the study of Man. All anthropology is contained in dress." The emphasis is on Spanish clothing, and since textiles are fragile, most of the exhibits are from the 18th, 19th, and 20th centuries. The fashion galleries rev up with circa-1906 evening gowns by the Granada-born Fortuny (1871–1949), who largely worked in Venice, and builds to Cristóbal Balenciaga (1895–1972), best known for his work in Paris.

Goya created a sequence of dramatic murals with scenes from the life of San Antonio of Padua on the walls and cupola ceiling of **La Ermita de San Antonio de La Florida** ✪ (Glorieta de la Florida 5; ☎ 915-42-07-22; www.munimadrid. es/ermita; free admission; Tues–Fri 9:30am–8pm, Sat–Sun 10am–2pm; Metro: Príncipe Pío). His final reward for the task was the mausoleum, where his remains have rested since 1919. Strategically placed mirrors obviate the need to lie on the floor to see the art. The chapel is a 5-minute walk from the Metro.

Spanish life. What had once been possible only abroad became possible at home. Gay Spaniards came out of the closet, and Madrileños began to experiment with alternative cultures and lifestyles—and they did it in Chueca and Malasaña. The neighborhood began to thrive as a territory of artists, writers, filmmakers, and the like. The Plaza Dos de Mayo became a rallying ground for the counterculture—and a likely place to score illicit drugs. In a familiar pattern, artists and the gay community have transformed Chueca/Malasaña into one of Madrid's most desirable barrios. Today it's filled with bars, restaurants, cafes, design shops, home furnishing stores, and boutiques.

The arch in **Plaza de Dos de Mayo** (Metro: Bilbao) marks the artillery barracks where Madrid's defenders rose up against the French on May 2, 1808, and the statue honors captains Daoíz and Velarde for their role in the futile uprising. The same spot became symbolic of another May 2 uprising in 1976 when a couple undressed on top of the statues to the delight of a crowd—an event often cited as the beginning of the *movida madrilena*. Those heady days are gone; today the plaza is skateboard turf by day and a center of cafe life at night.

West of calle de San Bernardo, the narrow working-class streets are technically in Universidad, not Malasaña, but the **Centro Cultural Conde Duque** (Conde Duque 9–11; ☎ 915-88-58-00; www.munimadrid.es/condeduque; Metro: Plaza de España) strikes a similar artistic and bohemian note, especially with the neighborhood's students. The city-owned cultural center's performance space hosts free concerts—line up well in advance to secure a seat. We're particularly impressed with the center's **Museo de Arte Contemporáneo** (free admission; Tues–Sat 10am–2pm and 6–9pm, Sun 10:30am–2:30pm). The curators don't shy from controversy, but they also don't seem to shock for the sake of shocking. All the displays have some connection to Spain, but they often include artists from elsewhere in Europe. The media range from digital art to graphic arts to video and photography to paintings on canvas.

Note: Two of the area's more interesting museums, the **Museo Romantico** (San Mateo 13; ☎ 914-48-10-71; http://museoromantico.mcu.es; closed for renovations; Metro: Tribunal or Alonso Martínez) and the **Museo Municipale de Madrid** (Fuencarral 78; ☎ 917-01-18-63; www.munimadrid.com; free admission; Metro: Tribunal or Bilbao) were closed for renovation as we went to press. The municipal museum is scheduled to reopen in late 2008; no date has been set for the return of the Museo Romantico.

ATTRACTIONS IN PLAZA MAYOR & LA LATINA

On a beautiful spring afternoon when the sun shines beneficently down on **Plaza Mayor** ✯✯✯, you'd think the grand square was built just to offer outdoor dining and arcade shopping. But the site was originally a food market just outside the city walls, and once the current square was built in 1619, it became the city's main gathering spot. People came to the plaza to see bullfights, attend political rallies, celebrate royal weddings, shop for bread and meat, watch hangings, and witness the torture-induced confessions of victims of the Inquisition. With apartments on the square, the royal family had ringside seats.

Now Madrileños come to the plaza for the Sunday coin and stamp market or the annual Christmas market, but it is no longer the city's principal gathering place. Plaza Mayor does teem with visitors, who perhaps best appreciate the 1992 **zodiac murals** decorating the Casa de Panadería (originally home to the all-powerful Bakers' Guild) on the north side, the austere brick of the Casa de Carnecería (where butchers stored and sold their meat) on the south. The plaza's acoustics can be quite extraordinary, and musicians often perform in the center beneath the equestrian statue of Felipe III.

Plaza Mayor was fully enclosed in 1854, creating the great arches that serve as gates. The most dramatic is the **Arco de Cuchilleros (Arch of the Knife-Sharpeners),** on the southwest corner, which leads to the street of the same name.

Walk This Way

The Madrid tourism office offers a surprising range of inexpensive walking and bicycling tours in either Spanish or English (with a few per week in French, Italian, and German) that are well worth taking. English-language tours emphasize history and architecture by exploring specific neighborhoods—such as "The Madrid of Cervantes." Tours are 3.30€. Ask for the schedule at the **Centro de Turismo de Madrid office** (Plaza Mayor 27; ☎ 915-88-29-06).

The "caves" under Plaza Mayor are occupied by tourist restaurants and bars of long standing. Spending too much for sour sangria in one of these atmospheric spots has been an essential rite of passage for visitors to Madrid since the days of Washington Irving. Every traveler should do it. Once. Of somewhat higher caliber is **Restaurante Botín** (p. 39), certified by the Guinness Book of World Records as the world's oldest restaurant.

Cuchilleros quickly splits into Cava Alta and **Cava Baja,** a street virtually synonymous with tapas-hopping (p. 38). The end of Cava Baja hooks to the right down calle Almendra, which leads to the front door of the **Museo de San Isidro** ★ (Plaza de San Andrés 2; ☎ 913-66-74-15; www.munimadrid.es/museosanisidro; free admission; Tues–Fri 9:30am–8pm, Sat–Sun 10am–2pm; Metro: La Latina). Installed in a former palace, the museum is located where tradition says that San Isidro Labrador (patron saint of Madrid) and his wife, Santa Maria de la Cabeza, lived in the 12th century. Their well (from which legend says prayer rescued their son) remains, and a few exhibits deal delicately with the stories of San Isidro and the political machinations of his canonization. Isidro's remains are in the Cathedral de San Isidro (Toledo 37–39).

The museum also delves into the prehistory and history of Madrid from the first humans who hunted along the Manzanares River some 300,000 years ago through Madrid's apotheosis as Spain's capital. Much of the story is told through reproductions of paintings—especially portraits of the artists, kings, poets, playwrights, and soldiers for whom city streets are named. Signage is all in Spanish. Two photographs summarize how quickly the city changed in the 19th century. One taken in 1865 shows open fields and vineyards. An 1872 photograph of the same spot reveals buildings instead of fields.

The immense **Basilica de San Francisco el Grande** (Plaza de San Francisco; ☎ 913-65-38-00; Tues–Sat 11am–1pm and 4–6:30pm; 3€ adults, 2€ students; Metro: La Latina) served as Madrid's leading church from the 19th century, when the old cathedral burned, until 1993, when Catedral de la Almudena was finished (p. 54). It's a church of relatively meaningless architectural superlatives (largest cupola in Spain, for example), but it also boasts some wonderful art, including the recently restored ceiling murals of Mary Queen of Heaven. Although you can tour during the museum hours, the art assumes more meaning when the faithful gather for Mass on weekdays at 8:30am, 9:30am, or 10:30am.

Don't Fight City Hall

Don't overlook **Plaza de la Villa** on calle Mayor between Plaza Mayor and La Almudena. Fragments of some of Madrid's oldest buildings are located here, notably the Mudéjar-style, 15th-century Casa Lujones and the 16th-century Casa Cisneros, built by the nephew of the powerful cardinal. The **Ayuntamiento** (town hall) is also found here, as the plaza has been the site of city government since medieval times. The building is a hodgepodge of styles. The original medieval structure was rebuilt in Renaissance classical style in 1645, and further modified when Spanish baroque became all the rage. A free tour is offered at 5pm on Mondays; it includes the grand staircase and some municipal treasures, such as the silver monstrance (receptacle for the Host) traditionally carried in the Corpus Christi procession.

ATTRACTIONS IN LAVAPIÉS

The long slope that fans out south of calle de la Magdalena between calles Toledo and Atocha has been Madrid's outsider barrio since the late 14th century. Until the 1492 expulsion of the Jews, it was the Jewish Quarter and has been the home of successive waves of newcomers, either from the Spanish countryside or from former overseas colonies. It was, and to some extent remains, the neighborhood where the dirty work of Madrid is done and where the poorest workers live. Writers and artists from Cervantes to Goya sought inspiration in Lavapiés, especially the butchers' row known as El Rastro, finding it a source of colorful characters. Lavapiés is still a fascinating place to wander, as most of the streets are little changed since Goya's day. Many of today's residents, however, are East Asian and North African, and you'll spot Chinese confectioners and *halal* butcher shops among the ancient taverns and convent buildings.

Should you find yourself in need of a length of vinyl tubing, antique brass plumbing fixtures, handmade silver earrings, an embossed leather belt, or music CDs of dubious origin, plan to wade through the crowds on Sundays and holidays at **El Rastro flea market** (Metro: Lavapiés), which is in full swing from midmorning to midafternoon. The market is a gently rocking sea of humanity; we've heard that as many as 1,000 vendors participate, but not even the tax man knows for sure. Goods range from cheap tools and clothing churned out by Chinese factories, to the contents of grandma's attic laid out on a folding table to make some ready cash. You might not buy a thing, but you'll get to mingle with bargain-conscious Madrileños for the day.

Safety note: Most people will suggest you take the Metro to either La Latina or the Tirso de Molina stop and walk over to Plaza de Cascorro. Since so many euro-loaded tourists do this, these lines are also very popular with pickpockets. We *strongly* suggest walking a little farther—from Plaza Mayor or Puerta del Sol—and keeping a close watch on your valuables at all times.

ATTRACTIONS IN SALAMANCA

After walking in the claustrophobic quarters of Madrid's Centro, Salamanca is literally a breath of fresh air. The Marquis de Salamanca, a legendary financier and bon vivant, began constructing the quarter in the 1870s as an elegant alternative to the cramped quarters of the Old City. By the time it was completed around 1920, Salamanca was Madrid's premier address. The neighborhood of broad, tree-lined streets laid out in an orderly grid is lined with elegant buildings, many girded with wrought-iron balconies. Situated east of Paseo de Castellana and north of Parque del Retiro, Salamanca was the first barrio to feature such modern conveniences as electric lights, elevators, and central heating.

Today it's a lot like contemporary Spanish fashion: a lively mix of classic formality and radical modernism. It's no accident that streets like Serrano, Goya, and Velázquez are home to the boutiques of Spain's top fashion designers as well as the usual international lineup of *prêt-à-porter* fashion labels.

Salamanca seems to have its own dress code: Well-coiffed women wear beautiful shoes and hide behind designer sunglasses. When the temperature drops below 10°C (50°F), they don fur coats.

We bet painter Joachín Sorolla (1863–1923) felt right at home when he had his Andalusian-style house and studio built in the northwest section of the barrio in 1911–17. Today the property is the **Museo Sorolla** ★★ (Paseo del General Martinez Campos 37; ☎ 913-10-15-84; http://museosorolla.mcu.es; Tues–Sat 9:30am–3pm, Sun 10am–3pm; 2.40€ adults, 1.20€ students and seniors, free Sun; Metro: Gregorio Marañon), and it captures one of Spain's sunniest painters at the height of his career. With unfinished paintings on easels, the studio seems as if Sorolla has just stepped out for tea with the family. If you've already visited the Prado, you'll see immediately how he was influenced by Velázquez, especially in his society portraits that often drew from the court painter's compositions. The remaining downstairs rooms, with their wonderfully corny fading sepia photographs, capture the family life of the rare artist who really seems to have had it all—fame, fortune, and love (not to mention talent). The upstairs galleries neatly encapsulate the career of Spain's foremost modern painter of light. Don't miss the folkloric paintings that served as studies for the mural Sorolla painted at the Hispanic Society of New York (1912–19), as well as the sun-drenched paintings of the beaches of Valencia, his native land. While principal signage is in Spanish, there's also good signage in English.

Strictly speaking, the Museo Sorolla isn't actually in Salamanca, as it lies west of the Paseo de Castellana. We like the contrast of walking from the museum back into Salamanca by heading south to calle Juan Bravo and crossing through the **Museo Arte Público** (beneath calle Juan Bravo bridge at Eduardo Dato; no phone; free admission; open 24 hours; Metro: Serrano). The sculptures add interest to what would otherwise be a rather dreary set of steps between calle Serrano and the busy Paseo. The works represent two generations of the Spanish avant-garde (a dangerous thing to be in the Franco years) including Joan Miró and the so-called Generation of 1950, a defiant group of artists who picked up the mantle of abstraction. Our favorite is the waterfall/fountain of alternating wave forms (it's called *Barandillas en "S"*) created in 1972 by Eusebio Sempere. You can't miss it— the rushing water makes you think that Madrid has suddenly sprung a leak.

Let's Talk

The name sounds like an arcane dance step, but the *tertulia* began in the city's cafes in the 1830s, when intellectuals met in discussion groups (the literal meaning of *tertulia*) to hash over the latest art, music, theater, politics, or even bullfights. One of the most famous, El Parnasillo, welcomed non-Spaniard Rossini to sit in when he came to Madrid in 1831 to stage the first production of the *Barber of Seville*. Tertulias flourished until the Civil War, when many of their host cafes were destroyed and it became hazardous to air opinions in public. Sporadic attempts are made in Madrid to revive the tradition, and some arts-minded bars will occasionally advertise a *tertulia* for a slow night.

After you climb the steps back to Serrano, the **Museo Arqueológico Nacional** (Serrano 13; ☎ 915-77-79-12; www.man.es; free admission; Tues–Sat 9:30am–8:30pm, Sun 9:30am–2:30pm; Metro: Serrano) is just a short walk to the right. Many of the galleries related to the early history of humans on the Iberian peninsula are closed for renovations until 2010 or later. But admission is free for now, and there are still a few incredible highlights, though it helps to read Spanish because English signs are usually just labels. If you're fascinated by burial tombs from the 5th century B.C., by all means visit the Dama de Baza in **Gallery 19.** The seated figure inside a sealed room was uncovered in 1971 near Granada. Otherwise, make your way around the stairwell to the Visigoth exhibits. The gem here is the Treasure of Guarrazar, uncovered in 1858 in the hills north of Madrid, spirited out of Spain, and stashed in the Cluny in Paris until 1940 or 1941. The collection of artifacts, made between 621 and 672, represents Visigoth goldsmithing at its height. History subsumes archaeology when the timeline reaches the era of the Muslim kingdom of al-Andalus, paralleled by the consolidation of Christian power in the northern fringes of Iberia. Some of the finest craftsmanship in ceramics, wood, and glass are the works of Mudéjar craftsmen, Muslims allowed to remain in Spain after the Christians reconquered parts of al-Andalus. On the way out of the museum, be sure to visit the re-creation of Cantabria's Altamira cave and its 15,000-year-old wall paintings. The "cave" has a separate entry between the museum's monumental steps and the equally monumental front gate.

Closed for an indeterminate period for renovations, **Museo Lázaro Galdiano** (Serrano 122; ☎ 915-61-60-84; www.flg.es; hours and prices to be announced; Metro: Rubén Darío or Gregorio Marañón) contains the personal collections of a financier who left them, along with his 35-room mansion, to the Spanish state on his death in 1947. His furniture, silverware, enamels, and sculpture rival the artwork, which includes several works by Goya, El Greco, and Velázquez.

THE OTHER MADRID

A big part of what makes travel fun, and sometimes even life-changing, is connecting with the locals wherever you go. We call this the "Other" Madrid, and it's really about finding the social settings where you can share the passions of the Madrileños on their own turf.

If you haven't guessed by reading the restaurant listings, Madrileños are social animals who play out much of their lives in busy bars and taverns, restaurants and *sidrerías* (places that sell hard apple cider). You'll be shoulder to shoulder with them, so you might as well strike up a conversation. It helps to speak Spanish, but many Spaniards speak some English, French, or Italian. You'll also find the locals at the flamenco shows detailed in the nightlife section (p. 72), as these are performances that cater to aficionados of the art form. You'll run into them (literally) at El Rastro flea market (p. 62), in the city's great museums, and at Parque del Retiro (p. 50) on Sundays.

That said, there are some places where Madrileños go and tourists often don't. Here's your ticket into life as it's lived in Madrid.

SOCCER

If you want to get to know a Madrileño, ask him what he's having for dinner— or which football (soccer to Americans) club he supports. The most elemental passions of Madrid are food and sport, and they often intersect.

A Madrid friend once told us that the only time she ever saw her grandfather cry was when Real Madrid lost a championship for the second year in a row. Despite such disappointments, Real Madrid was named "best team of the 20th century" by the Fédération Internationale de Football Association (FIFA) and claims the fervid loyalty of most Madrileños. In a sports lover's dream scenario, Real Madrid even has a crosstown rival, Atlético de Madrid, perfect for those who prefer to root for the underdog.

Going to see a match in person gives you a close-up on the passions of the fans. Atlético de Madrid plays in **Estadio Vicente Calderón** (Paseo de la Virgen del Puerto 67; ☎ 913-66-47-07; www.clubatleticodemadrid.com; Metro: Pirámides). Unless the match is against Real Madrid, tickets are often available at the stadium ticket offices on the day of the match.

On the other hand, tickets for Real Madrid's **Estadio Santiago Bernabéu**, (Paseo de la Castellana 144/Concha Espina 1; ☎ 913-98-44-00, ☎ 902-24-48-24 for tickets; www.santiagobernabeu.com; Metro: Bernabéu) sell out fast. "Go to the stadium, stand in line, and pray," we've been told.

The matches are also broadcast on pay-per-view TV channels and short of sitting in the stadium, you'll get the best communal experience of a match by claiming a seat in a smoky bar with TV sets. The fans watch every motion on the field with laser-like intensity, though they're surprisingly undemonstrative by American standards.

When Real Madrid is playing an away match, the **Real Cafe Bernabéu** (at entrance 30 of the stadium; ☎ 914-58-36-67; www.realcafebernabeu.es; 10am–2am, closed during home matches; MC, V; Metro: Bernabéu) is the definitive place to watch, broadcasting the contest on two flat-screen TVs, and on a giant projection TV in the stairwell leading up to a private dining room. The food is a revelation for a sports bar: pickled anchovies with cherry tomatoes or roast pork loin, chicken, and avocado on brioche. The cafe begins to fill up about a half-hour before the match begins. Other good places to watch include **Zahara Restaurante Cervecería** (Gran Vía 31; ☎ 915-21-84-24; Sun–Thurs 9am–1am, Fri–Sat 9am–2am;

MC, V; Metro: Callao) and **Restaurante Anonimato** (Alvarez Gato 4; ☎ 915-22-57-45; www.anonimato.com; 1:30–4pm and 8pm–1am; AE, DC, MC, V; Metro: Sevilla), near Plaza Santa Ana.

If you're in town when one of the teams clinches a big championship, head to the fountains along the Paseo del Prado and Paseo de Recoletos. Real Madrid team members and fans celebrate at Cibeles, while the Atléticos claim Neptuno.

BULLFIGHTING

We're conflicted about bullfights. In Spain, lithe (and, yes, sexy) matadors have all the celebrity of rock stars—and we certainly love a good spectacle. But as animal lovers, we've never attended a bullfight because we know that no matter how skillful and graceful the matador, we couldn't stomach the baiting, wounding, and eventual killing of the bull—even though we know that the animal is respected in death and that some of its meat is distributed to the poor.

Although many Spaniards, including the queen, dislike (or simply have no interest) in the sport, the *corrida* remains an essential element of Spanish history and identity. If you'd like to grapple with your own feelings about this confluence of culture and cruelty, tour Madrid's **Plaza de Toros Monumental de Las Ventas** (Alcalá 237; ☎ 915-56-92-37; www.las-ventas.com; 6€; tours in Spanish with some English translation Tues–Sun 10am–1:30pm except on days of *corrida*; Metro: Ventas). The grand Mudéjar-style concoction of red brick, tile, and ornate ironwork opened in 1931 and seats 24,000 people. It's not the largest ring in the world (that's in Mexico), but it is arguably the most important. The best bullfighters face the best bulls here—and the fans who pack the stands are among the sport's most passionate and knowledgeable.

The tour, which includes climbing one long flight of steps, goes into the stands for an overview of the hushed and empty arena and then onto the ring itself. It doesn't visit the chapel or infirmary, where seven medical specialists wait out every match. If you don't think that Spaniards harbor matador dreams, just watch as grown men take the measure and heft of a 17- to 22-pound red cape, give it a few tentative flourishes, and then grin sheepishly for the camera.

The bullfighter's greatest honor is to be awarded two *orejas,* or ears. The matador can claim the first by killing the bull with one thrust. The second is awarded by the crowd, with the consent of bullfight officials, for style and showmanship. Those so honored are carried through the Grand Portal by jubilant fans. "It opens the doors of all the bullrings in the world," the guide told us on our last visit. A top bullfighter can earn 5€ million to 6€ million a year. "It's like winning an Oscar in Hollywood—only much more dangerous."

If you decide to see a bullfight at Las Ventas, the season is March to October. The Fería de San Isidro, from the first week in May to the first week in June, is one of the sport's top events; tickets are scarce and prices soar on the black market. At other times, expect to pay 7€ to 36€ for reasonable seats; some of the best are in *tendidos* (rows) 9 and 10. Buy tickets at the box office or on the website.

A good alternative is to watch a match in a neighborhood bar. We were once drinking happily in a small-town bar when the broadcast of a bullfight began on TV. Surrounded by intense fans, we found it impossible not to watch and the whole event—played out as small images in black-and-white—was moving and unsettling at the same time. Then again, the best travel experiences make you think—and sometimes make you uncomfortable.

SPANISH SCHOOL

There's good reason why we say if someone knows something really well, he or she "speaks the language." Even if high school and college Spanish are far behind you, morning classes and afternoon excursions can make you reasonably fluent rather quickly. Director Angel Luis Piñuela and his brother have operated **Eureka Academia de Español** (Arenal 26, 3rd Floor; ☎ 915-48-86-40; www.eureka-madrid.com; bank transfer or cash) for more than 2 decades, and they're very hands-on in the school operations. Classes are small (rarely more than 8) and teachers are local. The 20-hour-per-week intensive Spanish classes (200€ per week, reduced rates for extra weeks) are a good combination of education and free time because classes end at 1pm on the theory that you can use the rest of the day to practice what you've studied. It's not all conjugating verbs and memorizing vocabulary—the school offers bonus afternoon and evening classes in Spanish cooking, music, and dance, and often runs short sightseeing excursions to the countryside. In short, they look after you like family. The school also owns its own studio apartments and shared student flats (several bedrooms sharing several baths) near Puerta del Sol. Students must be at least 16, but many are in their 40s, 50s, or older, and Piñuela recommends that the older students take the studio apartments for comfort and privacy. The neat but sparsely furnished units rent for 250€ per week (extra 50€ for non-student companion)—an utter bargain compared to conventional tourist lodging. It's best to reserve housing 6 to 8 weeks in advance.

MARKETS

There's almost nothing we like better than a good food market (and do we ever have the photos to prove it). But we finally wised up that the cameras put a barrier between us and the place. Busy vendors and shoppers don't need tourists with cameras getting in their way. Nobody is more discerning—or demanding—than a Spanish cook. Just watch as she insists that the butcher trim the last remnant of sinew from a turkey cutlet, sniffs suspiciously at a whole dorado at the fishmonger, and purchases precisely what she needs for a pot of soup: two carrots, three ribs of celery, and a third of a squash, all assembled cheerfully by the grocer. You may not be shopping to put dinner on the table, but assembling the ingredients for a picnic is a good way to take the pulse of the market. Public markets are generally open Monday through Friday 9am to 2pm and 5pm to 8pm and Saturday from 9am to 2pm. Here are a few with real neighborhood character:

Two levels of stalls at **Mercado de la Cebada** (Plaza de Cebada 15; Metro: La Latina) serve families in the immigrant and working-class neighborhood of La Latina. Pick up a hundred grams each of ham, cured sausages, and cheese, and a few pieces of fruit. Bread choices are limited, but you can select from more than a dozen kinds of olives—the vendor will scoop your choices from a big vat and seal them in a plastic bag.

You'll find a little more exotic produce and some packaged gourmet goods (crackers, pâté, and the like) at **Mercado Antón Martín** (Santa Isabel 5 at Atocha; Metro: Antón Martín), about halfway between the Museo Reina Sofía and Plaza Santa Ana. Like Cebada, it's a working-class market that emphasizes raw ingredients over ready-to-eat food.

The residents of Salamanca frequent **Mercado de la Paz** (Ayala 28 at Legasca; Metro: Velázquez) for fresh fish and shellfish that is misted every few minutes, organic meats, breads, decadent pastries, baby pineapples, asparagus tips, and good wine. It's also a natural for gourmet picnic fixings. You'll find the stalls of La Boulette by looking for the crowd waiting to buy Spanish artisanal cheeses, country-style pork pâté, or cooked chicken breast stuffed with foie gras mousse. Cold salads and fish dishes are the specialty at **La Alacena del Gourmet,** including *pulpo a la vinaigretta* (pickled octopus) or *salmon ahumado artesano* (smoked salmon). The olives at **Aceitunas San Miguel** are displayed in hand-painted ceramic crocks. This tidy little vendor also has the best prices we found on gift-size boxes of saffron (2 grams for 5.80€). If you're not in the mood for a picnic, eat lunch with the shoppers and grocers at one of the market cafes. **Bar El Segoviano,** for example, offers a menu of the day for 8€ to 9€ or a combination plate with a small beef filet, fried egg, and french fries for 5€.

ATTENTION, SHOPPERS!

As a big European city, Madrid is naturally awash in stores selling all the familiar European name-brand merchandise. But you'll often find those same goods just as cheap (or cheaper) at home. Concentrate your Madrid shopping on things that are truly Spanish—the ceramic dish for serving olives that includes a receptacle for the pits, flamenco CDs and sheet music, fine guitars, Spanish fashion, fabulous leather handbags, and equally fabulous Spanish shoes.

El Rastro Sunday flea market (p. 62) is touted for bargain hunters, but most merchandise is fairly predictable inexpensive clothing, and much of it comes from East Asia, not Spain. You might find some nice silver jewelry, leather goods, or even pashmina shawls. If you're looking for a funky fashion accessory, go ahead and bargain for the best deal. Otherwise, just enjoy the spectacle of the sprawling market (and watch your valuables).

For a look at Spain's fashion elite and the style trends, window-shop in the upscale barrio of Salamanca; but then do your serious shopping in the hip and up-and-coming Chueca neighborhood.

Most stores are open 10am to 8pm or later Monday through Saturday. But some smaller shops still close roughly between 1:30pm and 4:30pm and reopen until 8pm or so on weekdays; they tend to be closed Saturday afternoon and often are closed on Sunday. Larger stores are often open on Sunday but may close early.

ANTIQUES

You'd never know it when El Rastro flea market is in full swing, but the lower end of Ribera de Curtidores holds Madrid's greatest concentration of antiques dealers. At **Galerias Piquer** (Ribera de Curtidores 29), roughly 70 dealers cluster on several levels around a courtyard. You'll find a lot of late 19th- and early 20th-century Chinese and Indian furniture, knickknacks, and dishware, reflecting a long-passé Spanish passion for the East. Better bets are Spanish ceramics and paintings. Many shops, alas, are stuffed with the contents of abuelita's attic. Much the same mix can be found across the street at **Nuevas Galerias** (Ribera de Curtidores 12).

FASHION

If eyeing the Salamanca shops of Spain's top fashion designers has made you yearn for a piece of clothing that sets, rather than follows, the trends, check out

Make a Spectacle of Yourself

Spain is a great place to buy eyeglass frames. Spanish manufacturers excel at handmade acetate frames in great colors and patterns—you'll pay less and end up with something you won't find at home. (Pat's most prized pair of tortoiseshell frames were made by a Spanish designer who went on to work for Alain Mikli in Paris; his work is now out of our range.) There are several good shops near Puerta del Sol. Choices at **Federopticos Dorff** (Mayor 17; ☎ 913-66-08-26; www.federopticosdorff.com) include the Barcelona style setter Etnia. **Grand Optical** (Puerta del Sol 14; ☎ 917-01-49-80) stocks many ubiquitous European designers; look for their "Marca Exclusiva," including hip geometric shapes from Studio 123. **General Optica** (Preciados 22; ☎ 915-22-21-21) carries Italian designers not sold in the States. The Spanish line Oggi is one of the best bargains. Your local optician will (probably grudgingly) make lenses for your foreign frames.

Algarabia Outlet (Ayala 74, ☎ 915-75-62-91; José Ortega y Gasset 48, ☎ 914-02-97-60; www.algarabiaoutlet.com) for a choice selection of women's wear from up-and-coming Italian, French, and Spanish designers. "These designers focus on making quality goods, not getting media attention," the shop owner says. All prices are at least 50% below retail.

Most of us have to wait for fashion trends to trickle down to the masses. At least the Spanish retailer **Zara** (Preciados 14; ☎ 915-21-25-08; www.zara.com) accelerates the process by moving men's, women's, and children's clothing from design phase to store shelves in about 15 days. With interesting silhouettes and imaginative use of buttons and zippers, one piece can liven up a wardrobe. (Also at Alcala 161, ☎ 914-31-99-21; Fuencarral 126, ☎ 914-45-12-13; Gran Vía 47, ☎ 915-76-74-56; and Serrano 48, ☎ 915-75-48-55.)

We've certainly made the mistake of buying cool clothing abroad only to discover that our prize seemed a little costume-y at home. Still, there are certainly some iconic Spanish items that might be hard to resist if you have a flair of the exotic.

If you're a hat person, check out the classic Basque caps (more constructed than a French beret) at **La Favorita** (Plaza Mayor 25; ☎ 913-66-58-77; www.lafavoritacb.com). Clerk María José Iturbe says that the best are made by Elosegui in their factory near San Sebastián Toloso. Men favor the leather-lined wool caps on rainy days—but perky colors such as red, yellow, and blue are designed for women.

Capas Seseña (Cruz 23; ☎ 915-31-68-40; www.sesena.com) has been making wool capes for men and women since 1901, and in Madrid at least, they have never gone out of style. If you can carry off the look, this is a great investment piece. Check the display racks for the style and color you want; if it's not there, shop seamstresses can make it for you in a week or less.

MUSIC & MUSICAL INSTRUMENTS

At least one of the instruments that flamenco genius Paco de Lucia plays is a model handcrafted by **Conde Hermanos** (Atocha 53, ☎ 914-29-93-33; also Felipe V 2, ☎ 915-47-06-12; www.conde-hermanos.com), a family-run company that's been around since 1915. His custom model sells for 5,000€, but student guitars, either classical or flamenco, run 300€ to 600€ (professional instruments begin around 1,250€). Clerks might offer to let you try the instruments. It's good form to demur unless you're a fabulous musician, or you're really interested in buying. If you're a Saturday picker who's only dreaming, opt for a new set of strings, or consider a lower-priced model from **José Ramirez Guitarreria** (de la Paz 8; ☎ 915-31-42-29; www.guitarrasramirez.com), whose guitars begin around 150€ and top out around 2,000€.

A number of luthiers and musical-instrument shops dot the streets around Teatro Real. Perusing the sheet music at **Musical Opera** (Carlos III no. 1; ☎ 915-40-16-72; www.musicalopera.com) reveals that Madrid tastes run to flamenco and jazz. The shop sells all instruments from accordions to xylophones, but about 50 models of Spanish-made guitars dominate the displays.

If you're seeking flamenco sheet music, fake books, or recordings, head to **El Flamenco Vive** (Conde de Lemos 7; ☎ 915-47-39-17; www.elflamencovive.es). It's a hard shop for a non-Spanish speaker to navigate, as most of the staff speak no English. If you can get past that, they're a great resource for what's happening in the current flamenco scene.

SHOES & OTHER LEATHER GOODS

A Spanish friend claims that she can tell European women from American women by their shoes. We probably don't have to tell you who is more stylish. If you're looking for that European look—and this goes for guys, as well—head to the outlets on calle Augusto Figueroa in Chueca.

The Mallorcan firm Barrats, for example, has been making shoes since 1890. The fairly conservative styles are considered to be among the best in Spain. At the **Barrats outlet** ✪ (Augusto Figueroa 20; ☎ 915-31-65-37), men's and women's shoes are usually discounted 30%, sometimes up to 50%. At **Farrutx** (Augusto Figueroa 18; ☎ 915-32-02-40) new inventory is discounted about 40%; older styles often 60% or more.

Spanish-based **Camper Shoes** (Serrano 24, ☎ 915-78-25-60; Ayala 13, ☎ 914-31-43-45; Preciados 23, ☎ 915-31-78-97; Gran Vía 54, ☎ 915-47-52-23) have a cult following and their shops dot the city. The styles can be overly cute. But how much fashion can you expect in shoes that claim to be so comfortable that you'll forget about your feet?

The unassuming espadrille transcends fashion trends. At **Casa Hernanz** (Toledo 18; ☎ 913-66-54-50), outside Plaza Mayor, Jesus Hernanz carries on the family business started in 1865. A simple pair of espadrilles perfect for the beach are less than 5€; most are in the 10€ to 15€ range.

For the other extreme of handcrafted shoes, check out the gorgeous leather styles for men and women at **Gaytan** (Jorge Juan 15; ☎ 914-35-28-24) in Salamanca. Custom shoes, made in 2 to 3 weeks, can be shipped to the United States. They're a definite splurge, but you could amortize the cost over your lifetime.

Bargain Season

Among our favorite Madrid souvenirs are red shopping bags from El Corte Inglés department store with the word *rebajas* in big white letters. Translating loosely as "reductions," it's a word worth remembering. It signals the city-wide sales in department and specialty shops, when merchandise is marked down 30% to 70%. Sales take place in January and February and again in July and August.

Bernardo Jodar, who takes client's measurements, told us that European women wear their shoes cut much tighter than American women—stoic martyrs to fashion.

Enough on shoes? **Salvador Bachiller** ✷ (Gravina 11; ☎ 915-23-30-37; www.salvadorbachiller.com) is a Madrid institution for luggage, travel accessories, purses, and small leather goods. The firm's only discount outlet is near Plaza Chueca. We've found shoulder bags marked down from 45€ to 19€ or slim card holders reduced from 40€ to 19€. If our luggage was destroyed in transit, we'd head here for sturdy hard-sided canvas suitcases with wheels. Best bargains are on the wilder colors—red, turquoise, pink—but at least they stand out in a sea of black bags. Buyer beware: Look for flaws, especially broken zippers.

Near the Conde Duque cultural center, you can watch artisans at **Puntera** (Cristo 3; ☎ 915-41-33-60; www.puntera.com) handcraft leather purses, tote bags, and backpacks using soft leathers in rich browns and a range of bright colors. But you'll have to settle for just handling the goods at **Gracia Mazuelo del Hierro** (Cava Baja 6; ☎ 913-64-58-91) in La Latina. The beautiful leather purses are hand-painted in Menorca.

Never grab a leather glove by the bottom edge and yank it onto your hand. So say the clerks at **Guantes Luque** (Espoz y Mina 3; ☎ 915-22-32-87), just outside Puerta del Sol. Window displays of inexpensive woolen gloves seem unpromising, but the shop makes its own fine leather gloves. Rest your elbow on a leather pillow on the counter and the clerk will massage one onto your hand.

SOUVENIRS

El Corte Inglés ✷✷ (Preciados 3; ☎ 913-79-80-00; www.elcorteingles.es) complex in Puerta del Sol offers one-stop souvenir shopping. The electronics store has rack upon rack of CDs, including pop-rock and Latino-Español as well as flamenco organized by specialties such as rumbas, Las Sevillanas, *pasodobles* flamenco guitar or Nuevo Flamenco. (See "Music & Musical Instruments," earlier, for other shops.)

El Corte Inglés's large food shop is on the lower level of the building behind the electronics store. Spaniards claim that their saffron is the best in the world and a half-gram box for 2.65€ makes an impressive gift. (If you have time, you'll find cheaper at Mercado de la Paz; p. 67.) Much more reasonable—and a new favorite of North American chefs and foodies—are little tins of smoked Spanish paprika or "Pimentón de la Vera." If you've become hooked on Spanish hot chocolate, pick up some Valor cocoa powder for yourself and your friends.

Among the accessories on the street level are souvenir-grade embroidered Spanish shawls and damascene jewelry and other accessories made in Toledo (p. 83). The leather and metal jewelry by the Spanish company Una de 50 is much more hip—sort of tasteful punk-bondage.

Don't overlook the pharmacy aisles. Our friends love the large bars of Magno Classic black soap. The concentrated bath gel from Madrid's venerated **Perfumería Alvarez Gómez** (Serrano 14, ☎ 914-31-16-56; Paseo de la Castellana 111, ☎ 915-55-59-61) is great for travel. To see their complete line, visit the shop at Serrano 14.

If you must have a flamenco doll, leather wine flask, or Don Quixote figurine, check out **Objetos de Arte Toledano** (Paseo del Prado 10; ☎ 914-29-50-00; www.artetoledano.com); their upscale shop next door (Paseo del Prado 12) has fine porcelain including traditional Lladró and more modern Sargadelo.

You'll recognize **Antigua "Casa Talavera"** ★ (Isabel La Catolica 2; ☎ 915-47-34-17) off Plaza Santo Domingo by the beautiful tile facade depicting scenes from Don Quixote. Three small rooms are crammed with hand-painted pitchers, platters, mugs, olive servers, and more. Many are historic reproductions, and the owner knows all the families who carry on this tradition of fine handcraft.

When you stop on Plaza Mayor for a drink, check out **El Arco Artesania** (Plaza Mayor 9; ☎ 913-65-26-80; www.elarcoartesania.com) for a nice range of work made by contemporary Spanish craftspeople.

NIGHTLIFE IN MADRID

We know you thought dining was Madrid's major nightlife. But for a rundown on every conceivable form of entertainment from ballet to sex shows, pick up a copy of *Guia del Ocio,* published on Thursday and sold at every newsstand.

FLAMENCO

For our money, the city's best nightlife is flamenco. More than entertainment and atmosphere, it's a lifestyle. Don't expect performances to begin before 10pm. Flamenco's tangled musical roots sprout from Andalusia (p. 127), but the current artistic revival began in Madrid in the 1980s and not even the big cities of Andalusia offer as much variety. If you are going to take in just one performance in Madrid, go straight to **Casa Patas** ★★★ (Cañizares 10; ☎ 913-69-04-96; www.casapatas.com; Metro: Tirso de Molina or Antón Martín), which is co-owned by one of the founding members of the jazz-flamenco band, Pata Negra. You might see a newly discovered singer-guitarist duo—or members of the Amaya, Montoya, or Habichuela families (the royalty of flamenco). Either way, the performance will be top rate. The bar starts filling up with *flamencos,* as those who live the life of the music are called, about an hour before the nominal start time for a performance. Unshaven men sporting long black ponytails and dressed all in black nurse glasses of sherry amid the chic Madrileños in designer jeans tossing back Scotch on the rocks. Shows are 28€ Monday through Thursday, 31€ Friday and Saturday, including a drink. Reservations strongly recommended.

Flamenco was nearly moribund from the Spanish Civil War into the early 1980s and was kept alive in part by tourist dinner shows. A few of those old-fashioned and usually expensive *tablaos* still do a roaring business; just ask at your hotel and they'll eagerly book you into one to earn the commission. (Actually, don't do that; the flamenco is a pale version of the real thing.) But even the dinner-show market is evolving. Wherever you go, plan to dine elsewhere and just pay for the show admission, which always includes a drink.

Performers founded **Las Carboneras Tablao Flamenco** (Plaza del Conde Miranda 1; ☎ 915-42-86-77; www.tablaolascarboneras.com; Metro: Opera or La Latina) as a showcase for young talent. Some flamenco venues emphasize music—here dance is the focus, with long solo performances. You'll hear backstage tapping rhythms and an occasional guitar chord

> ❝To go to bed at night in Madrid marks you as a little queer. For a long time your friends will be a little uncomfortable about it. Nobody goes to bed in Madrid until they have killed the night.❞
>
> —Ernest Hemingway,
> *Death in the Afternoon*

before the lights dim, leaving the audience in flickering shadows from the candles on each table. Combined packages for dinner and show run 55€ to 68€; performance and one drink 29€. Reservations recommended.

Dancer Maripaz Lucena, who is well-connected in the tight-knit flamenco world, is the force behind **Espacio Flamenco** (Ribera de Curtidores 26; ☎ 912-98-19-55; www.espacioflamenco.es; Metro: Puerta de Toledo, Embajadores, or Lavapiés). Evening performances take place in a stylish space with gray walls and polka-dot underskirts on the tables. It's beneath a shop catering to musicians and dancers. (Try hefting one of those ruffled skirts to really appreciate how much effort is involved in the artistry.) Dinner and show 65€; performance and one drink 30€. Go for the latter. Reservations required.

With a strong subculture of musicians and dancers to draw on, several bars stage flamenco one or two nights a week. Calle Echegaray has long had at least one such establishment, and for the moment it's **Cardamomo Tablao Flamenco** (Echegaray 15; ☎ 913-69-07-57; www.cardamomo.es; flamenco Tues–Wed; Metro: Sevilla or Sol). Arrive at least a half-hour before the posted show time to get a seat at one of a dozen tiny tables with hard wooden stools. The performance will start when the air has turned blue from cigarette smoke and the crowd has finished the "free" beer or sangria that comes with admission. The musician-driven performances feature elaborate percussion, two guitarists, and a top-notch singer. Women dancers dominate, but you might also catch a young man with plucked eyebrows in a frenetic solo. Admission 10€.

Don't arrive too early at **Sala Juglar** (Lavapiés 37; ☎ 915-28-43-81; www.salajuglar.com; Metro: Lavapiés), as they don't roll up the corrugated metal door until after 9pm. For most of the week, this tiny Lavapiés club pumps late-night dance music and sometimes hosts jazz concerts. The Sunday evening *Juglar X Flamenco* show features ace guitarist Manuel Cavas, singer El Ciervo, as well as dancers and percussion. Grab a bottled beer at the bar and hang out in the back until the doors to the performance space open. Flamenco admission 7€.

Flamenco is a night owl's pursuit, and nowhere more so than at **Clan** (Ribera de Curtidores across from #30, just south of Ronda de Toledo; ☎ 915-28-84-01;

Making the Most of the Cheap Seats

Ready to see a show on a whim? More than 30 theaters scattered all across the city offer day-of-performance tickets at discounts up to 50%. Buy in person at **Taquilla Ultimo Minuto** (Plaza del Carmen 1; www.taquillaultimominuto.com; Wed–Sun 5–10pm; Metro: Gran Vía or Sol). Check the website for productions, which can range from Spanish-language versions of U.S. musicals to circus-like spectacles, to new plays by local companies.

---

www.osclan.com; Metro: Puerta de Toledo or Embajadores), where performances don't begin until midnight on Friday and Saturday. Don't be fooled by the modest stage in the front window or by the free admission. This isn't a dive bar like some near Sol that offer flamenco when they can't book anything else.

JAZZ

In addition to flamenco, Madrid has a pretty good jazz scene, led by **Central Cafe** (Plaza del Angel 10; ☎ 913-69-41-43; www.cafecentralmadrid.com; cover 8€–11€). Since 1982 this bar-restaurant-cafe has been programming live jazz with touring musicians from Europe and the U.S. Shows go on nightly between 10pm and midnight.

You'll also find a lot of jazz in the mix at the Malasaña mega-club, **Clamores** (Albuquerque 14; ☎ 914-45-79-38; www.clamores.es; Metro: Bilbao), though its real strength among the nightly concerts is the lineup of contemporary Spanish-language singer-songwriters.

THEATER, DANCE & CLASSICAL MUSIC

Popular music may have a strong presence in Madrid, but so do the fine performing arts, at least from September to June or July. (Even oboe players go on vacation in August.) You could go see a Spanish-language production of *Jesus Christ Superstar* or *Barefoot in the Park,* but if you're curious about *zarzuela,* which mixes sketch theater, opera, popular song, and spoken narrative, check out performances at the **Teatro Lírico National de Zarzuela** (Jovellanos 4; ☎ 915-24-54-00; http://teatrodelazarzuela.mcu.es; 10€–128€; Metro: Sevilla). Most Wednesday performances are half-price.

The city of Madrid operates the historic **Teatro Español** (Principe 25 on Plaza Santa Ana; ☎ 914-29-62-97; www.esmadrid.com/teatroespanol; Metro: Antón Martín or Tirso de Molina), which hosts performances of dance, orchestral, and chamber music, as well as live theater (in Spanish).

For opera or ballet, check **Teatro Real** (Plaza de Oriente; ☎ 902-24-48-48 tickets or ☎ 915-16-06-06 information; www.teatro-real.com; Metro: Opera). Student same-day rush tickets are discounted 90%.

The city's top symphonic orchestra, Orquestra Sinfónica de Madrid, makes its home at the acoustically splendid **Teatro Monumental** (Atocha 65; ☎ 914-29-12-81; www.osm.es; Metro: Antón Martín).

CINEMA

One of our guilty pleasures is watching first-run U.S. action movies in Spanish-speaking countries so that we can use the Spanish subtitles to learn new vocabulary that you rarely pick up in the classroom. Alas, in Madrid, most English-language films are dubbed into Spanish. But there are a couple of options. **Cine Doré** (Santa Isabel 3, across the alley behind the Mercado Antón Martín; ☎ 913-69-11-25; tickets 2.50€; Metro: Antón Martín) is a classic *filmoteca* or repertory house in an unusual Madrid example of modernismo built in 1922. Original language films, including many classics, are subtitled in Spanish. The nine theaters at **Cine Ideal** (Doctor Cortezo 6 in Plaza de Jacinto Benavente; ☎ 902-22-09-22; http://yelmocines.es; tickets Mon 5.60€, otherwise 6.90€; Metro: Tirso de Molina) screen current films in their original language (such as English, French, or Mandarin) with Spanish subtitles if needed.

DANCE CLUBS

Like a reversal of the Cinderella story, the central room at **Clamores** (above) is transformed from a sedate performance venue into a throbbing disco every night at 1:30am, with the action really starting around 2:30am and ending more or less at 5am.

Most of the time, though, disco is a weekend activity—always on Fridays, usually on Saturdays, sometimes on Thursdays. The physically largest and most-touted dance club (you'll find discount cards in every cheap hotel) is Puerta del Sol's own **Disco-Teatro Joy Eslava** (Arenal 11; ☎ 913-66-37-33; www.joy-eslava.com; cover 12€; Metro Sol). The action takes place in a cavernous 19th-century theater that used to stage the uniquely Madrileño form of light opera called *zarzuela*. Doors open at 11pm, but the party won't get going until 1am or later.

The main room at **Cool** (Isabel La Católica 6; ☎ 902-499-994; cover 10€–15€; Metro: Santo Domingo) is a hard-rock space, but side room "Sunflowers" specializes in salsa, Latin jazz, and house music for gay and straight dancers alike, while the other side room "Royal" offers predominantly gay dancing, often bare-chested, to tribal and house from midnight to 6am.

On Friday nights, the Flamingo Club (you really don't want to know) is transformed into **Ocho y Medio** (Mesonero Romanos, 13; ☎ 915-41-35-00; cover 10€–15€; Metro: Callao or Gran Vía), named for the Fellini movie. The scene favors indie pop with a heavy dose of New York and L.A. hip-hop, and draws a student-age crowd for meeting, greeting, and shaking between 1am and 6am.

For socializing a little earlier in the night, **Tupperware** (Corredera Alta de San Pablo 26; no phone; no cover; Metro: Tribunal) opens up around 10:30pm, reaches capacity around midnight, and closes at 3:30am. The bar is filled with American pop-culture kitsch and the soundtrack for dancing (or just swaying) is loud and often psychedelic. It's also a magnet for the Malasaña lesbian scene.

A Malasaña favorite for the boys is **Club Nasti** (San Vicente Ferrer 33; ☎ 915-21-76-05; cover 10€; Metro: Tribunal), where the synthopop, electroclash, and New York punk fuel the action on the crowded dance floor.

GET OUT OF TOWN

If you've visited the Palacio Real, you'll be forgiven if you think one royal palace is quite enough. But the Madrid countryside is dotted with other royal residences, thanks largely to the 16th-century efforts of Felipe II. They're all accessible either by bus or *cercanía* train.

Only 10km (6¼ miles) from the city, **Palacio Real de El Pardo** (Manuel Alonso; ☎ 913-76-15-00; www.patrimonionacional.es; 4€ adults, 2.30€ students and children 5–16; Oct–Mar Mon–Sat 10:30am–5pm, Sun 10am–1:30pm; Apr–Sept Mon–Sat 10:30am–6pm, Sun 9:30am–1:30pm) is a 15-minute ride on the 601 interurban bus from the Moncloa terminal. Monarchs began hunting here in the 14th century, and Emperor Carlos V (King Carlos I) began construction of a palace in 1553; it was completed in 1558 under his son Felipe II.

Like so much else, the palace gained its grandeur in the 18th century from the intercession of Carlos III, who, among other things, commissioned Goya to paint cheery country scenes as cartoons for a series of tapestries. After the Civil War, Franco made El Pardo his official residence and stayed there, surrounded by the trappings of monarchy, until his death in 1975. Though still used by visiting heads of state, El Pardo has become something of a curiosity. The guided tour includes the Generalissimo's office, state dining room, private sitting room, bedroom—and even his bathroom.

Although Felipe II made Madrid the capital of Spain and seat of the monarchy in 1561, he already had his eyes fixed on his death and legacy. Starting in 1562, he focused on the **Real Monasterio de San Lorenzo El Escorial** (Juan de Borbón y Battembergr; ☎ 918-90-59-02; www.patrimonionacional.es; 8€ admission; guided tours 10€ adults, 4€ students and children 5–16; Oct–Mar Tues–Sun 10am–5pm, Apr–Sept Tues–Sun 10am–6pm), which was completed in 1584. Set in the Guadarrama mountains about 50km (31 miles) northwest of Madrid (via C-8 train from Atocha or bus no. 664 or 661 from the Moncloa transport terminal), El Escorial can be surprisingly cooler than the city. The vast complex includes a palace, a monastery, a 40,000-volume library, and a basilica. Most monarchs from Carlos I and Felipe II forward are buried in the Pantheon of Kings beneath the chancel of the basilica.

Felipe II must have been a frustrated architect. In 1561 he ordered the construction of a summer palace at Aranjuez, yet another royal hunting ground. Although the **Palacio Real de Aranjuez** (Plaza de Parejas; ☎ 914-67-50-62; www.patrimonionacional.es; 5€ adults, 2.50€ students and children 5–16; Oct–Mar Tues–Sun 10am–5:15pm, Apr–Sept Tues–Sun 10am–6:15pm) wasn't completed until the 18th-century reign of Carlos III, Felipe would have certainly been thrilled with the grandeur of the so-called "Spanish Versailles." You can reach Aranjuez on the C-3 train from Atocha or the Madrid-Aranjuez bus from Estacion Sur on calle Mendez Álvaro. The best time to visit is in the spring when local strawberries and asparagus are in season. A museum on the lower level of the palace purports to pull back the veil on life in such grand surroundings, while a Barge Museum on the grounds shows the pleasure craft of the royals. The rich really do live differently. Be sure to allot time for a stroll through the elaborate gardens.

If you've had enough pomp and circumstance, take the C-7 train from Atocha to **Alcalá de Henares,** 30 kilometers east of Madrid. The town was established as

a center of learning in 1499 by Cardinal Cisneros, though most university buildings date from the 17th century. It's also the birthplace of Miguel de Cervantes. The **Museo Casa Natal de Cervantes** (Mayor 48; ☎ 918-89-96-54; www.museo-casa-natal-cervantes.org; free admission; Tues–Sun 10am–6pm) is located in the old quarter of town at the site where the creator of Don Quixote is believed to have been born in 1547. Furnishings in the two-story house with courtyard recreate domestic life of a well-off family (Cervantes's father was a doctor). The exhibit room displays copies of Cervantes's works published in 22 languages.

The ABCs of Madrid

American Express Located at Plaza de las Cortes 2 (☎ 913-22-55-00), next to the Palace Hotel.

Banks You can usually find a bank—or at least an ATM—wherever crowds gather in Madrid, especially in shopping districts and around major Metro stations. Most permit cash withdrawals via MC or V, and many are linked into international networks that will let you access your American bank account. Most offer a choice of language, almost always including English. Major banks include **Banco Santander, Caja Madrid, Banesto,** and **BBVA**.

Emergencies Dial ☎ 112 for any emergency. You can call an ambulance at ☎ 061, the national police at ☎ 091, or the municipal police at ☎ 092.

Hospital Both **Hospital General Universitario Gregorio Marañón** (Dr Esquerdo 46; ☎ 915-68-80-00) and **Hospital Universitario La Paz** (Paseo de la Castellana 261; ☎ 917-27-70-00) have emergency rooms.

Internet Most *hostales* and many hotels offer free Wi-Fi access if you have your own laptop, although as a rule of thumb, the more expensive the lodging, the more likely it charges for access. Many cafes also offer free access. Internet centers are almost as common in Madrid as hams hanging in bars. Look for them in areas frequented by tourists and immigrants (they're often coupled with long-distance telephone services). Expect to pay 1€ to 3€ per hour.

Police The Central Police Station (Leganitos 19) provides emergency services for foreign tourists (☎ 915-48-85-37 or ☎ 915-48-80-08). To report a crime, call ☎ 902-10-21-12, a 24-hour line.

Post Office The ornate architecture of the General Post Office (Plaza de Cibeles; ☎ 915-214-260), makes it a true Palacio de Comunicaciones. It's worth a visit, but you can also purchase stamps at tobacco shops.

Restrooms Pay toilet stalls (marked WC) can be found in high-traffic areas such as Plaza Mayor, Puerta del Sol, and Atocha train station. They cost 1€. More reliable are the clean restrooms in the city's many free museums (p. 48).

Telephones You can purchase phone cards at tobacco shops, although some phones also accept cash. Public phones, however, are on the wane in Madrid because many residents carry mobile phones.

Tourist Offices The **Madrid Tourism Centre** (Plaza Mayor 27; ☎ 915-88-16-36; Metro: Sol or Ópera) and **Colón Tourism Centre** (Plaza de Colón in the underground walkway between calles Génova and Goya; in-person inquiries only; Metro: Colón) are open daily 9:30am to 8:30pm. Check www.esmadrid.com and www.turismomadrid.es.

3 Central Spain

The crucible of Spanish identity

by Patricia Harris & David Lyon

AS YOU APPROACH THE CITIES OF CENTRAL SPAIN, IMAGINE THAT YOU ARE leading an invading army. After a long march across a flat plain with no place to hide, you finally reach the outskirts of Toledo, Cuenca, Segovia, or Avila. You crane your neck to look up at the walled fortress city high on the hill. Its defenders have watched your approach for days, and their swords are ready . . . It is the story of central Spain written over and over—only the names of the invaders and defenders constantly changed.

And whoever seized the plains of La Mancha or the hilltop aeries of the cities, they always acted audaciously. Roman engineers channeled water from distant mountains to make Segovia bloom. Centuries later, a string of rulers named Alfonso and Sancho and Ferdinand (Fernando) plotted power in the name of a Christian god and fortified the heights, giving the region its enduring name, Castilla, or land of castles. They carried the battle of the *reconquista* from castle to castle across the searing center of the peninsula, mustering the military might, religious fervor, and brilliant scholarship that made them the most powerful rulers in Iberia—and ultimately kings of Spain.

But Castilla is more than just battles and castles. It's hard to think of the region without envisioning Don Quixote tilting at the windmills of La Mancha and nursing his impossible dream of nobility, so eloquently articulated (and skewered) by Castilian native son Miguel de Cervantes. This region is a dreamer's world where Santa Teresa sought the ecstatic embrace of Christ in her hometown of Avila and ended up revitalizing the Catholic Church as a moral force. The painter El Greco conjured his fantastic images—swirling, elongated figures rising to the heavens like animate thunderheads—from the hilltop citadel of Toledo, a city of both prayers and swords. And in Salamanca, Christopher Columbus lectured to the young students (Hernán Cortes possibly among them), recounting his adventures in a new world. There may be more impressive fortresses, more richly decorated churches, and even more picturesquely sited cities in other areas of Spain, but none boast so many touchstones of Spanish identity in such close proximity.

DON'T LEAVE CENTRAL SPAIN WITHOUT . . .

Seeing Toledo through the eyes of El Greco.   Four centuries later, Toledo still shines on a hill as its most famous painter depicted it. See p. 83.

Savoring roast suckling pig.   The signature dish of central Spain reaches its apotheosis in Segovia. See p. 104.

Climbing an urban mountain that inspired an art movement.   Cuenca's soaring heights and dizzying angles fostered a generation of abstract artists. See p. 98.

Looking for storks nesting in the highest bell tower.   Storks return every year to nest in central Spain's bell towers and castle turrets.

Feeling dwarfed beneath the roman aqueduct in Segovia.   The soaring arches of Segovia's aqueduct form an enduring reminder of the Roman presence. See p. 109.

Walking the ramparts of a medieval wall.   Views from the ramparts of central Spain's fortified cities still command the surrounding countryside.

Basking in the glow of Spain's greatest university.   The golden sandstone of the University of Salamanca reflects 8 centuries of learning. See p. 122.

A BRIEF HISTORY OF CENTRAL SPAIN

The story of central Spain is a microcosm of the history of the Iberian peninsula. When the Romans arrived in the 2nd century B.C., they quickly conquered the chiefdoms of loosely organized Celtic tribes in central Spain. Direct Roman rule was spotty, as many towns remained under Celtic leaders who paid tribute to Rome, although such engineering feats as the Segovia aqueduct attest to an enduring Roman legacy. When the Vandals invaded Iberia in 407–409, Rome turned to the Visigoths, another Germanic tribe, for help. In return for defeating the Vandals, the Visigoths were encouraged to settle most of Iberia and what is now southern France. No great respecters of enervated Roman might, the Visigoths declared their independence in 475.

Although the Franks soon pushed them out of France, the Visigoths consolidated their power in the Iberian peninsula with Toledo as their capital. The conversion of the Visigoth kings to Roman Catholicism in 589 joined church and crown in a two-fisted control of the population, one of the most expansive kingdoms in early medieval Europe. By 711, when the Moors invaded Iberia, central Spain was already a polyglot culture of Celts, Romans, and Visigoths with a small but significant Jewish population. The Moorish conquest of Toledo in 712 accelerated the multiculturalism, bringing in large numbers of Jews and Muslims from throughout the Islamic world, but it also heralded the onset of nearly 5 centuries of warfare that left less-fortified areas of central Spain sparsely populated.

Late in the 8th century, the Christian kings of northern Iberia began to push southward to take back the Iberian peninsula from the Moors. They followed a two-pronged approach to regain territory: They fortified the heights, and they encouraged resettlement of depopulated areas by Christian subjects. Thus, Castilla was born—literally the land of castles.

Castilla's capture of Toledo in 1085 marked a turning point in the *reconquista,* establishing a Christian stronghold at the doorstep of Andalusia. By founding the University of Salamanca in 1218, the crown established Castilla as one of medieval

Europe's great centers of learning. Central Spain was secured after the Battle of Las Navas de Tolosa in 1212, when Alfonso VIII of Castilla led a Christian coalition through the mountains to Andalusia and took the Moorish Almohad army by surprise, leaving 100,000 men dead on the battlefield and turning the tide of the border wars. For the next 290 years, the Castilian kings of central Spain spearheaded the *reconquista.* Success at taking the main cities of Andalusia made them the strongest monarchy on the peninsula, especially when the 1469 marriage of Isabella I of

> " The stern tablelands that form the heart of Spain are like sounding-boards for the spirit. Though your voice often falls flat upon a dry soil, or is whisked away by the bitter wind, ideas seem to echo and expand, visions form in the great distances, and man, all alone in the emptiness, seems only the agent of some much greater Power. "
>
> —Jan Morris,
> *Among the Cities* (1985)

Castilla and Ferdinand II of Aragón (known as Isabel and Fernando in Spain) unified the crowns of the two largest kingdoms in Iberia. Later hailed as the "Catholic kings" by Pope Alexander VI, they completed the *reconquista* when they took Granada on January 2, 1492.

The strong-willed Catholic kings also launched the Spanish Inquisition in Castilla in 1477, initially as a tool against Jews and then Muslims. This heavy-handed religious cleansing—later turned against Protestants—lasted until 1834. It made Spain the most fiercely Catholic country in Europe and a center of the Counter-Reformation, the church's movement to clean up abuses of power and rediscover its religious roots. The teachings of central Spain's 16th-century mystics Teresa de Avila and Juan de la Cruz had a powerful impact throughout the country, but especially in Avila and Segovia, their home base.

In 1561, Felipe II moved the Spanish court to Madrid from Toledo, in part because the hilltop city was physically too small to support new construction. Although Toledo remained the ecclesiastical center of Spain, the city was thus spared Madrid's growing pains. In 1577, the Crete-born painter, Doménicos Theotokópoulos, better known as El Greco, arrived in Toledo from Rome to paint his first commissions and remained until his death in 1614. His work over nearly 4 decades still defines the city, which looks surprisingly as it did in his day.

The concentration of civil power in Madrid drew money and resources from the surrounding cities of central Spain. As a result, their historic cores look much as they did in the 16th and 17th centuries. Salamanca was something of an exception, as it was not contained as a fortress city and continued to grow into the 18th century, the period of its extraordinary Plaza Mayor.

LAY OF THE LAND

Central Spain, for the purposes of this chapter, consists of two modern autonomous regions that form a doughnut around Madrid: Castilla y León to the north, and Castilla–La Mancha to the south. Toledo is the historic administrative center of the seemingly endless plains of La Mancha, once the breadbasket of the

Central Spain

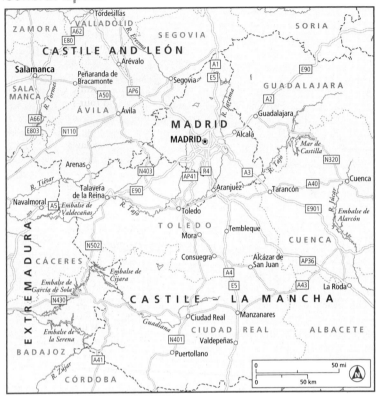

Roman Empire. It is flat country interrupted by rocky spurs that almost seem to jump out of the ground. Cuenca is also part of Castilla–La Mancha but lies in the midst of a small mountain range east of Madrid. The cities of Segovia, Avila, and Salamanca in Castilla y León occupy rolling hill country. Historically, they were the urban centers for a pastoral economy based largely on sheep.

Most overseas travelers to this part of Spain begin and end in Madrid—indeed, all the cities in this chapter can be visited from Madrid as day trips, though you won't see much in the few hours between trains or buses. Because Madrid is so central, travelers relying on public transportation will often find it faster to return to Madrid rather than wait for the next direct bus between the cities of central Spain.

If you plan to tour extensively, you may prefer to drive. Leave your car parked securely on the outskirts of each historic city while you explore on foot. Specific information on bus and rail service is detailed in the city sections below. For schedules and prices, check the website of the national rail network, **RENFE** (www.renfe.es). *Important:* Since distances are short and fares are cheap, it does not pay to squander days of a Spanish Rail Pass in this region.

TOLEDO ✮✮✮

Only an hour by car, bus, or train from Madrid, Spain's old capital seems centuries removed from its new one. It is as if hilltop Toledo has barely twitched a muscle since Felipe II ordered the court to pack up—lock, stock, and barrel—for a change of venue. It still stands as a citadel atop a promontory where the Río Tajo wraps a lasso around three sides. The tiny streets of the historic center (some barely more than shoulder width) are lined with three- and four-story buildings that ensure cool, deep shade even in the heat of summer. Native Toledanos expertly dart from shadow to shadow. There's hardly a building in the city that *isn't* historic, but most of what you see dates from Toledo's heyday as the Spanish capital—roughly A.D. 1250 to 1560—as Spain wrapped up the *reconquista* and moved onto the world stage as an imperial power.

GETTING TO & AROUND TOLEDO

Bus and train service between Madrid and Toledo is quick (about 1 hour) and inexpensive (9€ train, 4€ bus). The **RENFE train station** (Paseo de la Rosa; ☎ 925-223-099) and the **Toledo bus station** (Molinos de Viento; ☎ 925-220-300) are both serviced by city buses. To get into the center of the Old City, ask for a bus bound to Plaza de Zocodover. Don't even try driving in Toledo's Old City—even if you manage not to destroy your car, you'll never find a safe and legal place to park. If you do have a car, look for free parking along avenida Carlos III outside the Old City, or, failing that, bite the bullet and zip into the well-signed Recaredo Parking Garage (maximum of 16€ per day). It used to be daunting to walk uphill into Toledo, but the free Recaredo escalator, installed in 2000, now zips up six levels. You'll enter on the opposite side of the city from the cathedral, but just follow the signs for a 10-minute walk down narrow streets. The **Patronato Municipal de Turismo** (Pl de la Ayuntamiento; ☎ 925-254-030; www.turismocastillalamancha.com; daily 10:30am–2:30pm and Mon–Fri 4:30–7pm), on the plaza adjacent to the cathedral, has good city maps.

There are two ways to explore Toledo: Either follow the roads by the Old City walls (which will take you to most of the convents and the Jewish Quarter), or abandon yourself to fate and follow the interior streets. Most attractions are within sight of the main east-west corridor that keeps changing names: calles San Ángel, Santo Tomé, de la Trinidad, Hombre de Palo, and Comercio.

ACCOMMODATIONS, BOTH STANDARD & NOT

Although many visitors make the mistake of trying to see the city in a day, Toledo has a range of good hotel options. The following accommodations include air-conditioning, heat, phone, and TV unless otherwise noted, but the rates do not include Wi-Fi, tax, or breakfast unless specified. If you have a car (useful for exploring the countryside), we suggest opting for one of the lodgings outside of town, Hotel Béatriz or either one of the *cigarrales,* to make parking and highway access easier.

€–€€€   There's a longstanding tradition in Europe that a traveler may take refuge in the shadow of the church, and while these two lodgings aren't quite as cheap as the church doorway, they're a lot more comfortable. They're both just feet from Toledo's cathedral, in the heart of the attractions of the Old City. Only

Toledo

0   200 m
0   200 yds

LOS BLOQUES

Roman ■
Circus
(Ruins)

Carretera de Carlos III

Paseo del Circo Romano

Av. de la Reconquista

Av. de Duque Lerma

Calle del Cardenal Tavera

Calle de la Carrera

Glorieta de la
Reconquista

LA ANTEQUERUELA

Avenida de la Cava

Paseo de Recaredo

SANTIAGO

Esta. de la Granja

Puerta del Sol 18

C. de los Azacanes

Palacio
Benacazón

Calle de Gerardo Lobo

**Museo de
Santa Cruz**
20

Plaza de
la Merced

Convento
Carmelitas
Descalzas

Santo Domingo
el Antiguo 2

Plaza
Sta. Catalina

17

C. de los
Alfileritos

16

Plaza
Sta. Teresa
de Jesús

Plaza
San Juan
de los Reyes

Palacio de
la Cava

Casa de Mesa

Plaza de
San Román

Iglesia
San Román

Plaza de la
Magdalena

Cuesta de Carlos

Alcázar

19

**SAN
MARTÍN**

Monasterio
San Juan de
los Reyes
3

Museo de Arte
Contemporaneo

C. del Ángel

C. de los Reyes Católicos

Trinidad

Palacio
Arzobispal

14 15

Plaza del
Ayuntamiento

Catedral
13

21

Plaza
San Justo

LA CANDELARIA

JUDERIA
4

Iglesia
Sto. Tomé

C. San Tomé

9

5

10

7

Plaza
Salvador

San
Marcos

Taller del
Moro

12

11

Calle del Pozo Amargo

Conservatorio

Paseo de Cabestreros

← 6
← 8

Calle Los Descalzos

EL CALVARIO

Plaza
Santa
Isabela

Plaza
Santa
Catalina

Seminario

Plaza
San Ciprano

Carreras de San Sebastián

**SANTA
CATALINA**

Plaza de
los Infantes

Tagus (Tajo)

FRANCE

SPAIN
★ Madrid
● Toledo

PORTUGAL

ACCOMMODATIONS ■
Cigarral de Caravantes 6
Hotel Beatriz Toledo 1
Hotel Eurico 12
Hotel Los Cigarrales 8
Hotel Pintor El Greco 10
Hotel Santa Isabel 11

DINING ◆
Adolfo Collectión 14

Alfileritos 24 Taberna
  Restaurante 16
Cafetería Restaurante Alex 17
Cafetería Wamba 19
Cervecería Restaurante
  La Campana Gorda 15

ATTRACTIONS ●
Alcázar 21
Catedral 13

Convento de Santo Domingo
  El Antiguo 2
Mirador Barrio Nuevo 7
Monasterio de San Juan
  de los Reyes 3
Museo de Santa Cruz 20
Museo de Santo Tomé 9
Museo Sefardí 5
Museo Vittorio Macho 4
Puerta del Sol 18

open since 2006, **Hotel Eurico** (Santa Isabel 3; ☎ 925-284-178; www.hoteleurico toledo.com; MC, V) occupies a pair of late 15th- and early 16th-century houses that were joined in the 18th century. Most of the 23 rooms—arrayed around a central patio—are extremely simple with two beds pushed up against a wall-mounted headboard and a corner desk. But the bathrooms, which have both bidet and toilet, tub shower, and vanities constructed of marble, are much more sumptuous and modern than usually found in this price range. Think comfort, not luxury. Official rates for doubles are 120€ to 140€ but in practice go as low as 59€, even in the busy summer season. Slightly farther from the cathedral, the older **Hotel Santa Isabel** (Santa Isabel 24; ☎ 925-253-120; www.santa-isabel.com; MC, V) has 42 rooms fully renewed with gleaming hardwood floors and functional modern bathrooms with floor and walls covered with travertine. Unadorned traditional white plaster walls rule here as well, but some rooms also have exposed wooden beam ceilings. Room 215 is perhaps the nicest, with its glassed-in balcony, while slightly smaller 303, right above it, is next to the spiral staircase that leads to the roof terrace where guests can sit in the evening and watch swallows skim along the rooftops. Prices hold steady all year at 52€, including tax. Breakfast is an extra 5€, while underground garage parking (if you dare drive here) is 10€ a day.

€€–€€€€   You'll have to be a little lucky to get parking (12€) at one of the most romantic lodgings in the Old City, **Hotel Pintor El Greco** ✹✹ (Alamillos del Tránsito 13; ☎ 925-285-191; www.hotelpintorelgreco.com; AE, MC, V), as it has only 17 spaces and the hotel nearly doubled its size from 33 to 60 rooms in July 2008. The original section is a classic 17th-century Toledo house (and former bakery) of brick and stucco, inside and out. Carved wooden furniture upholstered in patterned woven fabrics, wrought-iron banisters and light fixtures, and sunny colors sponged on stucco walls conjure up fine living in old Toledo. The new addition is as ultra-modern as the original is traditional, with contemporary dark wood and leather furniture, bright splashes of saturated color in pillows and wall decor, white marble floors, and flat-screen TVs. Ironically, many guests prefer the older section for its historical ambience. The location on the west side of town near the Sinagoga del Tránsito and San Juan de los Reyes is quiet, but it's only a short walk to the cathedral. Prices range from 60€ for a standard double to 129€ for a small suite in the new section.

€€–€€€€   Although it's a five-minute drive outside the Old City, if you're traveling with children in the summer, be sure to check for web deals on the **Hotel Beatriz Toledo** (kids) (Ctra de Avila, Km 2.75; ☎ 925-269-100; www.beatrizhoteles. com; AE, MC, V). The large, nicely landscaped swimming pool is a huge amenity in the summer heat of La Mancha, and it's one of the few "resort" hotels that allows you to book without breakfast or other meals. (The meals, in our opinion, are not worth the price.) The hotel was built for large groups—conventions, bus tours, weddings, and the like—and when that business falls off in the summer heat, prices drop to as low as 60€ per night for a double, with extra beds at 12€. (Those same rooms can run 180€ during a conference.) The fact that the Beatriz is a newer, five-story highway hotel on the northern outskirts means less historic character, but much more space in the rooms, each of which boasts a small outdoor terrace.

Your Country Estate

El Greco painted his famous *View of Toledo* from the small hills across the Río Tajo from the southwest corner of the city. But the painter wasn't the only one to appreciate the view. High-society families of Toledo built their country estates, or *cigarrales,* amid the olive groves along the same hillside, and some of these properties have found new life as delightful small hotels. If you want a restful base from which to explore the city, our favorite two hotels are both on the no. 71 city bus line, which runs back and forth to Plaza de Zocodover every hour.

€–€€   The flat-out bargain of the two is **Hotel Los Cigarrales** ★ (Ctra Circunvalación 32; ☎ 925-220-053; www.hotelcigarrales.com; MC, V), where doubles are 59€, and doubles with an outside terrace (worth the upgrade for the El Greco view of Toldeo) are 68€, tax included. The blue-and-white-tiled walls in the stairways and hallways set a country house tone, while the 35 rooms are fairly spare—white stucco walls, carved dark wood furniture, and modest bathrooms with a small tub-shower. For a private patio without others adjoining it, ask for Room 220.

€€€   Each of the 22 rooms at **Cigarral de Caravantes** ★ (Ctra Circunvalación 2; ☎ 925-283-680; www.cigarraldecaravantes.com; AE, DC, MC, V) has a patio or terrace with a stunning view of Toledo beyond the hotel's own lush gardens and fountains. The wooden-beamed ceilings, large floor tiles, and extensive use of wrought iron for the furniture and architectural details evoke the era of Spain's colonial heyday. (Americans will find themselves reminded of design-conscious Santa Fe.) Although more expensive, Caravantes, which also has an outdoor pool, is also a great value at 100€ to 119€, tax included.

DINING FOR ALL TASTES

Toledo's cuisine relies heavily on mushrooms foraged from the river gorges, artichokes raised in the dry fields below the city, and wild game. The striking signature dish *perdiz a la Toledana* (partridge cooked with herbs, olive oil, and white wine) is widely imitated all over Spain.

€   When you're tromping the steep and narrow streets of the Old City, sometimes you simply need to fuel up. **Cafetería Wamba** (Comercio 2; ☎ 925-222-057; daily 8am–10pm; cash only) serves a range of quick combination plates that are too tasty and satisfying to be called fast food but nonetheless appear quickly at the table. Most of these plates feature a small steak, a grilled chicken breast, or two fried eggs complemented by crisp french fries, a small green salad, or, best of all, the house *pisto Manchego,* a cooked-down blend of red and green peppers, eggplant, and tomatoes. This healthy local food is almost priced like the Golden Arches: 4.50€ to 8€.

€€   **Cafetería Restaurante Alex** (Pl Amador des los Ríos 9; ☎ 925-223-963; daily 1–4pm and 7pm–midnight; MC, V) specializes in regional wild game, especially deer, quail, and partridge. Bypass the upstairs bar/coffee shop for the more

Tastes of Toledo

All over Spain, you'll see shops that sell *productos tipicos,* or "typical products." But at their best, their goods are anything *but* typical. Instead, they are local food specialties that get little distribution out of their home areas. **Casa Cuartero** (Hombre de Palo 5; ☎ 925-222-614) has been a great source in Toledo for *productos tipicos* since 1920. You'll find several cheeses from small producers and classic Iberian hams. Look for clear plastic cases of tangled threads of saffron in amounts that most non-Spaniards only dream about. (At last check, 20 grams of saffron, about the size of a deck of cards, sold for 55€; in the U.S., you could expect to pay anywhere from $100 to $150.) You'll also find tins of whole partridge packed in broth, as well as local pâtés made from rabbit, deer, or partridge. Anyone for a picnic?

gracious downstairs dining rooms with formal wooden furniture and cheerful checked table linens. By the same token, skip the cheap (11€) Menu Alex, which includes run-of-the-mill Spanish dishes, in favor of the menu del día (18€), with choices such as deer in a wild herb sauce or stuffed quail in wine sauce. Local Castilla–La Mancha wines are included in the menu price. The same dishes are also available a la carte (9€–12€), but the menu is a better deal if you're eating more than one course.

€€   Superchef Adolfo Muñoz's restaurants around Toledo cover a lot of gourmet ground, from fancy grill to white-linen Toledano cuisine. But you don't need to pay haute prices to sample the star chef's creative cooking (and some fabulous wines from central Spain) if you head to his bargain-priced **Adolfo Colleción** ★★ (Nuncio Viejo 1; ☎ 925-224-244; www.grupoadolfo.com; 11am–11:30pm; AE, DC, MC, V), a wine bar and shop that also serves food in a hip, casual setting. Again, game figures prominently, with such treats as rolled, stuffed venison with herbs (7.50€). It's also a good place to try the typical Toledan dish, *carcamusas,* which is a stewed meat casserole, in this case pork, tomatoes, and green peas, served with fried potatoes (7.50€). The menu del día (2 courses and dessert, but no wine) is only 12€.

€€–€€€   Perhaps the best deal in town on a menu del día is in the tavern side of **Alfileritos 24 Taberna Restaurante** ★ (Alfileritos 24; ☎ 925-239-625; www. alfileritos24.com; daily noon–4pm and 8pm–midnight; AE, DC, MC, V), where two courses, dessert, and choice of drink is only 9.90€. Starters could include a salad of tuna and white asparagus or mixed cheeses and dried fruits with a honey vinaigrette. For a main course, choose the deer tacos with mushroom salsa, if it's available. The tavern can get a bit rowdy on weekends, as it's one of the favorite watering holes for Toledo professionals. For a splurge, Alferitos 24 also has a fine dining restaurant with a quieter, more sophisticated vibe and more ambitious menu, such as grilled venison with spiced chocolate and caramelized red onion (17€).

€€–€€€ You'll find the Toledo shopkeepers having lunch of traditional specialties such as pickled partridge and vegetables (18€) in the dining room at **Cervecería Restaurante La Campana Gorda** (Hombre de Palo 13; ☎ 925-210-146; daily noon–4pm and 8–11pm; AE, MC, V) near the cathedral. The beer hall in the front room has a beautiful, long, curving marble bar, and serves a tapas/raciones menu where you can order plates of anchovies in vinegar (9€), wild mushrooms sautéed in butter (10€), or a version of jerky that's actually paper-thin slices of air-dried venison (17€).

WHY YOU'RE HERE: THE TOP SIGHTS & ATTRACTIONS

Although most of Toledo's medieval defensive walls have been taken down, the city still has the feel of a hilltop fortress. So approach it in that manner, beginning your visit with a circumnavigation of the roads that once lay just inside the walls, eerily marked by the preserved ceremonial gates, notably the Arabic archway of **Puerta del Sol** on the north side. To better understand how defenders could watch potential enemies as they approached, spend some time surveying the surrounding plain from **Mirador Barrio Nuevo** across the street from the Museo Sefardí at the Singoga del Tránsito (see below). Once you begin spiraling into the city interior, there are two key squares that are the centers of life in Toledo. You'll find Toledo children playing street soccer or learning to ride bicycles (as well as travelers visiting the tourist office) at the **Plaza del Ayuntamiento,** southwest of the cathedral. **Plaza de Zocodover,** northeast of the cathedral, is filled with outdoor cafes popular both with visitors and, at night, with young Toledanos. Both squares serve as reference points, as they represent transitions between neighborhoods within the city. The highest point of the city with the most commanding view, however, is off limits. The rugged Toledo **Alcázar** was virtually destroyed early in the Spanish Civil War but was rebuilt under Franco as a major military headquarters. Post-Franco redevelopment was supposed to convert it to a museum of the army, but opening has been delayed so long that many Toledanos suspect it will never come to pass.

Even after Toledo lost its temporal power, it remained the ecclesiastical capital of Spain, and its hulking **Catedral** ✦ (Cardenal Cisneros; ☎ 925-222-241; 7€, free Sat afternoon and Sun morning; Mon–Sat 10am–6:30pm, Sun 2–6:30pm) remains the physical hub of the city and the largest structure under a single roof. Oddly enough, you can't enter from any of the logical doorways that open onto broad plazas. The main entrance is off calle Hombre del Palo (look for the clock tower). In true Spanish fashion, the cathedral stands on the site of the Great Mosque, which displaced an earlier Visigothic church. The architecture is purely Gothic, befitting the 13th-century plans executed over several centuries, but the Gothic lines of the interior have been obscured by baroque decoration. The cathedral's heavily gilded main altar shows the influence of Moorish damascene art on what would become over-the-top Spanish baroque. The backs of the lower tier of the seats in the choir, carved by Rodrigo Alemán in 1495, depict the conquest of Granada just a few years earlier. His extraordinary carving of the seat arms in images of knights deep in prayer or thought (some of them hooded like Death himself) may be the most moving statues in a cathedral filled with statuary. Toledo's cathedral is somewhat overwhelmed with elaborately decorated VIP tombs (kings Alfonso VII, Sancho II, and Sancho III; Cardinal Mendoza; among

Ecclesiastical Confections

The nuns of Toledo began making the sugar and ground-almond confection known elsewhere as marzipan (but called *mazapán* here) in the early 13th century as a hedge against war-induced famine. (The candies were a way of preserving eggs and served as emergency rations.) The tradition still flourishes, but the nuns face stiff competition from small commercial operations. In fact, some of the best *mazapán* pastries in the city come from **Santo Tomé Obrador de Mazapán** (Santo Tomé 3, ☎ 925-223-763; Pl Zocodover 7, ☎ 925-221-168; www.mazapan.com). The company was founded in 1856 and its principal shop remains in the original location near the Santo Tomé church. Unlike the convents, which sell their pastries in prepackaged boxes, Santo Tomé allows you to assemble your own assortment from the display cases—or just buy one piece for a quick shot of sugar (1€–3€). The Plaza de Zocodover location is known for extravagant *mazapán* sculptures in the main display window.

others). The side chapels and Sacristy contain some of the cathedral's greatest artistic treasures in rooms small enough to get close to the work and study it. Be sure to visit the Sacristy to see the modest-sized El Greco portraits of each of the apostles, as well as his 1577–79 masterwork, *El Espolio (The Disrobing of Christ)*.

There are more El Greco canvases, of course, in the **Museo de Santa Cruz** ✪✪✪ (Cervantes 3; ☎ 925-221-036; free admission; Mon–Sat 10am–6pm, Sun 10am–2pm). In the fine art galleries, you'll find the 16th- and 17th-century paintings that once decorated many Toledo churches and convents. About a dozen of them are by El Greco, and the greatest of the lot is *La Asunción de la Virgen (Assumption of the Virgin)*, painted 1607–13. Stand about 18 inches from this late masterpiece and you'll be able to see how the paint flows like tiny rivers. You don't have to be religious—or even an art fan—to appreciate the electric excitement in this progenitor of "action painting." Nearby on the upper levels, the Carranza collection of ceramics of the Iberian peninsula is a thorough but not overwhelming survey of colorful Spanish and Portuguese tile work from the reconquest of Valencia in 1238 through the 19th century. And part of the interest in visiting here is simply to see the building itself. The immense halls of this 16th-century former convent feature elaborate carved and painted coffered ceilings and are devoted to changing temporary exhibitions, many of which are dwarfed by the space. *One note:* Don't be put off by the seemingly haphazard ground-level display of Roman, Visigothic, Moorish, and Mudéjar architectural fragments. (This is the museum's "archaeology" section.)

El Greco is ubiquitous in Toledo. He first came to the city in 1577 on a lucrative contract to paint nine canvases for **Convento de Santo Domingo El Antiguo** (Pl Santo Domingo El Antiguo; ☎ 925-222-930; museum 4€; Mon–Sat 11am–1:30pm and 4–7pm, Sun 4–7pm). They were to make his reputation, especially his early version of the *Assumption* that hangs over the altar. The painter's tomb is deep in the crypt below the convent church—the tour of the quirky museum includes the chance to gaze through the ultimately unsatisfying peephole in the floor at what is purported to be the underground tomb. Nor will you see the church interior if you go to see what many scholars consider El Greco's greatest work, *El Entierro del Conde Orgaz (The Burial of the Count of Orgaz),* in the **Museo de Santo Tomé** (Pl de Conde; ☎ 925-256-098; 2.30€; daily 10am–7pm). The painting is displayed in a foyer outside the church. Because it was the convention of the age to have nobility assist with burials of other nobles, the painting is a virtual who's-who of late 16th-century Toledo—a masterful gallery of portraits within a single composition. This small church was able to commission the work because El Greco was a parishioner and worked for a nominal fee.

The **"El Greco House" museum,** which was an early 20th-century attempt to replicate the quarters where the artist last lived, has been gutted and slated for rehabilitation as a modern museum dedicated to the painter. Meanwhile, the best of its paintings, *Vista y Plano de Toledo (View and Map of Toledo),* resides in a dedicated gallery at the **Museo Vittorio Macho** (Barquillo 10; ☎ 915-310-170; 3€ adults, 1.50€ seniors and students, children 11 and under free; www.realfundacion toledo.es; Mon–Sat 10am–7pm, Sun 10am–3pm). The gallery interpretation, which includes photographic blowups of painting sections, focuses on both the artistic qualities of the work and what it tells us about Toledo circa 1600. The remainder of the museum is devoted to sculptor and painter Macho, whose mature work in Art Deco and Streamline styles was largely carried out in exile after the Spanish Civil War. The vista from the gardens is alone worth the price of admission.

There are no El Grecos in the **Monasterio de San Juan de los Reyes** (San Juan de los Reyes 2; ☎ 925-223-802; 2.30€; daily 10am–6pm), just around the corner from the Macho museum, but the cloisters work their own kind of magic. Ferdinand and Isabella had the convent built to mark their 1476 victory over the Portuguese and originally intended to be buried in the monastery. (The symbolic importance of being buried in Granada, however, trumped that plan.) It is the epitome of a Franciscan retreat—the cloister's jungle-like central garden is filled with birdsong, and the high-vaulted Renaissance arches flood the arcades with reflected light.

Across the street from San Juan, the **Museo Sefardí** ✭ (Samuel Leví; ☎ 925-223-665; 2.40€ adults, 1.20€ seniors and students, free to all Sat and afternoons Sun; Feb 15–Nov Tues–Sat 10am–9pm, Sun 10am–2pm, Dec–Feb 14 Tues–Sat 10am–6pm, Sun 10am–2pm) fills the halls of Sinagoga del Tránsito, built in 1355 by Samuel Leví with a special dispensation from Pedro I. Leví definitely had some pull in the court, having served Pedro in a number of capacities, including as Royal Treasurer. It was the only Toledo synagogue untouched in the 1391 attacks on the city's Jewish ghetto. The building was Christianized after 1492, so little remains of the original scrollwork on the walls. It was partially restored in 1910, and the Sephardic Museum opened here in 1992 as a general education museum about Judaism in a country where Jewish presence has been minimal for 500 years. Cases chronicle the Jewish communities on the Iberian peninsula from the Roman era to 1492. One gallery deals with slow changes in 19th-century Spanish law, from the 1802 edict that allowed Jewish religious observances to the 1869 formal retraction of Ferdinand and Isabella's expulsion order.

THE OTHER TOLEDO

Toledo craftsmen were the first in Europe to rediscover the techniques that had made Damascus famous in antiquity for its weapons of hardened steel. A fine sword of "Toledo steel" was the standard for a crusading knight going to do battle in the Holy Land. Cheesy souvenir swords are ubiquitous in Toledo, but there are a handful of proud swordmakers still practicing the trade. Mariano Zamoraño's family has been making swords in Toledo since the late 19th century, and he continues hammering and honing fine steel at **Mariano Zamoraño Fábrica de Espadas y Armas Blancas** (Ciudad 19; ☎ 925-222-634; www.marianozamorano. com), just a few blocks from the cathedral. Visit the workshop Monday through Friday in the winter and you can see Zamoraño or one of his few fellow artisans heating steel bars red-hot on a bed of charcoal, then stretching and shaping the steel into the final blades. During the rest of the year, the swordmakers attend to less heat-intensive tasks, such as creating foils and tangs, sharpening blades, or painstakingly polishing the high-nickel steel into a mirror finish. (Unlike souvenir swords, Zamaraño's blades are not plated with chrome.) The shop produces everything from fencing rapiers to sabers and cutlasses to ceremonial presentation swords. They also make some kitchen cutlery. Every piece, Zamaraño points out with swelling pride, bears his stylized MZ mark.

ATTENTION, SHOPPERS

In addition to fine swords (see above), Toledo's artisans also rediscovered the ancient secrets of making damascene inlays of gold and silver threads on hardened, blackened steel, and their jewelry and decorative items have been justifiably famous for centuries. Practically every street corner in the city has a shop hawking souvenir swords and jewelry, pillboxes, picture frames, and plates made of steel incised with elaborate patterns in gold and silver. You probably don't have much use for a sword, but the same skill and craftsmanship goes into making fine cutlery. For one of the best selections of knives that will last a lifetime, check out **Artesanía Morales** (Santo Tomé 18; ☎ 925-216-172), which is also a good bet for reasonably priced damascene jewelry.

For a lesson in connoisseurship—and what we believe is the best damascene artistry in the city—head to **Damasquinados y Grabados** ✦ (Samuel Levi 3; ☎ 925-216-955). You'll probably see artisan Luis Navarro working at a small bench, painstakingly incising thin gold wires into pieces of steel to form elaborate geometric patterns that recall Toledo's Arabic heritage. Owner J. J. Simón Martin de la Fuente laments that there are few artisans left to practice this tradition and even fewer young people willing to take up the challenging craft. While all the items in their shop are made entirely by hand, much of the inexpensive damascene work that floods the souvenir shops is made by machine. "If you look at a handmade piece," says Vivian, "you will see the imperfections. One wire will be slightly thinner than another." Truly visible only with a magnifying glass, these variations are a sign of the maker's hand. Of course, fine craftsmanship carries a higher price. For a gift, Vivian Simon (the owner's English-born wife) advises buying the charming but simpler designs of birds and flowers, which are easier to make and, hence, less expensive. If you're thinking of investing in an heirloom piece for yourself, "buy something with elaborate wire work," she says.

GET OUT OF TOWN
Talavera de la Reina

Even if you've never been to Talavera de la Reina, you're almost certainly familiar with the city's most famous products, its painted ceramic tiles and tableware. Talavera tiles cover the facades of stores in Madrid and many other Spanish cities. Souvenir shops throughout the country abound with such Talavera ceramic tchotchkes as ashtrays and olive bowls, as well as elegant plates featuring historic and literary scenes. The graceful, elongated hares and deer that decorate everything from salad plates to coffee mugs are reproductions of a 17th-century style that flourished in Talavera. But even if you think you've seen it all, you haven't even scratched the surface until you visit the city that set the standard.

GETTING THERE

Talavera is a cinch to reach by car from Toledo, only 50 miles west on major highways. From Toledo, follow the N403 toward Avila, continuing on the A-40 at Maqueda. In 16km (10 miles), the road joins the A-5 and is well-signed to Talavera. Several buses a day run from Toledo (about 45 minutes, 2€).

TALAVERA CERAMICS

For an overview of the history of ceramics in Talavera, visit the **Museo Ruiz de Luna** ✫✫ (Pl de San Agustin 13; ☎ 925-800-149; .60€; Tues–Sat 10am–2pm and 4–6:30pm, Sun 10am–2pm). Among the archaeological displays in the basement—all objects discovered when converting an old convent into a museum—are original Moorish pottery from the 10th century, proving that someone has been making pottery in Talavera for more than 1,000 years. (It had long been thought that Talavera pottery did not begin until the 16th century.) The principal galleries trace the modern Talavera style back to 16th-century pieces of cobalt blue designs sponged over a white slip that covered the orange clay. The evolution of painted motifs was swift, and, by the early 17th century, Talavera artists had created stylized hares, deer, and partridges (the same game you'll find on many La Mancha menus), as well as standardized background scenes of cities in a distance and one saint or another in the foreground. As you follow the chronological exhibitions, the pieces become increasingly complex, reaching high points with the 1914 facade for the Talavera ceramic factory Ruiz de Luna, for which the museum is named, an extraordinary altar-sized Annunciation, and an entire altar of tiles depicting Santiago the Moorslayer in action. Alas, the museum's restrooms are a disappointment, as they're covered in unadorned utilitarian beige tiles.

The apotheosis of the Talavera ceramic style is found inside and outside the **Basilica de Nuestra Señora del Prado** ✫✫✫ (Los Jardines del Prado 6; no phone; free admission; Mon–Fri 7am–2pm and 5–9:50pm, Sat 8am–2pm and 5–9:50pm). This blocky, mostly Renaissance structure is so overwhelmed by colorful tiles that locals call it "the ceramic Sistine Chapel." Tiles on the entrance facade hint at the riches inside, depicting such biblical set pieces as Adam and Eve (complete with fig leaves), the Nativity, the baptism of Jesus by John the Baptist, and the Temptation in the Desert. Less traditional is an extraordinary frieze of an Adoration, with a line of women approaching Jesus from the left, and another line of Spanish soldiers approaching from the right. Inside, Old Testament figures

Gastronomic La Mancha

Driving *la meseta,* the tablelands of La Mancha south of Toledo, is a journey through an edible landscape. The barely rolling countryside along CM-42 and the A-4 motorway heading south toward Andalusia stretches into the distance with alternating plots of olive trees, low-growing grapevines, and huge squares of wheat. Closer to the villages you'll see shepherds leading their flocks of sheep. As sun-blasted and desert-like as this countryside appears, it nonetheless yields the bulk of Spain's wine (both routine plonk and some superb vintage wines), the wheat for its breads, rivers of intensely aromatic olive oil, the majority of the world's high-grade saffron, and Spain's signature sheep's milk cheese, Manchego.

Despite these lures, gastronomic tourism is still in its infancy here. But it is possible to seek out some key artisanal producers and learn how they live and work—and make products in demand by gourmets around the globe. We've highlighted three of the most accessible communities: Consuegra for its saffron (p. 94), Tembleque (just outside of Consuegra) for its cheese (p. 96), and Valdepeñas for its wines (p. 96).

It's not all sightseeing (or sight-tasting), either. By going to the source, you're cutting out the middlemen and can often buy gourmet delicacies at significant savings. As you drive the highways of *la meseta,* you'll find small producers along the road advertising their wares, sometimes with the equivalent of a makeshift farm stand. Stop at a highway rest area, and you'll find that the bar not only serves tapas and beer, but it also sells local honey, cheese, and olive oil from neighboring farms.

(including a weary Solomon playing his harp) line the left side of the nave, while New Testament scenes line the right.

Talavera ceramics remain a vital art form, as a walk through the adjacent city park, **Los Jardines del Prado,** demonstrates. Every few yards, glazed tile benches invite strollers to sit and enjoy the leafy shade. A central bandstand is likewise covered in decorative tiles, including glazed paintings of band instruments on the ceiling. There's even a tiled duck pond! As you walk through the city streets, you'll see butcher shops, pharmacies, taverns, and even *churrerías* (places that make the fried dough called *churros*) with tile facades that graphically depict the activities inside.

Unless you're entirely immune to the power of suggestion, you'll want to purchase a few pieces to take home. Most factories also have shops that sell their wares. A couple of the best smaller operations are **Cerámica Artística** (Santa María 4; ☎ 925-812-854), which is near the museum and specializes in finely painted scenes, and **Adeva** (Av. de Portugal 12; ☎ 925-802-797), one of the shops along the industrial avenida de Portugal on the west side of the city.

THE OTHER TALAVERA

Once in a while, you'll see someone sitting in a shop painting pottery, but it's really just for show, as most makers keep their shops and their factories separate. A fabulous exception to that rule is **Artesanía Talaverana** (Avda de Portugal 36; ☎ 925-802-909; Mon–Fri 8am–9pm, Sat 8am–2pm), the only place in the city where you can stroll from the showroom into the factory (no tour, no pressure salesmanship) and see the entire process of making Talavera ceramics. According to owner José Carlos Corrochano Godóy, his father and a business partner launched the company in 1966, and today it employs 16 artisans. Corrochano is among them, as he sometimes designs and paints the pieces. It all depends on the day you visit, but you're likely to see someone pouring clay paste into molds or forming pieces by hand on a wheel. It's almost certain that a few people will be hand-painting designs on vases, bowls, or plates, while a few other painters work away on large tile murals commissioned for restaurants, taverns, or other businesses. "We still do all the classic Talavera styles," Corrochano says, "or we can do any design that a client requests." A visit here will make you appreciate the hard work and artistry of that blue, white, and yellow mug from which you drink your morning coffee.

Consuegra

Propeller-like wind turbines spin slowly atop the small hills that rise above the gusty plains of La Mancha, pumping electricity into Spain's modern grid. But as you approach Consuegra, 65km (40 miles) southeast of Toledo on the CM-42, you'll be forgiven for thinking you've suddenly been thrust into the age of Don Quixote. **Eleven old-fashioned windmills** ★★ 🎈 and the imposing walls of a 12th-century castle stand on the long limestone ridge of Mount Calderico. They're so important to Consuegra's image (some say these mills inspired Cervantes to have his nearsighted knight tilt against one of these "giants") that the **Tourist Office of Consuegra** (Molino de Viento "Bolero"; ☎ 925-475-731; www. consuegra.es; Thurs–Mon 11:30am–2pm and 4:30–8pm) occupies a restored 19th-century mill on the hilltop. Once you've obtained a map, you can climb inside the mill to view the deceptively simple workings that the Spaniards used to grind wheat into flour. You can drive (or better yet, walk) along the ridge to see the other mills and appreciate the strategic advantages of a high point above the plains.

The city's technical school is restoring the **Castillo de la Muela** 🎈 (3€; Mon–Fri 9:20am–1:45pm and 4:40–6:45pm, Sat–Sun 10:40am–1:45pm and 4:40–6:45pm). Constructed on top of a modest Moorish fortress, the castle was more a military fortification than a domicile, which means that a lot of the area inside the walls is simply open space. It was the headquarters in Castilla for the crusaders known as the Order of St. John of Jerusalem, which survives to this day as the Knights of Malta. You can see the cisterns where the soldiers stored water (essential in a climate where it doesn't rain for months at a time) and visit the chapel. Children get the biggest kick out of climbing stone steps into three of the towers for extraordinary views.

ACCOMMODATIONS & DINING

€€   Paula Gutiérrez Roco and her husband bought the fine 19th-century Manchegan house now occupied by **La Vida de Antes** ★ 🎈 (Colón 2; ☎ 925-480-609; www.lavidadeantes.com; MC, V) in 2004 and worked for three years to restore and ready it as a *hotel rural* (a designation for small-town and village properties that reflect the local traditions). Nine rooms (7 with air-conditioning) on two levels—including one fully handicapped-accessible room—surround a tranquil central courtyard. Families tend to favor the two-room suites with a daybed and trundle bed for the kids as well as a refrigerator and microwave. Couples looking for a romantic getaway prefer the duplex rooms with a living area on the main floor and a sleeping loft above. These rooms also have refrigerators and microwaves. The name of the hotel translates roughly as "The Life Before," and the gracious decor adapts traditional Spanish elements (wrought iron, substantial dark wood furniture, leather and densely woven upholstery, original 19th-century tile floors) to a modern *Town & Country* look. Most of the year is high season here, with double rooms at 82€ to 88€ (19€ for each extra bed in the 2-room suites). Gutiérrez also has loaner bicycles for guests who want to pedal up to the windmills.

€€€   Consuegra cuisine leans heavily on small game, especially quail and partridge, but only one restaurant in town also plays up its use of the town's famous saffron. Look past the rather industrial architecture of **Las Provincias** (Ctra Toledo-Alcázar Km 58.5; ☎ 925-482-000; www.restaurantelasprovincias.com; daily 1:30–4pm and 8–11pm; MC, V), which is located on the outskirts of town along the highway. The formality of the dining room—white linens over red table covers—is punctured by a large, rather funny tiled mural of the classic scene of Don Quixote and his long-suffering sidekick, Sancho Panza, encountering windmills. The kitchen at Las Provincias is far more ambitious than you might expect from a highway restaurant, serving venison steak with a sauce of sweet squash and apples caramelized in beer (18€). The saffron dishes include roasted hake (13€) with an intensely orange saffron sauce and a version of crème brûlée with both saffron and marzipan (8€).

THE OTHER CONSUEGRA

If you'd like to understand why saffron is one of the most expensive spices in the world, simply head to Consuegra during the late-October harvest season. La Mancha produces about two-thirds of the world's culinary saffron—a bounty that is celebrated in the annual **La Fiesta de la Rosa del Azafrán,** or Saffron Rose Harvest Festival. It's usually the last full weekend in October. Consuegra's few lodgings book up quickly, so you may find it easier to make a day trip from Toledo. Just be forewarned that you'll have to leave early so that you can reach the fields outside town at dawn. During the last three weeks of October, the dry landscape turns a patchwork of purple as *crocus sativa,* the saffron crocus flower, bursts into bloom. In a scene barely changed since the Moors introduced saffron culture roughly a millennium ago, farmers wait in the fields for sunrise and then quickly harvest the blossoms before their scent is lost in the wind.

Despite the labor-intensive work, harvest season is also a time of high spirits. When we visited, farmers and their families looked up from their work to chat briefly and proudly gave us handfuls of bright flowers.

The scene in Consuegra's Plaza España is even more festive. Almost everyone wears a crocus flower pinned to his or her lapel and many dress in colorful regional costumes with elaborate black and white lace or embroidered flowers. While there are plenty of performances of folk music and dance, the festival's raison d'être is the crocus "stripping" competition. With bragging rights and serious cash prizes up for grabs, children and adults compete to see who can most quickly (and cleanly) remove the three bright red stigmas from 100 crocus flowers. The most nimble-fingered adults can complete the task in less than 3 minutes. Throughout the day and into the night, those prized stigmas are toasted on charcoal braziers—sending the spice's heady scent wafting through the countryside.

It's only a half-hour drive from Consuegra to visit **Finca La Prudenciana** ★★ (Km 100 Crtra A-4 south of Tembleque; ☎ 925-145-192; free admission; www.arte queso.com), one of the finest makers of Spain's greatest cheese, Manchego. Here you'll meet Alfonso Álvarez Valera, the fourth generation of this farming family that began making artisanal cheese in the early 1980s. Over the last decade, he has turned his Artequeso marque into one of the most prestigious in the Manchego region. From a herd of about 1,200 ewes on the 250-hectare (618-acre) farm, he and eight other staff produce about 40,000 wheels a year. The operation is shockingly small for a cheesemaker with such an international reputation. The "factory" and the century-old, thick-walled "caves" for aging the cheeses adjoin Álvarez Valera's home where he, his wife, and two children live in the summer. (The family lives in Toledo during the school year.) Call ahead, and he'll allow you to watch the production as staff turns raw milk of the day into curds, and then presses the curds into molds to make the wheels of cheese. The deeply refrigerated aging rooms are redolent with the sweet tang of Manchego (and the occasional sharper note of goat's milk cheeses, a minor sideline). The most popular form of Manchego, *semi-curado,* is aged a minimum of 4 months. The prestigious *curado* is aged a full year. The tour concludes with a tasting.

To get there from Consuegra, drive just over 5km (3 miles) south on the CM-42 to pick up the A-4 motorway northbound. The farm is located off the northbound side of the highway at Km 100. Take the exit, go past the gas station and restaurant, and turn right on the dirt road.

Valdepeñas

Castilla–La Mancha produces more wine than the rest of Spain combined, and the controlled denomination of Valdepeñas DOC (where the southern plains of La Mancha edge up against the foothills of the Sierra Morena mountain range) makes the best of Castilla–La Mancha's wines. As the name of the DOC suggests, the city of Valdepeñas is ground zero for wine lovers. So it shouldn't come as a surprise that gigantic terra-cotta vessels line the avenida de Viño (Avenue of Wine) from the A-4 highway into downtown Valdepeñas. Despite the prominence of the wine industry, Valdepeñas is hardly Napa Valley or even the Côtes du Rhône. Of more than 30 producers, only a handful are open for visitors. Stop at the **Oficina de Turismo de Valdepeñas** (Pl de España; ☎ 926-312-552; www.valdepenas.es; Mon–Fri 10am–2pm and 4:30–7pm, Sat 10am–2pm) for a map and schedule of visiting hours. We recommend concentrating your visit on the two following innovative producers who craft great wines and sell them at bargain prices.

Dionisio de Nova is the guiding spirit behind **Bodegas Dionisos** ★★ (Union 82; ☎ 926-313-248; www.labodegadelasestrellas.com; Mon–Fri 9am–2pm and 4–7pm). His 200-year-old home flows seamlessly into the bodega in back (complete with a patio for unloading grapes, large fermentation halls, and ancient cellars 7m below ground). De Nova, who lives here with his English-speaking wife Karina,

Grapes & History in Valdepeñas

They came, they saw, they planted vines. Yes, it was the Romans who first introduced the amphora method of wine production to this region some 2 millennia ago. And even 5 centuries of Moorish occupation couldn't fully wipe the industry out: Monks revived it in the 12th century by planting mostly Burgundian and Rhone valley grape varieties. By the late 1970s, the region had reached its peak production of about 78 million liters per year, more than half of them young white wines. Over the next two decades, Valdepeñas joined the international revolution in winemaking with a change of approach from quantity to quality, an emphasis on red wines (especially the native *tempranillo* grape), scientific control of the winemaking process, and judicious aging of the best reds in French and American oak barrels. Another, quieter revolution is fermenting here, as small artisanal winemakers shift their production to organically grown grapes from which they coax exquisitely balanced and distinctive wines.

says he is the last of the Valdepeñas producers with a combined home and bodega in the city, and we have no reason to doubt him. It's a unique look at the traditional lifestyle of a wine producer. He adheres to tradition in other ways as well, still using the ancient amphorae, or *tinajas,* for some fermentation. Although he grows all his grapes organically, de Nova produces two separate lines from them. One group of wines is created conventionally, but his best wines are made from hand-selected grapes grown, tended, and harvested in accordance with his personal theories based on phases of the moon and astrological signs. Despite a certain level of mumbo-jumbo, he makes great, prize-winning wines. The extended winery visit includes a sojourn inside de Nova's inflatable planetarium, where he makes the case for his theories. A basic visit and tasting can be had for 5€; visit with tasting and tapas is 18€ for six people or more; add extra 9€ for a visit to vineyard with a viticulture lecture.

Bodegas Real ✸ (Finca Marisánchez, Ctra a Cózar Km 12.8; ☎ 914-577-588; www.bodegas-real.com; visit and tasting 6€, free if you eat at the restaurant; Tues–Sun 11:30am and 1:30pm; reservations essential) produces 1.2 million bottles a year, 80% of them red wine, and a tour here highlights the future and massive industry of winemaking. A guide takes you around the extremely modern and scientific facility—stainless steel fermenters with cooling jackets, precision electronic monitoring. The scale dwarfs Dionisos, although Bodegas Real is a very small producer by Valdepeñas standards. The conclusion of this walking tour is the tasting room, where the guide usually pours a surprisingly superb un-oaked chardonnay and a smooth tempranillo (the major grape used here) that has spent 6 months in oak and a year in the bottle. You'll have to drive 12.8km (8 miles) east of Valdepeñas toward Cózar to visit this winery. After turning off, you'll drive almost 3.2km (2 miles) through vineyards, olive groves, and some patches of wheat to reach the bodega, which is centrally located to bring the harvested grapes in for processing as quickly as possible. (They pick the white grapes at night to keep them cool.)

Along with these bodegas, a small museum gives an overview of the 2,400 years of winemaking in the region. The **Museo del Viño** (Princessa 39; ☎ 926-321-111; free admission; Tues–Sat 10:30am–2pm and 6–8:30pm, Sun noon–2pm) is set in a 1901 bodega that operated into the 1970s and has much of its original equipment intact.

GETTING TO VALDEPEÑAS

Valdepeñas is an hour south of Tembleque (see "Finca La Prudenciana" above) or a half-hour south of Consuegra on the A-4 highway.

ACCOMMODATIONS & DINING IN VALDEPEÑAS

€€   For a fun change from staying in all those historic buildings converted to lodgings, **Hotel El Hidalgo** 🄺 (Autovía de Andalucía Km 194; ☎ 926-313-088; www.hotelelhidalgo.es; MC, V) is an honest-to-goodness 1960s-era motor hotel designed by Antonio Lamela, architect of the new Terminal 4 of Madrid's Barajas airport. As is the case with these types of motels, most of its 54 rooms open onto a small patio or balcony overlooking the courtyard (with pool). Here, however, in an innovative touch, the diagonal staggering of the room blocks guarantees that you don't see your neighbors and they don't see you. Although it's right off the highway, the hotel feels like a little oasis and is an extremely popular getaway for families. The bedrooms are spacious and roughly square, with a built-in iron and marble desk in one corner, a built-in armoire in another. Double rooms are 60€. You can add an extra bed for 19€.

€€€   You should time your visit to Bodegas Real (see above) so that you can enjoy lunch at **Restaurante El Umbráculo** ✦✦ (Finca Marisánchez at Bodegas Real; ☎ 926-360-323; Tues–Sun 2–4pm and 9–11pm; MC, V) in its new reception center. The bodega's wines are a stunning bargain (none costs more than 10€) and the gourmet restaurant is a comparable deal, with main dishes starting at just 14€. Organic vegetables on the menu come from the *huerta* (kitchen garden) behind the restaurant, and when the patch is at full production, the restaurant even offers an eight-course tasting menu for 65€. That's a bargain for one of the country's top dozen or so restaurants, but we've also spent the same sum on a more modest meal for two with wine and tip. All starters are designed for sharing, and *queso frito* (13€) concentrates three iconic Spanish flavors in one dish. It consists of Manchego cheese wrapped in paper-thin dry Iberian ham and then quickly deep fried. The chief flavor in the accompanying sauce is saffron. A signature main dish, *perdiz de la finca* (18€), features roasted wild partridge from the farm estate served in a sauce flecked with black truffles. The restaurant holds Spain's highest government ranking (four forks), and while the table settings tend to be formal, dress at lunchtime is merely smart casual, though prices are the same.

CUENCA ✦✦

The *casco antiguo,* or Old City, of Cuenca stands atop a high limestone spur between the Huécar and Júcar rivers, with dizzying views down at both riverbeds. Its street pattern dates from 714, when it was constructed as an Arabic fortress, but its buildings are late Gothic and early Renaissance. Cuenca's appeal, however, owes little to history and everything to abstract art. Although the city hemorrhaged population after the Spanish Civil War, it never lost its dramatic appearance as a

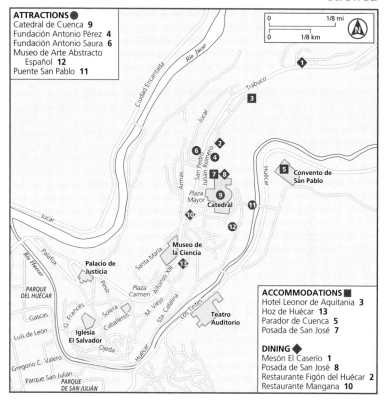

ATTRACTIONS ●
Catedral de Cuenca **9**
Fundación Antonio Pérez **4**
Fundación Antonio Saura **6**
Museo de Arte Abstracto
  Español **12**
Puente San Pablo **11**

Convento de San Pablo

Museo de la Ciencia

Palacio de Justicia

Iglesia El Salvador

Teatro Auditorio

PARQUE DEL HUÉCAR

PARQUE DE SAN JULIÁN

ACCOMMODATIONS ■
Hotel Leonor de Aquitania **3**
Hoz de Huécar **13**
Parador de Cuenca **5**
Posada de San José **7**

DINING ◆
Mesón El Caserío **1**
Posada de San José **8**
Restaurante Figón del Huécar **2**
Restaurante Mangana **10**

hilltop fantasy of angular vertical buildings built right to the edges of the gorges. In the 1950s, Spanish abstract artists who became known as El Grupo Paso discovered picturesque Cuenca. Where artists lead, vacationers often follow, and Cuenca has become a favorite weekend getaway for well-to-do Madrileños. The painters' legacy accounts for several museums, but most visitors come, as the artists did, for the heady ambience of Cuenca itself.

GETTING TO & AROUND CUENCA

The new city that sprawls at the base of Cuenca is of limited interest, except for its bus and train stations. The easiest way to get here—until the Madrid-Valencia AVE line stops at a Cuenca station (planned tentatively for 2011)—is by bus or automobile. Five to six buses a day run back and forth between Madrid and Cuenca. Round-trip express (2 hours) is 31€, or with multiple stops (3½ hours) 20€. A city bus from **Plaza de la Estación** to the casco antiguo is .70€. Driving into this medieval city is easier than in others, as the single main road to the top is broad enough for two vehicles to pass. If you're disinclined to drive to the top, watch on the left for the sign to **Aparcamiento San Pedro,** which has an elevator into the Old City. The rate is a reasonable 1.35€ per hour. If you're braver, you can park for free in the large lot at the pinnacle of the city on calle San Jerónimos, just outside the upper gate, Arco de Bezugo, a.k.a. "El Castillo." You'll definitely want to pick up a free city map at **Oficina de Turismo-Ayuntamiento Cuenca** (Alfonso VIII 2; ☎ 969-241-051; www.turismocastillalamancha.com; daily 9am–9pm), located just below the main arch entering the Plaza Mayor.

ACCOMMODATIONS, BOTH STANDARD & NOT

To fully appreciate Cuenca after the daytrippers have departed, you'll want to book a room in one of the lodgings in the *casco antiguo.* In keeping with their historic character, few have air-conditioning. But even in the heat of July and August, temperatures drop so low at night that it's more pleasant to sleep with the windows open. You might even find yourself reaching for a blanket in the middle of the night. And you'll definitely waken to the sound of roosters crowing in the valley below.

You'll get the feeling that you're a real Conquense (as people who live in Cuenca are called) if you're shopping and cooking and sleeping in your own flat. **Hoz de Huécar** ✹✹ 🅺 (Alfonso VIII 29; book through Posada de San José, Julián Romero 4; ☎ 969-211-300; www.posadasanjose.com; AE, DC, MC, V) opened in July 2008 with five apartments in a completely renovated ancient house just below Plaza Mayor. Each apartment occupies its own floor, which means that windows overlook both the main street and the Huécar gorge. (An elevator makes it easy to bring in luggage or groceries.) Those on floors 1 through 3 have two bedrooms and two baths, with wooden beamed ceilings, terra-cotta-tiled floors, simple modern furniture, marble and stainless steel kitchens, and baths with jet-massage showers. The first-floor unit also has a small balcony overlooking the main street. For more privacy, the "attic" unit has one bedroom on the main floor along with the large kitchen and living area, and two more bedrooms up a flight of stairs. Similarly, the "basement" unit has bedrooms on two levels below the main living area. This is also the only unit with a washing machine and dryer. In all cases, the living room couch can be unfolded to provide yet another double bed—making it possible to sleep up to eight in the attic apartment and up to six on the other levels. Per-night rates (no discount for longer stays) for the two-bedroom units range from 160€ to 180€; three-bedroom units, 180€ to 210€— that's high we know, but not too bad on a per-person basis, if you stuff 'em to capacity.

€€　The owners of the Hoz de Huécar apartments, Antonio and Jennifer Cortinas, have also operated an inn located in the 16th-century building of Colégio de San José near the cathedral since 1983. **Posada de San José** ✹ 🅺 (Julián Romero 4; ☎ 969-211-300; www.posadasanjose.com; AE, DC, MC, V) might be your best choice if you're traveling as a duo or only staying a night or two. Every one of the 31 rooms has a different configuration, though most are furnished with an almost monastic simplicity of plain wooden furniture and whitewashed walls relieved by abstract contemporary art from Cuenca painters. The public areas maintain an even more ecclesiastical air, with religious frescoes on the walls and statues of saints standing in corners. If you're willing to forgo a private bathroom, you can get a double room for 35€ to 38€, and if you're traveling with kids, a couple of these rooms that share one bath may be a good budget

Wi-Fi Alfresco

Owners of accommodations in Cuenca's *casco antiguo* treasure their properties' old-fashioned ambience—to the extent that many lodgings act as if they've never heard of the Internet, let alone the idea of offering wireless access to their guests. But one spot in the Old City has embraced the 21st century: the Museo de las Ciencias in the 18th-century former almshouse on Plaza Merced. Not only can you access the Internet inside, you can sit in the plaza with your own computer and connect via a free, strong, high-speed, open-access signal, even on days when the museum is closed.

option. If you're too squeamish to share a bath with strangers, try to get one of the rooms overlooking the Huécar gorge for the view, the cool night breezes, and the private bathroom. Rooms 23 and 24 fill the bill, while rooms 21 and 32 have the same view but with outdoor terraces. They're all 78€ to 86€. Should you feel the need for a large unit with separate sitting room, TV, and coffee bar, ask for Room 12 or Room 33 (which also has an outdoor terrace). They can accommodate an extra bed for a third family member. They cost 120€ to 132€. All prices include tax.

€€€   If you want some of the more typical hotel amenities (telephone, TV, and minibar in your room), you'll find them at **Hotel Leonor de Aquitania** (San Pedro 60; ☎ 969-231-000; www.hotelleonordeaquitania.com; AE, MC, V). Colorful floral drapes and bedspreads play off pastel walls and dark tile floors. The rooms are comparable in size to those at the Posada—large enough, but not exactly roomy. While you almost expect a prayer book next to the bed at the Posada, at the Leonor each room is equipped with a copy of *Don Quixote* (in Spanish, of course) on the bedside table. Double rooms are 99€ to 115€. If you're coming on a weekend, inquire about the weekend special of 216€ for two nights of lodging, two breakfasts, and dinner in one of the hotel's two restaurants.

€€–€€€€   Located in the former San Pablo convent across a footbridge from the Old City, the **Parador de Cuenca** ★ (Subida San Pablo; ☎ 969-232-320; www.paradores-spain.com; AE, DC, MC, V) is the city's most deluxe hotel, and you'll pay dearly for a double room (138€–242€) unless you can score one of the handful of rooms set aside for special promotions (see "Fit for a King—at a Bargain," p. 488). If you've purchased the 5-night card, for example, you might be able to get a double room for just 96€. Availability of the discounted rooms is limited, especially on weekends, but it doesn't hurt to ask. Rooms are spacious and decorated in classic Spanish style, with carved wooden headboards on the beds, high ceilings, and flowing floral draperies. One big advantage is that you can drive directly to the Parador and park in the outside lot. The Old City is a short walk across a footbridge (not for those with vertigo). The disadvantage of the Parador is its isolation from the daily life of the city. It can seem a long walk when you want to get out of the midday sun to lounge in your air-conditioned room.

DINING FOR ALL TASTES

The cuisine of Cuenca reflects its location at the border between the mountains and the plains of La Mancha. Wild game and foraged mushrooms figure prominently on most menus, and virtually every eatery offers two Cuencan specialties: *morteruelo* (a pâté of rabbit, partridge, ham, pork liver, pine nuts, clove, and caraway), and *ajoarriero* (a creamy pâté of potato, flaked codfish, oil, and garlic). Both are usually spread on bread or toast as a starter and one serving makes a fine appetizer for two people. Since this is sheep country, lamb appears on most menus. If you're adventurous, try the *zarajos,* or grilled lamb intestines. Chewy and richly flavored, they're usually served coiled around a vine shoot like a ball of yarn.

€–€€   You'll probably smell **Mesón El Caserío** ★★ (Larga 25; ☎ 969-230-021; Wed–Mon noon–4:30pm and 8:30pm–2am; MC, V) before you see it, as this casual restaurant at the top of the hill barely outside the walls of the Old City specializes in wood-grilled meat and vegetables. Seating is available at the indoor bar and dining room, but in nice weather almost everyone gravitates to the casual tables outside. If it's too crowded when you arrive, get a drink at the bar and carry it across the street to the scenic overlook for great views of the city while you wait for a table. If you want to sample *zarajos* (5.50€), you can do it here without much damage to your budget. But none of the savory, smoky meat is going to set you back too far. Beef sirloin steak (15€) or a plate of four lamb chops (12€) is about as expensive as it gets, and big plates of grilled asparagus (what did mother say about eating your vegetables?) are only 6.50€.

€€   While the area at the top of the hill hops with evening activity at Caserío and nearby bars, Plaza Mayor is always busy at mealtimes. With so many cafeterias and restaurants, it can be hard to choose, but the hands-down favorite for Conquenses looking for a good meal at a fair price is **Restaurante Mangana** (Pl Mayor 3; ☎ 969-229-451; Fri–Wed 1–4pm and 9–11pm; MC, V). In addition to the Cuencan specialties mentioned above, this is a great spot for the local salad (6.50€) of lettuce, tomatoes, green olives, sliced onion, hard-boiled egg, and flaked dark tuna. With a drizzle of olive oil and a few dashes of vinegar, it's the perfect restorative in the afternoon heat.

€€–€€€   The most desirable tables at the restaurant of **Posada de San José** ★ (Julián Romero 4; ☎ 969-211-300; www.posadasanjose.com; Tues–Sun 7:30–10:30pm; AE, DC, MC, V) are outside on the terrace surrounded by rose bushes and an olive tree. But the view of the Huécar gorge is just as impressive from the windows of the semiformal dining room. Like the rest of the inn, the restaurant strikes a fine contrast between simple, heavy, monastic furniture (set with white linens) and outstanding abstract graphic art by contemporary Spanish masters. There's a strong local flavor to the menu, and many diners start with a small plate of *zarajos* (3€) or share a bowl of *morteruelo* (6.50€). If you've grown tired of organ meats and wild game, order the pork tenderloin braised with apples in cider (10€). The restaurant is open to the general public, not just guests of the inn. Reservations are required, and the sooner you can make them for the weekend the better.

€€€   One of Cuenca's most elegant restaurants is next to the posada in the former home of singer José Luis Perales. Get dressed up to dine at **Restaurante Figón**

del Huécar (Julián Romero 6; ☎ 969-240-062; www.figondelhuecar.com; Tues-Sat 1:30–4pm and 9–11pm, Sun 1:30–4pm; AE, MC, V), as the staff wear dark suits and ties. Dining rooms are on two levels, and one occupies a book-lined library. Fine examples of contemporary art are key to the decor, and the most sought-after tables are those with views of the Huécar gorge. While the kitchen pays homage to tradition (*morteruelo, ajoarriero,* salad with pickled partridge—all 8€–12€ as starters), it brings modern creativity to Cuencan cuisine, with dishes like a creamed squash soup with a hint of cheese and parsley-infused oil (8€), or grilled veal sirloin with a Manchego cheese sauce (19€). The restaurant also offers a three-course menu del día with bread and wine at 27€.

WHY YOU'RE HERE: THE TOP SIGHTS & ATTRACTIONS

Practically the first thing Alfonso VIII ordered after wresting Cuenca from the Moors in 1177 was the construction of **Catedral de Cuenca** ✪✪ (Pl Mayor; ☎ 969-224-626; 2.80€ adults, 2€ seniors and students; Apr–Oct Mon–Fri 10am–2pm, Sat 10am–7pm, Sun 10am–6:30pm; Nov–Mar Mon–Fri 10am–2pm, Sat 10:30am–2pm and 4–7pm, Sun 10:30am–2pm and 4–6:30pm), which duly began in 1183 under Anglo-Norman craftsmen. (Alfonso's wife, Eleanor of Plantagenet, was an English princess.) The resulting High Gothic masterpiece with soaring alabaster columns is one of Spain's prettiest cathedrals. The audioguide provided with admission is perfect for a city whose people know a thing or two about art. It provides detailed art-historical explanation of 37 features within the church. Note that the stained-glass windows installed in 1990 were designed by Cuenca artists.

The three buildings that form the *casas colgadas*, or **"hanging houses,"** are perhaps the most famous of Cuenca structures, although they are largely 20th-century constructions on much earlier foundations. Their chief visual appeal is that they are cantilevered over the Huécar gorge and appear to be merely clinging to the rock on which Cuenca is built. They front on calle Canónigos but are best viewed from the **Puente San Pablo** footbridge over the gorge. One is a private residence, while the other two are occupied by a restaurant and by the **Museo de Arte Abstracto Español** ✪✪ (Canónigos; ☎ 969-212-983; www.march.es; 3€ adults, 1.50€ seniors and students; Tues–Fri 11am–2pm and 4–6pm, Sat 11am–2pm and 4–8pm, Sun 11am–2:30pm). The core of the museum's holdings are the personal collections of mid-century Spanish abstract art accreted by Cuenca artist Francisco Zóbel. The works are displayed in small but airy galleries on several levels of the "hanging house." Prominently featured among the artists is Antonio Saura, who saw fit to deposit some of his collections with the **Fundación Antonio Saura** (Pl de San Nicolas 4; ☎ 969-236-054; free admission; Thurs–Tues 11am–2pm and 5–7pm, Sun 11am–2pm). The organization opened its own museum in early 2008. The permanent exhibits focus on Saura, whose abstract paintings of crumpled, heavy, black lines seem to bring a modern frenzied energy to a compositional grace inspired by Goya's etching. Be sure to check out his work as a book illustrator illuminating the texts of *Don Quixote* and the poems of San Juan de la Cruz. Artist and collector Antonio Pérez created a similar repository for *his* art collection, the **Fundación Antonio Pérez** ✪ (Ronda de Julian Romero 20; ☎ 969-230-619; free admission; Mon–Fri 10am–9pm, Sat–Sun 11am–9pm, closes 1 hour earlier in winter). His taste also embraced Pop art (there are some pretty good Warhols in the collection) and found art, of which he was a practitioner. (His

Castrati, for example, is an installation of three bells without clappers.) You'll never look at trash the same.

ATTENTION, SHOPPERS!

Cuenca has a strong crafts tradition and you can find a good overview of work displayed at **Artesanía de Santa Cruz** (Santa Catalina; ☎ 969-233-184) in the soaring nave of the 16th- and 17th-century Santa Cruz church. Among the most original work are the brightly colored leather bags and purses of Carmen del Olmo and the embossed metal designs of Julia Díaz-Romeral Hermosilla applied to free-form glass objects or to wooden frames for mirrors. Cuenca is best known for a modern style of pottery created through a technique called *raspado*—incising through a black slip to reveal the red clay beneath. **Adrián Navarro** (Pilares 7; ☎ 969-212-828) is one of the masters of the art and his unique pieces recall both Greek redware and the erotic engravings of Pablo Picasso. At his eponymous shop, you can see work that ranges from souvenir to collection quality, along with pottery by his son Rubén, who is pushing the boundaries of the art form by introducing bright colors.

NIGHTLIFE IN CUENCA

Conquenses, by and large, don't stay home in the evenings. While there's not a significant music scene (unless you count the flamenco musicians passing the hat to tourists near the cathedral), you'll find the locals sharing drinks and conversation in bars that are modeled on the Spanish idea of an Irish pub—right down to the polished dark wood and the inevitable Guinness and Irish coffee. Since it opened in the late 1970s, **Taberna Jovi** (Colmillo 10; ☎ 969-214-284) has been a favorite watering hole for many artists and proudly claims that several members of El Paso, the first generation of Cuenca's abstract artists, used to hang out here. Another classic *bar para charlar* (roughly, a "bar for chatting") on the opposite side of the Plaza Mayor in the barrio San Miguel is **Pub Vaya Vaya** (Bajada de San Miguel; ☎ 969-235-487). The scenic overlooks of barrio San Miguel are also popular spots for Conquenses of all ages to gather on a hot night with cold beer from a nearby grocery store.

SEGOVIA ✿✿

Poor Segovia! Because the city's Roman aqueduct appears on every checklist of Spanish monuments, the city often suffers from drive-by tourism. It's easy to park near the aqueduct, take a picture, maybe stop for lunch, and then move on. But Segovia is more than just a pretty face. The relatively broad, not terribly steep streets of the old quarter make it one of the nicest strolling cities in central Spain, and behind the cheerful facade of a town seemingly devoted to eating and drinking lies a deep history of religious devotion and military might.

GETTING TO & AROUND SEGOVIA

By bus, train, or car, Segovia is roughly 2 hours from Madrid. To drive, follow the Autopista del Nordeste (A-6) north from Madrid. At the junction with CM110, follow AP-61 or N-603 into Segovia. Once you've spotted the aqueduct, head for the nearest parking lot and leave your car. Frequent trains from Madrid arrive at **Estación Renfe** (Paseo Obispo Quesada; ☎ 921-420-774; one-way ticket 5.90€).

Segovia

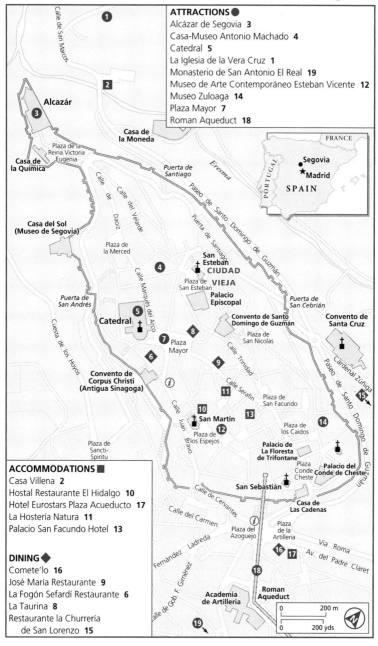

ATTRACTIONS ●
Alcázar de Segovia **3**
Casa-Museo Antonio Machado **4**
Catedral **5**
La Iglesia de la Vera Cruz **1**
Monasterio de San Antonio El Real **19**
Museo de Arte Contemporáneo Esteban Vicente **12**
Museo Zuloaga **14**
Plaza Mayor **7**
Roman Aqueduct **18**

ACCOMMODATIONS ■
Casa Villena **2**
Hostal Restaurante El Hidalgo **10**
Hotel Eurostars Plaza Acueducto **17**
La Hostería Natura **11**
Palacio San Facundo Hotel **13**

DINING ◆
Comete'lo **16**
José María Restaurante **9**
La Fogón Sefardí Restaurante **6**
La Taurina **8**
Restaurante la Churrería
   de San Lorenzo **15**

Equally frequent buses from Madrid arrive at **Estacionamiento Municipal de Autobuses** (Paseo de Ezequiel González 10; ☎ 921-427-707; one-way ticket 5.90€). From either station, hop a city bus (.75€) marked "Acueducto" to get to the aqueduct and Plaza del Azoguejo, a logical starting point for exploring the city. Segovia is shaped like a thick slice of cake on its side. The aqueduct is at the point, while the Alcázar stands atop the thick end above all the frosting. The cathedral and Plaza Mayor are in the middle. The **Centro de Recepción de Visitantes** (Pl del Azoguejo 1; ☎ 921-466-720; daily 10am–8pm) offers a free city map and sightseeing advice. Follow calle Juan Bravo toward Plaza Mayor where you'll find the regional **Oficina de Información Turística de Castilla y León** (Pl Mayor 10; ☎ 921-460-334; daily 9am–3pm and 5–7pm). This office's tourist map is easier to use. If you're going to visit Avila, ask for that city's map as well.

ACCOMMODATIONS, BOTH STANDARD & NOT

Lodging in Segovia offers such good value for the euro that you could be tempted to stick around long after you've seen the sights. While we like one older property (El Hidalgo) for its bargain price and convenience, all the other accommodations we recommend have opened in the last few years. Rates include air-conditioning, heat, telephone, and TV, but not breakfast or tax, except as noted.

The posh, modern apartments at **Casa Villena** ★ 🄺 (Marqués de Villena 2 and 4; ☎ 921-423-042; www.casavillena.com) could certainly lure you into making Segovia a base for touring with a car. The riverbank location just outside the Old City beneath the Alcázar is picturesque and countrified, despite being on a busy corner of one of the roads around the city. You can stroll up the riverside path to El Parral monastery. Moreover, the apartments are on the no. 8 bus line to the aqueduct (.75€ per ride, 10 rides for 4.70€). The five large apartments in the peach-colored stucco building sleep two to four people. Decor looks like a showroom for a high-end furniture store, mixing elegant traditional upholstered chairs and couches with such touches of contemporary style as glass coffee tables. Kitchens come fully equipped, which can be especially handy if you're traveling with kids or not fond of the local diet of pork and lamb. (There's a small grocery store around the corner.) The apartments mostly rent by the week (360€–480€ for the entire week) but are also available Friday through Saturday (180€–240€ for 2 nights), or Monday through Thursday (300€–400€ for 4 nights).

€   If you prefer bargain lodgings with historic character, take a look at **Hostal Restaurante El Hidalgo** (José Canalejas 4; ☎ 921-463-529; www.el-hidalgo.com; MC, V) in the heart of the medieval quarter and a short walk from most of Segovia's attractions. With dark wood and wonderfully aged tiles, the Renaissance-era central patio (devoted to a modestly priced restaurant) is the most striking feature of this restored 13th-century house. The 11 rooms upstairs are more spare, with simple wooden furniture, unadorned painted walls, and dim lighting. These are rooms for sleeping, not for hanging out. There's no elevator, but you can't beat the price (40€–50€ per night including tax, even in high season). For a further touch of history, ask to see the well where early residents used to dip water from the aqueduct.

€–€€   Similarly well situated in the former noble quarter, only 50m from the Plaza Mayor, **La Hostería Natura** ★ [kids] (Colón 5 and 7; ☎ 921-466-710; www.naturadesegovia.com; MC, V) kept the exterior of its 17th-century *palacio* intact but took a lot of creative liberties with the interior, ragging bright colors in textured patterns on the walls. The cheerful stylishness almost makes you forget that there's no elevator. Of the 17 rooms, nos. 101, 102, and 112 are the best bargains in high season (59€). These unusually large rooms are furnished with two twin beds, but their airshaft windows do not open. The most romantic rooms are 103 and 114, which are both 70€ during the week and 86€ on the weekends. Room 103 has a high, carved-wood four-poster bed; a little private balcony; and walls sponged a deep red. The walls in Room 114 are a soft salmon color, as is the canopy on the four-poster wrought-iron queen-size bed. The room doesn't have a balcony, but it does feature a hydro-massage tub. Families should consider Room 111, which easily sleeps up to five, costs 102€ per night (but families not needing all the beds may be able to wangle a discount), and has a privacy enhancing layout. Parents get a private bath and bedroom suite with a queen-size bed and a balcony overlooking the park next door. It's connected to a narrow interior room with three twin beds lined up along the wall and a separate bath for the kids. All prices include tax.

€€–€€€   A complete break from new hotels in ancient buildings, **Hotel Eurostars Plaza Acueducto** (Avda Padre Claret 2–4; ☎ 921-413-403; www. eurostarshotels.com; AE, MC, V) is an all-new hotel in a prime spot right on the eastern side of the Roman aqueduct and the Plaza del Azoguejo. The 72 rooms are the very model of a modern high-end hotel room: a king bed (or two oversize twins), a sleek dark wood and frosted glass desk with good working area and free Wi-Fi, plenty of space to walk around the furniture, and a travertine and white ceramic bathroom with full-size soaking tub and shower. The only thing that's missing is the high-end price. Doubles here dip as low at 59€ in the winter, to 79€ on weeknights, or 69€ on a weekend night in July. In September—prime time for tourism in Segovia—rates rise to around 110€. Underground parking is available for an extra 14€, a fairly bounteous breakfast for 11€.

€€€–€€€€   It's also possible to enjoy contemporary comfort and artful design with a touch of history. The colors of the rooms in **Palacio San Facundo Hotel** ★★ (Pl San Facundo 4; ☎ 921-463-061; www.hotelpalaciosanfacundo. com; AE, MC, V) are every bit as intense as those in Natura (see above), but their deep saturation and rich tones suggest an artist's palette rather than a color-swatch book. The glassed-over courtyard with soaring columns, where you might eat breakfast or hang out during the day, was originally the cloister of a convent taken over as a private palace nearly 5 centuries ago. (The current incarnation as a hotel dates from 2006.) The 33 rooms surrounding the cloister on the upper floors all have tub showers, glass-slab sinks on stained-wood bases, and flat-screen TVs. Headboards run either to wrought iron or padded dark brown leather, with soft leather trim on the decorative pillows. On the second floor, both 202 and 204 have small balconies with a view of the plaza out front. Many third-floor rooms have even more character, with exposed pine beams on the slanting ceilings and skylights with remote-controlled shades. One especially popular room is 306, with a large bed and decor in deep aubergine tones. Underground parking here can be a little steep (18€), but the rooms are a relative bargain at 99€ to 120€ during the week, up to 145€ on weekends for room, breakfast, and taxes.

DINING FOR ALL TASTES

Menus in Segovia vary surprisingly little. Although the dish is served throughout Spain, roast suckling pig reaches its apotheosis here, and the locals make a fetish of it. There's even a special certification for roast baby pig, *Marca de Garantía "Cochinillo de Segovia,"* indicating that the restaurant only uses milk-fed local pigs less than 21 days old that have been processed and cooked in accordance with a strict set of standards. Restaurants without a special oven will fry the piglet, a dish known as *cochifrito.* The other star entree is the local lamb, usually offered as *chuletóns de cordero,* or lamb chops. One classic starter is *sopa castellana*—a soup usually made with a chicken broth base to which chopped ham, bread, sweet paprika, and eggs are added. (The eggs end up poached.) The other common starter is *judiones de La Granja:* a dish of white broad beans (similar to lima beans), chorizo sausage, fresh ham, and onion.

€€   If you look hard enough, though, there are a few alternatives to piglets and lamb. The best bargain on healthy food in Segovia has to be the all-you-can-eat buffet at **Comete'lo** (Padre Claret 2; ☎ 921-436-281; www.cometelo.es; daily 12:30–5pm and 7:30–11:30pm; MC, V), on the west side of the aqueduct. You line up at the salad buffet (maximum value for the euro: white asparagus) and fill your first plate and choose a drink. Then you pay—9.90€ for most meals, 12€ Friday evening and all day Saturday and Sunday. Children 6 and under only pay 6€. You move on to the hot buffet, which usually includes roast chicken, some form of pasta, and fried fish. Desserts (soft-serve ice cream as well as pastries) and coffee, tea, or hot chocolate are also included. The buffet line and cafeteria tables hardly offer great ambience, but the food is freshly prepared and the value is hard to beat.

€€–€€€   At the other extreme for ambience, **La Fogón Sefardí Restaurante** ✯ (Judería Vieja 17 and 19; ☎ 921-466-250; www.lacasamudejar.com; daily 1:30–4:30pm and 8:30–11:30pm; AE, MC, V) is an elegant formal restaurant in muted reds and dark wood tones in a quiet interior courtyard. The kitchen is not exactly kosher (they do serve roast piglet), but chef Mariano Muñoz also offers a delightful vegetable and grain-intensive Sephardic menu. Vegetarians appreciate the eggplant stuffed with chopped vegetables, pine nuts, and almonds (9.30€). The curried lamb with paper-thin slices of eggplant and baby garden vegetables (6.50€) is the perfect antidote to otherwise heavy Segovian cuisine.

€€€   If you *do* want to try the specialties of Segovia (every visitor should, at least once), there are a couple of places that offer *raciónes* (entree-size plates without accompaniments) of both the *cochinillo* (roast baby pig) and the lamb. (Most other restaurants only offer the piglet as an entree and the lamb as an entree for 2 people.) We're fond of **Restaurante la Churrería de San Lorenzo** ✯ (Pl San Lorenzo; ☎ 921-437-984; daily 8am–4pm and 8pm–midnight) because it's in a separate neighborhood below the Old City that simply drips with character. San Lorenzo, named for its ancient, almost crumbling church, is about a 10-minute

Pastry with a Wallop

Although translating literally as "Segovian punch," the sweet delicacy known as *ponche segoviano* is not exactly the kind of punch you dip from a bowl at a party. It consists of sponge cake saturated with a lemon syrup thickened with egg yolks, and then completely enveloped in a thin layer of *mazapán*. While it's usually sold as a whole bar cake, the superb pastry shop **Limón y Menta** (Isabel La Católica 2; ☎ 921-462-141) also produces the confection in a single-serving size (3.50€). Try one before investing in a pricey whole bar.

---

walk from the aqueduct, and La Churrería is the most popular family restaurant on the plaza. Either roast piglet or roast lamb is 19€. The bar looks as if it could serve as a stage set for a tavern scene in *Man of La Mancha*. The gimmick of the menu at **La Taurina** (Pl Mayor 8; ☎ 921-460-902; daily noon–5pm and 8pm–midnight; MC, V), located right on Plaza Mayor, is that each course is organized by a stage in a bullfight. (One look at the bullfight tiles and the decor of matador memorabilia tells you that the restaurant, founded in 1939, belongs to the true church of the *corrida*.) Here you can get an unadorned plate of *cochinillo* for 17€, or roast lamb for 18€. The 21€ menu hits most of the culinary highlights: *sopa castellana, judiones de La Granja, cochinillo,* as well as bread, dessert, and a drink. On a nice night, sit outside and enjoy a view of the cathedral with your meal.

€€€–€€€€   Ask a Segoviano where the family goes for *cochinillo* and he or she will smile and start telling you about the crackling skin and succulent pork served at **José María Restaurante** ★★★ (Cronista Lecea 11; ☎ 921-461-111; www.rtejosemaria.com; daily 1–4pm and 8:30–11:30pm; MC, V). Chef-proprietor José María Ruiz is a legend in pig roasting circles. You'll pay dearly for the privilege of eating in the formal white-tablecloth interior dining room (*cochinillo* is 31€), but if you're going to "pig out," it should be on the world's best.

WHY YOU'RE HERE: THE TOP SIGHTS & ATTRACTIONS

Roughly 2,100 years ago, Roman engineers constructed a 15km (9½-mile) waterway to bring water from the Guadarrama mountains to Segovia. The graceful feat of engineering remains as impressive as it was in the age of the Caesars. While much of the original **Roman Aqueduct** ★★★ was a ground-level canal, the concluding segments arch high over the city and then continue underground all the way to the Alcázar. The entire structure was built of granite blocks without mortar, and supplied the city's water into the late 19th century. The highest of the 166 arches is 28.1m (92 feet), and seems even higher when you stand under it and look up. Follow the aqueduct uphill and you'll find pleasant residential neighborhoods where cats and kittens scamper along the much shorter arches. Perhaps the most striking vantage for photographing the aqueduct is from the overlook just off Plaza Avendaño, which places you atop the arches. The neighborhood surrounding this half-hidden mirador is the erstwhile noble quarter where wealthy clergy and nobles built many elegant in-town Renaissance palaces.

Constrained by geography, Segovia's layout is fairly simple, and most roads leading west from the aqueduct converge on lovely **Plaza Mayor,** bracketed by arcades, a grand theater, and the cathedral. Thursday is market day on the plaza.

Segovia's **Catedral** (Marqués del Arco; ☎ 921-462-205; 3€, free Sun 9:30am–1:15pm; Apr–Sept daily 9:30am–6:30pm, Oct–Mar daily 9:30am–5:30pm) was the last Gothic cathedral constructed in Spain. The city's old cathedral was destroyed in 1520 during the uprising of the Castilian cities. When Carlos V crushed the rebellion, he ordered the cathedral rebuilt in similar fashion. Construction began in 1525, and it was finally consecrated in 1768. Even on the brightest days, the interior is gloomy; the religious art is especially saturnine, focusing on martyrdoms and the Crucifixion rather than the more upbeat Assumption and Resurrection scenes. It's worth visiting, however, to see the swirling, gold-encrusted altar created by José Benito Churriguera (p. 124) for the Santisimo Sacramento chapel circa 1700.

Reconstruction is something of a theme in Segovia. After the 13th-century **Alcázar de Segovia** ✯✯ (Pl de la Reina Victoria Eugenia; ☎ 921-460-759; 4€ adults, 3€ seniors and students, additional 2€ to climb Torre San Juan; Apr–Sept daily 10am–7pm, Oct–Mar daily 10am–6pm) burned in 1862, it was "restored" to a late 19th-century romantic ideal of the Middle Ages that more closely resembles a storybook castle from 16th-century northern Europe than a messy fortress-castle of Spain's warrior monarchs of the 1300s. In effect, you see a museum of the nobler side of the *reconquista*. As you enter, the first thing you'll spy are suits of German plate armor for knights and two of their steeds—an image cultivated by Spanish monarchs ever since the Hapsburgs came to the throne in the 1500s, and, not coincidentally, a favorite image of most late 19th-century illustrators of books about chivalry. The castle was a favorite residence of Castilian monarchs throughout the medieval period, and the sumptuous decoration of tapestries, tiles, and Mudéjar woodwork conjures "days of old when knights were bold." Isabella took refuge in this fortress in 1474 when word came that her brother Enrique IV had died. A mural in the Galley Chamber tells the rest of that story: Having mustered the support of the royal army, she marched out of the Alcázar to Segovia's Plaza Mayor to be proclaimed queen of Castilla. The most dramatic room of the castle is the Hall of Monarchs, with its ceiling-level frieze in a style usually reserved for the depictions of saints. Each king or queen in the Castilian line from Pelagius of Asturias, credited with starting the *reconquista* in the 720s, to Juana la Loca, Isabella's mad daughter, is shown seated on a golden Gothic throne. It was commissioned by Juana's grandson, Felipe II, to cement his lineage's claim to the Spanish crown.

In recent years, Segovia has made an effort to emphasize its artistic heritage, and three excellent small museums show something of the range. **Museo Zuloaga** (Pl de Colmenares; ☎ 921-463-348; 1.20€ adults, seniors and students free, free to all Sat and Sun; July–Sept daily 10am–2pm and Tues–Sat 5–8pm, Oct–June daily 10am–2pm and Tues–Sat 4–7pm) occupies the medieval Iglesia San Juan, where ceramic artist Daniel Zuloaga based his family pottery studio starting in 1908. The firm made many of the scenic tiles that decorate the building facades all over Spain, and museum exhibits elucidate the entire artistic process, with an emphasis on the painterly artistry of the clan. The **Casa-Museo Antonio Machado** (Desamparados 5; ☎ 921-460-377; 1.50€, free Wed; guided tours Wed–Sun

11am, noon, 1pm, 4:30pm, 5:30pm, 6:30pm, closed Mon–Tues) is more a remembrance of the great Spanish poet (who lived in this boardinghouse from 1919 to 1932 when he taught French) than a true museum. Documents, drawings, and other mementos try to conjure the poet, but they aren't half as evocative as the little courtyard overgrown with flowering cacti and hollyhocks gone to seed where a canary sings as he flits from perch to perch in his cage. The newest of the group of artistic museums is **Museo de Arte Contemporáneo Esteban Vicente** (Plazuela de las Bellas Artes; ☎ 921-462-010; 2.40€ adults, 1.20€ seniors and students, free Thurs; www.museoestebanvicente.es; Tues–Fri 11am–2pm and 4–7pm, Sat 11am–7pm, Sun 11am–2pm), named for a chameleon-like modern artist who was part of the Madrid scene in the 1920s, fell in with Picasso and Raoul Dufy in Paris in 1929, and finally wound up in New York, where he had a fruitful career as an Abstract Expressionist painter. The museum collection is built around 150 works made throughout his long career. Temporary exhibitions place a strong emphasis on video.

Segovia has an equally vibrant religious history, and a visit to the **Monasterio de San Antonio El Real** ✪ (San Antonio El Real 6; ☎ 921-420-228; donation; Tues–Sat 10am–2pm and 4–7pm, Sun 10am–2pm) pulls back the curtain on the contemplative life of the cloistered Clarisa nuns, of whom only 11 remain at the site. When you enter through the church, you may see some of the nuns praying in a small chapel behind an iron grate, or hear them singing unseen behind the altar. Because their numbers have shrunk, the nuns have effectively turned over large parts of the monastery to a museum, and the tour through the rooms shows the contrast between some of the naïve religious art painted by the sisters and Spanish and Flemish religious art, mostly from the 15th and 16th centuries. The salon contains Segovia's only fully original carved and coffered wooden ceiling constructed by Mudéjar craftsmen (Moors who remained in Spain after the *reconquista* and practiced an artistic style informed by Muslim decorative traditions).

Outside the walls and constructed on the 12-sided pattern of the Church of the Holy Sepulcher in Jerusalem, **La Iglesia de la Vera Cruz** ✪ (Crtra de Zamarramala; ☎ 921-431-475; 1.75€; Tues 4–7pm, Wed–Sun 10:30am–1:30pm and 4–7pm) still resonates with the rough faith of the warrior monks who founded it. The shape, the style of the niches, and the fragmentary wall murals all had special significance in the mystic beliefs of the crusader order, Knights Templar, who built the church to house a piece of the True Cross. Consecrated in 1246 (1208 on the Gregorian calendar), the church's very existence illustrates the strong bond between military and religious life in Segovia. The site was abandoned when the Knights Templar were disbanded by Pope Clement V in the early 14th century. Fortunately, the structure has been partially restored under the care of the Knights of Malta.

THE OTHER SEGOVIA

Visiting churches and convents is often an exercise in art history rather than religious feeling. But two of Segovia's religious orders open their cloisters for world-weary pilgrims seeking a spiritual experience. Their modest lodgings are not bases for exploring the city, but rather rare opportunities to escape the modern hubbub for a brief sojourn into the contemplative life.

The 16th-century mystic and theologian, San Juan de la Cruz, founded and personally helped build the **Convento de los Padres Carmelitas Descalzos** (Paseo de Segundo Rincón 2; ☎ 921-431-961; centrosjc@ocdcastilla.org; donation; church open Mon 10am–1:30pm, Tues–Sun 10am–1:30pm and 4–8pm) in 1586. Upon his death in Úbeda in 1591, his body was returned here for burial, where it still rests in the left side chapel of the convent's church. One of the most significant theologians of the Counter-Reformation, the teachings of St. John of the Cross found new audiences among Roman Catholics in the late 20th century, and clergy in Segovia speak of him as if he was merely away for the weekend. His central axiom was that a person must empty his or her soul of "self" in order to be filled with God—a mystical tenet akin to Zen Buddhism. The monastery's Casa de Espiritualidad (House of Spirituality) offers an extensive program of themed spiritual retreats (conducted only in Spanish), housing men and women (and couples) in 32 private rooms (each with bath) arrayed around the convent's 16th-century courtyard. Courses include "The Road of Perfection" on using Santa Teresa as a model for one's own life, studies of the poems of San Juan de la Cruz, and theoretical and practical classes in the art of meditation. For more information, write or e-mail.

A more austere form of religious retreat is available at the Mother House of the Hieronymite Order, the **Real Monasterio de Santa Maria de El Parral** (Subida de El Parral 2, Segovia 40003; ☎ 921-431-298; donation; Mon–Sat 10am–12:30pm and 4:15–6:30pm, Sun 10–11:30am). This cloistered order, which emulates the hermit St. Jerome in its rejection of most physical comforts, welcomes men only for up to a week of prayer, reflection, and work helping to restore and maintain the property. Write for details. A large facility with extensive gardens, the facility once housed dozens of monks but now is home to only seven.

ATTENTION, SHOPPERS!

Segovia's prosperity is evident by the preponderance of jewelry stores along pedestrian avenida de Fernández Ladreda in the new city and along the streets leading from the aqueduct to the cathedral. But only a few shops carry products unique to Segovia. The upscale gift shop **Montón de trigo montón de paja** (Pl de la Merced 1, ☎ 921-460-769; Juan Bravo 21, ☎ 921-362-670), for example, carries a line of stylish T-shirts featuring images of internationally famous poet Antonio Machado and locally famous folklorist and musician Agipito Marazuela. Similarly, the handicrafts shop **Pink Elefant** (Marqués del Arco 30; ☎ 921-462-264) sells *tiles esgrafiado*, tiles that reproduce some of the geometric designs found on the stucco exteriors of Segovia buildings. The 10cm (4-inch) tiles make good hot pads. If you're buying for a youngster fascinated by the chivalric world of the Middle Ages, the shop at the **Alcázar** ★ (see above) has detailed cast-plastic "toy soldiers" of horses and knights in full regalia. For men, the same shop offers a selection of tasteful silk neckties with small repeat patterns of the insignia of Castilla y León, the arches of the aqueduct, or knights on horseback drawn from a manuscript owned by Charles III.

NIGHTLIFE IN SEGOVIA

During the summer, there are many free or inexpensive outdoor concerts throughout the Old City. Check at the tourist office for a schedule. You might find tango in Plaza San Lorenzo outside a 13th-century church, or jazz on the steps of the cathedral. On the flip side of the year, **Teatro Juan Bravo** (Pl Mayor;

www.teatrojuanbravo.org) programs a varied schedule of music, dance, variety shows, and children's entertainment.

Segovians, like most Spaniards, consider a night out to be tapas, dinner, and drinks, in that order. But a few spots emulate the British and American night scenes. Calle de la Infanta Isabel, for example, has several nightlife bars, including **Toys** (Infanta Isabel 13; no phone), which has foosball, a big-screen TV for sporting events, disco dancing nights, comedy nights, and everything else that a Spanish bar owner can imagine is American. If you can handle the Paris Hilton wannabes, you might want to check out the nightly karaoke at **Summum Disco** (Avda Fernández Ladreda 16; ☎ 921-462-611).

AVILA ✦

The centuries seem to roll away in Avila, where the 11th-century city walls are the main physical attraction, while the chief spiritual attraction is the legacy of Santa Teresa, the mystic reformer of the Catholic Church and co-founder (with San Juan de la Cruz) of the Carmelitas Descalzos (Barefoot Carmelites). She was born here in 1515, entered the Carmelites at 19, and began her reform of the order at age 45. Both a prolific writer and a brilliant organizer, Santa Teresa became the practical and political mover of the Spanish Counter-Reformation, while her compatriot San Juan de la Cruz tended to the inner spiritual life of the reform movement. Several sites associated with Santa Teresa remain in Avila, and the pious visit them as a pilgrimage.

GETTING TO & AROUND AVILA

From Madrid, the best travel choice is the roughly 2-hour trip by train, which arrives at **Estación del Renfe** (Avda José Antonio; ☎ 902-240-202; www.renfe.com). The one-way fare ranges from 6.50€ to 8.40€. If you're coming from Segovia, a better choice is the bus (4.90€), which arrives at **Estación del Autobus** (Avdas Madrid y Portugal; ☎ 920-220-1540) in around 2 hours. You can also drive here easily from Segovia in 1½ hours (just follow signs south of town) or from Madrid in just over 2 hours going northwest on the A-6. In any case, you'll want to pick up a city map at **Centro de Recepción de Visitantes** (Avda de Madrid 39; ☎ 902-102-121; www.avilaturismo.com; daily 9am–8pm). There are two options for exploring the city: Walk the perimeter streets, staying close to the city walls, or trust to luck, knowing the whole city tilts downhill from the cathedral. Driving? We think not.

ACCOMMODATIONS & DINING

While 1 day in Avila gazing at the walls and visiting a Santa Teresa site or two satisfies most visitors, others are sufficiently smitten to extend their trip. Here are two excellent alternatives for lodging, and two equally excellent places to dine.

€–€€   For photo-perfect views of Avila's walls, try to book a room from 103 through 105 at **Hotel las Murallas** (Ronda Vieja; ☎ 920-353-165; www.hotellas murallas.com; MC, V). Alternatively, Room 101 looks directly at the San Vicente bell tower across the street. A good choice for both drivers and bargain hunters, this modern 16-room hotel is located a short walk from the cathedral gate into the Old City and sits at the end of a long road with a lot of free parking. (Garage parking is also available at 11€.) Furnishings are simple, dark-stained wood, which goes well with the deep red or blue color schemes of the walls and the brown tile floors. Rooms 301 through 304 each have small terraces but lack the sweeping valley views. Rooms never exceed 75€ and dip as low as 55€.

€€€–€€€€   On weekends, the luxurious **Hotel Palacio de los Veladas** ✪ (Pl de la Catedral 10; ☎ 920-255-100; www.veladahoteles.com; AE, MC, V) offers rooms for the bargain rate of 105€, including the generous buffet breakfast (usually 13€ per person extra). As a bonus, you can survey the scene as wedding parties assemble for cocktails in the glittering central courtyard. You might find an even better deal in the dog days of August, when rooms sell for around 60€—a far cry from the official rate of 300€. (In practice, rooms rarely go over 200€.) This renovated 16th-century palace is one of Avila's top hotels, with a prime location next to the cathedral. Renaissance architecture frames subdued, sophisticated decor in the rooms—think Laura Ashley with a Spanish accent.

€€   After encountering so much pork and lamb in the rest of central Spain, it may come as a surprise that the meat specialty of Avila is the grilled *chuletón de Avila*, or T-bone steak. No one does it better than the stylish bar-restaurant **Chocolate** ✪ (Pl de Nalvillos 1; ☎ 920-211-679; daily 11am–4pm and 8:30–11:30pm; cash only), where 13€ gets you about a pound of meat served with roasted red peppers and oven-fried potatoes. Located in a quiet plaza outside the walls, Chocolate seems to have taken its decor from a candy box: dark brown walls, brown banquettes, chocolate brown napkins on the red plastic tables, and Philippe Starck red acrylic chairs. (There are even red "crystal" plastic chandeliers.) Essentially a playful bar with foodie aspirations, Chocolate's other house specialty is a massive hamburger (9.50€).

€€€   Far more self-consciously traditional in its decor, the white-linen dining room of **Meson del Rastro** (Pl del Rastro 1; ☎ 920-211-218; daily 1–4pm and 9–11pm; AE, DC, MC, V) also serves the local T-bone, though the menu is stronger on roasted rather than grilled meats. This spot is very popular with Spanish tourists who come to dine on saddle of lamb (19€) or pig's feet (15€). Since it's still Castilla, you can also get a wide variety of organ meats such as tongue, sweetbreads, or tripe. We have noticed that non-Spaniards often opt for the whole roast chicken (10€) with a sigh of relief.

WHY YOU'RE HERE: THE TOP SIGHTS & ATTRACTIONS

Avila is the perfect stage set of a Castilian city—a Cubist jumble of Gothic convents and palaces slumping down the top of a hill and entirely surrounded by imposing, castellated stone walls. It seems one great unified whole, making a greater impression than its individual parts. Among the best-preserved medieval fortifications in Europe, Avila's walls *(muralla)* were erected (1090–99) of blocks of brown granite atop earlier Roman walls. You can explore the **Muralla de Avila** ✪✪ ✪ 🧒 (entry points at Carnicerías, Alcázar, and Ronda Vieja; ☎ 920-255-088; 4€; Apr–Oct 15 daily 10am–8pm, Oct 16–Mar daily 11am–6pm) from the ramparts, walking along the top for about 40% of the 2.5km (1½-mile) circumference. Children seem to scurry along the walls like so many squirrels, but the less nimble should be aware that there are many rough stone steps and some tricky footing, and despite railings,

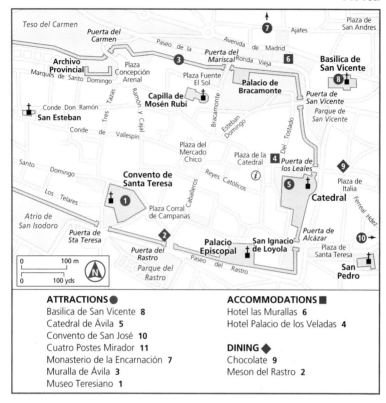

Teso del Carmen
Puerta del Carmen
Paseo de la
Plaza de San Andres
Ajates
7
Avenida de Madrid
Puerta del Mariscal
Ronda Vieja
3
6
Basilica de San Vicente
8
Archivo Provincial
Marqués de Santo Domingo
Plaza Concepción Arenal
Plaza Fuente El Sol
Palacio de Bracamonte
Puerta de San Vicente
Parque de San Vicente
Conde Don Ramón
San Esteban
Conde de Vallespin
Capilla de Mosén Rubí
Tres Tazas
Ramón y Cajal
Bracamonte
Esteban Domingo
Del Tostado
Santo Domingo
Plaza del Mercado Chico
Plaza de la Catedral
4 **Puerta de los Leales**
9
Plaza de Italia
Los Telares
Convento de Santa Teresa
Reyes Católicos
Caballeros
5
Catedral
Ferreal Hdez
Atrio de San Isodoro
Puerta de Sta Teresa
1
Plaza Corral de Campanas
Puerta de Alcázar
Puerta del Rastro
2
Palacio Episcopal
San Ignacio de Loyola
Plaza de Santa Teresa
10
Paseo del Rastro
Parque del Rastro
San Pedro
0 100 m
0 100 yds
N

ATTRACTIONS ●
Basilica de San Vicente **8**
Catedral de Ávila **5**
Convento de San José **10**
Cuatro Postes Mirador **11**
Monasterio de la Encarnación **7**
Muralla de Ávila **3**
Museo Teresiano **1**

ACCOMMODATIONS ■
Hotel las Murallas **6**
Hotel Palacio de los Veladas **4**

DINING ◆
Chocolate **9**
Meson del Rastro **2**

some fully exposed heights. Still, the views are unsurpassed, and it's a kick to imagine the frustration of invading armies thwarted by the soaring fortifications. The elevation also puts you on eye level with the many storks' nests on the city's towers.

In fact, about a half-dozen nests dot the heights of the **Catedral de Avila** (Pl de la Catedral; ☎ 920-211-641; 4€; Apr–Oct Mon–Fri 10am–6pm, Sat 10am–7pm, Sun noon–5pm [1 hour later each day mid-Jul to Sept]; Nov–Mar Mon–Fri 10am–5pm, Sat 10am–6pm, Sun noon–5pm), a dark and austere Romanesque/Gothic hulk literally built into the city walls. So heavy is the fortified church that a veritable forest of columns in the local mottled red and white stone supports it from within, obscuring many sight lines. Nine hundred years of entombments have filled every nook and cranny of the voluminous cathedral, though it's worth seeking out the beautifully sculpted tomb of "El Tostado," called "the toasted one" for his dark complexion. A prominent theologian of his day, he was the powerful bishop of Avila from 1454 to 1455. A side altar, naturally enough, honors local celebrity Santa Teresa. Be sure to stop in the Capilla del Cardenal to marvel at the polychrome wooden statues of saints created by anonymous artists in the 12th and 13th centuries.

Looking Back

When the intensely devout Teresa of Avila was only 7 years old, she ran away from home intent on seeking martyrdom by the Moors. Her uncle, however, tracked her down on a hilltop about 2.5km (1½ miles) northwest of the city on the Salamanca road and dragged her back to Avila. (The Moors had been kicked out of Spain 30 years earlier anyway.) A cross covered by a four-posted canopy marks the spot, known as **Los Cuatro Postes** (The Four Posts). Because it is a small shrine, there's a good roadside turnout—and it just happens to be the best place to photograph the walled city. Go late in the day, when the afternoon sun pulls the walls out of shadow.

Although it lies just outside the city walls, the **Basilica de San Vicente** (Humilladero; ☎ 920-255-230; 1.80€ adults, 1.40€ seniors and students; May–Oct daily 10am–6:30pm; Nov–Apr Mon–Sat 10am–1:30pm and 4–6:30pm, Sun 4–6:30pm) is a must-see for its insistence on pre-modern, pre–politically correct Christianity. It was built on the site where legend says that an 11th-century Jew was so frightened by his encounter with a talking serpent that he converted to Christianity. (The serpent's cave is in the cellar.) The centerpiece of the basilica is an elaborately carved sepulcher depicting the martyrdom of St. Vincent in gory detail (crucifixion, skull-crushing, and so on). The church is also a center of the cult of the Virgen de la Soterraña (Virgin of the Underground), a 1392 apparition of the Virgin still venerated today. Young Teresa of Avila was said to pray before the circa-1400 statue of the Virgen de la Soterraña to be martyred by the Moors.

The saint-to-be was born in Avila in 1515 on the site where the Convento de Santa Teresa now stands. Around the corner from the Plaza de la Santa entrance to the convent church (a favorite for weddings), is the **Museo Teresiano** ✦ (La Dama; ☎ 920-211-030; 2€; Apr–Oct Tues–Sun 10am–2pm and 4–7pm, Nov–Mar Tues–Sun 10am–1:30pm and 3:30–5:30pm); it actually lies *below* the convent, preserving the garden where Teresa recalled her childhood joy at playing with her siblings. Among some of the museum's more striking artifacts are painted portraits of Teresa by artists who were her contemporaries, as well as letters between Santa Teresa (vigorous, no-nonsense penmanship!) and San Juan de la Cruz (a more meticulous but rather florid hand). The museum does a good job of placing Teresa in the context of 16th-century Roman Catholicism, and then tracing the influence of her thought down to the present day.

The more personal side of the saint comes through at two other sites. The first Barefoot Carmelite convent that Teresa founded under her austere reforms was the **Convento de San José** (Las Madres 4; ☎ 920-222-127; 1.20€; Apr–Oct daily 10am–1:30pm and 4–7pm, Nov–Mar daily 10am–1:30pm and 3–6pm), east of the city walls. The convent's peculiar little museum, consisting of several rooms behind plate glass, holds personal artifacts of the saint, including her collarbone and the saddle on which she rode around Spain founding convents. One room recreates her original cell at the convent, including the window seat where she sat to write and a narrow bed with a log pillow. (You'll never complain again about twin-bedded hotel rooms after seeing it!) When you enter the tiny convent church, you might hear the disembodied voices of the cloistered nuns as they sing their prayers. For more than 30 years, Teresa's own home was the **Monasterio de la Encarnación** ✦ (Paseo de la Encarnación; ☎ 920-211-212; 1.70€; May–Sept Mon–Fri 9:30am–1pm and 4–7pm, Sat–Sun 10am–1pm and 4–6pm; Oct–Apr Mon–Fri 9:30am–1:30pm and 3:30–6pm, Sat–Sun 10am–1pm and 4–6pm), where she eventually served as prioress. The largely self-guided tour has a certain resonance, as this is the convent where Teresa took the habit in 1535 at age 20. As the ticket taker told us, she "entered the convent by this very door." Ironically, this convent did not adopt Teresa's reforms until the 20th century, so during her tenure, the nuns lived in surprisingly comfortable rooms, each with its own kitchen for cooking at a fireplace hearth. The tour has the appeal of seeing where church history happened—the *locutorios* (small receiving rooms) where Teresa and Juan de la Cruz jointly experienced being "lifted up in ecstasy," as they described it, or the statue that supposedly tattled on the nuns' misbehavior when Teresa returned from business trips.

SALAMANCA ✦✦✦

Don't look for an alcázar or fortified walls in Salamanca. A university city since 1218, it has always built its castles in the air and fortified itself with argument. What it lacks in medieval derring-do, it more than makes up for with wit and thought—they are even evident in the architecture and the sculptures that adorn building facades. The chief building material used in Salamanca has been a golden sandstone, and the softness of the stone permitted the evolution of an expressive, naturalistic carving style. You have to take Salamanca slowly so you don't miss the fine details.

GETTING TO & AROUND SALAMANCA

However you travel, it takes about 2½ hours to reach Salamanca from Madrid. The train arrives at **Paseo de la Estación** (☎ 902-240-202; www.renfe.es; 17€ one-way), the **Avanza** bus at **Estación de Autobuses** (☎ 902-020-999; www.auto-res.es; 9€ one-way). To drive, follow the AP-6 west to pick up the N-501 south of Segovia. When you reach Salamanca, turn right to cross the Enrique Estéban bridge and look for the **Reyes de España underground parking garage.** Parking is 2.15€ per hour (maximum 11€ per day), but it's an easy walk into the Old City, where driving is difficult and parking almost nonexistent. Maps and information are available from both the **Oficina de Información Turistica de Castilla y León** (Rúa Mayor at Casa de las Conchas; ☎ 902-203-030; mid–Sept to June daily 9am–2pm and 5–8pm; July to mid-Sept Sun–Thurs 9am–8pm, Fri–Sat 9am–7pm) and the **Oficina Municipal de Turismo de Salamanca** (Pl Mayor 32; ☎ 923-218-342; Mon–Fri 9am–2pm and 4:30–8pm, Sat 10am–8pm, Sun 10am–2pm).

ACCOMMODATIONS, BOTH STANDARD & NOT

To take full advantage of Salamanca, you'll want to stay within the Old City, which has been at peace since the 13th century and, thus, has most of its ancient buildings still intact. It's not uncommon to find even modest *pensiones* tucked into the upper levels of golden sandstone structures that date from the 15th through 17th centuries. A great deal of Salamanca lodging, however, is geared toward students who are planning to stay at least a month and as long as a semester, or in the case of Japanese students, up to a year. Unless otherwise stated, all the lodgings below have TV, telephone, heat, and air-conditioning.

€   While most apartment buildings are locked up with long-term student stays, you can get some of the advantages of an apartment—more space and kitchen facilities that enable you to live in a place rather than just visiting it—by opting for one of the small hotels that include apartments in their mix of rooms. Seven of the 16 rooms at **Hostal Sara** ✰ (Meléndez 11; ☎ 923-281-140; www.hostal sara.org; MC, V) are equipped with small kitchens (2-burner stove, refrigerator, and sink), which are useful for keeping snacks and cold drinks or even preparing your own breakfast. Depending on the season, they run 50€ to 58€. The largest of the kitchen-equipped rooms is known simply as the "Salon Social," but we'd suggest asking for either 303 or 304. They have tiled outdoor terraces where you can enjoy a cold glass of wine from your fridge while admiring the dome and bell tower of nearby San Martín church. While the decor is simple and traditional, everything, including the marble bathrooms, is fresh and new (the *hostal* opened in 2005). Each room, even those without kitchen, includes a pair of chairs, a good desk for working, and an ample armoire in lieu of a closet. Rooms without kitchenette are an even better deal: 42€ to 53€.

€–€€   Families traveling together will be pleased to discover the generous-sized apartments at **Apartahotel Toboso** 🧒 (Clavel 7; ☎ 923-271-462; www.hotel toboso.com; MC, V), steps from Plaza Mayor. While the building has 28 double rooms (which rent for 45€–52€ per night), the real attractions are the seven apartments that sleep three to five people each and have living/dining rooms and separate kitchens (with 4-burner stoves, refrigerators, and washing machines). New bathrooms finished in shining red marble add to the appeal, though the rest of the decor is rather simple, with modern furnishings including a soft, somewhat shapeless couch in the living room. The two-bedroom units are 76€; three-bedroom units are just 99€ per night. There are a couple of caveats about Toboso, however. Some of the double rooms sit above a cabaret/music bar and can be noisy; ask for one of the quieter apartments overlooking the interior courtyard instead. And none of the rooms has air-conditioning. That's rarely a big deal, as the building's thick stone walls maintain a constant, cool temperature. (There *is* central heat for the chilly winter.)

€€   If you're looking for a romantic lodging furnished with more contemporary panache (for a honeymoon perhaps?), **Microtel Placentinos** ✰ (Placentinos 9; ☎ 923-281-531; www.microtelplacentinos.com; MC, V) is the perfect spot. Somehow the designers managed to shoehorn six double rooms and three singles into a tiny 16th-century sandstone structure amid the looming blocks of the old university. Many rooms have at least one exposed stone wall where the windows are nearly a foot deep and can be closed off with heavy wooden shutters. The soft contemporary furniture carries through a muted palette. Although simple, the rooms are hardly spartan—bathrooms in doubles have whirlpool tubs, the flat-screen TVs carry digital satellite stations, and the bed linens are thick and

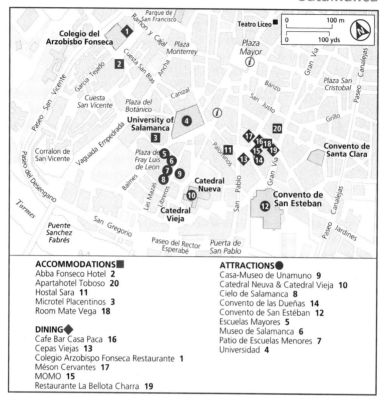

ACCOMMODATIONS ■
Abba Fonseco Hotel **2**
Apartahotel Toboso **20**
Hostal Sara **11**
Microtel Placentinos **3**
Room Mate Vega **18**

DINING ◆
Cafe Bar Casa Paca **16**
Cepas Viejas **13**
Colegio Arzobispo Fonseca Restaurante **1**
Méson Cervantes **17**
MOMO **15**
Restaurante La Bellota Charra **19**

ATTRACTIONS ●
Casa-Museo de Unamuno **9**
Catedral Neuva & Catedral Vieja **10**
Cielo de Salamanca **8**
Convento de las Dueñas **14**
Convento de San Estéban **12**
Escuelas Mayores **5**
Museo de Salamanca **6**
Patio de Escuelas Menores **7**
Universidad **4**

welcoming. Guests also share a large terraced Jacuzzi. Double rooms are 67€ on weeknights, but can go up to 92€ on weekends, though rates include breakfast.

€€–€€€   Contemporary style, of course, is the hallmark of the Room Mate group of boutique hotels, and the 38-room **Room Mate Vega** ✪ (Pl del Mercado 16; ☎ 923-272-250; www.room-matehotels.com; AE, MC, V), which opened in 2008, is no exception. The designer took inspiration from the city's muted sand tones, but enlivened the look with graphic patterned bed covers and large color art photographs. Vega is located near the public market about a minute's walk from Plaza Mayor. A single traveler should ask for Room 003 on the ground level. By accident of architecture, the small, sleek room with one twin bed has its own tiled terrace almost as large as the room itself. It's only 50€ to 60€. Most rooms, however, are doubles, with two full beds, sometimes pushed together like a king. Like other Room Mate hotels, Vega serves its generous breakfast (included in the price) until noon every day. Doubles are 60€ to 100€, though you can get an extra sitting area in an "executive" room for about 20€ more. Prices include tax.

€€–€€€ You'll give up the intimacy of a boutique hotel when you book into the 86-room **Abba Fonseca Hotel** ✦ (Pl San Blas 2; ☎ 923-011-010; www.abba hotels.com; AE, MC, V), but you'll gain lots of space to spread out and all the services of a business hotel at the price of something much more modest—as low as 68€ in the winter or late August, but rarely above 110€ even during the September festival season. Although the hotel adjoins a classic 17th-century university college and is built of matching sandstone, the rooms have the requisite deeply comfortable bed linens (maybe the best beds we've ever had in Spain), thick towels, a modern desk with power and computer network outlets, flat-screen TV, and a minibar with enough extra room for your own drinks. The hotel is on the edge of the Old City across from the university's Fonseca cultural center and about a 5-minute walk to the cathedrals.

DINING FOR ALL TASTES

While similar to the rest of central Spain, Salamantino cuisine has a few specialties: the thinly sliced dry mountain ham from Guijuelo; a spicy and crumbly sausage called *farinato;* and a pastry stuffed with cheese, sausage, and ham, called *hornazo.* Students traditionally feasted on these meat pies during Easter week to celebrate the return of prostitutes to the city after Lent, but the dish is now available year-round and is no longer eaten only by young men with flaming hormones. Tourist restaurants along **Rúa Mayor** offer acceptable if uninspired meals at slightly inflated prices, and the restaurants lining **Plaza Mayor** attract tourists and locals alike. To join Salamantinos in a more tranquil setting, walk up to **Paseo Carmelitas** between calle La Fuente and Puerta de Zamora. The leafy green park that lines the street is full of terraces that are popular for afternoon drinks and snacks.

€ Salamanca bars offer the most generous tapas that we've encountered in central Spain. For example, **Cafe Bar Casa Paca** ✦ (Pl del Peso 10; ☎ 923-218-993; www.casapaca.com; daily 1–4pm and 8:30pm–midnight; AE, DC, MC, V) is the casual side of one of Salamanca's finest restaurants. A drink at the bar might set you back 2.30€ to 3€, but each drink earns you a generous tapa such as farinato

---

A Handy Light Lunch

The quintessential cheap lunch in central Spain comes not from a restaurant, but from a bakery. The *empanada* is nothing more than a savory turnover in either a flaky, croissant-like pastry, or a more crumbly pie-dough pastry. Usually priced around 1€, empanadas come with a wide variety of fillings. The most common are *carne* (stewed meat in a spicy tomato sauce often with green or red peppers), *atún* (dark-meat tuna, usually with roasted red peppers and sometimes with cheese), ham and cheese, smoked salmon, or bacon and dates. Most bakeries sell them, and you'll find a good selection at the bakery shops in Salamanca's main food market, Mercado Abastos on Plaza Mercado, just off Plaza Mayor.

The Cool Spots

On hot summer nights, you'll find as many people eating ice cream as dining on Plaza Mayor. If you want a cone, join the line outside **Café Novelty** (Pl Mayor 2; ☎ 923-214-956; daily 8am–midnight; AE, MC, V). (During colder months, an arty crowd convenes in the Art Nouveau interior, and you might want to go in, just to have a look.) Local specialty cold drinks can be just as refreshing, and we like the plaza tables of **Cafetería Las Torres** (Pl Mayor 26; ☎ 923-214-470; daily 8am–midnight; MC, V) for sipping *leche helado* (a smooth concoction with hints of vanilla, cinnamon, and citrus rimmed with whipped cream) or *blanco y negro* (vanilla ice cream melting in a double shot of espresso).

---

sausage with scrambled eggs *(revuelto farinato)*, pig's ears in tomato sauce *(orillas)*, or a square of pastry filled with fresh goat cheese and quince jam. A similarly good deal is available at **Cepas Viejas** (Felipe Espino 6; ☎ 923-262-336; daily 1–4pm and 8:30pm–midnight; AE, MC, V), a snazzy wine bar a few blocks away. A glass of wine and a tapa cost 2€, a glass of beer and a tapa 1.50€. The "free" tapas are mostly bites of meat atop a thin slice of baguette: sliced pickled octopus, small fried sausages, breast of dove, or tuna topped with roasted red pepper. You'll probably have to eat standing up, but a few upended wine barrels serve as tables. An interior dining room offers a fancier, more expensive menu of roast meats and fish.

€–€€€   Salamanca may be a town of old traditions, but every so often you'll encounter a place that bursts that bubble with modern design and an innovative kitchen. Once you get past the decor of black walls, dark wood bar, zinc backsplash, and red painted highlights, the first thing you'll note at **MOMO** ★★ (San Pablo 13–15; ☎ 923-280-798; Mon–Sat noon–4pm and 8pm–midnight; MC, V) is that the TV over the bar is not tuned to football or bullfights. It's set on the cooking shows of the Spanish food network, and the dishes are suitable for prime time themselves. MOMO's stylish tapas, which have won a number of regional dining awards, tend toward small assemblages on thick slices of bread and, instead of giving them away, MOMO allows you to order them for .90€ at the bar along with a drink (good wine for 1.80€). Some of the restaurant's winners are the artichokes and fava beans with garlic mayo and melted cheese, or asparagus and serrano ham with the same aioli. The dining room officially opens at 9pm, and a good bet as a dinner entree (if you haven't filled up on tapas) is the smoked veal tongue smothered in roasted red peppers (16€).

€€   Combination plates are the mainstay of dining on Plaza Mayor, and **Méson Cervantes** (Pl Mayor 15; ☎ 923-217-213; www.mesoncervantes.com; daily 10am–midnight or later; MC, V) offers some of the best deals as well as some of the best food. You can get a small steak with two fried eggs and fried potatoes for 9€ or lamb chops with lettuce, tomato, and fries for 14€. After all the pork products of Spain, we're happy to sit at a plaza cafe table and dine on a generous vegetarian plate of white asparagus, green beans, peas, lettuce, tomato, marinated artichokes, and steamed squash (11€). The darkly atmospheric upstairs bar (the restaurant has no plaza-level dining room) is jammed at midday with locals drinking beer and eating such plates as rice-filled blood sausage with red peppers (11€) or scrambled eggs and farinato drizzled with honey (also 11€).

€€–€€€   You'll rarely find a tourist at **Restaurante La Bellota Charra** ✶ (Pl del Mercado 8–10; ☎ 923-219-657; daily 1:30–4pm and 8–11:30pm; AE, DC, MC, V), located next to a sausage store and across the street from the city food market. More casual than most Salamanca restaurants (basic blond wooden tables and chairs in a tile-floor dining room), it's also less expensive. Salamantinos swarm Bellota Charra for the bargain plates of top-notch local sausages (7€), sliced Iberian ham (14€), cured pork loin (13€), or a whole meal of meat pâtés and vegetable terrines (10€). Carry the tasting of local flavors one step further with a bottle of Abadengo, an intense but smooth red wine from the up-and-coming Arribes del Duero region (11€).

€€€   Every major college town has a spot like the **Colegio Arzobispo Fonseca Restaurante** ✶✶✶ (Pl Fonseca 4; ☎ 923-260-270; daily 1:30–4pm and 9–11:30pm; AE, MC, V). It's the university's restaurant where faculty and staff take guests for inexpensive meals in a fancy setting—in this case, a formal 16th-century court-yard. It's worth seeking out this off-the-beaten-path spot for its bargain *menu del día* (available both at lunch and dinner) and for the chance to rub elbows with the scholarly elite. The menu is an amazing 8€ for a choice of two first plates (typically a salad or a rice dish) and two second plates (sole or chicken, for example), along with wine, bread, and a pastry. On weekends the price goes up to 10€. The wine list is strong on Ribera del Duero reds (10€–22€).

WHY YOU'RE HERE: THE TOP SIGHTS & ATTRACTIONS

It's a pleasure to stroll in Salamanca because something always catches your eye. The heart of city life is the **Plaza Mayor** ✶✶✶, where the decoration is ostensibly baroque but the design is purely neoclassical. The proportions of the square and its graceful arcades—the least effusive major work by José Benito Churriguera (p. 124)—effectively form a picture frame around civic life. Salamantinos gather here morning, noon, and night to meet and greet, talk and sing, and, above all, eat and drink. You'll quickly identify other tourists: They're the ones studying the high-relief sculptural portraits above each spandrel of the arches. The cameos depict kings, queens, Spanish heroes, or illustrious figures from Salamanca's history, such as zarzuela composer Tomás Bretón on the east wall.

Roughly a quarter of the Old City is dominated by buildings of the University of Salamanca, which reached its apex of influence in the 15th and 16th centuries but has remained one of Spain's most significant centers of learning. Courtyards around university buildings are generally open to the public, and the **Patio de Escueles Menores** is a popular gathering point for tour groups as well as Salamantinos. A **statue of 16th-century poet and scholar Fray Luis de León** stands proudly in the center. More than four centuries after his persecution, he remains Salamanca's poster boy for intellectual freedom.

Given the importance of the school, it's a little disappointing that the only tour *inside* the **Universidad** (Libreros; ☎ 923-294-400 ext. 1150; 4€ adults, 2€ seniors and students, children 11 and under free, free for all Mon morning; Mon–Fri

9:30am–1:30pm and 4–7:30pm, Sat 9:30am–1:30pm and 4–7pm, Sun 10am–1:30pm) is a self-guided walk around the Renaissance arcades of the Escuelas Mayores, the original college of the university. Let your nose lead the way. The chapel has the lingering odor of sanctity (actually, frankincense), while the wonderful old library on the upper level smells of paper and old leather. You can visit the lecture hall of Fray Luis de León, who was imprisoned for four years by the Spanish Inquisition for the crime of translating the *Song of Solomon* from Hebrew into Spanish. When he was released, he returned to his university lectern and began his lesson, "Decíamos ayer . . ." ("As we were saying yesterday . . ."). The **facade of the Escuelas Mayores** ✶ is one of Salamanca's witty and puzzling sculptural marvels. About two-thirds of the way up on the right-hand side, a small frog is perched atop a human skull. Being able to spot the frog supposedly brings students good luck on their exams.

Miguel de Unamuno stole Luis de León's line ("decíamos ayer . . .") when he returned from six years of government-imposed exile in 1930 to resume his duties as rector of the university. The philosopher, poet, and novelist is well depicted in the university's **Casa-Museo de Unamuno** (Libreros 25; ☎ 923-294-400; 3€ adults, 1.50€ students and seniors; Tues–Fri 9:30am–1:30pm and 4–6pm, Sat-Sun 10am–1:30pm, closed Mon and Jul–Sept afternoons), his home during his first stint as rector (1900–24). The rooms are full of mementos, and just reading the titles of his personal library provides an intellectual portrait of the figure who, in the days leading up to the Spanish Civil War, famously championed "the resurrection of the man of thought who cries out against brute force and the failure of reason." Unamuno loved his adopted city deeply, once writing in a poem, "I keep your very soul in my heart. And you, my golden Salamanca, will keep my memory when I die." And so it has.

Don't miss one of the university's art treasures, the **Cielo de Salamanca** ✶✶ (Patio de Escuelas Menores; no phone; free admission; Tues–Sat 10am–2pm and 4–8pm, Sun 10am–2pm). Haunting and mysterious, the ceiling mural is all that remains of the 1473 mural by Francisco Gallego that once covered the vault of the university library. The astrological figures blend with astronomical observation—a very Renaissance convergence of art and science.

Only steps away, the **Museo de Salamanca** (Patio de las Escuelas 2; ☎ 923-212-235; 1.20€ adults, free for seniors and children, free to all Sat–Sun; Tues–Sat 10am–2pm and 4–7pm, Sun 10am–2pm) was founded in 1848 with art taken from monasteries and convents under the state's seizure of church property. The collections are predictably strong in 15th- to 17th-century religious art, with the highlight being an intricate golden Churrigueresque altarpiece crafted between 1697 and 1704. Several galleries also display contemporary art on loan from the Reina Sofía in Madrid.

Holding onto the old while emphasizing the new is very like Salamanca, a city that kept its old cathedral even after building a new one starting in 1513. The **Catedral Nueva** (Pl de Anaya; ☎ 923-217-476; free admission; Apr–Sept daily 9am–8pm, Oct–Mar daily 9am–1pm and 4–6pm) has been called "the last gasp of the Gothic style," and it is the largest and highest building in the city. The soaring spaces inside welcome pious contemplation, and if you stop in merely to see the art and architecture, you'll also observe believers progressing from chapel to chapel to light a candle and say a prayer. Many details of the New Cathedral are

One Twisted Family

It is an old pun in art history that the Spanish "go for baroque," but it's also true that Spanish baroque can make all other variations of the style look tame. The most extreme practitioners, one could say, carved out a name for themselves with a family style that owes a great deal to the forms assumed by twisted rope. **José Benito Churriguera** (1665–1725) and his brothers **Joaquín** (1674–1724) and **Alberto** (1676–1750) were stone sculptors who became architects. Their work in Salamanca, especially with altarpieces and the stucco work on building facades, spawned many imitators in Spain as well as in Mexico—hence the term, Churrigueresque.

Churrigueresque (see box), and with good reason—all three Churriguera brothers served as supervising architects of the cathedral's construction. The tradition of inspired carving continues. When the lower portion of the Puerta Ramos was rebuilt in 1992, the stonemason and restorers decided to update the carvings with the image of an astronaut floating in space and a monkey eating an ice cream cone! (Innocuous panhandlers will point them out for a tip.) The **Catedral Vieja** ✦ (Pl de Anaya; ☎ 923-217-476; 4.25€ adults, 3.50€ seniors and students; Apr–Sept daily 10am–7:30pm, Oct–Mar daily 10am–12:30pm and 4–5:30pm), entered through the New Cathedral, functions more as a museum than as a house of worship. It is effectively a Romanesque temple, begun in the 12th century but finished slowly enough that interior arches and vaults are in Gothic style. The 15th-century altarpiece is a tour de force of early Renaissance religious painting, with 53 panels relating the life of Christ and scenes of the Virgin Mary.

The religious and humanist strains of Salamancan thought converge at the **Convento de San Estéban** (Pl del Concilio de Trento; ☎ 923-215-000; 3€ adults, 2€ seniors and students; daily 10am–2pm and 4–8pm). Dominicans from this convent not only accompanied Columbus on his voyages to the New World to proselytize but also led the fight in Spain for the rights of indigenous people around the world. While the dignity of all humankind seems a no-brainer in the 21st century, it was a radical concept in the 16th, and the Dominicans of Salamanca suffered for it. Nonetheless, they persevered and continue to agitate for social and economic justice. Their convent is a pleasure to tour, highlighted by the José Benito Churriguera altar in the church and the stunning baroque choir with an illustrated hymnal big enough that all 118 monks could read the music from their seats. The nuns of the order are cloistered, but you can visit the nearby **Convento de las Dueñas** ✦✦ (Pl del Concilio de Trento; ☎ 923-215-442; 1.50€; Mon–Fri 10:30am–12:45pm and 4:30–6:45pm, Sat 10:30am–12:45pm) to enjoy the cloister arcades and strongly scented rose garden. The capitals on the arcade pillars represent some of the most inspired carving in the entire city, and any fan of gargoyles or modern graphic novels should make the effort to see them. They're a sample book of contorted human bodies, angels, griffons, devils, flying goat heads, winged horses, and other fantastic creatures.

THE OTHER SALAMANCA

One of the best ways to experience this city of scholarly pursuits is to settle in as a student for a week or more. You can do so at the Spanish language school **don Quijote** (Placentinos 2; ☎ 923-268-860; www.donquijote.org) set in a 16th-century monastery, which nestles among university buildings—and the restaurants, bars, and cafes essential to student life. Summer enrollment runs toward college students, but don Quijote attracts people of all ages and the school's attached cafe and grassy courtyard encourage socializing. Like most language schools, don Quijote keeps classes small (8 students maximum) and offers cultural enrichment programs (such as lectures on art or literature and film screenings). You can start with a 1-week intensive course (4 hours of study per day at 177€), or opt for a 2-week program that combines language study with cooking (560€) or wine tasting (520€). (It's amazing how well fluids aid fluency.) Check the website for specific dates. Cooking classes are held twice a week in a restaurant kitchen and students help prepare—and then dine on—such stalwarts of Spanish cuisine as gazpacho, paella, and tortilla Española (the potato omelet that everyone falls in love with when they visit Spain). The revolution in quality in Spanish wines is the talk of the world's wine fans. The wine-tasting course, led by a professional oenophile, meets three times a week so students can sample and learn to identify the unique wines from the country's different regions. Lodging with a host family starts at 140€ per week for a single room, 115€ for a double. Weekly rates for rooms in don Quijote's own student residence, close to the school, start at 145€ single and 110€ double.

NIGHTLIFE IN SALAMANCA

Plaza Mayor is the hub of Salamanca's public life. Indeed, a collective "ahhhh!" issues from the crowd at the cafe tables around the plaza when the lights suddenly come on about 20 minutes after sundown. People sit out here to talk and drink until the early morning, and the singing groups known as *tunas*—students in formal academic robes who accompany themselves with guitars, lutes, mandolins, and castanets—perform most evenings for tips.

For more formal evening entertainment, check out the musical and dance performances at the University of Salamanca's **Colegio Arzobispo Fonseca** (Pl Fonseca 4; no phone; ticket information at www.servidureo.com).

Chances are, you won't see too many students at the Fonseca, though, because they'll be making the rounds of the bars, which start opening around 8pm and close anywhere from 2am to dawn. The routine is to spend a little time in one bar, having a chat, a drink, and maybe a dance—and then move on to the next. The stretch of **Gran Vía** between Plaza Constitución and Plaza Concilio de Trento is popular with both Spanish and foreign students. Fortify yourself at **Vía Libre Cafe Bar** ★ (Gran Vía 47; ☎ 923-260-320) with an excellent choice of such free tapas as mushrooms sautéed with ham (drink and tapa around 2€). You may also end up here at the end of the night (or beginning of the morning) having *churros* and hot chocolate (3€). As you make the rounds, you'll find most bars equipped with a breathalyzer—put in a half-euro coin and blow into the machine with a straw to find out how impaired you are. (This becomes a competitive source of amusement as the night wears on.) **Espannola** (Gran Vía 51; no phone) is the place for superb rum-based cocktails, especially *mojitos* and *caparinhas,* amid Art Nouveau dark wood and silvery mirrors. During the academic year, you might even catch some live jazz on weekends. The music is always cranking at **Cafe Moderno** (Gran Vía 75; no phone), though it's usually recorded. American country music and some pop rock start the evening, but the progression gets louder and more discordant as the night wears on. Watch for band posters on walls around town—Moderno hosts local performers on no particular schedule.

By contrast, the entertainment is plotted a month in advance at **Medievo** (Gran Vía 93; no phone), and runs the gamut from '80s and Spanish music to erotic cabaret and wet T-shirt contests. The decor is pseudo-cave, with suits of armor mounted haphazardly around the room and a disco ball spinning overhead. Every night from Monday through Thursday, starting at 11pm, it's an open bar. Pay 4€ for a plastic cup and you get unlimited refills of beer, sangria, or a student favorite mix of red wine and Coca-Cola.

Signs at **Siglo I/Gran Cafe Centera** (Gran Vía 101; no phone) advise patrons, *"Pide tu mamadu,"* and if you ask the bartender what that might be, he'll tell you that if you have to ask, you're in the wrong place. The stylish cocktail bar side (Siglo I) follows a tasteful Roman theme, and it's popular with stylishly dressed older men, while Centera is the more happening side, with lots of vaguely Andy Warhol takeoffs (like Mona Lisa as Marilyn Monroe) in the artwork and well-tanned, heavily muscled young men at the bar. The house drink, the *mamadu,* is dark rum with coconut cream floating on top.

ATTENTION, SHOPPERS!

Just as the university dominates Salamanca's Old Town, its "official store," **Mercatus** ✪ (Cardenal Plá y Deniel s/n; ☎ 923-294-692) stands head and shoulders above the proliferation of souvenir shops that surround it. If you fell in love with the student singing groups, or *tunas,* on Plaza Mayor, you can purchase their CDs. Reproductions of the "cielo of Salamanca" painting on T-shirts, tote bags, puzzles, coasters, and silk scarves make good gifts, while polo shirts with the Universitas Studii Salamantini logo are classy and understated. Buy your budding scholar a bright green stuffed frog—the good luck talisman of Salamanca university students. If you really need good luck, **Joyero Artesano Baillo** (Palominos 13; ☎ 923-267-269) sells gold and silver frog charms as well as their own jewelry in Salamanca's distinctive filigree style.

4 Andalusia

Where all the clichés of Spain ring true

by Patricia Harris & David Lyon

ANDALUSIA (ANDALUCÍA) MOVES TO A FLAMENCO SOUNDTRACK. BRIGHT rhythms of a *bulería* burst from a market stall, a contemplative *soleá* sets the mood at a restaurant, hybrid flamenco hip-hop blares from the open window of a passing car. The trill of guitar arpeggios—faster, *faster, FASTER*—rings out from an open window. Like flamenco, Andalusia itself emerges from an overlay of cultures. It is simultaneously Roman, Arabic, and Spanish, a land so different from the rest of the Iberian peninsula that Spaniards themselves make a special pilgrimage to see and understand it. Even as Andalusia asserts its identity distinct from the rest of the country, it is also the birthplace of much that the world understands as Spanish. It is the land of the bullfight and sherry, the cradle of flamenco, the setting for opera's *Carmen,* and the stomping grounds of the lecherous Don Juan.

Certain archetypes recur in Andalusia, yet they never lose their power to surprise or delight. The cathedral is built on the ruins of a mosque, built in turn on the foundations of a Roman temple—every conqueror saw fit to set his altar on the ashes of the vanquished. Virtually every village is splashed in whitewash on stucco walls beneath orange roofs. Virtually every courtyard is tiled with splendid patterns that wed the Roman penchant for mosaic with the Arabic eye for decoration. Every home is hung with flowers, often as not the *gitanillas,* or "little Gypsies," as Andalusians are wont to call their favorite geraniums.

The desert Arabs left their stamp on Andalusia with their love of wells and fountains, of the sound of water tumbling in the shade as respite from the brilliant sun. When the guitars of Andalusia pause and everyone takes a breath, you can hear the sound wherever you are—the sound of water gurgling from fountains and streaming down the channels to irrigate the flowers.

DON'T LEAVE ANDALUSIA WITHOUT . . .

Being dazzled by lavish moorish decoration.   The artistry of the palaces and fortresses of long-ago al-Andalus live on though the Moors are long gone.

Internalizing the rhythms of flamenco.   Throughout the region, there's a song and a dance for every mood, from the aching loneliness of a *soleá* to the fiery passions of a *bulería* and the sultry rhythms of Las Sevillanas.

Succumbing to the hypnotic power of horseshoe arches receding into the distance.   The medieval mosque in Córdoba keeps alive the spiritual vitality of Europe's largest and most cultured medieval city. See p. 151.

Sipping a salt-tinged manzanilla sherry with a plate of shrimp.   Pull up a chair and feast. Andalusian shellfish is some of the world's best and most varied, and sherry is the perfect complement. See p. 198.

Sitting in a shady patio to listen to a bubbling fountain.   Like an oasis in the desert, the central courtyard of an Andalusian house is a cool respite from intense sun. The sound of water is the song of life.

Buying an embroidered shawl, flirtatious fan, or pair of dangly earrings.   Andalusia is the birthplace of Spanish style—channel your inner Carmen.

A BRIEF HISTORY OF ANDALUSIA

Maybe the best place to understand the tides of Andalusian history is in the archaeological exhibits of the **Museo de Cádiz** (p. 206). The artifacts here chronicle the region's progression of cultures from Paleolithic hunters on to Phoenician traders, Greek olive growers, Carthaginian warriors, and finally, around 200 B.C., Roman bureaucrats. The first Mediterranean cultures brought olive trees and grapevines—and the potter's wheel, making possible the amphorae to ship home olive oil and wine. The Romans came first to defend themselves against Hannibal's North African armies. They came, they saw, they conquered . . . and they settled.

Southern Iberia became Roman Bética, the most productive region of the empire outside Italy. Wheat and wine flowed from the Guadalquivir valley and the mountainsides yielded a river of olive oil. By 100 B.C., Córdoba was established as the capital. Rome gave Bética its language, its laws, its religion, and its roads, bridges, and aqueducts (some, like the Roman bridges in Córdoba and Ronda, still in service 2 millennia later). Bética gave Rome the philosopher Seneca and three emperors: Theodosius, Hadrian, and Trajan.

When Rome teetered in 410 and fell in 476, Andalusia, like much of Iberia, fell into the hands of the upwardly mobile Visigoths, who quickly adopted Roman ways. Other than a few architectural remnants—notably some of the columns and capitals on buildings in Granada—little remains of their reign in southern Iberia. A fight over royal succession led one party to make the culturally and strategically fatal error of seeking military assistance from the Berbers of Morocco.

In A.D. 711, general Tarik ibn Ziyad ferried 9,000 soldiers across the Strait of Gibraltar, but he helped himself, not the Visigoths. His army swept through the crumbling kingdom, aided by the Jews and Celtic Iberian slaves who bridled at the Visigoth yoke. It was both a conquest and a revolution. Within a year, Tarik solidified his control of the Guadalquivir valley and made Córdoba his own capital. Over the next 2 decades the Moors (as the Europeans called all Muslims, regardless of their origin) seized most of the Iberian peninsula and crossed the Pyrenees, only to be stopped in 732 at Poitiers by the Frankish king Charles Martel, the grandfather of Charlemagne.

The new Muslim lands were called al-Andalus—a name Hispanicized to Andalucía (Andalusia). In the pockets of northern Iberia still in native hands, the leaders retrenched, built their armies, called for aid from the pope and the kingdoms of northern Europe, and began the slow 7-century march of the *reconquista*, or reconquest. The Andalusian countryside is littered with reminders of this struggle in ruined fortresses on remote hilltops, but the prosperous cities of Seville (Sevilla), Córdoba, Cádiz, Málaga, and Granada remained far from the strife. The Moors built their greatest mosques and fortresses in these population centers, and except for Cádiz, each of those cities still bears a strong Moorish stamp.

From late 756 until 1031, the Umayyad dynasty ruled the entire region from Córdoba, first as emirs beholden to Damascus, then as independent caliphs. It was the golden age of al-Andalus, when Córdoban scholars preserved the learning of the ancient world, adding their own discoveries in mathematics, philosophy, and astronomy. La Mezquita, the largest mosque in Europe, was erected in Córdoba as the purest symbol of that age. But the overthrow of the caliphate in 1031 led to the political devolution of al-Andalus into independent *taifa* kingdoms ruled by local strongmen. The political scuffling left its mark—the alcázars of Málaga, Seville, and Jerez were all built in this time of war.

Seville managed to reunite al-Andalus again in 1162, but less than a half-century later, the allied armies of Christian kings from the north crossed the Sierra Morena and began the *reconquista* in earnest. Under the flag of Fernando III of Castilla (canonized by the Church for his efforts), victorious Christians took Córdoba in 1236 and Seville in 1248. Only the Nasrid kings of Granada held out by making a fragile peace in which they agreed in principle that they were vassals of the King of Castilla and would pay annual tribute. With this truce in place, Granada flourished until "the Catholic Kings" Ferdinand and Isabella (known as Fernando and Isabel in Spain) launched their personal holy war of reconquest in 1482. On January 2, 1492, they took Granada.

They also dispatched Christopher Columbus on his voyages of discovery, and the subsequent wealth that flowed to Spain from its colonies came through Andalusia. For the first 250 years, Seville was the axis of trade with the Americas, succeeded by Cádiz in the 18th century when the Rio Guadlaquivír became unnavigable by large ships. Andalusia's economic decline paralleled Spain's, as it returned to a largely agricultural economy after the Napoleonic invasion. The region opposed Franco in the Civil War, and the generalissimo established a practice of relocating Andalusian workers to other parts of the country to provide cheap labor. Agitation for independence, which began in the 19th century, was finally stilled in 1982 when the Spanish government was decentralized and Andalusia became an Autonomous Region governed largely by its own administration, the Junta de Andalucía.

LAY OF THE LAND

Geology has conspired to define Andalusia. Roughly the size of the island of Ireland, the region is an ellipsis of ancient limestone sea bed walled off on the north and east from the rest of Spain by the low, glacier-rounded cordillera of the Sierra Morena. Boasting long coastlines on both the Mediterranean and the Atlantic, much of Andalusia is drained by a single mighty river, the Río Guadalquivir that flows east to west through Córdoba and Seville and empties into the Bay of Cádiz. Granada is also a river city, but owes its prominence to the nearby mountains that (somewhat) protected it from military incursions, thus allowing Granada another 2 centuries to flourish after the rest of al-Andalus had fallen. The great Mediterranean port of Málaga, which rivals the Atlantic port of

Andalusia (Andalucía)

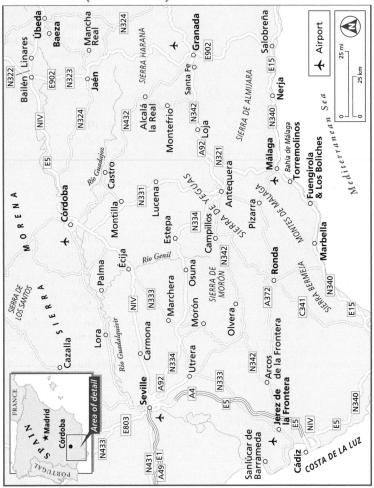

Cádiz for antiquity, grew up as the principal Roman port for shipping oil, wheat, and wine from Bética.

Most North Americans visiting Andalusia will begin either at Seville (thanks to its high-speed trains and good airport) or at Málaga, which has the larger airport and recently acquired high-speed rail service as well. Seville makes the better starting point for the classic Seville-Córdoba-Granada tour of Moorish monuments, and for heading west to Jerez and Cádiz. Málaga's coastal location makes it the gateway of choice for the Costa del Sol and a point of departure for visiting Granada.

For such a large area, Andalusia is remarkably easy to get around, thanks to good public transportation. Specific information on bus and rail service is detailed in the city sections below. For schedules and prices, check the website of the national rail network, **RENFE** (www.renfe.es). Depending on how many days you actually plan to travel, a Spanish Rail Pass from **Rail Europe** (www.rail europe.com) may save you money. Reservations are essential on the high-speed, long-distance trains. Buses are often even cheaper and more frequent. For complete schedules of bus service throughout Andalusia, see www.andalucia.com/travel/bus/home.htm.

SEVILLE (SEVILLA) ✪✪✪

Seville has been Andalusia's shining capital since Fernando III of Castilla tossed out the Almohad rulers in 1248. As one of the first major cities in the heart of Andalusia to return to Spanish hands, it has a markedly Christian countenance. The city is studded with churches and former convents, most of them in the high baroque style that reflects Seville's 16th- to 18th-century trade monopoly with the New World and the riches of the Indies that filled its coffers.

GETTING TO & AROUND SEVILLE

High-speed **trains** from Madrid and Córdoba arrive at Santa Justa station (Avda de Kansas City) in the city center. **Seville airport** (SVQ) has frequent service from most Spanish cities and many European destinations, but no direct service from North America. **Buses** run between the airport, train station, and Puerta Jerez (near the cathedral) every half-hour from 6:15am until 11pm. **Taxis** between the airport and central city cost about 25€. Seville is also easily accessed from the A4 highway, but driving and parking in town can be nightmarish. Fortunately, Seville is eminently walkable, especially if you use the 1€ city buses to get across town—otherwise an 8€ to 10€ taxi ride.

Pick up maps and useful information at the **Consorcio de Turismo de Sevilla** (Pl de San Francisco; ☎ 954-590-188; www.turismo.sevilla.org) and **Turismo de la Junta de Andalucía** (Avda de la Constitución 21B; ☎ 954-221-404; www.andalucia.org).

Most visitors orient themselves by the cathedral and adjacent Alcázar. South of these monuments lies Parque de María Luisa. Immediately north and east is the

The Eye Candy of Seville

Style matters in Andalusia's largest, most self-assured, and most sophisticated city. To see it at its best, spend a Saturday afternoon watching wedding parties come and go at the Basilica de Macarena near the ruins of the 12th-century Almohad defensive wall. Men in traditional suits or tuxedos escort women resplendent in elegant shawls and flamenco-influenced designer dresses that accentuate their feminine curves. The family grande dames add several inches to their height with elaborate hair combs and intricate mantillas. And when the happy couple rides off in their limousine, the Sevillanos in all their finery pack into a bar across the street for a celebratory drink—and another wedding party floods into the church.

old Judería, or Jewish Quarter, now called barrio Santa Cruz. The pedestrian length of Plaza de Constitución and calle Sierpes run north from the cathedral, separating Santa Cruz from Arenal. Farther north is the colorful working-class barrio Macarena, named for the church (not the pop-dance tune), and the bohemian quarter surrounding the Alameda de Hercules. The former fishing port of Triana stands on the opposite side of the Río Guadalquivir.

ACCOMMODATIONS, BOTH STANDARD & NOT

If you have 3 or 4 days to spend in Seville, consider a short-term apartment rental. Probably the most economical option, it will allow you a glimpse of how the fabulous Seville style translates into home decor, and may let you meet some of your neighbors in the residential neighborhoods on the edge of the tourist districts. While neither short-term apartment rental agency discussed here has exclusive listings of all the accommodations they handle, they do have a commitment to personal service that is often lacking in this nascent industry.

Office manager Manuela Stuhl of **Sevilla5** ★ (Sierpes 54, Edificio 1, 1st Floor; ☎ 954-226-287; www.sevilla5.com) has a background in hotel management, which gives her a good idea of travelers' expectations. "We don't just do the reservation," she says. "We match the apartment owner and the client." Stuhl, who speaks Spanish, English, French, and German, sometimes greets clients and is available by phone to help solve problems. Many of Sevilla5's apartments are in barrio Santa Cruz, though several are in the up-and-coming student and gay-friendly quarter of Alameda de Hercules, about a 20-minute walk from Santa Cruz and close to the working-class barrio Macarena. If you've visited El Rinconcillo (p. 138), you'll recognize the "storytelling" tiles in the entry to two apartments at calle Relator 25 just off calle Fería near the Macarena basilica. A recent building makeover also preserved the original tile floors and brick walls in the units, which have dark modern furniture, balconies facing the street, small bathrooms with tile showers, and modern kitchens. The two units (each 70€) share a rooftop terrace and a washing machine on the patio level, but the building does not have an elevator. Nine apartments at Apartmentos San Andrés are among the company's most popular, in part because the owner serves breakfast at his street level bar/cafeteria, which is also a handy spot for drinks and snacks all day. (Since it's open from early morning until midnight, someone is usually around in case of a problem.) The apartments surround a courtyard and share an elevator and washing machine. The older, traditional furnishings are in good condition though baths are small. The six one-bedroom and three two-bedroom units all have sofabeds. Rates are 85€ per night for two people and 120€ per night for four. With a few exceptions, Seville5 requires a three-night minimum stay. Rates per apartment are reduced after six nights; no additional cleaning fee is charged.

> ❝ Sevilla always appears to me essentially feminine; she is beautiful, languorous, dallying, coquettish, fickle, fragile, perhaps even a little cruel, a sultana, a jewel of great price. ❞
>
> —Paul Gwynne, *Along Spain's River of Romance* (McBride, Nast & Company, 1912)

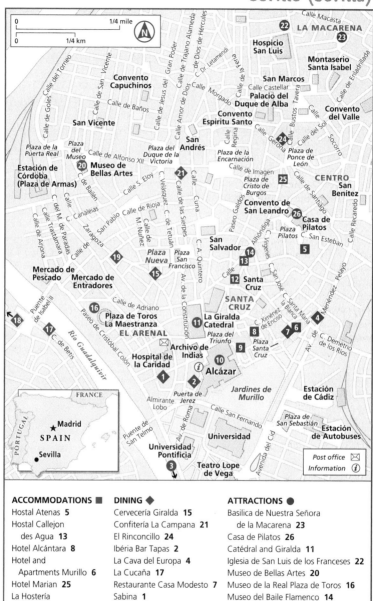

ACCOMMODATIONS ■
Hostal Atenas **5**
Hostal Callejon
  des Agua **13**
Hotel Alcántara **8**
Hotel and
  Apartments Murillo **6**
Hotel Marian **25**
La Hostería
  del Laurel **9**
YH Giralda **12**

DINING ◆
Cervecería Giralda **15**
Confitería La Campana **21**
El Rinconcillo **24**
Ibéria Bar Tapas **2**
La Cava del Europa **4**
La Cucaña **17**
Restaurante Casa Modesto **7**
Sabina **1**
Sol y Sombra **18**
Taberna del Alabardero **19**

ATTRACTIONS ●
Basilica de Nuestra Señora
  de la Macarena **23**
Casa de Pilatos **26**
Catédral and Giralda **11**
Iglesia de San Luis de los Franceses **22**
Museo de Bellas Artes **20**
Museo de la Real Plaza de Toros **16**
Museo del Baile Flamenco **14**
Parque de María Luisa **3**
Real Alcázar **10**

A Note on Accommodations

Whether in an apartment or a hotel, you'll have the chance to spend time in traditional Andalusian houses, some of which date back to medieval days. But unless otherwise noted, all accommodations in this chapter include the 21st-century amenities of heat, air-conditioning, television, telephone, and private bathroom. Prices quoted, unless otherwise noted, do not include breakfast or room tax.

Gronia Bryan is the Seville manager of **Friendly Rentals** ★★ (☎ 932-688-051; www.friendlyrentals.com), a U.K.-based company founded by her sister and brother-in-law. She often shops for essentials for families with small children, especially if they're arriving late, and once even made a late-night delivery of a corkscrew to young French women who had broken the one in their kitchen. "Then I stayed for a glass of wine," she says. Her agency currently lists about 30 apartments, most in the old city, but "I'll take some that are slightly outside if they are really nice," she says. "The first things I look at are the bathroom and kitchen, which, if they are not new, must be in really top condition." She also requires that owners stay in their apartments overnight to ensure all appliances (including the mandatory washing machine) work properly and that there's enough hot water for everyone to shower in the morning. Bryan handles "cheap and cheerful" apartments (75€ per night) only if they're located near major attractions. Otherwise, the company focuses on more upscale, larger apartments that range up to 200€ per night. Some of the best options combining price, style, and comfort are in the San Bernardo district, a residential neighborhood about a 10-minute walk from the cathedral. "It's a posh area now," Bryan says, "but a lot of bullfighters were born here." The owner of two rental units on calle Gallinato owns a home-furnishings shop and his apartments resemble boutique hotel suites. There's not a trace of IKEA amid the stylish modern furniture in muted colors and snazzy kitchens with intense red designer cabinetry. The one-bedroom unit with sleeper sofa fetches 110€ to 120€ per night; the two-bedroom unit, also with sleeper sofa, 180€ to 200€. Friendly Rentals requires a three-night minimum and charges a 40€ to 50€ cleaning fee. Discounts of 10% to 15% may be available on bookings of seven or more nights.

Hotels

Seville's larger hotels tend to be located on the periphery of the old city, which is good for arriving by car but means a bit of walking to reach the sights. The hotels included here are more convenient since they are embedded in the narrow streets of the old quarters, mostly in barrio Santa Cruz. If you're planning to drive in Andalusia, arrange to pick up your rental car when you leave Seville (or drop it off before you visit). Hotel parking is scarce. If your hotel choice doesn't have parking (and most don't), plan to leave your car at the Santa Justa train station parking lot and get a cab as close as you can to the hotel—cabs are allowed places where private cars are banned. Hotels throughout Andalusia reflect the regional tendency to spend most of one's time not in the bedroom, but in the courtyard. Thus, lobbies are often more lush than the rooms.

€€–€€€   Suits of armor, a carved wooden ceiling, and elaborate carved door in the lobby belie the modern style of **Hotel and Apartments Murillo** ✪✪ 🅺🅸🅳🅢 (Lope de Rueda 7–9 and Reinoso 6; hotel ☎ 954-216-095, apartments ☎ 954-210-959; www.hotelmurillo.com; AE, DC, MC, V), which holds down a corner of a narrow pedestrian-only street. (A cab can get you within about 20m.) There are 94 rooms in the main hotel and 17 apartments in adjacent buildings. Double rooms are 94€ and feature large closets and the cooling elegance of marble floors and bathrooms. Some have small balconies. The rooms are perfectly comfortable, but you can step up to a studio apartment with more space and a rudimentary kitchen (2 burners and a refrigerator) for only 99€. A larger apartment that can sleep three people is good for families at 109€ a day. Prices drop by the week and month and include tax.

€–€€   Walking down the long tiled hallway shaded by an arbor makes entering **Hostal Atenas** (Caballerizas 1; ☎ 954-218-047; www.atenashostelseville.com; MC, V) an event. Step through the elaborate wrought-iron gate, and you enter a larger, lavishly tiled patio that serves as the lobby—which is the heart of the house, where you'll find the only TV in the place as well as some vending machines. Built as a private home in 1824, the *hostal* has 20 smallish bedrooms where, alas, the tile ends and the white paint begins. Furnishings are monastically simple—save a picture or two on the walls—but everything is spotless and the rate is about as low as it goes in Seville for digs with private bathroom: just 59€ to 86€ with tax. And did we mention the location, right adjacent to the atmospheric Casa Pilatos (p. 142)?

€€   The tiled "santo" or image of Christ in the patio signals that **Hotel Alcántara** ✪ (Ximemez de Enciso 28; ☎ 954-500-595; www.hotelalcantara.net; AE, DC, MC, V) was once a convent. All 21 rooms overlook the patio and retain an air of tranquility with simple painted wooden headboards and bedside tables, crisp white bedspreads, and low-key striped fabrics on the chairs and stools. It's quite modern and stylish for 73€ to 87€ with tax. Wi-Fi is available in the lobby, and if you didn't bring your laptop, you can rent one for 1€ per hour. While there's no parking for autos, Alcántara does have dedicated free parking for bicycles!

€€   The architect who designed Plaza de España also designed the historic structure now occupied by **Hotel Marian** (Alhóndiga 24; ☎ 954-212-113; www.hotelmarian.com; MC, V); while you won't find that attraction's elaborate tilework

Do-It-Yourself Tapas

If you have a microwave in your apartment, look for surprisingly tasty **Tapas al minuto** in the refrigerated case of any grocery store. Choices include cheese or dates with bacon, mild or spicy chorizo sausage, or *morcilla* sausage (blood pudding) with rice. Each 1.55€ package provides 6 to 12 pieces, and a couple of packages and a bottle of wine make a quintessentially Andalusian quick meal.

at this modest hotel, you will find a formal design that gives this hotel an air of grace rarely found in this price class. All 23 rooms (doubles 62€–75€ with tax) look out on plant-filled patios, and the tiled rooftop terrace is a splendid spot for lying out to soak up the Seville sun. Half-paneled light pine walls are less somber than the usual dark oak and contrast nicely with red marble in the public areas and white marble floors in the rooms. Artificial lighting throughout the hotel is limited, although the high ceilings and abundant patios make it simultaneously bright and cool during the day. There's no particular architectural distinction to the ground level's friendly, guests-only bar, but it's a convenient spot to purchase simple breakfasts of juice, coffee, and baked goods and afternoon cold drinks. Favored by vacationing Spaniards, the hotel does have a strong tobacco aroma in the halls and patios.

€€–€€€   By contrast, **La Hostería del Laurel** ★★ (Pl de los Venerables 5; ☎ 954-220-295; www.hosteriadellaurel.com; AE, DC, MC, V) is light, airy, and smells faintly of lemons. Author José Zorrilla stayed here in 1844, and is said to have been inspired by the inn's romantic atmosphere to create his now-immortal character, the tragic womanizer Don Juan Tenorio. None of the 20 rooms—furnished with light wood furniture and painted either white or in bright pastels—suggests a licentious past. Still, they are well priced at 78€ to 104€ including breakfast. And the Laurel does have a lot of character, perhaps best appreciated in its attached restaurant with its low ceilings hung with hams. Breakfast is served in the restaurant, which is also a great place for an afternoon pickup of tapas at 2.20€ each.

€€   When you're walking on calle Abades, you'd never guess that **YH Giralda** (Abades 30; ☎ 954-228-324; www.yh-hoteles.com; AE, DC, MC, V) stands less than 100m from the Giralda (the famous bell tower of the cathedral), as the street is so narrow that you can't see the horizon. Located in an 18th-century former home of local abbots, the tall, slender building has rooms on three levels around a central courtyard. The rooms are intimate, but the wood-beamed ceilings and briskly whitewashed walls with brick-red details and trim give them a spacious feel. Paneled wooden doors hint at the antiquity of the building, but fully modern baths and new iron bedsteads in an historic style assure you that everything is very much 21st century, not 18th. Doubles range from 80€ to 93€ with tax.

€€–€€€   The 16 rooms in **Hostal Callejon del Agua** ★ (Corral del Rey 23; ☎ 954-219-189; www.callejondelagua.es; AE, MC, V) almost make up a tiny village in themselves. A narrow marble staircase winds around the central courtyard, and all the rooms have windows overlooking the courtyard, as well as windows looking out on the narrow alley-like streets. Like most hotels in barrio Santa Cruz, the rooms are on the small side, but they are carefully decorated with floral bedspreads, contrasting paint accents on the walls, and modern wrought-iron headboards with vine motifs. Nightly rates tend to swing from 70€ to 100€ but include tax and breakfast. You'll also find great tapas nearby on Plaza Alfalfa.

DINING FOR ALL TASTES

Dining categories in Seville are subtle. Restaurant dining tends to be for special occasions because the restaurants are too formal (and often too expensive) for a comfortable night out. But many of Seville's tapas spots are more like the Spanish equivalent of a French bistro than like a bar. They tend to serve limited selections of bite-sized tapas and many more choices of *media raciones* or full *raciones*, which are nearly the size of restaurant entrees. Sevillanos also love their sweets, which they tend to eat as snacks rather than dessert. There's a pastry shop on every corner; most specialize in pastry with an Arabic accent—lots of almonds, dates, and honey. While a few may also have the occasional sandwich (usually ham and cheese), they're not the one-stop dining and takeout shops like French patisseries. You can make a picnic (or shop for your apartment kitchen) at the *mercados de abastos,* or fresh food markets. Each neighborhood has its own, but two of the most colorful are the one on calle Féria in barrio Macarena and the Arenal market on calle Pastor y Landero near the bullring.

€   A steady crowd of people file out of **Confitería La Campana** ✦ (Sierpes 1 and 3; ☎ 954-223-570; 8am–10pm; MC, V) with packages of pastry wrapped in blue-and-white paper and tied with a string. Unlike most pastry shops, La Campana also does a bustling business in coffee drinks. Try to secure one of the outside tables (definitely a place to be seen) to sip a *café con leche* and sample such local delicacies (1.70€–2€) as *polvorones* (cookies made with almond flour), *yemas* (candied egg yolks), or *tortes de aceite* (crisp anise biscuits made with olive oil).

€   If Sevilla Fútbol Club is playing a match, you'll find a crowd of locals glued to the TV in one corner of **Ibéria Bar Tapas** ✦✦ (Almirante Lobo 7; ☎ 954-213-052; 7am–1am; 2.50€–6€ tapas and *media raciones*), an unassuming bar with some of the friendliest staff we've encountered. The tapas are also unusual and ambitious: croquettes of Iberian ham with a ratatouille-like salsa; pork steak with raisins and pine nuts and a sweet sherry sauce; or king prawns rolled up inside slices of eggplant (all 2.50€–3€). When we couldn't translate *jabalí* to figure out the kind of ground meat in the *albóndigas* (meatballs), the barman Francisco put his fingers on either side of his nose and scrunched up his face until we understood: wild boar!

€–€€   Located close to the Puente Isabel on the Triana side, **La Cucaña** (Betis 9; ☎ 954-340-131; 1–4pm and 8–11pm; DC, MC, V) sets out tables and umbrellas along the riverbank in nice weather, offering a splendid vantage on Seville. The food is straightforward fare like hot peppers stuffed with salt cod (2 for 7€), mixed salad with tuna (5.20€), or a pot of the tomato-bread puree called *salmorejo* with bits of ham and chopped egg mixed in (4.20€). Keep a watchful eye on the decorative Seville orange trees overhead, as you might have to dodge a dropping fruit or two.

€–€€€   Don't be fooled by the Milano style of hard stainless steel surfaces and lots of black everywhere at **La Cava del Europa** (Puerta de la Carne 6; ☎ 954-531-652; 8am–1am; AE, DC, MC, V). Contrary to the trying-too-hard decor, this is a multipurpose eatery, where you can get simple breakfasts like a plate of farm-fresh fried eggs with sausage and ham (6.60€) or come at night for inventive tapas, such as duck crepes or partridge pâté (either one 3.60€ or 12.30€ for a *racion*). The tapa of cold soup of pureed green beans and mint (2.40€) is an excellent complement to a light Andalusian white wine. The restaurant also sells olive oil and wines by the bottle for takeout.

€–€€€   Tourists drop by **El Rinconcillo** ✸ (Gerona 40; ☎ 954-223-183; 1pm–1:30am; MC, V) out of curiosity, since it traces its history back to 1670. But it's hardly a period piece. Hams hang from the ceiling above the bar and the barmen mark the tab in chalk on the wooden top as regulars eat spinach with chickpeas (2€), plates of aged cheese (2.20€–5€), and slices of *caña de lomo Ibérico* (a sausage made of the scrappier parts of expensive Iberian ham; 7€). If you can make your way through the crowd, you'll find two charming little dining rooms in the back with wonderful old tiles and vintage posters for the Sevilla fair decorating the walls, where entrees run 7€ to 15€. For a proper meal at a table, instead of snacking at the bar, try venison stew (9€) or scrambled eggs with wild mushrooms (7€).

€–€€€€   It was the crowd of Sevillanos that convinced us that we had been wrong to steer clear of **Cervecería Giralda** (Mateos Gago 1; ☎ 954-228-250; 9am–midnight; 3€–24€; MC, V) just because it is so popular with tourists. *Everybody* likes the tapas here. Slices of duck breast on mushrooms (3€) or pork sirloin stuffed with a slightly hot pepper sauce (3.50€) are several notches above the usual bar snacks. If you desire something more substantial, ask for a plate of grilled prawns wrapped in paper-thin slices of potato (16€). Unlike most Andalusian eateries, Giralda serves food continuously from morning until midnight—convenient if you haven't adapted to Spanish dining hours.

€€–€€€   The hotel restaurant at **Taberna del Alabardero** ✸ (Zaragoza 20; ☎ 954-502-721; www.tabernadelalabardero.com; 1–4pm and 8–11:30pm; 8€–14€ half and full *raciones;* AE, DC, MC, V) is a pretty posh space. Go midday for the bargain menu of 13€ and you'll jockey with downtown businessmen to get a seat, so dress appropriately. You can also eat reasonably priced and refined *tapas* in the lobby bar. Wontons filled with cheese, ham, and tiny onions, or rice with fish and king prawns are 8€ for a half *racion* or 14€ for a full. It's an elegant setting to sample some inventive cuisine while sipping a glass of Andalusian wine, of which there are nine choices priced around 2.50€ per pour.

€€–€€€   Ask any Triana native where to get tapas, and he or she will likely send you to the very antithesis of Alabardero's elegance. Every inch of wall space at **Sol y Sombra** ✸✸ (Castilla 151; ☎ 954-333-935; www.tabernasolysombra. com; 1–4pm and 8pm–midnight; MC, V) is covered with bullfight posters, and the ceilings are hung not just with hams, but also with nets of garlic and wine bottles. It's a madcap scene, with customers hunched knee to knee at the tables with a bottle of Rioja in the middle and plate after communal plate of garlic shrimp (13€), pork in a vinegar sauce (9€), and stewed oxtail (12€) arriving from the kitchen.

€€€   Located a block off avenida Constitución behind the Plaza del Cabildo, **Sabina** ✸ (Dos de Mayo 4; ☎ 954-562-547; Mon–Sat 2–4:30pm and 9pm–midnight; MC, V) can be hard to find but worth the effort. It's in a former *ataranza*—a shipyard building—with soaring, vaulted ceilings at least 30 feet high. It's not a restaurant for picky eaters, as it specializes in hearty Andalusian country fare such as braised pork trotters (12€), marinated partridge (12€), and squid cooked in their own ink (14€). The very substantial leg of lamb (17€) roasted with rosemary is probably the only dish you'd find on most American tables.

€€€–€€€€   When the weather is temperate, you'll find the outdoor tables swarmed at **Restaurante Casa Modesto** ☆ (corner of Cano and Cueto; ☎ 954-416-811; www.modestorestaurantes.com; noon–midnight; AE, MC, V), located at one corner of the lovely Jardines Murrillo. The 20€ three-course set menu varies daily but offers good value. Modesto is an ideal choice for a special dinner, try the lobster and monkfish stew (66€ for 2 people), or lamb sweetbreads with wild mushrooms (14€). If you're looking to keep the tab lower, opt for sweet and intense grilled scarlet shrimp (12€).

WHY YOU'RE HERE: THE TOP SIGHTS & ATTRACTIONS

As befits any capital city, Seville's major monuments are symbols of power and glory. Chief among them is the palace-fortress complex of the **Real Alcázar** ☆☆☆ (Patio de Banderas; ☎ 954-502-324; 7€ adults, free for students and seniors; Apr–Sept Tues–Sat 9:30am–7pm, Sun 9:30am–5pm, Oct–Mar Tues–Sat 9:30am–5pm, Sun 9:30am–1:30pm), where the gardens and one of the palaces rival Granada's Alhambra and Generalife. Remarkably, the sprawling complex manages to bring harmonious order to a series of buildings constructed from the 10th through 16th centuries under Moorish and Spanish rulers. It's been a royal Spanish residence since the 13th century, and since the king stays here on state visits to Seville, it's the oldest royal palace in Europe still in use. You probably won't see the king, but you will see lots of other travelers, so plan to be there at opening to avoid congestion in the smaller rooms.

After passing through the entry complex at the Patio del León, you'll find yourself in a large courtyard. To your right is the **Cuarto del Almirante (Admiral's Quarters),** notable mainly for the 16th-century altarpiece of the **Virgen de los Navegantes (Virgin of the Navigators)** blessing the royal navy— the military might behind Spain's domination of sea trade. To your immediate left, the **Sala de Justicia (Hall of Justice)** leads into the Patio del Yeso, the last trace of the 12th-century Almohad palace. It lay hidden under other construction until 1890, when it was discovered and restored. The graceful and tranquil spot conjures up the spirit of Moorish Seville.

The **Palacio Mudéjar,** straight ahead from the entry court, could have you wondering if you're in a Moorish fort or a Christian one. Islamic decorative motifs are everywhere in the carved plaster and stone, the delicate arches, and the calligraphic friezes. These same motifs continue inside the palace rooms (apart from the Italianate upper story added in the 16th century), with the addition of carved wooden ceilings and exquisite Moorish decorative tiles on the walls. Yet the palace was built by Christian King Pedro I (a.k.a. Pedro the Cruel) in 1362. Tradition says the same builders worked on Grenada's Alhambra, though historical evidence is scant. Look closely at the carved walls and you'll see traces of the original bright color pigments. The building is organized around the **Patio de las Doncellas (Courtyard of the Damsels),** with the official business rooms radiating from the sun-drenched plaza. Wander through the ground-story rooms, some of which have pedantic exhibitions on the history of tile-making in Seville, to find the quieter **Patio de las Muñecas (Courtyard of the Dolls)** off what were once the family bedrooms. (The patio got its nickname because it was where the royal children played.) Visitors often claim a bench near a small koi pond to sit and read as doves coo from beneath the elaborately carved eaves.

Pedro's digs are the highlight of the Alcázar, but don't sell the **Palacio Gótico** short just because it's a hybrid of vastly different eras. The building was erected under Alfonso X in the 13th century, remodeled by Carlos V in the 1500s, and heavily restored after the Lisbon earthquake of 1755. The structure and layout are clearly Gothic, but the interior decor celebrates the life and achievements of Carlos V, the Holy Roman Emperor and would-be conqueror of North Africa and much of southern Europe. If you enter this sector of the Alcázar through the gardens of the Patio del Crucero, you'll start at the great hall. The room is filled with immense tapestries woven at Madrid's Real Fábrica de Tapices to celebrate Carlos's conquest of Tunis in 1535. The most magical room of this otherwise plain palace is the Sala de Fiestas. The first of the Hapsburg kings, Carlos V had the immense, vaulted room decorated for his wedding to Isabella of Portugal, his first cousin, the union that began the dynasty's genetic problems posed by intermarriage. The hall is covered in painted, glazed tiles that epitomize the Seville *azulejo* style to this day. Look for matching portraits of the bride and groom flanking the doorways at each end.

The gardens of the Alcázar are even larger than the footprint of all the buildings. Some are Moorish in style, with prominent water features, while others embody the pure order of the Renaissance, and still others (with a spouting waterfall, no less), the baroque excess for which Seville became so famous.

In a city where the baroque is ubiquitous, it is ironic that only some side altars of Seville's **Catédral** ✪✪ (Puerta San Cristóbal; ☎ 954-214-971; 7.50€ adults, 2€ students and seniors, children 15 and under free; Jul–Aug Mon–Sat 9:30am–4pm, Sun 2:30–6pm, Sept–June Mon–Sat 11am–5pm, Sun 2:30–6pm) employ the style. The church itself is utterly Gothic, right down to the soaring pointed vaults, and its bell tower, the **Giralda,** is unmistakably Islamic, having been the minaret of the mosque destroyed in 1401 to build the cathedral. The church is so huge that it's impossible to appreciate its sheer bulk from the surrounding plazas. It's worth ascending a sequence of 34 ramps to reach the top of the 230-foot-high Giralda where you can peer down at the cathedral. Oddly enough, it *is* possible to grasp the ambition of the cathedral once you're inside. Space seems to extend skyward, disappearing into the dark recesses. The high altar is one of the artistic highlights, containing a virtual book of short stories in scenes depicting the lives of Christ and the Virgin Mary. Murillo's atmospheric *Vision de San Antonio* in the chapel named for the saint may be one of the largest paintings ever stolen. The thief was caught when he tried to fence it in New York in 1874. Sevillanas often pray for romance in front of the painting, since St. Anthony is patron of the lovelorn.

Just inside the Puerta de San Cristóbal, a 19th-century monument depicts Christopher Columbus's coffin. (Columbus's purported remains were brought here from Cuba in 1899.) The carved pallbearers underscore the importance of the year 1492—one thrusts his sword through a pomegranate, symbol of Granada, the last Moorish city to fall, while another holds an oar to row to the Americas. It's appropriate that the church honors the explorer—the gold that gleams all around came from the Americas.

That same gold built the convents and cloisters of Seville and hired the greatest painters of the age to decorate them. Second only to the Prado in the depth of its collections of Spanish painting, Seville's **Museo de Bellas Artes** ✪✪ (Plaza del

Of Love & Death

French and Italian composers alike had a penchant for setting their operas in Spain—after all, any country that embraces a primal struggle to the death between man and bull is operatic almost by definition. But few stage passions have captured the world's imagination like Georges Bizet's *Carmen*. The dark-eyed Gypsy of the title established the stereotype of the Spanish woman as the embodiment of smoldering sexuality and fiery temper. She worked in the Fabrica de Tabaco (now part of the university on calle San Fernando), where the first act of the opera is set, and perished at the bullring, or Plaza de Toros, when she was murdered by a former lover whom she had rejected for a bullfighter. (Any Sevillana worth her salt would take a bullfighter over a soldier any day.)

While *Carmen* does not paint the most flattering picture of the city, Sevillanos nonetheless embrace the story, and a buxom bronze statue of the cigar-roller stands on the riverbank across from the bullring. Alas, the statue has more life than the guides at the **Museo de la Real Plaza de Toros** (Paseo de Cristóbal Colón 12; ☎ 954-224-577; www.realmaestranza. com; 5€ adults, 4€ seniors, 2€ children 7–12; May–Oct daily 9:30am–8pm, Nov–Apr daily 9:30am–7pm), whose bland recitations barely hint at the charged history of these bloody sands. (We're not even sure they know who Carmen was, or her connection to the ring!) Try to lag behind the group to study the exhibitions, which are a good overview of the evolution of the spectacle from an equestrian sport in the 17th and 18th centuries to the *torero-á-toro* competition on foot we know today. Galleries feature paintings of famous bullfighters and display some of their beautifully embroidered ceremonial capes. While some, like El Córdobes, grow rich and famous, found their own wineries, and star in feature films, others—like José Gomez Ortega ("El Gallito")—die young and tragically. It might be said that there are no atheists in the bullring. Toreros stop to pray to the Virgen de la Caridad at the Capilla de los Toros before they enter the ring.

Museo 9; ☎ 954-786-500; www.museosdeandalucia.es; 1.50€ adults, students with ID card free; Tues 2:30–8:30pm, Wed–Sat 9am–8:30pm, Sun 9am–2:30pm) is housed in the former Merced Calzadas convent—a building that is itself an artistic gem. Fourteen galleries surround three patios where the walls are covered with local tiles made in the 16th and 17th centuries. The museum emphasizes religious art since its greatest masterpieces came from convents that were closed when Spain disenfranchised the Catholic church in the 19th century. The former church of the convent, Sala V, is laden with canvases by Murillo (including a gigantic version of one of his favorite subjects, the Immaculate Conception). The adjacent Sala VI contains a remarkable series of Mannerist portraits of the saints that Francisco Polanco executed in 1640 for Seville's Convento de Capuchinos. The holy folk are an expressive lot, from the harrowing madness in the face of St.

Paul to the unbridled enthusiasm of St. John the Evangelist, shown writing rather than boiling in oil. (Spanish painters are usually fond of showing St. John being boiled, an attempted execution he is said to have survived.) Another extraordinary sequence of portraits is the work of Francisco de Zurbarán. Those painted early in his career show saints and monks full of vigor and life, those painted later make the shadow of death palpable in their cyanotic flesh. The antidote to all this ethereal mysticism is the effusive romanticism displayed in the 19th-century galleries, with their depictions of society ladies out for a stroll and cigar-rollers at work in the tobacco factory.

With its long history of the reconquest, southern Spain always had a special relationship to the Holy Land, and one of Seville's finest noble palaces was inspired by the Jerusalem house of Pontius Pilate. Thus, it is called **Casa de Pilatos** (Plaza de Pilatos 1; ☎ 954-225-298; www.fundacionmedinaceli.org; 5€; inquire for hours of guided house tours, additional 3€; Apr–Oct daily 9am–7pm, Nov–Mar daily 9am–6pm). Despite the name, it's predominantly Mudéjar in style, encrusted in molded and carved plasterwork and gleaming glazed tiles. Unless you bemoan the cancellation of *Lifestyles of the Rich and Famous,* you can skip the house tour in favor of enjoying the courtyard and gardens, which hang with some of the most profuse bougainvillea we've ever seen.

Posters lining the stairway of the **Museo del Baile Flamenco** ★★ (Manuel Rojas Marcos 3; ☎ 954-340-311; 10€ adults, 8€ students, 6€ children; 9am–7pm) capture Cristina Hoyos in the full intensity of performance. One even proclaims her the "Queen of Flamenco"—not really an overstatement for one of the most famous dancers of the late 20th century, who performed in Antonio Gades's ground-breaking films of *Bodas de Sangre, Carmen,* and *El Amor Brujo.* Now director of Flamenco Ballet de Andalucía, Hoyos founded the museum in 2006 to cement her legacy and promote the art form. It's clearly a museum conceived by an artist, with an emphasis on music (specifically composed for the museum) and movement. Exhibits delve into the many cultures that influenced the evolution of flamenco, but the video clips explicating the seven most representative styles of flamenco are the most interesting and engaging, illuminating, for example, differences between the rumba and the *bulería.* The museum also mounts performances on Friday and Saturday nights (see "Nightlife in Seville," below). If you're inspired, staff will arrange an individual private dance class for 60€ for up to four people or 180€ for five to eight people.

Even if you have had your fill of churches, stop in **Iglesia de San Luis de los Franceses** ★ (San Luis; ☎ 954-550-207; free admission; Tues–Thurs 9am–2pm, Fri–Sat 9am–2pm and 5–8pm) for one magical moment. Completed in 1731 for Jesuit novices, the relatively measured baroque exterior hides an extravaganza of decoration inside, including several excellent Zurbarán paintings by the main altar. But the capstone is the cupola with its elaborately imagined paintings of heaven. Peer into the table-height round mirror placed on the floor beneath the cupola for a close-up view of cavorting muscular angels.

At the north end of the city, just inside the remains of the 12th-century walls, the **Basilica de Nuestra Señora de la Macarena** (Becquer 1; ☎ 954-901-800; free admission; Mon–Sat 9am–2pm and 5–9pm, Sun 9:30am–2pm and 5–9pm) might be the best-loved parish church in Seville. Constructed in the late 17th and early 18th centuries, the church's great dome is ornamented with Seville tiles. The

Freewheeling

Daunting traffic on main thoroughfares, a plethora of one-way streets, and virtually no parking make driving in Seville a challenge. But there's a good alternative for covering ground quickly.

SEVICI ✪ (☎ 902-011-032; www.sevici.es) provides access to bikes for only 5€ a week. The snazzy red bikes are parked in 250 areas all over the city, each with a kiosk where you can subscribe by credit card and pick up and deposit bikes. For your first outing, try the broad paths in Parque de María Luisa.

---

namesake of the church, and hence the entire neighborhood, is the elaborately carved 17th-century image of the Esperanza Macarena. She is mounted in a silver alcove, and the parade of the statue through the streets of this working-class barrio is one of the grandest spectacles of Holy Week in Seville.

One of the loveliest neighborhoods of central Seville, the extensive park system south of the cathedral, grew from the gardens of Palacio de San Telmo and a 1914 gift of the princess María Luisa de Borbón. Under landscape architect Nicolas Forestier the district quickly evolved into **Parque de María Luisa** 🔵. The lush, green oasis in the city center was chosen as the site for the Exposición Ibero-Americana of 1929, the king's plan to showcase Spain's transition to a modern country. Former colonies constructed neo-Mudéjar palaces and pavilions throughout the park (many of them are now consulates), but the collapse of the stock market and ensuing worldwide depression made the exposition a flop. The trees and gardens remain, as do two striking plazas constructed for the event. The Plaza de España might be the world's most expensive travel brochure. Baroque towers anchor each end of a long, curving arcade covered in *azulejos*. Its 54 tiled enclosures depict scenes from Spain's provinces. On Sundays, families often take to the surrounding canal in rowboats.

THE OTHER SEVILLE

Unlike language schools that offer flamenco courses as an enhancement, **Taller Flamenco** (Peral 49; ☎ 954-56-42-34; www.tallerflamenco.com) is a school of music and dance that offers Spanish lessons on the side. Office manager José David Gil explains that 90% of the students have already taken flamenco classes in their home countries, and they come to Seville for an in-depth immersion "where flamenco was born." Courses of study break down into separate disciplines of choreography, dance technique, flamenco guitar, flamenco singing, *compás* and *palmas* (clapping), and percussion. Most students sign up for 2 to 4 weeks (240€ for first week, less for additional weeks), though the school does arrange one-day tastes of flamenco dance for groups. They can also arrange private lessons in dance or guitar (42€ per hour, 378€ for 10 hours). Beginners can also sign up for the one-week dance class (240€). Students at Taller Flamenco tend to be ages 20 to 40, "but we've had ladies in their 60s," Gil says. (Older students, we've been told, are often adept at flamenco's complex rhythms.) Mostly women study dance and mostly men study guitar. The staff are largely professional performers, and class sizes are capped at seven. The school also arranges lodging for its students, usually in bedrooms in shared flats either with other students or with locals (125€ per week).

ATTENTION, SHOPPERS!

It's almost impossible to leave Andalusia without buying at least one elaborately patterned piece of ceramic ware, be it an *azulejo* tile to use as a trivet or a serving bowl for olives with a small compartment to hold the pits. **Cerámica Santa Ana** ★ (San Jorge 31; ☎ 954-333-990), a Triana factory and showroom that opened in 1870, may have the most broad and tempting selection in the region, but there are a number of other shops on surrounding streets. **Cerámica Triana** (Antillane Campos 3 and 4; ☎ 954-332-179) will even make personalized wall tiles in 2 or 3 days. Several individual ceramic artists display their work at **El Postigo** (Arfe; ☎ 954-560-013), where you'll also find leather pieces, jewelry, and even 8€ delicate silver hair combs. If you're really interested in Seville finery, hand-embroidered silk shawls can run as high as 1,500€ at **Artesanía Textil** (Sierpes 70; ☎ 954-56-28-40; www.artesania-textil.com), but the elegant women who run the shop take just as much care helping customers choose from their selection of attractive 35€ shawls.

NIGHTLIFE IN SEVILLE

The main entertainment for many Sevillanos is going out for drinks until dawn's rosy fingers creep up the sky. Among the bar concentrations are Plaza Alfalfa, the Triana riverfront on calle Betis, the Alameda de Hercules (just west of barrio Macarena), and, during the summer, the outdoor bars around the edges of Parque de María Luisa.

Clubbing

If you want to check out the limited scene of dance clubs and discos, head for Isla de Cartuja, where some of the pavilions of the 1992 World's Fair now house entertainment complexes. The largest and most successful is **Antique Theatro** (Matemáticos Rey Pastor y Castro; ☎ 954-46-13-28; www.antiquetheatro.com).

Flamenco

Every region in Andalusia has its own flamenco style, with Seville claiming the sultry Las Sevillanas. It's hardly the only style danced and played here, but the popularity of these complex pieces underscores Seville's prominence in both historic flamenco and the ongoing revival. In September and October of even-numbered years, the **Sevilla Flamenco Biennial** serves as a world summit of flamenco's leading artists, with more than 60 shows over a 4-week period. About a half-dozen *tablaos* (nightclubs) offer nightly *espectáculos,* highly choreographed flamenco performances with lots of musicians and dancers and lots of dazzling costume changes. Admission fees are 30€ and up.

Three other venues stage less showy performances that better capture the improvisational, emotional nature of the art form. The **Museo del Baile Flamenco** (p. 142) hosts performances of established but not yet internationally famous artists every Friday and Saturday at 7:30pm; admission is 25€. The patio setting at the center of the museum is far more traditional than the nightclub cabaret of the *tablaos*. Young and emerging artists are the headliners at **Casa de la Memoría** (Ximénez de Enciso 28; ☎ 954-560-670; www.casadelamemoria.es), which also sets up in the patio of an ancient Andalusian house in barrio Santa Cruz. The nightly performances begin at 9pm and cost 14€ adults, 12€ students. Located near the Plaza de Toros, **Casa Carmen Arte Flamenco** (Marqués de Paradas 30; ☎ 954-215-633; www.casacarmenarteflamenco.com) opens the doors at 8pm for shows at 9pm (16€ adults, 14€ students). Reservations are essential for all three venues, as they can only hold 30 to 80 spectators.

The flamenco bar scene is more fluid, with bars all over the city sometimes programming flamenco. Three gaudily tiled bars serving sherry, beer, and perfunctory *tapas* in Triana have a long history with the art form. Stop in for a late-night drink at **Casa Anselma** (Pagés del Corro 49; no phone), **El Rejoneo** (Betis 31A; no phone), or **Lo Nuestro** (Betis 31B; no phone) and ask if there will be a performance later on. (Music rarely starts before midnight.) Don't be surprised by limited or no shows during July and August, when performers try to head for cooler climes.

Performing Arts

Built for opera, the **Teatro de la Maestranza** (Colón 22; ☎ 954-561-535; www.teatromaestranza.com) next to the river has a grand auditorium seating 1,800 and a smaller music hall that seats 400. It is filled almost every night from December into June with classical music concerts and performances of opera, ballet, and zarzuela.

CÓRDOBA ✪✪✪

Visiting Córdoba is like a tantalizing glimpse of what might have been. A thousand years ago, Muslims, Christians, and Jews lived and worked together to create western Europe's greatest city of the age—a cosmopolitan center of poetry, art, music, philosophy, cutting-edge science and medicine, and far-ranging scholarship. Until the late 11th century, Córdoba was also the capital of western Islam; La Mezquita, the largest medieval mosque in Europe remains its star attraction. The city was demoted in status as Andalusia broke up into regional kingdoms, and became even less important under the Christian rulers. But the streets and whitewashed buildings of Andalusia's most intact Arabic city center still endure and visiting Córdoba is ultimately less about monuments and more about getting lost in the maze of cobbled lanes that bore witness to an ancient, harmonious world.

GETTING TO & AROUND CÓRDOBA

High-speed train connections from Madrid, Seville, and Málaga are the best way to reach Córdoba, though it also lies on the A4 (Madrid, Seville) and A45 (Málaga) highways. If you do drive, park your car for the duration, as most of Judería is a pedestrian zone and the rest of it should be. Pick up a walking map from the **Oficina de Turismo** (Torrijos 10; ☎ 957-355-179; Mon–Fri 9am–7:30pm, Sat–Sun 9am–3pm). Since the city is at its best in the cool and dusky evening, **Turismo de Córdoba** (Plaza de Las Tendillas; ☎ 902-201-774; www.turismodecordoba.org; 15€) offers a guided tour at 9:30pm.

ACCOMMODATIONS, BOTH STANDARD & NOT

Even if you don't take the city's tour, you should avoid the day-tripper syndrome that plagues Córdoba and stay at least one night in the Judería so that you can walk the streets after the bus groups have departed. Your footfalls will echo on the narrow streets and you will experience the city exactly as it was a thousand years ago. Before dawn or after dark, look up between the whitewashed walls: The skies over Córdoba turn an almost impossible shade of midnight blue.

Short-term apartments rentals are rare in Córdoba, but **Luna de Cristal** ★★★ (Pl de las Cañas 1; ☎ 957-492-353; www.lunadecristal.com; MC, V) makes up in quality (top-notch) for what's lacking in quantity (only 6 units). The golden facade with deep sea-blue paint outlining the windows and doors makes you feel good before you even step inside. The historic building where the northern edge of the Judería verges on Plaza de Corredera was remodeled into six apartments that preserve the traditional domestic arrangement of life around a central patio. Director Pilar Escribano Aguilar decorated the interiors to reference Moorish sensibilities as seen through the lens of *Architectural Digest*. Rippling tiled walk-in showers coexist with Wi-Fi, and the intensely saturated colors would fit right in to a North African souk. Apartments, which go for 100€ to 130€ a night or 650€ a week (except in May, when they soar to 175€/1,050€), feature large modern beds, contemporary bathroom fixtures, and kitchens that, while they're not set up with Gaggenau ovens and Sub-Zero freezers, are adequate for making breakfast (2 burners, microwave, and small refrigerator). Several rooms have unique architectural details, such as a beamed wooden ceiling or a medieval arch separating living room and bedroom. Unlike most old city spots, you can drive to it easily and parking is available, though it's only a short walk to La Mezquita.

€–€€   Long a popular choice for travelers on a budget, **González Hotel** ★★ (kids) (Manríquez 3; ☎ 957-479-819; MC, V) recently expanded into an adjacent building to add eight new rooms on the ground level, including a few that are handicapped accessible (except for a small threshold at the hotel entry). Not all rooms are served directly by elevator, so if that's important, ask for specifics when making your reservation. Decor is simple, dark-wood Spanish, and the availability of triple and quadruple rooms as well as rooms that can be combined into a suite makes González a good choice for families or travelers in a group. The combination of price (41€–66€ including breakfast) and quality is unbeatable in the heart of the Judería.

€€   All the double rooms at **Hotel Albucasis** (Buen Pastor 11; ☎ 957-478-625; MC, V) overlook the large courtyard, visible from the street through a wrought-iron gate. The feeling of spaciousness is striking for the crowded quarters of the Judería, and the hotel even has its own underground parking for drivers who brave the narrow streets. The rooms feature white walls, light-wood furniture, and traditional moss-green tiles in the all-modern bathrooms. But you won't find a TV—it's available on request but only receives a few Spanish-language channels. Rates range from 70€ to 85€ per night.

€€   One of Córdoba's newest lodgings, **Alma Andalusí Hospedería** ★ (Fernández Ruano 5; ☎ 957-760-888; www.almaandalusi.com; MC, V) has just nine rooms on three levels wrapped around a tall, narrow patio. The rooms are suffused with

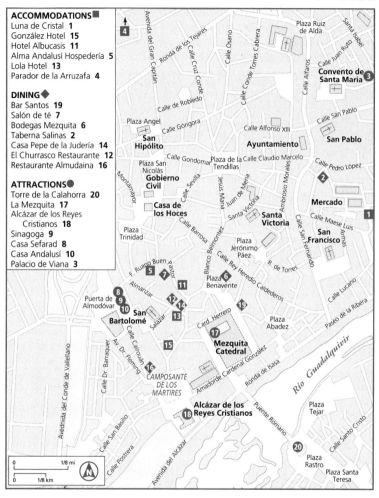

ACCOMMODATIONS ■
Luna de Cristal **1**
González Hotel **15**
Hotel Albucasis **11**
Alma Andalusí Hospedería **5**
Lola Hotel **13**
Parador de la Arruzafa **4**

DINING ◆
Bar Santos **19**
Salón de té **7**
Bodegas Mezquita **6**
Taberna Salinas **2**
Casa Pepe de la Judería **14**
El Churrasco Restaurante **12**
Restaurante Almudaina **16**

ATTRACTIONS ●
Torre de la Calahorra **20**
La Mezquita **17**
Alcázar de los Reyes
    Cristianos **18**
Sinagoga **9**
Casa Sefarad **8**
Casa Andalusí **10**
Palacio de Viana **3**

light and the design-magazine decor takes advantage of every square foot of this traditional medieval Judería house. Modular plastic cubes serve as bedside tables and as shelves for guests' belongings. Contemporary lamps provide a warm glow to the room. Alas, square feet are few, so luggage space is limited. But guests are encouraged to use the patio, where you can plug into the Internet via a cable. And prices are decent at between 70€ to 100€ including breakfast.

€€–€€€   The first room inside the door at **Lola Hotel** (Romero 3; ☎ 957-200-305; www.hotelconencantolola.com; MC, V) is named for an opera heroine (Aïda), a sure hint that Lola Carmona Morales has employed an bigger-than-life sensibility in decorating her eponymous hotel with such antiques as a circa-1910 brass-horn gramophone. Each of the eight sumptuous rooms is distinctly and theatrically decorated. Guests can eat breakfast in one of two nearby restaurants (it's included in the nightly cost of 83€–120€), but don't take the full meal plan (an extra 30€ per person), as you can do better on your own.

€€€–€€€€   Don't expect an historic building at the **Parador de la Arruzafa** (Avda Arruzafa; ☎ 957-275-900; www.paradores-spain.com; AE, DC, MC, V) about 3km (2 miles) outside the Judería. Though the site was once a summer palace of Abderraman I, that 8th-century Moorish structure is long gone, replaced by a modern 94-room hotel with long corridors flanked by spacious rooms decorated in low-key contemporary furniture. Balconies in most rooms catch the cool breezes and provide long vistas over the rolling countryside. The peaceful gardens, fountains, and a large swimming pool provide a sultan's respite from the city, especially in the heat of summer. Rates vary widely by season, from 104€ in the dead of winter to 166€ at holiday periods like Christmas and Easter. For most of the year, expect to pay around 125€.

DINING FOR ALL TASTES

Chefs in Córdoba draw more heavily from Arabic cuisine than anywhere else in Spain. You'll find a lot of beef and lamb and as well as the standard pork and shellfish. In addition to sweets, many savory dishes also incorporate dried fruits and nuts, and are seasoned liberally with cumin, turmeric, and cinnamon.

€   That's not to say that you won't find the staple of bar food—*tortilla española*—in Córdoba. In 1984, a local newspaper proclaimed that Francisco Santos Serrano made the best potato omelet in the city, and people have been coming to **Bar Santos** ★ (Magistral González Frances 3; ☎ 957-47-93-60; Fri-Wed 12:30-4pm and 8:30pm-midnight; cash only) ever since to test the claim. When we asked Sr. Santos, now in his 80s, the secret of his recipe, he said, "Good potato, good olive oil, and good hands to make it." The unusually thick and creamy tortilla is well worth 1.40€ a slice, but the bar has some other winners as well, such as tuna topped with roasted peppers (1.50€), or a bowl of *salmorejo* and slices of bread (2€).

€   Settle onto a padded bench in the flower- and fruit-filled courtyard of **Salón de té** ★★ (Buen Pastor 13; ☎ 957-487-984; daily 11am–11pm; MC, V), and you'll half expect to carry on a spirited conversation with the poet-philosopher Averroes, or at least his modern counterpart. This upscale tea room, devoid of the pretentiousness of its hookah-filled counterparts, has a dazzling selection of teas and infusions to accompany exquisite pastries based largely on figs, almonds, dates, pistachios, and honey (tea 2.30€–3.30€; pastry assortments 3€–6€). To relax here is to understand the sensual side of Andalusian life in Córdoba's heyday.

€€–€€€   While the Salón de té serves only nonalcoholic drinks, **Bodegas Mezquita** (Céspedes 12; ☎ 957-490-004; www.bodegasmezquita.com; daily noon-midnight; MC, V) focuses on Spanish wine, with an emphasis on bottles from Córdoba province. Its location, steps from La Mezquita, guarantees a lively tourist clientele, but Córdobans also favor the bodega for its broad selection of regional food available as a *tapa*, half *ración*, or full *ración*. The bodega does offer some

---

In the Soup

Most non-Spaniards know gazpacho (or think they do). It's the classic Andalusian cold soup of pureed tomatoes, green peppers, cucumber, garlic, and vinegar. If made traditionally, it will be bright red and taste like liquid salad. Less familiar is the *salmorejo* of Córdoba, which adds olive oil and bread to the ingredients to create a creamier, rose-colored mixture thick enough to use as a dip or a spread. Sometimes served as cold soup, *salmorejo* often appears as a sauce in bar tapas.

---

twists on tradition, dressing up the usual meatballs with a raisin sauce (3.15€–8.65€), or serving roast free-range pork in a cinnamon sauce (3.30€–8.95€). Wines by the glass are local, young, and fruity.

€€–€€€   Bodegas Mezquita (see above) is modeled on Córdoba's classic *tabernas,* such as **Taberna Salinas** ✹ (Tundidores 3; ☎ 957-480-135; www.tabernasalinas.com; Mon–Sat noon–4pm and 8pm–midnight; closed Aug; MC, V) which opened in 1879 near Plaza de Corredera, a few blocks outside the Judería. With rustic rush-seated chairs and paintings of dead game on the walls, it's changed little since. Unusual among bars, Salinas only offers full *raciónes,* or big plates. The signature dish is a salad of chopped oranges and codfish drizzled with olive oil (6€).

€€–€€€   Equally an institution, **Casa Pepe de la Judería** (Romero 1; ☎ 957-200-744; Mon–Thurs 1–4pm and 8:30–11:30pm, Fri–Sun 1–4:30pm and 8:30pm–midnight; AE, MC, V) looks like a corner bar from the street, but opens into a series of dining rooms and patios. Munch a few *menosabios,* or crispy chunks of codfish (4.05€ as a *tapa*), or indulge in a full-sized plate of puff pastries of goose liver with apples and goat cheese (18€), depending on whether you're drinking a young white from Moriles or a raisin-thick Pedro Ximenez *dulce.* You can also sample some other Arabic-influenced dishes, such as grouper marinated with almonds (5.05€ as a small plate, 8.85€ for a dinner entree) or a rich cheese salad with honey vinaigrette and pine nuts (9.50€ for a plate adequate for a light meal, 17€ for a huge plate to share among several diners as an appetizer).

€€€   Arabic influences also lend interesting flavors to the grilled meats at **El Churrasco Restaurante** (Romero 16; ☎ 957-290-819; www.elchurrasco.com; 1–4pm and 8:30pm–midnight; MC, V). Grilled pork sirloin (16€), for example, is served with *salsas arabes,* a gravy seasoned with cumin and cinnamon. But El Churrasco is also a good place to sample the Andalusian standard, *rabo de toro,* or stewed oxtail (18€), especially satisfying for those with hearty appetites. Entrees are all 14€ to 20€.

€€€   You can also get a rich *rabo de toro* at **Restaurante Almudaina** (Jardines de los Santos Mártires 1; ☎ 957-474-342; www.restaurantealmudaina.com; dining room 1–4pm and 8:30–11pm, bar 1–11pm; AE, DC, MC, V). Set into the old city walls near the Alcázar, Almudaina aspires to a more international style than

Convent Sweets

Many cloistered orders of nuns sell sweets through *retornos,* rotating counters set into walls to preserve the sisters' anonymity. They are generally open 10am to 2pm and 4 to 6pm. We've highlighted them in their respective cities. The recipes are closely guarded, and each convent's version of a particular cake or bun is distinct. Not only are they tasty, but the associated good cause provides a dispensation for breaking one's diet. Here are some of the most common *dulces de convento:*

Tocino de cielo, which translates literally as "bacon" or "lard of heaven." Andalusia's richest flan, it is made principally of egg yolks left over when the whites are sold to bodegas for clarifying wine.

Yemas, which are sweet cakes made from sugar and eggs. Sometimes *yemas* are whole egg yolks that have been poached in syrup and dried.

Mantecadas, a sweet of Moorish origin using great quantities of ground almonds. Sometimes *mantecadas* resemble a sponge cake, sometimes a shortbread, and sometimes a cookie.

Bollitos, or sweet buns.

Tortas almendradas, small almond cakes.

---

most Córdoban restaurants, offering its pork sirloin with truffle sauce (20€) and finishing swordfish steak in a brandy sauce with wild mushrooms (20€). But the kitchen also prepares some great regional classics, such as *flamequin,* a rolled fritter stuffed with cured ham (14€). The three-course menu with bread and wine is a good deal: 21€ for lunch and 25€ at dinner.

WHY YOU'RE HERE: THE TOP SIGHTS & ATTRACTIONS

If you've followed our advice and booked lodging in or near the Judería, you should still begin your visit on the other side of the Río Guadalquivir at the **Torre de la Calahorra** ✪ (Puente Romano; ☎ 957-293-929; 4.50€ adults, 3€ seniors and students; May–Sept 10am–2pm and 4:30pm–8:30pm, Oct–Apr 10am–6pm). As you cross the Puente Romano (constructed in the reign of Julius Caesar and rebuilt many times since), you'll see herons and egrets wading in the shallows and worshippers crossing themselves and leaving sprigs of rosemary at a small shrine to the archangel San Rafael at the midpoint of the bridge. The display rooms at the Torre, a 14th-century defensive tower built during an era of considerable squabbling among Spanish nobility, are often crowded with school groups, so arrive early. The one-hour audio tour (available in English, Spanish, French, and German) evokes Córdoba of the 9th through 13th centuries, and is as valuable for vacationers as it is for kids studying history. One room features likenesses of some of Córdoba's great thinkers, including Averroes, Maimonides, and Alfonso X. Through the headphones, you listen to them carry on a conversation with an unseen questioner. Just when it seems too much like an NPR interview, Averroes exclaims, "I've had enough of your questions. Think things out for yourself."

You could begin those contemplations in the Patio de los Naranjos on the north side of **La Mezquita** ✪✪✪ (Calle Cardenal Herrero; ☎ 957-470-512; 8€ adults, 4€ children; Mon–Sat 10am–7pm, Sun 2–7pm), Córdoba's famous mosque. Admission to the patio, where worshippers performed ritual ablutions before prayer, is free. The welcome shade of the orange trees, the sound of running water, and the rhythmic patterns of the gardens still work their magic.

The mosque is the pure expression of the spirituality of a desert people. The brown stone exterior impresses with its size—nearly equal to three football fields—but the interior inspires simple awe. A forest of red and white arches stretches into the distance like silk tents billowing at an ancient oasis. Some 40,000 worshippers could gather here, as light flooded in from open doors on all sides. Alas, when a Christian cathedral was built inside the mosque in the 16th century, the doors were sealed, cloistering the building in gloom ever since.

Many of the mosque's stones, columns, and capitals are recycled from the Visigothic church and Roman temple that preceded the mosque on this site. Fernando III of Castilla recaptured Córdoba in 1236, but he and his immediate successors treated the mosque with respect. A small Christian chapel was constructed by Mudéjar artisans in 1371, the **Capilla de Villaviciosa,** in a style complementary to the larger house of worship. The **Catédral Coro** and **Capilla Real,** finished in 1523, are another matter. Even Carlos V, who had authorized the work, later upbraided the archbishop for desecrating one of the world's great artistic buildings. But the cathedral does have an aggressive Renaissance beauty. Stop in, if only to look at the 18th-century carved mahogany choir stalls.

The Christians set about quickly to transform the Moorish fortress on the banks of the Río Guadalquivir into the palace-fortress now known as the **Alcázar de los Reyes Cristianos** ✪✪ kids (Campo Santo de los Mártires; ☎ 957-297-567; 4€ adults, 2€ students, free Fri; Tues–Sat 10am–2pm and 4:30–6:30pm, Sun 9:30am–2:30pm). Notably, their renovations retained the spa (the basement Moorish baths). While hardly as inspiring as La Mezquita, the Alcázar was the backdrop to a number of important historical events. Ferdinand and Isabella kept Boabdil, the last Moorish ruler in Andalusia, prisoner here. The regional branch of the Spanish Inquisition was based here from 1490 until 1821, and Franco later turned the fortress into a prison. Views from the ramparts and the dark tower rooms show just how secure the structure was. But the troubled past is behind it now, and the surprisingly small castle engages children, who enjoy the winding stairways and (very safe) walkways on the ramparts. Some of the larger halls display 3rd- and 4th-century A.D. Roman storytelling mosaics unearthed in Córdoba, while the formal 18th-century gardens hold ever-changing flower beds, long lines of sculpted cypresses, and fragrant orange trees. Statues at the center commemorate Columbus's audience here with Ferdinand and Isabella in which they agreed to underwrite his exploratory voyage of 1492.

That same year, the royal couple, seemingly immune to the spirit of tolerance that pervaded Córdoba in its heyday, booted Jews out of Spain. It wasn't the first such religious and ethnic cleansing. When Islamic religious extremists from North Africa took Córdoba in 1148, they destroyed the schools, executed the intellectuals, and expelled the Jews. (The Christians welcomed the Jews back in 1236.) One young son of Córdoba forced to flee was the 13-year-old boy who would become the philosopher and physician Moses Maimonides. He eventually settled at Fez in Morocco, but Córdoba reclaimed him long ago, mounting a bronze statue in his honor in a small plaza on calle Judíos, the "street of the Jews." Many a passerby has rubbed Maimonides's feet for luck, polishing them to a golden sheen. The street houses the **Sinagoga** (Judíos; ☎ 957-202-928; .30€; Tues–Sat 9:30am–2pm and 3:30–5:30pm, Sun 9:30am–1:30pm), built in 1315 and one of only three medieval synagogues left in Spain. Discovered during building renovations in 1884, the plasterwork on the walls uses the same decorative techniques as the Islamic plasterwork in the Alhambra palace in Granada—except that the figures are Hebraic script from the Torah.

One of the city's newest small museums, **Casa de Sefarad** (corner of Judíos and Averroes; ☎ 957-421-404; www.casadesefarad.com; 4€ adults, 2€ seniors and students; Mon–Sat 11am–8pm, Sun 11am–2pm) relates 11th- to 12th-century daily Jewish life in Córdoba, the de facto capital of Sephardic Jewry. At one level, the exhibits seek to explain some of the basic precepts of Judaism in a country where Jews have been largely absent for 500 years. For visitors from countries with intact Jewish culture, the rooms with the most resonance explore the traditional craft of making golden thread; highlight Sephardic musical and literary traditions; and celebrate Christian, Jewish, and Islamic women of Córdoba's heyday who were leading poets, philosophers, singers, and scholars.

Practically across the street, you can get a taste of how the Islamic neighbors lived. A small fountain strewn with roses provides a sensuous welcome to the ivy-draped main courtyard of **Casa Andalusí** (Judíos 12; ☎ 957-290-642; 2.50€; www.lacasaandalusi.com; 10:30am–7:30pm), which re-creates daily life in Córdoba during the 12th-century caliphate. Don't spend too much time studying the model of the mill on the Río Guadalquivir that produced paper for spiritual texts or reading the often heavy-handed interpretive notes. Instead, take a seat on a low chair, lean against an embroidered cushion, breathe in the scent of the flowers, and listen to the gurgle of the fountain.

The best way to experience the modern courtyards of Córdoba is during the May festival of patios (see below), but the **Palacio de Viana** (Pl de Don Gome 2; ☎ 957-496-741; 6€ full visit, 3€ patios only; Mon–Fri 10am–1pm and 4–6pm, Sat 10am–1pm) features 12 patios, each with a different style of garden. Skip the palace tour unless you're wild about chunky Córdoban furniture. The palace is about a 15-minute walk north of the Judería.

THE OTHER CÓRDOBA

Córdoba has a long history of hospitality. But despite welcoming Anglophones since the days when medieval Irish monks came here to study classical culture (which they spread to the benighted Europe of the Dark Ages), it's not one of the most fluent cities when it comes to English. There are a couple of ways to bridge the linguistic gap and take advantage of the openness of Córdobans to outsiders.

If you're like us, you won't be able to resist peering into the beautifully tiled and plant-filled patios at the heart of Córdoba homes. There's even a Córdoban etiquette governing this impulse: If the door to the courtyard is open, go ahead and look, but stay on the sidewalk and don't enter the doorway. It's a lot of work to maintain a lush, green oasis in a desert climate and Córdoba homeowners are proud of their patios.

So proud, in fact, that many of them open their patios to visitors during the annual **Concurso Popular de Patios Cordobeses, or Córdoba Patio Festival** ✪✪✪ (www.amigosdelospatioscordobeses.es; maps available from tourist office), when they also compete for prizes in several architectural and horticultural categories. (Look for hard-won plaques displayed on the whitewashed walls amid pots of geraniums.) We usually don't advise travelers to plan their itinerary around an event, but this one, which stretches over 2 weeks in May, is an exception. It offers an unprecedented chance to get more than a passing glimpse at how people really live.

Most of the people trekking from house to house are Córdobans and other Spaniards. Making the rounds is an annual social event, when neighbors catch up on gossip or exchange gardening advice and plant cuttings. We've been offered glasses of sherry and listened to impromptu songfests. Best of all, life as usual goes on as visitors stream in: Family members eat their meals, sweep the floor, greet their friends, or just sit in the dappled shade of a lemon tree and read the newspaper. While admission is free, it's customary to leave some change on the tip tray in each patio you visit.

You will also have more opportunities than usual to interact with local people if you study Spanish language at **Academia Hispánica Córdoba** ✪ (Rogríguez Sánchez 15; ☎ 957-488-002; 2-week course 320€; www.academiahispanica.com). Based in a traditional Andalusian-style home just outside the Judería, Hispánica also operates an English-language school for local people and encourages student to get to know each other. "Most Spanish-language students choose to stay with a family," says staff member Lindsay MacNeil, "and most of the time we place them with people who are studying English with us and really want to meet foreigners." (Host family lodgings 140€ single, 120€ double per week with half-board; 175€/159€ with full board; shared apartments 95€ single or 77€ double per week.) As in most schools, students range in age and study 4 hours each morning. "Then they can add the fun extras," says MacNeil. In addition to flamenco courses (399€ for 2 weeks of Spanish and 4 flamenco lessons), Hispánica also offers a cooking course (only available for language students), which is difficult to find in this part of Spain (389€ for 2 weeks of Spanish and 6 cooking classes). "The classes are held in the home of a local chef. The students help prepare an appetizer, main course, and dessert," says MacNeil, noting the cooking classes are limited to seven students. "Then they open a bottle of wine, sit on the terrace, and enjoy the meal."

ATTENTION, SHOPPERS!

Córdoba has a history of fine artisanry in leather and delicate gold and silver *filigrana* (filigree) and you'll find examples of both in the **Zoco** (Judío; no phone), a cluster of studios and shops in the heart of the Judería near the Sinagoga. For more choices, check **Meryan** (Callejon de las Flores 2; ☎ 957-475-902) where Alejandro and Carlos Lopez-Obrero make a range of leather goods or **Alminar** (Albucasis; ☎ 957-297-782) for investment-quality embossed and colored leather purses that would bring any outfit up a notch. **Herederos Luis Ramirez** (Judería 8; ☎ 957-475-356) has a large selection of filigree jewelry in traditional and modern styles.

GRANADA ✹✹✹

When Boabdil, the last king of Moorish Granada, was exiled to North Africa in 1492, he took the bones of his ancestors with him. But he left behind their fortress-palace, the Alhambra, and a legacy of nearly 8 centuries of Islamic culture. Ferdinand and Isabella may have won the war and completed the reconquest of Moorish al-Andalus, but in Granada they lost the history. Few people come to this beautiful city to see the solemn tombs of *los reyes catolicos*. They come for the joyous ornamentation of the Alhambra, the inextinguishably Arabic face of the Albaícin, and the haunting *zambras* echoing from the Sacromonte hills. As native son Federico García Lorca wrote, "Oh, city of Gypsies! Who could see you and not remember?"

GETTING TO & AROUND GRANADA

RENFE (Avda Andaluces; ☎ 958-271-272) offers **train service** from Córdoba, Seville, and Málaga. **Buses** are quicker and cheaper, but the station is about 3.2km (2 miles) out of town (Carretera de Jaén; ☎ 958-185-480). Driving is straightforward, with the A92 linking the city directly to Seville and, via the A45, to Málaga and Córdoba.

Granada itself is huge, but you'll want to concentrate on only a few districts: the central city anchored by the cathedral and Plaza Nueva, the hillside of the Alhambra, the facing hillside of the Albaícin Quarter, and the Gypsy hilltop neighborhood of Sacromonte. The nos. 30 and 32 city buses (1€) run continuously from Plaza Isabel la Catolica to the ticket office of the Alhambra, and the nos. 31 and 32 buses leave from the same spot for Sacromonte. Taxis are relatively inexpensive. Expect to pay about 5€, for example, from Plaza Nueva to the Lorca house. For tourist-office help, skip the office at Plaza Nueva in favor of the **Oficina Provincial de Turismo** (Pl Mariana Pineda 10; ☎ 958-247-128; www.turgranada.es).

ACCOMMODATIONS, BOTH STANDARD & NOT

We'll start again with short-term apartment rentals, as they not only give you a kitchen and extra breathing room but allow you to experience daily life in some of Granada's more residential neighborhoods (and they're fascinating areas to explore).

The most unusual accommodations in Granada—and perhaps all of Andalusia—are at **Las Cuevas El Abanico** ✹✹ (Verea de Enmedio 89; ☎ 958-22-61-99; www.el-abanico.com; MC, V), composed of five Gypsy caves carved into the Sacromonte hillside. They have been fashioned into contemporary apartments with whitewashed walls and low, rounded ceilings—rather like a very large igloo. Rates are stable at 70€ for a one-bedroom, 110€ for two bedrooms (able to sleep 4), with a 2-night minimum. Each has a minimal kitchen and small bathroom— and a space heater to take away the chill. No air-conditioner is necessary as the caves remain cool and slightly humid all year. Surprisingly, the caves all have Wi-Fi, but the owners decided against TV so the sound wouldn't disturb guests who truly want to get away from it all. The owners can arrange cheap parking (8€ per day) and will assist with your luggage, as it's a long, steep climb to this really special place. A shared terrace has striking views of the Alhambra.

Granada & the Alhambra

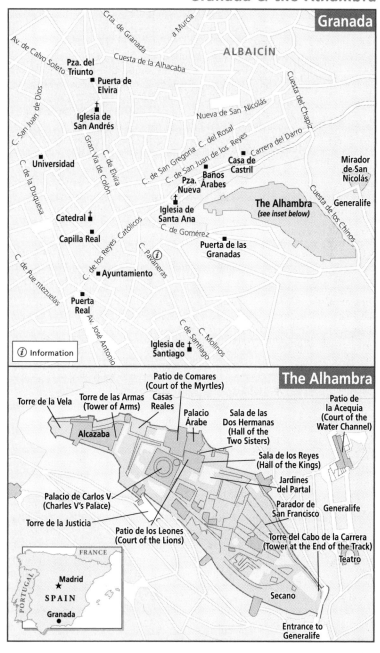

Granada

ALBAICÍN

Crta. de Granada
a Murcia
Av. de Calvo Soleto
Cuesta de la Alhacaba
Pza. del Triunto
Puerta de Elvira
C. San Juan de Dios
Iglesia de San Andrés
Nueva de San Nicolás
Cuesta del Chapiz
Universidad
Gran Vía de Colón
C. de Elvira
C. de San Gregoria
C. del Rosal
C. de San Juan de los Reyes
Carrera del Darro
Casa de Castril
Mirador de San Nicolás
C. de la Duquesa
Pza. Nueva
Baños Árabes
The Alhambra
(see inset below)
Cuesta de los Chinos
Generalife
Catedral
Capilla Real
C. de los Reyes Católicos
Iglesia de Santa Ana
C. de Gomérez
C. Pavaneras
Puerta de las Granadas
C. de Pue ntezuelas
Ayuntamiento
Puerta Real
Av. José Antonio
C. de Santiago
C. Mollinos
Iglesia de Santiago
ⓘ Information

The Alhambra

Torre de la Vela
Torre de las Armas (Tower of Arms)
Casas Reales
Patio de Comares (Court of the Myrtles)
Palacio Árabe
Sala de las Dos Hermanas (Hall of the Two Sisters)
Patio de la Acequia (Court of the Water Channel)
Alcazaba
Sala de los Reyes (Hall of the Kings)
Jardines del Partal
Palacio de Carlos V (Charles V's Palace)
Torre de la Justicia
Patio de los Leones (Court of the Lions)
Parador de San Francisco
Generalife
Torre del Cabo de la Carrera (Tower at the End of the Track)
Teatro
Secano
Entrance to Generalife

FRANCE
PORTUGAL
Madrid
★
SPAIN
Granada
●

155

If you want a more central location, Paloma Rodrigo and four colleagues manage three modern apartment buildings in rehabilitated old structures. **Apartamentos Santa Ana** ✫✫✫ (Puente Cabrera 9; ☎ 647-774-173; www.apartamentos-santaana.com) sits at the foot of the Alhambra hill—the reception desk is in a cave dug into the wall. Of the five units, the best is the attic apartment with a private patio and knockout view of the Albaicín (also visible through large windows when you sit up in bed beneath a silk patchwork bedspread). If that apartment isn't available, choose from the nine at **Apartamentos San Juan de los Reyes** ✫✫✫ (San Juan de los Reyes 31), just barely into the Albaicín. The attention to detail here is striking: a hand-carved, Mudéjar-style wooden ceiling in the patio and handmade wrought-iron light fixtures. The rustic-feeling rooms feature red tile floors and dark carved wood furniture. A shared rooftop sitting area has front-row views of the Alhambra. Some rooms will sleep four people. For either building, you'll want to take a cab, but you'll still have to carry your bags up cobbled streets and stairways. The third option, **Apartamentos Puerta Real** 🖼 (Padre Alcover 8), is near the cathedral. Though it's marginally more convenient, the apartments have less character, with IKEA-like modern furnishings and dim lighting. But two apartments on the third level are especially good for families. Each has one room with a double bed and one room with twin beds (in Three Right, the twin beds are up an iron staircase under the eaves). All choices are 75€ per night as doubles, 130€ for units sleeping three or four, with no extra cleaning fee.

Hotels

€   Granada's identity is intertwined with its Islamic history, including the tradition of the Arabic bath. Located at the edge of the Albaicín, **Arteaga Hostal** (Arteaga 3; ☎ 958-202-653; hostalarteaga@hotmail.com; MC, V) is conveniently connected to **Baños de Elvira Spa** (Arteaga 3; ☎ 958-208-841; 4:30–9pm), making it possible to pop in for a treatment without schlepping across town to some other baths. Hotel rooms are compact and simply furnished, as you'd expect with a nightly rate of 48€ to 50€ including tax, but they include a small refrigerator and cable Internet connection. Spa prices are likewise modest: A one-hour "Termal Basico" with hot pool, steam room, toning bath, and 15-minute massage is 25€. Sorry, no discount for hotel guests.

€–€€   It's equally relaxing to spend an evening with a bottle of wine and good company on the communal balcony on the top floor of **Hotel Los Tilos** ✫ (Pl Bib-Rambla 4; ☎ 958-266-712; www.hotellostilos.com; MC, V), looking out at the illuminated cathedral. Rooms are large considering they cost just 55€ to 80€ a night (with tax) and are brightly painted in luminous yellows, oranges, and tropical marine blue. Of the hotel's 30 rooms, 22 have views of the lovely but quiet plaza filled with good tapas bars and cafes. Book three nights through the website and the hotel throws in breakfast (otherwise, 7€ per person).

€€–€€€   Skip the 12€ supplement for a room with a "vista" at **Casa del Capitel Nazarí** ✫ (Cuesta Aceituneros 6; ☎ 958-21-52-60; www.hotelcasacapitel.com; AE, MC, V), since the views of the Alhambra are rather limited. Instead, study the lithographs in the lobby for ideas on how to photograph the Alhambra when

Granada

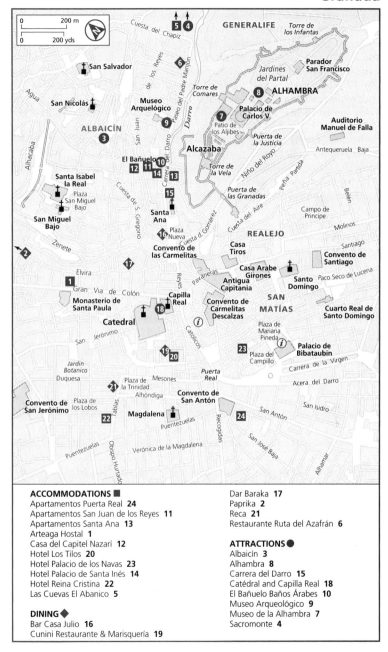

ACCOMMODATIONS ■
Apartamentos Puerta Real **24**
Apartamentos San Juan de los Reyes **11**
Apartamentos Santa Ana **13**
Arteaga Hostal **1**
Casa del Capitel Nazarí **12**
Hotel Los Tilos **20**
Hotel Palacio de los Navas **23**
Hotel Palacio de Santa Inés **14**
Hotel Reina Cristina **22**
Las Cuevas El Abanico **5**

DINING ◆
Bar Casa Julio **16**
Cunini Restaurante & Marisquería **19**

Dar Baraka **17**
Paprika **2**
Reca **21**
Restaurante Ruta del Azafrán **6**

ATTRACTIONS ●
Albaicín **3**
Alhambra **8**
Carrera del Darro **15**
Catédral and Capilla Real **18**
El Bañuelo Baños Árabes **10**
Museo Arqueológico **9**
Museo de la Alhambra **7**
Sacromonte **4**

157

you visit in person. The hotel takes its name from the original Nasrid capital that helps support the 16th-century building. Historic preservation precluded an elevator, but ground-floor rooms are available. You can expect to pay between 82€ and 110€ a night. Bathrooms are equipped with showers rather than tubs to maximize the living space in the bedchambers, which are large by Albaicín standards. The 17 rooms have carved wooden ceilings in the Nasrid style, cool white-plastered walls, creamy marble floors, and minibars—a luxury that even the emirs didn't enjoy.

€€€ For a more traditional Spanish style, with weighty wooden furniture in the bedrooms and glittering chandeliers in the public spaces, **Hotel Reina Cristina** (Tablas 4; ☎ 958-253-211; www.hotelreinacristina.com; MC, V) is the best choice. Granadinos gather in the restaurant for anniversaries, birthdays, and retirement parties. Poet, playwright, and composer Federico García Lorca lived in this building, then a private residence of a powerful politician who tried to protect him from Franco's men, for the last few months of his life. Rooms are a bit pricier than the others at 114€ to 132€ a night, but they include a hearty breakfast.

€€€ Calle Navas, a restaurant-lined street leading east from Plaza de los Reyes Catolicos, is also a principal processional street during Holy Week. Set at one of the sharp turns in the road ascending from the Centro to the Alhambra, **Hotel Palacio de los Navas** 🟊🟊 (Navas 1; ☎ 958-215-760; www.palaciodelosnavas.com; AE, DC, MC, V) offers 19 sumptuous rooms in an in-town *palacio*. The soothing beige and cream tones of the decor in this modestly priced luxury hotel (125€, tax included) take their cue from the limestone and marble that make up historical Granada—a style synthesized from eternal stone.

€€€ Striking an entirely different artistic tone, **Hotel Palacio de Santa Inés** 🟊🟊 (Cuesta de Santa Inés 9; ☎ 958-222-362; www.palaciosantaines.com; AE, MC, V) in the Albaicín features stunning if fragmentary 16th-century frescoes on the reception area walls. (They're attributed to a student of Raphael.) Interior balconies with wooden spindles and rails surround the glass-roofed, light-filled central courtyard. The hotel is decorated with boldly colored Tuscan plaster, and the rooms (which go for 115€ double, 140€ "superior") are simultaneously serene and richly decorated. The price difference is a matter of season and interior versus exterior view. If you're traveling during low season (July–Aug, Nov, and Jan–March), you might consider spending 150€ for the spacious and truly beautiful Alhambra suite, decorated as if one of the Nasrid nobility was coming to stay. (It's 250€ otherwise.)

DINING FOR ALL TASTES

Granada has the most generous free tapas served with drinks that we've seen anywhere in Spain. The plates tend to be appetizer sized, and usually vary with each successive drink. By the time you've consumed four drinks—even soft drinks or iced tea—you'll have eaten enough to skip a formal meal. In the mornings, vendors at Mercado San Augustin (behind the southwest corner of the cathedral) sell everything you need for a picnic: fresh fruit, bread, cheeses, and cured meats.

€   Arabic teahouses are popular in Granada, but many are jammed with hookah-sucking poseurs. For exquisite Arabic pastries, such as baklava and almond tarts, along with delicious mint tea, **Dar Baraka** ★★ (Elvira 20; ☎ 649-114-171; noon–2am; cash only) is a delightful exception—one of the friendliest, least pretentious, and least expensive places in the Albaicín.

€–€€   Barman Livan Soto is typical of folks you'll meet at **Reca** (Plaza Trinidad; ☎ 958-228-826; 10am–3am; cash only), where a plate of *arroz con pollo* (rice with chicken and spicy sausage) is likely to be your first free tapa. This trendy watering hole on Plaza Trinidad draws university faculty, local fashionistas, and a prominent gay clientele. Soto is from Cuba, where he studied law; now he's taking a master's in gender studies and pouring aged Cuban rums at the bar. Reca's substantive *raciones* (mostly 10€) include fava beans stewed with pork, or goat cheese with fresh tomatoes, fried eggs, and *morcilla* sausage. The music is flamboyant and loud—alternating between progressive jazz and contemporary flamenco.

€–€€   You'll find the stylistic antithesis of Reca if you bypass Plaza Nueva's doner-kebab houses and make the first left onto calle Hermosa on the square's southwest corner to seek out **Bar Casa Julio** ★ (Hermosa at Elvira; no phone; 1–4pm and 8pm–midnight; cash only). This narrow sliver of a bar, covered in historic tiles, has some of Granada's best cheap seafood tapas. Order a drink and you'll probably get a small taste of octopus stewed in wine sauce. In addition to pickled anchovies (5.50€) and small squid cooked in their own ink (5.50€), you'll find such delicacies as diced shark in a spicy pepper-tomato sauce (5€).

€€–€€€   Bebop jazz and rotating art exhibits signal immediately that **Paprika** ★ (Cuesta de Abarquares 3; ☎ 958-804-785; www.paprika-granada.com; Tues–Sat 1–4pm and 8pm–midnight, Sun 1–4pm; MC, V), a colorful bar/cafe/restaurant dug into one of the old city walls, is far from a traditional Granada haunt. The kitchen follows the trends of contemporary Spanish cooking, with simple but inventive combinations such as vegetarian paella studded with cashews (7.50€) and codfish served in a sumptuous lemon sauce (9.50€). The lunchtime *menu del día* is just 12€.

€€€   The liveliest tapas scene in Granada is **Cunini Restaurante & Marisquería** ★★ (Pl de Pescadería 14; ☎ 958-25-07-77; Mon–Sat 12:30–4pm and 8:30pm–midnight; MC, V), where the marble bar undulates in a wave pattern and the unflappable bar staff in crisp white shirts and black bow ties somehow keep up with the crowd without breaking a sweat. The free tapas with drinks are varied and large, but you might want to spring for such fish plates as monkfish in white wine (17€), half a dozen oysters (14€), or a big serving of fried red mullet (12€).

€€€–€€€€   Set along the river at the edge of the Albaicín, the elegant **Restaurante Ruta del Azafrán** (Paseo del Padre Manjón 1; ☎ 958-226-882; www.restauranterutadelazafran.com; Sun–Thurs 1–11pm, Fri–Sat 1pm–midnight; AE, MC, V) has striking views of the Alhambra and contemporary cuisine with a strong North African accent. Budget travelers can opt for pink salmon (13€) in a sauce of sweet-and-sour oranges, or the chicken (11€) or lamb (13€) couscous dishes. For a treat, try the veal sirloin with wild mushrooms and a foie gras mousse (22€). The extensive, largely Spanish wine list includes a small selection of Granada province wines.

WHY YOU'RE HERE: THE TOP SIGHTS & ATTRACTIONS

There's much more to Granada than the Alhambra. To discover some of the lesser-known sights, we highly recommend the audio tour from **this.is:Granada** (available at kiosk on Pl Nueva; ☎ 958-210-239; www.thisis.ws). It will take you on several routes through the city, that include, but are not limited to, the Alhambra and the cathedral. A player with two headsets for five days is a good value at 15€. If you'd prefer not to have someone talking in your ear the entire time, we suggest you travel independently to the following spots.

Crowning the city on its northeastern hillside, the palaces and gardens of the **Alhambra** ✹✹✹ (☎ 902-441-221; www.alhambradegranada.org; 12€ adults, 9€ seniors and students, children 11 and under free, 6€ gardens only; Mar–Oct daily 8:30am–8pm, Tues–Sat 10–11:30pm Nasrid palaces and Generalife only; Nov–Feb daily 8:30am–6pm, Fri–Sat 8–9:30pm) represent the high-water mark of Moorish culture. All the power, money, and artistry of the kingdom of Granada were mustered to construct the Palacios Nazaríes (the living quarters at the heart of the complex) over the course of the 14th century. The results were so awe inspiring that every conqueror has treated them with respect (even Napoleon, who showed less deference to the defensive fortifications). The palaces are actually three separate buildings linked by passageways. Each building is organized around a stunning patio. Among them, they are the models to which every Andalusian patio, however humble, aspires. If you're in the first wave of visitors for the day, get ahead of the pack by scooting through the square council chamber to the **Patio de Cuarto Dorado (Patio of the Golden Quarter).** The south wall encapsulates the decorative elements of the entire palace: geometric tiles, borders carved with Arabic inscriptions, a frieze of carved plaster, and panels carved with leaves and vines. It's almost as dazzling as the adjacent room, with its carved plaster walls, wooden ceiling, and vistas of the Albaicín.

A long, narrow pool is the central feature of the **Patio de los Arrayanes** (Myrtles), leading into the Sala de Barca, where Nasrid coats of arms and Arabic inscriptions cover the walls. The adjacent **Salon de Embajadores (Hall of Ambassadors)** may be the most beautiful room in the complex. The marquetry

---

Photo Ops

The terraced gardens between the Nasrid palace and the defensive walls are a good spot for shooting photos with the city of Granada as backdrop. Like much at the Alhambra, the towers along the walls are under restoration for the foreseeable future.

The long pool lined with water jets, the Patio de la Acequia, in the Generalife Gardens is also one of the complex's most famed photo ops.

Strategizing the Alhambra

When King Ferdinand stormed the Alhambra, he didn't need a timed admission ticket. To minimize congestion, only 1,500 visitors at a time are allowed into the Alhambra—and they have only a half-hour window to enter the Nasrid palaces. You can often purchase a ticket on the day of your visit, but we recommend that you make a reservation—especially since the first time slot of the day is the best time to visit without congestion. You can place your ticket order up to 3 months ahead with a credit card (☎ 934-923-750 from abroad, ☎ 902-888-001 from Spain, or www.alhambra-tickets.es). There's a 1€ surcharge on each ticket, but it's a small price to pay to guarantee your slot—and avoid waiting an hour or more at the box office. You'll get a reservation number to use when you pay for and pick up your actual tickets at Servicaixa machines throughout Spain—and at the Alhambra itself. People with reservations get priority at the ticket machines, and once you have the actual ticket in hand, skip the long box office line and walk down to the entry point for the Nasrid palaces—a 15-minute hike—to make sure you're on time.

dome is inlaid with thousands of pieces of multicolored wood representing the seven heavens of the Koran, while the walls feature colored-tile paneling, carved plaster with both geometric and vegetative motifs, and more inscriptions over the doors and niches.

The final courtyard, the famed **Patio de los Leones,** is one of the oldest sections. The 11th-century fountain at the center, supported by 12 stone lions, is undergoing restoration to reverse some of the processes that have obscured the delicate medieval carvings. A re-installation is scheduled for late 2009 or early 2010. The surrounding rooms have a delicate beauty that belies their violent history. Be sure to see the unusual star-shaped lantern cupola in the Sala de los Abencerrajes. This room off the patio is named for a noble family implicated in a plot to overthrow Boabdil. On learning that his wife was meeting secretly with a man from the Abencerrajes family, Boabdil had the entire clan slaughtered in this room and piled their heads up in the fountain.

Important note: The route of the tour through the palaces is well marked and, once you leave the buildings, you cannot reenter. Before you head downstairs to the royal baths, decide if you want to revisit any of the rooms or patios. If you backtrack against traffic, the guards will frown and even point out the tour directional arrows, but just say, *"Disculpame"* (diss-*cool*-pah-may; forgive me), look embarrassed, and keep going.

Walk through garden terraces above the Nasrid palaces to visit the **Palacio de Carlos V,** which would be an architectural highlight anywhere else. The structure, designed by Michelangelo student Pedro Machuca, exudes the power of empire, yet the no-nonsense geometry of the European Renaissance suffers in comparison to the decorative Orientalism of the Nasrid palaces. Skip the **Museo de Bellas Artes** on the upper level if you're pressed for time. The lower-level **Museo de la Alhambra** (Palacio de Carlos V; ☎ 958-027-900; free admission; www.alhambra-patronato.es;

Lorca the Artist, Lorca the Man

Labeled by critics variously as a Symbolist or a Surrealist, Federico García Lorca (1898–1936) was an artistic polymath. He is best remembered today as a powerful poet (*Gypsy Ballads* and *Poet in New York*) and playwright (*Mariana Pineda* and *Blood Wedding*). But in his brief lifetime, he was also celebrated as a composer, pianist, and painter, and was closely allied with friends Luis Buñuel, Salvador Dalí, and composer Manuel de Falla. He was a controversial figure for his outspoken democratic views in ultraconservative Granada, and a target for his homosexuality. The circumstances of his death at the hands of the Falangists at the outset of the Spanish Civil War remain a mystery. Lorca's work remained out of print in Spain until 1953, and uncensored versions did not appear until after Franco's death.

Granada has embraced him in recent decades, and his family's 1926–36 summer home on the south side of the city, **Huerta de San Vicente Casa-Museo Federico García Lorca** (Virgen Blanca; ☎ 958-258-466; www.huertadesanvicente.com; 5€ adults, 1€ children, free on Wed; Mar–Oct Tues–Sun 10am–12:30pm and 5–7:30pm, Nov–Feb Tues–Sun 10am–12:30pm and 4–6:30pm), functions as a museum. Lorca returned here from Madrid at the outset of the Civil War, living in the house for a few weeks before fleeing to the Rosales family house (now Hotel Reina Cristina), where he was arrested. Given that Lorca was such a free spirit and original thinker, it is ironic that his home epitomizes the taste of the early 20th-century middle class.

Tues–Sat 9am–2:30pm), however, is a must-see. Exhibits chronicle both the technology and the artistic evolution of Moorish pottery; glazed tiles; wood and plaster carving; and work in stone, bronze, and gold. Until the reinstallation at the Patio de los Leones, the museum also displays one of the restored lions and a detailed exhibition about the restoration process.

You might want to detour to the **Alcazaba,** the original fortress of the complex, to climb the late 8th-century Torre de la Vela for a panoramic view of the Nasrid palace on one side and the city on the other. Otherwise, follow the signs for the **Generalife** gardens that are located on a small plateau above the Alhambra fortress. Water channels cut throughout the terraced gardens here create an idyllic setting around the small building sometimes called the "summer palace" (it was actually a hunting lodge).

Ferdinand and Isabella readily grasped Granada's symbolic importance as the final prize of the *reconquista,* and they authorized the construction of the massive **Catédral** ✸ (enter on Gran Vía de Colón; ☎ 958-222-959; 3.50€ adults, 2.50€ seniors, children 9 and under free; Mar–Oct Mon–Sat 10:45am–1:30pm and 4–8pm, Sun 4–7pm, Nov–Feb Mon–Sat 10:45am–1:30pm and 4–7pm, Sun 4–7pm) on the site of the Moorish city's main mosque. Construction didn't begin until 1518 and continued sporadically for another 2 centuries. As intended, visitors feel cowed in the presence of the Christian god, and there's no denying the majesty of the high altar or the stirring tones of the organ pipes. The most prominent of many side chapels is dedicated to Santiago the Moorslayer, depicted on horseback, and recurring images of Santiago and San Miguel (Archangel Michael, usually shown sticking it to Satan with his sword) emphasize Christian triumph at sword-point.

Perhaps because its intentions are more modest, the adjacent Royal Chapel, or **Capilla Real** ✪✪ (enter on Gran Vía de Colón; ☎ 958-229-239; 3.50€ adults, 2.50€ seniors, children 9 and under free; Mar–Oct Mon–Sat 10:30am–1pm and 4–7pm, Sun 11am–1pm and 4–7pm; Nov–Feb Mon–Sat 10:30am–1pm and 3:30–6:30pm, Sun 11am–1pm and 3:30–6:30pm) is more inviting. Ferdinand and Isabella commissioned it as their burial site, and their daughter Juana la Loca (Juana the Mad) and her husband Felipe el Hermoso (Philip the Handsome) joined them here in death. The likenesses of the famous monarchs are carved on their mausoleums and the adjacent museum displays some of their royal trappings: Isabella's scepter and crown, Ferdinand's sword and robes, and their family collection of religious paintings, including extraordinary works by Rogier van der Weyden and Hans Memling.

The broad street Los Reyes Católicos runs from the plaza by the same name, where a statue commemorates the monarchs receiving Christopher Columbus, up through tourist-filled Plaza Nueva and smaller Plaza Santa Ana. The Río Darro divides the two hillsides of Granada, and a stroll along the banks on **Carerra del Darro** passes several ancient stone bridges. You'll also pass **El Bañuelo Baños Árabes** (Carrera del Darro 31; ☎ 958-027-800; Tues–Sat 10am–2pm; free admission), 11th-century Moorish baths that are among the best-preserved in Spain. It's easy to imagine soaking off the grit of the day in the vaulted subterranean rooms beneath the star-shaped skylights. The past is less palpable at the **Museo Arqueológico** (Carrera del Darro 43; ☎ 958-575-408; 1.50€; Apr–Oct Tues 2:30–8:30pm, Wed–Sat 9am–8:30pm, Sun 9am–2:30pm), but it's worth a visit to this small institution in a Renaissance palace for its account of the successive civilizations of the Iberian peninsula. After nods to the Paleolithic, the exhibitions crank into high gear at the 9th century B.C. with Egyptian alabaster vases, and then move into the ancient Iberians, who came to Spain in the 6th through 1st centuries B.C. A circa–500 B.C. stone bull shows the Greek influence on their culture as well. These early artifacts were all recovered in excavations over the last 150 years. The architectural columns and capitals from Roman, Visigoth and Moorish eras were never buried—most of them have been recycled for centuries in Granada buildings.

Near the archaeological museum, calle Gloria rises into the **Albaicín** ✪✪✪, Granada's most famous neighborhood. At the Convento de San Bernardo (Gloria 2), you can pause at the *retorno* to purchase a half-kilo of honey- and almond-based cookies (6.50€) made by the nuns. Plan at least a half-day to simply wander the maze of narrow streets and tiny plazas. Most of the city's Moorish population lived here after the Reconquest and the Albaicín retains an Arabic flavor even today. (A new mosque opened in 2003, the first since 1492.) The steep alleyways of **Calderería Vieja** and **Calderería Nueva,** off calle Elvira, have the atmosphere of a souk, with merchandise spilling out of little shops and a preponderance of tea-houses and couscous joints. The neighborhood becomes more interesting and less

Coming Clean in the Hammam

As surely as the Christian conquerors built cathedrals and churches on top of mosques, they obliterated the *hammam,* or Arab bath. In many cases, the baths were literally destroyed but in all cases they were closed because they had been social centers of Islamic life. Getting rid of the baths destroyed the gathering places for potential rebellion and undercut what many had seen as a social necessity. (It was said that a beggar in Córdoba would spend his last bit of money on a bath rather than food.) For years, travelers were reduced to marveling at the rich architectural detail and graceful arches of historic ruins while reading interpretive plaques about the links between cleanliness and spirituality—interesting in the abstract, but ultimately unsatisfying. Fortunately, the baths are enjoying a revival, with modern facilities that recapture the sensuous delight of pools of water and hushed surroundings where you can soak, relax, and sip mint tea. While they're not as central to Andalusian lifestyle as they were in Islamic days, they've become a popular pastime for tourists in particular, as well as for those Spaniards who can afford them as a serene alternative to a night of drinking and dancing. Facilities are usually segregated by gender and tend to be open from around 10am until well after midnight. Expect to pay about 17€ to 24€ to soak in the cool, warm, and hot waters and linger in the relaxation rooms. If you need to de-stress even further, most baths also offer aromatherapy treatments and massages.

Here are our suggestions. Your weary feet will thank us.

Seville: Aire de Sevilla (Aire 15; ☎ 955-010-024; www.airede sevilla.com)

Córdoba: Hammam Baños Árabes de Córdoba (Corredidor Luis de la Cerda 15; ☎ 957-484-746; www.hammamspain.com)

Granada: Aljibe Baños Árabes (San Miguel Alta 41; ☎ 958-522-867; www.aljibesanmiguel.es)

Málaga: El Hammam Baño Mágico (Tomás de Cozar 13; ☎ 952-212-327; www.elhammam.com)

commercial the higher you climb. The **Mirador San Nicolas,** a terrace in front of the church of the same name, has a number of small cafes where you can sip coffee or a cold drink and watch the sunset reflect off the Alhambra.

THE OTHER GRANADA
Gypsy Granada

Traditionally, Granada's Gypsy Quarter, the sacred mountain, or **Sacromonte,** rises above the Alabaicín. Whether or not you decide to sleep in the former Gypsy caves at El Abanico (see above), spend some time here to get to know this tightknit community with its own traditions and art forms. Most of the dwellings on the hillside high above the city were carved out of the hard-packed lime soil between the late 19th and mid-20th centuries as inexpensive, quickly constructed housing for people relocating from the countryside. In 1950, Sacromonte had more than 3,600 inhabited caves, though many were abandoned after a major flood in 1963.

"Today there are about 200 inhabited caves, in the lower part of Sacromonte," estimates Carmen Barabel, "and then a few barefoot young hippies who live high up in the hills." Barabel helps oversee the **Museo Cuevas del Sacromonte** ✪✪ (Barranco de los Negros; ☎ 958-215-120; www.sacromontegranada.com; 5€; Apr–Oct Tues–Sun 10am–2pm and 5–9pm, Nov–Mar Tues–Sun 10am–2pm and 4–7pm), an institution that signals a new sense of pride and openness within the largely self-sufficient Roma (Gypsy) community. Exhibitions are spread over several caves clustered around herb and vegetable gardens. It's a rare chance to examine these tidy dwellings with tile or packed-earth floors, whitewashed walls, and low ceilings. The community is known for its weaving, metalwork, pottery, and basketry; if artisans are demonstrating these skills, be sure to strike up a conversation.

Sacromonte's Gypsies are also credited with developing *zambra* flamenco. The son of leading *zambra* artist María La Canastera, Enrique, operates a small museum in a memorabilia-filled cave, **Zambra de María La Canastera** (Sacromonte 89; ☎ 958-121-183; donation; www.granadainfo.com/canastera). The hours tend to be irregular, but if you happen to catch him, he provides personal, tender insight into the community's song and dance traditions. Flamenco performances are no longer held outdoors around the fire, but they do take place almost nightly in several of the caves—a highly evocative setting. (See "Nightlife in Granada," below.)

Schools for Language & Other Arts

In all of Andalusia, our favorite place for immersion in Spanish culture and language is the **Escuela Montalbán** ✪✪ (Conde Cifuentes 11; ☎ 958-25-68-75; www.escuela-montalban.com; MC, V), founded by Margret Fortmann and several fellow teachers in 1986. "We're a cooperative," she says, "we're still the same, just getting older." Classes are held in a 1930s house in the Realejo neighborhood. "When Lorca lived in this neighborhood, he lived in a house like this," Fortmann says. "But there are only about 10 of them left—the rest were torn down to put up apartment blocks." The school coordinates with other studios for courses in flamenco dance (100€ per week) or private guitar lessons (30€ per lesson), and has a strong cooking program (110€ per week). "Now that Spanish cuisine is so well known, we have many inquiries from people who want to do Spanish courses and cooking every day," says Fortmann. The flamenco, guitar, and cooking classes are available without enrolling for Spanish language instruction, but it's not a good idea unless you're already fluent. One highlight of Montalbán's language instruction (160€ per week) is that students are paired with locals who are studying English so they can swap stories as they practice language skills. The school can arrange for rooms with a host family (23€ single, 20€ double per day with breakfast) or in a student residence (25€ single or 22€ double per day with breakfast). In both cases, half- or full-board is available. Private apartments are also available (120€ per week single, 100€ per week double).

ATTENTION, SHOPPERS!

It seems as if every visitor to Granada sports a bold checked scarf, woven bag, or brass bracelet purchased at one of the shop's in the Albaicín's souk-like streets. If you want to step up to a serious souvenir, check out jeweler **Rafael Moreno** (Reyes Católicos 28A; ☎ 958-229-916) for sterling silver and enamel pins, pendants, and cufflinks based on tile designs from the Alhambra. Not all Granada designs are Moorish. The striking logo of the University of Granada depicts two entwined eagles. Check the school bookstore **La Bóveda** (Pl Isabel la Catolica 4; ☎ 958-224-676) for logo-embossed caps, T-shirts, and bags that make practical but unusual gifts.

NIGHTLIFE IN GRANADA

Of the Sacromonte caves offering flamenco shows **Venta El Gallo** (Barranco Los Negros 5; ☎ 958-228-476; www.ventaelgallo.com; 22€ for show, 52€ for show and dinner, additional 6€ for transportation from hotel; daily 9:30pm) is dug deep into the hillside with the stage at the far end. It's moody and comfortable, and the flamenco shows are first-rate—everything that Granada *zambra* is cracked up to be. Book for the show and not the dinner, however—you can eat better and more cheaply elsewhere. City buses stop running at 11pm, so it's advisable to pay the extra charge for the mini-bus transportation.

Flamenco probably wouldn't be enjoying a revival today without the efforts of clubs like **Peña La Platería** ★★ (Placeta Toqueros 7; ☎ 958-210-650). Launched in 1949, it was Spain's first flamenco enthusiasts' club, founded to give exposure to young artists and to build an audience for the art. They accomplish this neatly on Thursday nights (Feb–July 10:30pm; 8€; cash only) by opening the club to the public for performances by up-and-coming artists. Easily one of the friendliest places to enjoy flamenco, the performance space feels a bit like a church hall with a raised stage on one end. The last time we visited, the host told the packed house, "Flamenco has four parts: the music, the rhythm, the dancing, and the audience. An artist must have an audience."

(Mostly) Gay Bars & Dance Clubs

Despite some heinous history under Franco, Granada today is extremely friendly to gay, lesbian, bisexual, and transgendered people. Gay nightlife is a largely local scene, but travelers are welcome to join the fun. On warm summer nights, you'll find some of the most attractive young gay Granadinos sitting out on the wall along the Carerra del Darro. In effect, they're cruising the stretch between two of the city's most popular and classiest bars catering to a predominantly gay and lesbian clientele: **Al Pie de la Vela** (Carrera del Darro 135; ☎ 958-22-85-39) and **El Rincón de San Pedro** (Carrera del Darro 12; no phone). Both places open late afternoon as cafes but crank up the music for dancing for about 4 hours beginning around midnight. Cover charges are infrequent but usually run the cost of a drink (3€–5€). One of the most popular dance and cabaret bars for visitors—expect lines outside on weekends—is tiny **Fondo Reservado** (Cuesta de Santa Inés 3; ☎ 958-221-024; 5€ cover), where doors rarely open until after midnight. The best established gay dance bar in Granada is **La Sal** (Santa Paula 11; no phone; no cover), where the house music begins at 11pm and doesn't stop until 3am on weekdays, 4am on weekends. Originally a lesbian hangout, nowadays La Sal attracts both women and clean-scrubbed preppy men. If you're bent on both dancing and hooking up, **Perfíl** (Rosario 10; no phone; 4€ cover) rocks with rave music and attracts a hot-dressing young crowd that's about half-straight, half-gay. The music starts around midnight and ends at 5am.

MÁLAGA ✪

Málaga seems to prove the adage that flamenco styles reflect their birthplace. Andalusia's second largest city is as deeply nuanced and improvisational as the *malagueña*. Yet travelers often give it short shrift as they rush from the airport or train station to the Costa del Sol resorts, not realizing that Málaga has superb beaches of its own, historic sites, and a strong identification with native son Pablo Picasso. If you want to have it all, base yourself in Málaga, use the train to spend a few hours a day on a Costa del Sol beach, and return to the vibes of a real Spanish city by nightfall. The city of weekday commerce changes into a grand tapas-hopping scene in the evenings and a beach community on the weekends.

GETTING TO & AROUND MÁLAGA

Most flights from outside of Europe to **Málaga Airport** (Avda Garcia Morato, ☎ 952-048-838) are routed through Madrid. On the other hand, more than 20 U.K. and four Irish cities have direct Málaga flights, often at extremely reduced rates on such airlines as Ryanair, Monarch, Globespan, and easyJet. The quickest route into the city is on the C1 line of the local *cercanía* trains. When it reopens (late 2009), get off at the last stop, Centro-Alameda, rather than the main RENFE station (de la Explanade de la Estación) to avoid a 20-minute walk or 5€ cab ride to the old city center. The high-speed AVE train (www.renfe.es or www.raileurope.com) from Córdoba, which arrives at the main station, is another good option. Central Málaga is eminently walkable, but you'll save a lot of time by hopping local buses (1€) from Alameda Principal to reach the beach at Pedregalejo (bus nos. 11, 33, 34) and the Gibralfaro (bus no. 35). Málaga is building a city Metro line, but it's unlikely to start running before 2010.

   Málaga Turismo (Pl de la Marina; ☎ 952-122-020; www.malagaturismo. com; Mon–Fri 9am–6pm, Sat–Sun 10am–6pm), provides standard maps and literature. Staff speak good English and, though they're unlikely to volunteer information, they can be very helpful if you're persistent with questions. Orient yourself by calle Marqués de Larios, a pedestrian mall, which runs from the port up to Plaza de la Constitución. It's the city's main shopping street, though choices are fairly predictable, and most dining and lodging is located nearby.

ACCOMMODATIONS, BOTH STANDARD & NOT

Although many Málaga hotels cater primarily to business travelers, vacationers can find a good range of reasonably priced lodgings both in the city center and near the beach. In-city hotels are often cheaper on weekends.

€   Technically a "youth hostel," **Picasso's Corner** ✪ (San Juan de Letran 9; ☎ 952-212-287; www.picassoscorner.com; MC, V) has facilities for almost everyone.

Backpackers tend to book the shared dormitories (large rooms with 4 or 6 small cots), while middle-class couples and older travelers snap up the small but cheerfully bright private double rooms. All rooms are located on upper floors with narrow stairs—not a good bet for those with impaired mobility. The large common room on the ground floor is a convivial gathering spot, but the presence of travelers of all ages tends to keep the scene from becoming a loud party. Facilities include free Wi-Fi, shared computers, and inexpensive (3€/load) laundry. Reflecting the hostel's friendly nature, nightly dinners of paella or barbecue are available for 4€ to 5€. Two hammocks on the rooftop terrace provide the perfect respite from the bustle of the city. And the prices? Six-bed rooms are 18€ per person, and four-bed rooms are 19€ per person; double rooms with single beds are 44€ per room, and triple rooms are 60€. (All prices include breakfast and tax.)

€   If you'd rather stay near the water, **Hostal El Nogal** ✿ (Avda Juan Sebastián 62; ☎ 952-295-558; www.hoteleshijano.com; MC, V) is only a block from Pedregalego beach on the east end of the city. Although it's on a busy street, the 15 guest rooms (58€ including tax) cluster around two patios and seem far removed from the traffic. Tile floors are cool underfoot and the rooms have a rustic charm with rough plaster walls and carved wooden headboards and doors. But the patios are the real gems, with lounge chairs for sunbathing and a hot tub on the upper level and lush greenery on the ground level.

€€   Back in town, it's about a 5-minute walk from **Hotel Kris Tribuna** (Carretería 6–10; ☎ 952-122-230; www.krishoteles.com; MC, V) to Plaza de la Constitución at the head of Marqués de Larios. The 42-room hotel sits on remains of an 11th-century wall, visible behind glass in the attached cafe. The rooms are small but have attractive wrought-iron headboards and tiled bathrooms and are fairly priced at 70€ to 80€ per night. Large street-side windows can let in noise. A quiet option is the bright interior Room 105, which has a full-size tub instead of the shower found in many other rooms.

€€€   A few extra euros buys a lot of extra space at **Hotel Don Curro** (Sancho de Lara 7; ☎ 952-227-200; www.hoteldoncurro.com; MC, V)—rooms average 105€ to 115€ a night (VIP rooms are a bit more). Just off Marqués de Larios, the family-run hotel was built in 1933 but has been thoroughly updated. Large hallways lead to 128 spacious rooms with new parquet wood floors, marble bathrooms, and very large closets. A mezzanine dining area for guests offers a 9€ breakfast buffet, and a 20€ *menu del dia*. A lounge and bar with giant TV is located next to the dining room.

€€–€€€€   A lodging pioneer on the port side of Málaga's Alameda Principal, **Room Mate Lola** ✿ (Casa de Campos 17; ☎ 952-579-300; www.roommatehotels. com; AE, MC, V) is in a rapidly gentrifying neighborhood where sex shops hint at its shadier past. That said, it's a clean and safe area, convenient to the central city. The decor is fashion forward, a melding of Art Deco styling, with intense shades of blue, green, and purple, and such modern touches as large padded headboards, flat-screen TVs, and black vinyl easy chairs. Lola includes free Wi-Fi and a generous buffet breakfast (served until noon) in the rate, which can range from 85€ to

PERCHEL · Calle de Cárreterias

LA MERCED · Teatro Cervantes

Los Mártires

C. de Alamos · C. Méndez Núñez

Plaza de la Merced

Calle de la Victoria

Pasillo de Natera · Pasillo de Guadalmedina · Río Guadalmedina · Pasillo Santa Isabela · Calle Compañía · C. Especería

Plaza Constitución

CENTRO · Nueva · Calle Marqués de Larios · Calle de Molina Larios

Calle de Granada

Palacio Episcopal · Museo Picasso Málaga

Mercado Central

Catédral

Calle Altarazanas

Alameda Principal

Calle Córdoba

C. del Campos

Av. Manuel Agustín Heredia

Palacio de la Aduana

Plaza de la Marina

Calle Alcazabilla · Teatro Romano

Alcabaza del Málaga

Castillo de Gibralfaro

Jardines de Puerta Oscura

C. Guillén Sotelo

Ayuntamiento

Paseo del Parque

Paseo de Cintura del Puerto

Puerto de Málaga

Estación Marítima

0   200 yds
0   200 m

ACCOMMODATIONS ■

Hostal El Nogal **19**
Hotel Kris Tribuna **2**
Hotel Don Curro **6**
Málaga
  Centro Hotel **1**
Room Mate Lola **3**
Picasso's Corner **16**

DINING ◆

Bodegas
  Quitapenas **5**
Cafe Central **8**
El Pimpi **12**
Restaurante
  El Cabra **20**
Strachan **7**

ATTRACTIONS ●

Alcazaba de Málaga **15**
Antigua Casa de Guardia **4**
Casa Natal de Picasso **17**
Castillo de Gibralfaro **18**
Catédral **9**
Iglesia de Santiago **10**
Museo del Málaga **13**
Museo Picasso Málaga **11**
Teatro Romano **14**

160€, though usually you'll pay around 100€ to 110€. Underground parking is 14€ per night, but determined drivers can often find on-street parking.

€€–€€€€   On the west side of the Río Guadalhorce, **Málaga Centro Hotel** (Mármoles 6; ☎ 952-070-216; www.salleshotels.com; AE, MC, V) is about a 10-minute stroll from Plaza de la Constitución. The 147 rooms are geared for business travelers: small but functional, with a table, two chairs, and desk in traditional dark wood. But you get the amenities of a big hotel, with a grand marble lobby and bar, large lounge area with flat-screen TV, a small fitness room, and an indoor pool with striking views of the Catédral and Alcazaba. Rates range from 70€ to 170€, with the higher rate reflecting holiday periods and business conventions. Expect to pay 100€ to 120€ most of the time.

DINING FOR ALL TASTES

The line between tapas bar and restaurant is blurred in Málaga, and many establishments serve two menus, even in the sit-down dining room. As a general rule, the best dishes are small plates of local seafood. Don't worry about getting a seat (or a place to stand) at the busy tapas spots. Since Malagueños are avid about

Vino, Old Style

The Málaga region has a winemaking tradition at least as old as the Greeks and probably the Phoenicians. The best place in the city to sample about 20 different varieties straight from the cask is **Antigua Casa de Guardia** (Alameda Principal 18; ☎ 952-214-680; Mon–Sat 9am–10pm; MC, V), founded in 1840. Place your order and the barman will chalk your tab on the worn wooden counter in front of you. The sweet versions are usually the best, such as Pajarete 1908. If you insist on dry, try Seco Trasañejo. They're only 1.30€ per glass, but watch out: Málaga is fortified to 18% to 20% alcohol.

tapas-hopping, and may visit half a dozen an evening, if you don't see an opening at the bar, just wait a minute. Someone will move on shortly.

€   Most of the tapas at **Bodegas Quitapenas** (Marín García 4; ☎ 952-602-357; noon–4pm, 8pm–midnight; cash only) are displayed behind glass at the indoor bar, so you can simply point if your menu Spanish is weak. But locals prefer to gather around wine barrels outside where they share plates of tiger mussels, fried baby squid, breaded fried shrimp, or crab fritters (1.30€–4.50€).

€   Even when you're jet-lagged and dog-tired, a hot coffee isn't quite the right pick-me-up in balmy Málaga. Probably the best way to cool off and get a hit of caffeine is the popular *granizado de cafe,* a sort of espresso slush. You can sample it at the venerable **Casa Mira** ★ (Larios 5; ☎ 952-212-422; daily 10:30am–midnight; cash only) on the main pedestrian drag. Work your way through the crowd to the bar, and when you think it's your turn, speak up! For a double treat of smooth and icy, ask for a granizado *con helado* (with ice cream). Either the *crema de cafe* (coffee) or the *flan de caramelo* (caramel) is a perfect counterpoint to the strong coffee (1.60€–2.10€).

€–€€   People with shady pasts are often the most interesting, and so are bars. According to local legend, **El Pimpi** ★ (Granada 62, also enter via plaza on Alcazabilla; ☎ 952-228-990; noon–2am; MC, V) has a back exit so wastrels could dodge their creditors. Today it's a hangout for everyone from British tourists to local families, including film star Antonio Banderas when he's visiting his Málaga relatives. Giant barrels of Málaga wine dominate the indoor patio, and every celebrity from bullfighter El Córdobes to designer Paloma Picasso has inscribed a greeting on one. It's worth visiting just for a drink at the bar surrounded by aging posters of the Málaga Feria and vintage Franco-era tourism posters touting the then-new Costa del Sol. The bar offers a 10€ tapas sampler at all hours.

€–€€   We almost dismissed **Cafe Central** ★ 🧒 (Pl de la Constitución 11; ☎ 952-224-972; wwwcafecentralmalaga.com; 8am–11pm or midnight in summer; cash only) because of the generic signboard touting paella (a tourist come-on) and the poseurs holding down the outdoor tables. But we're glad that locals encouraged us to head inside to the cozy dining room with walls covered with black-and-white photos of the plaza over the decades and a slot machine in one corner. The food is simple and filling, such as filets of pork in an onion-mushroom-carrot sauce (a Málaga specialty), or grilled red mullet, each only 6.50€. The cafe also has a kid-friendly menu with offerings such as lasagna or meatballs for 5.50€. Be sure to have a coffee, since owner José Prado is credited with standardizing seemingly limitless ways to order. A big tile plaque on the wall explains the difference between a *solo* and a *largo* or a *corto* and a *mitad*.

€€€   While seafood figures heavily in Málaga cuisine, grilled meat is also popular. And **Strachan** (Strachan 5; ☎ 952-227-573; noon–midnight; AE, MC, V) is the place to go for that. It offers expertly cooked pork sirloin (13€); lamb chops (19€); or a brochette of chicken, pork, chorizo, beef, and morcilla sausage (16€). You can sit outside and watch the crowds heading to and from the Marqués de Larios shops, but for a more decorous meal, take a marble-topped table in the main salon and admire the ornately carved woodwork.

WHY YOU'RE HERE: THE TOP SIGHTS & ATTRACTIONS

Like every municipality in Andalusia, Málaga has its Moorish ruins. But the city seems more tied to its modern artist than its Moorish past, identifying strongly with native son Pablo Ruiz Picasso, born here in 1881. Following his childhood footsteps gives you an intimate experience of the city. To do so, you may want to pick up one of the **free audio tours** on offer from Málaga Turismo (p. 167). Or hit the Picasso-centric spots described below.

Begin where the artist did: at the **Casa Natal de Picasso** ✪ (Pl de la Merced 15; ☎ 952-060-215; www.fundacionpicasso.es; 1€ adults, free for seniors and children 16 and under, free for all Sun; 9:30am–8pm), the house where Picasso was born. His father, José Ruiz Blasco, was an art teacher and a seminal influence on the gifted young Pablo, who by all accounts began drawing and painting as soon as he could hold a pencil and brush. The house museum displays Picasso prints as well as photographs of the artist over the years, but its real appeal is as a touchstone of the place where the artist began his remarkable life. Like relics of a saint displayed in a cathedral's treasure room, glass cases display the baby Picasso's cloth umbilical band and the tiny cotton shift that served as his baptismal outfit.

Blue-and-white tile markers on the Plaza de la Merced and nearby streets identify other Picasso sites, such as the family's second house at no. 17 on the plaza, and the building at calle Granada 75 where his father used to gather with friends to shoot the breeze. Picasso was baptized at **Iglesia de Santiago** (Granada 62; free admission; 9am–1pm and 6–8pm). The parish church is gorgeously simple on the outside, retaining a Moorish horseshoe doorway from the mosque that first stood on the site. The church's interior, including the 18th-century main altarpiece, is so encrusted with baroque detail that it's easy to imagine young Pablo staring around during Mass thinking, "Simplify! Simplify!"

Toward the end of his life, the artist expressed the wish that his work be displayed in the city of his birth. Several decades later, that wish became reality with the opening of the **Museo Picasso Málaga** ✪✪✪ (Palacio de Buenavista, calle San Agustin 8; ☎ 902-443-377; www.museopicassomalaga.org; 6€ adults, 3€

A Perfect Málaga Beach Evening

€€–€€€   It takes about an hour to stroll along Playa de la Malagueta from the port to Playa Pedregalejo. You'll pass fishermen casting in the surf, colonies of feral cats living in the rocks, and on a Saturday afternoon, barefoot brides having their pictures taken on the beach. Fish-house restaurants line the beach just above the tide line at Pedregalejo. Typically, they're little more than rooms opening onto an outdoor eating porch with tables inside for bad weather. One of the value spots is Manuel Cabra's **Restaurante El Cabra** ★★ (Playa Pedregalejo 17; ☎ 952-251-595; Tues–Sun 2–6pm, 8pm–midnight; MC, V). His specialties include grilled sardines on a wooden stake (4.50€) and a *fritura Malagueña* of mixed fried fish, including squid, scallops, sardines, red mullet, calamari, and cuttlefish (9€). You can linger as long as you want and then walk 2 blocks up from the beach to avenida Juan Sebastian Elcado to catch the no. 11, 33, or 34 bus back to Alameda Principal.

seniors and students with ID, free for children 18 and under, free for all after 3pm last Sun of the month; Tues–Thurs and Sun 10am–8pm, Fri–Sat 10am–9pm). Set in the 16th-century Palacio de Buenavista (former home of the Museo de Bellas Artes), its lower level houses ruins from the Phoenician, Roman, and Moorish occupations of the city (which was founded about 1100 B.C.), which were turned up by builders renovating the space. Above, 12 beautifully lit galleries contain 155 works donated by Picasso's daughter-in-law and grandson. The collection is just large enough to tease out the artist's multifaceted genius. At the same time that he was making abstract Cubist portraits, for example, he also drew a delicate portrait of his lover so realistic that it could be a photograph. An additional gallery hosts temporary exhibitions of Picasso's works from other collections or works by his contemporaries. (When you live to age 92, you accumulate a lot of contemporaries.)

Some of Picasso's women have strange visages, but none of them is known as *La Manquita,* or the "one-armed lady." Because its second bell tower was never finished, that's the nickname for Málaga's **Catédral** (Molina Lario; ☎ 952-060-215; 3.50€; tours Mon–Fri 10am–6pm, Sat 10am–5pm), which collapses a lot of history in one hulking mass of stone. It sits more or less at the foot of the Alcazaba, the old Moorish fortress-city, on the former site of the mosque. The symbolism of obliterating an Islamic house of worship to construct a Catholic one was not lost on the Spanish royalty, who only managed to take back Málaga from the Moors in 1487. Construction of the cathedral didn't begin until 1528, and the builders finally threw up their hands in 1782. Skip the guided tour, but step inside briefly to see the 17th-century choir stalls carved of mahogany and cedar. The 40 images of saints are largely the work of Pedro de Mena, one of Spain's most celebrated sculptors in wood.

Picasso bumped the municipal art museum from its long-time home, but the **Museo del Málaga** (Palacio de la Aduana, Alcazabilla 2; ☎ 952-218-382;

www.museosdeandalucia.es; free admission; Tues 3–8pm, Wed–Sat 9am–8pm, Sun 9am–2pm) draws from its collection to mount temporary exhibits to remind people that Picasso wasn't the only artist who hailed from this region. In fact, the collection is strong on Spanish painters of Málaga and the Costa del Sol who never achieved international reputations (as well as some who did, such as José Moreno Villa). It's a good place to get out of the sun and see some art for free before ascending the hill to the Moorish monuments.

Pause before the climb at the ruins of the **Teatro Romano** adjacent to the Alcazaba. Built in the 1st century A.D., the theater, the best hunk of Roman architecture in Málaga province, was not uncovered until 1951. Now enclosed behind bars, it's still occasionally used for theatrical productions—Antonio Banderas performed here early in his career.

While Granada's Alhambra palace represents the lifestyle of the Moorish rich and famous, the **Alcazaba de Málaga** ✪ (Alcazabilla; ☎ 952-128-860; 2€ adults [or 3.30€ combined with Castillo de Gibralfaro], .60€ seniors, students, and children, free for all Sun after 2pm; Tues–Sun 9:30am–8pm [until 7pm in winter]) tells the story of the warrior potentates of the Taifa period in Andalusia, when the central Moorish empire had disintegrated into small kingdoms. The combination fortress and palace does not occupy the highest ground in Málaga, but it does command an irregular rocky spur that towers above most of the city. Begun shortly after the Arab conquest of 711, the largest sections were built between the 11th and 14th centuries. Just as the Catholic churches often reused stones from Moorish buildings, the Alcazaba is filled with fluted Greek-style columns with acanthus capitals from 300 B.C. to 200 B.C. and occasional blocks of Roman stones with Latin inscriptions still visible. Military history buffs will find the fortifications an interesting study in creating a defensible city, but the well-preserved interior palace retains a palpable air of domesticity and is the most evocative part of the complex. Water gurgles from fountains as gardens of oranges and palms provide lush greenery in what is essentially a maritime desert climate. The main entrance to the Alcazaba is up a long series of steps on Plaza de la Aduana. But there is an elevator entrance behind the Ayuntamiento (city hall) at the corner of Guillén Sotelo and Francisco Bejarrano Robles.

That's also where you'll find the shortcut to and from the **Castillo de Gibralfaro** (☎ 952-227-230; 2€ adults [3.30€ combined with Alcazaba], .60€ seniors, students, and children, free for all Sun after 2pm; 9am–8pm). At the Alcazaba, staff members direct would-be walkers to follow Paseo de Don Juan Tamboury to the Gibralfaro. That walk is long and slippery on steeply graded inclines, but it affords a good view into Málaga's bullring. It's easier to climb the rock steps that begin in the Jardines de Puerta Oscura, also behind the Ayuntamiento. Easier still is bus no. 35 from Alameda Principal. The Gibralfaro was constructed by the Granada king Yusef I in the early 14th century, but alas the hilltop castle is not as well preserved as the Alcazaba. The view from the ramparts down to the harbor, however, is spectacular.

THE OTHER MÁLAGA

Come to Málaga (or any other city in Andalusia) the week before Easter, and you'll experience an utterly different place. Nighttime processions of religious brotherhoods dominate the city. In amazing feats of devotion and endurance, the brothers carry weighty thrones bearing religious images through crowd-lined streets.

Even if you miss the processions, you can get insight into this primal ritual by visiting one of the societies' museums, such as the **Museo Casa Hermandad Nuestro Padre Jesús Cristo del San Sepulcro y Nuestra Señora de la Soledad** (Alcazabilla 5; ☎ 952-602-150; 1€; Mon–Fri 9:30am–1:30pm and 5–7pm). The brotherhood was founded by the bishop of Málaga in 1893 and is the "official brotherhood" of the city. Its two gigantic thrones rest in this modest facility and you can walk around them and even put your shoulder under the support poles to imagine what it would be like to heft your share of the weight. The brotherhood's statue of the Virgin is carried on a 16×13-foot throne covered with engraved silver plate and enormous candelabras on each corner. It weighs 10,800 pounds and is carried on the shoulders of 220 men. The throne for the figure of the recumbent Christ was designed by Picasso's first drawing teacher. Made of wood, it weighs "only" 8,150 pounds and is carried by 164 men. Málaga's Good Friday procession, which features 52 such thrones, begins at 9pm and usually lasts about 6 hours, creeping through the streets to a dirge-like march. The *portadores* must carry the thrones for the entire procession—no substitutions—although they can rest along the way. "One of our *portadores* is 75 years old," a member of the brotherhood told us. "Last year the procession took 6 hours and 34 minutes," he recalled. We believe that they count every minute.

You'll embrace the sunnier side of Málaga if you decide to study Spanish language at **Cervantes Escuela Internacional** ★ (Avda Juan Sebastián Elcano 69; ☎ 952-295-378; www.escuelacervantes.org). Founded in 1986, the school occupies an historic building a block from Pedregalejo beach. Students spend 4 hours in language study in the morning, take a break for lunch (and maybe the beach), and then take flamenco classes with a professional dancer in the afternoon. "We teach Spanish language and culture together," says Melanie Izmiryan, adding that the school usually arranges evening activities, which can range from museum visits to tapas hops. One-week courses are 150€, but the school encourages students to spend at least 2 weeks. "After 1 week students are just getting comfortable with the language," says Izmiryan. Most classes have five or six students, none more than nine. While classes attract students of all ages, Cervantes recently introduced a "Golden Age" course (570€ for 2 weeks) for students 50 and over with a greater emphasis on cultural activities and lectures. The school will arrange lodging with host families or in shared student apartments. For adults, Izmiryan recommends a single or double room in the school's own residence building, a large house on a hill above town with an ocean view, swimming pool and garden, and shared cooking facilities (singles 165€ per week, doubles 145€ per week; room with private bath 30€ extra). From Cervantes, it's only about a 15-minute ride by city bus to downtown Málaga to put that Spanish into practice.

If you prefer to be in the heart of things, **Instituto Picasso Málaga** (Pl de la Merced 20; ☎ 952-213-932; www.instituto-picasso.com; 2-week course 265€) is located in a 150-year-old building next door to Picasso's birthplace. Four classrooms have large windows on busy Plaza de la Merced, where students congregate at cafes between lessons. Like Cervantes, Picasso limits classes to no more than nine students and offers four hours of instruction per day. With plenty of diversions right outside the door, Picasso has a less ambitious schedule of cultural activities.

Best but most expensive lodging choice for adults are small apartments for one or two people (475€ for 1 person for 2 weeks, 590€ for 2 people), right in the heart of Málaga, less than a 5-minute walk from the school.

NIGHTLIFE IN MÁLAGA

Málaga's most unusual late-night attraction is the **Santísima Trinidad** (Puerto de Málaga, Muelle 3; ☎ 952-221-346; www.naviosantisimatrinidad.es), a replica of a 1769 three-masted bark that took part in the Battle of Trafalgar. By day it lures in curious tourists, at night it turns into a *discoteca* (10€), opening at 12:30am and closing at 7am. If you prefer a parlor-like setting and earlier hours, **Cafetería-Restaurante El Jardin** (Cañón 1; ☎ 952-220-419; www.eljardinmalaga.com; 6€ minimum consumption) near the cathedral gardens offers a curious but lively mix of piano music, tango, and flamenco from 9:30pm to 2am. The shop **Flamenka Vive** (Pasillo Santa Isabel 5; ☎ 952-214-778) is the hub of Málaga's flamenco network. Artists usually sing and play in a casual atmosphere on Thursday nights beginning at 9pm. Visitors are welcome to join the scene at no charge. More conventional international fare in the performing arts (concerts, plays, modern dance, opera, and ballet) is presented at **Teatro Cervantes** (Ramos Marín; ☎ 952-224-100; www.teatrocervantes.com).

GET OUT OF TOWN

Málaga is a good base to explore one of Andalusia's most dramatic natural areas as well as one of its most picturesque mountain towns.

El Torcal de Antequera ✫

Just 19 miles north of Málaga on the A45, the parched hills of water- and wind-sculpted limestone known as **El Torcal de Antequera** 🐸 might as well be another planet. Designated as a Paraje Natural in 1929 (the first natural area so protected in Andalusia), El Torcal's astounding rock formations make the imagination run riot. But they're part of a natural process. Starting about 20 million years ago with the tectonic plate shifts that gave rise to the Alps, the limestone of the sea floor was compressed, deformed, and fractured—then slowly lifted up in a process that still continues. This soft rock is especially vulnerable to erosion, leaving bits of harder limestone like the skeleton of a mountain range. Several easy-to-reach overlooks afford broad overviews of the park and two walking routes circle through the natural area. Both have well-marked, packed-earth paths, some rock steps, and a few boulder scrambles. The easier route is about a mile, while the slightly more difficult route is almost twice as long and extends into the heart of the park. Be on the lookout for rabbits and foxes, eagles and falcons. But whatever you do, do *not* leave the path—it's almost impossible to find your way through the maze of rocks.

The best driving route to El Torcal is to follow A45 north to Antequera, A343 south from Antequera, then local road 3310 to El Torcal (watch for brown signs). You can also get there by public transit on the weekends late May to mid-September by taking the early-morning Casado bus (☎ 952-315-908) to Antequera, then hopping the free bus at Plaza de Coso Viejo at 10:30am. (Return bus from El Torcal to Antequera leaves at 2pm.) Bring your own food and water, as the vending machines at the visitor center are rather limited.

Mijas Pueblo ✮

It's inevitable that tourists have discovered Mijas, given its stunning mountainside location—and the ready availability of public transportation from Málaga (4 buses a day) as well as the Costa del Sol (buses every half-hour). When making your travel plans, be sure not to confuse Mijas Costa (vast vacation housing tracts farther down the mountain) with Mijas Pueblo. Arrive at the right place and you'll find an old-fashioned mountain village where families have known each other for generations.

ACCOMMODATION IN MIJAS

€   Mijas Pueblo has plenty of resorts and time-share apartments on the hillside leading down to Fuengirola, but to live like a Mijan, your best bet is **Hostal Posada Mijas** (Coin 47; ☎ 952-485-310; cash only). Josepha, the red-haired grandmother of the Posada clan, oversees the family-owned lodging while keeping an eye on the grandkids. She has five rooms to sleep two people on single beds and three apartments that sleep four and include kitchens. There's heat for the winter but no air-conditioning (and little need of it at this altitude). Well-made country furniture is simple and spare—just like the town—and most rooms have sweeping views over the village and down to the sea. It's about a 5-minute walk to the Peña or 3 minutes to the town museum. Rates are 35€ to 45€.

DINING IN MIJAS

€–€€€   When the crowds arrive for the Saturday bullfight, much of Mijas takes a holiday, including **El Olivar** (Av Virgen de la Peña 4; ☎ 952-486-196; Sun–Fri 11am–4pm and 7–10pm; AE, DC, MC, V). But for the rest of the week, this polished restaurant with fabulous views is the best place for a meal. The kitchen is built around a wood-burning grill and the menu is strong on local products, including grilled trout (8.60€) and grilled lamb chops (12€).

ATTRACTIONS IN MIJAS

The quaint **donkey taxis** (15€) of Mijas grace many a postcard. Most visitors opt for a half-hour sightseeing tour of the village in one of the rustic donkey-pulled carts, but it's as easy to walk from the bus stop and the view from the nearby *mirador* is much better than the view from behind a plodding donkey. (A sign just beneath the overlook, where condos are being built, warns in English, "The view will last forever. Your opportunity to own it won't.") Shaded benches line the small park at the overlook, where the **Ermita de la Virgen de la Peña** (dawn to sunset) occupies a cave excavated by a Carmelite monk in the mid–17th century to hold an image of the Virgin kept hidden (or so the legend goes) from the Moors for 5 centuries. A single main road leads uphill into town. On the lower of the town's two hilltops, the shopping square of Plaza de la Libertad is dominated by the **Casa Museo Ayuntamiento de Mijas** (Pl de la Libertad 2; ☎ 952-590-380; free admission; 10am–2pm and 4–7pm). Devoted to the history of the village, it includes exhibitions of old olive mills and other food specialties of the region, including pine nuts, yellow cherries, and honey. At the very top of the town, the **Plaza de Toros** (☎ 952-485-852; tour 3€; Sun–Fri 10am–2pm and 5–7pm), a lovingly maintained oval bullring, was constructed in 1900. (People bus in from all over the Costa del Sol for the Saturday *corridas* from May through October; plan accordingly to avoid the crowds.) Next to the bullring, the parish church of **Immaculada Concepción** ✮ (free admission; Mon–Sat 10am–5pm), built 1540 to 1645, incorporates a Mudéjar tower from the former mosque as its bell tower. The cooing of doves under the eaves echoes through the small sanctuary. Eight 17th-century frescoes of the Apostles were discovered during a 1992 restoration of the church.

ACTIVE MIJAS

Like many mountain villages, Mijas radiates rural walking paths once used by residents to get from town to town. Check with the **Oficina de Turismo** (Pl Virgen de la Peña; ☎ 952-589-034; www.mijas.es; 10am–7pm) for maps. At 10am every Wednesday and Saturday April through June, **free walking tours** in the countryside depart from the tourist office. They last 2 to 5 hours and are limited to 20 participants. Guides are students in the rural guide course of a tourism school based in Mijas—the perfect chance to get to know some of the locals.

COSTA DEL SOL

You'll find some of Spain's finest beaches—and worst traffic congestion—on this 50-mile stretch of sand and sea west of Málaga. High-rise hotel development ran rampant here in the 1960s, and it continues as new villa communities pop up every year. But there's good reason why millions of travelers ignore the ugly architecture and brave the traffic jams. The Costa del Sol climate is balmy, the long brown-sand beaches are impeccable, and the sun shines an average of 325 days a year. It's best to know yourself before you go. Do you want to simply bake on the beach? Do you crave nightlife? Do you long to hobnob with the beautiful people? Or do you hanker for the least built-up fishing village? There's an option for everyone.

Whatever you choose, there's a strategy to enjoying the Costa del Sol. When you leave the highway and enter a thicket of unattractive concrete buildings, keep heading toward the water and look for the old city center, where narrow, twisty streets have defied development.

GETTING TO & AROUND COSTA DEL SOL

The coastal N340 highway links the towns of Costa del Sol, though drivers who don't want to stop at every streetlight are better served by the A7 inland toll highway. The coast roughly divides into three sections. Starting just west of Málaga's industrial port, the beach communities of Torremolinos and Fuengirola form an almost continuous line of concrete resort hotels and apartment blocks across a two-lane street from the beach. West of a rocky point, Marbella, home of the 1950s jet set, is an enclave of great wealth and glamour. Farther west, the fishing village of Estepona anchors a quieter, more contemplative stretch of Costa del Sol. Cheap (1.30€) and frequent bus service from Málaga makes it easy to stay in the city and day-trip to the

> " To the Moors, Andalusia was an earthly paradise. To the travel agents it still is. To the rest of Spain it stands in rather the relationship of some flibbertigibbet but undeniably charming cousin—of whom indulgent elders say you really needn't worry, John's the kind that always falls on his feet. "
>
> —Jan Morris, *Spain* (Oxford University Press, 1979)

beaches at Torrie or Fuengirola. Cercanía trains (1.20€–2.60€) are even faster and less crowded.

HIGH-RISE COSTA DEL SOL

The towns just west of Málaga along the coast are only a small part of the Costa del Sol, yet they are the most densely packed of the beach communities, which is why we've grouped them together as "high-rise" Costa del Sol. British pensioners flock to Torremolinos and Fuengirola during the winter and you'll find lots of places offering "Full English Breakfast," where you'll get a choice between ham-'n'-egg or bacon-'n'-egg and between orange pekoe and Earl Grey. You'll hear a lot of English spoken here, but you can sort the Spaniards from the visiting Brits because the Spaniards schooled in English have more formal accents and speak in complete sentences. The huge inventory of apartments and hotel rooms means that bargains are often available. Good maps and piles of promotional literature are available from the excellent local tourist offices: **Oficina de Turismo** (Pl Blas Infante 1, Torremolinos; ☎ 952-379-512; 9am–2pm and 5–8pm) and **Oficina de Turismo** (Jesús de Rein 6, Fuengirola; ☎ 952-467-457; Mon–Fri 9:30am–2pm and 5–7pm, Sat 10am–1pm).

The Sun in Box: Package Deals to Costa del Sol

The Costa del Sol used to be prime package-deal territory, but now that most travelers can easily book their own flights and hotels online, the packaging market has moved on to other beach destinations where the dollar hasn't been so beaten down. (Many former Spain specialists now concentrate on Cancún and the Riviera de Maya in Mexico, or on the Dominican Republic.) Similarly, packagers in the U.K. work on trips with very short notice, usually advertising in the London Sunday papers.

The basic package includes airfare and hotel, with the option of adding rental cars, airport transfers, tours, sports activities, and travel insurance for less than the price of purchasing them separately. Contrary to common wisdom, the percentage of savings over published rates booked separately tends to be greatest during high season because competing airlines add seasonal service, and sharply elevated room rates allow more room for discounting.

Lodging available through travel packages ranges from generic all-inclusives to exclusive luxury resorts, varying by company, season, and availability. Travel agents can book package trips, and have access to some deals from wholesalers that aren't available to individual travelers. The Spanish National Tourist Office publishes a list of **Spain specialist travel agencies** on the Web: **www.okspain. org/ssprogram/ssp1.asp**.

Some packagers consistently offer better savings than others, and within each company some deals are better than others. There's only one way to determine how much of a bargain any particular deal is: Compare the total package price—including taxes and fees, which often aren't quoted upfront—with prices available directly through the hotel's and airline's websites. Even when the saving is minimal, you'll benefit from the convenience, access to an agent if something goes wrong when you're on foreign soil, and any extras the company includes, such as airport transfers. For greatest savings, look for last-minute deals and other specials.

Vacation packages are available from specialized vacation companies, some airlines, and the Big Three online booking agencies (Expedia, Orbitz, and Travelocity). The listings that follow are all established, reputable firms, and their deals run the gamut from great values to overpriced. They appear in order of average savings per night for a couple, based on our research of air-hotel packages offered from New York in fall through spring, compared with the cost of booking the same flights and rooms separately on airline and hotel websites.

All three of these vacation companies offer the best deals on Costa del Sol packages, often at savings of $200 to $300 per couple over making the same bookings yourself. Note, however, that all packages are limited to the January-through-March season. **ClubABC** (888/TOURS-ABC; www.clubabc.com) offers several dates on a 7-day tour that includes airfare and 5 nights in a choice of pretty good beach hotels with breakfast and dinner. Note that airport transfers are extra and you have to join Club ABC ($30 per household for a year) to book any of its packages. **Gate1Travel** (☎ 800/682-3333; www.gate1travel.com) has several dates as well on an 8-day tour to Torremolinos with breakfast only. In some ways the best deal is through **Abreu Tours** (☎ 800/223-1580; www.abreu-tours.com), which uses the Bajondillo apartments right on the beach in Torremolinos for

Parsing Packages

Not all packages are created equal. So it's extremely important to read all the fine print and make comparisons before booking. Some suggestions on how to proceed:

- **When looking at different companies online, make sure that you're making an apples-to-apples comparison.** Go all the way through to the booking page to get the true rate. Prices on the initial search page usually don't include mandatory taxes and fees.
- **To save the most, don't futz around with the package.** If you search for a different flight than the one included in the initial offer, it often increases the cost. Upgrading to a better room category certainly will; initial price quotes are always for the most basic rooms.
- **Carefully reread the package inclusions before turning over your credit card number.** Some packages include airport transfers or some form of travel insurance at no extra cost, but most don't. An insidious ploy of some packagers is to add these or other extras, along with their additional charges, by default. If you don't want the extras, it's up to you to remove them.
- **Move quickly.** The price you're looking at is good only for that instant in time. Because of changes in airfares or hotel occupancy rates, you could see a different price if you go back to the site an hour later; the price might even be updated while you're looking at it. A package can disappear altogether if the hotel has filled up. Since different packages are based on different flights, the best deal one minute can be a runner-up the next. Once you've narrowed down the contenders, run a quick double-check—then grab it.

lodging. No meals are included. Searching on **Expedia** (☎ 800/397-3342; www. expedia.com, or www.expedia.co.uk in the U.K.) yields paltry savings on packages from the U.S. ($70–$100 at best, and then for questionable hotels). Virtually the same packages at virtually the same prices turn up on **Orbitz** (www.orbitz.com) and **Travelocity** (www.travelocity.com). Searching through the British version of **Expedia** (www.expedia.co.uk), however, uncovers some of those last-minute deals otherwise advertised in the London Sunday papers.

Accommodations on High-Rise Costa del Sol

Located at Los Boliches, a quarter-mile from Fuengirola's chaotic downtown, **Aparthotel La Jabega** 🧒 (Paseo Maritimo at Jaen, Los Boliches, Fuengirola; ☎ 952-475-354; www.jabega.com; 42€–84€; MC, V) is one of the best maintained and most pleasant of the "self-catering" lodgings that attract the northern European winter-pensioner market. Each of the 133 units has a small balcony and at least a partial ocean view. Cooking facilities are limited to two burners, a tiny under-counter fridge, toaster oven, and electric tea kettle. In the smallest units, two twin beds are arranged at right angles along one corner to double as a couch, but if you've come for the beach, you won't spend much time indoors anyway. The two-room units will sleep four, making a decent option if the kids are along. If you want to experience Semana Santa (Holy Week) in Andalusia, sleep here and take the train to Málaga. Studio apartments are only 59€ a night during a time period that commands premium prices almost everywhere else.

€€–€€€   For a splurge, ask for an upper-level corner room on the front at **Hotel Isabel** ✪ (Paseo Maritimo 47, Playamar, Torremolinos; ☎ 952-381-744; www.hotelisabel.net; 85€–130€; AE, MC, V). Room 606 (126€–174€), for example, has two balconies and stunning views. Across the street from one of the nicest stretches of Playamar Beach, Isabel is set slightly apart from the massive hotels and apartment blocks. A recent overhaul transformed the cookie-cutter beach lodging into a gleaming full-service hotel with 70 airy rooms, sparkling lounges, and pretty gardens.

Dining on High-Rise Costa del Sol

Where you eat lunch almost always depends on which patch of sand you've claimed. The *chiringuitas* (beach snack shops) have interchangeable menus of fried fish, fish and chips, fried potatoes, and grilled sardines—it's best to avoid the usually soggy tourist paella.

€–€€   When the sun goes down, the action shifts from the beach to the sidewalk tapas bars, such as Fuengirola's **El Bolichito** (Avda Jesús Cautivo; ☎ 952-478-546; MC, V), where the most popular dish is grilled shrimp (11€) but arguably the best is grilled fresh octopus (9.70€).

€–€€   For serious seafood, head to the section of the beach called La Carihuela in Torremolinos. Although locals tout it as the fishermen's quarter, those erstwhile sailors are too busy running restaurants to haul nets. A perfect example is **El Roqueo** (Carmen 35; ☎ 952-384-946; cash only), where the three-course midday menu is 5.50€. The tart house wine perfectly balances the strong flavors of grilled fresh anchovies (4.50€) or a dish translated as "seafoam" (7.20€)—a plate of mixed tiny fish flash-fried in tempura batter.

Attractions on High-Rise Costa del Sol

If you don't love lying on a sandy beach and baking in the sun, you have no business here. Although each section has a local name bestowed by developers trying to differentiate their real estate from the rest, the **beach** ✪✪✪ 🧒 is a nearly 10-mile continuous swath of brown sand from Málaga's western city limits through Torremolinos and Fuengirola, where it ends at a few rocky outcrops. Only the occasional marina or private club interrupts public access, and the towns provide public restrooms and changing rooms every half-mile or so. Like much of southern Europe, these are topless (or top-optional) beaches and people of both genders—regardless of age or physical fitness—seem to welcome the chance to wear as little as possible. The Paseo Maritimo roadway separates the strand from the hotels and shops, and the entire length has a wide promenade for strolling or jogging the length of the high-rise world.

Hokey amusements line the beach—from merry-go-rounds to a full-blown fake medieval castle. The **Fuengirola Zoo** (kids) (Camilo José Cela 8–10; ☎ 952-666-301; www.zoofuengirola.com; 14€ adults, 10€ seniors and children 3–9; daily 10am–sunset [July–Aug until midnight]) is the winner of the lot. Dispensing with cages and bars, this modern zoo groups animals by habitat within its tropical forest and protects them from visitors with glass walls. Some of the glamorous headline animals are here (gorillas, leopards, tigers, orangutans) but the most charming may be the Lesser Malay Mousedeer, a ruminant the size of a rabbit.

Nightlife on High-Rise Costa del Sol

The village of Benalmádena Pueblo, about 2.4km (1½ miles) from the beach, is the center of the dance scene for young English-speaking tourists. Five discos surround **Plaza Solymar** (a.k.a. The 24-Hour Square) in the village center on the N340. Thanks to recent police crackdowns, the nickname is no longer accurate. The bars open about 8pm, dancing starts around 11, and it all closes up between 2am and 3am. The wildest dance scene is at **Silver** (no phone), which doesn't open until 11pm, while the friendliest drinking scene is on the terrace of the **Dutch Inn** (no phone), which extends above the McDonald's.

MARBELLA

Marbella is a universe removed from the high-rise holiday scene. In the late 1940s and 1950s, the Prince of Liechtenstein established the Marbella Club as a winter beach getaway for his jet-set friends, and legendary luxury resort Los Monteros soon followed. In the 1980s, Puente Romano eclipsed them both, and numerous Arabian Gulf millionaires began building their own compounds. Twice daily the amplified bells of the mosque that King Fahd of Saudi Arabia built next to the yacht harbor in Puerto Banús (about 6.4km/4 miles west of the town center) call the faithful to prayer. While Marbella is clearly gilded around the edges, it retains a vibrant old center just a few blocks from the beach. From the wide stone promenade along the beach, you simply climb a set of marble stairs past a sequence of Salvador Dalí bronze statues, and cross the Alameda, a leafy park with tiled benches. Suddenly you're in a tangle of medieval streets and whitewashed houses hung with pots of geraniums. Should you succumb to the urge to rent a Rolls-Royce while you're here, you can find the relevant information (and everything else) at the **Oficina de Turismo** (Glorieta de la Fontanilla; ☎ 952-771-442; Mon–Fri 10am–6pm, Sat–Sun 10am–3pm). Because shopping is good primarily for standard international labels and Marbella's best nightlife is by invitation only to private parties, we've eliminated those sections of the text.

Accommodations in Marbella

Some of Marbella's most famous accommodations often cost more per night than most readers of this book plan to spend for a week. But if you book carefully, there's no need to spend $1,000 a night to bask in its reflected glamour.

If beachfront location is your primary goal, you can lease a small flat by the night at **Aparthotel Puerto Azul** (entrances on Paseo Marítimo and Camila José Cela 3; ☎ 952-765-681; www.puertoazul.net; AE, DC, MC, V), across the promenade from Playa de la Fontanilla and next to lush Parque de la Constitución. The immediate neighborhood is filled with small ethnic restaurants and it's a short stroll to the marble stairway into the old town. The price ranges here are wide, but have more to do with the directness of the view than the accommodations. Studios with excellent angled views from their balconies run from 70€ to 90€, one-bedroom apartments for two or three people are 80€ to 150€, and one bedroom apartments with full beach view can run anywhere from 120€ to 190€. Kitchens are very basic and the studio units are so small that the round dining table doubles as a nightstand. But when you're not asleep or at the beach you'll spend all your time on the balcony (furnished with a plastic table and a couple of chairs) anyway.

€   If you prefer charm to ocean views, opt for **Hostal Enriqueta** ✭✭ (de los Caballeros 18; ☎ 952-827-552; cash only), in the old city about a 5-minute stroll to the beach. Juan García Parra and his wife, Enriqueta Gonzalez Claros, have operated the Enriqueta for about 40 years, but you'll probably be greeted by their daughter, María del Mar. Many of the 20 rooms are grouped around an enchanting flower-filled courtyard. Alas, the courtyard is for the family's use only. Rooms 208 (a triple) and 202 (a double) have balconies where guests look out on the courtyard while they catch the sun. Stairs are steep and narrow and there is no elevator, but there are four rooms at ground level. Every room has a ceiling fan and María says guests rarely turn on the air-conditioner because "these old houses stay very cool." Rooms here go for 50€ to 60€ double, 70€ to 80€ triple.

Dining in Marbella

€€–€€€   Many of the restaurants set in the sea wall at Playa La Fontanilla are only open for lunch, but **Basilio Bar Restaurante** ✭ (Playa La Fontanilla 4; ☎ 952-777-504; MC, V) serves from noon to midnight daily. Like most eateries in Marbella, the specialties are local seafood, including delicious starters of tiny squid (*puntillitas* for 7€) and slabs of swordfish (11€) or whole sea bass (14€) grilled on a wood fire built right on the beach. Tourist-area paella is often disappointing, but Basilio's mixed paella (small local shellfish with a few pieces of sausage and chicken) brims with authenticity for only 16€.

€€–€€€€   Away from the beach, restaurants ring the orange-scented Plaza de los Naranjos in the old city, although many rely on indifferent paella as their main offering. **Restaurante Mena** (Pl de los Naranjos 10; ☎ 952-771-597; 11:30am–11pm; MC, V) attracts more dapper and knowledgeable Marbella vacationers who savor good Spanish wine on the patio along with large plates of monkfish with shellfish (22€); whole dorado roasted in a salt crust (22€); or clams sautéed with onion, garlic, and a little fresh tomato (15€). Some dishes go as low as 10€, if you're watching your budget.

Marbella's One Noteworthy Attraction

The Costa del Sol was a haven for artists before it became a destination for tourists. When you need a break from the beach, check out the extensive collection of works on paper by the likes of Picasso and Miró at the **Museo del Grabado Español Contemporáneo** (Hospital Bazán; ☎ 952-765-741; www.museodel grabado.com; 3€; 10am–2pm and 6–8:30pm), housed in the spacious rooms of a former hospital.

ESTEPONA ✯

Estepona is our favorite place on the Costa del Sol because it is more town than resort. The restaurateurs grumble that, except at the peak of high season (the first 2 weeks of Aug), it lacks the crowds of the rest of the coast. What's bad for them is good for the rest of us. The air here smells of the sea, and on a cool night, a thin salty fog settles on the old town. What's more, Estepona is still an active fishing port—see the local catch at the Mercado Abastos on Plaza Cañada. You'll even get a history lesson, as you look down into the archaeological excavation of 10th-century Arabic ruins beneath the plaza.

Accommodations in Estepona

€   It's hard to beat the combination of charm and price at **Hostal El Pilar** ✯ (Pl de los Flores 10; ☎ 952-800-018; www.hostalelpilar.es; MC, V) in the center of the old town. The 1750 home became a hotel in 1995. All of the 12 double rooms (36€–50€), two quadruples (65€–90€), and three singles (22€–28€) have solid wood furniture and new bathrooms, albeit with smallish corner showers. Although there is no air-conditioning, terrazzo floors and crisp white walls make the rooms feel cool. Unlike many small lodgings, El Pilar has a spacious lobby with comfortable chairs.

€–€€   Stand on the long beach just across the street and **Hotel Buenavista** (Paseo Marítimo 180; ☎ 952-800-137; www.buenavistaestepona.com) looks a little like an ocean liner—a popular architectural style in the 1950s when this hotel claimed the best spot on the beachfront boulevard. Although the rooms have new baths and furniture and are painted every year, there's no getting around their compact size. Spacious balconies help expand the living space and the prices aren't too painful at 50€ to 70€ for a double, including tax. Twenty of the 38 rooms have a sea view where you can take a sunrise photo that you can brag about when you get home. Ask for one when you reserve, but they're especially tight in July and August when many Spanish families return to the same room every year.

€€   Estepona is easily the most G-rated town on Costa del Sol, and **Hotel Altamarina** 👶 (Avda San Lorenzo 32; ☎ 952-806-155; www.hotelaltamarina. com; MC, V) cultivates a family clientele. Many rooms in this fully refurbished 1950s hotel sleep three or four, charging between 75€ and 129€ (doubles are 61€–84€). The furniture is solid enough to hold up to toddlers, though the larger rooms lack balconies. Rates include a buffet breakfast, which is laid out in a sunny cafe-restaurant at ground level, where you can also elect to take other meals.

Dining in Estepona

€€–€€€   Estepona is a fishing town and a good place to get a taste of the local catch is at **Bar Simon** ✯✯ (Avda San Lorenzo 40; ☎ 952-791-455; Mon–Sat noon–4pm and 8–11pm; MC, V), where fresh fish are displayed on crushed ice. The specialties of the house are grilled fish and grilled or steamed shellfish (9€–18€), especially the smooth, tiny clams known as *almejas Esteponas,* and razor clams, or *navajas*). Also recommendable: the grilled bass, mackerel, red mullet, sardines, and sea bream. The outdoor patio is a lively gathering spot for locals, who drop by to snack on a few clams or mussels with a pint of beer.

€€–€€€   If you want to try the local specialty fisherman's rice stew—a dish that's halfway between a wet paella and a dry bouillabaisse—go to **La Rada** (Avda España, Edificio Neptuno; ☎ 952-791-036; Tues–Sun 1–4pm and 8pm–midnight; MC, V) for the *arroz caldosa*, priced at 13€ per person. Other dishes range in price from 7€ to 18€. The front bar might look unpromising, but there's a large, semi-formal dining room in the back with pink tablecloths and comfortable seating. Most people opt to dine outside on the patio just across the wide street from Estepona's central beach.

€€–€€€   The decor at **Meson Cordobés** (Pl de las Flores 15; ☎ 952-800-737; Tues–Sun 10am–4:30pm and 7pm–midnight; MC, V) is full of character—straight-backed wooden chairs, old iron paella pans and stew kettles hanging on the walls—but in nice weather, everyone wants to dine outside on the plaza next to a gurgling fountain. Again, the house specialties are grilled and fried small fish (7€–16€) landed at the Estepona beach. But the kitchen also does a good job with grilled pork (12€) and beef sirloin steaks (16€), which are best accompanied by the sturdy Rioja house wine.

€€–€€€€   If you want a great view with your steak, stroll eastward along the promenade to **Punta Sur** ✪ (Edificio Jacaranda, bajo playa; ☎ 952-807-854; Tues–Sun 1–4pm and 7:30–11:30pm; AE, MC, V), nearly a mile from central Estepona. Brothers Fabian and Miguel Molinero from Argentina serve grilled local fish (most at 15€–16€), but more customers stream in for their deeply flavorful and ultra-tender Argentine beef (16€–24€). We like to arrive in time to watch the sunset over the long expanse of beach while dining on small thick-crust pizzas (7€–8.20€) with a glass of wine.

RONDA ✪✪

In 2,000 years, no one has been able to improve on Pliny the Elder's epithet for Ronda: "the glorious." The city sits high on a limestone cliff dramatically divided by the gorge *(El Tajo)* cut by the Río Guadalevin. If you're prone to vertigo, Ronda's high aerie could feel as if the city were built on a spinning plate atop a circus clown's pole. Located at the eastern edge of the mountain ridges that separate the Costa del Sol from the Cádiz plain, Ronda is the gateway to the *serrania*—the serrated ridges that harbored mountain bandits and political rebels from the age of Caesar through the days of Franco.

GETTING TO & AROUND RONDA

You can drive to Ronda on the A378 from the Costa del Sol, but **Portillo** (☎ 902-143-144) also provides good bus service to the center of town from Costa del Sol, Málaga, and Cádiz. **RENFE** (avenida Andalucía, ☎ 952-871-662) trains also service the city, though connections are limited and the station is a 5€ to 7€ cab ride from the historic city.

The twisting streets of the Ronda's old town and most of the historic sites and monuments sit on one side of the gorge. The "new" town, or *Mercandillo,* is on the other, with the lion's share of restaurants and shops on streets laid out on a grid. Three bridges connect past and present: the low Puente Arabe in the valley west of the gorge; the Puente Viejo (built 1616) at the west entrance to the gorge;

and the main auto bridge, the Puente Nuevo, built in 1793 at the top of the gorge, 400 feet above the river. The city map provided at the **Oficina Municipal de Turismo** (Paseo de Blas Infante; ☎ 952-187-119; www.turismoderonda.es; Mon–Fri 10am–7:15pm, Sat–Sun 10:15am–2pm and 3:30–6:30pm) will help you find your way.

ACCOMMODATIONS, BOTH STANDARD & NOT

Lodging in Ronda usually divides between places with a view (from your room or from a shared terrace) and those without (usually less expensive).

€ Nowhere near the gorge, despite its name, **Hotel El Tajo** (Cruz Verde 7; ☎ 952-874-040; www.hoteleltajo.com; 45€–60€, tax included; AE, MC, V) does have marble floors and Mudéjar-style decor in the lobby to give it an air of elegance. The rooms, however, are small, in-room TVs even smaller, and the traditional furniture is well worn. Pluses are the extremely friendly staff, reasonably priced on-site parking (10€/night) and a large lobby with TV and comfortable sitting areas. Save your room for sleeping and spend your spare time here.

€€ Just a block from the Puente Nuevo, you'll find views galore from the rooftop patio at **Hotel Ronda** ✪✪ (Ruedo Doña Elvira 12; ☎ 952-872-232; www.hotelronda.net; 65€–90€, tax included). There are wonderfully nostalgic family photos in the lobby of this private home now converted to a five-room hotel, and with a little prodding the now senior Señora Lara Nieves will point out herself as a young girl in the pictures. Spacious Room 5, which has a double bed, used to be the stable, while slightly smaller twin-bedded Room 3 was where they kept the birds. From the rooftop, you'll see Ronda's "new town" as well as a distant vista of the Sierra Nieves mountain range. "Guests like to come up here with a bottle of wine in the evening," she says.

€€ The gorge is at your window in 20 of the 30 rooms at **Hotel Restaurante Don Miguel** (Pl de España 4 and 5; ☎ 952-877-722; www.dmiguel.com; AE, DC, MC, V), which perches on the edge of El Tajo next to the bridge. The low-key decor employs a limited palette of beige and brown, and the traditional solid-wood Spanish furniture is essentially unremarkable. But in Ronda, views are everything, and you get astounding ones here at just 85€ to 100€ a night with breakfast. Room 208 is exceptionally large and has a private balcony.

€€ Outdoor restaurant tables almost obscure the entrance to **Hotel Restaurante Don Javier** (José Aparicio 3; ☎ 952-872-020; www.hoteldonjavier. com; AE, DC, MC, V), which has just a dozen rooms in the narrow building sandwiched between Ronda's main street and the narrow pedestrian calle José Aparicio. One of the best is spacious Room 122, decorated in a deep rose the color of a matador's vest. Perfectly functional antique telephones give a touch of whimsy to the Victorian decor. And rooms are slightly less expensive than at Don Miguel (see above) at 70€ to 85€ with breakfast.

€€ A timeless elegance pervades **Hotel San Gabriel** ✪✪ (Marqués de Moctezuma 19; ☎ 952-190-392; www.hotelsangabriel.com; AE, MC, V), a private

Ronda

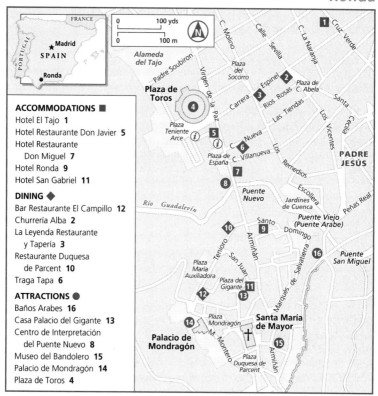

ACCOMMODATIONS ■
Hotel El Tajo **1**
Hotel Restaurante Don Javier **5**
Hotel Restaurante
  Don Miguel **7**
Hotel Ronda **9**
Hotel San Gabriel **11**

DINING ◆
Bar Restaurante El Campillo **12**
Churrería Alba **2**
La Leyenda Restaurante
  y Tapería **3**
Restaurante Duquesa
  de Parcent **10**
Traga Tapa **6**

ATTRACTIONS ●
Baños Arabes **16**
Casa Palacio del Gigante **13**
Centro de Interpretación
  del Puente Nuevo **8**
Museo del Bandolero **15**
Palacio de Mondragón **14**
Plaza de Toros **4**

enclave of 21 rooms around several patios on a side street in the old city. Hushed and romantic, the hotel has a library of fine books as well as a tiny movie theater furnished with rescued theater chairs and a DVD projection screen. It's worth splurging the 150€ to 165€ for suite *Luna de Miel* (Honeymoon), with its proper Victorian salon as a living room and its sumptuous bedroom behind velvet curtains. Room 1 on the lower level, a cozier love nest, looks out on a small patio and costs just 82€ to 92€ (as do the other doubles in the hotel). Free parking a few blocks away next to the police station is a bonus.

DINING FOR ALL TASTES
Casual restaurants do a bang-up business with the crowds day-tripping from Costa del Sol, but Ronda also has one of Spain's top restaurants and a number of chefs committed to innovative cuisine at affordable prices.

€ If your hotel doesn't serve breakfast, **Churrería Alba** (Espinel 44; no phone; daily 8am–3pm; cash only) is a good choice for coffee or hot chocolate with churros (3€). You can be served at a table upstairs, but stand at the bar instead to watch the cook fry the dough.

€€   If you're a late riser, try **Bar Restaurante El Campillo** ✫ (Pl María Auxilladora 1; ☎ 952-878-652; Mon–Sat 10am–6:30pm, food until 4pm only; MC, V), on a quiet plaza where a classical guitarist often performs and sells CDs. By afternoon, the sun floods the cafe tables and people spend as much time catching the rays as sampling such local specialties as *patatas mondragón,* a baked dish of potatoes, ham, prawns, raisins, pine nuts, onion, and sweet red peppers (12€).

€–€€€   Chef Benito Gómez of Restaurante Tragabuches is one of Spain's most celebrated chefs and the tasting menu at Tragabuches costs 85€. Fortunately, Gómez is also a leader in redefining tapas, and **Traga Tapa** ✫✫ (Nueva 4; ☎ 952-877-209; open noon–4pm and 8pm–midnight; MC, V), with its gleaming modern decor and minimalist design, is the casual spot to try his creations. The single spear of grilled asparagus (1.65€) topped with grated cheese and accompanied by a square of quince paste is delicious, if a little precious. Most tapas come in more generous portions, including cubed grilled chicken immersed in a vinaigrette (1.50€). Traga Tapa's *raciones*—good for a dinner portion or to share—include plates of sautéed clams (9.50€) or roast piglet (11€). **La Leyenda Restaurante y Tapería** (Los Remedios 7; ☎ 952-877-894; 1–4pm and 8pm–midnight; cash only) takes a cue from Traga Tapa by offering more inventive bar food. But Leyenda's strength remains its inexpensive (12€) three-course menu offered all day long except on Friday and Saturday.

€€–€€€€   You expect to pay a premium for a restaurant with a great view, but **Restaurante Duquesa de Parcent** ✫ (Tenorio 12; ☎ 952-871-965; 11am–11pm; MC, V) surprises with a great value 13€ three-course menu all day. You probably won't be handed that menu if you arrive for dinner, but ask and wait staff will bring it. Choices run the likes of gazpacho or cream of vegetable soup as a starter, roast chicken or hake with clams and shrimp as main courses (most mains are 9€–22€). The dining room is marvelously formal, with fine crystal and linens, and features attentive, professional service. Some tables have views of the gorge and sunset behind the mountains. The theater of watching the staff open and debone a whole sea bass baked in salt is worth the 18€ price.

WHY YOU'RE HERE: THE TOP SIGHTS & ATTRACTIONS

The landscape is Ronda's top attraction. Most visitors are happy just circling the city through the terraced gardens along the lip of the gorge, pausing to peer down into its depths, and then looking out toward the surrounding mountains. But don't ignore Ronda's winding streets and hidden plazas. Start at the **Centro de Interpretación del Puente Nuevo** 🧒 (Pl de España; ☎ 649-965-338; 2€ adults, 1€ seniors and students, free for children 13 and under; Mon–Fri 10am–7pm, Sat 10am–1:45pm and 3–6pm, Sun 10am–3pm) for an overview of the geography of Ronda's high escarpment and the engineering achievements of the so-called "new bridge." The bridge was authorized in 1542, but it took another 2 centuries for the technology to advance enough to finish it in 1739. The center is actually inside the bridge, where windows provide dazzling views and the small chambers echo with the slightest noise—which can become intense when several children are squealing with excitement about feeling suspended over the gorge.

Stand & Deliver

The mountains leading southwest from Ronda to the Straits of Gibraltar haven't always been a magnet for tourists. From Roman times into the late 19th century, this was bandit country where brigands robbed travelers at will. By the late 19th century, many of these larger-than-life characters acquired the status and colorful names of folk heroes—Pasos Largos (Longshanks), Cabeza Torcida (Twisted Head), and the horse thief and stickup artist, El Tempranillo (A Little Early). Using old weapons, yellowed newspaper clippings, garish comic books, and marvelously hokey dioramas, the **Museo del Bandolero** kids (Arminar 65; ☎ 952-877-785; 3€ adults, 2€ students; 10am–8pm) takes the subject of banditry very seriously, explaining the desperate economic circumstances that led men to crime, and praising the Guardia Civil, which was created in 1844 to clean up the mountains. Even apart from the educational content, small children (boys in particular) seem to get quite a kick out of the guns, costumes, and der-ring-do.

Follow the terraced gardens on the Mercandillo side of the gorge to cross the Puente Viejo and walk through the 1742 arch to enter the old city. A set of steps on your left descend to the **Baños Arabes** (Barrio de Padre Jesús; ☎ 656-950-937; 3€ adults, 1.50€ seniors and students, free Sun; Mon–Fri 10am–6pm, Sat 1–1:45pm and 3–6pm, Sun 10am–3pm). Recently restored as a museum only (no bathing—sorry), the 13th-century baths are some of Andalusia's best preserved, with their brick columns, horseshoe arches, and barrel vaults with star-shaped skylights.

You'll find more evidence of Moorish Ronda at **Casa Palacio del Gigante** (Pl del Gigante; ☎ 678-631-445; 2€ adults, 1€ seniors and students), a small in-city Nasrid palace built in the 13th through 15th centuries. The visit to this inter-pretive center includes a short film that begins with the geological forces that created Ronda and its gorge. Exhibits move swiftly through various ages of human habitation, concentrating on the 10th- and 11th-century urban explosion that shaped today's city. The most interesting deal with the restoration of the house, which has many of the same decorative features as Granada's Alhambra, but on a much smaller scale.

The exhibitions on history, ethnography, and environment at **Palacio de Mondragón** ✪ (3€ adults, 1.50€ seniors and students; Mon–Fri 10am–7pm, Sat 10am–1:45pm and 3–6pm) are well-intentioned but a little too pedagogical. No matter—the palace itself (which is also Ronda's city hall) says everything you need to know. The tiled walls, carved ceilings, fountains, and gardens create a picture-perfect setting where brides and grooms often pose for their wedding photos.

Aficionados of the *corrida* rank Ronda's **Plaza de Toros** ✪ (Virgen de la Paz 15; ☎ 952-871-539; www.rmcr.org; 6€ adults, 5€ college students, 4€ children 15 and under; Nov–Feb 10am–6pm, Mar and Oct 10am–7pm, Apr–Sept 10am–8pm) as one of the most important rings in the history of bullfighting. It was home base for legendary matador Pedro Romero, who killed more than 5,000 bulls over 6 decades before he died of natural causes in 1839. His austere and formal style is the basis of the Goyaesque bullfight, named for the 18th-century formal bull-fights depicted in Goya's paintings and revived as a tradition in Ronda in 1954. Once inside, you can stand in the arena and walk along the catwalks above the pens where bulls and horses are kept. The **Museo Taurino** is packed with photographs and memorabilia that evoke, as one display calls it, "the oscillation between luck and death" in the life of a matador.

ATTENTION, SHOPPERS!

You can buy the same souvenir bullfight posters at tourist shops throughout Spain. But the **gift shop at Ronda's Plaza de Toros** sells copies of the artist-designed posters for the city's yearly Goyaesque corridas. These works of art capture the beauty of the ring, the matador's sense of anticipation, or even the still moment as the matador and bull face each other. They're a steal at 3€ to 5€.

Tourist shops abound in Ronda. For something different, check out the bowls, pitchers, platters, and salad serving sets carved of local olive wood at **Los Arcos** (Armiñan 8-A; ☎ 952-874-623). In one of the vanishing traditions of southern Spain, nuns at the **Convento de Carmelitas Descalzas** (Pl Merced; 10:15am–1:15pm and 4:45–6:45pm) sell their pastries through a small revolving door in the wall (called a *retorno*) where you speak with, but never see, the cloistered sisters. Buttery *mantecadas* sell by the quarter-kilo (2.50€) and half-kilo (5€).

GET OUT OF TOWN

Parque de Grazalema ✪

It would take months to visit all the villages that seem to drift like snow on the rugged hills of the Sierra de Grazalema range west of Ronda. The highest ridges of the mountains are such critical habitats for wildlife and rare plants that they are protected under the Parque Natural Sierra de Grazalema. Of the villages in and around the park, Grazalema is especially well-equipped for visitors who want to survey the mountain scenery, hike, or simply savor a slower way of life. It is feasible to drive to Grazalema on A372 (less than a half-hour), and Portillo buses (☎ 902-143-144) run a couple of times a day from Ronda's Plaza de Toros to Plaza de España in Grazalema.

Most towns of the sierra have Roman origins, but Grazalema was founded in the late 8th century A.D. by Berbers from Saddina, an apparently peaceful lot who chose a green valley over an arid peak and never fortified their town. It lies deep in a pocket between soaring hills, so Grazalema comes as a surprise when you round a turn and first spot it settled in the verdant valley of the Río Guadalete. The small **Oficina Municipal de Turismo** (Pl de España 11; ☎ 956-132-073; 10am–2pm and 4–8pm) has hiking trail maps and serves as a clearinghouse for guide services. Its shop sells scarves, shawls, and blankets woven from local lambs' wool in rich shades of brown and beige.

ACCOMMODATION & DINING

To stock your apartment kitchen, **Panadería Todo Sierra** (Pl Andalucía 23; ☎ 956-132-415; 9am–8:30pm) has aged mountain cheeses (stupendous when drizzled with the local wildflower honey), fresh bread and pastries, local meats and sausages, olive oil, and sherry.

€–€€   Operated by Cadiz provincial tourism, **Villas Turísticas de Grazalema** ⭐⭐ 🧒 (Carretera Olivar; ☎ 956-132-213; www.tugasa.es; MV, V) is one-stop shopping for lodging. The complex sits about .8km (½ mile) north of the village center and includes a rural hotel with 24 rooms, a spacious dining room, and 38 apartments. All the hotel rooms and most of the apartments look out on pretty little Grazalema center. The hotel rooms are 59€ (including breakfast) and feature the mountain-standard of heavy rustic furniture, as well as a small refrigerator. The villas have either one or two bedrooms (68€ or 118€, respectively), a full kitchen, and a wood-burning fireplace. The views from rooms 29 through 38 are unobscured by other buildings. If you're offered one of the few duplex buildings, ask for the upper-level unit to get the best views (nos. 9–12 and 14).

€–€€   The restaurant at the **Villas Turísticas** (daily 9–11am, 1–4pm, and 9–10:30pm) isn't the only food in town, though it may be the only full-fledged restaurant, and the only spot with a three-course 16€ daily menu featuring roast boar and wild mushrooms (if you just want a main course expect to pay 7€–17€). Village center bars also do a fine job with simple country fare. A typical dish of pork chop, fried egg, and potatoes only runs 4.50€ at **Bar Zulema** (Plaza Andalucía; ☎ 956-132-402; 1–4pm and 8–11pm; MC, V), and most entrees are in the 3€ to 9€ range.

ACTIVE GRAZALEMA

A moderate hiking trail (about 20 min. each way) leaves from behind Camping Tajo Rodillo just west of town and climbs gradually to the 3,600-foot peak of Llano del Endrinal for outstanding views. Experienced outfitter **Horizon Grazalema** (Corrales Terceros 29; ☎ 956-132-363; www.horizonaventura.com) operates a shop for outdoor gear and offers all kinds of outings in the park, from hikes to kayaking, caving to rock climbing (13€–70€).

JEREZ DE LA FRONTERA ⭐

Like Kentucky with its thoroughbreds and its bourbon, Jerez is defined by its Andalusian horses and its sherry. Just take a walk down pedestrian calle Larga and through Plaza Arenal and you'll see what we mean. Fashionable young women all wear knee-high black boots with tight pants as a nod to the city's equestrian tradition. And the umbrellas on the cafe tables are emblazoned with the logos of Tío Pepe, Don Patricio, or El Gallo instead of the Cruzcampo beer. The soundtrack, naturally enough, is flamenco's quick-paced *bulería*.

GETTING TO & AROUND JEREZ DE LA FRONTERA

The most frequent **bus service** to Jerez from Seville is via **Linesur** (☎ 954-988-222; www.linesur.com), and **RENFE** (www.renfe.es) runs several trains between the two cities.

The Jerez **airport,** located 4.8km (3 miles) out of town, is also a viable option, with regular flights from Madrid, Barcelona, and London. Get into town on the M50 or M51 bus (.85€); or use the same buses to go to and from Cádiz.

With nearly 200,000 inhabitants, the city sprawls across an open plain, but the old quarters are compact and walkable. The most interesting shopping and dining radiates from pedestrian calle Larga, or is found northwest of Plaza Arenal in the twisting, medieval streets of barrio Santiago. Most of the larger sherry houses have facilities near the Alcázar and cathedral. The **Oficina de Turismo** (Alameda Cristina, Edificio Los Claustros; ☎ 956-338-874; Mon–Fri 9am–3pm and 4:30–6:30pm, Sat–Sun 9:30am–2:30pm) provides maps.

ACCOMMODATIONS, BOTH STANDARD & NOT

Luxury hotels catering to the sherry and horse-breeding trades are located on the outskirts of the city. Bargain hunters will find lodgings with the right mix of price and convenience in the older downtown neighborhoods.

€–€€   Ángel de la Orden grew up behind the reception desk of **El Coloso** ✪ 🅺🅸🅳🆂 (Pedro Alonso 13; ☎ 956-34-90 08; www.elcolosohotel.com; MC, V), the hostelry a few blocks east of Plaza Arenal that his family has owned for 40 years, and he is both a gracious host and a knowledgeable guy (take his advice on where to dine and shop; he has yet to steer us wrong). The property has 25 hotel rooms for 55€ to 95€, tax included, all of them cool and restful with white stucco walls and white tile floors. But the real prizes are the four apartments, each of which costs two people just 65€ per night, 350€ for a week. They have well-equipped kitchens, including washing machines. The ground level units (rooms 21 and 22) are the best bet, since the patio right outside the door extends the living space. Room 22 has a small sitting area with table and sofa bed, while Room 21 is "more like a hotel room with a kitchen," as de la Orden puts it.

€   It's hard to find a decent hotel at a lower price (35€ with private bath, 30€ with shared bath, tax included!) than **Hostal Las Palomas** (Higueras 17; ☎ 956-343-773; www.hostal-las-palomas.com; MC, V), which the staff claims is the oldest hotel building in Jerez. Certainly the spectacular 19th-century tiles in the reception area and stairwells support the claim, as does, unfortunately, the lack of elevator or air-conditioning. Still, it's a friendly place to stay and meticulously well maintained. Rooms are small, simple, and very white—from the whitewashed walls to the well-bleached cotton bedspreads. More than half have private bathrooms with small shower stalls. The shared rooftop terrace is a great spot for cooling off in the evening with a glass of chilled wine (BYOB).

€€   Just a two-minute walk east from the Gallo Azul statue at the foot of calle Larga, **Hotel Doña Blanca** ✪ (Bodegas 11; ☎ 956-34-87-61; www.hoteldona blanca.com; AE, DC, MC, V) sits back from the street on its own little cul-de-sac. Decor is very traditional, with solid wood furniture and coordinating floral bedspreads and draperies, but the immaculate rooms, which go for 77€ a night, are large—it was built in 1992. Many rooms have a small couch along with comfortable armchairs, and all have minibars. Comfort, convenience, and modest prices make it a good buy.

€€   We've never felt safer than at **Hotel Bellas Artes** ✪✪ (Plaza del Arroyo 45; ☎ 956-348-430; www.hotelbellasartes.com; AE, MC, V), which adjoins the regional police headquarters. An actual refurbished palace, it's close to the cathedral—you can study the architecture from the hot tub on the shared rooftop terrace. Don't be put off by the worn furnishings in the lobby. The high-ceilinged guest rooms with exposed beams and soft pastel decor are downright romantic

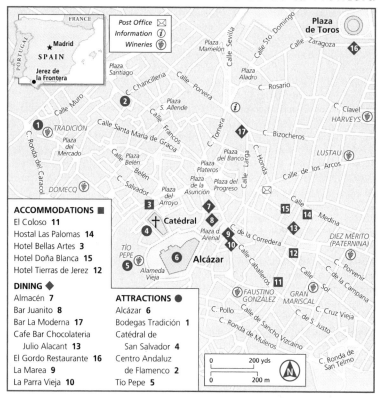

FRANCE

SPAIN

★ Madrid

Jerez de
la Frontera

PORTUGAL

Plaza
de Toros

Plaza
Mamelón

Calle Sevilla

Calle Sto. Domingo

Calle Zaragoza

16

Plaza
Santiago

Plaza
Aladro

C. Rosario

C. Chancilleria

Calle Porvera

Calle Muro

Plaza
S. Allende

2

Calle Santa Maria de Gracia

Calle Francos

C. Tornera

ⓘ

C. Clavel

HARVEYS 🍷

17

C. Bizocheros

TRADICIÓN

1

Plaza
del
Mercado

C. Ronda del Caracol

Calle Plaza
Belén

Belén

C. Salvador

Plaza
del
Arroyo

Plaza
del Banco

Calle Larga

C. Honda

LUSTAU 🍷

Calle de los Arcos

DOMECQ 🍷

Plaza
Plateros

Plaza
de la
Asunción

Plaza del
Progreso

✉

Plaza
del
Arroyo

Catédral ✝

3

4

7

8

Plaza d.
Arenal

9

10

C. de la Corredera

Calle

15

14

Medina

13

DIEZ MÉRITO
(PATERNINA)

🍷

TÍO
PEPE

5

Alameda
Vieja

6 Alcázar

Calle Caballeros

12

C. de Porvenir

C. de la Campana

Calle Sol

11

FAUSTINO
GONZÁLEZ

🍷

GRAN
MARISCAL

C. Cruz Vieja

C. Pollo

Calle de Sancho Vizcaino

C. de S. Justo

C. Ronda de Muleros

C. Ronda de
San Telmo

0   200 yds

0   200 m

ACCOMMODATIONS ■
El Coloso **11**
Hostal Las Palomas **14**
Hotel Bellas Artes **3**
Hotel Doña Blanca **15**
Hotel Tierras de Jerez **12**

DINING ◆
Almacén **7**
Bar Juanito **8**
Bar La Moderna **17**
Cafe Bar Chocolateria
   Julio Alacant **13**
El Gordo Restaurante **16**
La Marea **9**
La Parra Vieja **10**

ATTRACTIONS ●
Alcázar **6**
Bodegas Tradición **1**
Catédral de
   San Salvador **4**
Centro Andaluz
   de Flamenco **2**
Tío Pepe **5**

and a reasonable buy at 90€, tax and breakfast included. (Wedding parties often book all 18 rooms.) Room 6 has a small private balcony and stunning cathedral view.

€€   All the rooms at Bellas Artes are contemporary and warm, but you should definitely ask for one of the rooms in the new addition if you book at **Hotel Tierras de Jerez** (Corredera 58; ☎ 956-346-400; tierrasdejerez@intergrouphoteles. com; AE, DC, MC, V). The hotel recently expanded into an adjacent building, swelling from 30 to 50 rooms. All doubles are the same price, 95€ a night, but the new rooms are 50% larger, far more contemporary in their decor, and have hardwood floors. Best choices are rooms 206, 207, and 208, which have private patios.

DINING FOR ALL TASTES
Cooking in Jerez tends to emphasize the local products. The Bay of Cádiz is only a few miles away, so shellfish often tops the menu. If you order meat, don't be surprised if it arrives in some form of sherry-based sauce.

€   Jerezanos line up to buy churros to go (1.80€ for about a half-pound wrapped in a paper cone) at **Cafe Bar Chocolateria Julio Alacant** (Doña Blanca 24; ☎ 616-145-055; 8am–1:30pm and 5–9:30pm, closed Sat afternoon and Sun; cash only), but it's better to sit at a table in the plaza or stand at the bar so that you can dunk the long, thin churros into thick hot chocolate (2€), served in a small glass.

€–€€   Local people will tell you that they never visit the extremely popular **Bar Juanito** ★★ (Pescadería Viejo 8-10; ☎ 956-334-838; 1–4:30pm and 9–11:30pm; MC, V) because it's too expensive, but every time we've visited, everyone is speaking Andalusian Spanish at the outside patio tables, inside bar, and dining room. True, you pay a small premium for the quality of the food and the atmosphere of the old fish market, about 4.50€ to 7€ for most dishes, but it's worth a little extra to enjoy fresh tuna loin salad in sherry vinegar (1.80€), meatballs in oloroso sherry sauce (4.50€), or the dark and juicy sweetbreads *al Jerez* (4.50€).

€–€€   Half the people at **Bar La Moderna** (Larga 67; no phone; Mon–Sat 7am–11pm; cash only) were introduced to this Jerez institution by their grandfathers. It might have seemed "modern" many decades ago when Gonzalez Byass sponsored the tiled plaque out front, but the bar has aged gracefully, with fading sherry posters and grainy black-and-white bullfight photos covering the walls. There is a beer tap, but fino sherry is the beverage of choice with a 1.80€ tapa of *carne con tomate* (beef with grated fresh tomato). Same for a tapa of anchovies, foie gras, and roasted pepper (1.80€). La Moderna is closed on Sunday. "It's the day for God," says the bartender.

€–€€   While La Moderna is open to the street, **Almacén** (Latorre 8; ☎ 956-187-143; 8:30pm–1am; MC, V) hides its elaborate interior of concrete arches and Moorish-style filigree behind a plain exterior. Expect a youthful tapas scene with a good buzz and some of the most unusual small plates in Jerez, such as vegetable couscous drizzled with the prune-like sweet wine, Pedro Ximenez (6.50€).

€€–€€€€   Jerezanos crowd the bar at **La Marea** ★ (San Miguel 3; ☎ 956-320-923; 11:30am–4pm and 8:30–11:30pm; MC, V) to drink fino and share plates of shrimp, barnacles, and crab legs, so it's usually fairly easy to score a table outside on the narrow street or in the dining room. Most prices are by the kilogram based on the market price, expect to pay about 25€ for the meal. The best deal is grilled yellowfin tuna at 15€ per kilo.

€€–€€€   Tapas-style dining is not for everyone. An Irish acquaintance living in Spain told us that when her father comes to visit he doesn't want to share small plates of tapas with a crowd. He wants his own plate—preferably topped with a big piece of meat. Just off Plaza Arenal, **La Parra Vieja** (San Miguel 9; ☎ 956-335-390; 8am–11pm; AE, MC, V) would be his kind of place. The cooks throw the occasional fish on the grill (gilthead for 12€, cuttlefish for 9€), but the highlights are meats, like a thick slab of beef sirloin (15€) or a pork sirloin of Iberian black pig (10€). Start with artichokes in oloroso sauce with cured ham (7€) while you admire the 19th-century tiles covering the walls.

€€–€€€   Our choice for prettiest dining room is **El Gordo Restaurante** (Zaragoza 38; ☎ 956-169-080; Tues–Sat 1–4:30pm and 9–11pm, Sun 9–11pm; MC, V), about a block from the bullring. You can walk around the Plaza de Toros and study the tiles immortalizing noble and brave bulls before you head to dinner, but you won't find the usual bullfighting memorabilia at El Gordo. Instead, the tables are set with white tablecloths and blue napkins to accentuate the blue-and-white tiles on the walls. Owner Manuel García López is called "El Gordo" (a more affectionate version of "Fatso") and is known for his baked rice dishes, such as the *arrroz negro* (black rice) made with squid ink (12€). He's also famed for the quality of his Bay of Cádiz seafood, such as grilled sea bass or monkfish braised in tomato broth (16€).

WHY YOU'RE HERE: THE TOP SIGHTS & ATTRACTIONS

In many ways, Jerez is Andalusia in miniature, with just enough Moorish heritage to lend an air of exoticism; just enough religious architecture to remember the Reconquest and the power of the church; and a distinctive local culture of music, dance, food and drink.

Even Jerez's **Alcázar** ★ 🛝 (Alameda Vieja; ☎ 956-326-923; Alcázar only 3€ adults, 1.80€ students; with camera obscura 5.40€ adults, 4.20€ students; guided tours additional 3€ per person; May 1–Sept 15 Mon–Sat 10am–8pm and Sun 10am–3pm, Sept 16–Apr 30 Mon–Sat 10am–6pm and Sun 10am–3pm) is the region's most straightforward example of a Moorish palace-fortress. Built in the 12th century as a frontier country fort, it has all the essentials: an austere mosque, extensive blooming gardens, and the remains of Moorish baths. You can tour the complex in a half-hour, catching such highlights as the intact prayer niche in the mosque (which has been consecrated as a Catholic church since 1264) and the well-signed baths. (They're the first historic baths we've seen where you can view the boiler system and understand how the complex actually worked.) The gardens are extensive, though the courtyard gardens and some of the surrounding walls are off-limits until 2010 for restoration work.

Parts of the fortress are dedicated to "cultural" exhibits that have little to do with the Alcázar itself. But kids generally love the two ancient olive oil mills—all that remain from the 32 active mills of the 1700s, when sherry overtook olive oil as the city's dominant industry. The odd structure inside the fort is the Palacio Villavicencio, a rich family's home constructed between the late 1600s and 1927. A camera obscura in a tower room projects images of the city, but unless your kids have never seen such a device, it's hardly worth the extra fee.

The other weighty monument to the past is the nearby **Catédral de San Salvador** (Pl de la Encarnación; ☎ 956-348-482; free admission; Mon–Fri 11am–1pm), a pastiche of Gothic, baroque, and neoclassical styles built on the site of the main mosque. It's open limited hours, but worth peeking in to see the Zuburán portrait of the Virgin as a sleeping child. The cathedral turns lively during the fall harvest when the first sherry grapes are crushed on the stone stairs of the entrance.

But the city's identity is not tied exclusively to sherry. Jerez is one of the self-proclaimed birthplaces of flamenco and the **Centro Andaluz de Flamenco** (Plaza de San Juan 1; ☎ 856-814-132; www.centroandaluzdeflamenco.es; free admission; Mon–Fri 10am–2pm) holds the largest public archive of the art form. Books,

Ay, Caballero!

Horses have fascinated Spaniards since Stone Age artists painted images of steeds in the caves outside Ronda 20,000 years ago. The museum at the **Fundación Real Escuela Andaluza del Arte Ecuestre** ✪✪✪ (Av. Duque de Abrantes s/n; ☎ 956-318-015; www.realescuela.org) traces the evolving bond between man and beast, placing its emphasis on horsemanship skills and the breeding of what the English-speaking world calls the Andalusian horse, but which Spaniards call *Pura Raza Española,* or "pure Spanish race." The top bloodlines were first established at Carthusian monasteries in the late Middle Ages.

The Real Escuela, founded in 1973, trains horses and riders and operates a breeding farm. Performances of the exquisitely trained, so-called "dancing horses" (usually Tues and Thurs at noon; 18€–24€) are a great spectacle. But spend less and see more by touring the facility on non-performance days (10am–2pm; 10€ includes guided tour), when you can watch the training in the main arena from 11am to 1pm. Arrive at opening to have time to view a short video, visit the museum, and watch artisans make and restore traditional tack in the Saddlery before the workout starts. (If you have tickets to the Tues or Thurs show, you'll have to pay the additional admission to tour the grounds.)

Even during practice, most horses and riders are a polished team. But the last time we visited, we watched three trainers encourage a nervous horse to perform the signature chorus-line prances. Every few minutes, the trainers stopped to speak softly to the horse, rub his nose, and pat his flanks. It was a revealing glimpse at the hard work, patience, and persistence behind the dazzling artistry.

music scores, and videos are a great resource to scholars. Even if your interest is only casual, stop in to see the engravings and paintings on the walls around the former palace's central courtyard. Videos are screened every day in the auditorium and, each week, the music of a different artist provides the soundtrack to a visit. Staff can provide leads on occasional performances held in the *peñas,* or clubs of aficionados, as well as a listing of more formal *tablao* performances.

THE OTHER JEREZ DE LA FRONTERA

If you want to know Jerez, you must first learn sherry. "I was born in Jerez," says Lola Jekeler, a tour guide at **Tío Pepe** (Gonzalez Byass at Manuel María González 12; ☎ 956-357-046; www.bodegastiopepe.com; 10€, or 15€ with tapas served with tasting; tours in English 11:30am–5:30pm). "When we are born in the middle of the grapes, we don't drink milk as a child." She's joking—we think—but there's a grain of truth in the jest.

The word *sherry* is simply a corruption of *Xérès,* the Arabic name for Jerez, and for the last 400 years, the wine and the city have been inextricably linked.

Phoenicians, Romans, and Arabs all planted vineyards here, and Alfonso X continued the tradition when he conquered the area. The Tío Pepe tour includes a small vineyard of Palomino grapes (used in 95% of sherry production). Moist, moderating winds off the Atlantic combine with a dry climate and chalky hardpan soil to create the precise conditions for making an oxidized, high-alcohol wine with distinctive *terroir*.

Tío Pepe is the world's top selling sherry and the tour sometimes verges on a sales pitch. But it does provide a clear overview of what 23-year-old Manuel María González Ángel started when he left his bank job in 1835 to make wine. Visitors pass the grand bodega designed by Gustave Eiffel and González's tennis court. "It was the first in Spain," says Jekeler, "so Sr. González could play tennis with his English distributors." In 1844, González bought Arab stills to make brandy from year-old sherry, and in the same year named his best fino after his uncle: Tío Pepe. The now-classic logo of the bottle with hat, jacket, and guitar was designed in the 1930s. Tío Pepe may sell in 115 countries on 6 continents, but Jerezanos are the most avid consumers. "We drink dry fino with all the tapas," says Jekeler, "with ham, cheese, fish. We even drink fino with lunch, always cold from the refrigerator."

The fifth generation of the González clan still works at González-Byass, but there are other, more intimate sherry houses in Jerez. To get closer to the modern sherry aristocracy, reserve a tour at **Bodegas Tradición** ✪ (Plaza Cordobeses 3; ☎ 956-168-628; 15€; tours Mon–Fri 9:30am–5:30pm). Joaquin Rivero, a construction magnate whose family roots in the sherry business date back to the 17th century, founded the bodega in 1998 to specialize in the rarest and most expensive sherries. One cellar master, his son, and another employee (the firm has just 7 employees) blend old sherries from other producers to create VOS (Very Old Sherry—aged at least 20 years) and VORS (Very Old Rare Sherry—aged at least 30 years). "We label the bottles by hand and they are all hand-numbered by the cellar master," explains Sabrina Melcher.

Owner Rivera favors the Tradición amontillado, an exceedingly dry and nutty sherry with an average age of 37 years. It's easy to imagine him sipping it as he contemplates his private collection of Spanish art from the 15th through 19th centuries, including a pair of portraits by Goya. "It's a very nice hobby," Melcher says. The bodega gallery displays a portion of the collection for visitors to admire—a glimpse of the world of sherry privilege.

For insight into the manzanilla sherry subculture, see Bodegas Romero in Sanlúcar (p. 200) and Bodega de Mora in El Puerto de Santa María (p. 209).

ATTENTION, SHOPPERS!

If *zoco* conjures up images of crowded Arabian markets, you'll be surprised by the **Zoco de Artesanía** ✪ (Pl Peones; no phone; Mon–Fri 10am–2pm and 5–8:30pm, Sat 10:30am–2:30pm), a large and light-filled space, opened in March 2008 with stalls for 22 shopkeepers. You might find some of the merchandise in other shops, but the *zoco* does gather good-quality merchandise under one roof: *repoussé* metal boxes and picture frames, recycled and embellished denim jackets, handmade fans, leather goods, beautiful glass tea cups, painted ceramic *tagines,* and hand of Fatima brass door knockers. You might also encounter Mercedes Jimenez shaping sculptures from clay, Manuel Ramos Jiménez forming small sherry casks from strips of oak, or David Cosano wearing a white lab coat as he meticulously crafts a violin. Milagros Barrosa has been designing and making flamenco garb for 30 years and you'll probably find her bent over her sewing machine. Ask her how long it takes to make an elaborate ruffled dress and she'll just shrug her shoulders. "I don't keep track of the hours," she says. "It's enough."

NIGHTLIFE IN JEREZ DE LA FRONTERA

The city operates the striking **Teatro Villamarta** (Pl Romero Martínez; ☎ 956-350-272; www.villamarta.com), a grand hall that presents concerts, operas, and zarzuelas (a uniquely Spanish form of light opera) September through June. Performances are usually on weekends, but they run daily during the Feria del Caballo, or horse festival, in late April and early May. Prices tend to range from 15€ for a local musician in concert to 50€ and up for opera seats.

Nightclubs aren't big in Jerez, but **Didimos Cafe** (Zaragoza 35; ☎ 635-018-127; 4pm–2am) on the north side of town turns its upstairs room over to dancing late every evening. Programming varies but usually includes Latin dance nights (with free instruction) and Argentine tango.

Apart from the bar scene, nightlife in Jerez usually means flamenco. More than a dozen *peñas* scattered through barrios Santiago and San Miguel host performances on an irregular schedule—check the Centro Andaluz de Flamenco (see above) for details. The city also hosts two of the world's largest flamenco festivals: the Jerez International Flamenco Festival (Feb–Mar), and the Bulería Festival (Sept). Of the nightclub-style tablaos, good options in barrio Santiago are **La Taberna Flamenca** ✸ (Angostillo de Santiago 3; ☎ 956-323-693; Nov–Apr Tues–Thurs and Sat 10pm, May–Oct 2:30pm) and **El Lagá de Tío Parilla** ✸ (Pl Mercado; ☎ 956-338-334; Mon–Sat 10:30pm), which is operated by master guitarist and recording artist Juan Parrilla. In either case, skip the expensive dinner and opt for tickets for the show and a drink.

GET OUT OF TOWN
Sanlúcar de la Barrameda

It's easy to travel by **Linesur bus** (☎ 954-988-222; www.linesur.com) between Jerez and **Sanlúcar de Barrameda** ✸, a dreamy little fishing town turned resort village on the left bank of the mouth of the Río Guadalquivir. Buses leave on the hour either direction from 7am to 9pm weekdays, and on weekends every 2 hours from 9am to 9pm from Jerez, returning every 2 hours 8am to 8pm. By car, it's a 20-minute drive on the A480. You might want to visit one of the town's bodegas to compare the distinctive salty local *manzanilla* (also made in El Puerto de Santa María) to the sherry of Jerez. But Spaniards are drawn to Sanlúcar's 19 miles of soft, brown-sand beaches and the extraordinary shrimp, king prawns, and rock lobster found near the mouth of the river. So follow their example and take in the sun, swim at the beaches, eat shellfish, and drink manzanilla.

Sanlúcar remained a ducal property from the Reconquest until the 17th century, and the old part of the city, which rises on a hill, has the usual mix of much-altered Renaissance and baroque architecture. Stop at the **Oficina de Turismo** (Calzada del Ejército; ☎ 956-36-61-10; Mon–Fri 10am–2pm and 5–7pm, Sat 10am–2pm, Sun 11am–2pm) for a map. The two areas of most interest to visitors are the Plaza del Cabildo (the central square of the lower town), and the sandy strand of Bajo de Guia, about .8km (½ mile) away.

ACCOMMODATIONS IN SANLÚCAR DE LA BARRAMEDA

€–€€ If you decide to stay overnight, the best deal (58€–76€ a night), is **Hotel Las Helechos** (Pl Madre de Dios 9; ☎ 956-361-349; MC, V). Although the high-ceilinged rooms are spacious (with 2 beds, a desk, and an armchair with table), you'll want to spend as much time as possible in either the ground-level patio filled with flowers and a burbling fountain, or on one of the spacious, tiled sun decks shared by rooms on the upper two levels. For full sun exposure with both table and chair sets and lounge chairs, ask for rooms 201 through 206.

DINING IN SANLÚCAR DE BARRAMEDA

Sanlúcareños assemble for lunch at the bars and cafes of **Plaza del Cabildo,** the lively center of the lower town away from the beaches. Follow their example and place your order inside before grabbing a table on the plaza. Your food will be delivered to you when it's ready. One word of caution: Be careful how much you drink. Restrooms can be hard to find in Sanlúcar, even in bars and restaurants, perhaps explaining why people only sip small glasses of sherry rather than taking big glugs of water, soda, or beer.

€–€€€ Just don't ask for Tío Pepe at **Bar La Gitana** (Pl del Cabildo 15; ☎ 956-382-014; 11am–11pm; 6€–18€; MC, V), which is owned by Hidalgo, maker of La Gitana manzanilla. In fact, the specialties of the house—fried and grilled fresh shellfish—are the perfect match for a chilled glass of manzanilla. Grilled shrimp are usually priced per kilo (50€–70€, depending on season), but you can get a half *ración* of lightly battered fried shrimp for 5€. Don't even try to peel them—just snap off the heads and crunch up the rest, shell and all. The larger prawns (another species of shrimp) wrapped in bacon and grilled will only set you back 6€. No restrooms.

€–€€€ If you're looking for a more bustling scene, head to **Casa Balbino** (Pl del Cabildo 11; ☎ 956-360-513; 11am–11pm; MC, V), where a virtual army of bar-men yell orders to the kitchen and chalk up tabs on the bar. You'll pay about a third more for the same dishes served at Bar La Gitana, or you can order grilled meats (beefsteak for 12€, pork steak for 11€). The advantage might be the atmosphere (complete with hams hanging from the ceiling and bullfight photos on the walls), the house manzanilla (1.20€ a glass), and bathrooms for the customers, something La Gitana lacks.

€€–€€€€ If you'd rather eat at Bajo de Guia, the stretch of beach closest to the fishing port, **Restaurante Mirador de Doñana** ★ (Bajo de Guia; ☎ 956-364-205; www.miradordonana.com; 1–11pm; 9€–30€; AE, DC, MC, V) rules over this section of town like a queen. The upstairs dining room has two walls of windows to look out to sea and across a small estuary to Parque Doñana (see below), but on a sunny afternoon, Spanish families prefer to cluster around the outside tables at the beachfront. As perhaps the largest restaurant in the city, Mirador de Doñana also offers the broadest menu, bringing in large fish, like tuna and swordfish, from the coast south of Cádiz to augment the local shrimp. The budget-minded can

Crustacean Confusion

Spanish names for crustaceans differ—sometimes confusingly—from French and Italian names for the same creatures. English menu translations only make matters worse. From small to large:

Camarón: A prawn or shrimp, usually about 2½ inches long, known as *crevette rose* in France. Those of Sanlúcar de Barrameda are famous.

Gamba roja: A larger prawn sometimes called *langostino moruno,* known as *crevette rouge* in France.

Gamba: Also a prawn, red-orange when live with a violet belly, and slightly larger than the *gamba roja.* The French call it *crevette rose du large.*

Cigala: The "Norway lobster," best known to the world by the Italian moniker, *scampi.* The French call it *langoustine,* reserving *cigala* for the rock or "flat" lobster, which Andalusians call *cigarra.*

Langosta: The spiny lobster, called *langouste* by the French.

Bogavante: The European true lobster, *homard* in French; shows up on luxury menus but has been air-freighted from more northern fisheries.

opt for a plate of shrimp sautéed with garlic (10€), but if price is no object, get a half-kilo of steamed *langostinos de Sanlúcar* (the crunchy and sweet giant prawns) for the table for around 45€.

€€–€€€   If the weather is good, you can enjoy the local shellfish at a significant discount—about 8€ to 19€ for a full meal—at the outdoor tables of nearby **Casa Juan** (Bajo de Guia; ☎ 956-362-695; noon–11pm; MC, V) or **Casa Bigote** (Bajo de Guia; ☎ 956-362-696; daily 1–11pm; MC, V). Casa Juan offers a daily menu (24€–26€) with three courses of shellfish (usually a soup, a small baked dish of shellfish and beans, and a fried shellfish plate) in addition to bread, wine, coffee, and dessert.

THE OTHER SANLÚCAR DE BARRAMEDA

Many Sanlúcar manzanilla makers offer guided tours of their facilities, but the fixed hours will almost certainly interfere with your beach or lunch plans. So visit **Bodegas Pedro Romero** ★ (Trasbolsa 84; ☎ 956-360-736; www.pedroromero.es; 9am–8pm, phone only until 2pm) which has a free audioguide tour available whenever the shop is open. Hand over a credit card or ID, and they literally give you the key to the kingdom and a map. The tour covers three different buildings and explains the sherry-making process from start to finish. You can walk through the working operation at your own pace—just be prepared to jump out of the way, for example, when a few strong men roll a full 600-liter barrel from one location to another. We prefer the audioguide to the bodega's guided tours (6€, including a tasting) at fixed hours (Tues–Sat noon, Tues–Fri 6pm, in July and Aug nighttime visits are available Tues–Fri 8:30pm for 10€). Similarly, invest in the wine-tasting course (noon Tues, Thurs, Sat; 20€; must be reserved in advance) only if you want to make some serious purchases. It includes a tasting of the entire product line, including some of the VOS and VORS bottles.

ACTIVE SANLÚCAR DE BARRAMEDA

Sanlúcar's harbor was once so deep that Columbus launched his third voyage to the Americas here, but the delta spreading from the mouth of the Guadalquivir clogged the harbor with sand bars in recent years. Andalusia's environmental agency spent much of 2008 and early 2009 dredging the harbor and reshaping and remodeling the beaches to restore the area as both a blue-flag beach and a pleasure-boat harbor.

Environment is everything in Sanlúcar—the estuarine system sustains the shell-fishing and creates the perfect climate for making sherry. At Bajo de Guia, the old ice house **Fábrica de Hielo** (☎ 956-381-635; free admission; daily 9am–8pm), has been converted into an interpretive center for **Parque Doñana,** the vast nature pre-serve around the mouth of the Guadalquivir. Displays introduce visitors to the marshes, shifting sands, and stabilized sands of this vast ecosystem and are a per-fect prelude to **riverboat voyages** ✹✹ kids (16€ adults, 8.10€ seniors and chil-dren, 33€ families; Nov–Feb 10am, Mar–May and Oct 10am and 4pm, June–Sept 10am and 5pm) into the highly protected park. Doñaña is a major stopover for migrating birds from Europe and North Africa and is also rich with resident storks, flamingos, egrets, herons, and songbirds. The 2½-hour journey includes two stops for guided walks through the park.

CÁDIZ

Residents of this seaport city on the Atlantic coast are a forward-thinking lot, yet they still call themselves Gaditanos, a reference to the Phoenician trading post founded here about 1100 B.C. As Western Europe's oldest continuously inhabited city, Cádiz fell under the successive sway of Athens, Carthage, Rome, and finally the Visigoths and Moors. All traces of that storied past were obliterated in the 1755 earthquake that also leveled Lisbon, and the Cádiz of today was conceived as an Enlightenment city with long, straight boulevards and now-abandoned for-tifications to protect the galleons of new-world trade. Its stately pastel buildings are a welcome relief from the somber browns of Jerez.

GETTING TO & AROUND CÁDIZ

Most travelers arrive, appropriately enough, by **ship.** But it is possible to **drive** into the city on the A4 from Jerez de la Frontera (about an hour), or to take the M-050 or M-051 **buses** operated by the Bahía de Cádiz Transportes (www.cmtbc.es) from the Jerez airport. Train service on RENFE (www.renfe.es) is available from Seville and Málaga.

To appreciate this lovely city, you'll want to walk whenever possible. If you're in a rush, the no. 1 bus runs up and down the peninsula along the central avenues. Pick up a city map at the **Oficina de Turismo** (Paseo de Canalejas; ☎ 956-241-001; Mon–Fri 8am–6pm, Sat–Sun 9am–5pm), which also provides the well-researched Paso a Paso MP3 audio guides (12€), with an annotated map, a player, and two sets of headphones.

ACCOMMODATIONS, BOTH STANDARD & NOT

As a smallish city of about 130,000, Cádiz is not richly endowed with lodgings. Several small properties cluster around the main port of the old city, but you'll also find a few along the seaside boulevards on the west side. Distances are not great on this narrow peninsula, so either location makes a fine base for exploring.

€–€€   Located a few streets from the passenger port, both **Hostal San Francisco** (San Francisco 12; ☎ 956-221-842; MC, V) and **Hostal Canalejas** (Cristóbal Colón 5; ☎ 956-264-113; MC, V) represent the best in low-price lodging in Cádiz. The first will run you about 50€ to 65€ a night, tax included, while Canalejas tends to come out 5€ more. Clean and well kept, they offer smallish rooms with two twin beds, an armoire, and a small writing desk. Think of them as bedrooms for sleeping, not accommodations for hanging out. That said, they are cheerful and attractive. San Francisco has a beautifully tiled lobby and stairwells, and the rooms feature beds with wrought-iron headboards. Canalejas, by contrast, has the heavy, dark-pine furniture so common in Spanish lodgings.

€€   The name of **Hotel de Francia y Paris** (Pl de San Francisco 6; ☎ 956-212-319; www.hotelfrancia.com; AE, MC, V) might be French, but the rooms are decorated in modern Spanish taste with cherry-toned wood furniture, white walls, and floor-to-ceiling draperies that accentuate the 12-foot ceilings. Most rooms hold two twin beds, a small desk, and one or two chairs and cost between 74€ and 98€ a night. The best rooms have small balconies overlooking the plaza, which bustles by day but is relatively quiet by evening. If you visit in the spring, request Room 108, which looks out on flourishing orange trees. Leave your windows open and you'll sleep in the perfume of orange blossoms and not even notice that the carpets are overdue for replacement.

€€–€€€€   No need to worry about carpets in **Hostal Hospedería Las Cortes de Cádiz** ✪✪ (San Francisco 9; ☎ 956-212-668; www.hotellascortes.com) because all the floors are marble. Each room is named for an event or personality associated with the Constitution of 1812—Spain's first liberal government, proclaimed in Cádiz. That government failed but cemented Cádiz as a bastion of liberty. Three floors of rooms circle a glass-roofed patio with a black-and-white checkerboard floor. With a color scheme of warm oranges, salmons, and pinks, as well as floral bed covers and Victorian-style spindled headboards, the rooms have a gracious, feminine ambience. Expect to pay between 78€ and 138€, including breakfast.

€€–€€€€   Set along the harbor drive next to Parque Génoves, the architecture of **Parador Hotel Atlántico** ✪✪ (Av. Duque de Nájera 9; ☎ 956-226-905; www.parador.es) won't charm anyone, but the rooms are spacious, modern, and extremely comfortable and cost between 70€ and 141€, including breakfast. (The high rates reflect business conferences and holidays, while the low rates are dead-of-winter discounts. Generally, expect to pay 85€ to 110€, depending on the view.) One of Spain's first *paradores,* the modern complex overlooking the Bay of Cádiz was rebuilt in the 1980s. The bounteous breakfast buffet features fresh fruits and superb pastries. Official rates always seem high, but deep discounts are

Cádiz

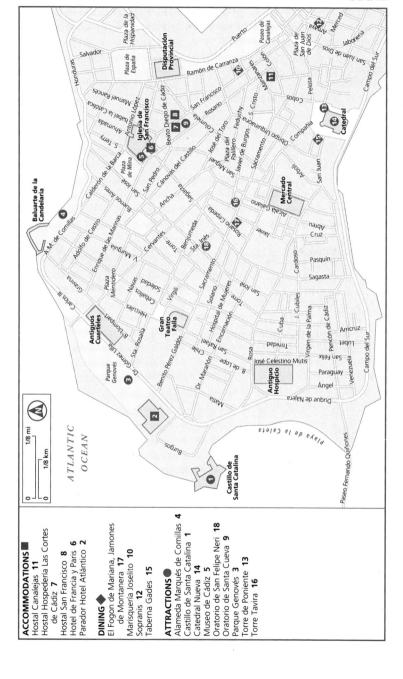

ACCOMMODATIONS ■
Hostal Canalejas **11**
Hostal Hospedería Las Cortes
de Cádiz **7**
Hostal San Francisco **8**
Hotel de Francia y París **6**
Parador Hotel Atlántico **2**

DINING ◆
El Fogón de Mariana, Jamones
de Montanera **17**
Marisquería Joselito **10**
Sopranis **12**
Taberna Gades **15**

ATTRACTIONS ●
Alameda Marqués de Comillas **4**
Castillo de Santa Catalina **1**
Catedral Nueva **14**
Museo de Cádiz **5**
Oratorio de San Felipe Neri **18**
Oratorio de Santa Cueva **9**
Parque Genovés **3**
Torre de Poniente **13**
Torre Tavira **16**

203

available all year for travelers age 20 to 30 and 60 and over (and their compan-ions of any age) through the website, where monthly specials are usually posted for the rest of us.

DINING FOR ALL TASTES

Cádiz is surrounded by the sea, so it's no surprise that seafood (especially shrimp from the mouth of the Guadalquivir river) dominates the menus. To accommo-date cruise-ship passengers, many restaurants cluster near the port. The ships usu-ally haul anchor by nightfall, so dining is busiest at midday and tends to be rather casual.

€ If you want to eat with the Gaditanos, look for an establishment where smok-ing is permitted, as only tourist bars and restaurants are smoke-free. Tiny, smoky **Taberna Gades** (San Juan 38; ☎ 856-076-904; 11:30am–4:30pm and 7:30–11:30pm; MC, V) opened on a back street near the cathedral in 2004, but feels as if it's been here since Hannibal made Cádiz his base to conquer the Iberian penin-sula. Everyone gravitates to the back where a large-screen TV is usually tuned to sporting events. You can eat lightly on tapas such as potatoes with garlic sauce (1.40€), or more heavily on a full plate of fried squid (6.90€) or stewed beef (6€). Good greens can be hard to find, but Gades prepares a healthy salad with tuna and chopped hard-boiled egg amid the lettuce, tomato, green peppers, and corn kernels (7.50€).

€–€€ Essentially a fishmonger, **Marisquería Joselito** ✹✹ (San Francisco 38; ☎ 956-266-548; noon–4pm and 8pm–midnight, closed Sat and Sun evenings; MC, V) also cooks the catch and serves it at tables in the bar-like interior or on the out-side patio just a block from the fishing piers. Many dishes are priced by the mar-ket that day, but you can always count on a plate of large shrimp sautéed with garlic (9.70€), or grilled shrimp with a little olive oil (4€). The real treat, though, is grilled fresh tuna (8.70€) landed at Barbete, one of the world's most famous tuna ports a few miles south of Cádiz. Pescaphobes are out of luck—there's not a meat dish on the menu.

€€ The carnivore's complement to Joselito is **El Fogon de Mariana, Jamones de Montanera** (Sacramento 39; ☎ 956-220-600; noon–5pm and 8pm–midnight; cash only), a combination butcher shop and bar/restaurant that specializes in both fresh and cured pork from the nearby Sierra Aracena, where pigs graze on acorns in forests of cork oaks. There are only a couple of tables, so you'll have to settle for one of the few wooden stools at the high marble bar or gathered around big sherry casks. Sherry, of course, is the drink of choice, and plates of cheese and *jamón Iberico* (8€–15€) are the perfect match. This is one of the few places we know where you can also feast on fresh pork roast (9.80€) from the Iberian pigs most famous as cured hams.

€€–€€€ For a departure from casual dining, join the young sophisticates at **Sopranis** (Sopranis 5; ☎ 956-284-310; www.sopranis.es; Tues–Thurs 1–4pm and 8:30–11:30pm, Fri–Sat 1–4pm and 9pm–midnight, Sun 1–4pm; MC, V), where you can pull up a minimalist stainless-steel bar stool at the raised communal table and join in the conversation. The contemporary, international look carries through into the cooking. Tapas tend to be light and less fatty than at most places, with simple dishes like vegetable quiche (2€), a tiny casserole of fried egg with spinach (2.25€), or big prawns with a hot cocktail sauce (2.50€). For a full meal, try roasted cod on a bed of eggplant and ratatouille (17€). Even the desserts depart from the creamy norm—try the pear poached in caramel and drizzled with chocolate (4.50€).

WHY YOU'RE HERE: THE TOP SIGHTS & ATTRACTIONS

The leading attraction of Cádiz is the city itself. Its melodic nickname, *Tacita de Plata* (little silver cup), describes a near-island connected to the mainland by a slender stem. The seaside promenades provide a seamless transition between the urban world and the timeless ocean, while the parks have a 19th-century grace. The trees of **Parque Genovés** are sculpted to create artful patterns and the park's outdoor theater often hosts free plays and music in the summer. The adjacent leafy **Alameda Marqués de Comillas** also dates from the 19th century but is less formal and, therefore, more welcoming. You'll always find more people sitting around in the Alameda, just as most people gravitate to the kitchen rather than the formal parlor. The wide oceanfront sidewalks pass the silent remains of the Cádiz fortifications. They were constructed with good reason. In 1587, Sir Francis Drake attacked the harbor and waylaid the Spanish Armada, and in the 1590s, Anglo-Dutch invaders set Cádiz to the torch. The Spanish crown responded by erecting a series of fortifications around the knob of the city. Only **Castillo de Santa Catalina** 🧒 (Antonio Burgos at La Caleta beach; no phone; free admission; March–Oct 10am–8:30pm, Nov–Feb 10am–7:45pm) remains more or less in its original condition and kids love to climb the ramparts. In place of cannons, the fortress now mounts cultural exhibitions and hosts craftspeople for limited residencies.

The blocky sandstone base of **Catédral Nueva** ✸ (Pl Catédral; ☎ 956-286-154; 4€ adults, 2.50€ seniors and children; Mon–Fri 10am–6:30pm, Sat 10am–4:30pm, Sun 1–6:30pm) looks more like a defensive wall than a church, but the handsomely decorated main entrance and gilded brick dome give the building a redeeming air of importance. The so-called "new" cathedral replaced an older building burned in 1596. Started in the 1720s, it wasn't finished until the 1850s, so it bridges both baroque and neoclassical styles. The highlight is the beautifully carved baroque choir stalls from a Carthusian church in Seville that were installed here in the 19th century. Two of the city's 20th-century artistic giants rest in the crypt below: composer Manuel de Falla and poet and novelist José María Pemán. The **Torre de Poniente** 🧒 (3.50€ adults, 2.50€ seniors and children; June 15–Sept 15 10am–8pm, Sept 16–June 14 10am–7pm), the cathedral's late 18th-century bell tower provides splendid views of the city and coastline.

In the late 18th century, when Cádiz handled three-quarters of Spain's commerce with the Americas, the city was dotted with more than 150 watchtowers to monitor the comings and goings of ships in the harbor. The sole survivor is **Torre Tavira** 🧒 (Marqués Real Tesoro 10; ☎ 956-212-910; 4€ adults, 3.30€ students and seniors; May 15–Sept 15 10am–8pm, Sept 16–May 14 10am–6pm). Exhibitions on two levels (a chance to pause in the tiring climb of winding stairs) tell tales of

We, the People

The **Oratorio de San Felipe Neri** (Pl San Felipe Neri; ☎ 956-211-612; 2.50€; Mon–Sat 10am–1pm) happens to contain a huge and important painting of the *Immaculada* by Murillo on its main altar. But the building is more a shrine to liberty than to the Virgin. In 1812, when Napoleon still occupied Spain, representatives from around the country met here as the Cortes (or Parliament) of Cádiz and issued a Declaration of Independence on the square outside. The Cortes also framed Spain's first liberal constitution, though its implementation would not occur until decades later. Plaques sent from other countries in support of Spain's independence still line the walls.

the trading heyday of Cádiz, but the real payoff is the rooftop view of the city, its harbor, and the surrounding seas. Every half-hour, a camera obscura with rotating aperture casts images of the city on the round walls of a viewing chamber.

The best perspectives on the city's past, though, are the archaeology exhibits at the **Museo de Cádiz** ✹✹ (Pl de Mina; ☎ 956-203-368; 1.50€; Tues 2:30–8:30pm, Wed–Sat 9am–8:30pm, Sun 9:30am–2:30pm), which boasts the best collection of Phoenician artifacts anywhere in Europe. In 1887, a 5th-century B.C. sarcophagus of a Phoenician man was excavated beneath the city—a discovery that led to the museum's founding. A century later, his female counterpart was discovered nearby and the two carved burial vessels have been united in an impressive and rather touching display. The Phoenician settlement later passed to the Carthaginians, and then to the Romans in the 2nd century B.C. In fact, Julius Caesar held his first public office here. More Roman artifacts survive than Phoenician (though the Phoenician gold work is worth examining closely), and some of the sunny, dramatic rooms of the museum are literally filled with broken statuary and cases of coins, mosaics, and ceramic vessels.

Don't linger too long on the Roman collections, as the museum's art galleries include a masterful series of paintings created by Zurbarán for a Carthusian monastery in Jerez. Both sides of the painter's nature are on display in these paintings of sweet boyish angels with rouged cheeks and mystic saints with haunted dark faces. A separate gallery holds the ancient scenery and marionettes of Cádiz's unique Tía Norica puppet theater. Some of these historic pieces serve as models for annual performances of the revived company (see "The Other Cádiz," below).

Not all the great art in Cádiz is in the museum. The top-floor chapel of the baroque-style **Oratorio de Santa Cueva** (Rosario 10; ☎ 956-222-262; 2.50€ adults, 1.50€ seniors and students; Thurs–Fri 10am–1pm and 4:30–7:30pm, Sat–Sun 10am–1pm) features three striking frescos by Goya, including an unusual Last Supper in which Christ and his disciples recline on cushions on the floor.

THE OTHER CÁDIZ

There's no more charming way to connect with people than to share their beloved amusements. If you're in town during the limited performances of **Teatro La Tía**

Norica ★ 🧒 (Baluarte de Candelaría on Alameda de Apodaca; ☎ 956-808-472), you'll find yourself in the company of squealing toddlers and doting grandmothers and everyone in between. Generations of families have watched the tribulations of Gaditana grandmother Tía Norica as she contends with her impish, ill-behaved grandson Batillo. Their adventures lead them into every corner of the city, from the bullring to the bars, from the back alleys to public plazas—all shown with changing painted backdrops. The excitement seems as fresh as when the marionette company (which is often credited with pioneering Spain's modern theater) was founded in 1790. In its oldest form, it retells Bible stories, and the modern company still presents the Nativity during the holiday season. But the marionette shows evolved over the years to meet changing political circumstances, using children's entertainment as a medium for social and political satire as early as the Napoleonic occupation. The original company closed in 1959 but was revived in 1984 under puppet master Pepe Bablé. Company members can sometimes be seen creating new marionettes at the waterfront theater. The company also performs during the annual book fair, which takes place between March and May.

ACTIVE CÁDIZ

Two blue-flag beaches are within city limits. Sandwiched between rocky reefs, **La Caleta** 🧒 (Avda Duque Najera; ☎ 956-258-646) is a pocket beach only a short walk from the center of the old city. The main city beach, 3.2km-long (2-mile) **La Victoria** 🧒 (Avda Fernandez Ladreda; ☎ 956-258-646), is about 3.2km (2 miles) farther south and is best reached by the no. 1 (beach route) or no. 7 (central avenue route) city buses (.90€). Get off at Plaza Ingenerio La Cierva. This is a good place to join a pickup volleyball game before grabbing a bite at a beachfront snack bar.

ATTENTION, SHOPPERS!

If you come away from the Museo de Cádiz craving a Roman or Phoenician ring or amulet, check out the reproductions in bronze and silver at **islahAbitada** (Sacramento 24; ☎ 956-213-457). Alas, the artists in the small studios at **Galería el Populo** (San Antonio Abad 14; ☎ 699-101-157) keep irregular hours, but it's worth stopping in to see if Manos Gaditanas is open. Their tote bags and purses made from the city's vinyl advertising banners make great—and environmentally friendly—souvenirs. **El Potro** (Companía 8; ☎ 956-225-673), the outlet of a company based in the nearby leather-working town of Ubrique, has elegant leather goods and the company's horse-head logo gives many pieces a vaguely Louis Vuitton–like look.

NIGHTLIFE IN CÁDIZ

Cádiz nightlife is geared almost entirely to Gaditanos, since most of the tourists are safely tucked into their cruise-ship bunks by the time the shows begin.

Nightclubs

The most amusing and eclectic nightclub in town is **Café Teatro Pay-Pay** (Silencio 1; ☎ 956-252-543; Wed–Sat 10pm–2am), located in the Barrio del Pópulo behind the cathedral. The small and smoky room features local flamenco artists every Wednesday. On other nights, you might find a magic show, avant-garde monologist, or drag-queen cabaret. The leading disco, **dmclub** (Cánovas del Castillo 29; Thurs–Sat 10pm–4am), shakes it on weekends when the resident DJ plays a blend of house, progressive, and techno-pop.

Theater & Music

At the other end of the cultural spectrum, the Cádiz city government operates **Gran Téatro Falla** (Pl Fragela; ☎ 956-220-834; www.telentrada.es; 4€–30€), an imposing brick building of the neo-Mudéjar style popular in the late 19th century. The facility presents everything from contemporary and classic theater pieces to star flamenco singers and guitarists, modern dance, opera, and philharmonic orchestras. In May each year, the theater hosts an international music festival of classical music, including the works of local composer Manuel de Falla.

Flamenco

Cádiz is the home of *tangos,* a flamenco style only tangentially related to the Argentine dance music of the same name. One of the last of the great *tangos* guitar masters, Juanito Villar, operates **Peña Flamenca Juanito Villar** ✸ (Avda Campo del Sur; ☎ 956-225-290) at La Caleta beach, where his company performs on weekends during the summer. Throughout the year, you can catch credible performances of lesser-known artists near the port at **La Cava Taberna Flamenca** (Antonio López 16 bajo; ☎ 956-211-866; www.flamencolacava.com; 22€; flamenco Tues, Thurs, Sat 9:30pm), where the audience sits inches from the performers. A private club and school of flamenco aficionados, **Peña La Perla de Cádiz** (Carlos Ollero; ☎ 956-259-101; www.perladecadiz.com) offers an annual program to the public, the Concurso Nacional de Baile por Alegría, between April and June. The club takes its name from one of the city's great Gypsy flamenco singers, who died in 1975, and showcases many dancers, singers, and musicians who are not well known outside of Spain.

GET OUT OF TOWN

El Puerto de Santa María

Located just a few miles north on the Bay of Cádiz, **El Puerto de Santa María** makes a splendid day trip from the larger city. Hop one of the frequent catamaran ferries operated by Bahía de Cádiz Transportes (www.cmtbc.es; 2€ each way) that dock across from the Palacio de Congresos. It's a 25-minute ride through gentle waters lined by sandy beaches to the town known for its soft and subtle manzanilla sherries and its extraordinary seafood. As the boat pulls into harbor you'll see fishermen scrubbing the decks of their vessels or taking on a load of ice before they head out to the fishing grounds.

Columbus's flagship on his 1492 voyage, the *Santa María,* hailed from this small port and its owner, Juan de Cosa, was the explorer's pilot. He and other local mariners who participated in the epic voyages are memorialized in a plaque on the town's most striking building, the 12th-century **Castillo de San Marcos** 🅺 (Pl Alfonso X El Sabio; ☎ 956-851-751; 5€ adults, 2€ children, free Tues; Tues–Sat 10am–2pm). The base of the small fort with impressive watchtower was built between 1257 and 1260, when Alfonso X (a.k.a. "The Wise") was putting the squeeze on the Moors as he sought to retake southern Spain. It was restored in the

Fino vs. Manzanilla

Spain's most popular sherry style is the fino, produced from palomino fino grapes, and lightly fortified when the fermentation is complete. A cake of yeast called the *flor* settles on the top of the wine in the task, imparting the characteristic "fresh bread" taste to the wine. In Jerez, the *flor* dies back over the winter, allowing the wine to resume oxidizing. But *finos* produced in Sanlúcar de Barrameda and El Puerto de Santa María, where the sea moderates the winter cold, remain sealed beneath a thick *flor* throughout their aging. The finos of these two towns are known as *manzanilla,* a style with delicate, nutty notes and a hint of salt from the sea air and coastal soil.

1940s. The best part of the tour is the harbor view from the ramparts, where children like to feign medieval swordplay.

If you're not planning to tour sherry operations elsewhere, you may want to visit El Puerto's **Bodega de Mora** (Los Moros; ☎ 956-869-100; www.osborne.es/rrpp; 3€), which produces manzanilla for Osborne (the company that dots the Spanish hillsides with giant cutouts of black bulls). One-hour tours in English are offered Monday through Friday at 10:30am and Saturday at 11am and require reservations by phone or e-mail (visitas.bodegas@osborne.es).

Truth be told, we really visit El Puerto to eat. The entire town closes promptly at 2pm for lunch and those who don't go home for a siesta proceed directly to **Romerijo** ✦✦ (José Antonio Romero Zarazaga 1, at Ribera del Río; ☎ 956-543-353; www.romerijo.com; 11am–midnight; AE, DC, MC, V), which has been in the shellfish game since 1952. The shellfish market cum bar cum restaurant sprawls half a block in either direction from its intersection and spills out into the nearby park with a large contingent of tables and awnings. A look at the cases in the market will reveal more varieties of shrimp then you probably knew existed. Regulars choose what they want, have it cooked on the spot, and repair to an outdoor table to order a bottle of chilled white wine. First-timers can get a good sampling with an assorted plate (13€–30€) that could include half-inch-long white shrimp (eaten whole), small sweet *camarónes,* larger meaty *gambas,* and *cigalas* (saltwater crawfish). Some plates also include edible barnacles.

5

València, City & Region

Its song, *fiestas,* and cuisine are world renowned, but Valencia the city has been largely ignored . . . until recently

by Peter Stone

SPAIN'S GREAT LEVANTE CAPITAL HAS LONG BEEN ASSOCIATED WITH TWO of Spain's great attractions—the ebullient *Fallas* celebrations (see below) and the rice dish known as *paella.* But for a long time, those two items were the only ones of any interest to outsiders, at least those considering visiting the city of València. That all has changed and how! What was once an unkempt burg has been cleaned up, but more important, modernized. To put it bluntly, it's "done a Bilbao," inviting world-class architects to stretch the bounds of their art with important new buildings. Connoisseurs of architecture, as well as those who are simply drawn by "the next big thing," have been coming to the city ever since.

The rest of the province is a lush Mediterranean world of orange orchards, vineyards, rivers, lakes, wooded hills, wild inland mountains dotted with tiny hamlets, and the extremely popular beaches of the Costa Blanca and Costa del Azahar, all enjoying one of the best year-round climates in Spain. The second-largest city in the region, Alicante, a magnet for visitors in its own right, wows 'em with a beautifully preserved Old Town and one of the most sophisticated beach scenes in Spain. Visit València, city or province, and you may just come away humming that catchy old tune.

DON'T LEAVE VALÈNCIA WITHOUT . . .

Gazing at the future of architecture.   Just as the Guggenheim is now a must-visit in Balboa, València's "City of Arts and Sciences" is a not-to-be-missed envelope pusher in its own right. See p. 220.

Scaling the Miguelete Tower.   It's a giddy hike up the cramped and dimly lit medieval stairway that spirals heavenward inside the distinctive conical tower, but the view of the city's rooftops and blue domed churches you get from its circular platform at the top makes it all worth it. See p. 219.

Shopping in the great covered market.   Built in the 1920s at the peak of modern site fervor, it's one of the Spain's greatest food emporiums, traditional, colorful, packed with the riches of the great Valèncian *horta* (orchard) and its lagoons, including the largest eels you're likely to see anywhere. See p. 223.

Boating across the Albufera lagoon.   The calm glittering waters, tall reeds waving lethargically in the breeze, the swish of the rower's oar—it's a magical experience, especially at sunset.

Downing horchata in a traditional tiled taberna.   The delicious milky-hued almost coconut-flavored beverage (actually made from *chufas,* or tiger nuts) can still be sipped in a number of vintage city bars *(horchaterías)* like Daniels's in the appropriately named avenida de la Horchata.

Singeing your eyebrows at the Fallas de San José.   Those famed March festivities in which giant satirical effigies of political and other public-eye figures, lovingly and expensively created over the preceding months, are summarily burnt in minutes on huge bonfires throughout the city are a sight you'll never forget. (València is probably the noisiest city in Spain at fiesta times; rockets, giant bangers of bomb-like decibels, and ubiquitous *macletas* [strings of smaller fireworks linked on a line like tiny items of washing] explode anarchically in the days preceding the Fallas.) See p. 476.

VALÈNCIA (THE CITY)

València's bravely innovative 21st-century architectural changes have suddenly put it on the world map much like the Guggenheim Museum did for Bilbao. Here, the starring attraction is the Ciutat de les Arts i de les Ciències (City of Arts and Sciences) designed by architects Santiago Calatrava and Félix Candela, with its evocative array of waterways, domes, spheres, arches, bridges, and surrealistically angular rooftops resembling the bleached skeletal ribs of some prehistoric creature. At night, its illuminated buildings gleam at the Mediterranean end of a former river bed like an earthbound space station. Closer to the city are more eye-popping buildings: the Palacio de Congresos designed by Norman Foster and Catalán Ricardo Bofill's Palau de la Música. Today, it's a twin city, part medieval, part jet age, continuously burgeoning and enjoying the best of both worlds.

A BRIEF HISTORY OF VALÈNCIA

Of all the region's early settlers—from Iberians, Greeks, and Carthaginians to the Romans who first named the city *Valentia*—it was the Arabs who most influenced its early agricultural lifestyle. They ruled for 500 years, setting up an intricate network of irrigation channels and planting huge citrus orchards in the surrounding countryside. After being defeated by El Cid in 1094, the Moors almost immediately retook the city, but Jaime I finally managed to claim it for Christianity for good in 1238. And with this change in religion came a fundamental shift in the way locals—now looking beyond basic agriculture—earned their daily bread. A golden age of international trade, business, and the arts followed, and by the 16th century it was the financial capital of a Mediterranean empire, even more prosperous, at one stage, than Barcelona.

Its subsequent fall can be attributed to three grave mistakes made over the next 3 centuries. The first was ethnic, involving the expulsion of the *Moriscos* (Moors converted to Christianity) in 1616—a short-sighted economic error as they comprised over a third of the inhabitants, and it was mainly their business acumen that had made the province rich. The second and third were political gambles in which they twice backed the losing side and suffered consequent reprisals. After supporting the Archduke of Austria instead of the ultimately victorious Philip V (for which they were punished with the abolition of charters and province's autonomy or *fueros*) they took the side of the Republicans in the Civil War against Franco's Nationalist forces and had to endure subsequent decades of repression. There were other ups and downs. A 19th-century economic revival (thanks to successful agricultural, ceramic, and silk production) was undercut in 1957 by one of the most disastrous floods in Spain's history, after which the river was rerouted round the city.

In the wake of Franco's death, the city slowly recovered its self-esteem. In 1982, an *estatut* (statute) was passed giving València more autonomy. Six years later, an innovative Metro system—with chic lightweight trains—was launched, and the following year IVAM, one of Spain's top modern art museums, opened its doors to the public. The former river bed running through the center was next turned into attractive parklands with cycle trails and sports facilities. The greatest architectural change came when the new millennium saw the birth of the aforementioned City of Arts and Sciences, one of the most dazzlingly imaginative buildings in Spain. Its ambitions are echoed by the still embryonic Port America's Cup development which curves round the beautiful inlets between the main commercial harbor and long restaurant-lined Malvarrossa beach, attracting further world interest in the city as a business and touristic center.

LAY OF THE LAND

The city lies at the center of Spain's Mediterranean coast beside a lush plain, known as the *huerta* or *horta*, filled with a veritable green sea of citrus orchards (a legacy of the Arabs) and ringed by inland purple-gray mountains. To the north stretches a seemingly endless sequence of fine sandy beaches lined with popular tourist resorts that mainly attract Spanish holiday makers. To the immediate south of the city is the reed-flanked Albufera lagoon bordered by towns like Sueca where much of the local rice is grown, while inland to the west a long fertile valley extends to the twin towns of Utiel and Requena, whose joint vineyards produce large quantities of quaffable table.

GETTING TO & AROUND VALÈNCIA

For city information contact the **Oficina de Turismo** (calle Paz 48; ☎ 963-98-64-22; www.comunidad-valencia.com; Mon–Fri 9am–6:30pm and Sat 10am–6:30pm).

Arriving by Air

Though there are few international air connections with València airport (far more flights go from Europe to Alicante; p. 230), regular **Iberia flights** operate from main Spanish cities like Madrid, Barcelona, and Málaga. There are also flights between Palma de Mallorca and València. For flight information, contact the **Iberia Airlines** (☎ 902-40-05-00; www.iberia.com). The airport is 15km (9 miles) southwest of the city and aerobuses run from here to València's town center every half-hour during the day (a one-way ticket costs 2.50€). For more info, call ☎ 961-500-082. A taxi ride from the airport into town will cost you about

València

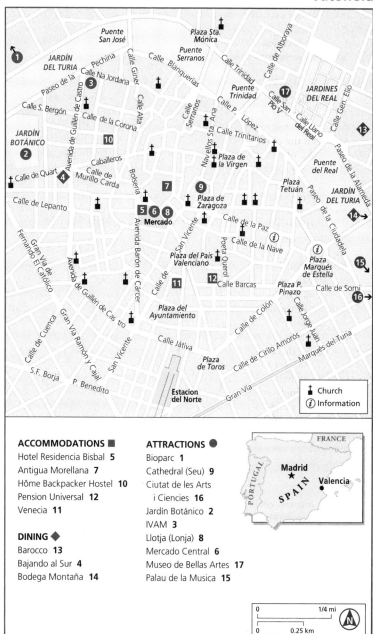

ACCOMMODATIONS ■
Hotel Residencia Bisbal **5**
Antigua Morellana **7**
Hôme Backpacker Hostel **10**
Pension Universal **12**
Venecia **11**

DINING ◆
Barocco **13**
Bajando al Sur **4**
Bodega Montaña **14**

ATTRACTIONS ●
Bioparc **1**
Cathedral (Seu) **9**
Ciutat de les Arts
  i Ciencies **16**
Jardín Botánico **2**
IVAM **3**
Llotja (Lonja) **8**
Mercado Central **6**
Museo de Bellas Artes **17**
Palau de la Musica **15**

16€. Taxis park in the rank just outside the arrival hall, but if you arrive late at night or very early in the morning and find none are available, two emergency taxi services you can contact are **Radio Taxi València** (☎ 963-70-33-33) and **Teletaxi** (☎ 963-57-13-13), both based in the city.

Arriving by Train

The high-speed **Alaris** and **Talgo** train services have greatly shortened traveling times between major Spanish cities and València. Thirteen trains arrive daily from Madrid (the Alaris: 44€ one way) and eight from Barcelona (the Talgo: 40€ one way). They take 3½ hours and 3 hours, respectively, though by 2010 even faster services should cut the journey times to an amazing 2 hours traveling at a top speed of 300kmph (200 mph). (The Alaris and Talgo already reach maximum speeds of 227kmph/137 mph.) The train journey from Málaga station, on the other hand, still takes 8 to 9 hours and costs 50€ one way. The arrival point is the **Estación del Norte** (North Station), calle Játiva 2, close to the city center. Check with **RENFE** (☎ 90-224-02-02; www.renfe.es; Mon–Fri 8am–9pm) for timetables and fares.

Arriving by Bus

Thirteen buses a day, at least one every hour, from Madrid (journey time 4 hr.; 30€–35€ one way), 10 buses daily from Barcelona (journey time 5 hr.; 40€ one way), and 5 buses from Málaga (journey time 10 hr.; 47€ one way) arrive at València's **Estació Terminal d'Autobuses** (Av. de Menéndez Pidal 13; ☎ 963-46-62-66). From here, it's a 30-minute walk or a 5-minute bus ride (no. 8; 1.20€) to the central Plaza del Ayuntamiento.

Arriving by Car

If you're coming by **car** the A-7 motorway approaches the city from Barcelona in the north, and the E-901 national highway from inland Madrid to the west. The toll fee on the latter route is 20€. If you're coming from Andalusia, the roads are longer, more difficult, and not connected by express highways. You can drive from Málaga north to Granada and cut across southeastern Spain on the 342, which links with the 340 into Murcia. When you reach Alicante from Murcia, take the fast E-15 highway for the final stretch into València.

Ferries

Ferries sail from València port to and from the Balearic Islands. Check with the **Transmediterránea** office (☎ 902-45-46-45; www.trasmediterranea.es) for summer and winter timetables and tariffs. You can buy tickets there or from travel agents in town. Islands covered directly are Mallorca (6 hr.) and Ibiza (winter services limited to 1 a week). To reach the port, take bus no. 4 or 19 from the Plaza del Ayuntamiento. Ferries from Majorca to València leave from Estació Marítim 2, Palma. Call ☎ 902-45-46-45 for details.

Local Transportation

València is well served by its inexpensive and efficient public transport system. The **bus** is best for navigating the central parts of town, as it offers numerous routes and is likely to take you exactly where you want to go in the minimum of time. City buses depart from the Plaza del Ayuntamiento 22 and a single fare for a journey anywhere within the city limits is 1.20€. You can also buy a 10-ticket combination for 9.50€. Get a map of bus routes from the **EMT** office (calle Correo Viejo 5; ☎ 963-15-85-15; Mon–Fri 9am–2pm and 4:30–7:30pm).

If you're looking to go a little farther out (to Malvarrossa for example) then the **Metro** (www.Metrovalencia.com) and **FGV** services, with their higher speeds and fewer stops, are a better bet. Tariffs are the same as for the bus routes. There's also a tram that goes from the Pont de Fusta (Wooden Bridge) to Malvarrossa Beach.

Chances are, you won't need a **taxi** except in an extreme emergency—as the Metro and bus systems run so frequently and are so well organized. They're also, of course, a lot cheaper. If you do need a taxi, check out the two city-based taxi companies—Radio Taxi València and Teletaxi—in the "Arriving by Air" section, above. However, bear in mind that if you hail a street taxi there are three tariffs: one for city areas between 6am and 11pm; another for city areas after 11pm and on Saturdays and Sundays in and out of the central Metropolitan area; and a third for Saturdays, Sundays and fiestas outside of the city limits.

ACCOMMODATIONS, BOTH STANDARD & NOT

Staying in well-equipped apartments right in the city center allows those who like to spread out to do so without "splashing out." Full apartments, usually with several bedrooms, regularly cost the same as a small, standard hotel room. To find the right digs, contact local company **Accommodation València** (☎ 963-382-384; www.accommodation-valencia.com; Mon–Fri 11am–2pm and 4–8pm), which represents 45 well-tended apartments (the agency takes care of the cleaning and maintenance and inspects its properties often). The amenities and ambience shift from apartment to apartment, as they're all individually owned, so you might find yourself in a modern building with access to a swimming pool and full gym or in an older property that nevertheless boasts a state-of-the-art kitchen (all brushed steel), flat-screen TVs, and glowing hardwood floors. This being a style-conscious city, I found the level of decor to be pretty high in most of the places I saw. Nearly all of this agency's offerings are two-bedroom apartments which average around 80€ per night.

Though I do think that these apartments offer great value, you need to tally up all the extra costs before booking: Linens and towels are extra, and you'll need to either hire someone to clean the place through the agency (35€) or leave it just as you found it to avoid incurring an even greater cleaning fee. The cancellation fees, as at many rental agencies, are also stiff, so be sure you understand what you're getting into before booking. There's a 3-night minimum for stays, deposits of 30% are required for bookings, and guests are requested to pay the rest of the fee in either cash or by check. A further security deposit of at least 300€—refundable on departure provided no damage costs are incurred—is also required.

€   On to standard hotels. Your best ultra-budget choice in town, beyond the hostels (see below), is the family run **Pension Universal** (calle Barcas 5-2º; ☎ 963-51-53-84; MC, V) right in the heart of the Old Quarter and a short walk from the Colon Metro stop. The compact rooms here are rather basic but clean and have en suite shower rooms—a really good value at 45€ per double.

€–€€   Also hidden away in a narrow lane in the Old City, opposite the great covered market (another primo location), the friendly **Hostal Residencia Bisbal** (Pie de la Cruz 9; ☎ 963-91-70-84; AE, MC, V) has a with-it husband-and-wife team at the helm, and offers rooms (60€–70€) that are again on the small side, but tidy and spotless, with tiled floors, simple wooden furnishings, and, most key, comfortable beds. Each has its own bathroom with shower. The English-speaking staff do their very best to make guests feel welcome.

€€   **Hostal Antigua Morellana** ✦✦ (En Bou; ☎ 963-91-57-73; MC, V) is a slice of old València set in a particular atmospheric corner of town. Charmingly converted from an 18th-century house, the Morellana offers good-size rooms, peppily furnished in reds and yellows, with private bathrooms (doubles cost 60€–80€). Though the decor is not particularly traditional, the hospitality here is, and the desk staff is unusually gracious and hospitable. It's located close to the Lonja and huge central market, in a bustling area of restaurants and bars that can get noisy (ask for a back room).

€€   Directly overlooking the scenic Town Hall Square, the immaculate **Hotel Venecia** ✦✦✦ (En Lop 5; ☎ 963-52-42-67; www.hotelvenecia.com; AE, MC, V) is located in a large, turn-of-the-century house, right in the center of the action. It offers small, but smart, well-lit rooms with mellow fine wood furnishings, en suite bathroom and shower stall for 75€ to 100€ per double. (Bargain rates come up occasionally, so ring the hotel first to see what's on offer; that's what I did last time I went and came up with a price a third lower than the standard rate.) An added bonus is soundproofing, which stops you from hearing your neighbors stomping around but, alas, doesn't block the sounds of late-night revelers outside in the main square (ask for a rear room if you're a light sleeper, a front one if lovely vistas are more important to you). The team of young receptionists is helpful, and the Venecia has won several awards from industry monitors for its efficient service. A small adjoining salon has a single Internet connection for clients' free use. Self-service buffet breakfasts are also available (in a corner room with great views of the Plaza del Ajuntament) for 5€ to 7€.

Hostel Accommodations

€   Just as València's "City of Art and Science" (p. 220) is moving architecture along, so the **Hôme Backpacker hostels** ✦ (located inside the Old Quarter at La Lonja 4, ☎ 963-916-229; Cadires 11, ☎ 963-914-691; and Plaça Vicente Iborra, ☎ 963-913-797; www.likeathome.net; MC, V) are offering a new, groovier twist on the hostel concept. Along with providing cheap dorm rooms (beds 15€–18€ per night), this trio of lodgings offers hammocks with a view (when the weather permits), strung on atmospheric terraces. Guests sink into them, happily buzzed after attending one of the three parties that are thrown weekly (including the occasional paella soiree). Other perks: free Internet access at computers in the lobby, DVD rentals, a fully equipped communal kitchen for guest use, and dorm rooms that are spacious and significantly cleaner than most hostels. Dorms are either female-only or mixed; if you want to come for the Fallas fiestas in March, you must book for a minimum of 5 nights.

DINING FOR ALL TASTES

€   Sandwiches, or *bocadillos,* are the specialty at the popular **Bajando al Sur** (Doctor Montserrat 32; ☎ 963-92-50-86; Mon–Sat 8–11pm; MC, V) and they cover the spectrum from hearty *jamon Serrano* (mountain ham) to mixtures vegetarians take a shine to, like *requesón* (cottage cheese) with dill, tomato, and slices of *cogollos* (lettuce hearts). Salads, crepes, and desserts are just as tasty here, and you can usually get out paying just 5€ to 7€ a dish (less for desserts) whether you sit down in this bright and airy little eatery or buy your sandwiches to go. It's located quite close to the Botanical Gardens.

€–€€   You know a place is going to be cheap if students eat there, but in the case of **Barocco** ✯ (calle Artes Gráficas; ☎ 963-61-36-43; daily 1:30–4pm and 8–11:30pm; V), it happens to be darn good as well. Tasty Mediterranean fare of all kinds is served in the vast barn like nosh spot just around the corner from the city's university. Never mind the noise: just tuck into a dish of *all i pebre* (12€) or (what else) paella (25€ shared between 2) and enjoy the highly quaffable low-cost house wine. *All I pebre* literally means "garlic and pepper," but it's a rich blend of eel (full-grown variety and not those baby *anguilas*), potatoes, garlic, chili peppers, and parsley, all cooked in olive oil. Unlike the famous paella, this dish is virtually unknown outside of València (so do try it if you get a chance while here; it's a real treat).

€–€€   If you're just out for tapas, don't miss the **Bodega Montaña** (Casa José Benlliure 69; ☎ 963-67-23-14; daily 1–4pm and 8pm–midnight; cash only), a *taberna*-cellar established in 1836 and still furnished with hoary old wine barrels and hanging mountain hams. Top tidbits here are the rich *anchoas* (anchovies) and *pimientos asados* (roast peppers). Accompany them with a couple of *copas* of Valèncian *tinto* (try Morverdre), and it'll set you back around 10€ tops.

€€–€€€   It should be against the law to leave València without sampling paella at least once, and you should do so at the estimable **l'Estimat** ✯ (Av. de Neptuno 16, Playa de la Arenas; ☎ 963-711-018; www.lestimat.com; Wed–Mon 2–4pm and 8–11:30pm, closed mid-Aug to mid-Sept; MC, V). Located right on the city's main Paseo Marítimo beside a beach that adjoins the long sandy Malvarrossa, it stands head and shoulders (or should I say "fins and scales"?) above its neighboring rivals in a zone that's particularly noted for high seafood standards. Choose either the *ciega* (literally "blind," with the shells of all the shellfish removed for easy, crunch-free eating) or the *banda* (cooked very slowly so as to totally absorb all the fish flavors; you'll have to wait a bit for this one) style of paella here. Both these paella choices cost around 30€ shared between a minimum of 2 people (that is, 15€ per head) and entrees range from 7€ for a gazpacho to 8€ for a mixed salad. Best value, though, are the three-course menus with wine, which cost from 25€ to 40€ per person. One suggestion: Though the inside of the restaurant is large and delightfully nautical in its looks (hanging nets and coastal navigation maps), pick an outside table for the uninterrupted sea views.

Viva la Paella

València is the home of Spain's most famous dish, the rice-based paella. Originally the name of the pan the rice dish was cooked in, over the years the word *paella* transformed into the name of the dish itself, and the cooking utensil in turn became known as a *paellera*.

Usually referred to simply as *arroz* (rice) on its home ground, paella (the dish) may be served *a banda* (rice on its own—*a banda* means "apart"—cooked simply in a fish broth), *ciega* ("blind," as it has been stripped of any shells or bones that might choke you), or *negra* (*black* in English, *negre* in Valenciano, meaning that the dish is cooked in squid's ink). A non-marine variant is *al horno* (cooked in the oven with bacon, blood sausage, chickpeas, and tomato among the flavoring ingredients), and other versions may contain lamb, partridge, or rabbit.

Like many a popular national or regional dish, from the French *cassoulet* to Mallorca's *Frito Mallorquín* (see chapter 10), it has humble origins, mainly based on economical use of the cheapest ingredients available. Legend has it that paella was invented when servants of the reigning Moorish kings used rice still left after one of the palace's prodigious feasts to create this new simple unadorned dish. Later on, other trimmings like *gambas* (prawns), *mejillones* (mussels), *guisantes* (peas), and slices of *pimiento rojo* (red peppers) were added to enhance it.

The rice is grown in the swamplands around the Albufera lagoon. The hot, humid summer months provide the ideal conditions for the production of this traditionally eastern crop. In spring, the paddy fields are dried out and the rice is planted. In May, the fields are manured to speed up the growth, and in July and August, the whole great golden expanse resembles a sea of waterlogged corn shoots. The crop is collected in the middle of September, and during the first fortnight of that month a special fiesta is held in the area's biggest town, Sueca. Highlights include paella contests and the *calbalgata de arroz*. On the first of November, called the *perellonà*, the three exit channels to the sea are closed and the zone is flooded until the following January.

WHY YOU'RE HERE: THE TOP SIGHTS & ATTRACTIONS

València's most important religious building, built on the site of a former mosque, is the huge **Seu (Cathedral)** ★★ (Plaza de la Reina; ☎ 963-91-81-27; Cathedral free admission, Museo de la Catedral 3.50€; Cathedral daily 7:30am–1pm and 4:30–8:30pm, Museo de la Catedral Mon–Fri 10am–1pm and 4–7pm). Like many cathedrals, its long construction phase means you'll see a hybrid of architectural styles at each of its three portals (the first stone was laid in the 13th century). Most impressive of these is the main Gothic entrance, its facade lined with statues of the apostles, though the oldest is the Romanesque Puerta de Palau, which features a particularly attractive rose window. Amid its surprisingly bright and elegant interior—none of your medieval gloom here—inside a small glass cage in one of the chapels you can see its most treasured exhibit, the *Caliz de Oro* (Golden Chalice) which—it is claimed—is the Holy Grail that Jesus drank from at the Last Supper, brought here from Jerusalem by Christian Crusaders. Also prized are Goya's two portraits of San Francisco de Borja, one of them showing him attempting to eject horrifying fanged devils in a style prefiguring his later nightmarish *pinturas negras* (black paintings).

The cathedral's octagonal 47m-high (154-ft.) **Miguelete Tower** (2.50€; Mon–Fri 10am–12:30pm and 5:30–6:30pm, Sun 10am–1pm and 5–6:30pm) provides the best panoramic views of the city if you don't mind the lung testing climb up a steep spiral stairway (207 steps) to get to the top. Time it right and you could also be deafened by the loudest bells in València (the biggest weighs 11,000 kilos/24,251 pounds).

Connected to the cathedral by a Renaissance arch and passageway used only by priests is the **Basilica de Nuestra Señora de los Desamparados,** a comparative youngster of 350 years whose interior boasts a richly bejeweled Virgin and a huge oval cupola painted by Antonio Palomino in 1701. The nearby 15th-century **Torres del Quart** is one of two surviving medieval stone archways that provided entry points to the Old City, the other being the equally impressive **Torres de Serrano** to the north near the riverbed park area.

A rare example of secular Gothic architecture, the **Lonja** ✪✪, or Commodity Exchange, is a beaut, especially its serene, high-ceilinged Hall of Columns (also known as the Contract Hall) with its grotesque gargoyles; horizontal and vertical naves; twisted columns resembling ships' ropes; and black, white, and brown marble floors. Constructed in 1498 for mercantile transactions and given the additional name of **Lonja de la Seda** (Silk Exchange) in recognition of the then highly lucrative silk trade, it was declared a world heritage monument by UNESCO in 1996 and is open daily to the public. On Sundays it's also a popular venue for exchanging stamps and coins.

Outstanding among the city's great wealth of religious buildings are the **Monastery of San Miguel y Los Reyes** (Av. Constitución 284; ☎ 963-87-40-00; free admission; Sept–July Mon–Fri 9am–8:30pm, Sat 9am–1:30pm, Aug 9am–2:30pm) a 16th-century renaissance building, which is now the headquarters of the Valèncian Library, and **San Juan del Hospital** (calle Trinquete de Caballeros 5; ☎ 963-922-965; free admission; Mon–Sat 9:30am–1:30pm and 5–9:30pm, Sun 11am–2pm and 5–9:30pm; free pre-booked guided visits Mon–Fri 9:30am–1:30pm), which was founded by the military religious order of St. John of Jerusalem and is the oldest building in València.

Beyond lovely architecture, there's plenty in town for art lovers to enjoy. By far the best of the traditional galleries is the **Museo de Bellas Artes** ✪✪ (San Pío V 9; ☎ 963-87-03-00; free admission; Tues–Sun 10am–8pm), with its Bosch, Velázquez, Van Dyck, and El Greco masterpieces. My favorites here are Van Dyck's rather moody self-portrait in which the great Dutch artist seems to be defiantly staring down the viewer, and—in direct contrast—Joaquín Sorolla's joyous *On Side Saddle,* in which a young couple, dressed to the nines for a fiesta, are riding an almost equally dolled up horse together in the leafy countryside. València's modernist pride and joy, meanwhile, is the 21st-century **IVAM** ★★ (Instituto Valenciano de Arte Moderno, calle Guillém Castro 118; ☎ 963-86-30-00; www.ivam.es; 2€ adults, free for children 9 and under; Tues–Sun 10am–8pm), vanguard of all that's innovative in today's art world. As well as permanent exhibitions ranging from Tapiès to Klee, the museum has some extraordinary metal sculptures by Catalán Julio González, who influenced Picasso in the 1930s and used oxy fuel welding to create bizarre masterpieces like *Monsieur Cactus.*

A highly personal curiosity that I find charming is the **Vicente Blasco Ibañez' Casa Museo (House Museum)** ★ (calle Isabel de Villena 149; ☎ 963-56-47-86 or 963-52-54-78; free admission; Tues–Sat 10am–2pm and 4:30–8:30pm, Sun 10am–3pm), located at the northern end of Malvarrossa Beach in the very villa the popular Valèncian novelist lived and worked for many decades. Here you can see the study where he wrote *Blood and Sand* and *The Four Horsemen of the Apocalypse* (among his most successful works), photos of him on his many worldwide travels, and preserved handwritten accounts from his diaries.

Among the city's many parks, the oldest is the **Jardín Botànic (Botanical Garden)** (calle Quart 80; ☎ 963-15-68-18; www.jardibotanic.org; free admission; winter daily 10am–6pm, summer daily 10am–9pm), which was originally founded by the University of València in 1567, was re-created by the eminent naturalist Antonio José Cavanilles in 1802, and today contains a huge greenhouse with tropical plants and over 300 species of trees from around the world.

The most recent giant fun attraction to hit the city (opened Apr 2008) is the $94-million state-of-the-art **Bioparc València Zoo** ★★ 🧒 (Av. Pío Baroja 3; www.bioparcvalencia.es; 20€ adults, 17€ seniors, 15€ children; winter daily 10am–6pm or 7pm, summer daily 10am–8pm or 9pm; closed Jan 1–Feb 27). Its 25 acres accommodating over 250 different worldwide species of animals—4,000 in all are located on the northern side of the Old City just beyond the gardens lining the former Turia riverbed. A self-styled "total immersion" zoo, its specialty lies in concealing any man-made constructions behind a carefully created "natural" world of savanna grasslands, water holes, rocky heights, and lush equatorial forests, backed up by recorded "sounds of the wild" to give it authentic atmosphere.

City of the Future

The extraordinary **Ciutat de les Arts y de les Ciències (City of Arts and Sciences)** ★★★ (Autopista del Saler; ☎ 902-10-00-31 for all 4 buildings; www. cac.es; Bus: 19, 35, 40, or 95 to Centro Comercio de Saler) has done for the city what the new port developments did for Barcelona and Guggenheim Museum did for Bilbao. That is to say, put it firmly on the international map. Glass windows and steel struts and supports merge in a series of humpbacked designs (inspired by animal skeletons) by the visionary architect Santiago Calatrava; it embodies the forward-looking, 21st-century València. The educational complex extends over a 36-hectare (90-acre) site amid lush landscaped gardens and tranquil lagoons (it adjoins the seaward end of the Turia Gardens) and contains a dazzling quartet of attractions. You can buy individual tickets for each section (below) or save money by getting a combined city pass giving you access to all four at a slightly reduced price for each.

The largest building is the gleaming white **Museo de las Ciencias Príncipe Felipe** ✦ 🧒 (www.cac.es; 7.50€ adults, 5.80€ seniors, students, and children 16 and under; Mon–Thurs 10am–8pm, Fri–Sun 10am–9pm), which resembles an intergalactic space station with its soaring roofs and the juxtaposition of its transparent glassy northern face and opaque south side. Its wide selection of interactive "hands-on" scientific displays are imaginative enough to satisfy kids of all ages, covering everything from the "Big Bang" to advances in space exploration and the workings of the body.

Adjoining it is **L'Hemispheric** ✦ (7.50€ adults, 5.80€ seniors, students, and children 12 and under; shows held Mon–Thurs 10am–8:30pm, Fri–Sun 11am–10:15pm). Its easily comprehensible, multilingual program of "images, sound, and the cosmos," focusing on the solar system and the universe, is shared out between a **Planetarium,** a **Laserium show,** and a huge **IMAX movie house** with a 84 sq. m (900-sq.-ft.) concave screen. Book well ahead for any of these shows. Combined tickets are available.

A highlight of the nearby 8-hectare (20-acre) **Oceanogràfic** ✦✦ 🧒 (24€ adults; 18€ seniors, students, and children 12 and under; Mon–Fri 10am–6pm, Sat–Sun 10am–8pm) is its massive **aquarium**—the largest in Europe—containing no less than 45,000 fish and sea mammals. It's no surprise that the most popular section is the dolphinarium with its high-IQ team of performing dolphins; the scariest is the enclosed walkway you can take amid shoals of menacing sharks. There are also sleek white Beluga whales, hefty brown walruses, and sociable crowds of pert black "dinner jacketed" Antarctic penguins to gaze at. You can even eat underwater here in the glass-covered restaurant!

Last to open—in 2003—was the **Palau de les Arts,** less showy than the other three but becoming quite famous for the superb acoustics of this whale-shaped structure of glass and metal. There are two indoor auditoriums, one with a large stage for special orchestral performances and a huge outdoor auditorium on the upper section of the building for up to 2,500 spectators.

The impressively "green" fifth member of this new world is the **Umbracle,** a large glass covered structure with trellis-like metal archways designed by Santiago Calatrava. It's a sort of 21st-century "Winter Garden" filled with palms, bitter orange trees, sweet-scented honeysuckle, bougainvillea creepers, and herbs like rosemary and lavender. Outside on the granite covered *paseo* is an open-air gallery of sculptures by contemporary local and international artists (including Yoko Ono).

THE OTHER VALÈNCIA

Right behind the city's main Malvarrossa beach (below) is the well-preserved former fishing area of **El Cabanyal,** which has so far defied the (ever-present) threat of modern developments—apart from a tastefully designed cultural center built a few years back—that would have destroyed its sleepily traditional character. Incorporated into València proper as late as the 19th century, El Cabanyal still retains the semi-independent "town within a city" atmosphere it had before, and its **Santa María Church**—the best Renaissance building in the city—has virtually the status of cathedral (at least in the eyes of the Cabanyal inhabitants) and forms the nucleus of this still highly individual barrio. Attend mass here amid the black-shawled women and somber men if you want to get some idea of the traditional values of this tightknit community. You can get here easily by *tranvía* from the *Pont de Fusta* (Wooden Bridge) on the north side of the Turia Gardens.

Learn to Cook, València-Style

Whether you're a beginner or an accomplished cook you may be interested to know that you can join small groups at the **Escuela de Cocina Eneldo** (Carrer Joaquín Costa 45; ☎ 963-955-457; www.cocinaeneldo.com) to learn how to prepare a variety of delights, ranging from traditional local fish and rice dishes to tapas and summer buffets. Groups are small and there's lots of emphasis on presentation. The school tries to fit in with whatever schedule suits you, whether it's morning, afternoon, or evening. Only one snag: Each course is spread over a 3-month period (total cost of 320€, plus 30€ for the certificate you get at the end) with just one 3-hour lesson per week. (Ten lessons in all.) Far too long for most holidaying visitors. So if you're interested and want to get a taste of the proceedings the best thing is to contact the school and see if you can attend just one or two classes. (You should have a reasonable working knowledge of Spanish to be able to fully participate.) If there's a space they're usually happy to oblige. Cocina Eneldo also arranges express cooking courses, creative cooking courses, and *cursos monograficos de cocina de autor,* or highly individual courses concentrating on a single dish. (*Eneldo,* incidentally, is Spanish for "dill.")

ACTIVE VALÈNCIA

For details on a wide variety of outdoor sporting activities in the València area, check out the website www.valencia.angloinfo.com.

Swimming & Beaches

València has easy access to a wide variety of long, gently shelving beaches offering excellent—and mainly safe—swimming for all ages. The best is the city's very own **Malvarrossa** ✹, immediately north of the port and easily reached directly by *tranvía.* A fine sandy stretch backed by a palm-lined promenade, it shelters some of the city's best fish restaurants at its harbor end and the celebrated **Casa Museo** (House Museum, p. 220) at the other.

Two more once-splendid beaches to the south are **Cullera** and **Gandía,** both alas now grossly overgrown tourist resorts. You can reach them by frequent FGV *cercanías* train from València's central station.

Scuba Diving

Equipment, including oxygen tanks and wetsuits, can be rented out for around 20€ per day from the **Escuela de Buceo Casco Antigua València** (calle Ayora 31; ☎ 963-822-565; www.buceovalencia.com). They also arrange Initiation Courses (350€) and Advanced Open Diver Courses (285€) for beginners and serious divers. Costa Blanca beaches down the coast have much clearer waters than, for example, València's neighboring Malvarrossa beach, and the school makes special arrangements for you to carry out your diving there.

Golf

The par-72, 18-hole **El Saler** (Av. de los Pinares 151; ☎ 961-61-11-86; www.parador.es) is the nearest and finest course, ideally located next to the sea and a nature reserve and magnificent "El Saler" Parador (a government-run luxury inn) just south of the city. Built in 1968 by leading golf architect Javier Araña, it's considered one of the best in Spain because of its challenging and stylishly planned greens and its magnificent location. Clubs can be rented. Green fees range from 100€ in the low season (Nov–Feb, Jul–Sept) to 110€ in the high season (Mar–June, Oct).

Horseback Riding

La Hipica (calle Jaca 23; ☎ 963-61-53-63) in the Trinitat district of València (accessible via Metro lines L3 and L4) rents horses for 1-hour trail rides for just 16€.

Bike Rental

The whole city of València lies on a flat level, making it ideal for getting around by bike. There are various city cycling trails, one of the most attractive being the Turia Gardens route (see above). Best contact if you want to hire a bicycle is **Orange Bikes** (Santa Teresa 8; ☎ 963-91-75-51; Mon–Fri 9:30am–2:30pm and 4:30–7:30pm; www.orangebikes.net). It rents out city and mountains bikes at 8€ to 10€ per day or 55€ to 70€ per week.

ATTENTION, SHOPPERS!

València's top shopping areas are in and around **calle Don Juan de Austria, calle Colón,** and the **Plaza del Ayuntamiento.** On Sundays—from 8:30am onwards—the **Rastro** (Flea Market) on avenida de Suecia near the soccer stadium is a great spot to seek out the odd bargain, especially in denim and leatherwear.

But the one unmissable shopping opportunity—and such a wonderfully rich cultural experience that we wrestled with whether we should include it in the sightseeing section as well—is the huge, covered, 1920s-built **Central Market** ✪✪✪ (calle Vieja de la Paja s/n; www.mercadocentralvalencia.es; Mon–Sat 7:30am–2:30pm), one of the most striking food emporiums in Europe. Packed with stalls selling all manner of local Mediterranean produce from huge eels netted in the Albufera lagoon to the freshest of fresh oranges plucked from the surrounding *huerta,* it recently underwent a 2-year revamp—finished in 2008—and is today better and brighter than ever before: Its wrought-iron roof and mosaic encrusted glass dome literally gleam. Behind it, in modest contrast, the circular **Plaza Redonda**—resembling a midget bullring with well-worn covered market stalls instead of bulls and *toreros* and an encompassing ring of equally weathered mid-19th-century facades in place of tiered aficionados' seats—offers the fascinating spectacle of small traders selling everything from pet monkeys to Manises ceramics.

The **Mercado de Colón** ✪ (Jorge Juan 19; ☎ 963-52-54-78; www.mercado colon.com; Mon–Sat 7:30am–2:30pm)—not your usual mall thanks to its Gaudí-influenced design—hosts a variety of interesting shops and cafes, though classy food shops predominate. Look out especially for **Manglano** (☎ 963-52-88-54), which is built in an exotic moderniste style and sells traditional local fare like blood sausage, rice, and almonds. Around the corner, you'll find chocolate delights at the **Cacao Sampaka** (calle Conde de la Salvatierra 19; ☎ 963-53-40-62).

Ceramics and **pottery** are both top Valenciano specialties. Within the city itself, you'll want to browse through **Las Añadas de España** (calle Játiva 3; ☎ 963-53-38-45) for its colorful selection of bowls, plaques, and kitchenware. But if you're willing to head out of town, you can visit the small towns where, since the Middle Ages, the area's luminous blue-and-white ceramics and *azulejos* (tiles) have been created. The industry was introduced into the area by the Moors and you can still see that Islamic influence today. The town of **Manises,** about 9km (5½ miles) from València, has been one of the most important centers for ceramics and boasts a number of well-priced retail outlets, including **Angeles Botet** in avenida Blasco Ibañez and **Tarin** in Carrer Maestro Guillem. It's also worth visiting **Paterna,** 6.5km (4 miles) northwest of València, as its numerous pottery stores sell ceramics at lower prices than those you'll pay in the capital. Both these towns are easily reached from the center by regular and frequent buses.

Another uniquely Valenciano creation is **Lladró porcelain.** These intricate and sometimes overly twee ornamental creations are sold widely in a number of locales. They're most reasonably priced at its main shop in **Calle Poeta Querol 8** (Querol 9; ☎ 963-51-16-25), though you'll find the best bargains in the northerly suburb of **Tavernes Blanques** 5km (3miles) north along the CV 315 and CV 3001 roads, at **Casa de Lladró** (Carretera de Aloborraya; ☎ 963-18-70-00), the retail outlet of the adjoining factory. Some of the lowest-priced items have slight flaws.

Fans are also top buys. Century-old **Abanicos Carbonell** (calle Castellón 21; ☎ 962-41-53-95), makes hand-held fans as beautiful as you'll find anywhere in Spain.

NIGHTLIFE

Because València's bustling nightlife scene is always shifting, use this chapter in concert with the *Qué y Dónde,* an excellent local periodical you can purchase from any news kiosk (1.20€) for listings of the new "in" spots.

That being said, the liveliest year-round zones are the Old Quarter around the central **Plaza del Ayuntamiento** and the nearby bohemian district of **Barrio del Carmen.** The latter's **Calle Alta** is a good place to start a crawl of the local *tascas* (pubs). In summer, head for breeze-cooled **Playa de Malvarrossa.** Open-air bars patronized by most age groups play music, often have dance floors, and are open from late May through September. Drinks usually cost 3€ to 5€. Of the discos in this part of town, the liveliest as I write this is **Akuarela Playa** (calle Eugenia Viñes 152; ☎ 963-859-385; cover 10€–13€).

Another fashionable dance spot, **La Indiana** (calle San Vicente 97; ☎ 963-820-891; www.laindiana.es; cover 12€; 11pm–5am) is a chic three-floored club where top DJs play a wide range of sounds, from salsa to funk. One of our favorite dawn-till-early-hours spots is **Barcas** (calle Barcas 7; ☎ 963-52-12-33) opposite the Estación Norte, which starts the day serving breakfast at 7am and ends it with nightcaps—or very-early-morning-caps—around 2am. It's not so much a regular nightspot as a post-music and dancing place to recharge yourself with nosh and beverages, especially as the night recedes and daylight approaches. Drink prices start at 1.60€ and tapas cost 4€ to 6€.

Gay *visitantes* can have a ball at a number of places, including **Donna Donna** (calle Portal Valldigna 2; no phone; Wed–Sat 8pm–2am) and **Sala Mogambo** (La Sangre 9; no phone; Thurs–Sun 11pm–4am). The hottest news on what's currently going down (so to speak) can be found at **Lambda** (calle San Dionisio 81; ☎ 963-912-084), and the most outrageous spot is **La Guerra** (calle Quart 47; ☎ 963-913-675), which has five action-packed floors, a labyrinth, and so-called "Californian movies" you wouldn't want mother to see, nightly from 8pm to 3am (until 4am Fri–Sat).

Theaters & Movies

The elegantly pillared greenhouse-style **Palau de la Música** (Paseo de la Alameda 30; ☎ 963-57-50-20; www.palaudevalencia.com) is a mecca for classical-music lovers. Designed by award-winning architect José María de Paredes, it offers over 200 programs a year featuring a combination of local and international orchestras. Ticket prices range widely—from 9€ to 60€ depending on the performance.

The city also boasts plenty of **cinemas,** one or two with films shown in their original language with Spanish subtitles (instead of following the usual practice of being dubbed in Spanish). Movie buffs delight is the **Filmoteca** at the IVAM modern art museum, with its constantly changing choice of programs, often featuring pretty esoteric fare from countries as culturally varied as Iran or Iceland. Check at the museum for individual programs and prices (usually 5€–6€).

DAY TRIPS FROM VALÈNCIA CITY

The valley around València is marked by rice paddies and orange groves that hide peaceful lagoons and nature parks, while the inland hills are dotted with charming towns noted for their colorful fiestas, dramatic hilltop castles, and lush neighboring vineyards. Most of these sites can be easily reached in well under an hour from the city by regional train or bus.

La Albufera

Just a few kilometers to the west of town, the limpid, circular lagoon of **La Albufera** has become quite popular in recent years with bird watchers and fishermen. But it's a lovely place for plain old sightseeing, too, with its reed-fringed channels, handful of surviving *barraca*-style houses with their thatched, high, V-shaped roofs (now virtual showpieces), rice paddies, and small cultivated fields filled with a cornucopia of Mediterranean fruits and vegetables. The area was immortalized—though hardly romanticized—by Vicente Blasco Ibáñez in his gritty Zola-esque novels *Cañas y Barro* and *La Barraca,* which depicted the hard life of 19th-century peasants working there. The central area is known locally as *el lluent,* "the most luminous," and Arab poets, who first gave the region its name, referred to it as the "mirror of the sun." The lagoon is dissected by labyrinthine canals, which you can explore in a long, low draft boat (or *barquet*) navigated by a gondolier-style fisherman.

Just under a mile from La Albufera's lagoon, beside the coastal crossroads, which lead south to the fishing village of Perelló or southwest to El Palmar, you'll find a well-equipped information and migratory-bird-watching center, the **Racó de l'Olla** (Carretera El Palmar s/n; ☎ 961-627-345; www.cth.gva.es), which is

Buñol & Its "Tomatina" Fiesta

Inland, west of València, the tiny town of **Buñol** tumbles picturesquely down a gorge just out of sight of its two ugly neighboring cement factories. It boasts an archeological museum in the remains of its old Arab fort and a traditional blue-domed Valenciano church (**San Pedro**). But its main attraction comes on the last Wednesday of August when a tomato throwing orgy known as the *tomatina* literally paints the whole town red. Best not to be wearing your most stylish summer outfit if you're visiting the place between 11am and around 6pm, that day. This manic display of tomato abuse started in 1940 just after the end of the Civil War, so you just might interpret it as a darkly ironic send-up of the bloodletting that took place then—or simply a fun event in which you can let off steam. It's great fun, and the whole mess is cleared up surprisingly quickly by the local fire brigade, which miraculously transforms the town back to its original state in just a couple of hours, as if nothing had ever happened.

For additional information, check with the **València-Paz Tourist Office** (calle Paz 48 in València; ☎ 963-986-422).

To get there, take the C3 *cercanías* railway line, which operates a regular service from València directly to Buñol.

now home to a small, silver-hued, freshwater fish called the *samaruc.* This wee creature, and the less fortunately named *fartet,* another former lagoon resident, were both in severe danger of extinction due to the pollution of the waterways. But now, thanks to the care and attention of dedicated local conservationists (who have helped cleanse the area), the dynamic duo are able to dart happily amid weeds in crystal-clear water, just as they used to in more halcyon days in the lagoon itself. Daily tours are offered by the center.

El Palmar is the tiny, cul-de-sac capital of this small region where you can eat *all i pebre* (a rich eel and potato dish) or paella in a score of waterside restaurants that are very crowded on the weekends with Spanish tourists. In spite of its great attraction, it's surprisingly difficult to get to by public transport—buses are few and far between—so this is one occasion where car rental is useful. Another option is to club together in a group of four or more for a taxi.

For more information on the Albufera, see www.albuferavalencia.com.

Xàtiva Castle

Xàtiva (Játiva in Castilian) lies some 60km (37 miles) south of València amid a sea of vineyards and olive groves. Birthplace of two notorious Borgia popes and of the great Valenciano artist Ribera, the town is filled with old mansions and twinkling fountains. Its greatest attraction is the huge, magnificently restored hilltop castle; its battlements and watchtowers offer fine panoramic views. Put aside some time for the comprehensive information center, which includes a video recounting its early history. And do take the winding walk up though pines past the Sant Feliu Romanesque Chapel if you're feeling fit. Also here is the **Cova Negra** (Black Cave), which boasts wall etchings dating back 8,000 years.

For more information, contact the local **Tourist Office** (Alameda Jaume I, 50; ☎ 962-273-346; www.xativa.es). To get there, take the 40-minute C2 *cercanías* train trip direct from Valèncìa to Xàtiva station. From there it's an invigorating 15-minute walk uphill to the castle.

Wine Lands of Utiel & Requena

The Valèncìa region has a long history of wine production, and vineyards have traditionally provided large amounts of workaday, low-cost *vino* that's ideal for quaffing with your paella or *pescado frito*. Today the standards and prestige of many of those wines have risen considerably, and if you want to sample some of these newer, highly improved vintages it's worth an inland trip by *cercanías* train to the laidback townships of **Utiel** and **Requena.** The latter, with its museums, 16th-century palaces and old wine warehouses is the more interesting of the two, but **Utiel** has a wider selection of *bodegas* (where you can sample top tipples such as the prize-winning Mustiguillo). Inside the bodegas are wineries or small shops where you can buy a bottle or two of whatever takes your fancy.

For more information, contact the **Tourist Office** (calle Puerta Nueva 9, Utiel; ☎ 962-171-103). The C3 *cercanías* line runs a service directly from Valèncìa to both Utiel and Requena, a total journey of just over an hour.

Sagunto (Sagunt)

A few kilometers north of Valèncìa are the remains of **Sagunto** (Sagunt in Valenciano; ☎ 962-66-55-81; Tues–Sat 10am–2pm and 4–6pm, Sun and fiestas 10am–2pm). The original city was built by Romans who occupied it, after the Carthaginians, under Hannìbal, had besieged and defeated its stubborn Iberian residents in 218 B.C. Highlights are the **Forum,** a compact amphitheater—controversially over-restored by architects Giorgio Grassi and Manuel Portaceli—and now under threat of semi-demolition by the Valèncìan cultural authorities—and a line of **watchtowers** from which you get great views of the green surrounding countryside, inland mountains, and sea. There's also a little **archeological museum** where you can see a modest collection of ceramics and statuettes dating back to Iberian times. Less interesting is the drab little township of modern Sagunto that nestles in its shadow.

To get here, take the C6 *cercanías* train to Castelló from Valèncìa; it stops at Sagunto after a half-hour journey.

Costa del Azahar & El Maestrazgo

Between Valèncìa and the city of Castellón an almost continuous string of long sandy beaches lines what is locally called the *Costa del Azahar* (orange blossom coast) because of the vast orange groves that extend behind it. Along it are a chain of rapidly booming and already overbuilt resorts. **Windsurfing** and **sailing** are the two most popular aquatic activities (rent the equipment for both at the **Real Club Nautico de Castellón** (Dique del Poniente; ☎ 646-88-00-36). **Scuba diving** can be arranged at the **Azahar Club** (Puerto Deportivo 7, Benicalssim; ☎ 964-31-23-13).

Levante Thirst-Quenchers

Recommended wines for purchase or just to quaff while in the region:

Morvedre and **Castillo de Liria:** Friendly, highly drinkable table *vinos*. These affordable tipples (widely available in supermarkets at 2.50€–4€ a bottle and in restaurants at just over double that) are made mainly from Malvasia and Macabeo grapes if they're white and Monastrell, Merlot, and Pinot Noir grapes if they're red. Both are refreshingly modest in their alcoholic strength (11%–12%).

Utiel's Bodega Mustiguillo: Classier—and far more expensive (about 15€–20€ a bottle). This vintage uses the almost black-hued *bobal* grapes blended with the softer *tempranillo*. The vineyard is located 850m (2,790 ft.) above sea level and avoids the oppressive summer heat of lower regions, which tends to make wines flabby.

Mustiguillo from Bodega Casa del Pinar: Utiel's quality competitor in the large Utiel-Requena wine zone, named after its two main wine-producing towns. Its vineyards lie some 20km (14 miles) from **Requena** and its innovative wines have actually beaten prominent Riojas such as Muga in recent London tastings. They only produce around 16,000 bottles a year using a dark *bobal* grape, which gives the product its rich color and spicy flavor. The bodega's **Sanfir Crianzas** (vintages) are tempered in oak *barriques* and blended with *tempranillo*, Cabernet Sauvignon, Merlot, and Syrah grapes to obtain a perfect balance, and these range in cost from 10€ to 20€ a bottle.

If your tastes are nonalcoholic try **horchata,** a refreshing summer beverage that looks like coconut milk and is made from roots. Local *horchaterías* specialize in the real thing, as opposed to the synthetic bottled versions found in many bars. Beware of a drink called **Agua de València,** usually served in a jug, which sounds nonalcoholic and tastes innocuously refreshing but is, in fact, a deceptively lethal combination of spirits and white wine.

Inland, but truly a world away, are the craggy peaks, Templar built castles, and undisturbed, walled hamlets of El Maestrazgo, of which Morello (below) is the most interesting for visitors. For more information on both coastal and inland towns in this area check www.castellon-costaazahar.com.

Vall d'Uixò Caves

A mesmerizing sequence of subterranean water-filled tunnels, the **Grutas de San José** ✪ (☎ 964-69-67-61; www.riosubterraneo.com; daily 11am–1:15pm and 3:30–5:45pm; 9€ adults, 4€ children) are well known to Valèncianos but still a novelty to outsiders. You tour them by boat for several kilometers and during your 40-minute mini-voyage view 15,000-year-old cave-wall paintings, and a wealth of torch-lit stalagmites and stalactites. The caves are located 20km (13 miles) south of Castellón at Vall d'Uixó, near the small town of Nules.

Peñíscola

Peñíscola ✯ served as the setting for València in the 1961 movie *El Cid*. It's superbly set on a rocky promontory topped by a 14th-century Templar's fort (now a very modest history and art museum), and its tiny lanes are still a delight to explore off-season, though the isthmus road linking it to the "mainland" is tastelessly overbuilt and in high summer gets terribly congested with tourists.

    Autos Mediterraneo (☎ 961-401-936) run 10 buses a day to Vinarós (1 hr. 25 min.) from where it's a further 20-minute ride by frequent local bus service into Peñíscola. Trains also run from Castellón to Benicarló where you can catch the half-hourly summer shuttle bus to Peñíscola. In winter, you'll have to take a taxi (around 7€–8€).

Morella

For many years, **Morella** ✯✯ was a secret kept tight to the vest by the happy few visitors who were aware of its existence. Today this walled Gothic city of vertiginous streets crowned by an impressive, if ruined, castle and set high up in the Maestrazgo mountain range is gradually becoming more widely known, though so far it's managed to preserve its natural character and not become just another trinket- and souvenir-filled tourist pueblo. The natural beauty of the place is remarkable, surrounded by wooded slopes and brilliant red poppy fields, its streets crammed with historic churches and monuments. Top sight (and sound): the dazzling, blue-domed, 15th-century **Basilica de Santa María la Mayor** (Plaza Arciprestal; daily noon–2pm and 4–6pm), the ancient organ of which plays a major part in the August Festival of Baroque Music held here. Loveliest views are from the tiny plaza in the ruins of the high **Castillo** (1.50€ adults, free for children; Easter–Oct 9am–8pm, Nov–Easter 10am–6:30pm), reached via the adjoining 800-year-old **Convento de Sant Francesco** (free admission). From there, you'll get a bird's-eye view of the well-preserved Gothic aqueduct way below. At the nearby (6km/4 miles) ancient site of **Morella la Vella** (☎ 964-173-051 to book a visit), you can view 10,000-year-old prehistoric cave paintings.

    For information on the town, check its **Tourist Office** (Plaza San Miguel; ☎ 964-173-032; www.morella.net).

    If you decide to stay overnight, look no further than the very hospitable **Hostal La Muralla** (calle Muralla 12; ☎ 964-160-243), which provides spruce and spotless double rooms with TV and en suite bathroom for just 40€ per night.

    Autos Mediterraneo (☎ 964-220-536) runs a twice-daily bus service at 8:30am and 3:30pm from Castellón, Monday through Friday, with just one bus on Saturday, departing at 1:30pm (no buses on Sun). The journey lasts about 2½ hours and costs 7.45€ one-way.

ALICANTE

Alicante is one of the brightest stars on the Mediterranean coast. Its white buildings, fine hotels, shop-laden avenues, *azulejo-* (tile-) covered esplanade, radiant yacht-filled harbor, and curving palm-tree-lined beach—all overlooked by a huge ochre castle perched atop a white rocky peak—combine to convey the impression of an affluent, sun-drenched paradise where lotus eaters can enjoy "the good life" year-round.

A BRIEF HISTORY

Alicante stands on the site of *Lucentum*—founded by Romans who were followed in turn by Visigothic and Arabic occupants. The next centuries saw a three-way tussle between Castile, Catalunya, and Aragón for ownership of the province before it finally became part of the Christian Kingdom of València in 1296. Two hundred years later, Alicante was given the official title of town, but in the 17th century it suffered a crippling plague and in 1706 was temporarily occupied by Archduke Charles's troops, who disputed the right of Philip V to the Spanish throne. In more modern times, its most notorious moment came in 1936, at the beginning of the Civil War, when José Antonio Primo de Rivera, founder of the extreme right-wing Falangist party, which supported Franco's military invasion, was shot by the Republicans. The past three decades have seen a gradual growth of prosperity, thanks in no small way to tourism, and the city now enjoys one of the highest standards of living in the country.

LAY OF THE LAND

Alicante rises gently above a bay enclosed by Cape Santa Pola and Cabo de las Huertas. Around the city is a dusty gray ocher landscape that would seem to have more in common with North Africa than Spain. Tawny arid mountains loom high inland, while along the coast an almost endless array of beaches and headlands extends in both directions, merging into more green and fertile regions after Benidorm to the north and Elche to the south.

GETTING TO & AROUND ALICANTE

Flights arrive at **Alicante International Airport** (☎ 966-91-90-00), which is located 9km (6 miles) south-southwest of the city. There are as many as 11 daily flights from Madrid, which can cost anything from 130€ to 300€ one-way (not the most economical option!), and 3 weekly flights from Barcelona, which start more reasonably at around 60€ one-way. A large number of charter flights—especially during the summer months—arrive from European towns and cities, mainly bringing tourists heading for the Costa Blanca resorts (see below). These can be extremely good value if you avoid high season (from as little as 60€ one-way from London with operators like easyJet). Buses run every 40 minutes daily between 6:15am and 11:10pm from the airport into the center of Alicante, and the fare is 1€.

Up to 12 **trains** a day run from València (1½–2 hr.; 26€ one-way) and Madrid (4 hr.; 41€ one-way); and 8 times a day from Barcelona (up to 6 hours; 50€ one-way). Information and timetables are available at **RENFE offices** (Estación Alicante, avenida Salamanca; ☎ 902-24-02-02; www.renfe.es).

Long-distance buses also run to Alicante from those three cities and their traveling times and one-way fares are as follows: València (2 hr.; 18€), Madrid (4 hr.; 35€), and Barcelona (5 hr.; 40€–45€). Locally there's a regular **bus** service to and from main Costa Blanca towns (from 2€ to the nearest, La Vila Joiosa, up to 9€ to Denia, the most distant), as well as to inland Alcoy (1 hr. 40 min.; 7.35€) and southerly Elche (45 min.; 3.50€). Additional information is available at the

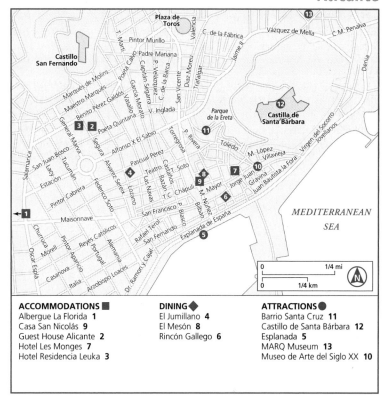

ACCOMMODATIONS ■
Albergue La Florida **1**
Casa San Nicolás **9**
Guest House Alicante **2**
Hotel Les Monges **7**
Hotel Residencia Leuka **3**

DINING ◆
El Jumillano **4**
El Mesón **8**
Rincón Gallego **6**

ATTRACTIONS ●
Barrio Santa Cruz **11**
Castillo de Santa Bárbara **12**
Esplanada **5**
MARQ Museum **13**
Museo de Arte del Siglo XX **10**

Alicante Bus Station (☎ 965-13-07-00). The best budget way to visit Costa Blanca is by the **FGV Tramway** (www.fgv.es), which was inaugurated in 2006 and runs a remarkably low-cost **rail** service northward along the coast, covering all towns and villages from Alicante up to Denia at fares ranging from 1.80€ to 11€ round-trip. Since 2008, a faster L 9 service has linked the city with Benidorm, covering that part of the trip in just over an hour. See www.fgvalicante.com/tram for timetables or visit their office (Plaza Puerta de Mar s/n; ☎ 900-720-472).

If you enjoy sea travel, fast **ferries** operated by **Balearia** (www.balearia.com) run between **Denia** and **Ibiza,** mainly in summer but with a limited service in winter. Arrival and departure point is Denia port's **Estació Maritim** (☎ 966-42-86-00) and the 2-hour crossing costs from 38€ at night to upwards of 46€ during the day year-round.

A final public transportation option is long-distance **bus** services from Madrid (5–6 hr.) and València (4 hr.). They arrive at the **Alicante Bus Station** (calle Portugal 17; ☎ 965-13-07-00). There is almost hourly service from Benidorm.

For those arriving by car from València, take the coastal E-15 Expressway southward. If you're coming from Andalusia or Murcia take the N-340 running northeast.

Local Transportation

Taxis are plentiful in the city and to travel from, say, the railway station to Castillo Santa Barbara, just under 2km (1½ miles), costs around 4€ to 5€. If you need to book a taxi urgently or in advance, call **Tele Taxi** (☎ 965-101-611), but expect to pay up to 50% more than the standard taxi rate.

Should you decide to drive yourself, there are **car rental** agencies galore. A reliable local company is **ATESA** (☎ 965-68-25-26), which may also be the most economical at 200€ to 240€ per week.

For info on the city's amenities and getting around in general, visit the **Oficina de Turismo** (Rambla de Mendez Nuñez 23; ☎ 965-20-00-00; www.alicante turismo.com or www.comunitatvalenciana.com; Mon–Fri 10am–7:30pm, Sat 10am–2pm and 3–7:30pm, until 8pm in summer). The www.aboutalicante. com website also gives a wide range of details on the city.

ACCOMMODATIONS, BOTH STANDARD & NOT

Though the neighboring Costa Blanca (below) has a wide choice of apartments to let, most of them are high priced and block-booked throughout the summer months and then closed or used by their owners in winters. The city itself has relatively few self-catering properties, but those that are available tend to be quite competitively priced. Here are my two favorites:

€   Actually four studio apartments, **Casa San Nicolas** (calle San José 5, ☎ 965-140-112; www.casasannicolas.com; MC, V) is right opposite the San Nicolas cathedral, so you have location, location, location in your favor. You'll also appreciate the sensible layouts: Each unit boasts an open-plan living area complete with a double bed and convertible sofa, TV, fully equipped kitchen, and separate white-tiled shower room. Three of them face the street and tend to suffer from traffic noise, so I recommend you try to book the more peaceful unit at the rear, which also has its own coolly tiled patio and sun loungers. Minimum stay is 3 days; rates are reasonable at 50€ to 60 € a night, payable in advance. A third person can be accommodated for an additional 20€ to 22€ per night. Cleaning is provided 3 days a week between 9am and noon (not including the kitchen).

€   Opened in 2003 in a peaceful corner of the Old Town, the small and welcoming **Guest House Alicante** ★ (calle Segura 20 bajo; ☎ 650-718-353; www. guesthousealicante.com; MC, V) is the project of savvy local Antonio Gonzalez. Wanting to keep his prices low, he decorated the rooms in what I'd call a "chic-spartan" style, by which I mean all the essentials are here, but no more than those. (Vibrant splashes of color soften the minimalist look.) However, as at the Casa San Nicolas (above), essentials include cooking facilities in the studio apartments (a boon for penny pinchers), allowing guests to prepare their own coffee or perhaps an omelet in the morning. Another genuinely lovely plus: tiny terraces off each room, overlooking a secluded and flower-filled central patio (also open to guests). Rooms are intimate (read: small) and prices range from 43€ to 48€ per unit throughout the year (with none of the shocking high-season rises you get in properties along the coast).

€ A summer-only option for travelers on a strict budget, **Alberge Juvenil La Florida** (Av. Orihuela 59; ☎ 965-113-044; cash only) is a surprisingly cushy dorm for college students during the school year, transforming into a hostel July through mid-September. Most beds are in private, single rooms (unusual for a hostel and at a good price: 8€–10€ per night), making up for the fact that the Alberge is a good 2km (1¼-mile) hike from the center of town. All rooms share bathrooms. *Note:* As we went to press, it was closed for renovations, but it should be reopened by the time this book is published.

€–€€ Business travelers are the core guests at **Hotel Residencia Leuka** (calle Segura 23; ☎ 965-20-27-44; www.hotelleuka.com; AE, DC, MC, V), so it's best to book a stay here on weekends when these briefcase toters are back home and you can enjoy both tranquility and lower prices (except in midsummer when rates don't shift much). Coolly comfortable, with double beds and pristine, in-room bathrooms nightly stays go from 60€ to 80€ for a double. They're in easy reach of the bus and train stations and a 15-minute walk from the seafront. Ask for a room above the third floor if you want a castle view.

€–€€ An antidote for the standard, bland hotel room, **Hostal les Monges** ✪✪✪ (calle San Agustín 4, or Monjes 2-1; ☎ 965-21-50-46; www.lesmonges.net; DC, MC, V), is a place with a soul, albeit a deeply eccentric one. In the common areas, surrealistic paintings (including a small one by Dalí—not an original) and ornate hanging lamps are side by side with time-weathered antiques (some with an Oriental or pseudo-Arabic cast), trendy modern furniture and colorful *azulejo-* (ceramic tile–) covered walls. Guestrooms are as delightful: Some have tradition- ally restored stone walls, roof beams, and iron bedsteads; others feature white- washed walls and polished wooden floorboards. Most have some kind of elegant period furnishing, be it a writing desk, a bedside table, or a small armchair, though all now also boast 21st-century conveniences like satellite TV, minibar, and Internet connection. Standard rooms are 70€ to 75€ a night and the star attraction—a Japanese-influenced suite with Jacuzzi and sauna—goes for 90€. The owners couldn't be more helpful, and there's even private parking.

DINING FOR ALL TASTES
€–€€ If you're trolling for tapas, head straight for Alicante's Casco Antiguo and either **El Mesón** (calle Labradores 23; ☎ 965-20-48-46; daily 1–4pm and 8pm–midnight; V) or **El Pote Gallego** (Plaza Santísima Faz 6; ☎ 965-20-80-84; daily 1:30–4pm and 9pm–12:30am; MC, V). The Muelle de Puerto's **Bar Potato** (no phone; Mon–Sat 1–3:30pm and 9pm–midnight; cash only), down beside the sea, is another small-plates mecca. Well-prepared tapas at all three are in the 3€ to 7€ range (from, say, mini tortillas up to *gambas pil pil*) and glasses of wine cost just 1.50€ to 2.50€.

€–€€ It may sound like it's a bit far from home, but the **Rincón Gallego (Galician Corner)** (Plaza Ayuntamiento 7; ☎ 965-140-014; daily 1:30–4pm and 8–11:30pm; AE, DC, MC, V) brings some toothsome but very modestly priced Atlantic seafood dishes to the Mediterranean seaboard. *Pulpo* (octopus: one of the dearer dishes at 14€) and *Ribeiro* white wine (14€ a bottle) are recommended choices here, though the best value is the 12€ inclusive lunch menu.

€€–€€€   A 5-minute walk south into the town lies a vintage eating spot that was a wine bar before the Civil War and evolved into a restaurant immediately afterward. A Hemingway-esque time warp, **El Jumillano** ✪ (César Elguezábal 62-64; ☎ 965-212-964; Mon–Sat 1–4pm and 8pm–midnight, Sun noon–4pm; AE, DC, MC, V) is delightfully nostalgic with faded bullfight posters and Old Town photos lining the walls and solid wooden furnishings that don't seem to have changed in more than half a century. All dishes from *merluza a la plancha* (grilled hake, 18€) to pig's trotters (12€) are cooked in a mouthwatering traditional style, their quality checked and ensured by the original owner's sons (Miguel and Juan José Pérez Mejías), who now run the place.

WHY YOU'RE HERE: THE TOP SIGHTS & ATTRACTIONS

The city's magnificent **Explanada d'Espanya** ✪, extending around part of the yacht harbor, boasts the loveliest mosaic-floored and palm-lined promenade on the Spanish Mediterranean coast. Towering high above it on the stark chalky hill of Benacantil, known as Akra Leuka (White Rock) by the Greeks, the stately **Castell de Santa Bárbara** ✪✪ (☎ 965-26-31-31; free admission; summer daily 10am–8pm, winter daily 9am–7pm) seems almost to float above the city. Romans and the Arabs used original defenses erected earlier by the Carthaginians in 400 B.C. and today the fort is still a maze of tunneled entrances, cisterns, underground storerooms, powder stores, barracks, high breastworks, and deep dungeons, all surrounded by moats and drawbridges. You can get up to the castle by elevator or by car on a curving upward road. Board the elevator at the **Explanada d'Espanya** (admission 2.50€ round-trip). When the elevator isn't working a minibus, leaving every hour between 10am and 6pm, takes you up and back (also for 2.50€) from the inland side of the roundabout near the small city beach.

On the southern slopes of the castle descending to the cathedral is the attractive **Barrio de Santa Cruz** ✪, a handsome district of wrought-iron window grilles and lush flowers that boasts a swell view of the entire harbor. This part of the **Villa Vieja (Old Quarter)** is becoming increasingly gentrified with trendy eating spots and tastefully renovated old houses gradually replacing the old run-down barrio. It still has a long way to go, though.

Right opposite the magnificent old Church of Santa María is Alicante's center for the modern arts, the **Museu de Arte del Siglo XX Asegurada** ✪ (Plaza de Santa María 3; ☎ 965-14-07-68; free admission; Jun–Sep Tues–Sat 10am–2pm and 4–8pm, Sun 10:30am–2:30pm, Oct–May Tues–Sat 5–9pm). It started life in 1977 with the donation of a private collection by the painter and sculptor Eusebio Sempere, which included works by Miró, Cocteau, Dalí, Picasso, Chillida, and Tàpies (as well as by Sempere himself). Today that collection has been added to, and you'll see notable works by Braque, Chagall, Giacometti, Kandinsky, and even a musical score by Manuel de Falla. The Museu is housed in the town's oldest building, a sleekly modernized 17th-century granary.

A recent addition to the Alicante cultural scene, the **MARQ (Museu Arqueológico Provincial de Alicante)** ✪✪ 🄺 (Plaza del Doictor Gómez Ulla; ☎ 965-159-006; www.marqalicante.com; free admission; Tues–Sat 10am–8pm, Sun and fiestas 10am–2pm) is certainly the antithesis of your stuffy old-fashioned repository of historical artifacts. Declared European Museum of the Year in 2004, it's gimmicky, noisily echoey, and effect-conscious, but children love it and you have to admire the huge inventive effort put into it. Its various rather eerily lit sections are filled with high-tech interactive exhibits that take you through various stages of Alicante's history, including information on the recently excavated Ibero-Roman city of Lucentum close to the Albufereta beach.

THE OTHER ALICANTE

Inland from Alicante is a spectacularly mountainous landscape, though its aridity—in contrast with the fertile coast—has forced local inhabitants to forsake farming and turn to private industries to survive. So one town has gone into textile and paper productions, while two others manufacture toys and still another shoes. The town of **Xixona** (Jijona, 20km/14 miles north of Alicante), meanwhile, derives its income mainly from *turrón,* a Spanish version of nougat; its ingredients include honey, egg white, and locally grown almonds. If you enjoy seeing how things are made—and really, there is a Wonka-like appeal in seeing candy created—you can visit the **Turrón Museum** (Jijona-Busot road Km 1; ☎ 965-610-225; Mon–Fri 10am–8pm, weekends and fiestas 10am–1pm) to learn a bit about the centuries-old history and manufacturing processes of Spain's almond and honey-based version of the French nougat, including traditional hand molds and almond grinders that are still used today. The guided tours that take place every hour not only cover the museum, which provides you with an overview of the different types of *turrón,* from the soft yellow-brown marzipan and hard white almond centered versions to the wickedly delicious chocolate variety, but also let you have a gander—from an overhead balcony—at the working factory that produces the famed "El Lobo" brand. (One of the museum's most popular attractions, incidentally, is a vintage Rolls-Royce delivery truck advertising the factory's ultra-classy "1880" premium brand, a firm Christmas favorite in Spain.) And, of course, there are tastings at the end of the tour.

While you're in the vicinity for the tour, take a drive to a nearby town or two. Some of these small industrial backwaters like **Sax, Biar,** and **Castalla** are topped by vintage castles that belong in storybooks. It's a totally different world from the coastal circus, which prospers on mass tourism and—apart from a certain amount of agriculture—little else. Visit these towns and you'll find the old ways of life still largely surviving. Few concessions are made to the pampered tourist, and you still get an authentic feel of the region. And though the surrounding wild landscape doesn't lend itself well to farming, it's rich in natural parks and walking trails—a haven for ecologically minded travelers. Buses run, with varying frequencies, to all of them from the main Alicante bus station (see "Local Transportation," above).

ACTIVE ALICANTE

While the Costa Blanca to the north has by far the widest all-around selection of sports in the area, from horseback riding and tennis to sailing and scuba diving, there are a number of sporting facilities in the city itself:

Swimming & Weight Training

Alicante's best all-around sports complex is the **Parque Deportivo Monte Tossal** (calle Tossal; ☎ 965-24-61-78; 3.40€) at the back of the town. Amenities include a gym, football stadium, jogging track, and two large swimming pools:

one (covered) open from October through May, the other (open air) from June through September.

Sailing

In Alicante's inner harbor, you'll find the **Real Club de Regatas (Royal Regatta Club)** (Muelle de Poniente 3; ☎ 965-921-250; www.rcra.es) set in a modern building that happens to be one of the oldest nautical clubs in Spain. Nonmembers can book hour-long sailing courses in groups of four for 12€ a head, or in groups of just two for 30€ a head. (Four-hour courses cost 50€ per person for 4 and 100€ per person for 2.)

Golf

Nearest to the city, just 10 minutes up the coast beside Playa San Juan beach, is the **Alicante Golf Club** (avenida Locutor Vicente Hipólito, Playa San Juan; ☎ 965-152-043; www.alicantegolf.com) an 18-hole course designed by former Spanish champion golfer Severiano "Seve" Ballesteros. Greens fees are 71€ year-round (or 47€ for just 9 holes).

Tennis

At the back of the town near the Villafranqueza district you'll find the attractive **Club de Tenis Alacant** (Camino Font de Sal; ☎ 965-662-252; www.puntodeset. com), which has seven hard-surface courts. Nonmembers pay 6.80€ per person for an hour's play. (Members pay 2.40€, but as memberships cost 33€ a month it's hardly a practical option for a short stay.)

ATTENTION, SHOPPERS!

Those two hoary old souvenir standbys, **leatherwear** and **ceramics,** can be found at the all-purpose **Fran Holuba** (calle Jaime Segarra 16; ☎ 965-24-45-95). If, on the other hand, you enjoy totally original (and unclassifiable) ornamental creations visit the stylish little studio of **Pedro Soriano** ✯✯ (Plaza San Antonio 2; ☎ 965-20-78-54), and check out Pedro's handmade plaster-of-Paris statuettes of mythological figures and other highly personal, fantasy-inspired subjects.

The newest event on the Alicante shopping scene is the huge two-story **Panoramis mall** (www.panoramis.com) right beside the sea at the end of the Paseo Marítimo, which, in addition to banks, amusements arcades, movie houses, and a largely Americanized choice of restaurants (McDonald's, Foster's Hollywood, and so on), has pretty well every kind of shop you'll need, from sporting goods stores to bookshops.

NIGHTLIFE

The two liveliest nocturnal areas of Alicante are calle Labradores and the Plaza Santísima Faz in the **Casco Antiguo (Old Quarter),** clustered around the Catedral of San Nicolas, and **La Zona** located directly behind the Explanada.

At **Celestial** (San Pascual 1; no phone; daily 10pm–4am; cover 10€) a somewhat arty—and not too young—crowd enjoy listening or dancing to Las Sevillanas, flamenco, and rumba sounds amid some wacky kitsch decor. Its weekend fiestas are legendary and the service is very professional.

Another spot specializing in Latin-Spanish music is the **Callejón Pub** (Plaza Quijano 6; ☎ 965-143-727; Thurs–Sat 10pm–4am; cover 12€ including drink) where aficionados are egged on by ultra-hip DJs.

Disco-lovers should, in turn, head for **Cienfuegos** (Cienfuegos 8; ☎ 965-217-299; 11pm–5am; cover 8€), which gets a noisy and enthusiastic young crowd who rave to house- and techno-oriented beats.

Gay clubbers are also well catered for in town. The most lively and outrageous rendezvous is La Zona's **Caníbal Pub** (Cesar Elguezabal 26; no phone; weekdays 10pm–3am, weekends until 5am; entrance 10€).

GET OUT OF TOWN: THE COSTA BLANCA

The **Costa Blanca (White Coast)**—so named because of the luminous quality of its soil and rock and perennial year-round sunshine—extends north of Alicante from **La Vila la Joiosa (Villajoyosa)** up to **Denia,** taking in **Altea, Benidorm, Calp (Calpe),** and **Xàbia (Javea)** en route. Much of this coast has endured a positive orgy of building—well-planned in resorts such as Benidorm (see "'Ere we Go! Benidorm," below) but anarchically haphazard in others like Calp. (After the latter's destructive flooding in the fall of 2007, some said—not wholly unseriously—that they couldn't see anything different with the place.) All these coastal towns can be reached via the FGV Tramway service that operates between Alicante and Denia (see "Getting Around," above). For more information, see www.infocostablanca.com.

La Vila Joiosa can justly claim to be the most tastefully developed of all the coastal towns. Its unusual blend of ocher-, blue- and orange-hued houses give it a Portofino or even Venetian look. Visitors tend to be more sedate, and the laid-back cafe life along its palm-shaded seafront adds to its sophisticated Italianate appeal. Capital of the area known as the Marina Baixa, the town also hosts the most unusual of the many *Moros y Cristianos* (Moors and Christians) fiestas that take place in Alicante province (see "Moros y Cristianos," below). For more information check the **Tourist Office** (Costera de la Mar s/n; ☎ 966-851-371). It's located 35km (22 miles) from Alicantea, and the trip takes about 50 minutes.

Elche (Elx)

Just 21km (13 miles) southwest of Alicante across dusty arid countryside is the town of **Elche** which—thanks to its huge palm-tree forest (the biggest in Europe)—gives you the initial impression that you've crossed the Mediterranean and are somewhere in North Africa. (The one disappointment: The dates sold in local shops don't come from the lush local groves of date palms, but from Tunisia.) Apart from the great oasis, it's famous for its shoe and sandal production and a unique annual religious show known as the **Misteri d'Elx (Mystery of Elche).** The latter—Europe's oldest dramatic liturgy—celebrates the Assumption of the Virgin in the 18th-century **Basilica Menor de Santa María** and has been performed every August 14 and 15 for the past 6 centuries. Admission is free, but it's hard to get a seat unless you book in advance through the tourist office. It's all sung in a very early version of Catalán, so if you do actually manage to get in, don't expect to understand a word.

'Ere We Go! Benidorm

A true hedonistic phenomenon, the resort town of **Benidorm** (43km/27 miles from Alicante) tells you everything you need to know about Spain's Mediterranean tourist boom of the past 3 decades or so. A former fishing village of a few hundred inhabitants, it has mushroomed into a sea of high-rise hotels and apartments that spread far inland. Now the home of Spain's tallest edifices, it hosts a summer population of over 200,000.

To knock the place would be churlish, in spite of its 1970s and 80s reputation as a trashy/tacky resort. Compared with the chaotic development that's taken place in many other Med resorts—which shall be nameless—Benidorm is a well-planned, well-run holiday machine. Its avenues are systematically laid out, its twin crescent beaches (naturally sheltered by 2 headlands) are kept immaculately clean, and its amenities cover everything a visitor or resident could want. And stringent efforts are being made to change its down-market image (which stars loutish Northern European youths drinking Guinness, watching soccer matches on huge-screen satellite TVs, and yelling "'ere we go!" at the top of their lungs). Admittedly, the attempt is still just that, but it's spawning innovative improvements in the cultural offerings here, most notably in the development of Aiguera Park with its amphitheater and jazz, choral, and classical music shows.

One thing Benidorm is not short of is **hotels,** though most of them are perennially booked solid by European charter companies. The place is easily accessible from Alicante by coastal train (p. 230) and a day visit is usually enough, but if you do feel compelled to stay the night, check with the discounter **Benidorm Spotlight** (www.benidrom-spotlight.com) to see what's available. Avoid the months of July and August at all costs! Distance from Alicante: 45km (30 miles); traveling time 1 hour 10 minutes.

But the town's perennial attraction is the huge **Palm Forest** ✪✪ of 600,000 high, swaying trees, originally planted by Greek or Phoenician sailors, and irrigated by a system set up by their Moorish successors a thousand years back. The most well-known section is the **Huerto del Cura (Priest's Grove)** ✪✪ (daily 9am–6pm) where you can see an ornate rock and shrub garden overflowing with tropical flowers and cacti and dotted with tiny ponds. Keep an eye out for the extraordinary 19th-century **Palmera del Cura (Priest's Palm),** which has seven large branches sprouting up from its base that are so thick that they resemble separate trunks. Also serenely tucked away amid the greenery is the famed *La Dama de Elche (Lady of Elche)* or rather a replica of the 2,500-year-old Iberian limestone bust discovered in 1897. (The original is on display in the National Archaeological Museum in Madrid.)

The town's rich history is explored in its newish museum, **Museo Arqueologico y de Historia de Elche** (Diagonal del Paulau s/n; ☎ 966-61-53-82;

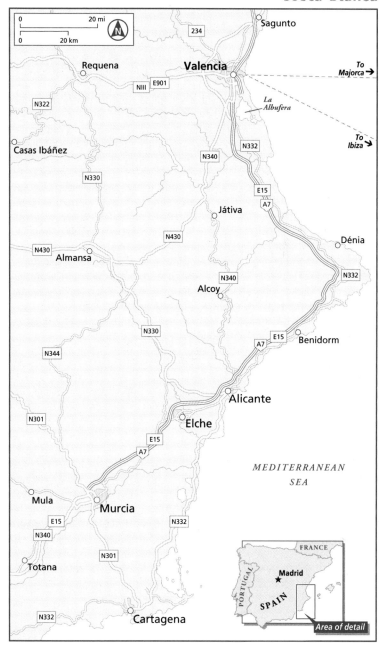

Moros y Cristianos

Though the Arabs ruled Southern and Eastern Spain from Andalusia to València for several centuries, it's only in the Alicante region that you'll encounter the uniquely lavish "Moors and Christians" festivities, which are celebrated with an enthusiasm that stuns the unsuspecting visitor. The locals, brought up on this tradition since birth, live these fiestas intensely. The best two shows are put on at **Alcoy,** a spirited independent Alicantino town located high above arid inland gorges, and at coastal **La Vila Joiosa.** The latter has—uncharacteristically—a completely nautical flavor. In this spectacular reenactment, which begins annually on the dawn of July 28, the "Moors" attack by sea and are repulsed on the beaches with alcohol-fueled, Churchillian enthusiasm by the "Christian" locals. Alcoy is a more typical solidly land-based example, starting the weeklong extravaganza with a huge parade—lasting up to 4 hours—of lavishly dressed Christian and Moorish troops brandishing scimitars or lances and accompanied by brass band or drum-playing groups, on foot or horseback, and accompanied by even more lavish floats portraying various activities relevant to the region (such as one I recently saw in Castalla which featured floats celebrating the area's wine harvest, complete with a tubby Bacchus surrounded by tempting nymphs who are inviting him to drink from bulging leather skins containing the local *vino*).

free admission; Apr–Oct daily 10am–10pm, Nov–Mar Tues–Sun 10am–10pm), which combines artifacts and interactive exhibits (all well signed in English) to get the job done. Recommended.

WHERE TO STAY & DINE

€   You'll only be able to savor the sleepy, almost North African atmosphere of this charming town once the last tour bus has departed, so it's a good idea to stay overnight here if you have the time. You can do this easily and economically at the **Hostal Residencia Candilejas** (calle Doctor Ferran 19; ☎ 965-46-45-12; www.hostalcandilejas.com; MC, V), which has compact yet comfortable twin or double bedrooms (45€ a night) that are attractively decorated with bright yellow– or cream-colored walls, tiled floors, built-in wardrobe space, and modernized en suite shower rooms. The hotel is near the center and about a 5-minute stroll from the Palm Forest. Even cheaper, but more spartan, is the **Hotel Faro** (Cami dels Magros 24; ☎ 965-46-62-63; cash only), where double rooms start at 30€.

€   First-rate weekday fixed menus for a mere 10€ are the lure at local's choice, **Mesón el Tozal** (calle Arbres 22; ☎ 965-460-904; daily 1–5pm and 8pm–midnight; MC, DC, V). A la carte specialties are available later in the day; for adventurous eaters, I recommend *pimientos de piquillo* (spicy peppers; 12€).

GETTING THERE

Train and bus services operate hourly from Alicante. Trains arrive at Elche's Estación Parque (avenida del Ferrocarril; ☎ 965-45-62-54 for schedules); and buses arrive at the town's Estación de Autobuses avenida de la Libertat (☎ 966-61-50-50).

If you're driving, simply take the N-340 highway southwest from Alicante; the turnoff for Elche is clearly marked. For general information check at the **Elche Tourist Information Office** (Parque Municipal; ☎ 966-65-81-96; www.elche.es; Mon–Fri 10am–7pm, Sat 10am–2:30pm, Sun 10am–2pm).

6 Barcelona

A tirelessly creative city of exhilarating contrasts

by Peter Stone

BARCELONA'S STILL A YOUNGSTER IN THE INTERNATIONAL TOURISM STAKES compared with other major European favorites like Paris, London, and Rome. Up to a decade and a half ago—so the word goes—relatively few people outside Spain knew, or wanted anything to do with, the place. Outsiders who did come before then encountered a grungy port city, one of the largest and busiest in the Med, its neglected seafront lined with wilting palms, oily canisters, and rusting containers, and its old, narrow-laned Gothic Quarter so grime covered you could hardly see the color of the buildings (gray as it happened). Add to that a muggy climate reinforced by the omnipresent Garbí wind (its humidity encouraged pollution) and you had a decidedly off-putting aura.

Then came the 1992 Olympics and everything changed. A tidal wave of civic projects swept away the containers and canisters, as well as the creaking wooden *chiringuitos* (still much missed down-to-earth seafood eateries) that had lined the then-grit-covered Barceloneta beach; they were replaced by spruce new "acceptable" eating spots (their delicious seafood identical to what came before, but pricier), an immaculate promenade lined with avant-garde statues and artworks, a freshly sanded shore, and chic yachting marinas. It didn't quite sweep away the muggy air—and now, alas, increasing pollution—but the whole place sure looked neater. Semi "no go" areas like Poble Nou zone on the northern coastal outskirts now boasted parklands and stylish eating spots, while still earthy Raval on the western side of the Barri Gótic evolved into a multicultural melting pot with some of Europe's best modern-art museums.

> " More than any other city in the world (Marseille and Naples are near rivals) Barcelona gives an impression of tempestuous, surging, irrepressible life and brio. "
>
> —Rose Macaulay

But wait just a sec. Let's not accept too readily this glib—if superficially accurate—appraisal. The city didn't really change overnight. All that pre-Olympics grunge merely put an apparent shroud over the city's instinctive dual talent for avant-garde creation and practical accomplishments: A seemingly conflicting blend of common sense and impulsiveness has long epitomized the Barcelonan temperament. The city may have been outwardly more rough edged before, but at heart it wasn't that different from what it is today. The canny Cataláns have ever been ready to adjust and go with the flow, to combine the brilliant originality of their arts (Gaudí is a prime example) with a will to build empires and make money, just as they did in their respective medieval

Golden Age and 19th-century Industrial Revolution eras (see "A Brief History"). They've seen good times and bad times, been on top and been oppressed (most recently during the Franco dictatorship), but always ready to soar like a phoenix when the opportunity presented itself. It did, and today they're riding high once more, the most dynamically inventive city in Spain and number one on any visitor to Europe's list.

DON'T LEAVE BARCELONA WITHOUT . . .

Going gaga for Gaudí.   Especially the famed trio of edifices at the Manzana de la Discordia and the knobbly-spired Sagrada Familia temple. Appreciation of such moderniste buildings has varied over the decades: George Orwell in the 1930s thought the latter was the ugliest building on Earth. Today it's revered as a masterpiece. You decide. See p. 284 and 288.

Drinking from the 19th-century Font de les Canaletes (Fuente de las Canaletas).   If you imbibe the slightly chloroformy water from this small artichoke-shaped fountain at the upper part of avenida La Rambla near Plaça Catalunya, they say you'll return to the city again. So if you believe that, just push one of the encircling brass taps, take a sip or two, and look forward to your next visit.

Savoring a concert at the Palau de la Musica.   The Oscar Tusquets–designed "Music Palace" is a magnificent sight, especially the sculptures of world-famous composers on the opulent facade. If you can swing it, consider splashing out on a top concert here (or just tour the place—it truly is eye-candy). See p. 282.

Admiring the colorful produce at the lively Boqueria Market (Mercat de Sant Josep).   Here the day's deliveries come in and top city chefs come to pick their goods—so colorfully and artfully displayed it seems almost a shame to buy anything and spoil the overall effect.

Taking the dizzy cable car ride (Teleféric).   Sway high above the harbor from Barceloneta to Montjuic in the Transbordador Aeri del Port (to give it the full name). Savor the exhilarating ride—broken briefly at three towers en route where you can relax and take photos—and the bird's-eye views of the city and harbor. See p. 291.

Enjoying the panoramic view from Tibidabo Hill.   This is where the Devil is supposed to have tempted Christ. (*Tibi dabo* means "I give you" in Latin and refers to the Evil One's supposed offer to Jesus to give him all that he could see below him if he would renounce his faith and follow him—the Devil, that is.) The sweeping urban and coastal vista is as evocative as any you'll encounter in the Mediterranean. Never mind the noise from the funfair—or the slightly tacky aspect of the would-be Sacre Coeur Church. See p. 246.

A BRIEF HISTORY OF BARCELONA

An appealing myth is that Barcelona was founded by Hercules, but it's generally agreed that the first settlers here were peaceful Celtic-Iberians who established a primitive outpost they called Laie in the lush lowlands between the Llobregat and

Besós rivers where today's Catalán capital stands. Greek and Phoenician traders followed, and the region's subsequent Carthaginian occupants were ousted in the 2nd century B.C. by the Romans who built a small, fortified township they named Barcino. Roman domination eventually succumbed to the destructive tidal wave of Visigoths that swept across Europe in the 5th century A.D., though—as in most parts of Spain, even their onetime capital Toledo—few architectural or cultural traces of warrior king Athaulf's race remain even after a 3-century occupancy. (Much of the layout of the old Roman burg can, on the other hand, still be viewed in the subterranean section of the History of the City Museum, see p. 277.) The Moors replaced the Goths but their century-long stay—a mere passing visit compared with their indelible, lengthier sojourns in southerly cities like Córdoba and Granada—likewise left little or no relics or monuments.

For Barcelona, the real change came with the next residents, who created the bulk of what you'll want to see in the city today (especially in the mesmerizing Barri Gótic, one of the largest repositories of medieval architecture in all Europe). This historic conglomeration began its life between the 9th and 12th centuries when, after a brief Frankish occupation by Charlemagne's son—whose introduction of French regional languages like Provençal sowed the seeds for today's Catalán tongue—successive counts united to make Barcelona their capital city, absorbing surrounding fragmented earldoms by marriages or inheritances. While inland Zaragoza and southerly Valencia and Andalusia were still Muslim-dominated, Barcelona, united also by a royal marriage with the neighboring kingdom of Aragón, launched its own Christian empire eastward into the Mediterranean conquering the Balearic Islands, Sardinia, Naples, Tunis, Malta, Sicily, and even Athens.

Political milestones achieved during the city's Golden Age—which reached its height in the 13th and 14th centuries, when both business and the arts flourished—were the drafting of the *Usatges,* or first Catalán Bill of Rights, in 1064, and founding of the autonomous city government (or Generalitat), known as the Consell de Cent, 2 centuries later. Coinciding ironically with the latter, the devastating Black Plague halved the city's inhabitants in a decade and was followed by a famine that put increasing pressure on the city's already stretched coffers, which had been poured into a delirium of magnificent buildings that included the great cathedral, royal palace, Santa María del Mar church, and Drassanes (the former shipyards that now house the imposing harborfront Maritime Museum; see p. 293). More funds were swallowed up maintaining its sizeable Mediterranean fleet and overseas possessions, and costs eventually outran income. One by one the possessions—Balearics excepted—were lost.

Then Ferdinand married Isabella (they're known as Fernando and Isabel in Spain) and the monarchs founded the new united country of Spain, bringing the hitherto independent Catalunya under its yoke, while subsequent regent Charles V forbade Barcelona to trade with the New World discovered by Columbus in 1492. Frustrated, the Cataláns rebelled unsuccessfully against the state in the Guerra dels Segadors (Harvesters' War) and lost their lands north of the Pyrenees to France. Further humiliations followed. After backing the losing Hapsburg side in the War of Spanish Succession the city was punished by victorious Bourbon prince Philip V who banned the Catalán language and closed all universities in the province, and from 1808 to 1814 the city was occupied by invading French forces.

Signs of regeneration followed—in spite of the intervening Carlist Wars and anarchic uprisings in support of Catalán autonomy (during which churches were burned and bombs thrown at the Liceo Opera House)—when Barcelona adapted to the Industrial Revolution with characteristic fervor, building the first steam-driven factory and creating the new wide-avenued "Eixample" section of the city. In spite of the general instability ambitious exhibitions of architecture, art, and industry in 1888 and 1929 put the city on the international map.

The end of the devastating 3-year Civil War in 1939 saw Barcelona sink to its lowest ebb when, after his victory, General Franco suppressed the Catalán language and culture, strictly censured writers and the arts, abolished the Generalitat, and even executed the province's president Lluis Companys. But after the fascist ruler's death, the city rejoiced and enjoyed an initially cautious resurgence, which has steadily gathered momentum. In 1979 the city was granted autonomous rule by King Juan Carlos; in 1992 came the famed Olympics; and in 2004 socialist president José Luis Zapatero requested that the Catalán language be regarded as one of the working EU languages. In 2006 a new *estatut* totally updated the 1979 version. Today the pendulum has swung so much the other way that Catalán is more used in schools—and in some offices—than Castilian (which some hardcore regionalists refuse to speak).

> ❝We're the perfect mixture, a fusion of Phoenician, Greek, Roman, French, Aragonese, Catalán, with a sprinkling of Musulman and Jew. Better than any other group in Spain, we're able to see the world as a whole, especially Europe. ❞
>
> —Barcelona resident and authority Dr. José María Poal talking to James Michener

LAY OF THE LAND

Barcelona divides cleanly into two main distinct areas: the narrow-laned medieval **Ciutat Vella** and wide-avenued 19th-century **L'Eixample** separated in the middle by the circular **Plaça de Cataluña**—the city's spiritual and geographical center. Most visitors will spend the majority of their time in these two areas, making visits as well to the harbor/Barceloneta area and Montjuic.

Tops on any traveler's list, of course, is the Old City (Ciutat Vella), a labyrinthine warren of slim streets (great for shopping and strolling) through which **La Rambla**—also known as Les Ramblas—cuts as its main artery. La Rambla winds its busy way (along a former riverbed) to the **Plaça Portal de la Pau,** with its 49m-high (161-ft.) monument to Columbus, right opposite the port.

To the west of La Rambla, behind the famed Boquería market, is the polyglot **El Raval** district, an interesting area that few visitors reach. On La Rambla's eastern side is the important, highly popular **Barri Gòtic (Gothic Quarter)** home to the city's famed cathedral.

Below the Old City, across the harbor on the peninsula, is **Barceloneta,** a former fishermen's quarter turned populist playground. Here you'll find dozens of seafood restaurants tucked away in the quarter's narrow streets and marinas that sprawl northward along the beach-lined coast. Just past the Port Olimpic is **Poble**

Nou an earthier but increasingly sought-after zone where you'll find some secretive "in" eating spots.

The **L'Eixample** (literally, the Extension), created in the 19th century, is home of many prized buildings of the modernisme period, including key works by Antoni Gaudí. You'll find it north of Plaça Catalunya. (Rambla is one of the main thoroughfares here, too, but it's known as Rambla Catalunya in this part of town; another important street, the Passeig de Gracia, runs parallel to it.)

At the northern border of the L'Eixample, across the road called Diagonal, is the chic, laid-back barrio of **Gràcia,** once a small town in its own right and now popular with artists and writers. Above Gràcia and to the west spread the stylish airy suburbs of **Sarrià, Sant Gervasí,** and **Pedralbes.**

The whole city is enclosed by hills on two sides. Southwest, above the Ciutat Vella, looms verdant park-filled **Montjuïc,** accessible by cable car, bus, or foot, and home of some of the city's top museums at its summit. Its hilltop stadium was the setting for the principal events of the 1992 Summer Olympic Games.

High behind the city to the northwest of L'Eixample, **Tibidabo** hill enjoys great views of the city and the Mediterranean from its pine-backed 503m (1,650-ft.) summit. It also has a veteran amusement park and a kitsch pseudo-Gothic church with a huge statue of Christ on top—a fabled landmark that can be seen from miles away. (More recently erected—and almost as high as the church, though it's several hundred meters away—is a Norman Foster tower that, intentionally or otherwise, resembles a huge hypodermic needle and is said by cynics to reflect certain activities that take place in the surrounding woodlands.)

GETTING TO & AROUND BARCELONA

Transport into the city is frequent and efficient, whether you come by road or rail, and once you're in the center, a further first-rate transportation network ensures you can find your way around the Catalán capital with the greatest of ease.

GETTING TO BARCELONA

Barcelona's main airport is **El Prat,** located 13km (8 miles) from the city center and offering easy access into town by bus, train, or taxi. Travelers arriving from within the European Union on budget airlines such as Ryanair may land at **Girona** airport, 103km (64 miles) northeast of Barcelona, or **Reus,** 110km (68 miles) to the west of the city.

Bus and **train** transport from all these airports is practical and economical. The **Aerobús** (☎ 934-15-60-20) from El Prat leaves just outside all three terminals every 15 minutes from 6am to 11:15pm. The journey takes about 20 to 25 minutes (leave a few more minutes for the return journey, as the bus takes a slightly different route) and costs 3.45€ each way. Alternately, El Prat has its own train station, just a short walk from the airport terminal. Trains leave every 30 minutes from 6am to 11:44pm, and the 25-minute journey costs 2.50€.

From Girona airport, the best way to travel into the city is by **Barcelona Bus** (☎ 902-361-550). The arrival point in the city is Passeig de Sant Joan, 52, and there are also stops at Plaça Espanya, Plaça Universitat, and Plaça Catalunya, all of which are major hubs with Metro (subway) connections. One-way tickets cost 12€. Round-trip tickets (which must be purchased inside the terminal) cost 21€.

Journey time is 1 hour 10 minutes. It may be slightly cheaper to ride the bus to the train station in either Girona or Reus (one-way tickets will range from 6€ all the way up to 20€ depending on whether the train is a slower standard model or a high-speed Talgo). However, I'm not sure the extra hassle of changing from buses to trains and the time that involves is worth it.

From Reus airport, the bus into Barcelona costs 11€ one way and 18€ round trip. The same advice on train travel (see Girona, above) applies here.

A **taxi** from El Prat into the center (Plaça Catalunya area) should cost 16€ including the airport surcharge. From 9pm to 7am and on Saturdays, Sundays, and fiesta days, the price rises to 17€. Luggage that goes in the trunk is charged at .90€ per piece. *Warning:* Make sure the meter is on when you hop in and that you are not being taken the long way around to your destination. *Also, very important:* Though you can take a taxi from Girona or Reus airport directly to Barcelona, it's not advised. The trip could cost you as much as 100€!

GETTING AROUND BARCELONA
Walking

If ever a city was made for exploring on foot, it's Barcelona, especially in the old Barri Gòtic where a new monument or church awaits you around every corner. At night it's even more evocative, especially on hot summer evenings when the tiny squares—gently illuminated—often echo to the laughter and music of seemingly impromptu young musicians.

Bicycles

An increasingly popular form of transport in the city is the bicycle. There are a number of bicycle lanes in the center of the city and few firms that rent them, including **Un Coxte Menys (Esparteria 3; ☎ 932-68-21-05)**, and **Biciclot (Verneda 16; ☎ 933-07-74-75)**. Rental rates average 18€ per day. You are not required by law to wear a helmet, and it's not necessary to pay a deposit if you leave your passport details. The first firm we mention also runs fascinating bike tours of the city from April through mid-September (a much more interesting alternative to the hop on bus tours, see p. 249). See the website www.bcn.es/bicicleta for a map of cycling routes and a more comprehensive list of bike rental outfits.

Public Transportation

Getting around the city is fairly easy thanks to an excellent inexpensive network of subway and surface trains, modern trams, buses, and even cable cars. One type of ticket covers the Metro, the city's buses, and the FGC (see below) and it costs 1.25€ for a **single (*senzill* or *sencillo*) ticket.** If you're going to make several journeys, a more economic option is to get a **T-10** ticket for 7.20€, which offers 10 journeys that can be shared by two or more people in central zone 1. (For journeys to outer zones 2 through 6, the card cost rises to 14€–31€, but the central zone 1 card is all you're likely to need for sightseeing purposes.)

Another option is a **T-Día** for unlimited 24-hour transport in central Barcelona for 5.25€. You can also buy Travel Cards of 2 and 3 days for 10€ and 14€, respectively, and there are more price-reduced tickets for longer periods.

The Barcelona Card

The cheapest and easiest way to get around is to buy a **Barcelona Card** at tourist offices, El Prat airport, Sants railway station, the Estació Nord bus station, and various branches of the Corte Inglés. It's well worth the outlay if you're staying more than just a day. Adults pay 25€ for 2 days, 30€ for 3 days, 34€ for 4 days, and 40€ for 5 days; for children 4–12 the card costs 4€ less on all options.

The 24-hour card covers unlimited travel on all public transport, includes a free walking tour, and offers discounts of 20% to 100% in museums, bars, restaurants, and certain shops. There are also discounts on certain theaters and shows, plus attractions such as the aquarium and the Golondrinas pleasure boats. For travelers 65 and over, a **T-10 or T-Día** pass (see "Public Transportation") is a better value, since seniors and pensioners already get those discounts for museums and galleries.

To sum up, for most short visits the T-10 offers the best value, with the T-Día a useful backup when things get really busy.

An activated *senzill* ticket can be used for up to 75 minutes on different forms of transport if you have to do a combined Metro/bus trip.

METRO

Barcelona's first-rate underground public transport system, the Metro (☎ 933-18-70-74; www.tmb.net), covers most areas of the city. Its five color-coded and numbered lines radiate from the heart of Barcelona. Stations are clearly identifiable by a red diamond-shaped sign with the letter M in the center; you can get maps either at the stations or tourist information offices. The Catalunya, Sants, and Passeig de Gràcia Metro stops connect with RENFE or surface trains. Tickets can be purchased either from vending machines or in-station ticket offices. (There's no difference in price between the two.)

The Metro operates from 5am to midnight Sunday through Thursday and 5am to 2am Friday and Saturday. Metro stops are often a mere 5- to 10-minute walk apart, so walking is a practical option if you don't want to keep hopping on and off during your sightseeing outings.

BUSES

A comprehensive and efficient bus service covers all corners of the city, though the day service doesn't run as late as the Metro, and rush hour traffic often wreaks havoc on the official schedules. Many routes have stops at the Plaça Catalunya, which is also the final dropping-off point for the Aerobús (see "Getting to Barcelona from the Airports," above) and the Bus Turístic (see below). After dark, the highly useful—and safe—**Nitbus** (night bus) runs from 11pm to 4am and is often your only option, as taxis can be hard to come by between 2am and 3am. These are bright yellow, clearly marked with an "N," and their main departure point is Plaça Catalunya. Travel Cards and other TMB passes can't be used on nitbuses: You have to buy your tickets for them (1.30€ one-way) from the driver.

A summer-only bus, but a useful one to know about, is **Tibibus T2,** which takes a circular route from the Plaça de Catalunya, via Passeig de Gràcia, Park Güell and the Vall d'Hebron up to Tibidabo. Buses run half-hourly and only in the warmer months when the park is open. The one-way fare is 2.50€ for adults, 24€ including entrance to the park (10€ for children under 1.2 meters/3 ft. 11 in.). Check the city hall's information hot line (☎ 010) for times.

A pricey bus tour, complete with multilingual commentary, **Bus Turístic** (☎ 933-18-70-74; www.tmb.net/en_US/turistes/busturistic/busturistic.jsp) is one of those popular double-deckers. Personally, we think you'll see more if you travel independently; Barcelona's more cost-effective public transportation is a snap to use. But for those who enjoy bus tours, trips cost 20€ for the 1-day pass (12€ children 4–12) and 26€ for the better-value 2-day pass (16€ children 4–12). Buy your ticket on the bus or at the Plaça Catalunya's underground Tourist Information Office. The service follows two different routes: the north (red) version covering L'Eixample and Tibidabo hill; and the south (blue) route around Ciutat Vella (Old Town) and up to Montjuïc. The service runs daily (except on Christmas Day and Jan 1) between 9am and 9:30pm.

TRAMS (OLD & NEW)

Hardly any genuine old-style trams are left in Barcelona today, though a notable exception is the century-old Tramvía Blau (Blue Streetcar), an atmospheric museum piece that grinds gutsily up the hill from Plaça de John Kennedy in Sant Gervasi district above Gràcia to Plaça de Doctor Andreu from where the funicular climbs to Tibidabo (see "Funiculars and Cable Cars," below).

Barcelona's newest forms of tram-style public transport are the comfortable Tramvíabaix and Trambesos services: sleek, modern mini-trains that cover five lines throughout the city: (numbered T1 through T5) extending along the coast from Port Olimpic and the Forum to San Adriá de Besós and inland up to the Palau de Pedralbes. Hop on at Port Olimpic or Plaça Francesc Macia respectively for these destinations. More trains are due to enter service, and by 2010 it's (conservatively) estimated they will transport 10 million passengers a year.

HEADING UP: FUNICULAR RAILWAYS & CABLE CARS

To get to **Tibidabo,** catch the steep **funicular railway** (☎ 010 or 906-42-70-17) operating from the end of the Tramvía Blau line (see above) when the Fun Fair is open. Opening times vary according to the season and the weather conditions. As a rule, the funicular starts operating 20 minutes before the Fun Fair opens, and then every half-hour; the usual schedule is mid-June through mid-September daily from 10am to 8pm and 10am to 6pm on weekends during the rest of the year. During peak visiting hours, it runs every 15 minutes. Fare is 2.50€ one-way (3.50€ round-trip) for adults and 1.50€ one-way (2€ round-trip) for children 4 to 12.

For full information on getting up to **Montjuïc,** see the box on p. 291.

Taxis

Taxis are everywhere and still a pretty good value. A ride from the Plaza Catalunya to, say, the Parc Guell will cost about 5€ or 6€ (rush hour traffic—8–10am and 6–8pm—can double that amount, however). If a green light is switched on, you know they're available. Their meters have a day rate (Tariff 2, which starts at 1.75€) and a slightly dearer, after-8pm night rate (Tariff 1, which starts at 1.85€, the amount initially registered on the meter, and incurs a further *extra* charge of 2€ midnight–6am on weekends), so check your watch—and the day of the week—before you get in. Kilometer rates are .80€ for Tariff 2 and 1€ for Tariff 1. Any further costs and surcharges are (by law) shown on the back passenger window. There is, inevitably, the odd con artist around (especially if you're coming in from one of the airports), so make sure the meter is switched on before you start your trip. You can prebook a taxi at the **Institut Metropolità del Taxi** (☎ 932-23-51-51), which can also provide wheelchair-adapted taxis.

Driving

Three words for you: Just say no. You really don't want to get behind the wheel of a car in Barcelona unless it's absolutely essential—negotiating the congested streets can be a nightmare. Buses and Metro trains run so frequently and regularly that they usually suffice, and if you're in a desperate hurry, there are always taxis. Parking is also scarce. If you do decide to have a car during your hotel stay, check to see whether on-the-spot parking is available. Hotel staff will direct you to a garage if it isn't. Expect to pay anything between 15€ and 25€ for 24 hours.

REGIONAL TRANSPORTATION

Cercanías or *rodalies* (in Catalán) services of **RENFE** (☎ 902-24-02-02; www.renfe.es) operate six lines from Sants station as follows, each colored differently on the RENFE Rodalies map.

   Line 1 (blue) goes east via l'Hospitalet to Maçanet; while **Line 2 (green)** takes you west to Sant Vicent de Calders and east via Granollers also to Maçacet. Both these lines have connecting or continuing services to Girona and Port Bou on the French border from Maçanet. **Line 3 (red)** goes west to l'Hospitalet and northeast to Vic, where further services operate to Puigcerdá in the Pyrenees. **Line 4 (yellow)** goes west to Sant Vicent de Calders and east to the Montcada Bifurcació, where it doubles back east again to Manresa, from which there are continuing services to Lleida. From Sant Vicent de Calders there are further services to Tarragona and Tortosa. **Line 7 (brown)** runs first east then west via the Montcada Bifurcació to Martorell. **Line 10 (purple),** inaugurated in 2006, provides a regular service to the airport (west) and the Estació de França (east).

ACCOMMODATIONS, BOTH STANDARD & NOT

Though most of the lodgings listed below are conventional hotels and pensions, there are several forms of accommodations that help make a stay in Barcelona more interesting and individual: traveler's rather than tourist's choices. We'll start with these:

SELF CATERING APARTMENTS

Aparthotels and short-term rented apartment accommodations are a boon for vacationers in search of a more authentic travel experience. Located in residential barrios across the city, they give you independence, a kitchen where you can cook for yourself, and the pleasing sensation of living like a local, if only for a week or so. They're a particularly good value compared with hotels for those planning longer stays. Most stipulate a deposit of one night and sometimes a security deposit. Look out for hidden costs for items like cleaning and extra people.

Below is a list of apartment rental agencies that I've given the once-over. In addition to interviewing them and their customers, I visited numerous apartments they represent. Because the agencies that service Barcelona tend to specialize in various areas of town, I've divided my recommendations geographically.

In the Old City

The Ciutat Vella probably has the largest selection of studios and apartments, especially in the Barri Gòtic where many old houses and mansions have been split up into small residential units, which are rented out by the day (normally a 3-day minimum), week, or month.

My favorite properties in this area are rented out by **Bcn Houses** (☎ 933-179-472 or 659-866-431; www.bcnhouses.com). Its specialty is compact (often 20-sq.-m/215-sq.-ft.) studios, complete with open-plan kitchenette and separate bath/shower room, that will accommodate between two and four people (a convertible sofa serves as a bed for larger groups). Prices per night range from 65€ to 110€. The lower-priced properties are often interior (either no windows or windows opening on a courtyard); the dearer ones are not only exterior but include lofts with small terraces from which you can enjoy views of the Old Town's towers and rooftops. As nobody actually lives in these properties—they serve purely to be rented out to visitors—the furnishings are functional with no personal touches or particularly individual character. But they're clean and cheery. Cancellations are accepted up to 3 days before arrival with no extra fees incurred.

Even smaller accommodations (only about 10 sq. m/108 sq. ft. living space!)—but ones that are blessed with a great location—are provided by **Soho Rooms** (☎ 630-08-82-44 www.sohoroomsbcn.com). It manages seven renovated units set on a medieval lane just three streets back from the port and surrounded by trendy boutiques. These tasteful little cubby holes, which can accommodate one or two guests, have retained the building's original floors and ceiling beams, giving them some welcome flair. Price-wise, they're similar to Bcn Houses (66€ per night in winter, 71€ per night in summer) and have their own en suite bath/shower room and a kitchenette with microwave. Their only real drawback is their size. Ask for an exterior unit—complete with a tiny terrace—if you don't want to get claustrophobia.

If you want more range and flexibility of choice—and you're ready to splash out a bit—then I recommend you call on **Friendly Rentals** (☎ 932-688-051; www.friendlyrentals.com). The mainly young staff are most obliging and only too happy to show you any number of studios or apartments in your price range throughout the city. All properties on their books are noted for their architectural character (moderniste, Impressionist, or Art Deco) but are mainly situated in the Old Town. Their wide and classy repertoire embraces everything from small to medium-size (30–40-sq.-m/322–430-sq.-ft.) studios at 90€ to 120€ per night to spacious (up to 150-sq.-m/1,614-sq.-ft.) five-roomed units, such as its elegant Reloj apartment (145 sq. m/1,560 sq. ft.)—with its wood beam ceilings, and curlicued, forged iron beds—that will set you back around 280€ per night for six people or 380€ for ten. (The latter may sound like a lot, but if you're traveling in a big group, it's actually a better value than staying in an equivalent standard

Barcelona Accommodations & Dining

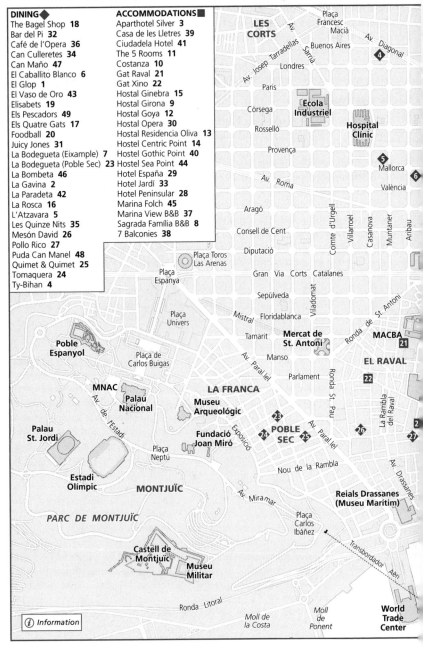

DINING◆
The Bagel Shop **18**
Bar del Pi **32**
Café de l'Opera **36**
Can Culleretes **34**
Can Maño **47**
El Caballito Blanco **6**
El Glop **1**
El Vaso de Oro **43**
Elisabets **19**
Els Pescadors **49**
Els Quatre Gats **17**
Foodball **20**
Juicy Jones **31**
La Bodegueta (Eixample) **7**
La Bodegueta (Poble Sec) **23**
La Bombeta **46**
La Gavina **2**
La Paradeta **42**
La Rosca **16**
L'Atzavara **5**
Les Quinze Nits **35**
Mesón David **26**
Pollo Rico **27**
Puda Can Manel **48**
Quimet & Quimet **25**
Tomaquera **24**
Ty-Bihan **4**

ACCOMMODATIONS■
Aparthotel Silver **3**
Casa de les Lletres **39**
Ciudadela Hotel **41**
The 5 Rooms **11**
Costanza **10**
Gat Raval **21**
Gat Xino **22**
Hostal Ginebra **15**
Hostal Girona **9**
Hostal Goya **12**
Hostal Opera **30**
Hostal Residencia Oliva **13**
Hostel Centric Point **14**
Hostel Gothic Point **40**
Hostel Sea Point **44**
Hotel España **29**
Hotel Jardí **33**
Hotel Peninsular **28**
Marina Folch **45**
Marina View B&B **37**
Sagrada Família B&B **8**
7 Balconies **38**

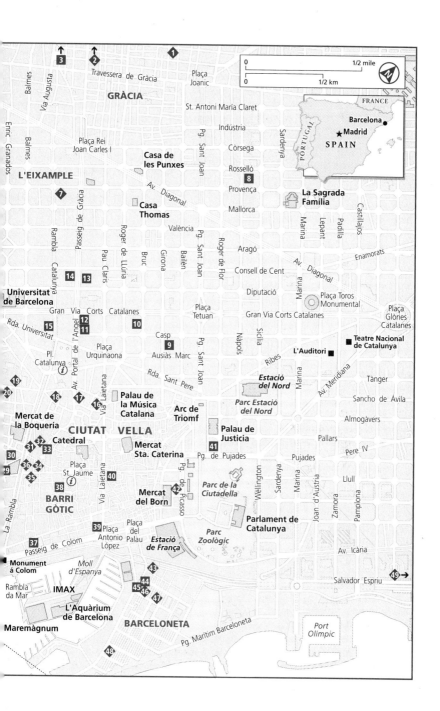

GRÀCIA

Travessera de Gràcia

Plaça Joanic

St. Antoni María Claret

Indústria

Còrsega

Rosselló

Provença

La Sagrada Família

Mallorca

L'EIXAMPLE

Plaça Rei Joan Carles I

Casa de les Punxes

Av. Diagonal

Casa Thomas

València

Aragó

Consell de Cent

Diputació

Plaça Toros Monumental

Universitat de Barcelona

Gran Via Corts Catalanes

Plaça Tetuan

Gran Via Corts Catalanes

Rda. Universitat

Pl. Catalunya

Plaça Urquinaona

Casp

Ausiàs Marc

Rda. Sant Pere

L'Auditori

Teatre Nacional de Catalunya

Plaça Glòries Catalanes

Estació del Nord

Parc Estació del Nord

Mercat de la Boquería

CIUTAT VELLA

Palau de la Música Catalana

Arc de Triomf

Palau de Justicia

Catedral

Mercat Sta. Caterina

Pg. de Pujades

Pujades

Pallars

Pere IV

Almogàvers

Plaça St. Jaume

BARRI GÒTIC

Mercat del Born

Parc de la Ciutadella

Plaça Antonio López

Plaça del Palau

Estació de França

Parc Zoològic

Parlament de Catalunya

Av. Icària

Passeig de Colom

Monument á Colom

Moll d'Espanya

Rambla da Mar

IMAX

L'Aquàrium de Barcelona

Maremàgnum

Salvador Espriu

BARCELONETA

Pg. Marítim Barceloneta

Port Olímpic

FRANCE

Barcelona

★ **Madrid**

SPAIN

PORTUGAL

0   1/2 mile

0   1/2 km

hotel.) A nonrefundable deposit of 25% is required to confirm the booking. Refunds of between 50% and 80% can be given on cancellations made more than 30 days before the reserved date, but after then no refunds are possible so it's best to cover yourself with an insurance policy.

Even more elegantly original, and a particular delight if you're a bookish person like me, is the **Casa de les Lletres (House of Letters)** (Plaça de Antonio López 6; ☎ 932-263-730; www.cru2001.com), a century-old mansion divided into half a dozen tasteful and highly individual apartments overlooking one of El Born's classic squares. Each unit is dedicated to a scribe who had literary connections with the city, such as George Orwell (author of the Spanish Civil War classic *Homage to Catalunya*) and revered regional chronicler Josep Pla (whose former home in Palafrugell is now a museum. Nice touches include the chilled glass of *cava*, flowers, and basket of fruit that greet you in the apartment on arrival, plus a bedside book giving a very personal view of the city and a bottle of wine to sip as your read it. All properties are equipped with satellite TV, cushy duvets, separate kitchen, and even a washing machine and tumble dryer. This is not a budget place, but you do get quality and value for your money. Costs per night are 150€ for a basic one-bedroom unit, 185€ for an *atico* (loft) with rooftop vistas, and 225€ for a two-bedroom unit.

Barceloneta

Barceloneta, just below El Born, is a good choice if you want to be close to the city's Mediterranean beaches. Though apartments here tend to be simply furnished, they're neat, clean, and reasonably priced: ideal for families with kids or younger, budget-conscious travelers.

The **Come2 Bcn agency** (Rambla del Caputxins 50; ☎ 934-81-35-77, toll-free U.S. calls 877/505-9161; www.come2bcn.com; daily 10am–9pm) not only covers a huge choice of properties throughout the city from Raval up to L'Eixample (where they tend to be large and expensive) but also—more interestingly—offers the most affordable and comprehensive choice of small (30–40-sq.-m/98–131-sq.-ft.) units in Barceloneta. Their sunny studios and two-bedroom apartments, set back from the beach in featureless low-level modern blocks (no elevators), all have private bathrooms and open-plan kitchens, and usually some stylish touches such as a wall painted Granny Smith green, shiny mod wood furnishings, or an arched brick ceiling. Expect to pay around 60€ per night in winter and 100€ per night in summer for a unit sleeping two people, and 80€ in winter and 125€ in summer for a unit sleeping four. Additional costs include a cleaning fee of 40€. Note that, in cases of cancellation, no refunds are made on prepayments.

Gràcia

An increasingly popular area just above L'Eixample is the villagey Gràcia just below the Güell park. It's fairly easy to reach by bus and Metro, and it has a relaxing and compact atmosphere. With its low-rise apartments, intimate plazas, slightly bohemian aura, and small but stimulating selection of bars and restaurants, it's one of Barcelona's most interesting and rewarding corners. Hotels here are few and far between, so it's an ideal spot to rent an apartment for a week or more and briefly get to be part of the local lifestyle.

A self-catering agency that provides really good value accommodations in this zone—as well as many other parts of the city—is **desigbarcelona** (☎ 934-676-774; www.desigbarcelona.com). It offers three main categories of properties. It's so-called "basic" studios for two people start at 60€ per night, while their "design" units start at 65€ and their "elegant" properties kick off at 80€. The difference between the three is mainly in style and size, the "basic" being functional and slightly cramped, often with futons rather than real sofas, and cheery if mass-produced furnishings; the "design" properties are larger and tend to be brighter, with such niceties as open-plan steel-topped kitchen areas and terraces; the "elegant" apartments are even more spacious, comfortably furnished, featuring notable extras like flat-screen plasma TVs, downright chic furnishings, and quirky works of art. The "elegant" apartments are also the ones that are blessed with large windows (and terraces). Still, if you're just looking for clean and convenient, any category should do (as I said earlier, the values offered here are high).

No refunds are made on prepayments, though dates can be changed up to 20 days beforehand with no extra charges incurred.

HOTELS & B&B'S

Barcelona is such a popular destination these days that it's essential to book before you come, no matter how modest the hotel you have in mind. If you don't, you may well find yourself scouring the often unappealing outskirts in search of a bed, and that's not exactly what you've come for. This is a year-round situation and not just true of the summer months, so be sure to get lodgings sorted out beforehand.

And don't forget to consider B&B accommodations. Virtually unheard of until two or three years ago, these family-run guesthouses (often no more than 2 or 3 rooms) offer a highly personal and cheap alternative to standard hotels. We list some of these below.

Hotels in Ciutat Vella

The Ciutat Vella (Old City), with its central Barri Gòtic (Gothic Quarter) and neighboring El Raval, La Ribera, and El Born districts, is good for hotels, *hostales* (not to be confused with hostels), and cheaper guesthouses. You can generally eat out less expensively here than in other parts of Barcelona and save money on transport, as most sights are within walking distance. *A word of warning:* Though instances of violent crime are rare in these areas (especially the Barri Gòtic and El Raval), it's best to watch your bags and be careful when returning to your hotel late at night.

€€   After visiting the trendy Gats (see box), I feel I'm stepping back into the past whenever I stay at the **Hostal Opera** (Sant Pau 20, El Raval; ☎ 933-18-82-01; www.hostalopera.com; MC, V; Metro: Liceu). It's a friendly place, though its slightly rough-edged and worn atmosphere echoes El Raval's down-to-earth personality (for all the good and bad that implies). I'd recommend it to travelers who want a private bathroom and air-conditioning at a good rate . . . while still maintaining a sense of adventure (doubles range from 58€ to 90€ according to the season). It also boasts a splendid location just around the corner from the restored Opera House (p. 278) and the Metro stop. The 69 rooms—all with phones for

Cool Gats

The bright and breezy Gat (Catalán for "cat") chain of hotels were designed by the hot, local architectural firm of BOPBAA, with the express purpose of bringing a touch of élan to budget-priced accommodations. They transformed these two older properties into hip hangouts, creating lodgings that are cheap but never chintzy.

€–€€   The more economical of the two choices—especially if you choose a room without private bathroom—is the **Gat Raval** ✸ (Joaquín Costa 44, 2ª; ☎ 934-81-66-70; www.gataccommodation.com; MC, V; Metro: Universidad). Here a mod decor—lots of white with cat's-eye green accents, comfy beds, and paintings from the local art school on the walls—is meant to hide the fact that the rooms are, at heart, pretty basic. (They're tiny, with concrete walls and floors.) Still, the place is highly social, thanks in part to the communication facilities in the lobby (including Wi-Fi) and a very gracious young staff. The hotel is also close to the MACBA and CCCB modern-art galleries, which is a plus if you want to gaze at some of the latest avant-garde exhibits. Most of the 24 doubles just have a washbasin plus TV and share a bathroom (average 55€), so if you want to have your own bathroom (75€) it's best to book ahead. **Downside:** Be prepared for noise—walls aren't soundproofed and the clientele here likes to party.

€€   Launched in 2004, the classier but still affordable **Gat Xino** ✸✸ (Carrer Hospital 149–155; ☎ 933-24-88-33; www.gataccomodation.com; MC, V; Metro: Liceu) is aimed at a slightly more adult and well-heeled visitor. It's a modicum quieter than the Gat Raval (they were installing double-paned windows when I last visited, which will help) with similar decor but a few additional relaxing perks such as a breakfast room that opens onto a wood-decked balcony and a lovely roof terrace where you can sunbathe in summer. Internet-enabled computers are available for use in the lobby. All rooms have air-conditioning, flat-screen TVs, and bathrooms with showers. Doubles average around 75€ to 80€.

receiving calls only—vary quality-wise between spacious standard ones and tiny basic picks, so if you haven't booked beforehand try to have a look around before you decide to stay. Those at the rear with private shower rooms are your best bet, as perennial round-the-clock revelers tend to parade along the street out front. It's a sound choice both financially and in terms of positioning but not, alas, aurally (the walls are thin, so bring something to stuff in your ears).

€€–€€€   The atmosphere is a bit more flamboyant just a hop and a skip away in the **Hotel España** (Sant Pau 11, El Raval; ☎ 933-18-17-58; www.hotel espanya.com; AE, DC, MC, V; Metro: Liceu), a genuine moderniste gem built in

1902 by famed architect Doménech i Montaner, who also designed the Palau de la Musica. (The creaky but quaint elevator that serves the four floors is also from another era.) The fact that the period character you find in the foyer and elaborately tiled dining room isn't echoed in the rooms—furnishings and decor are blandly motel-like—doesn't matter so much in view of the bargain prices you pay; I've seen doubles here for as little as 70€ from PlanetHoliday.com, though its published rates range from 90€ for a single to 110€ for a double (singles and doubles both include breakfast). So it's a good choice for visitors of all ages who are watching their shekels. Also, the España's in a prime central location between the Boquería market and Opera House (p. 278), and conveniently close to the Metro stop. Another plus: The friendly staff are moderately multilingual.

€–€€   Farther down the same street as the España, the 70-room Art Nouveau–style **Hotel Peninsular** (Sant Pau 34–36, El Raval; ☎ 933-02-31-38; www.hotelpeninsular.net; MC, V; breakfast included; Metro: Liceu) is yet another hotel with genuine character. Renovated at the beginning of the 1990s, it's standard moderniste in style with high ceilings and long corridors. The whole place was built inside the walls of a former monastery once linked by a tunnel to Sant Agustí church, and it still features the original tiled courtyard, lined with colorful plants and flowers and attractively filled with wickerwork furnishings. Half the clean, comfortable bedrooms have en suite bathrooms with showers, while the other half share one of the bathrooms on each floor. Rooms accommodating one to five guests are available and range from 55€ for singles to 80€ for doubles and on up to 140€ for quintuples. Communal facilities include a breakfast bar.

€€–€€€   In contrast with the coolly moderniste delights above is a far more intimate little hideaway on the other side of La Rambla. Called the **7 Balconies** ✪✪ (Cervantes 7; ☎ 654-23-81-61; www.7balconies.com; MC, V for room deposit only, room payment in cash only; Metro: Liceu), it's been run by the same friendly and hospitable family for more than a century. Traditional touches in this wee gem, set in the narrow-alleyed heart of the Barri Gòtic (just minutes away from the Metro stop), include a cozy tearoom, antique furnishings, Art Deco tiling, and faded family photos on the walls. There are just three rooms, one a suite that's a favorite of honeymooners (120€). The suite has an adjoining bathroom, while the other two rooms (80€) share a second bathroom. Each has its own TV, fridge, and safe. Make your reservation early, as many guests return yearly.

€€   A renovated old house tucked away in a cafe-lined square above the renowned (and separately owned) Bar del Pi—where students, artists, and fascinated visitors alike have long mingled—**Hotel Jardí** (Plaça Sant Josep Oriol 1; ☎ 933-01-59-00; hoteljardi@retemail.es; MC, V; Metro: Liceu) has a location that just can't be beat. And the views! The hotel directly overlooks the lovely medieval church of Santa María del Pi and the bustling square that fronts it. Those are the selling points, and they're good ones, especially when you consider the nightly rates (80€ interior, 90€ exterior). I'll also add that all rooms have air-conditioning and private bathrooms, 26 have small balconies, and some up the ante with private terraces (100€). Furniture is simple and wooden, floors are tile and very clean, and beds are generally comfortable. But some may dislike the over-enthusiastic lighting, the coffin-size shower stalls, pretty compact rooms, and the noise that wafts up from the ground-floor bar. (Book a room higher up if you can.)

€€   The great advantage of staying over on the northeastern edge of the Ciutat Vella at the relaxed family-run **Ciudadela Hotel** (kids) (Paseo Lluis Companys 2, esquina Pasaje Pujols 5; ☎ 933-09-95-57; www.ciudadelaparc.com; MC, V; Metro: Arc du Triomf) is that it's right next to the leafy, fountain-filled Ciutatela (Ciudadela) Park. So you can limber up with a leisurely pre-breakfast jog amid the palms, ponds, and swans if you're in the mood; and if you feel like some action, lively La Ribera district's bars, shops, and art galleries are a mere 5-minute walk away. The park's also home of the city zoo and zoological museum (p. 284), so it's a really good choice for families with children. Meals are taken in the hotel restaurant, and on warm summer days you can unwind with a drink on the terrace of the neighboring cafe. Private parking is available (15€ per day) should you feel reckless enough to drive. The white-walled rooms, with their rather functional wooden furnishings, all have free Internet access and private bathrooms with tub and shower. Prices are 75€ for an interior room and 90€ for an exterior. The closest Metro stop is the Arc de Triomf, right beside Barcelona's own smaller version of the Parisian icon.

Hotels in L'Eixample

In the wide-avenued L'Eixample district north of Plaças Catalunya and Urquinaona and centered around the Passeig de Gràcia and Diagonal, you'll find a mix of hotel styles. Some have been built from the ground up just to house tourists while others are tastefully converted late 19th-century moderniste houses, with the decor, elevators, and, alas, plumbing of that stylish era. What do they have in common? With the exception of those listed below, they tend to be on the pricey side. Still, this is a good home base. First-rate shops and restaurants are within easy access, as well as some splendid monuments and galleries. Those spacious boulevards do, however, increase the amount of traffic noise.

€–€€   You wouldn't expect to find a tiny, inexpensive, family-run bed-and-breakfast guesthouse set in the heart of pricey L'Eixample right next to one of Barcelona's most emblematic monuments. Yet the **Sagrada Família B&B** ✦ (Nápols 266; ☎ 651-89-14-13; www.sagradafamilia-bedandbreakfast.com; cash only; Metro: Diagonal) is just that. Nicely converted from a century-old house, it nestles alongside the distinctive knobbly towers of Gaudí's Sagrada Familia. Individual touches—like the open fireplace that makes wintertime visits to the Catalán capital more snug and cozy—go down well with older couples and family groups. As does the sunny balcony where, in summer, guests can relax over their morning coffee or even prepare their own drinks and snacks as the mood takes them in the communal kitchen. The genial owner also provides breakfast for 5€. The three comfortable, very simple double rooms (70€) are all equipped with queen-size beds and small private balconies.

€–€€   As I said, the Sagrada Família has a home-spun touch, but Barcelona purists often prefer to stay in lodgings that couldn't possibly be anywhere else but in the Catalán capital. Located southwest of the Sagrada Familia and just a short walk away from more central Plaça Catalunya and its Metro station, the **Hostal Girona** ★★ (Girona 24 -1º-1ª; ☎ 932-65-02-59; www.hostalgirona.com; MC, V; Metro: Catalunya) takes you back into golden age of modernisme. Designed by key architect Ildefons Cerdà in 1860, it's one of the most atmospheric hostelries in town. The main reason it's managed to keep its low cost is that the smaller rooms have to share bathrooms, which may deter some visitors. The charming decor includes multicolored Oriental rugs, twinkling glass chandeliers, and framed portraits and landscapes. The 19 brightly furnished bedrooms—all featuring air-conditioning and TV—range from singles with shared bathrooms to more ornate doubles with balconies and private facilities containing tub/shower combos (costing around 40€ and 80€, respectively).

€€   Whenever I stay at the **Hostal Ginebra** ★★ (Rambla Catalunya 1-3º-1ª; ☎ 932-17-10-63; DC, MV, V; Metro: Catalunya)—and I've been coming here on and off for nearly two decades—I feel I'm in a corner of a huge private apartment privileged with particularly fine views of Plaça Catalunya. Not that the rooms themselves (average 75€ double) are particularly big, but they are extremely clean, with plain but comfortable furnishings, and all have compact en suite bath/shower rooms. The big bonus may be the sturdy double-glazed panels that enable you to shut out the 24-hour noise from the hyperactive square. You couldn't wish for a better city base. The hotel's on the third floor of a vintage building, and you get there via an equally old lift. But the staff is extremely friendly and helpful, and there's a discreetly lit lounge with a 19th-century aura where you can sit and read or write as the mood takes you.

€€   Head north of Plaça Catalunya just a short way up L'Eixample's widest and finest avenue, and you'll find one of the best bargains in town, the well-worn **Hostal Residencia Oliva** (Passeig de Gràcia 32; ☎ 934-88-01-62; www.lasguias.com/hostaloliva/homepageingles.htm; cash only; Metro: Passeig de Gràcia). Nothing too fancy here, mind you—just honest, comfortable accommodations where you can spend a night in high-ceilinged rooms of basic character without breaking the bank as you might at neighboring ultra-stylish hotels. Doubles here average 60€ per night without a private bathroom—there's a shared communal one on each floor—and 80€ per night with private bathroom. To get the best out of staying here, ask for a room overlooking the Passeig de Gràcia boulevard, rather than one of the dingy interiors. They're a tad louder (though there can be noise from room to room so none is particularly quiet), but the sight of the ever-changing panorama of life outside compensates.

€€–€€€   If your tastes lean toward modern, pick the trendy, boutique-style **Constanza** (Bruc 33; ☎ 932-70-19-10; www.hotelconstanza.com; AE, MC, V; Metro: Urquinaona) on busy Plaça Urquinaona, bordering L'Eixample Dreta to the north and the Ciutat Vella's La Ribera district to the south. Its white-furnished lobby and sunny flower-print-decorated breakfast room create an infectiously youthful ambience and the bright and breezy air-conditioned rooms (125€–150€) all have Internet access and en suite bathrooms with showers. The lower-priced rooms are on the small side: Pay more and you'll get your own private terrace (though avoid those at the front if you want to get a peaceful night's sleep). For drivers, there's private parking close by, though in this area it doesn't come cheap (20€ more a day).

€€–€€€   The classiest bed-and-breakfast in L'Eixample is undoubtedly **The 5 Rooms** ✸✸ (Pau Claris 72; ☎ 933-42-78-80; www.the5rooms.com; DC, MV, V; Metro: Urquinaona), an atmospherically cosy place, with—you guessed it—five guestrooms, run by charming hostess Jessica Delgado. She not only provides a truly welcome personal touch but is also a font of local information and can keep you up to date on Barcelona's bustling art scene. The feeling you're staying in a particularly tasteful and civilized house is enhanced by the book-filled lounge and smartly-equipped rooms, urban oases of white brick, shiny light wood floors, and beds cushioned in fresh white linens. Original works of art grace the walls. At 120€ to 140€ per double, the rooms are not particularly cheap, but you certainly get quality and comfort for your money. Breakfasts are served virtually round-the-clock.

€€–€€€   Right next door, the equally friendly **Hostal Goya** (Pau Claris 74; ☎ 933-02-25-65; www.hostalgoya.com; MC, V; Metro: Urquinaona) is a darn sight noisier. It tends to attract a pretty hedonistic crowd, the type prone to letting off steam in the early hours (ask for the Principal wing as it's much quieter). Decor and size of rooms varies, but they all have a high-design sheen, with stark white walls setting off massive, colorful cushioned headboards or boldly patterned throw pillows. Best among the rooms (and all 19 have air-conditioning and en suite shower rooms) are the doubles with large, sunny balconies (100€–110€), so request one of them and avoid getting fobbed off with a darker interior room, which is often the fate of single visitors (70€). In the Nordic-style TV lounge, hot beverages (including tea, coffee, and hot chocolate) are dispensed free of charge. Book well ahead.

An Apartment Hotel in Gràcia

There are few hotels in this villagey corner of Barcelona at the northeast corner of L'Eixample, and those that are here tend to be small and unpretentious, in keeping with Gràcia's laid-back character.

€€–€€€   The **Aparthotel Silver** 🄺🄸🄳🅂 (Bretón de los Herreros 26; ☎ 932-18-91-00; www.hotelsilver.com; AE, DC, MC, V; Metro: Fontana) is a good example. An all-studio hotel, its furnishings never rise above the level of standard motel. But the crack staff here keeps them super-tidy, the front desk personnel couldn't be more helpful, and all rooms come with kitchenettes—small fridge and electric stove—handy for whipping up a meal if you have a picky kid in tow (or just want to save a bit on restaurant meals). Prices are a bargain compared with similar conventional hotel rooms, and range from 85€ for fairly compact "Budget" studios overlooking an interior patio up to a maximum of 145€ for spacious, brightly refurbished "Superior" rooms, which have larger kitchen units and their own terrace. Other perks: an on-site cafeteria and bar, private lawned garden, and parking facilities.

Hotels in Port Vell

€€–€€€   The bustling Port Vell (Old Port) that extends on either side of the famed Columbus statue at the end of La Rambla has never been a spot for real budget finds. The choice is mainly between traditional cheap but hardly cheerful ultra-basic *pensioni* (of an indeterminate age and dubious plumbing), and the high-priced four- and five-star business hotels of the modern harborside World Trade Center. There is, however, at least one glowing affordable alternative in the **Marina View B&B** (Passeig de Colom s/n; ☎ 609-20-64-93; www.marina viewbcn.com; MC, V for reservations, cash only for stay; Metro: Drassanes), a renovated 19th-century building, which directly overlooks the colorful yacht-filled harbor. From here, you can wander the alleyways of the Barri Gòtic just behind the hotel, or visit the nearby aquarium and explore the miles of beaches that extend north. Each of the five compact but cheery bedrooms (105€–130€)—think *lots* of yellow—bears a name with nautical or historic connotations (Columbus, Pier, and so on) and all have Internet access plus private bathrooms with shower. Obliging host José María will also lay on breakfast in bed if you're feeling lazy. Book well ahead.

Hotels in Barceloneta

Accommodations of any sort are hard to come by in this former fishermen's quarter which has recently experienced a wave of gentrification. It's more tranquil than the bustling city center, an area where the salty Mediterranean air blows along the Neapolitan-style narrow streets. Find the rare right spot here—like the Marina Folch below—and you can enjoy a totally different kind of Barcelona sojourn.

€€   The intimate **Marina Folch** (Carrer del Mar 16; ☎ 933-10-37-09; AE, DC, MC, V; Metro: Bareloneta) offers you a chance to be right on the Barceloneta seafront without paying the prohibitive rates you would in Port Olimpic just up the coast. It's just a few strides from the beach or back into the straight-laned barrio's tempting array of fish restaurants and tapas bars. Nothing flashy about the accommodations—just 10 clean, sea-blue bedrooms, each with air-conditioning, TV, and private bathroom with shower (singles 60€, doubles 75€). The only minor hassle is the restaurant below (same management), which can get noisy at lunch and in the evening. If you want to get out and about, the Barceloneta Metro station is several minutes' walk away and the hotel has parking facilities.

HOSTEL OPTIONS

The attractive **Equity Point chain** (Provença 332 entlo, Mezzanine Floor; ☎ 932-31-20-45; www.equity-point.com; Mon–Fri 8am–6pm) has a youth-oriented trio of hostels located in different corners of the city. All three charge for linens and towels at 2€ per item and include free continental breakfast and Wi-Fi Internet connection.

€   Let's start with the hyper-economical **Hostel Sea Point** (Passeig Joan de Borbó; ☎ 932-24-70-75; MC, V; Metro: Barceloneta), by far the most enticing option for visitors who enjoy being close to the Med, as it's a mere stone's throw from the main Barceloneta beach. What will put off many, though, is the fact that there are no individual rooms, only dormitories. Still, the dorms are large and clean, if spartan, and contain up to eight beds (nightly rates run 17€–24€ per person including breakfast). Among the facilities is a loud, fun-filled common room with TV, bar, and great sea views.

€–€€ Ciutat Vella's sprightly and sociable **Hostel Gothic Point** (Carrer Vigatans; ☎ 932-68-78-08; MC, V; Metro: Jaume I), is located in narrow-laned La Ribera close to the Picasso Museum and a host of chic local bars and nightspots. It provides basic accommodations, alleviated by ultra-bright decor, and—scoring over Sea Point—offers the choice between staying in independent single or double rooms (40€–55€) and eight-bedded dormitories (20€–24€). The spacious lounge has TV and vending machines and is a popular meeting point.

€–€€ The slightly classier counterpart to the above duo, located in L'Eixample's stylish Manzana de la Discordia area, is the **Hostel Centric Point** ★ (Corner of Passeig de Gràcia and Consell de Cent; ☎ 932-15-65-38; MC, V; Metro: Passeig de Gràcia), which provides the same type of bargain accommodations as its compadres, only this time in a splendidly refurbished moderniste building with a wide choice of both independent rooms and dormitories. Rates range from just 17€ to 25€ for a bed in a dorm to 100€ to 130€ for a double with en suite facilities. Independent singles with bath range from 80€ to a high of 120€ in summer. Like the others it has a sociable common room where guests congregate and have fun, and out in the wide avenues you have a nearly endless selection of shops, bars, and terrace cafes.

DINING FOR ALL TASTES

Barcelona has a culinary tradition that's all its own. In the opinion of many "foodie" critics, it's even surpassed its Gallic neighbors in inventiveness and quality, and top chefs like Sergi Arola and Ferran Adrià now rate high in Michelin awards thanks to their mold-breaking fusion dishes, which imaginatively blend both regional and international specialties.

Yet, even before its recent fame, Catalunya was highly regarded in the world of food and wine, producing simple classics like *pa amb oli* (white bread rubbed with tomato pulp and garlic and soaked in olive oil—with mountain ham as a possible deluxe extra). *Xamfaina* (a variant on Gallic rataouille) and *esqueixada* (a salt cod–based entree). The *cavas* and *vinos* of the Penedés area south of the city are among Spain's finest.

Vegetarian restaurants are denting the hearty protein-filled world of old Spanish cuisine, see Juicy Jones (p. 264). International cuisine is also making a stronger impression than in the past, especially in multi-ethnic districts such as El Raval, where inexpensive eateries run by Pakistanis, Moroccans, and South Americans offer a colorful change. Less progressive is the air-quality situation: Smoking is still widespread in eating spots in spite of a 2006 law that offered restaurateurs a chance to ban it if they saw fit. Ninety-nine percent didn't, though places over 100 square meters (1,076 sq. ft.) must have a small no smoking zone.

Finally, meals don't have to be expensive. Even though the cost of living in Barcelona is now the highest in Spain (alongside the Basque country's San Sebastián—another foodie heaven) you can still eat well more cheaply here than anywhere else in the country. Lunch hours are usually 2 to 4pm and dinner after 9pm. Make the most of the lunchtime *menú del día* (lunch of the day) which comprises three courses plus wine for somewhere between 10€ and 15€. Some places add the 7% IVA (sales tax) separately, but there is no service charge as in, say, France. A 10% tip maximum is recommended. In bars, for drinks and tapas, tip about the same.

CIUTAT VELLA

€   A functional locale that focuses, as you'd imagine, on its proclaimed "tasty chicken." **Pollo Rico** (Sant Pau 31; ☎ 934-41-31-84; www.polloricosl.com; Sun–Tues and Thurs–Sat 10am–1am; cash only; Metro: Liceu) offers little finesse in terms of ambience. But you do get what you pay for: a delicious, large-sized, freshly cooked fowl (they twirl and crackle on spits all day behind the zanily painted front window), which you can sample downstairs at the long zinc bar or in one of two tiled but mercilessly lit *salones* (one smoking, one no smoking). Or simply take a slightly smaller one away. Fishy dishes, including salmon and squid, are also available, and you can wash down whatever you eat with the restaurant's alcoholic piece de resistance: a knock-'em-cold sangria. No need to spend more than 10€ to 12€ a head, all in.

€–€€   Unobtrusively concealed in a tiny street near Plaça Catalunya, **La Rosca** (Juliá Portet 6; ☎ 933-02-51-73; Sun–Fri 9am–9:30pm, closed Aug 20–Aug 30; cash only; Metro: Catalunya) is a rustic-style blast from the past, with fading photos of old Barcelona lining its aging walls. Run by dedicated owner Don Alberto Vellve, it's been a hit with locals since the Franco era, thanks to its bargain blend of Catalán and Castilian dishes from *habas saltaedas con jamón y botifarra* (white beans sautéed with ham and Catalán sausage, 9€) to *calamares en su tinta* (squid cooked in their own ink, 10€). The three-course luncheon (10€) is the best value here, and for a semi-splurge try the *rape a la plancha* (grilled monkfish, 12€). Get in early, as the 60-odd tables fill up quickly.

€–€€   For a cheap lunch deal in central Raval just a short stroll from Plaça Catalunya, try **Elisabets** (Carrer Elisabets 2-4; ☎ 933-17-58-26; Mon–Fri 2–4pm and 7–11pm, Sat 7:30–11pm, closed 3 weeks in Aug; cash only; Metro: Catalunya). Its hearty, inclusive, 9€ menu includes the likes of lasagna and *escalope* plus wine. Evenings are an altogether different matter with mainly only tapas available (except Fri, when a fairly pricey dinner is served). The place also provides good sandwiches, but that bargain lunch is the thing to go for.

€–€€   If you enjoy delicious salty things like *mariscos* (shellfish) and *mero* (grouper) in a fun atmosphere, try the lively and understandably crowded **La Paradeta** ✸ (Comercial 7; ☎ 932-68-19-39; Tues–Fri 8–11pm, Sat 1–4pm and 8pm–midnight, Sun 1–4 pm; cash only; Metro: Arc de Triomf) close to the Arc de Triomf above the Ciutadella Park. Whatever you choose from the array of plastic tub containers at the counter is weighed in front of you and served in two shakes on a platter. There are no waiters, only the quicksilver counter staff, which probably accounts for the saving on costs. Most dishes are from 7€ to 12€, so expect to pay around 18€ to 20€ for a modest blowout. Wines—even the usually prohibitive Albariños from Galicia—are a good value, too. On weekends it becomes a bit too jostly, so avoid it then if you can.

€–€€   Speed and economy are the essence of **Les Quinze Nits** ✸✸ (Plaça Reial 6; ☎ 933-17-30-75; daily 1–3:45pm and 8:30–11:30pm; AE, MC, V; Metro: Liceu),

"Verde Que Te Quiero Verde"

Was the poet Lorca, subconsciously or otherwise, thinking of vegetarian grub when he wrote that line? (literally—with apologies for the clunkiness of the English translation—"Green, I want you green?"). If so he would be pleased to see the changes that have taken place over the last decade in the Catalán capital, where there are now well over 30 officially "green" establishments. Vegetarian-friendly dishes, like omelets, peppers, eggplants, *pisto* (like *xamfaina,* another Spanish version of ratatouille), and *patatas bravas* have been around for some time in traditional eating spots. But now the choice has become far more international and imaginative, not least due to the increasing numbers of Arabic, Chinese, Indian, and Greek restaurants—with their traditional couscous, rice and noodle-based dishes—that have sprung up in areas like Raval. For a comprehensive list, see www.sincarne.net/barcelona-vegan-restaurants.htm. In the meantime check out these four veggie hot spots:

€–€€   A delightful refuge in the heart of the Barri Gòtic is the friendly Danish-owned **Juicy Jones** ✦ (Cardenal Casañas 7; ☎ 933-02-43-20; daily noon–midnight; cash only; Metro: Liceu), the only 100% genuine vegan (as opposed to merely vegetarian) restaurant in town. Vivid cartoon-style images cover the walls and the youthful, extremely laid-back waiters are friendly even if they give the impression they're just passing through. Main dishes (6€–10€) include *escalivada* (grilled aubergine, onions, and peppers) and couscous and there's an affordable weekday menu of around 10€. Healthy beverages include delicious mango and pear juices, alcohol-free beer, and organic wines. If you're not in a hurry, go past the narrow bar with its long counter and settle down in the semi-basement dining area at the back.

€   You may have to queue for a while to get into **L'Atzavara** ✦ (Muntaner 109; ☎ 934-54-59-25; Mon–Sat noon–11pm; V; Metro: Hospital Clinic), but once you do cross the portals of this 100% veggie haven, you'll find yourself in one of the best value spots in all L'Eixample. It's down to earth,

a seriously popular locale in the Barri Gòtic's most emblematic square and one of several such establishments in the city. The decor and setting look relaxing (potted palms, non abrasive lighting), but the ambience is more in keeping with a fast food joint, as frantic waiters weave their way between the eager hordes of noshers who cram in—usually after queuing—to be quickly replaced by new arrivals. (Perennial lines outside are something you have to put up with before you can get in.) The prices and quality of the food are the reasons for the almost nonstop turnover. Here you can enjoy mouth-watering dishes like *dorada con esparragos* (bream with asparagus, 12€) and *botifarra con habas* (spicy Catalán sausage with broad beans, 8€) for far less than you'd pay for similar-quality food in classier basic, and often noisy, but who cares: What you're here for is the excellent constantly changing 10€ three-course lunch menu, which includes colorfully inventive salads and a wide choice of non-animal-fat dishes ranging from mushroom cannelloni to pine nut and raisin crepes.

€   They may not be quite New York style, but the goodies served in **The Bagel Shop** (Canuda 25; ☎ 933-02-41-61; daily 12:30–11:30pm; cash only; Metro: Liceu), a bright little cafe just off the top end of La Rambla (near the Metro stop), will certainly do if you're craving a taste of New York. The service is friendly and multilingual, and the bagels contain all the standards from sesame to poppy seed, plus a few European extras like black olives. Fillings range from honey to salmon and cream cheese. There are also over a dozen slightly dearer (5€–6€) vegetarian versions, including international items such as hummus, as well as pancakes with real maple syrup and a particularly tasty cheesecake selection. For those who prefer to eat on the move, a takeaway option is available for everything on the menu.

€   The name may sound like a Catalán attempt to describe soccer, but **Foodball** (Elisabets 9; ☎ 932-70-13-63; daily noon–11pm; cash only, Metro: Catalunya) is, in fact, a hip, low-budget, nonsmoking locale specializing in eponymous wholegrain rice balls (5€–6€) stuffed with veggie and macrobiotic treats like organic mushrooms, chickpeas, *seitan* (wheat gluten), tofu, and seaweed, and healthy beverages such as mineral water, hemp beer, or fresh fruit juices. Located near the Raval's MACBA and CCCB museums, it combines cafe and take-away amenities. Sit inside on cement chairs with straw cushions and watch soothing TV-screen images like rippleless ponds, or check out the colorful walls lined with holistic flyers, all designed by idiosyncratic Catalán Martí Guixé, who is also responsible for the decor of many of Camper's shoe shops (they own the joint). Or go outside with your (recyclable!) cardboard container and nosh wherever strikes your fancy.

establishments. There are a few glitches: For example, Paella is occasionally less up to scratch—given the time factors in such a place—but by and large you won't be disappointed. The 12€ weekday set lunch is a real save for this area, but don't expect to linger over your meal.

€–€€   Set between a couple of the Barri Gòtic's most charming squares, opposite an imposing Gothic church, the **Bar del Pi** (Plaça Sant Josep Oriol 1; ☎ 933-02-21-23; Mon–Fri 9am–11pm, Sat 9:30am–10:30pm, Sun 10am–10pm; cash only; Metro: Liceu) is one of the city's most emblematic watering holes. It's not a bad value either, as long as you stay inside beside the packed bar or at one of the rather cramped tables. Of course it's much nicer—and correspondingly costlier—outside where you can sit in the sun or in the shade of the single plane tree (contrary to what its name suggests—*pi* means "pine" in Catalán—there are no pine trees here). Sample the array of tapas and canapés (which usually cost 3€–7€ each); sip an *horchata* (a tigernut milk beverage originating from Valencia) or something stronger, like the heady house sangria; and listen to the street musicians.

€–€€   It's not exactly cheap for anything other than a morning coffee, but you'd kick yourself if you missed a visit to the **Café de l'Opera** ✦✦ (La Rambla 74; ☎ 933-02-41-80; Mon–Fri 8:30am–2am, Sat–Sun 8:30am–3am; cash only; Metro: Liceu), one of the handful of period waterholes that's survived the merciless advance of the twee and characterless franchises throughout the city in recent years and that for some developers—and let's face it, some members of the public—represent "progress." Located on La Rambla opposite the Liceu Opera House, it still manages to conjure up a time when well-clad aficionados of Tosca and Verdi would get together for a pre-performance *manzanilla*. It has been renovated over the years, but only in order to preserve its original Belle Epoque decor of opulent murals, decorative mirrors, and cast-iron columns. Service from the bow-tied waiters is not particularly warm, but you wouldn't want it to be in such a dignified setting, would you? The cakes and tapas (3€–6€) are both very good, if you get hungry people-watching through the windows. (You can also sit outside on the pavement terrace, but then you'll miss that unique interior atmosphere.)

€€   There's something of the atmosphere of Left Bank Paris in this legendary *moderniste* locale **Els Quatre Gats** ✦✦ (Montsió 3; ☎ 933-02-41-40; www.4gats.com; restaurant daily 1pm–1am, cafe 8am–2am; AE, DC, MC, V; reservations required; Metro: Urquinaona), which literally means "Four Cats," but idiomatically in Catalán slang means "just a few people." It was once frequented by the likes of (a very young) Picasso and composer Albéniz, and though the decor of beams, tiles, and mezzanine still conjures up a bit of a bohemian aura, you'll see more tourists than artists around today, enjoying the rather corny evening music program. Best to come for morning coffee or at lunchtime when the fixed-price 17€ menu (2 courses plus wine and dessert) often includes seafood dishes such as *rape* (monkfish) and *merluza* (hake) freshly obtained from the market. There's also a great selection of beers.

€€   Every city has at least one restaurant that's regarded as a living legend, and Barcelona's is **Can Culleretes** ✦✦✦ (Quintana 5; ☎ 933-17-64-85; www.culleretes.com; Tues–Sun 1:30–4pm, Tues–Sat 9–11pm, closed July; MC, V; Metro: Liceu), which started life modestly in 1786 as a *pastelería* (pastry shop). Hidden away—if a place as well known and publicized as this one can be described as "hidden away"—in one of the Barri Gòtic's most dank and stygian alleys, it looks the part of Barcelona's official "oldest eating spot." The three dining rooms—with their ornate tiles, iron chandeliers, and walls covered with autographed photos of bullfighters, flamenco stars, and international celebs—combine to create a suitably colorful and authentic ambience, and the service is nice and old fashioned. But with all those fellow tourists around, you may wonder, is the food any good? The short answer is yes, though you'll find none of that fancy Ferran Adrià stuff here. Just solid traditional fare like *civet de jabalí* (wild boar) and *butifarra con habas* (Catalán sausage with beans) alongside other well-prepared Spanish regional dishes such as *Fabada Asturiana* and *Merluza Vasca*. Reckon on 20€ to 25€ a head for two courses plus wine, unless you want to double that with the special *pica pica de pescado*—three separate fish courses including mussels and lobster. Don't even think of going without reservations.

L'EIXAMPLE

€   You'll be tempted to overeat at **Ty-Bihan** 🧒 (Lluis Pellicer 13; ☎ 934-10-90-02; Mon 1:30–3:30pm, Tues–Fri 1:30–3:30pm and 8:30–11:30pm, Sat 8:30–11:30pm; V; Metro: Hospital Clinic), which serves up scrumptious Breton crêpes and blini in a pseudo-rustic setting. The 6€ to 7€ crepes, known as *galettes*, are light and buttery, made from buckwheat flour, and the famed suzettes are flamed with Grand Marnier. The 10€ set lunch is top value, and kiddies are well cared for with the Petite menu. Cider—adults only—is the thing to drink here, served Breton-style in a bowl. The restaurant is at the eastern end of L'Eixample.

€–€€   Sharing its name with another highly regarded bodega bar over in the earthier Poble Sec barrio (p. 270), **La Bodegueta** (Rambla de Catalunya 100; ☎ 932-15-48-94; Mon–Sat 7am–1:30am, Sun 7pm–1am, closed Aug 8–22; cash only; Metro: Diagonal) is an authentic old (well, 1940) wine tavern adrift in a sea of franchised, and notably pricier, nosheries within walking distance of the Diagonal Metro. Well worth sampling the goods if you enjoy a raucous, student-filled atmosphere and robust tapas of cholesterol- and calorie-charged non-veggie items like *butifarra* or Catalán sausage (look elsewhere if you're on a diet). Accompany them with either *vermut* or cheapo (that is, more or less drinkable) wines, both served from the barrel. You should be well satisfied for 14€ a head.

€€   Seafood is rarely cheap in L'Eixample, but the popular, traditional **El Caballito Blanco** (Mallorca 196; ☎ 934-53-10-33; Tues–Sat 1–3:45pm and 9–10:45pm, Sun 1–3:45pm, closed Aug; AE, DC, MC, V; Metro: Hospital Clinic or Diagonal), halfway between the Hospital Clinic and Diagonal Metro stops, offers good values. Atmosphere—not enhanced by stark neon lighting—takes second place to the food. The varied choice of dishes, which includes *mero* (grouper), *mejillones* (mussels), and *gambas ajillo* (prawns in garlic) is highly affordable considering the excellent standard of the dishes—say 25€ a head for two courses with wine—providing you don't order *langosta* (lobster), *centollos* (spider crab) or, God forbid, the tiny but astronomically priced *percebes* (goose barnacles). Though fish is the main reason for coming here, meat dishes like grilled lamb cutlets are also on the menu, and you can kick off with a choice of pâtés or salads. Whet your pre-lunch whistle with a *fino* (dry sherry) at the adjoining bar.

GRÀCIA

€€   How can you resist a restaurant with a name like **El Glop** 🧒 (Montmany 46; ☎ 932-13-70-58; Mon–Sun 1–4pm and 8pm–1am; MC, V; reservations recommended; Metro: Joanic), which means "swallow" or "gulp" and, when enunciated, seems to epitomize all that's pared down and to the point about the Catalán tongue? Yet there's nothing pared down about this warmhearted Gràcia favorite, with its friendly service and down-home ambience (exposed beams, tranquil interior patio). One of the most lively eating spots in the city, it's a great place to bring the kids, not because they have any special kiddies' amenities, but because most of the regulars here are families with lively young offspring who fill the place with anarchic noise and play. To the point, though, are its highly affordable—if not exactly bargain-basement cheap—dishes like oven-cooked *caracoles* (snails, 11€), *rape aioli* (monkfish in garlic sauce, 12€), and, as a snack, *torrades* (toasted rustic bread rubbed with tomato and, optionally, garlic, and topped with ham). The best deal, as in so many establishments, is the fixed-price three-course lunch (12€).

€€ If you have a passion for pizzas and want to see the best that this fair city can offer in that department, then you must sample the goods at Gràcia's quirky and highly popular **La Gavina** ✿ 🅺🅸🅳🆂 (Ros de Olano 17; ☎ 934-15-74-50; July–Sept daily 1pm–1am, Oct–June daily 6pm–1am; cash only; reservations recommended; Metro: Fontana), whose menu covers everything from the standard tomato and mozzarella type to more exotic seafood and even caviar versions. The delicate homegrown *payes* model comprising paper-thin slices of potato, rosemary, and olive oil is also not to be missed. Prices are reasonable rather than downright inexpensive, but the produce is top notch. Aim at 12€ a head for a filling repast.

A Peix Dinner

First rate *peix* (pronounced pesh, which is fish in Catalán) is a hallmark of the Barcelona culinary scene. In a city where Mediterranean waves lap against port and coastline, and the tangy scent of ozone still tends to dominate the oft polluted air, a first-rate seafood dish is, for me, a worthy splurge.

€€€–€€€€ My favorite pescatorial eatery is **Els Pescadors** ✿✿✿ (Plaça Prim 1; ☎ 932-25-20-18; www.elspescadors.com; daily 1–3:45pm and 8:30pm–midnight, closed Easter week; AE, DC, MC, V; reservations recommended; Metro: Poble Nou). Set in a former tavern, it stands behind the Poble Nou shore just above Port Olimpic in a small square with three ombu trees around which 19th-century fishermen and industrial workers used to meet. The dining room has retained the original marble tabletops and wooden beams, service is genteel and unobtrusive. The fish—bought fresh daily by Esteve Monti from Arenys de Mar market up the coast—is impeccably prepared with a blend of the traditional and inventive. You might start off with *sopa de puerros con mejillones* (leek soup with mussels); for the main course, try *kokotxas de bacalao con arroz* (slender melt-in-your-mouth portions of cod in rice) or *lubina al horno con almejas y habas blancas* (baked sea bass with clams and small white beans). The cellar has over 150 wines to choose from and there's a smashing choice of desserts. Expect to pay about 50€ per person, including wine (less if you don't imbibe). Enjoy!

A bonus touch is the fun decor: images of angels, cherubs, deities, virgins, and other religious entities dangle everywhere—a heavenly kitsch fantasy. This place is very popular, so go before 8pm if you want to avoid queueing. *Note:* Don't confuse this place with the identically named but far more expensive eating spot in the portside Palau del Mar building.

BARCELONETA

€–€€ Probably the most raucous and popular eating spot in Barceloneta, **Can Maño** ✪ (Baluard 12; ☎ 933-19-30-82; Mon–Fri noon–4pm, Sat noon–5pm, closed Aug; cash only; Metro: Barceloneta) is the local equivalent of a working man's caff (with, of course, better grub). Cramped—you can hardly move between tables—with a totally ignored TV in the corner blaring banalities, cursory rapid service, and a constant hubbub of heated chat, the place comes up trumps both cost- and quality-wise, with the food—especially the fresh fish dishes like *salmonetes* (red mullet, 10€) and *calamares* (squid, 9€). It opens at the unusually early time of noon for lunch (the best time to come to avoid the rush).

€€–€€€ One of the best places to join the locals when they eat out in Barceloneta is **Puda Can Manel** ✪ (Passeig de Joan de Borbón 60; ☎ 932-21-50-13; Tues–Sun 1–4pm and 7–11pm; AE, DC, MC, V; reservations required; Metro: Barceloneta), which is by far the most authentic spot on the touristy marina. How good is it? There's usually an orderly queue of Cataláns trying to get in while other establishments are still more or less empty. *Fideuàs* (noodle-based versions of paella, 20€) and *arrroz negre* (rice cooked in black squid's ink, 25€) are two of the top delights here; they aren't cheap, but they're an extremely good value in view of their quality.

€–€€ It's worth popping into the "Glass of Gold" or **El Vaso de Oro** (Balboa 6; ☎ 933-19-30-98; daily 9am–midnight; MC, V; Metro: Barceloneta), if only to enjoy the wacky experience of ordering your tapas in one of the narrowest bars you'll find anywhere. The wisecracking staff make the cramped quarters more bearable, as do the tasty tapas (4€–8€ per small dish) ranging from *pimientos del Padrón* (small green peppers—some very hot) and *solomillos* (pint-size chunks of sirloin steak) to *atún* (tuna). Make sure the very daintiness of these succulent morsels doesn't make you eat too many, as the cost can mount up. It's best suited for a quick call on your way to another locale (like La Bombeta, below) if you're planning a tapa bar crawl in Barceloneta.

€–€€ A renovated tavern where traditional tastes, and a predominance of local clientele, still prevail, is **La Bombeta** ✪ (Maquinista 3; ☎ 933-19-94-45; Thurs–Tues 10am–midnight; MC, V; Metro: Barceloneta), a byword in Barceloneta tapas bars. The place specializes in *bombas,* which are not bombs—as it says in your dictionary—but deep-fried balls of fluffy mashed potato served in a spicy red *brava* sauce. Seafood attractions, as befits its marine setting, range from delicious *mejillones al vapor* (steamed mussels) and *gambas a la plancha* (grilled prawns) to chewy *rabas* (chunks of squid fried in olive oil). Dishes vary in price from 7€ to 12€ apiece. Wine there is aplenty. Try a jug of their tip-top in-house sangria before tottering off along the shore.

POBLE SEC

€   If you don't mind sharing a table in a rumbustious, no-holds-barred eatery that makes few touristic concessions on its mainly Galician menu, and may even expect you to sing with fellow diners and parry earthy quips with the waiters, then **Mesón David** ★ (Carretas 63; ☎ 934-41-69-34; Thurs–Tues 1–4:30pm and 8pm–midnight; AE, MC, V; reservations recommended; Metro: Paral•lel and Sant Antoni) is the place for you. It'll also save you a whole lot of dinero as it's one of cheapest eating spots in town. Here, amid an almost totally intact working-class ambience, you can enjoy dishes like *caldo gallego* (cabbage broth, 6€), *trucha navarra* (trout stuffed with serrano ham, 9€), or *lechazo* (roast pork, 8€). The 9€ set lunch is, as usual, the best value, and it's advisable to get here well before 2pm if you want a seat (let alone a table of your own).

€–€€   One of the most noisy and original restaurants in the city, **La Tomaquera** (Margarit 58; no phone; Tues–Sat 1:30–3:45pm and 8:30–10:45pm, closed Aug; cash only; Metro: Poble Sec) makes a positive virtue of its eccentricities. The service is almost determinedly offhand, and only meat dishes are served (8€–12€). There's not even a wine list; it's the house wine (10€ a bottle) or nothing. So why do people come? Have a meal here and you'll find out. And get there early because it's invariably packed!

€–€€   Ideal for folks who are into dairy products, the **Quimet & Quimet** (Poeta Cabanyes 25; ☎ 934-42-31-42; Mon–Fri noon–4pm and 7–10:30pm, Sat noon–4pm, closed Aug; MC, V; Metro: Paral•lel) specializes in cheeses, lots of them, at between 5€ and 8€ per item. Run by the same family for five generations, this tiny bar's repertoire includes *cabrales* (Asturian pungent blue cheese), *idiazabal* (Basque), *manchego* (La Mancha's famed goat cheese), and *nevat* (another goat's cheese, but from Catalunya). Other treats: preserved seafood (mussels, clams) and *montaditos* (inventive tapas served on bread). You can choose to have four or more such ultra-filling varieties on a plate, perhaps adding something with that little bit extra such as *tou dels tillers* (cheese blended with caviar or truffles and fish roe). The well-stocked wine cellar also provides some affordable and palatable local *vinos* (10€–14€ a bottle) alongside the more expensive Riojas, Ribera del Dueros, and Priorats (2€–4€ a glass).

€–€€   Don't confuse **La Bodegueta** (Blai 47; ☎ 934-42-08-46; Mon–Fri noon–4pm and 7–10:30pm, Sat noon–4pm, closed Aug; MC, V; Metro: Poble Sec) with the identically named tapas mecca in L'Eixample's Rambla Catalunya (p. 267); here, the surroundings are somewhat different. A highly popular bar thanks to the efforts of longstanding owner Eva Amber, it's located close to the Poble Sec Metro in what is still largely a working-class district. Nicely renovated, it retains original features like its rose petal–tiled floor. While tapas are the thing, ranging from standard no frills *jamon serrano* and *tortilla de patatas* (3.50€–4.50€) to *torrades* (toasted bread with charcuterie; 3€), the bodega also serves up hearty *comida casera* fare such as *lentejas con chorizo* (lentils with pork sausage) and *chuletas a la brasa* (grilled cutlets) at around 7€ and 12€, respectively.

WHY YOU'RE HERE: THE TOP SIGHTS & ATTRACTIONS

Barcelona is a treasure chest of historical and aesthetic delights. Brooding Gothic edifices fill its condensed labyrinth of medieval lanes and squares in the center, while lavish moderniste buildings of an unparalleled eccentricity line the outlying 19th-century boulevards. Its "reborn" port and beach-lined waterfront areas are as vibrant as any other barrios in the city, and its ubiquitous, relaxing parks pleasantly surprise unsuspecting visitors with their richly contrasting characters.

SUGGESTED ITINERARIES

If You Have Only 1 Day

Get up fairly early so you can devote the morning to the **Barri Gòtic.** Start at the **Plaza Cataluña** and meander from there down **La Rambla,** pausing halfway down to pop into the **Boquería market** for coffee and churros at one of the many stalls. Now you're ready to check out the Barri Gòtic's main attractions: the **Catedral** (p. 275) and **Pla de la Seu** square, central **Plaça Sant Jaume** (p. 279), and, last but not least, the 18th-century **Plaça Reial**. To round off the morning, head for **Mirador de Colón** (p. 278) statue beside the port and, from there, meander along the **Port Vell** waterfront with its molls (not gangsters' chicks but large jetties) and restaurant-lined yacht marina.

After a (light) lunch and short siesta, tackle the wide-avenued **L'Eixample** district north of Plaça Catalunya for your required intake of avant-garde architecture. The first must is the **Sagrada Familia** (p. 284)—Antoni Gaudí's great eponymous (and still unfinished) church. Then the **Manzana de la Discordia** to view (from the outside only today) the three great moderniste buildings: **La Pedrera, Casa Battló,** and **Casa Lleo-Morera** (p. 289). There won't be time to go inside the two that are open to the public now, but if you're here for three days or more, you'll be exploring their interiors on the third day (see below).

Take a deep breath and head up to **Parc Güell** (p. 289), where you can see Gaudí's fairy-tale buildings, statues, and decorations; wander the woodland paths at the back and enjoy the city views.

If you still have any energy left, you won't want to miss out on a sample of the fabled Barcelonanan nightlife. Have another quick nap after dinner and head for **Otto Zutz** (p. 304) or **El Tablao de Catmen** (p. 303), depending on whether you like dancing to the latest modern sounds or watching flamenco. (If you're here for longer than a day, save that outing for the 2nd or 3rd night.)

If You Have 2 Days

On your first day, follow the itinerary described above (with or without the nocturnal action). On the second day, take things easier with a morning stroll through the pond- and garden-filled **Parc de la Ciutadella** (p. 284), maybe including a visit to the **zoo** or **Museu de Geologia.** Then check out the narrow laned barris of **La Ribera** and **El Born** that border the park to the west, admiring the sumptuous facade of the **Palau de la Musica,** wandering around state-of-the-art **Santa Caterina market** and—queues permitting—visiting the **Picasso Museum** (p. 283) in Carrer Montcada. In the Paseo El Born, admire the high ceilings and

Barcelona Attractions

CaixaForum **2**
Casa Amatller **31**
Casa Batlló **32**
Casa de la Ciutat **19**
Casa Lleo Morera **30**
Casa Vicens **36**
Casa-Museu Gaudí **37**
Centre de Cultura Contemporània **11**
Conjunt Monumental de la Plaça del Rei
    (Museu d'Història de la Ciutat) **18**
CosmoCaixa (Museu de la Ciència) **38**
Fundació Joan Miró **6**
Galería Olímpica **4**
Gran Teatre del Liceu **14**
La Catedral de la Santa Creu i Santa Eulàlia **16**
La Mercè **21**
La Pedrera (Casa Milà) **33**
La Sagrada Família **34**
L'Aquarium de Barcelona **22**
L'Hospital de la Santa Creu i Sant Pau **35**
Mirador de Colom **12**

Monestir de Pedralbes **40**
Museu Barbier-Mueller Art Precolombí **25**
Museu d'Arqueologica de Catalunya **5**
Museu d'Art Contemporani de Barcelona (MACBA) **10**
Museu de Ciènces Naturals de la Ciutadella **28**
Museu de les Arts Decoratives/Museu de Ceràmica **41**
Museu d'Història de Catalunya **23**
Museu Frederic Marès **17**
Museu Marítim **8**
Museu Militar de Montjuïc **7**
Museu Nacional d'Art de Catalunya **3**
Museu Picasso **26**
Museu Tèxtil i d'Indumentària **24**
Palau de la Generalitat **20**
Palau de la Música Catalana **27**
Palau Güell **13**
Parc d'Atraccions Tibidabo **39**
Parc Zoològic **29**
Poble Espanyol **1**
Sant Pau del Camp **9**
Santa Maria del Pi **15**

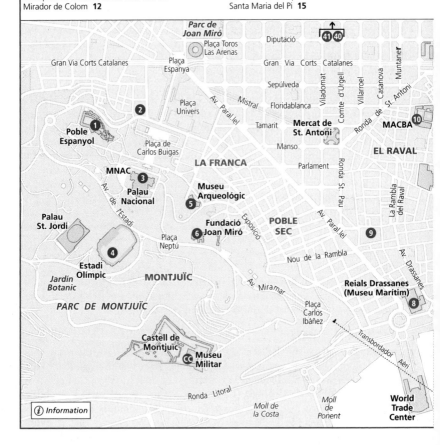

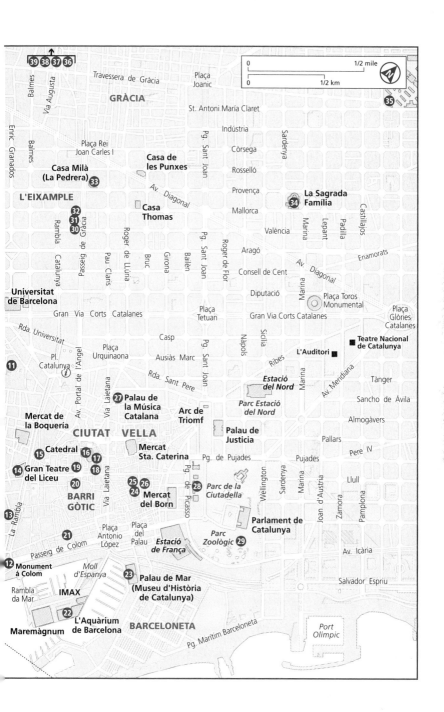

39 38 37 36

Balmes

Via Augusta

Travessera de Gràcia

Plaça Joanic

GRÀCIA

St. Antoni María Claret

35

0   1/2 mile

0   1/2 km

Enric Granados

Balmes

Plaça Rei Joan Carles I

Casa de les Punxes

Pg. Sant Joan

Indústria

Còrsega

Rosselló

Sardenya

Casa Milà (La Pedrera) 33

Av. Diagonal

Provença

La Sagrada 34 Família

L'EIXAMPLE

Casa Thomas

Mallorca

Marina

Lepant

Padilla

Castillejos

32
31
30

Rambla

Passeig de Gràcia

Pau Claris

Roger de Llúria

Bruc

Girona

Bailèn

Pg. Sant Joan

Roger de Flor

València

Aragó

Consell de Cent

Av. Diagonal

Enamorats

Catalunya

Diputació

Plaça Toros Monumental

Plaça Glòries Catalanes

Universitat de Barcelona

Gran Via Corts Catalanes

Plaça Tetuan

Gran Via Corts Catalanes

Rda. Universitat

Casp

Pg. Sant Joan

Napols

Sicilia

Teatre Nacional de Catalunya

11

Pl. Catalunya *(i)*

Plaça Urquinaona

Ausiàs Marc

Ribes

L'Auditori ■

Av. Portal de l'Angel

Via Laietana

Rda. Sant Pere

Marina

Av. Meridiana

Tànger

27 Palau de la Música Catalana

Estació del Nord

Sancho de Ávila

Mercat de la Boqueria

Arc de Triomf

Parc Estació del Nord

Almogàvers

CIUTAT VELLA

Palau de Justicia

Pallars

Pere IV

15 Catedral 16
17

Mercat Sta. Caterina

Pg. de Pujades

Pujades

14 Gran Teatre 19
del Liceu 18

Via Laietana

20

25 26
24 Mercat del Born

28

Parc de la Ciutadella

Wellington

Sardenya

Marina

Joan d'Austria

Zamora

Pamplona

Llull

BARRI GÒTIC

13

La Rambla

21

Plaça Antonio López

Plaça del Palau

Estació de França

Pg. de Picasso

Parlament de Catalunya

Passeig de Colom

Parc Zoològic **29**

Av. Icària

12 Monument á Colom

Moll d'Espanya

23 Palau de Mar (Museu d'Història de Catalunya)

Salvador Espriu

Rambla da Mar

IMAX

22

L'Aquàrium de Barcelona

BARCELONETA

Maremàgnum

Pg. Marítim Barceloneta

Port Olímpic

magnificent stained-glass windows of the imposing **Santa María del Mar church** (p. 280), and walk down to the old (but gentrified) maritime quarter and beach-front of **La Barceloneta,** with its modern adjoining Port Olimpic area. This is an ideal spot for an atmospheric seafood lunch (check menu prices first, though).

In the afternoon, explore the regenerated El Raval district—taking in the **MACBA** (p. 281) modern art gallery and truncated palm-lined **Rambla del Raval** with its large black marble gat (cat) sculpture and pungent array of Greek, Turkish, Indian, and Middle Eastern eating spots. Then take the funicular to the top of **Montjuïc** (p. 291) for a fine view of Barcelona and its harbor form the castle ramparts. Make sure you include a visit to the **Museu Nacional d'Art de Catalunya (MNAC)** (p. 292) on the hill's northern slopes near Plaça España for a glimpse of the finest collection of Romanesque relics in Spain. As night falls, you may be in time to see a colored fountain exhibition just below MNAC, at the Fuente Mágica (Magic Fountain), where twinkling waters constantly change their hues as they rise and fall.

If You Have 3 Days

Spend the first 2 days as described above. On Day 3, make a more leisurely return to L'Eixample via Barcelona's widest avenue, the Paseo de Gracia, and revisit the Manzana de Discordia zone to explore Gaudí's **Casa Batlló,** Puig i Cadafalch's **Casa Amatller,** and Domenech i Muntaner's **Casa Lleo Morera** (p. 289) in more detail. Check out nearby **Casa Mila** (p. 288, popularly known as La Pedrera) and be sure to visit the roof, with its surrealistic chimneys and great city views. While still in the neighborhood, pop into the famous design emporium **Vinçon** (p. 301) and then head for the semi-bohemian district of **Grácia** (p. 289) at the northern edge of the Eixample. Stroll around its villagey squares, especially the **Plaça de Rius i Taulet** with its 19th-century clock tower, and then have lunch in a local restaurant.

In the afternoon, after a siesta, head across to **Pedralbes** to relax and unwind at its peaceful time warp monastery and palace, and then—by way of contrast—proceed up to brash, noisy **Tibidabo** (if you're traveling with kids, they'll just love the funfair) for the best overall panoramic views of the city and coast stretching north toward the Costa Brava. Unwind once again with a final stroll along tree-fringed trails into the adjoining Collserola Park, still high above the city.

If You Have 4 or More Days

Follow the itineraries above for your first 3 days, then take in the amazing mountaintop **Monastery of Montserrat** (p. 306), **the Colonia Güell** (p. 305), or the nearby stylish seaside resort of **Sitges** (p. 307) on the fourth. Or even head north to historic **Girona** (p. 320).

LA CIUTAT VELLA

The historic heart of the city (La Ciutat Vella) abounds with fine churches, world-class museums, and splendid architecture; its artistic and architectural heritage is among the richest in the world. Highlights here include the Museu Picasso, the Gothic cathedral, and La Rambla (also known as Les Ramblas), the vibrant, bustling tree-lined promenade that dissects the heart of the Metropolis. (Its name comes from the Arabic word for "stream." Funny to think that this people-packed and opera house–lined boulevard was once the drainage ditch that bordered the central city.)

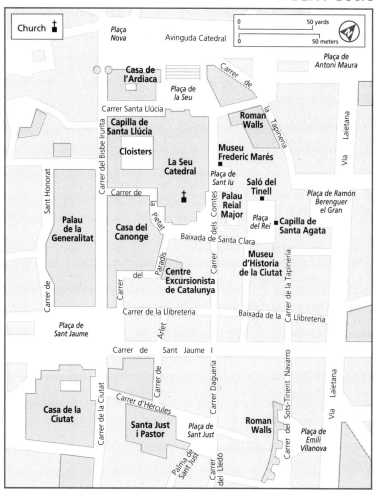

Legend on map:

Church ✝

Plaça Nova

Avinguda Catedral

0 — 50 yards
0 — 50 meters

Plaça de Antoni Maura

Casa de l'Ardiaca

Plaça de la Seu

Carrer de

Carrer Santa Llúcia

Roman Walls

Capilla de Santa Llúcia

Carrer del Bisbe Irurita

Cloisters

La Seu Catedral

Museu Frederic Marés

Via Laietana

Carrer de la Tapineria

Sant Honorat

Plaça de Sant Iu

Saló del Tinell

Plaça de Ramón Berenguer el Gran

Carrer de

la Pietat

Palau Reial Major

Carrer dels Comtes

Plaça del Rei

Capilla de Santa Agata

Palau de la Generalitat

Casa del Canonge

Baixada de Santa Clara

Paradis

Centre Excursionista de Catalunya

del

Carrer

Museu d'Historia de la Ciutat

Carrer

Carrer de la Tapineria

Carrer de

Carrer de la Llibreteria

Baixada de la Llibreteria

Plaça de Sant Jaume

Arlet

Carrer de Sant Jaume I

Carrer de

Carrer Dagueria

Via Laietana

Casa de la Ciutat

Carrer de la Ciutat

Carrer d'Hércules

Santa Just i Pastor

Plaça de Sant Just

Roman Walls

Carrer del Sots-Tinent Navarro

Plaça de Emili Vilanova

Palma de Sant Just

Carrer del Lledó

BARRI GÒTIC

The **Plaça de la Seu** has been the spiritual center of the city ever since ancient Roman times (a pagan temple stood here, followed by a mosque). Today the highlight of any visit here is one of Spain's most imposing religious buildings, **La Catedral de la Santa Creu i Santa Eulàlia** ✪✪✪ (Plaça de la Seu s/n; ☎ 933-15-15-54; daily 9am–1pm and 5–7pm, cloister museum daily 10am–1pm and 4–6:30pm; free admission to cathedral and cloister; Metro: Jaume I or Liceu).

Construction on this massive edifice began in 1298 under Jaume I; it was completed over 200 years by several generations of builders (the only recent addition is the west facade, dating from the 19th century), and—by sheer luck or divine interference (you decide)—managed to survive the ravages of the Civil War

Dancing in the Streets

No one knows when the *Sardana,* Catalunya's circular folk dance, came into being, though most historians agree that it became a touchstone of celebrations in the 16th century. Today, you'll see it performed every Sunday at noon in the plaza in front of the cathedral; dancers are passers by of all ages and backgrounds, who simply drop their belongings in the center of the circle, join hands, and engage in this potent symbol of Catalán unity. (The mere act of grabbing a stranger's hand and dancing is a powerful one, but for locals dancing has an even deeper meaning as Franco, in an attempt to stamp out Catalán culture, banned the *Sardana* during his time in power.)

If you feel an uncontrollable urge to join in with all those light-footed locals don't simply break into the circle of dancers and grab hands. Ask politely first and they just might let you join this sociable hoedown. I'd recommend simply watching however, as the steps are complex, and dancers get annoyed when a bumbling newcomer breaks the rhythm. The dancing is accompanied by music played by a *cobla* (group) made up of brass instruments, a *flaviol* (a piccolo style flute) and a *tambor* (a small drum). You may sometimes also see the *Sardana* performed here at 6pm on Saturday nights.

when many churches in the city were destroyed by anarchic groups protesting against Catholic buildings (which they saw as symbols of a repressive totalitarian state).

As you enter via the cathedral's sole remaining Romanesque doorway you're greeted by a serene little cloister; its forged iron grilles enclose "the loveliest oasis in Barcelona" (to quote historian and city chronicler Alexandre Cirici i Pellicer). Here, in a world apart from the bustle outside, orange and palm trees encircle a fountain and pond filled with 13 white geese. Why the fowl? Legend has it that the Cathedral's patron saint, Eulalia, was only 13 when she was subjected to 13 forms of torture for refusing to renounce her Christian faith. She was dragged into the town square naked (a fortuitous snowstorm preserved her modesty, according to legend), put in a barrel punctured with knives and rolled down the street, crucified on an X-shaped cross, and more, before the final torture, decapitation, ensured her martyrdom. The honking geese are a testament to the fortitude of this patron saint of sailors. Down in the crypt of the Cathedral is Eulalia's alabaster sarcophagus, decorated by Pisan sculptors. The stone slabs surrounding the cloister cover the tombs of leading members of the city's medieval guilds.

The massive interior of the cathedral is a masterful blend of Renaissance and Gothic styles, comprising a central nave, soaring arches, apse, high altar, beautifully sculptured choir, two aisles, and 28 side chapels (look out especially for the Romanesque Chapel of Santa Llucia to the right of the main facade, and Chapel of Sant Benet behind the altar with its magnificent 15th-century interpretation of the crucifixion by Bernat Martorell). Another treasure here is the small but amazingly lifelike effigy of the Virgin known as *La Pietà*. Sculpted by 15th-century artist Bartolomé Bermejo, this alabaster masterpiece is discreetly located on the wall on the northern side of the chapter house museum.

If you visit on any day but Sunday, you can take an elevator up to the roof (an extra 2€) for a bird's-eye vista of the whole Barri Gòtic. I highly recommend you do so before leaving the cathedral.

Just behind the cathedral in an historic palace, the **Museu Frederic Marès** ✿✿ (Plaça de Sant Iú 5–6; ☎ 933-10-58-00; www.museumares.bcn.es; Tues–Sat 10am–7pm, Sun 10am–3pm; 3.50€ adults, free for children 11 and under, free for all first Sun of month and Wed 3–7pm; Metro: Jaume I) houses one of the biggest repositories of medieval sculpture in Catalunya. Marès was a sculptor himself, and he obsessively amassed this stunning collection of religious sculpture and imagery that crosses the ages. Ground-floor exhibits date from the 3rd and 4th centuries to Romanesque and Gothic polychromatic crucifixes and statues of the Virgin Mary. Upstairs, the collection continues with baroque and Renaissance works before veering into another topic altogether: everyday life in Barcelona for the past 2 centuries. The "Entertainment Room," for example, is filled with toys and automatons; the "Women's Quarter" has Victorian fans, combs, and other "feminine use only" objects. This portion is known as the Museu Sentimental.

Next up is the 16th-century Gothic mansion of Casa Clariana Padellàs now the **Conjunt Monumental de la Plaça del Rei (Museu d'Història de la Ciutat and Palau Reial Major)** ✿✿✿ (Plaça del Rei s/n; ☎ 933-15-11-11; June–Sept Tues–Sat 10am–8pm, Oct–May Tues–Sat 10am–2pm and 4–8pm, year-round Sun 10am–3pm; 5€ adults, 3.50€ students, free for children 15 and under; Metro: Liceu or Jaume I), a museum and palace that comprise a unique twin monument. It's the first part of this duo—the **Museu d'Historia de la Ciutat (Museum of the History of the City)**—that will really bowl you over. Beneath its surface, one level down from the temporary exhibitions on Iberian and Mediterranean culture (which include a permanent virtual-reality display on the history of the city), is what's said to be the most extensive subterranean excavation of any city in

Follow the Dancing Egg

Eggs seem to play a key part in the Catalán heritage. Salvador Dalí was obsessed by them and had two large artificial ones on the roof of his Port Lligat house. At Corpus Christi time in June, the cathedral itself is the setting for a small-scale surrealistic event that could have been invented by Dalí, though it actually originated in the 17th century. An empty eggshell is placed on top of the cathedral cloister's gushing fountain—to the mild consternation of the geese—in a Catalán tradition known as *L'ou com balla* (the egg that dances). The bobbing up and down of this empty oval shell has supposed fertility connotations: representing either the Eucharist or continuity of life.

Europe—a remarkably intact section of Barcino, the old Roman settlement. An intricate network of walkways has been built over the unearthed relics and foundations, which include the forum, streets, squares, shops, and even laundries and huge vats used for wine production. Look out in particular for beautiful mosaics in the remains of some family homes.

The adjoining **Palau Reial (Royal Palace),** though highly impressive, is less of a surprise in this essentially medieval corner of Barcelona. After visiting the world of Julius Caesar, you're now time-capsuled forward to an epic Catalán era that began in the 10th century, when the counts of Barcelona made it their home, later to be followed by the kings of Aragón. King Ferdinand and Queen Isabella are said to have received Columbus at the top step of its sweeping entrance after he returned from the New World. The Chapel de Santa Agüeda, just inside, has temporary exhibitions, and the adjacent towering 14th-century Saló del Tinell (a key work of the period) features the largest stone arches to be found anywhere in Europe. It began life as the seat of the Catalán parliament. Also worth a peek: the 16th-century, five-floored Mirador del Rei Martí (King Martin's Watchtower) built by the eponymous monarch to keep an eye out for sea invaders and the local peasant revolts that often took place in the square below.

Nearby is the church of **La Mercè (Our Lady of Mercy)** (Plaça de la Mercè 1; ☎ 933-15-27-56; daily 10am–1pm and 6–8pm; free admission; Metro: Drassanes), notable for its magnificent baroque facade (the only one on any church in the city). Look up: the prominent rooftop statue of the city's beloved female patron saint, Mercé herself (who's said, among her many other accomplishments, to have thwarted a 17th-century plague of locusts). Set in an elegant square with a central fountain of Neptune, the church was built in her honor in 1775 and has ever since inspired the main fiesta in her name on September 24. A high number of Barcelona-born females are named after her, while the male population in turn abounds with Jordis—or George—Catalonia's other patron saint.

Many of the major sights you'll see in Barcelona were built by private interests, rather than the monarchy, the Catholic Church, or the city itself. A good example is the **Gran Teatre del Liceu** ★★ (La Rambla, 51–59; ☎ 934-85-99-00; www.liceubarcelona.com; unguided tours 4€, guided tours 8.50€, tours may be cancelled when private functions are scheduled; Metro: Liceu). It was paid for by a group of local businessmen in 1847 and its plush velvets and marbles, its studied exoticism, and perhaps most important, its lack of the usual royal box, mirrors the tastes and aspirations of that class and generation. Modeled on La Scala in Milan, Italy, it can house 4,000 spectators, making it one of the largest opera houses in Europe. What you see today, however, is not the original: That burned down . . . twice! In 1893, bombs thrown by an anarchist killed 22 people; 99 years later a stagehand accidentally incinerated the place with his blowtorch. Everything was gutted except the facade and members room. The new version was finally completed in 2000. Seeing an opera here is the ideal way of experiencing this grand space, but as that can be pricey (tickets are 20€–80€) the on-site tour is a good second option.

It's no secret that Spain was darn proud of its role in discovering the New World. One of Spain's many homages to the great Genoese explorer Christopher Columbus, known in Spain as Cristobal Colom, the **Mirador de Colom (Columbus Watchtower)** (Portal de la Pau s/n; ☎ 933-02-52-24; June–Sept 9am–8:30pm,

Sightseeing That Will Float Your Boat 🧒

Hokey but fun, year-round boat trips are available from **Las Golondrinas** (www.lasgolondrindras.com); its boats depart at the harborside close to the Columbus monument. The 35-minute port trip costs 6€ for adults and 3€ for kids 4 to 10, while the 2-hour-long port and coastal trip by seafaring catamaran costs 12€ for adults and 5.50€ for kids 4 to 10.

Oct–May 10am–6:30pm; 2€ adults, 1.30€ children 4–12; Metro: Drassanes) was erected in 1888 to celebrate the Universal Exhibition during Barcelona's Industrial Revolution; it's modeled after London's Nelson column right down to those four little lions at the base. Look also for the eight bronze bas-reliefs on the plinth (copies of the destroyed originals) depicting Columbus's principal feats. The capital boasts representations of Europe, Asia, Africa, and America—all linked together. That's all well and good, but in reality there's only one thing most visitors care about when it comes to this monument: If you take the tiny elevator inside up to the mirador at the top, you get the best views of the harbor and Villa Vella from any land-based building in the city—I'm not counting the *teleféric* (p. 291) because that's airborne.

From that bird's-eye perch in the Columbus Watchtower, you'll likely notice the rectangular flagstoned **Plaça Sant Jaume (St. James' Square)** ✠ set in the heart of the Barri Gothic. That central location and the buildings on its flanks have made it the political nerve center of Barcelona, so you may be looking down on an organized protest, a raucous celebration, or some sort of oddball activity like the erection of *castellers* (human towers).

On one side of the square is the late 14th-century **Casa de la Ciutat** (Plaça de Sant Jaume s/n; ☎ 934-02-70-00; office Mon–Fri 8:30am–2:30pm, guided tours Sun 11am–3:30pm; free admission; Metro: Jaume I or Liceu), home of the *ajuntament* (town hall) and a fascinating place to visit if you believe, as many do, that European democracy was reborn here, and not in England. In the oldest part of the building, the towering 15th-century Salò de Cent (Room of 100 Jurors), Barcelona's famed Council of 100 presided. Constituted in 1274 it was, many argue, Europe's first real parliament. They had a magnificent space from which to adjudicate, with gigantic arches supporting a beamed ceiling bordered by the semicircular Salò de la Reina (Queen's Room) and the black marble Salò de las Croniques (Room of the Chronicles). Take a gander at the 1928 murals by Josep Maria Sert (the Catalán artist who went on to decorate Rockefeller Center in New York); these can be viewed during the Sunday guided tours only (see above).

On the other side of the square is the **Palau de la Generalitat** (Plaça de Sant Jaume s/n; ☎ 934-02-46-17; guided tours available every 30 min. 10:30am–1:30pm on the 2nd and last Sunday of each month, Apr 25, and Sept 24, other visits arranged weekly Mon and Fri 9:30am–1pm and 4–7pm by appointment; free admission; Metro: Liceu). A magnificent Gothic building, it just about defines the term *staying power*. It's one of the few medieval buildings in all of

Europe that's still being used as a seat of government (it's the seat of Catalunya's autonomous government) and even rarer, by the same group that created the building. Beyond that tasty tidbit, it boasts some of the most eye-popping Gothic adornments in the Old Town in the form of a 14th-century bas relief of Sant Jordi (St. George) erected by Pere II (above the calle Bisbe side entrance). Inside, the supreme highlight is the first-floor Pati de Tarongers (Courtyard of Orange Trees) an elegant interior patio, with pink renaissance columns topped with gargoyles of Catalonian folkloric figures; it pioneered a style that was much imitated in later Barcelona courtyards. Take note too of the richly detailed 17th-century Flemish tapestries covering the walls of the Gilded Hall, and Catalán architect Marc Safont's masterpiece, the Capella de Sant Jordi (Chapel of St. George), where splendid furnishings and motifs glorify the patron saint.

Built in a typical Catalán Gothic style between the early 14th and late 16th centuries, **Santa Maria del Pi (St. Mary of the Pine)** (Plaça del Pi 7; ☎ 933-18-47-43; daily 9am–1pm and 4–9pm; free admission; Metro: Liceu), gets its name from the huge pine tree in the charming ever-lively square outside its main entrance. It's one of the very finest Gothic churches in the city, yet it's strangely ignored by visitors who are perhaps sidetracked by all the sprightly activity going on outside (cheese and artisan fairs Thurs–Sat, street musicians, outdoor cafes, and so on). But there are reasons to go inside: Santa María's charms include the gigantic rose window located above the main entrance and a wide, single nave supported by an ingenious stone arch that spans nearly two-thirds of the handsomely austere interior.

RAVAL

Not so long ago El Raval was one of the roughest inner-city neighborhoods in old Barcelona. In recent years, it's undergone a striking transformation and is now home to two of the city's most famed modern-art museums, a flurry of international—mainly Asian—eating spots, and a seemingly nonstop upsurge of new hotels and apartments. But though the whole area is constantly being transformed, there's still enough of an edge to make it of more than just blandly "trendy" interest. Prostitutes vociferously ply their trade in some of the narrow lanes, just as they've done for as long as anyone can remember, and in others it's still best to watch your back after certain hours; the gentrification to date remains skin deep. In quarters like the notorious Barri Xino (Lower Raval), you don't have to scratch much to see that the whole seedy Rabelaisian world of yesteryear still rumbles just below the surface. One thing is sure: It ain't dull.

By far the most impressive example of El Raval's cultural transition is the **Centre de Cultura Contemporània (CCCB)** ✪ (Montalegre 5; ☎ 934-12-08-10; Tues and Thurs–Fri 11am–2pm and 4–8pm, Wed and Sat 11am–8pm, Sun and holidays 11am–7pm; 4.50€ adults, 4€ students, free for children 13 and under; Metro: Catalunya or Universitat), which was ingeniously converted in 1994 from a former *casa de caritat* (poorhouse). Located in the heart of the district, it's one of the largest of all Spain's cultural and exhibition centers and is remarkable for its use of space and light. The steel and glass exterior walls support a huge mirror that reflects the surrounding rooftops, and you enter the place through a charming patio that was part of the original building. Exhibitions here tend to focus on photographers, modern painters, politically oriented writers, and cultural movements such as situationism or Parisian surrealism, though the center has been accused of placing production values higher than content. If you feel that's true after visiting, and you're ready for more culture, the renowned MACBA (see below) is virtually next door. Things get especially lively here in mid-June when Sonar, the annual dance music festival, stages its daytime events here; other mini festivals such as alternative film and the plastic arts are also part of its vibrant calendar. Barcelona's modern-art showpiece is the **Museu d'Art Contemporani de Barcelona (MACBA)** ✦✦ (Plaça dels Angels 1; ☎ 934-12-08-10; www.macba.es; Mon and Wed–Fri 11am–7:30pm, Sat 10am–8pm, Sun 10am–3pm; 7.50€ adults and 6€ students for entrance to both permanent and temporary exhibitions, free for children 13 and under, Wed 3.50€ for adults and students and free for children 13 and under; Metro: Catalunya or Universitat), a gleaming white building illuminated by natural sunlight and designed by American architect Richard Meier. When it first opened, the building, with its dazzling three-level atrium and gently rising ramp access, attracted more interest than its mundane exhibits. Things have improved since, and the ever-growing permanent collection has added works by contemporary giants like Broodthaers, Klee, and Basquiat, as well as contemporary Catalán artists. A real pain, though, is the proliferation of skateboarders who constantly zoom up and down the MACBA's ramp and around the large square outside the entrance.

Tucked away in the anarchic, higgledy-piggledy cityscape of the inner Raval just behind the MACBA, is a compact, weathered stone–built building that looks as if it's been time-warped in from the early Middle Ages. This unexpected rose amid a sea of thorns is the tiny Romanesque **Sant Pau del Camp** ✦✦ (Sant Pau 99; ☎ 934-41-00-01; 2.50€ cloister; Mon–Fri noon–2pm and 5–8pm; Metro: Paral•lel), Barcelona's oldest church. Its name—"St. Paul of the Countryside"—comes from the time when it was, in fact, surrounded by fields. Though you can still make out the remains of the 9th-century building on the capital and bases of the portal, most of what you now see originates from the 11th and 12th centuries when the church was rebuilt in the form of Greek cross with three apses. On its western exterior door is a remarkably well preserved Latin inscription referring to Christ, St. Peter, and St. Paul; inside, view the somber 10th-century tomb of Wilfred the Hairy's offspring, Guífre Borrell (who himself became Count of Barcelona) in the 14th-century chapter house. Most memorable of all, though, is the diminutive cloister with its Moorish arches and central fountain.

Down La Rambla towards the port, on the corner of a busy narrow street just off to your right, you'll find **Palau Güell** ✦✦ (Nou de la Rambla 3–5; ☎ 933-17-39-74; see below for current opening hours and entrance fee; Metro: Drassanes), one of the few private homes that Gaudí built that is open to the public, and a UNESCO World Heritage Site. Even by the master's standards, this grandiose mansion is a real eye catcher, its Venetian style facade emerging from this dowdy, cramped street in a fashion that's totally unexpected. It was placed here so that it could be next to Güell's father's home, even though the location was considered rather tawdry at the time of its construction (1885–89), thanks to a notorious cathouse on the corner. Two huge arched entrances, protected by intricate forged iron gates and a shield of Catalonia (a testament to both Gaudí's and his patron Güell's patriotism), combine to make the place look like a fort.

It was, in point of fact, meant to be a showplace, a marble-swathed mansion in which Güell, an art loving industrialist, could entertain in style. And that he did, even giving horses the royal treatment in a basement stable accessed by two curving ramps (one for the beasts and one for the grooms) sided by Gaudí's signature columns with their mushroom-topped capitals. On the elegant first floor, four Moorish-style salons are cleverly illuminated by natural light, which filters through a constellation of perforated stars inlaid in a parabolic dome above the central hall. One of Gaudí's primary challenges was using natural light to make the house seem less "hemmed in" on the street than it actually was, and his solutions were ingenious, often involving mirrors, skylights, and long, screened galleries. His other mission was, as I said, to make the home as sumptuous as possible, and you'll see ornate touches everywhere, from the first-floor wooden ceilings, which are decorated with plant motifs that graduate from buds to full-bloom stage across four rooms, to the superb Art Nouveau fireplace in the dining room, to the sumptuous marble staircase. But the roof, with its warrior-like, *trencadís*-covered chimneys—a run up to his later La Pedrera in L'Eixample—is what knocks out most visitors. (One chimney bears a fragment of the Olympic mascot Cobi, included after a 1990s overhaul.)

Important note: As we go to press, only the renovated ground floor and basement of Palau Güell are open (free admission; Tues–Sat 10am–2.30pm). It's scheduled to reopen fully to the public in January 2009, when a new timetable and entrance fee will be announced.

LA RIBERA & EL BORN

On the right-hand side of the busy Via Laietana, the former merchant's district of La Ribera, prized for its moderniste Palau de la Musica and state-of-the-art Santa Caterina market, blends coastward into its twin neighborhood of El Born. The latter is highlighted by the museums of Carrer Montcada and towering Gothic church of Santa María del Mar. In both quarters, narrow streets house a multitude of stylish cafes, restaurants, and artisan workshops. El Born also hosts a handful of chic after-dark locales.

The most stylishly upmarket of all these is Domenech i Muntaner's extravagantly moderniste **Palau de la Música Catalána** ★★★ (Carrer de Sant Francesc de Paula 2; ☎ 932-95-72-00 for info, 902-442-882 to buy tickets; www.palaumusica.org; 9€ adults, 7.50€ students; guided tours daily, every half-hour 10am–3:30pm; Metro: Urquinaona), which was declared a UNESCO World Heritage site in 1997. Built between 1905 and 1908, originally as a home for the Orfeu Catalá (Catalán Choral Society), this "Palace of Music" is a sensual feast. Its sculptured facade pays lavish homage to musical giants from Beethoven to the then-darling of the concert-going public, Wagner. Inside, brilliant mosaic colonnades line the foyer, and the dazzling first-floor auditorium is topped by a stained-glass, reverse dome surrounded by 40 female heads representing a choir. More figures of fair species, the *trencadís*- (broken mosaic images) and terra-cotta-designed Muses del Palau, line the rear wall of the stage, which is framed by a Pau Gargallo proscenium. On one side of the proscenium is a painting of the Orfeó's director Josep Clavé emerging from the "Flowers of May" (a tree representing a popular Catalán folk song) and on the other side by Beethoven peering through a host of Wagnerian Valkyries. Prices for tickets vary considerably according to the program: It's worth keeping an eye out for possible bargains. Best to book ahead, though, as this icon of culture is understandably popular.

If you fancy looking at some ancient pre-Columbian exhibits from the American continent for a change, head east across the Barri Gòtic to one of El Born's most emblematic streets, where you'll find the **Museu Barbier-Mueller Art Precolombí** ✴ (Montcada 12–14; ☎ 933-10-45-16; 3.50€ adults, 2€ students, free for children 15 and under, free for all on first Sun of month; Tues–Sat 10am–6pm, Sun 10am–3pm; Metro: Jaume I). All objects on display in this 15th-century Gothic mansion (the restored Palau Nadal) were leased here in 1996 by the main Geneva museum, which contains one of the most important collections of pre-Columbian art in the world. The exhibition here is smaller, comprising just 6,000 pieces of tribal and ancient art, of which Josef Mueller (1887–1977)—who founded both the Swiss and Catalán museums—acquired the first pieces by 1908. The themes are religious, funerary, and ornamental, with stone sculptures and ceramic and jade objects from cultures as varied as the Olmec and Mayan. Gold adornments from Peru and pottery work from the Amazon are also included.

Situated right next to the Museu Barbier-Mueller Art Precolombí (see above), in the imposing Gothic-style Palau de les Marquesos de Llió (Palace of the Marquises of Llió), is the **Museu Tèxtil i d' Indumentària** (Montcada 12–14; ☎ 933-19-76-03; 3.50€ adults, free for children 15 and under; Tues–Sat 10am–6pm, Sun 10am–3pm; Metro: Jaume I), the city's top display of clothing and fabric making techniques across the centuries. The first floor ranges from the Gothic to the crinoline skirts and ultra-tight bodices of the Regency period. Upstairs you enter the 20th century, with exhibits from the likes of Paco Rabanne and Basque-born Cristóbal Balenciaga. Even folks not especially interested in clothing tend to find this fashion trip through the ages a fascinating experience.

No fewer than five adjoining medieval mansions, just a few paces up the street, comprise the **Museu Picasso** ✴✴✴ (Montcada 15–23; ☎ 933-19-63-10; 9€ adults [5.80€ temporary exhibitions], 6€ students 25 and under [2.90€ temporary exhibitions], free for children 15 and under and for all first Sun of month; Tues–Sat 10am–8pm, Sun 10am–3pm; Metro: Jaume I, Liceu, or Arc de Triomf), a hugely popular museum devoted to—what else?—the work of the young Pablo Picasso (1881–1973). The artist spent his formative years from the age of 14 in the Catalán capital savoring the bohemian lifestyle and often depicting its seedier aspects. His secretary and friend Jaume Sabartés donated some 2,500 of Picasso's paintings, engravings, and drawings to the museum in 1970. The collection is particularly strong on his Blue and Rose periods, and some works clearly demonstrate the artist's debt to giants like El Greco and Rembrandt. Highlights are his 59 versions of Velázquez's *Las Meninas* and *The Harlequin,* showing the influence of his Ballet Russes sojourn in Paris. His sketches of Barcelona city life and characters are chronologically arranged to follow his quicksilver progress as an artist, ever looking for new ideas. Surprisingly to some, Picasso was a supreme portraitist and did many traditional representational works before going down his own unique and eccentric road. Works in "The Last Years" section, that include ceramic and collage pieces, were donated by his widow.

L'EIXAMPLE

The district above Plaça Catalunya and the Ciutat Vella is known as L'Eixample (or Ensanche in Castilian), which simply means "expansion." Built under the supervision of military engineer Ildefons Cerdà in the 19th century, its grid

Park It Here: Parc de la Ciutadella

Laid out on the site of a former 18th-century citadel, the **Parc de la Ciutadella** ✪✪ 🧒 (Entrances on the Passeig de Picasso and Passeig Pujades; free admission; daily sunrise–sunset; Metro: Arc de Triomf) is the city's most enchanting green area, a small wonderland of lakes, flower beds, and palms, with an Italianate fountain and several lampposts attributed to the young and ever ubiquitous Gaudí. The park hosted a prestigious World Fair in 1887, shortly after its opening, and ever since it has been a refuge for visitors of all ages seeking calm and beauty. On the Passeig de Picasso, which borders the park to the west, you'll find the bizarrely named *Hivernacle* (an English-style hothouse for tropical plants) and *Umbracle* (a misnamed glass house with brick and wooden louver facades). On calle Wellington, which runs along the park's eastern side, is the old arsenal from its citadel days, now home of the Catalán parliament.

Indisputable high spot for children of all ages, in the leafy midst of the Parc de la Ciutadella, is the **zoo or Parc Zoològic** ✪ 🧒 (Parc de la Ciutadella; ☎ 932-25-67-80; 15€ adults, 9.30€ students and children 3–12; summer daily 10am–7pm, off season daily 10am–6pm; Metro: Ciutadella or Arc de Triomf); its former star attraction, Copito de Nieve (Snowflake)—the only albino gorilla in captivity in the world, now alas deceased—left two generations of blond descendents. In his memory there's an exhibition on the extinction of gorillas from the time he was captured in Equatorial Guinea in 1966 through his rise to celebrity status as the city's mascot. The garden setting is beautiful, and many enclosures are without bars and only separated by moats. (That said, these small "island" spaces don't give the mountain goats, llamas, lions, bears, hippos, huge primate

system of crisscrossing avenues aimed at easing the congestion in the center following the removal of the latter's ring of oppressive medieval walls. Today, L'Eixample boasts the largest number of moderniste buildings in Europe.

L'EIXAMPLE DRETA

Begun in 1882 and still unfinished at the architect's death in 1926, Gaudí's inimitable masterpiece, **La Sagrada Família (The Church of the Holy Family)** ✪✪✪ (Mallorca 401; ☎ 932-07-30-31; www.sagradafamilia.org; 8€ adults, 5€ students, 3€ guide/audioguide, 2€ elevator to the top; Nov–Mar daily 9am–6pm, Apr–Sept daily 9am–8pm; Metro: Verdaguer or Sagrada Família), is the city's most idiosyncratic and symbolic moderniste creation, generally more admired today than it was when it was first erected. Its knobby quasi-phallic towers—four original and four completed by modern architects in recent years—rise like calloused fingers above the gray and characterless cityscape, cocking a metaphorical snoot at architectural convention.

community, and dozens of other species enough room to move around freely.) Other attractions include a dolphin show and a reptile enclosure.

Enter the Parc de la Ciutadella (see above) from its western side and you'll immediately come across the **Museu de Ciències Naturals de la Ciutadella (Geologia and Zoologia)** kids (Parc de la Ciutadella, Passeig Picasso 1; ☎ 933-19-68-95 for Museu de Geologia, ☎ 933-19-69-12 for Museu de la Zoologia; 3.70€ adults [for both] or 5.30€ adults [including Botanical Gardens], free for children 15 and under; Tues–Sat 10am–7pm, Sun 10am–3pm; Metro: Barceloneta or Arc de Triomf), a duo of museums that jointly form the city's Natural History Museum.

By far the favorite with families is Domenech i Muntaner's *Mudéjar* (mock-Arabic) style **Museu de Zoologia** , whose crenellated towers embossed with ceramic heraldry have helped give it the nickname Castell de Tres Dragons (Castle of the Three Dragons). It was originally intended as a cafe for the 1887–88 World's Fair, but it wasn't completed in time for this role. Inside, behind Victorian-style wooden and glass cabinets, is a suitably grotesque assortment of specimens such as Goliath frogs and giant crabs, plus a down-to-earth section on Catalán flora. The more soberly neoclassical **Museu de Geologia**—Spain's very first Scientific Museum—still boasts the largest geology collection in the country, thanks to the efforts of devoted collector Francesc Martorell. In its left wing, you'll find plenty of rocks: granite, quartz, and naturally radioactive stuff; more interesting for most is the right wing's selection of fossils accompanied by 1950s Jules Verne–style depictions of prehistoric life.

The church, which was commissioned by a staunch right-wing faction of the Catholic Church, became an obsession with the intensely religious Gaudí. With plenty of money available and no deadline (perhaps it would have been better if there had been), Gaudí was content to say "My client [God] is in no hurry." (Recent additions, however, including four new towers designed by modern architects—the original Gaudí plans were destroyed by anarchists—have been criticized by some of the more vociferous local traditionalists as shallow, trivial, and even comic-strip trashy.)

In its layout, it follows the design of a classic Gothic church, with transepts, aisles, and a central nave. But all similarity to what's come before ends there. The interior and exterior are festooned with a riot of stone carvings, with eight (to date) elongated towers: four above each of the three facades (representing the apostles) at 100m (329 ft.) high with four more (the evangelists) reaching a lofty 170m (558 ft.). The last tower, being built over the apse, will be higher still and dedicated to the Virgin Mary. The Nativity Facade on the Carrer Marina was the

Gaudí, Modernism & the Reshaping of Barcelona

by Pauline Frommer

Physics tells us that for each action there is an equal and opposite reaction, and for the artists of Europe in the 1890s, their reaction to the Industrial Revolution was a retreat back into nature. As factories spewed out mass-produced goods and the lifestyle for many Europeans was transformed from an agrarian one into one centered around assembly lines and gritty cityscapes, architects, designers, painters, and sculptors started banning right angles and straight lines from their works and studying plants, wave patterns, clouds, and animal shapes for their inspiration. In Britain and many other parts of Europe, this new style was called, appropriately enough, Art Nouveau. In Spain, it was (and is) called mondernisme. Its "ancestral home" is Barcelona, and one of its leading proponents was famed architect Antoni Gaudí i Cornet.

Born in 1852 into a family of metalworkers, Gaudí trained at the Escola Tècnica Superior d'Arquitectura. When he graduated, the director of the school, while signing his diploma, is said to have mused aloud, "Who knows if we are giving this diploma to a nut or a genius." The jury on that question was out for many years as Gaudí created extraordinarily inventive and idiosyncratic works of architecture. His detractors, including George Orwell, bemoaned the lack of symmetry in his work (a hallmark of classical architecture), deplored his innovative use of fragmented multicolored

only one to be completed while the architect was alive and represents the birth of Jesus. Its molten wax–styled Holy Family figures and flute-bearing angels have at their center the "Tree of Life," a cypress tree scattered with nesting white doves (nature was Gaudí's passion).

Facing it, the controversial Passion Facade by Catalán sculptor Josep M. Subirachs added stylized, elongated, figures not really in keeping with the Gaudí section; it's been ridiculed by the likes of formidable critic-cum-author Robert Hughes. It's hoped that the church will be finished by 2026 (the centenary of Gaudí's death); the work is being funded entirely by visitors and private donations. The next step toward this goal is the projected roofing of the cathedral in 2010, when work on the vaults of the transepts and apses is due to be completed.

Admission includes a 12-minute video on Gaudí's religious and secular works. Don't forget to visit Gaudí's Neo-Gothic burial crypt, which amazingly survived the 1909 Semana Trágica's ravages, which started with a worker's revolt protesting Spain's involvement in a war with Morocco but degenerated into an anarchic riot of urban destruction in the course of which many churches were totally destroyed.

It may strike you as a bit odd to see a medical center included on the list of places to check out in L'Eixample, but this one was striking enough to get itself declared a UNESCO World Heritage Site in 1997 and is well worth an investigative gander.

mosaics *(trencadis)* on the surfaces of benches and walls (most notably the Parc Guell), and claimed that he had inspired the English word *gaudy*. But he and his moderniste colleagues—who included such luminaries as Lluís Domènech i Montaner, Josep Puig i Cadalfach, Josep Junol (he was the actual designer of lovely mosaics on the benches in the Parc Guell), Salvador Valeri, and Joan Rubio i Bellver—kept on creating. Among their signatures was the bold blending of disparate materials—wrought iron, stained glass, hand-painted floral motifs, medieval bricks, *trencadis,* and faux-Arabic (neo-Mudéjar) archways. And what they did with prosaic materials like concrete (which they curved, bent, and twisted like rubber) is awe inspiring even today.

Oddly enough, it was the industrial revolution that allowed these architects to flourish. Money was flowing into the city at a rapid clip and the economic boom coincided with the return of entrepreneurs who had made their bundle in the Americas and wanted to show off their wealth in eye-catching villas both in the capital and in nearby towns like Tarragona, Reus, and Sitges. The new L'Eixample district's wide avenues, in particular, were catnip for architects eager for a spacious canvas on which to work. So they created the flamboyant mansions and churches, you see today, utterly transforming the city in the process.

Located on the elegant avenida Gaudí but designed not by the great man himself but by his close and highly talented competitor Domènech i Montaner, **L'Hospital de la Santa Creu i Sant Pau** ★★★ (Sant Antoni María Claret 167–171; ☎ 934-88-20-78; www.santpau.es; 6€ adults, 3€ students, free for children 14 and under; guided tours Sat–Sun 10am–2pm; Metro: Hospital San Pau) is one of L'Eixample's lesser-known moderniste masterpieces. Commissioned at the beginning of the 20th century by wealthy banker Pau Gil i Serra, who wished to create a hospital based on a vegetation-friendly "garden city" model, it abounds with colored pavilions and a profusion of leafy trees and flower-filled areas, softening the overall effect of the buildings. Also known as the Hospital San Pau, it's only slightly less flamboyant than the architect's better-known Palau de la Música Catalána (p. 282) and is rich with Byzantine and Moorish-inspired facades and decor, which range from gargoyles and angels to fauna and blossoming flora. Only the largest of its eight completed pavilions, the Administrative Pavilion, is open to the public, while the others are reserved for research and education purposes. (The last of its patients and their doctors moved to a brand-new functional but characterless hospital in 2006.) The building's facade glows with mosaic murals telling the history of hospital care, and inside are beautiful columns with floral capitals and an opulent rose pink tiled ceiling. The initial building was completed in 1911, and after funds ran out and

Gil i Serra died in 1930, subsequent work was carried out by his son. It's not essential to take the guided tour, and you can walk around quite freely on your own if you want to.

Highly unorthodox even by Gaudí's standards and greeted with widespread ridicule on its first appearance, **La Pedrera (Casa Milà)** ★★★ (Provença 261–265 on corner of Passeig de Gràcia; ☎ 934-84-59-80 or 934-84-59-00; 8€ adults, 4.50€ students, free for children 11 and under; daily 10am–7:30pm, tours Mon–Fri 6pm; Metro: Diagonal) acquired its nickname from its supposed resemblance to a stone quarry. Today, public and critics alike view it as a superlative example of modernista architecture but—rather tongue in cheek—the original name has stuck. Molded in sinuous limestone waves that sharply contrast with the design of its neoclassical Passeig de Gràcia neighbors, the building is a mass of curves both inside and out, and its cavern-like appearance famously inspired the French president Georges Clemenceau to report after a visit that in Barcelona they make caves for dragons.

The building was commissioned by wealthy developer Pere Mila i Camps and occupies a whole corner block. When it was restored in 1996, a small and highly personal museum, covering the works and life of Gaudí, was installed in the attic, and the entire first floor now also serves as an exhibition space for works of the likes of Dalí and Chillida. The apartments (many of them still private homes) are centered on two courtyards, their walls decorated with subtle, jewel-like murals. One of them has been refurbished in their original early 20th-century style. The highlight for most is the visit to the rooftop, where restored centurion-like chimneys cluster surrealistically on the undulating surface: Between them you get great views of the nearby Sagrada Família and distant port. Jazz and flamenco performances take place here in summer. Admission is included in the entry fee; English-language tours are offered Monday through Friday at 6pm.

> ❝ The Catalán lives artwardly. When there is a fantasy in his head he turns it into action, into stone. ❞
>
> —V. S. Pritchett

L'EIXAMPLE ESQUERRA

The three works by the three master architects of the modernisme movement—Josep Puig i Cadafalch, Lluis Domènech i Montaner, and Antoni Gaudí—on Passeig de Gràcia between Consell de Cent and Aragó, offer a brilliant condensed study of different moderniste styles.

Designed by Puig i Cadafalch in 1900 in a cubical style that blends a Flemish gable with Catalán ceramic and wrought iron, **Casa Amatller** ★★ (Passeig de Gràcia 41; ☎ 932-16-01-75; free admission; ground floor open to public Mon–Sat 10am–7pm; Metro: Passeig de Gràcia) was the very first building on the block. The architect's love of animals is reflected in the Eusebi Arnau sculptures of creatures blowing glass and taking photos.

Undisputed star of the triumvirate is the adjoining **Casa Batlló** ★★★ (Passeig de Gràcia 43; ☎ 934-88-06-66; 17€ adults, 13€ children and students, free for children 4 and under; Mon–Sun 9am–8pm; Metro: Passeig de Gràcia) designed by Gaudí in 1905. With its facade of sensuous iron and stone curves and luminous *trencadis* (collage of broken tiles and ceramic), the building portrays the legend of St. George (patron saint of Catalonia) and his dragon. (You can glimpse the saint in the turret, his lance crowned by a cross.) Imposing skull-like formations supported by columns that protect the balconies represent the dragon's victims, while the spectacular roof is the dragon's humped and glossy scaled back. The building was only opened to the public in 2004 and the sheer sumptuousness of the interior, with its Gaudí-designed furnishings, curving staircases, flowing wood paneling, and stained-glass gallery supported by more vertebrae-like columns, justify the comparatively high admission cost.

Last of the three, Doménech i Montaner's flamboyant but flawed **Casa Lleo Morera** (Passeig de Gràcia 35; Metro: Passeig de Gràcia) stands on the corner of Carrer del Consell de Cent. Built in 1906 in an international Art Nouveau style, it features a tiered wedding cake–type turret and a collection of bizarre ornaments that range from a light bulb and telephone (both inventions of the period) to a lion and mulberry bush (after the owner's name: in Catalán, lion is *lleó* and mulberry is *morera*). Alas, the lower part of the facade has been inexplicably replaced by plate glass by the building's cavalier tenant. (The similarly ruined interior of the shop is the only part of the building open to the public.)

GRÀCIA & PARC GÜELL

There are two very good reasons to visit this compact district just north of L'Eixample Dreta. One is that you're in easy walking distance of the magical Parc Güell (see below). The other is that it allows you to explore a corner of the city that's quite different from either the cramped, crowded Ciutat Vella or expansive L'Eixample. In the 19th century, Gràcia was actually a separate town, and today that individual atmosphere lives on in its tiny squares and friendly shops, attracting in recent times a creative blend of bohemian and artistic inhabitants. Its central calle Verdi and Plaça del Sol both buzz with cafe life, particularly during the lively summer fiestas.

As in both the L'Eixample (to the south) and Parc Güell (to the north), Gaudí's ubiquitous touch is on display again here, first in the form of a very early Art Nouveau work, the privately owned **Casa Vicens** ★★ (Carrer de les Carolines 18–24; Metro: Fontana), which was built for tile manufacturer Manuel Vicens i Montaner in 1883. Though not open to the public, its striking facade of brilliantly colored tiles and opulent minarets and corbels (Gaudí's interests were Eastern oriented at the time) makes it well worth a look. The well-photographed interior, which alas you can't visit, features exotic influences from Ottoman to Andalus.

Then, second, comes the one Gaudí attraction guaranteed to make the whole family happy: his marvelous **Parc Güell** ★★★ **kids** (Carrer Olot 7; ☎ 934-24-38-09; free admission; daily 10am–sunset; Metro: Lesseps, then either a 15-min. walk or take bus no. 24) located high among woodlands behind Gràcia and enjoying fine city views. Originally intended as a garden city for his wealthy patron Eusebi Güell, it became a park when the city took over in 1926. Its many fairy-tale corners begin with two gingerbread-style gatehouses decorated with broken mosaic collage topped with mushroom-shaped chimneys at the park's entrance. (These were created, so it's said, when Gaudí was under the hallucinatory influence of his Hansel and Gretel set designs for the Liceu Opera House.)

Just to the right of the park's entrance stands an eccentric little building, which gives you a unique insight into creator Gaudí's private life: the Ramón Berenguer–designed **Casa-Museu Gaudí** (Carrer del Carmel 28; ☎ 932-19-38-11; 4€ adults, 3€ students; daily 10am–6pm), which the reclusive genius made his home-cum-retreat for some years. Here you can see his original furniture, drawings, and other personal effects.

After you enter the park, its main steps lead past a spectacular tiled lizard to the covered Sala Hipóstila (marketplace), which supports a platform with 86 Doric columns connected by shallow vaults and a roof embellished with four sun-shaped disks representing the seasons. Above, in the elevated palm-tree-lined square, a long bench elaborately crafted with broken multi-hued shards of glass, crockery, and ceramic by Gaudí and craftsman Josep Marià Jujol curves around the perimeter. You can then wander the 3km (2 miles) of rustic pathways and explore the surrounding Mediterranean parkland, where sculptures and figurines greet you at every turn.

MONTJUÏC

Montjuïc is one of the two best vantage points from which to enjoy the Barcelona panorama (the other is Tibidabo). It has hosted two famous international events: the 1929 World's Fair and 1992 Olympic Games. Both fit quite easily into what is Barcelona's largest green zone, an area that's long been favored by joggers and cyclists. In recent years, the city council has installed more walkways, planted more trees and flowers, and extended the cable-car route up from Poble Sec to reach the castle itself. The multitude of gardens on Monjuic include the superb **Jardí Botànic (Botanical Garden)** ✹ (Doctor Font i Quer s/n, Parque de Montjuïc; ☎ 934-26-49-35; 4€ adults, free for children 15 and under; Mon–Sat 10am–5pm [until 8pm July–Sept], Sun 10am–3pm; see the box "The Way Up" for transportation info), created in 1999. Nestling behind the Castell de Montjuïc, it's been internationally praised for its imaginative and carefully ordered layout. The richly varied flora—all of which thrive in the Mediterranean climate—comes from areas as far afield as Australia and California. Top museums such as the Miró Foundation and the MNAC (see below) are further reasons to make the climb up here.

A good place to get the full lowdown on this and all the other Montjuïc parks and green zones is the charming information center at the nearby Puig i Cadafalch–designed **Font del Gat** (Passeig Santa Madrona 28; ☎ 932-89-04-04), which has also converted its once-fashionable cafe into a modern restaurant.

Most people head up to the hilltop **Museu Militar de Montjuïc** ✹ (Parc de Montjuïc s/n; ☎ 933-29-86-13; 2.50€ museum and castle, 1€ grounds, free for children 13 and under; Nov to mid-Mar Tues–Sun 9:30am–5:30pm, mid-Mar to Oct Tues–Sun 9:30am–8pm; see the box "The Way Up" for transportation info) to enjoy the out-of-this-world city and Mediterranean views rather than for the interesting but somewhat somber museum. You see these vistas from the terraces, walkways, and high points of this star-shaped *castell*, which dates back to 1640 but was rebuilt and extended 200 years later. Its Stygian cells served as a military prison during the Civil War. Franco's horseback statue was quietly removed a couple of decades back, but other vaguely projected plans for the fort's more peaceful future use remain on the shelf for the time being.

The Way Up

You have several ways to scale Montjuïc:

One is by **combined funicular railway and cable car** (or telefèric) trip from the district of Poble Sec. First, catch the funicular, which links with subway line no. 3 at the Parallel Metro stop on Avinguda Paral•lel and takes you up to avenida Miramar on the green slopes of the hill. The fare is 1.25€ each way. From there continue on the *telefèric,* which was renovated in 2007 and now goes right up to the castle/military museum at the top. This operates daily from 9am to 8pm in winter, 9am to 10pm in summer, and costs 4€ one-way and 6€ round-trip.

The other route to Montjuïc is by exhilarating *telefèric* ride from Barceloneta across Barcelona harbor up to the lower part of Montjuïc. Also known as the **Transbordador Aeri del Port,** it operates every 15 minutes and makes stops at three towers, where you can take photographs of the port, beaches, and the tree-lined Rambla avenue way below. The fare is 8€ one-way (10€ round-trip) for adults, and 5€ one-way (7€ round-trip) for children 4–12.

The museum itself contains paintings of military events and collections of armor, uniforms, weapons, and war instruments through the ages. A lighter touch, in Room 8, is the collection of thousands of miniatures forming a Spanish division. The easiest route here is the funicular from Paral•lel Metro station; its new final adjoining stop was opened in 2007.

Down on the northern side of Montjuïc, close to the Plaça Espanya, you'll find one of the city's very best private collections of contemporary art at CaixaForum ✦✦ (Av. Marquès de Comillas 6–8; ☎ 934-76-86-00; free admission; Tues–Sun 10am–8pm; Metro: Espanya), an ultra-modern gallery opened in 2002 in Puig i Cadalfach's Casaramona building, which in the past was first a textile factory and then a police barracks. For years it remained derelict and empty, until its 21st-century rebirth as a highly imaginative Art Nouveau "fortress," complete with a striking redbrick facade and singular turret, to which the Japanese architect Arata Isozaki (who designed the St. Jordi musical venue farther up the hill) added a walkway, courtyard, and entrance. Inside, past Sol Lewitt's giant abstract mural, are three interlinked levels of constantly changing exhibitions, highlighted past and present by Rodin and Turner masterpieces. No two visits are the same, and works by major artists such as Tapiès regularly appear. There's a lively calendar of events, music, and modern-dance performances, plus a first-rate bookshop.

But Montjuïc's undisputed mecca for modern-art lovers is the **Fundació Joan Miró** ✦✦✦ (Parc de Montjuïc s/n; ☎ 934-43-94-70; 7.20€ adults, 3.90€ students, free for children 13 and under; July–Sept Tues–Wed and Fri–Sat 10am–8pm, Oct–June Tues–Wed and Fri–Sat 10am–7pm, year-round Thurs 10am–9:30pm and Sun 10am–2:30pm; see the box "The Way Up" for transportation info), which contains works by one of the greatest masters of contemporary Catalán art, Joan Miró. Built in the early 1970s for Miró by his close friend and co-worker Josep Lluis Sert (who also designed the artist's workroom in Majorca) in a series of stark white galleries with terra-cotta floors, the museum is an ideal setting for the master's surrealist images and abstract forms. On permanent display are over 10,000 paintings, graphics, and sculptures (only a part of the whole collection) naturally lit by *claraboias* (skylights). Temporary additional exhibitions are also held, and in summer there are garden concerts.

Two high spots are the first gallery's 1979 Foundation Tapestry and Mercury Fountain (designed by American sculptor Alexander Calder). Early pieces from Miró's student days—expressing his horror at the civil war—include the visceral *Man and Woman in Front of a Pile of Excrement* (1935) in the Pilar Juncosa Gallery. More serenely dreamlike are his constantly recurring images of the sun, moon, and other celestial bodies, as seen in *The Gold of the Azure* (1967) in the same gallery: a hypnotic blue cloud on a gold background with dots and strokes for the planets and stars.

Stepping further back into the past for an exploration of the early influences on Barcelona is the **Museu d'Arqueologia de Catalunya** ✪ (Passeig de Santa Madrona 39–41 Parc de Montjuïc; ☎ 934-24-65-77; 2.40€ adults, 1.80€ students, free for children 15 and under; Tues–Sat 9:30am–7pm, Sun 10am–2:30pm; Metro: Espanya), located in the former Palace of Graphic Arts (built for the 1929 World's Fair). Beginning with prehistoric Iberian artifacts, the collection covers the Greek, Carthaginian, and Roman periods with an exceptional range of artifacts from the ancient Greco-Roman city of L'Empúries (p. 331). The Roman range of glassware, lamps, grooming aids, utensils, and splendid floor mosaics dating from their 218 B.C. arrival is not to be missed.

Even more richly redolent of the past is my favorite Barcelona museum, the **Museu Nacional d'Art de Catalunya (MNAC)** ✪✪✪ (Palau Nacional, Parc de Montjuïc; ☎ 936-22-03-60; www.mnac.es; 8.50€ valid for 2 days, 12€ for combined MNAC/Poble Espanyol ticket, 30% reduction for students and youths 15–21, free for children 14 and under and adults 66 and over; Tues–Sat 10am–7pm, Sun 10am–2:30pm; Metro: Espanya), which houses the greatest collection of Catalán art in the world. Ambitiously renovated in 2004, its star attraction is still the unique world-beating collection of simplistic but vividly colored Romanesque sculptures, icons, and frescoes taken from dilapidated Pyrenean churches and restored and mounted here in expertly reproduced domes and apses. These include the mesmerizing Apse of Santa María de Taüll (in Ambit [Gallery] V) where a serene, doe-eyed Christ is surrounded by the apostles who stand against an intense lapis lazuli–hued background. Exhibits in the next galleries range from the early Middle Ages to the Italian- and Flemish-influenced Gothic periods, dominated by Catalán genius Jaume Huguet's luminous carvings and paintings. Don't miss his colorful, highly detailed *retablos* (altarpieces) in Room XIII. Next comes an imposing collection of works by grand Old Masters such as Titian, Rubens, El Greco, and Goya, all generously bequeathed by local businessman Francesc Cambó. The MNAC's more recently acquired 19th- and 20th-century exhibits—which cover the neoclassical, moderniste, and *nou-centista* (or *fin de siècle*) periods—include furniture by Gaspar Homar, who combined ebony, jacaranda, cherry, sycamore, and ash wood in his dazzling marquetry work.

If sport turns you on more than art, head to the **Galería Olímpica** (Passeig Olímpic s/n, Estadí Olímpic; ☎ 934-26-06-60; 2.70€ adults, 1.50€ children and seniors; Apr–Sept Mon–Fri 10am–2pm and 4–7pm, Oct–Mar Tues–Sat 10am–1pm and 4–6pm; Metro: Espanya, then either a 15-min. walk or take bus no. 13 or 50 from Plaça Espanya; see the box "The Way Up"). Here, in a display celebrating the 1992 Olympic Games, you can browse photos, costumes, and memorabilia, reflect on the colorful pageantry of the event, see video recordings of athletic events, and vicariously savor the fame that changed the city forever. There's even audiovisual coverage of the drastic building programs that prepared the city for the onslaught.

After Olympic nostalgia, you'll find another kind of nationalistic fervor in the **Poble Espanyol** ★★ 🔵 (Av. Marquès de Comillas s/n, Parc de Montjuïc; ☎ 935-08-63-00; 8€ adults, 12€ for combined MNAC/Poble Espanyol ticket, 5€ children 4–12, free for children 3 and under, 20€ family ticket for 2 adults plus 2 children, 6€ students and adults over 65; Mon 9am–8pm, Tues–Thurs 9am–2am, Fri–Sat 9am–4am, Sun 9am–midnight; Metro: Espanya, then either a 10-min. walk uphill or take bus no. 13 or 50 from Plaça Espanya; see the box "The Way Up"). Built for the 1929 World's Fair, this lovingly re-created Spanish village displays no less than 100 styles of Spanish vernacular architecture ranging from Levantine to Gallego, Castilian high Gothic to the humble whitewashed Andaluz dwellings of the south. Whether you view it as a kitsch pastiche of faux Spanish architectural styles or (like me) simple Disney-style fun, it's hardly likely to leave you feeling indifferent, especially if you're a kid. Within many of the buildings are craft shops where you may see artists printing fabric, making pottery, and blowing glass. After-dark venues include the Tablao de Carmen flamenco *taberna* (p. 303) and a couple of other trendy nightspots. The Poble Espanyol's essentially touristy image received more hard-line cultural cred with the opening of the **Fundació Fran Daural** (daily 10am–7pm) a few years back. Check out its collection of contemporary Catalán arts, with works by Dalí, Picasso, Barceló, and Tàpies.

THE HARBORFRONT: PORT VELL & BARCELONETA

The renovation of the city's port and coast has been the most radical and enhancing change Barcelona has experienced in many decades. From the Columbus Monument at the busy harbor end of La Rambla you can now follow boardwalks and esplanades from Port Vell's modern yacht-filled marinas, past the gentrified former fisherman's district of La Barceloneta, alongside half a dozen beaches sheltered by stone breakwaters as far as Port Olimpic with its jetties, seafood restaurants, and famed Frank Gehry fish sculpture. (Most of the big sights are at the western Port Vell end.)

The real historic gem here, of course, is the city's Maritime Museum or **Museu Marítim** ★★★ 🔵 (Av. de les Drassanes s/n; ☎ 933-42-99-20; 6.50€ adults, 5.20€ students 11–25 and adults 66 and over, 3.25€ children 7–10; daily 10am–7pm; Metro: Drassanes), which is actually housed in the port's original former Drassanes Reials (Royal Shipyards)—a huge medieval structure, which is the best preserved of its kind in Spain and possibly the world. Though Barcelona's powerful seafaring rivals Venice, Genoa, and Valencia all had impressive shipyards in their medieval heyday, only vestiges of them remain. In contrast, the majestic arches, columns, and gigantic vaults of this high-ceilinged edifice are gloriously intact. Formerly located right on the seashore, the building was used to dry-dock, construct, and repair ships for the Catalán-Aragonese empire. The shipyards declined in the 18th century and served as an army barracks up to the time of the Civil War, eventually opening as a museum in the 1970s. A family highlight is "The Great Adventure of the Sea" collection honoring Catalonia's maritime history. It's centered round the *Galería Real* (Royal Galley or ship) of Don Juan of Austria, which was reconstructed in celebration of the vessel's finest hour: 400 years earlier at Lepanto, where it victoriously headed a combined Spanish, Venetian, Maltese, and Vatican fleet against the Turks, thus ending their Mediterranean domination. Onboard, visitors view a first-rate film re-creating the battle and admire the galley's elaborate hull, hold, and deck with its manned 59 oars. A wide variety of sailing and fishing vessels are also on display, ranging from caravels (four-masted sailboats of Portuguese origin) to sloops (smaller single-masted vessels known in their military naval version as frigates). You can also see models of the Compañía Trasmediterránea's fleet (which still operates to the Balearic islands) and a tiny version of *Ictíneo,* one of the world's earliest submarines, designed by marine pioneer Narcís Monturiol.

A more recent marine-oriented favorite, particularly with families with children, is **L'Aquarium de Barcelona** ✮✮ 🧒 (Moll d'Espanya-Port Vell; ☎ 932-21-74-74; www.aquariumbcn.com; 16€ adults, 13€ adults 61 and over, 11€ students and children 4–12; July–Aug daily 9:30am–11pm, Sept–June Mon–Fri 9:30am–9pm, Sat–Sun 9:30am–9:30pm; Metro: Drassanes or Barceloneta) just a 10-minute walk from the bottom of La Rambla. Opened in 1995 on one of the port's new jetties, it's one of Europe's best aquatic leisure and education centers, and each of the 21 glass tanks inside contains a different marine species from seagoing worms to sharks and a huge "oceanarium" showing the Mediterranean as a self-sustaining ecosystem. You view it from inside a glass-roofed, glass-sided 80-meter (262-ft.) tunnel while fish, eels, and sharks swim around you. Kids especially love the Explora section, with its collection of highly tactile exhibits on the Costa Brava and Ebro Delta.

The **Museu d'Història de Catalunya (Catalán History Museum)** ✮ (Plaça de la Pau Vila 3; ☎ 932-25-47-00; 4€ adults, 2.50€ children 7–18 and students; Tues and Thurs–Sat 10am–7pm, Wed 10am–8pm, Sun 10am–2:30pm; Metro: Barceloneta), provides an in depth (even exhausting) look at eight different aspects of the region's past from ancestry and Catalán-Aragonese sea trade to the Industrial Revolution to the modern age from Franco to modern democracy (the most entertaining section). The museum uses multimedia, re-creations, models, and other interactive devices to tell its stories (explanations are in Catalán, but English speakers are given a book with translations). Temporary exhibitions on the ground floor cover such areas as Mediterranean cultures and the notorious Federico García Lorca and Salvador Dalí poet-artist relationship.

UPPER BARCELONA

At the back of the city you'll find the quieter more affluent barris of Sarrià, Pedralbes, and Sant Gervasí, where period mansions still sit among the more modern array of apartment complexes and villas with gardens. Above them towers the infinitely less stylish and serene world of Tibidabo, its vulgarity luckily compensated for by its great views (see below).

The cheapest way to savor the apparent rural calm of a secluded monastery, without even leaving Barcelona, is to head for the **Monestir de Pedralbes** ✸✸ (Baixada del Monestir 9; ☎ 932-03-92-82; 5.50€ adults, 3.50€ seniors and students, free for children 15 and under; Tues–Sun 10am–2pm; FGC: Reina Elisenda), in the attractive confines of residential Pedralbes. Founded in 1326 by Elisenda de Montcada, queen of Jaume II, the monastery first housed the nuns of the Order of St. Clare (who now reside in a smaller adjacent building), and then, after the king's death, the queen herself. Her tomb, surrounded by angels, can be seen in the neighboring Gothic church. Its tranquil cloister with its central fountain, stone well, and verdant herb gardens enclosed by nearly two dozen elegant arches, really makes you wonder if you're still in a city. Adjoining it is another small treasure: the Chapel of St. Michael, exquisitely decorated with murals of the Passion of Christ by the 14th-century artist Ferrer Bassa.

In the original nuns' residence is an exhibition recreating 14th-century life, which takes guests through the day chambers, pulpit, kitchen, refectory, and communal dining room where the Mother Superior would break her vow of silence with mealtime Bible readings. In the renovated nuns' dormitory, a further treat awaits you: 70 outstanding works by Rubens, Titian, and Velázquez from the Thyssen-Bornemizca collection, as well as sculptures and Renaissance and baroque paintings.

To be frank, it's the setting that is the star at the **Museu de les Arts Decoratives/ Museu de Ceràmica (Museums of Decorative Arts and Ceramics)** ✸ (Av. Diagonal 686; ☎ 932-80-16-21; 3.50€ adults, 2€ students, free for children 15 and under; Tues–Sat 10am–6pm, Sun 10am–3pm; Metro: Palau Reial), which jointly occupy the Palau de Pedralbes and can be seen together. This neoclassical palace was first the property of King Alfonso XIII, who handed it over in 1930 to the local government, which subsequently made it an exhibition space for the decorative arts. During the dictatorship, General Franco lived there when he visited Barcelona. It finally metamorphosed back into a museum in 1960. Inside, the palace halls—decorated with gilt, marble, and vivid frescoes—form an opulent setting for the many objects of the Decorative Arts Museum (from Romanesque right up to Art Deco), and the regionally ordered collection—highlighted by Andalusian Mudéjar and metallic inlay work and Castilian baroque and Renaissance pieces—of the Ceramics Museum.

Since its total renovation and expansion in 2004, the **CosmoCaixa (Museu de la Ciència)** ✸✸✸ 🄺🄸🄳🄳 (Teodor Roviralta 55; ☎ 932-12-60-50; free admission to museum, 3€ planetarium, 2€ Toca Toca; Tues–Sun 10am–8pm; FGC: Avinguda Tibidabo then either a 10-min. walk or bus no. 17, 22, 58, or 73) can justly claim to be the top high-tech Science museum in Europe. It still occupies a converted moderniste poorhouse at the foot of Tibidabo, but its exhibition space has been increased to 3,700 sq. m (39,826 sq. ft.) to incorporate a new bioresearch center and revised permanent collection. The largest information area is the "*Salón de Materia* (Matter)," which is divided into separately titled sections: "Inert Matter," dealing with the Big Bang up to the first signs of life; "Living Matter," which covers life on Earth up to the birth of mankind; "Intelligent Matter," which examines the development of human intelligence; and "Civilized Matter," covering history and science from pioneers to the computer age. Far away favorite, though, is the "Flooded Forest" section, a totally re-created Amazonian rainforest, which contains over 100 species of animal and plant life. In the Toca Toca (literally, "Touch, Touch") section, kids can get up close and personal with rats, frogs, spiders, and the like, and are even allowed to pick up and handle some of them. There is also a 3-D planetarium and "Geological Wall," which explains, interactively, the history of the world from a geological viewpoint.

Wild, wacky, and seemingly unfazed by its incomparable setting, the time warp amusement park **Parc d'Atraccions Tibidabo** ★★ (Plaça Tibidabo 3; ☎ 932-11-79-42; 24€ unlimited rides, 7€ children under 1.2m (4 ft.), free for children under .90m (3 ft.), 9€ adults over 60; summer daily noon–10pm, off season Sat–Sun noon–7pm; Bus: 58 to Avinguda Tibidabo Metro, then take the Tramvía Blau, which drops you at the funicular, p. 249) stands atop the city's highest point, a popular escape point for Barcelonese since 1868 when a road was built connecting it to the center. Recent novelties like the blood curdling Dragon Khan roller coaster compete with more old-fashioned rides like the creaky 1928 L'Avio, a flight simulator replica of the first plane to operate a Barcelona–Madrid service. A long-time favorite is the hair-raising Aeromàgic cable car ride, which manages to intersperse exhilarating views of the Mediterranean world below with scary sorties through tunnels lined with effigies of witches and demons. Famed as a landmark visible from afar, is the adjoining Temple de Sagrat Cor, a tacky 1902 building crudely attempting to emulate Paris's Sacré Coeur.

THE OTHER BARCELONA

There are two Barcelonas—the one the tourists see and the one in which the inhabitants go about their daily business. For a genuine taste of the latter, pay a visit to **Poble Nou,** a former fishing and industrial district near Port Olimpic. Though more bourgeois in mood these days, the district still preserves reminders of its working-class background in the form of factory chimneys and warehouses, and although a modest number of them have been converted into studio lofts a la London's Docklands and New York's SoHo, this mild gentrification has barely changed the traditional, workaday atmosphere of the place.

You'll see locals pouring out of the central Santa María del Taulat Church after a morning service, shopping for Mediterranean produce in the distinctly untouristy Mercat Unio (Union Market), relaxing in the barri's squares and increasing number of open green zones, and strolling down the 1886-built Rambla de Poble Nou—far less packed and commercialized than the city's circus-like main *paseo*. Here, people have more time to stop and chat and look on the still relatively rare foreign visitor with a blend of surprise and friendly interest.

You may even get intimations of the afterlife in the district's huge 18th-century Cementeri de l'Est—where Barcelonans have been laid to rest over the years—if you take a walking tour of its macabre but fascinating Gothic tombs. At the cemetery's entrance, you can obtain a leaflet, or a more detailed but expensive (20€) guidebook, both describing a route that takes in the most important monuments here.

BE A CATALÁN CHEF FOR A DAY

There are several places in Barcelona where visitors can learn to cook the famed cuisine of Catalonia, but for my money the best organized outfit is **Cook and Taste** (La Rambla 58—3º; ☎ 933-02-13-20; www.cookandtaste.net), which is run by the charming English-speaking Begoña Sánchez (who has had a long involvement in the world of gastronomy herself, both as a cook and as a restaurant administrator). Her professional team of English-speaking—though mainly Spanish—chefs give lessons to would-be Ferran Adriàs in the finer points of producing a serviceable gazpacho, paella, or even a *zarzuela* (a richly complex seafood dish not to be confused with the similarly named Gilbert and Sullivan–style comic opera). Classes are usually in groups of no more than four, and participants tend to be foreign visitors rather than resident Spaniards. Courses are run twice a day at 11am and 5pm, last around 3½ hours, and are priced at 60€ a head. "We mold our courses around the type of dishes our participants have jointly agreed they want to do," says Begoña. "We'd advise anyone interested in booking to do so by e-mail as soon as they know the dates they want, as we tend to be booked up for months ahead." The cooking school is located very close to La Boquería market, where the students go first to choose their ingredients.

FLAMENCO CLASSES

Although flamenco originates from southerly Arabic-influenced Andalusia, some of its finest exponents are to be found in the big northerly cities like Barcelona and Madrid. So if you're a great fan of *soleas, bulerias,* and *alegrías* (different versions of joyous Andaluz songs), and you're tired of just sitting around watching and listening, here's your chance to dive in and learn how to play the guitar or click your heels with the best of them. You'll need a working knowledge of Spanish at both of the following institutes as no English is spoken during the classes.

Joaquín Herrera (Carrer Artà 11-13; ☎ 933-54-30-00; www.joaquinherrera.com; weekdays 9:30am–1:30pm and 5:30–9:30pm; Metro: Llucmayor) from Cádiz province started playing the guitar when he was 9. Courses vary in length. Many enroll in a 10-hour (5 days at 2 hr. a day) program where you learn to play pieces by both classical and modern composers (it's possible, of course, to devote less time). Usually there are one to three people per class, and costs vary from 20€ to 40€ per lesson, accordingly. *Compás* and *soniquete* (rhythm and handclapping) techniques are also taught.

Light-of-foot visitors can enroll in flamenco dancing classes at the **Alicianet Academy** (in Poble Nou, Carrer Salvador Espriu 27 bajos; ☎ 933-103-878 or 670-267-276; www.alicianet.net; Metro: Poble Nou). Launched by former flamenco artist Cristina Castellvi in 2005, it boasts a highly proficient team of professional dancers, including Venezuelan Angela Espanidero, who was coached by the legendary choreographer Cristina Hoyos, and the locally renowned Antonio Mouriño, who trained in classical ballet and has taught postural education classes for many years. Both give in-depth classes to all levels of participants. Its singer-tutors include Francisco Contreras (popularly known in Spain as "El Niño de Elche"), and *palillo* (castanet) trainers include Inma González who's appeared widely in festivals in France and Japan. Prices for 6-hour courses range from 75€ for groups of 8 to 12 up to 145€ for groups of 4. "We have students from all over the world," says Cristina. The academy is so successful that she'll also shortly be opening branches in Seville and Madrid.

See also www.flamencobarcelona.com and www.barcelonaflamenco.com for details of other schools that offer flamenco classes, long or short term.

CATALÁN LANGUAGE COURSES

Addressing a Barcelonan in Catalán will, after the initial jaw dropping expression of disbelief, draw an almost disproportionately warm and helpful response. If you can actually understand and answer his reply, you are decidedly "in."

So why not have a go at trying to master the language the Barcelonans have spoken for centuries? Catalán is a clipped no-nonsense lingo with guttural intonations and linguistic origins in Latin, Provençal, and Castilian. **C2 Barcelona** (Carrer Valencia 282; ☎ 932-72-16-34; www.c2-barcelona.com) arranges intensives in Catalán from 1 week for 160€ (4 lessons of 45 min. each per day). They can also arrange very cheap host family accommodation if you enroll.

ACTIVE BARCELONA

When you get tired of looking at Gothic monuments and moderniste buildings and want to unwind with some healthy sporting activities you'll find plenty going on: from swinging a club on a world-class golf course to cantering on horseback though the woodlands above the city.

GOLF

One of the city's very finest courses, **Club de Golf Vallromanes** (Afueras s/n, Vallromanes; ☎ 935-72-90-64; www.golfromanes.com), is a 20-minute drive north of the city. Established in 1972, it is the site of one of Spain's most important golf tournaments. Nonmembers who reserve their tee times in advance are welcome to play. The greens fee is 98€ on weekdays, 160€ on fiesta days and weekends. Amenities include a putting green, swimming pool, and restaurant. There's also a kiddies' tennis school.

First opened in 1954 and recently moved from its original El Prat location to Terrassa (24km/15 miles from Barcelona), the **Reial Club de Golf El Prat** (Carrer Plans de Bon Vilar; ☎ 937-28-10-00), is a prestigious club that admits nonmembers who have a handicap confirmed by the governing golf body in their home country, and who can prove membership in a golf club at home. Its two 18-hole par-72 courses were designed by Greg Norman. On-site is also a public school with its own 9-hole course. Other facilities include a sauna, pool, restaurant, and a supervised playroom for small children Nonmember greens fees are 114€ Monday through Friday, but a prohibitive 228€ at weekends.

For more general information on golf around Barcelona see www.barcelona golf.com. Alas, finding cheap golfing facilities here—or anywhere else in Spain for that matter—is difficult.

SWIMMING

Originally built for the 1992 Olympics, **Piscina Bernardo Picornell** (Av. de Estadí 30–40, on Montjuïc, adjoining Olympic Stadium; ☎ 934-23-40-41; Mon–Fri 7am–midnight, Sat 7am–9pm, Sun 7am–4pm) incorporates two magnificent swimming pools (1 indoors, 1 outdoors) which were custom-built to the highest international standards for the Olympic Games in 1992 (many records were broken here). If you get a full-day ticket (8€ adults, 4€ children) you can also use the gym, sauna, and whirlpools. The easiest way to get here is by the frequent no. 61 bus service from the Plaça d'Espanya.

The veteran **Club de Natació Atlètic Barceloneta** (Plaça del Mar, Barceloneta; ☎ 932-21-00-10; www.cnab.cat; Mon–Fri 6:30am–11pm, Sat 7am–11pm, Sun and fiesta days mid-May to Sept 8am–8pm and Oct to mid-May 8am–5pm), which reached its centenary in 2007, is located right between the port and seafront. It has three pools—two outdoors and one inside—plus a sauna, gym, and court for *frontón* (a high-powered Basque version of squash). Open year-round, it allows nonmembers daily or monthly membership. Bus nos. 17 and 39 stop close by, and the Barceloneta Metro station is a short walk away. Prices for one day's swim: 10€ adults, 7.50€ 65 and over, 5.85€ children 4–10, 3.10€ children 2 and under.

TENNIS

The top spot for tennis is the **Centre Municipal Tennis Vall d'Hebron** (Passeig Vall d'Hebron 178; ☎ 934-27-65-00; Metro: Montbau), which has been the training ground for some of the country's top players. It offers 20 clay and 7 grass courts set over beautiful grounds, but you'll need to bring your own racket and balls. Nonmember rates are 13€ per hour for grass courts and 10€ per hour for clay courts, but there are usually generous reductions—especially for the latter—after 3pm on Sundays.

Up on Montjuïc Hill are two prime tennis locations: the **Club de Tenis Pompeya** (Foixarda 2-4; ☎ 933-25-13-48), which has only 7 clay courts (so be prepared for a possible wait) and the **Club de Natació Montjuïc** (Carrer Segura ☎ 933-318-288), which has 10 clay courts and 1 grass court. The Pompeya reduces its rates drastically if you can find a member to play with. Get there by bus no. 50. The Club de Natació's tennis courts are also open to nonmembers, with slightly dearer rates at weekends. Note that nonmembers can only play between 2pm and 5pm on weekdays and 1pm and 10pm at weekends. Also be prepared for a longish walk from the Plaça España—unless you want the added expense of a taxi—as buses don't stop near here.

HORSEBACK RIDING

Montjuïc is the setting for the city's best riding school, the **Escola Municipal d'Hípica La Foixarda** (Av. Muntanyans 1; ☎ 934-26-10-66; Metro: Espanya), which gets riders of all ages and levels up on horseback. Classes and outings take place only on Sunday mornings between 9am and 1pm and must be reserved beforehand. Rates are 18€ per hour. To make bookings and obtain more information, contact their offices between 4:30pm and 9:30pm weekdays. The school is located directly behind the Pueblo Español on Montjuïc hill and you get there by bus no. 50 from Plaça España.

ATTENTION, SHOPPERS!

The Barcelonans are very fashion conscious, and you'll find some of the most trendy clothes shops in all Spain in the wide, Parisian-styled **Passeig de Gràcia.** In particular, look out in and around this stylish neighborhood for homegrown success stories like Zara and Adolfo Dominguez, whose respective mold-breaking womenswear (there's some menswear, too) sell like veritable hot cakes. Leather coats, handbags, belts, and shoes are also major quality buys thanks to the professionalism of the craftsmen who produce them in Catalunya and the nearby island of Mallorca. (Shops like Camper and Muxart lead the field here; it's obviously best to avoid the street vendors who hawk dubious-looking, made-in-the-Orient versions in tourist-packed areas like La Rambla . . . unless you enjoy getting ripped off.) The city's natural bent for innovative design, encouraged and backed by their local government, also ensures there's a wealth of housewares products from ceramic dishes to ultra-innovative lamps and furnishings, especially in places such as **Vinçon**—an emporium in the heart of L'Eixample that you can admire with the awe you'd extend to a modern-art museum.

The compact **Barri Gòtic** is, in turn, more noted for its one-of-a-kind retailers, which you'll find tucked away in the narrow lanes like **Portal d'Angel** and **Portaferrisa.** Near the Passeig de Gracia, Consell de Cent is the place to head for those interested in antiques and original works of art (though prices are high).

Opening hours are generally Monday through Saturday 9:30 or 10am to 1:30 or 2pm and 4 or 4:30pm to 8:30pm. Few places, except the specifically tourist oriented, are open on Sundays.

ANTIQUES

The best places to shop for antiquities are around the Barri Gòtic's Plaça de Pi and up in the L'Eixample's Carrer Consell de Cent. Open markets selling bric-a-brac and such are held Thursdays outside the cathedral and on weekends in the Port Vell. Among the many stores dealing in antiques I'm partial to **Angel Batlle** ✪✪ (Palla 23; ☎ 933-01-58-84; Metro: Liceu), which specializes in frame-worthy old posters covering everything from travel to old sherry ads to music and sports. Postcards, engravings, maps, and prayer cards are also on sale.

Quality period clothes—sequined dresses, pretty petticoats, and more—can be found at **Olde Worlde L' Arca de l' Aviva** (Banys Nous 20; ☎ 933-02-15-98; Metro: Liceu). Additional items include lace and linen bedspreads and curtains.

Run by the fourth generation of the eponymous Artur Ramón family, **Sala d'Art Artur Ramón** (Palla 23; ☎ 933-02-59-70; Metro: Jaume I) is one of the city's best spots for paintings, sculptures, engravings, decorative objects, porcelain, and glassware. Prices are high at this three-level emporium, but so is quality.

BOOKS

A combined cafe and bookshop specifically aimed at foodies, **Buffet y Ambigú** (Parada 435), is tucked away at the back of the Boqueria market. Many of the books are in English, and the selection includes everything from favorite tapas recipes to top chefs' manuals including an El Bulli's encyclopedia explaining famed chef Adrià's techniques.

Up in the L'Eixample above Plaza Catalunya is another much larger bookshop, the **Casa del Llibre** (Passeig de Gràcia 62; ☎ 932-72-34-80; Metro: Passeig de Gràcia), offering a fine selection from novels to travel and technical books, some of which are in English.

By far the best English language *librería* (which, incidentally, means "bookshop" and not "library" in Spanish) is **Hibernian Books** (Carrer Montseny; ☎ 932-17-46-96; www.hibernian-books.com; Metro: Fontana), a Gracía institution with a wide range of quality secondhand books, a cozy old-world atmosphere, and info on Anglo-Irish social and theatrical happenings in town. Other pluses include a kiddies' corner, tea and coffee service, plus armchairs where you can relax and browse before you buy.

CLOTHING

Fashionably frilled and form-fitting duds are the specialty at Spanish clothing chain Mango. It tends to appeal to fit young things who like their patterns bold and their cuts trendy. Its usually hectic **Mango Outlet** (Girona 37, between Ausia March and Gran Via del Corts; ☎ 934-122-935) is perennially chockablock with unsold or remaindered clothing. There are some real bargains to be picked up here.

Other discount temptations are available just outside the city at the huge 50-shop **La Roca Village complex** (no. 12 exit on Barcelona-Girona highway; ☎ 938-42-39-00; www.larocavillage.com; Mon–Fri 11am–8:30pm, Sat 10am–10pm). Here you can get top-brand goods like Versace and Camper at generally affordable prices. A bus from Carrer Fabra i Puig in Barcelona makes the round-trip four times a day (3 times a day in Aug) and costs 2.45€ each way. The journey time is 50 minutes.

Another mecca of Catalán design **Textil i d'Indumentaria** (Montcada 12; ☎ 933-10-74-04; Metro: Jaume I) is the showroom section of the Museum of Textile and Fashion (p. 283); it sells locally made accessories for men, women, and children—from sportswear to handbags—each devised by up-and-coming Cataláns like Antonio Miró and clothing guru Lydia Delgado.

DEPARTMENT STORES

In the world of large Spanish stores that sell everything from smart clothes to colorful ceramics, the undoubted king is the **Corte Inglés** (Plaça de Catalunya 14; ☎ 933-06-38-00; www.elcorteingles.es; Metro: Catalunya); its central branch sells just about everything you could need, from sweets to sweaters. Also on-site: a restaurant and a travel agent. Open Monday through Saturday from 10am to 10pm. There are two other branches in avenida Diagonal.

DESIGNER HOMEWARES

Launched by a group of leading Catalán architects (including Oscar Tusquets) and located in a key moderniste building, **BD Ediciones de Diseño** ✫✫ (Casa Tomás, Mallorca 291; ☎ 934-58-69-09; Metro: Passeig de Gràcia) is a bastion of design culture selling stylish kitchenware and furnishings alongside reproductions of Gaudí, Dalí, and the like.

A Barcelona byword in style, **Fernando Amat's Vinçón** ✫ (Passeig de Gràcia 96; ☎ 932-15-60-50; Metro: Diagonal) sells everything from small household items to the ultimate in contemporary furnishings. Located in the former home of early Picasso contemporary Ramón Casas, it constantly surprises with its innovative ideas.

JEWELRY

No fewer than 50 designers display their jewelry and silversmith work in tiny cubist cases in **Forvm Ferlandina** (Ferlandina 31; ☎ 934-41-80-18; Metro: Liceu and Catalunya), a shop that feels like a contemporary gallery. Bouquet brooches, rings, hair ornaments, and other items are produced in the back workroom.

Quality silverware at an affordable price is the attraction at **Platamundi** (l'Hospital 37; ☎ 933-17-13-89; Metro: Liceu). Goods are imported or made by local designers like Ricardo Domingo, head of the jewelry wing of FAD, the city's design council. Other branches are at Montcada 11 (Metro: Jaume I), Plaça Santa María 7 (Metro: Jaume I), and Portaferrisa 22 (Metro: Liceu).

LEATHER

Directed by top designer José Enrique Ona Selfa, Barcelona's biggest branch of the prestigious leather-goods chain **Loewe** ★ (Passeig de Gràcia 35; ☎ 932-16-04-00; Metro: Passeig de Gràcia) is located in one of the top moderniste buildings in town. These excellent goods are exported to several continents. The elegant showroom and immaculate service may well justify the high prices here.

Another "in" place to buy luxury leather items is chic minimalist silver and white **Lupo** ★ (Majorca 257, bajos; ☎ 934-87-80-50; Metro: Passeig de Gràcia). Bags and belts are fashioned here by molding and folding leather into amazing shapes. Innovative dyeing techniques are used to create their vivid colors. The word is out, and exports now extend to the U.S., Japan, and the rest of Europe.

Economical alternatives to the goods for sale in the above two shops can again be found at **Mango Outlet** (p. 301) and **La Roca Village** (p. 301).

PORCELAIN

If you're a Lladró fan, the spacious **Kastoria** (Av. Catedral 6–8; ☎ 933-10-04-11; Metro: Plaça de Catalunya) near the cathedral offers a large selection of the famous porcelain. It also stocks many kinds of leather goods, including purses, suitcases, coats, and jackets.

POTTERY

Close to the Picasso Museum in El Born is **Artesana i Coses** (Placeta de Montcada 2; ☎ 933-19-54-13; Metro: Jaume I), an agreeably messy locale specializing in thickset pottery and porcelain from all over Spain. Practical goods range from dishes and soup bowls to tea pots and coffee mugs (for as low as 3€), while genial souvenir items for putting on the sideboard at home may include secondhand cheap and chunky facsimiles of those delicate Lladró figurines of doggies.

Touristy it may be—both in its location and in the goods for sale—but the sheer range of pottery and ceramics for sale at **Art Escudellers** (Escudellers 23–25; ☎ 934-12-68-01; Metro: Drassanes) makes it well worth a visit. The store offers a kaleidoscopic selection of hand-painted blue, brown, green, and yellow earthenware, which tantalizes the eye. Some pieces are utilitarian; others, far more exotic. If you find something you like, the store can ship goods to anywhere in the world.

SHOES

If you take your shoes seriously, then **Casas** ★ (La Rambla 125, ☎ 933-02-75-52; Portaferrisa 25, ☎ 933-02-11-32; or Portal de l'Angel 40, ☎ 933-02-11-12; Metros for all three branches: Catalunya and Liceu) is the name to look for in Barcelona. It's a footwear mecca where you can buy Camper, Vialis, Dorotea, and other prominent Spanish brands, alongside key import names like Clergerie, Rodolfo Zengari, and Mare. There's also a good choice of sports and walking gear.

You'll find the essence of feminine style at **Muxart** ✦ (Rosselló 230; ☎ 934-88-10-64; Metro: Diagonal), where owner Hermenegildo Muxart creates elegant cutting-edge footware with individual features like jet-black stilettos with a red disc on the toe or metallic silver and electric blue leather plaited together with straw to form an intricate tapestry. Wear these if you want to be in the vanguard of footie fashion, though be prepared to pay upwards of 100€ a pair. You'll find another branch at Rambla de Catalunya 47 (☎ 934-67-74-23; Metro: Passeig de Gràcia).

NIGHTLIFE IN BARCELONA

The choice of after-dark venues in Barcelona is positively daunting. Most tastes and budgets are catered to, from opera and ballet to flamenco and jazz to round-the-clock discos and pop concerts featuring major current artists.

CLASSICAL MUSIC & OPERA

If your taste is classical, then head for the renovated Belle Epoque–style **Gran Teatre del Liceu** (p. 278) or the ultra-moderniste **Palau de la Música Catalána** (p. 282). Standards of all performances are very high. The former's program includes both international and national operas from Mozart's world-famous *Marriage of Figaro* to the lesser-known Manuel de Falla's *Retablo de Maese Pedro*, performed mainly by Spanish companies. The Palau offers a similar global range of purely orchestral works most frequently performed by the Spanish Orquestra Simfónica de Vallés. Occasional *Sardanas* (Catalonia's national dance, p. 276) are also performed by local *coblas* or musical groups (on a more polished scale than those impromptu displays you'll sometimes see outside the cathedral).

L'Auditori (Lepant 150; ☎ 932-47-93-00; www.auditori.com; 20€–25€; Metro: Glòries), designed by the award-winning Spanish architect Rafael Moneo, is a lesser-known modern concert hall with state-of-the-art acoustics. Here the program ranges from Wagnerian cycles to esoteric medieval chants.

If you think small is beautiful, there's **La Casa dels Músics** (Encarnació 25; ☎ 932-84-99-20; 22€; Metro: Fontana), where pianist Luis de Arquer has established a small chamber company in his charming 19th-century Gràcia home. More informally grand is the palatial **Espai Barroc** ✦ (Montcada 20; ☎ 933-10-06-73; 15€–20€; Metro: Jaume I) located in an old Gothic where on Thursdays singers belt out a roster of arias from assorted operas.

On another totally different cultural level, lively pop concerts are regularly held at the **Palau Sant Jordi** (Passeig Olimpic 5-7; ☎ 934-26-20-89)—main indoor sports pavilion during the 1992 Olympics on Montjuïc—between May and October when artists from Queen and Bon Jovi to local favorites like Miguel Bosé and the warbling duo Amaral appear.

FLAMENCO

Though Flamenco is hardly a Catalán tradition, there's an active Andalusian population and dancers as flamboyantly colorful as any you'd find farther south. The touristy but good **El Tablao de Carmen** ✦✦ (Poble Espanyol/Spanish Village de Montjuïc; ☎ 933-25-68-95; dinner and show 64€–87€ or drink and show 34€; Metro: Espanya) features top flamenco artists and newcomers who strut their somewhat "sanitized" stuff here in stylish, entertaining performances that, for true aficionados, tend to lack the earthiness and passion of the real thing.

Older (est. 1963), more traditional, and more reasonably priced is **Los Tarantos** ✦✦ (Plaça Reial 17; ☎ 933-18-30-67; cover including 1 drink around 20€; Metro: Liceu); its ever-changing roster of performers include many names from Granada and Sevilla. Make sure you eat beforehand, as no meals are served here.

MUSIC CLUBS

Jazz and cabaret enthusiasts will find plenty to keep them happy. An all-time favorite is the **Harlem Jazz Club** ✦ (Comtessa de Sobradiel 8; ☎ 933-10-07-55; free admission Mon–Thurs, 7€ and 1-drink minimum Fri–Sat; closed 2 weeks in Aug; Metro: Jaume I), where an appreciative audience enjoys an eclectic range of vibrant sounds from jazz and blues to tangos and Brazilian rhythms.

Jamboree (Plaça Reial 17; ☎ 933-01-75-64; 9€–14€ cover, including 1 drink and show; Metro: Liceu) is another top Ciutat Vella rendezvous for blues and jazz, featuring artists such as the Fringe and Miguel Zenón quartet, plus occasional flamenco groups like Paño Moruno.

Formerly an early 20th-century music hall, the plushly atmospheric **Luz de Gas** (Montaner 246; ☎ 932-09-77-11; cover including 1 drink 20€–25€; Bus: 6, 27, 32, or 34) is more into Latin sounds—not to mention pop, soul, rhythm and blues, salsa, and bolero. The lower two levels open onto the dance floor and stage. For privacy, head for the top tier, which has a glass enclosure. Come prepared for the attitude of the snooty staff.

DANCE CLUBS & BARS

Trendy dance clubs operate in nearly every major district of the city. High in the upper town it's worth tracking down **Bikini** ✦ (Deu i Mata 105; ☎ 933-22-00-05; cover if there's no concert 16€ including 1 drink; Metro: Les Corts). Its multiple rooms feature live music, Latin rhythms, or disco rock; and **Otto Zutz** ✦ (Lincoln 15; ☎ 932-38-07-22; cover 10€; Train: FGC Gràcia) a classy VIP venue where chic movers and groovers show off their assets. *Note:* Both these spots are a fair way from the Old Town, so be prepared for the extra outlay on taxi costs to get back to your hotel.

Down in the more accessible Ciutat Vella, Raval favorite **Moog** (Arc del Teatre 3; ☎ 933-01-72-82; entrance 9€ including 1 drink; Metro: Drassanes) pounds with primitive techno sounds, but the natives are friendly. The trendy **Café Royale** (Nou de Zurbano 3; ☎ 934-12-14-33; Metro: Drassanes), adjoining the Plaça Reial, combines a classically stylish (subtle gold lighting) ambience with hot music from a satisfactorily hyper DJ. *Warning:* The bouncers are picky.

Two indispensable locales for gay clubbers are **Metro** (Sepulveda 185; ☎ 933-23-52-27; cover 12€; Metro: Universitat), where, among other things, you can watch men of all ages elegantly dance Las Sevillanas together (tip-off: the bathrooms have videos installed in unusual places); and **Salvation** (Ronda de Sant Pere 19–21; ☎ 933-18-06-86; Metro: Urquinaona) the most exuberantly flamboyant joint in town, noted for its Adonis-like waiters. Beware the highly selective door staff.

The party continues outside in the summer months. After dark the **beaches** between Barceloneta and Poble have lively *chiringuitos* (water's-edge music bars and eating spots) and other open-air night spots where you can live it up in the balmy seaside air.

GET OUT OF TOWN

If you don't fancy going too far afield, but you would like to see something else new in the immediate Barcelona area, I suggest you take the short (20-min.) suburban rail trip out to **Colonia Güell** ✪✪ (Claudi Güell s/n; ☎ 936-30-58-07; 4€ adults, free for children 9 and under, guided tours 6€–8€; Mon–Sat 10am–2pm and 3–7pm, Sun 10am–3pm; FGC: Colonia Güell), where the highly industrious Gaudí did yet more inventive work for his wealthy benefactor Eusebi Güell. This grotto-like building, set in the midst of pinewoods on the outskirts of town and originally intended as kind of utopian colony for laborers working on Güell's textile mill, was to contain a hospital, library, theater, and even a church: a self-contained mini town. In the end, Gaudí only managed to complete the crypt, which is fascinating enough on its own and another of his amazing fantasies converted into apparently malleable stone, with its ribbed ceilings, outrageously curving walls, and cavernous interiors. Private ceremonies are sometimes held here, so check ahead to see if it's convenient to visit.

For day trips a bit farther afield, try the following:

THE PENEDÉS: CATALUNYA'S LAND OF "CAVA"

The Penedés area at the western end of Barcelona province has long been competing with France's illustrious Champagne zone in the production of clean crisp sparkling wine (here called *cava*). While lacking perhaps that final touch of Gallic subtlety, it's pretty damn good, and only a third of the price of the estimable French product. Sampling this delicious bubbly is the main reason you visit this area (though the green, rolling countryside, with its vineyards and pine groves, certainly adds to the experience). You used to be able to perform this enjoyable task in a nice musty old cellar, but today everything's a bit more neat and organized than it was a few decades back, and you'll likely find yourself in a clinical, pristine, brightly lit building with no cobwebs. The *cava* is still a pleasure to guzzle, of course; in fact, it's even better than before, if what the local winemakers tell you is true.

For tastings, head to the town of **Sant Sadurní de Noia,** a picturesque little hamlet which produces no less than 90% of Spain's entire *cava* output. The town's top tasting spot is an architectural charmer: the moderniste-style Puig i Cadafalch–designed **Codorníu winery** (Av Cordoniu, Sant Sadurni de Noia; ☎ 938-18-32-32; www.grupocordorniu.com; 2.20€; Mon–Fri 9am–5pm, Sat 9am–1pm). Here, the much sought-after fizzy beverage—Codorniu is the top seller in all Spain—is stored and aged in 15km (9 miles) of subterranean tunnels, and once you've arranged your visit a mini-train whisks you around the estate, including the vineyards, and along many of those tunnels. The trip ends with a tasting of the different varieties, which range from brut through semi-*seco* to *dulce.* If your taste is for the very dry *brut,* the best version to try is *Non Plus Ultra,* Spain's favorite Christmas standby to accompany the traditional *turrones* (almond and honey-filled nougat) that are avidly consumed after the main meal then.

Trains leave hourly from Barcelona's main Sants station between 6am and 10pm and cover the journey in 40 to 50 minutes.

MONTSERRAT

The **Benedictine monastery of Montserrat** (Plaça de Montserrat s/n; ☎ 938-77-77-00) looms at 1,200m (3,937 ft.) atop a surrealistic mass of curving rocks—as if Gaudí himself had lent a hand in shaping the work of nature—56km (34 miles) northwest of the city. Its Catalán name Montserrat—or, saw toothed mountain—has been interpreted as referring to its jagged outline, about which many a writer and poet has waxed lyrical. *"Amb serra d'or els angelets serraren eixos turons per fer-os un palau"* ("With a golden saw the little angels cut these turrets to make you a palace"), wrote local 19th-century scribe Verdaguer in his epic poem "Virolai." Wagner's *Parsifal* is said to have been based on it, after the great composer was inspired by a brief visit he made here, and other Teuton luminaries captivated by its soaring grandeur included Goethe and Schiller.

The monastery itself looks dauntingly severe. ("A bit like a Tibetan Buddhist Lamaserie," observed James Michener, succinctly.) It's the religious center of Catalunya, where thousands of pilgrims come annually to see the tiny Romanesque statue of **La Moreneta** (Black Virgin, see box) whose face has been blackened by years of candle burning and who is set up high in the dimly lit interior on a throne beside a silver gilt *reredos* (the ornamented screen behind the altar).

Today, newlyweds in particular regard it as good luck to get the Madonna's blessing. *Two tips:* Don't come on a Sunday as the crowds are impossible, and wear warm clothes as it can get cool here even in summer.

And another tip: A treat for the ears is the 50-member Escolanía or boys' choir, who at 1pm daily (noon on Sun) sing "Salve Regina" and the "Virolai" (hymn of Montserrat) in the basilica in a religious tradition dating back to the

---

Lost & Found: Tales of the Black Virgin

One explanation of this strange figure's origins is that it was carved by none other than St. Luke in 50 A.D.—presumably in between his writing of the Acts—then later brought to Spain and hidden in what's known today as the Santa Cova or Holy Grotto (see below) during the Moorish invasion, where it stayed until shepherds found it 200 years later. Another more fanciful version of how it was discovered is that two young boys exploring the area in the 12th century saw a strange light descending the mountain and illuminating a cavern. As they approached the spot, they heard music and canticles. A week later, after much cajoling on the part of the boys, the whole town turned out for the next appearance and followed the Bishop of Manresa in a long procession to find the cave. A fragrant aroma combined with the lights and they entered it to find the statue of the Virgin peacefully reclining against a damp inner wall. They set off to Manresa cathedral with it but didn't get very far. On reaching nearby Montserrat, they found they could move no further. So it was decided that this (Montserrat) was the spot it was intended to rest, and here it remains to this day. And so the cave became a holy shrine.

13th century. The basilica is open Monday through Friday from 7:30am to 7:30pm and Saturday and Sunday from 7:30pm to 8:30pm. Admission is free.

Art lovers in turn will relish the **Museu de Montserrat's** (Plaça de Santa María; ☎ 938-777-745; Mon–Fri 10am–6pm, Sat–Sun 9:30am–6:30pm; 4.50€ adults, 3€ students and children) collection of eclectically varied ecclesiastical paintings, including works by Picasso, Caravaggio, Dalí, Monet, Sisley, Degas, and El Greco. There's also a bizarre exhibition of ancient artifacts including a 2,000-year-old crocodile mummy.

The 9-minute climb by **funicular car** (Aeri de Montserrat: www.aeride montserrat.com; 8€ round-trip, 5€ one-way) up to the spectacular Sant Joan peak runs approximately every 20 minutes daily from 9:25am to 1:45pm and 2:20 to 6:45pm March through October, and 10:10am to 1:45pm and 2:20 to 5:45pm (6:45pm on public holidays) November through February. From the summit, on a clear day you can see not only most of Catalunya but also the purple-gray Pyrenees and—if there's no haze out at sea—the distant Mediterranean islands of Majorca and Ibiza.

There's an exciting additional trip—halfway by funicular, halfway on foot—that you can make to the cross-shaped 17th-century **Santa Cova (Holy Grotto),** where it's said the Black Virgin was found (see box). The grotto is open year-round daily from 10am to 1pm and 2 to 5:45pm and the funicular operates every 20 minutes daily from 11am to 6pm at a cost of 2.60€ adults, 1.35€ children round-trip. (See www.cremallerademontserrat.com.)

For more information, contact the **tourist office** (Montserrat's Plaça de la Creu; ☎ 938-777-777; daily 8:50am–7:30pm). They can also give you details and itineraries of local walks available.

Getting to Montserrat

You can reach Montserrat by regular train or once-a-day bus services. The hourly Ferrocarrils de la Generalitat de Catalunya train departs from Plaça d'Espanya, connecting on arrival at Montserrat with a high-tech funicular (Aeri de Montserrat; see above), which climbs up to the monastery itself every 15 minutes. Autocares Julià buses leave from near the Estació de Sants on the Plaça de Països Cataláns at 9:15am, returning at 5pm from September through June and at 6pm in July and August; the round-trip ticket costs 10€ on weekdays and 12€ on weekends. Contact the Julià company (☎ 934-90-40-00).

If you're driving, follow the Avinguda Diagonal west, then take the A-2 (exit Martorell). The signposts and exit to Montserrat will be on your right. From the main road, it's a spectacular 15km (9-mile) drive up to the monastery through eerie rock formations and wild scenery.

SITGES

There's a lot more to Sitges (40km/25 miles south of Barcelona) than its simplistic image as a gay mecca would suggest. In fact, it casts a much wider touristic net, drawing in a blend of day-trippers from Barcelona, mixed groups, young and old, families with kids, honeymooners, and singles (both straight and gay). Fine beaches, chic waterside restaurants, lively nightspots, a wide range of artistic events (from modern gallery exhibitions to an annual movie festival) and a rich

Sardines & Flowers: Fiesta Time

Sitges's most colorful fiesta, complete with fancy dress outfits and ornate floats, is the 100-year-old **Carnaval** which begins on the Thursday before Lent with the arrival of the king of the Carnestoltes and ends with the "Burial of the Sardine" on Ash Wednesday. The action peaks with celebrations on Sant Bonaventura.

The origin of this eccentric event, known in Spanish as the *Entierro de la Sardina*, can be traced back to the 18th century when a cargo of these fish destined for the Lent festivities arrived in such a putrefied state that the reigning monarch Charles III ordered them all to be buried. Sardines had been chosen as they symbolized the end of "Carnaval" hedonism and advent of Lenten fasting, fish being the recommended diet for this period. So, in memory of their tragic premature demise 2 centuries ago—which caused the Madrid populace to be deprived of their abstinence diet for the next 40 days—it was decided they—the sardines—should be mourned henceforth in style. Hence the *Entierro* ceremony (banned, by the way, under General Franco's dictatorship, partly because of its irreverent nature and partly because it allowed folks to wander freely about in disguise—something that could absolutely not be tolerated in those rigid times). It caught on elsewhere more for its novelty value than for anything else and is now celebrated in other provinces as far flung as Murcia.

In June, during Corpus Christi week, carpets of flowers are laid in the narrow streets of Sitges's old center, just as they are in towns all over Spain from Sevilla to Zaragoza during this period. Their purpose is purely decorative, aimed at creating joyfully colorful patterns in honor of the occasion, though sometimes they more ambitiously emulate local shields and insignias. The great pity is to see them trampled under foot as the processions pass over them, destroying in minutes what has taken hours, even days, to lay out. On the night of June 23, the feast of **Sant Joan (St. John)**, considerably noisier events take place, when the beach is the dazzling setting for fireworks and bonfires. (These festivities are a common feature at many other towns along the Catalán coast.)

Beyond fiestas (see box), those who visit during the quieter periods enjoy the beaches and a trio of waterfront museums located in the converted 16th-century house where Santiago Rusiñol lived and worked (he bequeathed them to the town on his death in 1931).

profusion of moderniste buildings—especially in the charming old narrow alleyed center—are just some of the reasons for its all-round appeal.

The 19th-century Catalán art nouveau movement began here, and creative artists like Santiago Rusiñol (the playwright and Bohemian dandy whose bust stands near the Passeig Maritim), Salvador Dalí, and the poet Federico García

Lorca created a brief pre–Civil War "golden age" of culture in the town. At around the same time, middle-class industrialists began to settle in the town and emigrant traders known as *indios* (who'd made their fortunes in the Americas) returned to build the often flamboyant houses that still line the seafront.

The **Museu Cau Ferrat** ✪ (Carrer Fonollar s/n; ☎ 938-94-03-64; 3.50€ adults, 1.75€ students, free for children 11 under, combination ticket for all 3 museums 6.40€ adults, 3.50€ students; June 15–Sept Tues–Sun 10am–2pm and 5–9pm; Oct–June 14 Tues–Fri 10am–1:30pm and 3–6:30pm, Sat 10am–7pm, Sun 10am–3pm) contains a variety of Rusiñol's works plus other paintings by Spanish artists ranging from Ramón Casas and Zuloaga to Picasso (including the latter's small *Corrida de Toros*). It's worth it to go just to view two supreme masterpieces by El Greco: *The Tears of Saint Peter* and *Penitent Mary Magdalene.* There's also an ornate selection of wrought-iron objects and some dazzlingly vivid Mediterranean tilework.

Adjoining Museu Cau Ferrat and divided into two parts, which are located on either side of a narrow street and linked by a small bridge, is the delightful **Museu Maricel** (all details as for Cau Ferrat). This small moderniste "palace" was created in 1912 by local architect Miquel Trujillo—who formed part of Rusiñol's "creative circle"—to accommodate the art works of a millionaire American and Catalánophile, Charles Deering, who had decided to settle in Sitges. Today, it's a charming art museum filled with Gothic and Romantic sculptures and paintings, including a striking allegorical depiction of World War I by José María Sert. Also in the collection are some fine Catalán ceramics, period furniture, and glass and porcelain exhibits from medieval to modern times.

Completing this cultural trio, the nearby **Museo Romantico** or Can Llopis (Sant Gaudenci 1; ☎ 938-94-29-69; all other details as for Cau Ferrat), former home of a wealthy wine merchant called Bernardi Llopis i Pujol, atmospherically re-creates 19th-century Sitges family life in a house filled with period furniture and household objects. Upstairs is a charming display of 400 antique dolls from a wide variety of countries, collected by writer-artist Lola Anglada, who died in 1984.

For more information, contact the **tourist office** (Carrer Sínea Morera 1; ☎ 938-10-93-40; www.sitges.org; June 1–Sept 15 Mon–Sat 9am–8pm, Sept 16–May Mon–Fri 9am–2pm and 4–6:30pm, Sat 10am–1pm).

Getting to Sitges

The *cercanías* (or *rodalies*) regional train is your best bet: The service is very frequent from Barcelona-Sants and Passeig de Gràcia to Sitges, and the trip takes a leisurely and comfortable 40 minutes. (Call ☎ 902-24-02-02 in Barcelona for exact times.) If you're driving, you have the choice between the A-7 express highway, which passes through the Garraf Tunnels, and the scenic C-246 coast road, which can see severe holdups on the weekends when all and sundry head out of Barcelona for the beaches.

Accommodations & Dining

€€ Although Sitges is very close to Barcelona, it's well worth staying the night if you want to sample the uniquely lively after-dark action—be it gay or hetero. If you do, the most economical accommodations available are at the centrally located **Hotel El Cid** (San José 39 bis; ☎ 938-94-18-42; MC, V; closed Oct–Apr) a mock Castilian-style hostelry complete with wood-beamed ceilings and hefty wrought-iron chandeliers. The compact rooms (60€–80€ double) are modest but comfortable, and all have an en suite bathroom containing shower stalls. Breakfast is the only meal served.

Also recommended is the moderniste gem **Hotel Noucentista** (Isla de Cuba 21; ☎ 938-11-00-70; www.elxalet.com; AE, DC, MC, V), just a 10-minute stroll from the beach. The small- to medium-size rooms (80€–120€ double) are cozily furnished, and there's a tranquil courtyard garden where you can relax.

€€–€€€   Top pick for grub is the very nautical **Mare Nostrum** ✠ (Passeig de la Ribera 60; ☎ 938-94-33-93; closed Dec 15–Feb 1; AE, DC, MC, V; reservations required), located on the Sitges waterfront directly overlooking the Mediterranean (in sunny weather, summer or non-windy-winter, you can sit outside). Nicely converted from a 19th-century house, it specializes in pescatorial delights like *merluza al vapor* (steamed hake cooked in cava) at around 18€ to 20€. The adjoining cafe has come up with a uniquely refreshing champagne and fruit sangria as an alternative to the usual red wine version.

Nightlife in Sitges

Once the sun goes down, you should relax in the way the locals do: Stroll along the waterfront *paseo*, settle down at one of the countless open-air terrace cafes, and savor a leisurely coffee or something stronger before retiring around midnight.

If you want to extend the action until the early hours, gay locales tend to outnumber the straight ones. A well clued-up rendezvous, the **Parrot's Pub** (in the Plaza de la Industria), can actually provide a map that shows you the hottest spots, or you can download the information on www.gaymap.info. Carrer Sant Bonaventura (near the Museu Romàntic) offers the widest choice of such disco/bars. Largest and liveliest (especially in high summer) is the **Mediterráneo** (at number 6; no phone), a renovated 1690s house with a garden, a pool room, and a covered terrace.

7 Catalonia

With its own language and culture, the lush province of Catalonia is a country in miniature

by Peter Stone

THE REGION SURROUNDING THE DYNAMIC CATALÁN CAPITAL BARCELONA IS one of the most richly varied in Europe. Historically, politically, and geographically it's in a class of its own. The province began to assert its own unique identity in the 10th century when Count Guifre el Pelos (Wilfred the Hairy to his friends) defeated the Moorish invaders and established a powerful chain of castles and religious strongholds. Almost simultaneously, it evolved its own earthy language from a blend of Latin, Provençal, and Italian.

Now an autonomous state with increasing powers of independence, Catalonia (or Catalunya, in Catalán) feels more European than purely Spanish. Its stimulating contrasts range from medieval Girona to Roman Tarragona, from compact Romanesque monasteries to towering Gothic churches, and from the classic coast of the Costa Brava to the snow-capped peaks and national parks of the Pyrenees.

DON'T LEAVE CATALONIA WITHOUT . . .

Seeing Tarragona's Roman highlights. Encircled by Cyclopean city walls, its forum and aqueduct are remarkably well preserved, and in the amphitheater you can still almost hear the crowds as they cheered on their favorite gladiators. See p. 316.

Monastery hopping. The Santa María del Poblet, Santes Creues, and Vallbona de les Monges near the picturesque town of Montblanc are as magnificent a trio of Cistercian religious buildings as you'll find in Spain. See p. 319.

Strolling Girona's "call" quarter. In the city's Villa Vella, the intricate cobbled lanes and handsome medieval houses date from its Jewish ghetto days. See p. 321.

Visiting the Costa Brava town of Cadaqués. One of the most beautiful seaside spots in Spain, this whitewashed former fishing village was Salvador Dalí's home and source of inspiration for many decades. See p. 330.

TARRAGONA

In its Roman heyday, Tarragona was one of the two most important cities in Spain, ruling half the country. That's a distant memory now, but so many vestiges survive almost intact—like its remarkable aqueduct and amphitheater—that UNESCO named it a World Heritage City in 2000. Today the city plays a more modest role as one of Catalonia's three provincial capitals (the other 2 being Girona and Lleida—see below). The newer town, with its lively student atmosphere, is centered round the wide **Rambla Nova (New Boulevard),** while the mainly medieval walled quarter, bordered by the **Rambla Vella (Old Boulevard),** stands on a rocky bluff from whose **Balcó del Mediterráni (Balcony of the Mediterranean)** visitors enjoy the sights and sounds of the sea below. In summer, you can swim from the nearby sandy bays of Platjes del Miracle and del Cossis; year-round, wander about the colorful Serrallo fishing port area.

A BRIEF HISTORY OF TARRAGONA

It's hard, even today, to avoid being reminded of Tarragona's golden Roman era, which began around 218 B.C. when the city was known as *Tarraco* and housed up to 1 million people behind its 64km-long (40-mile) walls. Capital of a region known then as *Hispania Citerior* (roughly half the Iberian Peninsula) and governed by the likes of Julius Caesar, the city enjoyed several centuries of glory before Goths, Franks, and Moors, respectively, took turns in pulverizing it. Repopulated by Normans in the 12th century, it slowly dwindled into provinciality only to be besieged by Philip IV 500 years later and ravaged by Napoleon during the Peninsula War. Shaken but stirred, it finally saw its industrial and mercantile fortunes initiated by 19th-century traders who arrived by sea from various European countries and set up shop. Today, tourism has added to its attractions, and the city has a comfortably prosperous—if still provincial—feel.

LAY OF THE LAND

Tarragona's landscape is flatter than in the rugged north of the province. Its long straight coast is lined with a succession of fine, sandy beaches, and its gently undulating inland countryside of meadows and valleys is rich with pine woods and vineyards (see "The Other Tarragona," below). The presence of cypress trees along the roadsides, unusual in Spain, gives the area an attractively Tuscan look.

GETTING TO TARRAGONA

For town **information** contact the **Oficina de Turismo** (calle Mayor 39; ☎ 977-250-795; www.tarragonaturisme.es; summer daily 9am–9pm, winter daily 10am–2pm and 4–7pm, closed Sun 4–7pm both in summer and winter); and for coastal information the **Costa Dorada Tourist Office** (Carrer Major 39; ☎ 977-25-07-95; www.costadorada.org; July–Sept Mon–Fri 9am–9pm, Sat 9am–2pm and 4–9pm, Sun 10am–2pm; Oct–June Mon–Sat 10am–2pm and 4–7pm, Sun 10am–2pm).

And if you want to know more about the whole province, visit the **Oficina de Turisme de la Generalitat de Catalonia** (calle Fortuny 4; ☎ 977-233-415; www.catalunyaturisme.com; Mon–Fri 9am–2pm and 4–6:30pm, Sat 9am–2pm).

An hour-long **train service** (www.renfe.es; ☎ 902-24-02-02) operates every 15 to 45 minutes to and from the Barcelona-Sants station and costs 5.40€ one-way. There's also a regular Talgo service from Madrid via Zaragoza and Lleida that takes between 2½ hours (an extra-fast AVE service introduced in 2008; one-way tourist class 71€) and 5 hours (normal service; one-way tourist class 37€). One snag: The extra-fast service stops at Camp de Tarragona, 12km (7½ miles) out of town, and from there you have to catch a bus into the center; all other services stop at the main central Tarragona station.

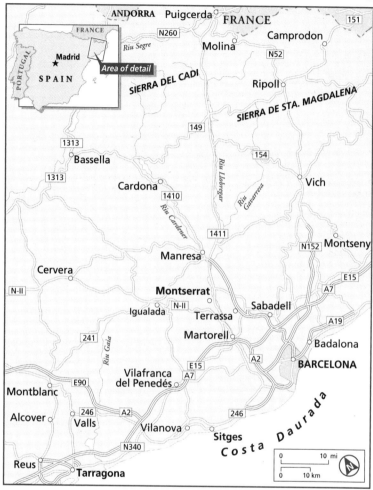

Catalonia

The Plana and Hispania **bus** companies run regular daily 1½-hour services to Tarragona (from just outside Barcelona's María Cristina Metro station. For schedule information, contact the Tarragona bus station (Plaça de la Imperial Tarracu s/n; ☎ 977-229-126).

If you're **driving,** take the A-2 southwest from Barcelona to the A-7, via Vilafranca.

ACCOMMODATIONS, BOTH STANDARD & NOT

Let's start with a word of praise for the rural rental properties of the Tarragona countryside, as they're an ideal choice for the vacationer seeking an away-from-it-all break. Groups of three or more are the key beneficiaries of this sort of

Tarragona

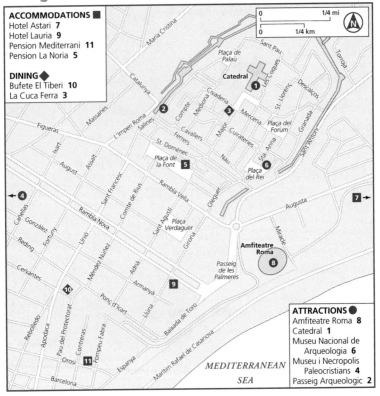

ACCOMMODATIONS ■
Hotel Astari **7**
Hotel Lauria **9**
Pension Mediterrani **11**
Pension La Noria **5**

DINING ◆
Bufete El Tiberi **10**
La Cuca Ferra **3**

ATTRACTIONS ●
Amfiteatre Roma **8**
Catedral **1**
Museu Nacional de
  Arqueologia **6**
Museu i Necropolis
  Paleocristians **4**
Passeig Arqueologic **2**

MEDITERRANEAN SEA

setup—the more people you have in your party, the less you pay per person. I've seen properties where you can pay as little as 25€ per head per night for a property that's located either in a village or in the open countryside, with abundant privacy for all. One of the best sources for finding these deals is through **Casas Rurales Tarragona** (☎ 616-707-485; www.casasruralestarragona.com), which represents 23 well-chosen properties in the region.

An example of its offerings is **El Clos** (Carretera de Rocafort 12; ☎ 977-898-021; www.elclos.com; MC, V) in the village of Conesa, which is rustic with a capital *R*; it's the sort of place where farm implements hanging as decoration on the outside walls don't look in the slightest bit goofy. Set in the midst of the Conca Barbera wine growing area north of Tarragona, this tastefully converted old farmhouse contains three separate apartments housing groups of three, four, and six, respectively. These lucky folks lodge in a setting that would seem lifted from the last century—rough-hewn stone walls, real fireplaces, exposed-wood ceiling, solid dark-wood furnishings—if it weren't for the well-equipped modern kitchens and bathrooms. Costs per person are from 27€ per night. A six-sleeper apartment, again as traditional looking, in the center of the little town of Pauls, goes for just 17€ per person per night through this agency.

€ If you'd prefer to stay in Tarragona town itself, a bargain base that's just 2 minutes from the rail station is the immaculate little **Hostal Mediterrani** (calle Osorio 11-B; ☎ 977-249-353; MC, AE, V) run by a hyper, helpful, local lady and her two assistants (gracious young women from South America). It's on the first floor (the elevator's slow, so best to climb) of a nicely renovated building and the cream-colored rooms are bright and slightly triangular shaped with mock-wicker-style bedsteads, generous wardrobe space, TV, and a compact but quite adequate shower room. At just 45€ a night for a double, including a modest breakfast (coffee and croissant or toast), this is a real value. Not so good, alas, are the thin walls; bring earplugs. The town center's an easy (uphill) 10-minute walk away.

€ Staying in the very heart of town doesn't have to be expensive, either. Right near the cathedral is the old-world **Pension La Noria** (Plaça de la Font 53; ☎ 977-238-717; MC, V), which has the happy ambience of a much lived-in house. Its rather moodily lit rooms occupy several floors and all have tiled floors, high windows, dark-wood wardrobes, and compact en suite bath or shower rooms for just 45€ to 50€ per night. The very friendly downstairs bar serves inexpensive snacks and breakfasts.

€€ Upping the comfort—and price—stakes is the welcoming **Hotel Lauria** ✫ (Rambla Nova 20; ☎ 977-23-67-12; www.hlauria.es; AE, DC, MC, V) located on a tree-lined *paseo* overlooking the Mediterranean. The main entry is particularly attractive: You pass through a hallway lined with original paintings and topped by a high glass-covered atrium; its immediate neighbors are a small swimming pool and a sunny cocktail terrace (yup, there's a bar). Each of the 72 small to medium-size rooms (70€–75€ for a double) features comfortable good-size beds, mellow wood bedsteads and tables, and carpeted floors, and each has its own tub/shower combo. A room at the back will give you a sea view but at an additional cost (80€–85€). Nearby parking is also available.

€€ A really great place to stay if you're thinking of hiring a car to explore the area is the modern **Hotel Astari** ✫ (Vía Augusta 95; ☎ 977-23-69-00; www.hotel astari.com; AE, DC, MC, V), which offers free parking. The hotel is a short (10-min.) walk away from the center in a northern residential avenue close to the sea. Its smart, comfortable rooms (70€–80€ double) boast such niceties as plasma TVs, and bright marble-surfaced bathrooms, and each has its own individual balcony with Mediterranean views. There's also a communal terrace beside the outdoor swimming pool where you can relax in the shade among geraniums, willows, and scented orange trees after your trips.

DINING FOR ALL TASTES

€–€€ The name may sound Roman, but the grub is definitely Catalán at the **Bufete el Tiberi** ✫✫ 🧒 (Carrer Martí d'Ardenya 5; ☎ 977-23-54-03; www. eltiberi.com; Sun–Mon 1:30–4pm, Tues–Sat 1:30–4pm and 8–11:30pm). Decorated and furnished like a country house (love the wall ceramics), this self-service restaurant is devilishly tempting in the range and variety of local food on offer from main course *fabes* (tasty local beans) or *galtas de porc* (pig's cheek) to exquisite *crema catalana* and pears in wine for dessert. The main problem is avoiding overeating; there's no restriction on how many times you fill your plate for the 10€ inclusive lunch (the extra drinks are a bit pricey, though). Staff are on hand to explain what some of the dishes are if you can't identify them.

€€ Over on the other side of the Rambla Vella, just below the cathedral, you'll find **La Cuca Fera** ★ (Plaça Santiago Rusiñol 5; ☎ 977-24-20-07; Wed–Mon 2–4pm and 8:30pm–midnight; MC, DC, V), by far the most affordable quality seafood spot in Tarragona. (Avoid at all costs the enticing but, alas, very pricey Serrallo port area.) It's cavern-like and low-ceilinged, and it features eccentric touches. (You may be startled by the two Oriental-looking statues standing sentinel on either side as you enter.) Particularly recommended here is the sumptuous *suquet* (a popular Catalán seafood stew), which occasionally appears on the excellent-value three-course lunch menu (12€). A la carte delights like *merluza vasca* (Basque-style hake), cooked to perfection, cost around 18€ a dish.

WHY YOU'RE HERE: THE TOP SIGHTS & ATTRACTIONS

Perched on a clifftop, overlooking a beach, Tarragona's **Amfiteatre Romà** ★ (Parc del Milagro s/n; ☎ 977-24-25-79; 2.10€ adults, 1€ seniors and students; Mar–Sept Tues–Sat 9am–9pm, Sun 9am–3pm; Oct–Feb Tues–Sat 9am–5pm, Sun 10am–3pm; closed Dec 25, Jan 1, and Jan 6) has drama to spare. And that's not just in its architecture. Back in the tumultuous 2nd century A.D., some 13,000 spectators would gather here for bloody gladiator battles and other games. (A monument on the walk to the site declares, "Many innocent lives were taken in this amphitheater.") The tiered seats they sat upon are the same that you'll see today.

A short walk away from Ben Hur territory is a youngster of a monument by Spanish history standards: the handsome 12th-century **Catedral** ★★ (Plaça de la Seu s/n; ☎ 977-23-72-69; cathedral and museum 2.40€ adults, 1.50€ seniors and students, free for children 15 and under; Mar–May daily 10am–1pm and 4–7pm, June–Sept daily 10am–7pm, Oct–Feb daily 10am–2pm). The great attraction here is the enormous vaulted entrance with its Gothic portals and Romanesque doors—an example of the unusually effective transition from one period's style to the other. Inside be sure to peer up at the cloister's Gothic arches and sculpted columns—one, bizarrely, depicts a procession of rats attending a cat's burial. Also look out for Pere Joan's superb 15th-century altarpiece of **Santa Tecla**, Tarragona's patron saint.

Back near the seashore, the **Museu Nacional Arqueològic** ★ (Plaça del Rei 5; ☎ 977-23-62-09; museum and Museu i Necròpolis Paleocristians, below, 2.40€ adults, 1.20€ students, free for seniors and children 17 and under; June–Sept Tues–Sat 10am–8pm, Sun 10am–2pm; Oct–June Tues–Sat 10am–1:30pm and 4–7pm, Sun 10am–2pm), founded in 1844, is the oldest archeological museum in Catalonia and a very fine one at that. The focus is Roman, and in many ways intensely local—many of the pieces you'll see preserved here (sculptures, ceramics, coins) were found accidentally, dug up as the city was creating its modern port and urban center. The museum's "Mona Lisa" is a fierce mosaic *Head of Medusa*.

In conjunction with—and on the same ticket as—the archaeological museum (joint prices are listed above) you can also visit the nearby **Museu i Necròpolis Paleocristians** ★ (Av. de Ramón y Cajal 80; ☎ 977-23-62-09; June–Sept Tues–Sat 10am–1:30pm and 4–7pm, Sun and holidays 10am–2pm; Oct–May Tues–Sat 10am–1:30pm and 3–5:30pm, Sun and holidays 10am–2pm). One of the most important burial grounds in the country, it was used by the Christians from the 3rd through the 5th centuries, and its **Museu Paleocristià,** contains astonishingly well-preserved sarcophagi and other artifacts found during the excavations. The site is located just outside town next to a tobacco factory, the construction of which led to its discovery in 1923.

Yet another reminder of Roman times, complete with an ancient archway entrance, is the **Passeig Arqueològic** ✰✰ (El Portal del Roser s/n; ☎ 977-24-57-96; 2.10€ adults, 1€ seniors and students, free for children 15 and under; Oct–Mar Tues–Sat 9am–7pm, Sun and holidays 10am–3pm; Apr–Sept Tues–Sat 9am–9pm, Sun and holidays 9am–3pm), a 8km-long (½-mile) walkway at the far end of the Plaça del Pallol, which takes you along the 2,000-year-old ramparts that the Romans skillfully contrived to build on top of huge boulders. Though the walkway's been subjected to a few structural changes over the centuries—particularly in the Middle Ages—it still looks pretty authentic and offers plenty of sea and country views as you stride along it.

THE OTHER TARRAGONA: IN VINO VERITAS

The undulating, green Tarragona countryside has a very long tradition of winemaking. Its big sellers today—after lapsing for many decades into obscurity—are the hearty, high-alcohol (and high-price) *tintos* of **Priorat**—made from vines first planted by 11th-century monks in need of physical as well as spiritual sustenance. Their vineyards are near the Montblanc trio of Cistercian monasteries (see below), and the wine produced from them has a quality all its own.

Take a visit to a bodega, have a tipple, and experience the Bacchus-inspired afterglow. One of the most delightful vineyards, **Cellers Scala Dei** (Carrer La Morera s/n Cornudella de Montsant; ☎ 977-827-027; on the C-242 road 25km/17 miles north from Reus) arranges tours round the bodegas by appointment, preferably in the mornings, during which they give you a comprehensive account of the entire winemaking process, following the grapes' route from vineyard to storage vat and finally maturation in oak casks. There's no charge for the visit, but expect to pay a minimum of 5€ to sample a couple of vintage wines. (One drawback: Buses are few and far between, so you'll need to rent a car.)

ATTENTION, SHOPPERS!

You'll find plenty of brassware—jewelry, ornaments, antique knickknacks, and bric-a-brac—all at highly affordable prices (you may even pick up the odd real bargain) at the **Antique Market** (Sun 9am–2pm); its stalls stretch from just outside the cathedral every Sunday to the arcades that line calle Merceria.

Though it's less atmospheric and certainly less traditional, the huge 100-shop **Parc Central** (Mon–Sat 10am–10pm) mall between the Parc de la Ciutat and River Francolí does have a terrific selection of competitively priced leather, ceramic, and carved olive-wood goodies. They're not necessarily indicative of the local market—in fact, the goods come from all over Spain—but you'll pay less to get these items here than you will in the larger cities.

NIGHTLIFE

Modest compared with Big Brother Barcelona, the city nevertheless has enough of a nocturnal buzz to make a weekend stay here worthwhile. Lively venues range from the subterranean **El Cau (The Cave)** (Carrer Trinquet Vell; ☎ 977-231-212; daily 10pm–4am; cover 10€), with its alternative musical groups, to **Groove** (Cervantes 4; daily 10pm–2am; cover 10€), where the vibe is more funk and blues. (Yes, there are live shows.) Younger visitors tend to prefer the trendy but paradoxically named **L'Antiquari** (calle Santa Ana 3; daily 10pm–3am; entrance 12€ including first drink), a dance club with a DJ, though it occasionally features live international bands such as Herbie Christ and the Rhythm Kings.

The whole town comes to life between June and August when the annual **Festival d'Estiu (Summer Festival)** unleashes a barrage of cinematic, theatrical, and musical programs. Check with the town's information office (see above) for details.

GET OUT OF TOWN
Tarragona's "Golden Coast": The Costa Dorada

The mainly flat Tarragona coastline is a swimmer's paradise, with fine-sanded **beaches**—many of them fringed by beautiful pine-covered headlands—extending on both sides of the capital. Two of the most attractive nearby towns on the **northern** stretch of the coast are boisterous **Torredembarra** (10km/6 miles), with its dominant castle and superb yachting marina and—nearer Barcelona province—the more sedate **Calafell** (28km/19 miles). To the **south,** the main attractions are big bustling **Salou** (10km/6 miles), the coast's biggest beach resort and a veritable mecca for international, family-oriented package tourism (it's close to sprogs' paradise Port Aventura; see above), and—further down—the more relaxed fishing town of **Cambrils** (20km/12 miles), backed by gray-green mountains and famed for its great portside seafood restaurants.

For Parents with Cranky Kids in Tow

Spain's answer to Disneyland, **Port Aventura** ✿ 🌟 kids (Av. Pere Molas Km 0.2; ☎ 977-779-090; www.portaventura.es; 44€ adults, 35€ seniors 60 and over and children 4–10, free for children 3 and under, including all shows and rides; mid–Mar to mid–June and mid–Sept to mid–Jan daily 10am–8pm, extended hours mid–June to mid–Sept daily 10am–midnoght opened in 1995 and just keeps getting bigger and bigger . . . and pricier. At present, covering 809 hectares (1,998 acres), planned further expansions will make it the largest entertainment area in Europe. Nevertheless it's heaven on earth for wee ones, consisting of a microcosm of five differing "worlds," with full-scale classic village re-creations ranging from Polynesia to Mexico to China to the old American West. As you might expect, it's also bristling with roller coasters and white-water rides, plus a lake you can cross on the deck of an oriental junk. The park lies 10 minutes southwest of Tarragona between the inland town of **Vila-Seca** and coastal resort of **Salou** and is easily reached by local trains and buses.

These coastal towns are easily reached by frequent *cercanías* train services from Tarragona in anything between 30 and 45 minutes, with one-way fares ranging from 2€ to 3.50€, making them ideal for a day—or even a half-day—visit.

Montblanc & the Cistercian Monasteries

Of all the evocative religious centers in Spain—and there are many—few compare in ambience and sense of mystery with this trio of small but exquisite monasteries founded in the 12th century by French Benedictine monks near the walled medieval town of **Montblanc** (30km/20 miles inland from Tarragona).

Set amid poplar-wooded hills, the oldest and largest of them, **Santa María de Poblet** (☎ 977-87-12-47; 4.50€; Mon–Fri 10am–12:30pm and 3–6 pm, closed at 5:30pm winter), was founded in 1151, and its subsequent architectural styles incorporated Romanesque (the 13th-century St. Catherine's chapel) and Gothic (the 15th-century St. George's chapel). Former kings of Cataluña and Aragón are entombed in its high vaulted chapterhouse and the still active (but out of sight) community of monks—originating in 1945 when the Poblet Brotherhood was created—enjoy a lifestyle of simple austerity detached from material concerns.

Close by in a secluded valley beside the River Gaia, the smaller **Monestir de Santes Creus** (☎ 977-63-83-29; 4€; Mar 15–Sept 15 10am–1:30pm and 3–7pm, Sept 16–Jan 15 10am–1:30pm and 3–5:30 pm, Jan 16–Mar 15 10am–1:30pm and 3–6pm) was founded 7 years later than Poblet and similarly updated over the centuries. Notable here is the 14th-century Gothic cloister with its striking Romanesque octagonal pavilion created by the English mason Reinard de Fonoll.

Last but not least of this mystical trio—which, in fact, lies farther north just inside neighboring Lleida province—is a convent. Established by the Cister's feminine branch in the 12th century, the **Monasteri de Vallbona de les Monges** (☎ 973-33-02-66; 2€; Tues–Sat 10am–1:30pm and 4:30–6:45pm, weekends and fiestas noon–1:30pm and 4:30–6:45pm) started life as a home for daughters of Aragonese noble families and today still houses over 30 nuns (well out of the public's eye). Key architectural features to look out for are the superb Romanesque-style north transept doors and tranquil cloister with its vines and flowers shrouding the somber tomb of Jaume I's Hungarian-born wife, Violant.

For **information** on both the town and its monasteries, check in at the very obliging **Montblanc** *Turisme* **Office** (☎ 977-861-733; www.montblancmedieval. org; Mon–Sat 10am–1:30pm and 3–6:30pm, Sun 10am–2pm). In addition to giving you information on the monasteries, it also lists several countryside walks you can make in the area.

GETTING THERE

Frequent trains from Tarragona to Lleida stop at **Montblanc** (one-way fare 7.50€), so it's easily accessible. Buses also run three times daily (except Sun) from Tarragona directly to **Poblet** en route to Lleida, stopping right outside the monastery walls. One-way fare is 5€; check with the Tarragona Tourist Office for timetables. The other two monasteries are harder to reach by public transport, so you'll need a rental car to visit them. For **Monestir de Santes Creues,** take the N-240 main road north to Valls, and then the C-51 east to meet the TP-2002, a minor road that leads north again, passing the monastery en route. For **Vallbona de les Monges,** take the same route to **Valls** and, from there, follow the C-14 north and turn left after Solivella onto a signposted minor road west, which eventually leads you past Rocallaura to the monastery.

Tortosa & the Ebro Delta

Just over an hour's train ride (12€ round-trip) from Tarragona in the southern part of the province lies little-known **Tortosa** (90km/60 miles), a historic gem of a town straddling the wide Ebro river as it flows east into a flat marshy delta, which fans out into the Mediterranean. It's famed for its medieval quarter, which has traces of its former Jewish and Arab occupants, and a fabulous Gothic cathedral, as well as another eye-catching clutch of moderniste buildings. Among these, the standout riverside *Escorxador*—an ornately decorated 1908 structure with a combined redbrick and sky blue facade, and multicolored ceramic decorations—was originally, of all things, a slaughterhouse. At its summit the former Arab fort of La Zuda has been converted into a sumptuous *parador* (government-run inn) where you can sip a coffee as you enjoy the great views of the surrounding lush plains. If you book a room online here (www.parador.es), you can stay in a double room at certain times of the year for as little as 80€ a night (that's per room and not per person, a remarkable deal for a place this flat-out lovely and historic).

For nature lovers, the high point of this area is the 483-sq.-km (188-sq.-mile) **Parc Natural del Delta del Ebre** (www.ebre.info/delta; free admission), a wide lowland area of marshes and rice paddies dotted with salty lagoons, and bordered by isolated beaches backed by breeze-swept dunes. This ecologically protected area has a haunting beauty all its own, and you can relax and cycle along the reed-flanked trails or go boating along the channels. The abundant bird life makes it a haven for ornithologists, amateur or otherwise. (***Note:*** Insect repellent is essential during the warmer months!)

At the tiny town of **Deltebre,** call in at the **Centro de Recepción y Documentación del Parque Natural del Delta del Ebro** (Plaça 20 de Maig; ☎ 977-48-96-79; daily 10am–2pm and 3–6pm), which has a series of exhibits showing the geographical layout and history of the park. At the center, there's also an aquarium filled with samples of park flora and fauna (including a wide range of fish and amphibians). You can also pick up a map of the whole park, with cycling and walking routes clearly indicated. Bicycles are rented out by **Delta Llover** (☎ 977-48-93-42) for 12€ for a full day (9am–7pm) or 7€ for a half-day (9am–2pm); rowing boats from **Garpi** (☎ 977-48-93-42), for around 8€ an hour. Both companies are within a 5-minute walk of the information center.

For more information, visit the **Oficina Municipal de Turismo de Tortosa** (Plaça Carrilet 1; ☎ 977-44-96-48). Staff here arrange city walks and river trips.

GIRONA

Increasingly popular today with visitors who, in the past, ignored it and headed straight for the Costa Brava beaches, provincial capital Girona is at last being appreciated for its wonderfully preserved old quarter—part 10th-century Jewish, part medieval Gothic. The city stands among the wooded countryside of the Lower Ampurdán region, and the high trees of its Parc de la Devesa rise above the junction of three rivers. Largest of these is the central Onyar, which runs through the heart of the city, crossed by bridges made of stone (Pont de Pedra) or iron (by Gustave Eiffel, of Eiffel Tower fame no less) and flanked by rows of Italianate

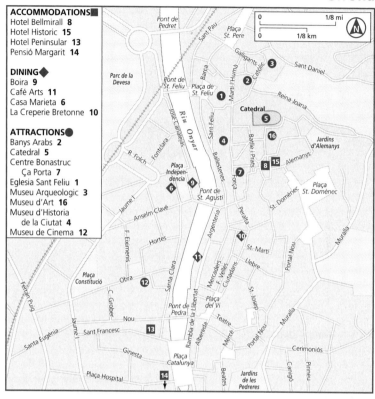

ACCOMMODATIONS■
Hotel Bellmirall **8**
Hotel Historic **15**
Hotel Peninsular **13**
Pensió Margarit **14**

DINING◆
Boira **9**
Café Arts **11**
Casa Marieta **6**
La Creperie Bretonne **10**

ATTRACTIONS●
Banys Arabs **2**
Catedral **5**
Centre Bonastruc
  Ça Porta **7**
Eglesia Sant Feliu **1**
Museu Arqueologic **3**
Museu d'Art **16**
Museu d'Historia
  de la Ciutat **4**
Museu de Cinema **12**

ocher- and russet-hued houses the colors of which reflect in the waters below. Dominating the whole scene are the imposing towers of Sant Feliu church and the emblematic Romanesque-Gothic Cathedral.

A BRIEF HISTORY OF GIRONA

If ever a town suffered . . . Originally called Gerunda by the ancient Iberians, Girona has been occupied by Romans, Visigoths, Moors, and French and besieged no fewer than 25 times over the ages, most notably in the 8th century when it was captured from the Moors by Charlemagne's son, Louis. Philip the Bold's assault 500 years later was another touchstone of its history, as was the successful 7-month attack by Napoleon's troops in the early 1800s. Final ignominy was the assault by Spain's own General Prim less than 50 years later. One of its greatest peacetime cultural influences was by Jewish immigrants who founded the now immaculately preserved early medieval Call Quarter and made a great commercial contribution to the city until they were expelled by the Catholic Kings on their accession in 1492. The original city walls, which were largely destroyed in the 19th century to make way for new buildings, have recently been rebuilt, and now constitute one of the city's major draws.

LAY OF THE LAND

Girona is in the heart of the richly varied region known as the Lower Ampurdán—in many ways Catalonia's most seductive face. At its center is a sylvan array of green fields lined with poplars, vineyards, and olive groves; along the coast, an idyllic blend of rocky headlands, intimate coves, sandy beaches, and coastal walks; way inland a mountain zone of lakes, pine forests, and rugged peaks.

GETTING TO GIRONA

For **information,** visit the **Oficina de Turismo de Girona** (☎ 972-226-575; www.ajuntament.gi; Mon–Fri 8am–8pm, Sat 8am–2pm and 4–8pm, and Sun 9am–2pm), which is located in an attractive modern building on the Call district side of the river at Rambla de la Libertat 1.

More than 26 **trains** per day run from Barcelona-Sants main rail station or the Passeig de Gràcia Metro station to the Girona station, which adjoins the city's Plaça Espanya (☎ 972-20-70-93 for general information). The journey takes between 1 and 1½ hours and one-way fares range from 5.90€ to 6.70€.

A **bus** regular service operates from Barcelona's Estació del Nord, with buses stopping at the Girona autobus station right beside the rail station. Buses (Aerobus A1) also run frequently from Girona airport every 7 to 15 minutes from 6am to 1am daily. One-way fare is 4.05€.

If you're **driving** from Barcelona, take the A-7 at Ronda Litoral and head north via the A-7.

ACCOMMODATIONS, BOTH STANDARD & NOT

Girona province has a wealth of *casas rurales* (country houses and cottages) where you can either stay in a room as you would in a *pensione* or small hotel, or rent a fully equipped house. Many of the latter accommodate large family groups of up to 10 or 12, but some are subdivided into apartments accommodating smaller parties of 2 to 6. Rates are generally higher than those of similar properties in Tarragona province (and even in neighboring France, the famed *gîtes* of which are far more commonplace and have been a more affordable option for decades), but you can be assured of a controlled high standard. To find these opportunities, look at both **www.turismegirona.com** and **www.casasrurales girona.com**. Both sites provide open listings but don't actually inspect the properties themselves, so be sure to ask a lot of questions before booking. Here are two from these sites that I was able to inspect:

€   A *casa rural* offering room-only accommodations, **Casa Monell** ✦ 🔟 (☎ 972-19-02-95; www.masmonell.com) is a lovely, restored 17th-century stone-built *masia* (Catalán country home) with a spacious garden and swimming pool in the inland volcanic park of **La Garrotxa** (a great walking area). The six spacious double rooms come in a number of configurations, from rooms with bunk beds and double beds (for family visitors) to those just big enough for two. Some have private bathrooms (50€–66€ a night), while the cheaper ones share (44€–60€). The furnishings may not match, and a wall may be an odd shade of blue, but you can rest assured that the mattresses will be restful, often set within classic wrought-iron bedsteads, the wood floors will be buffed to a high sheen, and all will be spic and span. A traditional-style dining room serves three meals a day (for an additional cost). There's also an outdoor barbecue area where alfresco meals can be arranged. In addition to the rooms, there's a similarly furnished adjoining self-contained **apartment** complete with lounge/dining area, kitchen, two bedrooms, and a bathroom. It accommodates four to six and charges 210€ for a weekend, plus 75€ for each extra day. Because of its out-of-the-way location, a rental car would be ideal here. Get there via the *salida* (exit) 6 from the A7 Girona highway, and then at Banyoles turn south onto the country road leading to the village of Mieres where you turn right toward the next village of El Torn. After 2km (1¼ miles), a lane appears on the right leading to the house 200m (656 ft.) away.

€ Another prime example of a peaceful self-catering property **Mas Pereta** (☎ 972-76-93-61; www.maspereta.com) is set amid gentle green countryside at Fonolleras near the village of Parlava in the **Lower Ampurdán** area, 20 minutes from Girona town. This large former working farm has been converted into four separate apartments, each with one double and three single bedrooms, vaulted brick ceilings, solid traditional furnishings, and a fully equipped open-plan kitchen complete with washing machine. There's also a large communal garden with a swimming pool. Each apartment costs 80€ to 100€ per night, working out to 20€ to 25€ per person for four or five people; a great saving over similar standard accommodations in a hotel. See www.casasruralesgirona.com for a wide range of other similar self-catering selections. Again, this website is purely a listing. It's up to the interested parties to contact the properties themselves to make the booking.

€ My favorite low-cost "find" in Girona town itself is the **Pensio Margarit** ★ (Carrer Ultónia 1; ☎ 972-20-10-66; www.hotelmargarit.com; MC, V), which actually offers its guests several types of "buys" depending on their needs. Solo travelers who are just looking for a place to crash pay between 32€ and 37€ for a night in a cozy (read: small) single, whereas doubles can opt for either a tidy, tiny "junior" room (38€–50€), a standard with a bit more elbowroom (47€–60€), or a superior that has enough space to lay your luggage down flat on the ground and a small inner terrace overlooking a tiny sunken Japanese-style garden (58€–70€). None go beyond the simple in the decor—prefab furnishings and bare wooden floors are the norm here—but they're kept spotlessly clean, and that includes the adjoining bathrooms. A generous breakfast buffet is part of the deal, and the location is primo. The fact that it's family run shows in the informal chumminess of the young staff. There's also a computer with an Internet connection right next to the reception.

€€ The five-floored **Hotel Peninsular** ★ (Nou 3, 17001 Girona; ☎ 972-20-38-00; www.novarahotels.com; AE, DC, MC, V) has been in business for over 150 years, though you'd never know it thanks to a thorough recent renovation. Now a prize-winning member of the Novara chain—which is known for its very high service standards—it provides warmly carpeted, soundproofed rooms with TV, wood-paneled walls, a good-size wardrobe, comfortable beds, and an en suite bathroom with shower, all for just 75€ for a double. A comprehensive buffet breakfast (extra 8€) is served in the bar and a host of eating spots are all around you when you step out.

€€   Cross the Pont de Pedra (stone bridge) on the east bank of the River Onyar, walk into the heart of the Call district, and you'll find one of the most historically atmospheric hotels in town: the enchanting **Bellmirall** ✫✫ (Carrer Bellmirall 3; ☎ 972-20-40-09; cash only; free parking; closed Jan–Feb). This time-warp treat provides highly atmospheric accommodations in a 14th-century house that's been imaginatively restored by your charming and hospitable host Christina Vach. The small to midsize bedrooms are individually (some might say eccentrically) decorated with antiques, paintings, or ceramics, each with its own small bathroom with shower. In warm weather, you can have breakfast outside on the patio. It's all very charming and well worth the 65€ to 75€ per night (breakfast included) that you pay for a double room here.

€€–€€€   Just across the road from the Bellmirall, another dazzlingly renovated period gem, the **Hotel Historic** ✫ (Carrer Bellmirall 4a; ☎ 972-22-35-83; www.hotelhistoric.com; MC, V), offers the best of both worlds. You can either stay in one of its six individually styled double rooms (120€ per night) or cater for yourself in one of its seven immaculate apartments (96€–130€ per night for 2–4 people). Both types of property retain original features like stone walls, roof beams, and tiled floors, and offer a blend of warm traditional pine-wood decor and coolly comfortable modern furnishings. The apartments have one or two double bedrooms with private bathrooms, a lounge dining area, and a fully equipped kitchen—plus TV and Internet access.

DINING FOR ALL TASTES

€   Eating at the riverside **Boira** ✫ (Plaça de la Independència 17; ☎ 972-20-30-96; Mon–Sat 1:30–4pm and 8–11:30pm; V) is a classic Girona experience, as the food is pure traditional Catalán and the setting delightful, with some tables right on the colonnaded square and others overlooking it. Hearty delights like *galtas de porc* (pig's trotters) and *conejo* (rabbit) feature on the a la carte list of the natty upstairs restaurant menu. More money saving, though, is the chummy down-to-earth bar on the ground floor where the starter tidbits include *tortillas* (omelets), *anchoas* (anchovies), and *queso manchego* (Manchegan cheese) at 3€ to 5€ each, and the top value-for-money lunch menu (9€) at the sociably close tables next to the bar regularly includes paella.

€   Across the river in the old Call Quarter, crepes are the best thing—value- and taste-wise—to go for in **La Creperie Bretonne** (Cort Reial 9; ☎ 972-21-81-20; daily 1:30–4pm and 8–11pm; MC, V), a welcoming French-owned eating spot that also serves delicious vegetarian dishes. Crepes range from 6€ to 8€ and the veggie *platos* from 7€ to 10€. Wash down your meal with pungent Gallic cider.

€–€€   I can't resist including the nearby bright and charming **Café Arts** ✫✫ (Rambla Llibertat; ☎ 972-227-084; daily 9am–10pm; MC, V), though many think of it as essentially a coffee and croissant rendezvous where you can savor your breakfast with a view of the river on one side and a bustling old-town avenue on the other. Having sampled both its breakfasts and its full meals (which tend to consist of omelets, salads, and pasta dishes), I'd say its appeal is broader. Café Arts serves quality grub, the decor is quietly chic, and the service is downright charming. Can you tell I like this place a lot?

€€   Though its meals are full at Café Arts, they're still light. If you're looking for fare that's a bit more substantial, there's hearty grub aplenty at the city's oldest (ca. 1892) eating spot **Casa Marieta** ★★ (Plaça Independencia 5; ☎ 972-20-10-16; www.casamarieta.com; Tues–Sun 1–3:30pm and 8–10:30pm, until 11pm in summer; DC, MC, V), a favorite culinary watering hole for *gerundenses* (locals). The low-ceilinged, wooden-floored time warp of a dining room is divided into five separate areas, each with its own distinctive decor and motifs, which vary from rural to nautical. Photos of early 20th-century Girona dot the walls and artifacts and sculptures decorate the place. The best way to sample the richly varied menu is through its *prix fixe* of three solid courses with wine, which you can pick from an a la carte list that includes *trinxat* (a more-delicious-than-it-sounds blend of ham, cabbage, and potatoes), *butifarra* (Catalán pork sausage), *calamares a la plancha* (grilled squid), and *graellada de peix i marisc* (grilled seafood) for a total per head of 25€ or more. (This is a particularly good value as it offers more variety of choice than the standard set menu you'll find in most restaurants.)

WHY YOU'RE HERE: THE TOP SIGHTS & ATTRACTIONS

Dominating everything in the town is Girona's stupendous 14th-century Catalán baroque **Catedral** ★★★ (Plaça de la Catedral s/n; ☎ 972-21-44-26; free admission to cathedral; nave cloister and museum 4€ adult, 3€ seniors and students, free on Sun; cathedral daily 9am–1pm and during cloister and museum visiting hours; cloister and museum July–Sept Tues–Sat 10am–8pm and Sun 10am–2pm, Oct–Feb Tues–Sat 10am–2pm and 4–6pm and Sun 10am–2pm, Mar–June Tues–Sat 10am–2pm and 4–7pm and Sun 10am–2pm). Its nave, at 23m (75 ft.), is the widest in the Gothic architectural world (and it's second widest for all types of Catholic churches, after St. Peter's in Rome). The approach to the main entrance up 90 stone steps is also suitably impressive, as are the 17th-century Romanesque-Gothic facade and bell tower above, crowned by a dome with a bronze angel weather vane. Inside, the must-sees are **Tapestry of the Creation,** a rare piece of 11th- or 12th-century Romanesque embroidery showing humans and animals in the Garden of Eden, plus depictions of seasonal activities (Apr, for example, is illustrated by a farmer plowing a field), and the just-as-rare 10th-century *Códex del Beatus,* an illustrated manuscript of commentary on the Revelation. The cathedral has several semi-hidden corners. Pass though the **Chapel of Hope** doorway and you're suddenly in a 12th-century **Romanesque cloister** with a bizarre trapezoidal layout, while the **Cloister Gallery,** with its double colonnade, shows off its superb biblical scenes—the pinnacle of Catalán Romanesque art.

Not far behind the cathedral in style, size, and character is the nearby 14th- to 17th-century **Església de Sant Feliu (Sant Feliu Church)** ★ (Pujada de Sant Feliu s/n; ☎ 972-20-14-07; free admission; daily 8am–7:45pm); its huge eight-pinnacled **bell tower** is one of the Girona skyline's iconic sights. Though the main facade of the church is baroque, it also has pillars and arches in the Romanesque style and a Gothic central nave. Make a beeline for its 16th-century **altarpiece,** a masterpiece of intricate tableaux, and an especially luminous 14th-century alabaster *Reclining Christ.* Also remarkable are the 1,800-year-old eight pagan and Christian **sarcophagi** set in the walls of the presbytery, one depicting Pluto carrying Persephone off to the depths of the Earth.

As you'll note, there's lots to see and do in Girona, but don't penny-pinch and skip the **Museu d'Art** ✮ (Pujada de la Catedral 12; ☎ 972-20-38-34; 2€ adults, 1.50€ students, free for seniors and children; Mar–Sept Tues–Sat 10am–7pm, Sun 10am–2pm; Oct–Feb Tues–Sat 10am–6pm, Sun 10am–2pm; closed Jan 1, Jan 6, Easter, and Dec 25–26), located right next to the cathedral in a former Episcopal Palace. It's a genuine treasure trove of over 8,000 objects created in the Girona region and emblematic, therefore, of the unique Catalán style. The **altarpiece**s of **Sant Pere of Púbol** by Bernat Martorell and of **Sant Miguel de Crüilles** by Luis Borrassa in the Throne Room, both from the 15th century, are considered among the finest examples of Catalán Gothic painting anywhere; *Our Lady of Besalú,* from the same period, is one of the most accomplished depictions of the Virgin carved in alabaster. Along with the older sculptures, paintings, and tapestries are such unusual pieces as stained-glass tables, jewel-toned 15th-century miniatures depicting the lives of the martyrs, and even 20th-century works of important Catalán symbolist and Impressionist painters.

Girona's past is just as colorful as the art pieces created here. For the lowdown on all the juicy goings on, head to **Museu d'Historia de la Ciutat (Museum of the History of the City)** (Carrer de la Força; ☎ 972-22-22-29; 2€ adults, 1€ seniors and students, free for children 16 and under; Tues–Sat 10am–2pm and 5–7pm, Sun 10am–2pm). The building alone is of great historic value. Originally a 15th-century Gothic mansion that was later transformed into a convent—you can still see the original cloister, cellar, and Capuchin cemetery—it also contains the remains of a 2nd-century Roman wall in its basement. Exhibits are displayed not only throughout the building but also in galleries in the nearby Placeta de l'Institut Vell and Pujada de Sant Feliu (at no. 2). They begin with Neolithic flints, tools, and ceramics and samples of Roman pavement mosaics and continue though medieval and 19th-century *noucentiste* (moderniste) architectural times right up to post-Franco democratic Spain, using a blend of paintings, sculptures, photos, posters, and multilingual descriptions to portray the latter periods. Temporary exhibitions are also worth a peek. In the past, they've covered subjects as widely diverse as the Peninsula War and Charlie Chaplin.

A small but indelible reminder of the Moorish presence in Girona—hidden in the warren-like old quarter of the city—is the 12th-century **Banys Arabs (Arab Baths)** ✮ (Carrer Ferran el Catolic s/n; ☎ 972-21-32-62; 2€ adults, 1€ students, free for seniors and children 15 and under; Apr–Sept Mon–Sat 10am–7pm, Sun 10am–2pm; Oct–Mar Tues–Sun 10am–2pm; closed major holidays). Wonderfully evocative in spite of having been heavily restored in 1929, they're highlighted by the *caldarium* **(hot bath),** with its tiled floor, and the *frigidarium* **(cold bath),** an octagonal pool surrounded by pillars supporting a prism-like structure in the overhead window.

Jews also played a prominent part in Girona's history, and the **Centre Bonastruc Ca Porta** (calle La Força 8; ☎ 972-21-67-61; www.ajuntament.gi/call/eng/mus-coleccio.php; 2€ adults, 1.50€ seniors 61 and over and students, free for children 15 and under; Mon–Sat 10am–8pm, Sun 10am–3pm) in the heart of El Call, explores their medieval life and customs, with a special emphasis on the cohabitation of Jews and Christians. In addition, the center offers an ever-changing program of photos, paintings, and sculptures by modern Jewish artists, plus organized guided strolls around the quarter (usually free).

There are two very good reasons for popping into the **Museu Arqueològic** ✸ (Sant Pere de Galligants, Santa Llúcia 1; ☎ 972-20-26-32; 2€ adults, 1.50€ students, free for seniors and children 15 and under; Oct–May Tues–Sat 10am–2pm and 4–6pm, Sun 10am–2pm; June–Sept Tues–Sat 10am–1:30pm and 4–7pm, Sun 10am–2pm), which you'll find tucked away in a tiny valley on the northern side of the cathedral. For a start, it contains some of the most important Paleolithic and Visigothic relics ever found in Catalonia. Second, the 11th-century monastery cloister in which it's housed ranks as one of the best examples of Catalán Romanesque architecture. In the cloister, look for the Hebrew inscriptions from gravestones of the old Jewish cemetery.

Then hop across the river for something really different. It's not exactly historical—except in a very short-term sense—but of unique interest to movie buffs: the **Museu de Cinema** ✸✸ (Sèquia 1; ☎ 972-41-27-77; 3€ adults, 1.50€ seniors and students, free for children 15 and under; May–Sept Tues–Sun 10am–8pm; Oct–Apr Tues–Fri 10am–6pm, Sat 10am–8pm, Sun 11am–3pm; closed holidays) is the only museum in Spain devoted entirely to the "Seventh Art." Its inimitable Tomàs Mallol collection of some 25,000 cinema artifacts covers movies dating from its silent beginnings up to the 1970s, and you get to see the pioneering Lumière brothers' original camera. Other attractions include a range of photographs, posters, engravings, drawings, and paintings, around 800 films of various styles and periods, and a comprehensive library of film-related publications.

ATTENTION, SHOPPERS!

One of the best ways to pick up a local bargain is simply to wander around the medieval quarter of **El Call** in the Old Town. You're likely to find several shops specializing in the truly charming ceramic ware crafted in the nearby inland town of **La Bisbal**. The same area's calle La Força also has several design and object stores, of which the most famous (and worthwhile) is **Emporium BD** (calle La Forca 10; ☎ 972-22-43-39). You can also pick up a souvenir such as a handmade ceramic plaque or olive-wood salad bowl at one of the town's open-air artisan markets on Saturdays, either at the Pont de Pedra (stone bridge) or in the central Plaça Miquel Santaló and Plaça de les Castanyes.

NIGHTLIFE

You don't come across many clubs located in a converted convent, but **La Sala del Cel (The Salt Cellar)** (Pedret 118; ☎ 972-21-46-64; daily 11pm–4am; cover 10€) is just that. A riotous "techno palace" featuring the latest sounds played by top DJs from all over Europe, it also retains a secluded garden area from quieter and more reflective times. The place gets terribly busy on the weekends, so be prepared for lines.

Slightly less flamboyant and outrageous is the **Sala de Ball (The Ballroom)** (calle Riu Güell 2; ☎ 972-201-439; Fri–Sat 11pm–5:30am, Sun 6–11:30pm; cover 12€), an elegant, old-style dance hall close to the Devesa Park, which covers a range of music styles from hip-hop to house and salsa, depending on the night, and features regular live performers.

THE COSTA BRAVA

The scenic Mediterranean paradise known as the **Costa Brava** ★★ (for my money, the most handsome coastline in mainland Spain) begins 70km (43 miles) north of Barcelona and extends as far as the French border. En route it takes in a multitude of former fishing villages that were virtually unknown till the 1950s and have long since blossomed into popular tourist towns—some still attractive, others shamelessly overbuilt. In July and August, the whole coast is impossibly crowded as northern European tour groups tend to block-book hotels, and in winter, freed of tourists, its seaside villages and towns sleep a deep sleep.

It's easy to get to many parts of the coast in well under an hour from Girona either by train or bus—and if you happen to be staying in Barcelona, it's also possible to make day trips from there in summer when a frequent and efficient bus service covers most main resorts. Car rental is *not* a relaxing option in high summer; the whole area is chockablock with rental cars.

The first town at the southern end—where the long flat stretches of the Maresme coast above Barcelona disappear and the cliffs and coves begin—is **Blanes** (41km/27 miles south of Girona), with its great fishing port and inimitable Botanical Gardens (see "Faust's Garden of Eden," below). After Blanes comes **Lloret de Mar** (7km/4 miles north), a crass monster resort ruined by developers. Just around the headlands 6km (4 miles) to the north, its smaller neighbor **Tossa de Mar** has managed to blend its original character with a fun ambience. In the summer, you can swim from two main beaches, **Mar Gran** and **La Bauma,** or take a glass-bottom boat trip and explore the crystal waters in nearby cliffside caves. (See "Pandora & the 'Blue Paradise,'" below.)

The next town, reached after 12km (8 miles) of countless (some say a thousand!) exhilarating scenic bends, is the Italianate-style Costa Brava capital **Sant Feliu de Guíxols,** least changed of all the coast's resorts and still—tourism apart—earning a modest living from sardine catching and cork production. (Cork forests line the inland hills.) Its attractive tree-lined *paseo,* backed by moderniste buildings, stands beside a sheltered harbor enclosed by rocky headlands, and along the coast north between here and S'Agaró—site of one of Spain's oldest luxury hotels, La Gavina—is as magnificent a coastal walk as you'll find anywhere

---

Faust's Garden of Eden

There are few lovelier lovelier paeans to nature than Blanes's 16-hectare (40-acre) **Jardí Botànic Marimurtra** (Passeig de Carles Faust 9, Blanes; ☎ 972-33-08-26; www.botanicmarimurtra.org; 5€; Mon–Fri Apr–Oct 9am–6pm [until 8pm Jul–Aug], Nov–Mar 10am–5pm; weekends and fiestas year-round 10am–2pm), whose flower-lined trails and white-domed sun terraces look down on the blue Mediterranean from a cliffside vantage point. Founded over a hundred years ago by biologist Karl Faust, it now contains more than 200,000 colorful species of plants and shrubs from all corners of the globe and has been declared an Area of National Cultural Interest. (*Marimurtra,* incidentally, means "sea and myrtle.")

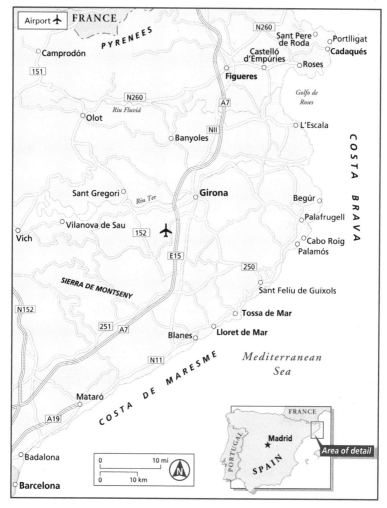

in the Mediterranean, undulating its scenic way past clear-watered inlets and superb crescent beaches like San Pol and La Conca before petering out just short of the overblown resort of **Playa de Aro.** For ambitious walkers, the 40km-long (25-mile) trail that extends all the way there from Girona center into Sant Feliu de Guixols is a seriously delightful trek through fields, woodlands, olive groves, and a number of small villages (where you can hop a bus if you find your ambitions were outmatched by blisters). Full information on this walk can be found at www.ajuntament.gi.

Some 20km (14 miles) beyond here the idyllic resort of **Calella de Palafrugell**—epitomizing the very best this inimitable "wild coast" has to offer—stands out as another pearl of Mediterranean perfection amid the continuing mini panorama of tiny summer resorts, coves, pines, caverns, and translucent blue waters. The most rewarding towns of all, however, are **Cadaqués** (below) and **Empúries** (see "Empúries: Greeks, Romans & Nature in the Wild," below).

GETTING TO THE COSTA BRAVA

There are regular year-round services by **Sarfa bus** (☎ 902-302-025; www.sarfa.com) from **Girona Bus Station** to **Tossa de Mar** (5.25€), **Sant Feliu de Guíxols** (4.95€), and **Palafrugell** (4.50€), where there's a minibus connection (1.50€) to nearby **Calella de Palafrugell** (3km/2 miles). There are also buses to these towns from **Blanes,** which can be reached directly by bus (5.50€) and *cercanías* train (5€) from Girona.

SALVADOR DALÍ & CADAQUÉS

Cadaqués ✶✶ (70km/45 miles from Girona) is like no other town on the Catalán coast. If you approach it by sea (as I did when I first saw it—entranced—

Pandora & the "Blue Paradise"

Tossa de Mar has long appealed to artists. With its 12th-century walls, maze-like old quarter, and curving bays, the town is a painter's delight and the coast north and south has a rugged beauty unequalled anywhere else in Mediterranean Spain apart from northwest Mallorca (p. 426). It was the setting for the 1951 Ava Gardner and James Mason movie *Pandora and the Flying Dutchman* and a life-size bronze statue of the screen goddess herself in evening dress, built in 1998 and facing a stone inscription of an Omar Khayam quote from the movie, overlooks the bay from a high vantage point in the Ciutat Vella. In the mid-1930s it was a secret haunt for writers and painters, one of whom, Marc Chagall, christened it a "blue paradise." (You can see samples of his work in the seaside museum.) This was a period of dashed hopes for many artists who'd come from northern Europe to escape the growth of Nazism only to find themselves confronted with the destructive rumblings of the Spanish Civil War. Their expectations that this new "Shangri-La" would be sufficiently isolated to escape the unpleasant repercussions and events of the real world proved false. Fervently socialist Catalonia quickly became one of the main battlegrounds in the struggle against Franco's 1936 military takeover bid.

The best means of getting there on public transport is via the Sarfa bus service from Barcelona's Estació Sud. The 90-minute trip has daily departures from 8:15am to 8:15pm (9.85€ one-way). For a timetable, call ☎ 902-26-06-06 or 932-65-65-08, or visit www.sarfa.com. If you're driving, take the A-19 highway north and look for the clearly marked signs to Lloret de Mar, from where a final short winding road brings you around a pine-wooded headland into Tossa. The **Tourist Information Office** is at Av. El Pelegrí 25 (☎ 972-34-01-08; www.infotossa.com).

Empúries: Greeks, Romans & Nature in the Wild

Roman and Greek ruins litter the Mediterranean, but it's unusual to see the remains of both civilizations—and such well-preserved ruins at that—so clearly at one archeological site. In fact, the history of **Empúries** goes back even further than the Greeks. The first settlement here, founded in 600 B.C. by the Phoenicians, was called Paleopolis, and its ruins are now covered by the sea. Next came the Greeks, who built a port they called Neapolis, which flourished until the Romans arrived in A.D. 2 and built the town of Empúries alongside it. As Barcino (Barcelona) and Tarraco (Tarragona) assumed more importance, this Greco-Roman hybrid began to decline. Today you can clearly see traces of the Greek agora harbor and fish salting area, and, further back, the impressive Roman walls, amphitheater, forum, and Paleo-Christian basilica. Its crumbling pillars, fading mosaics, and paved walkways are a poignant reminder of how even the most powerful empires eventually wither and die. Check the website www.cbrava.com/empuries for details on touring this active archeological site. (Only about 20% of the Roman City has yet been excavated.)

Half an hour's drive south from Empúries, 1.6km (1 mile) off-shore from the small fishing port–turned–pop resort of **Estartit**, are the **Illes Medes**, a miniature limestone archipelago of seven islets and one lighthouse whose surrounding waters are a protected ecosystem where divers can explore the pellucid waters for coral and rich aquatic life that includes lobsters and octopus. (Don't believe all they say about the Mediterranean being polluted and fished out.) **"El Rei Del Mar"** (Avinguda de Grecia 5; ☎ 972-75-13-92) charges 31€ for organized scuba-diving expeditions including equipment rental. For those who don't dive, in summer, **glass-bottom boat** tours are offered from Estartit; contact **Nautilus** (Passeig Maritim 23; ☎ 971-751-489; www.nautilus.es) for full information. Medas Island visits cost 14€ to 16€ for adults, 7.50€ to 9€ for children 4 to 11. You can take a longer trip up the coast to Cadaqués (see p. 330) for 22€ (12€ for children 4–11). There are also several **scuba-diving schools** in Estartit. For more information about the Medas islands see www.isleasmedas.com.

Getting there: Empúries is close to the fishing port of L'Escala, a 20-minute stroll along the shore of the wide Bay of Rosas. Year-round bus service is available from Girona bus station to Estartit (for l'Illes Medes) from AMPSA (☎ 972-21-63-53; 4.75€ one-way) and to l'Escala, for Empúries, with Sarfa (☎ 972-20-17-96; www.sarfa.com; 5.50€ one-way).

on a boat trip from Estartit), its jagged outline of dazzling white houses, topped by a dominant church and gleaming in reverse silhouette against a backdrop of dark, olive-tree-covered hills, has a faint Greek-island look. Wander its narrow

Hello, Dalí!

At one time, Dalí was one of the most sought-after painters, not only in Europe, but also in the United States, and so devoted to self-promotion that the surrealist poet André Breton baptized him with the anagram "Avida Dollars." (*Avida,* or *avido,* means "greedy" in Spanish.) Dalí is said to have once smashed windows along a New York City avenue to draw attention to his works.

Whatever you think about his PR methods, it's undisputed that he had serious artworks to promote; his *Persistence of Memory* (the painting with the melting watches) is an iconic work of surrealistic art, as are many of his phantasmagoric paintings.

But while much of his oeuvre depicted objects that came straight from his imagination, it's clear that this tiny coastal corner of Catalonia was also major inspiration for him. The cobalt blue waters and rocky headlands of Port Lligat feature in a large number of his works. And in this region—the Upper Ampurdán—the bone-dry Tramuntana wind blows most of the year, creating images so clear that it appears as though there's no air or space between the viewer and a distant object such as a rock protruding from the sea or a boat on the horizon. This compressed and airless perspective also makes an appearance in his work.

So next time you're staring at his flying tigers, spindly legged elephants, or melting watches, examine the hard-edged backdrops as well, and think back to your trip to Dalí's hometown.

souk-like alleyways and you could almost be in North Africa or in one of the tiny Andaluz pueblos of Granada province. Radiantly and impossibly picturesque, beloved by countless artists and writers over the decades, it basks at the tip of the northern Costa Brava's wild Cape Creus headland surrounded by gray-pebbled, transparent-watered coves, a 10-minute stroll down a winding lane from its tiny neighbor **Port Lligat**—where the extraordinary surrealistic painter **Salvador Felipe Jacinto Dalí i Domènech** (1904–89) lived and painted on and off for 40 years between his international travels.

His large cream-colored house **Casa-Museu Salvador Dalí Portlligat** ★ (☎ 972-25-10-15; www.salvador-dali.org; 10€ adults, 8€ seniors and students, free for children 8 and under; mid-Mar to mid-June and mid-Sept to Jan 6 Tues–Sun 10:30am–6pm, mid-June to mid-Sept daily 10:30am–9pm) overlooks an inlet of clear turquoise waters and surrealistic rock formations, very much like the landscapes you'll see in his paintings. Outsize effigies of white eggs adorn the roof while, inside, eclectic collections of Dalían objects, art, and icons thrown together in seemingly haphazard fashion clutter the labyrinthine sequence of rooms. The swimming pool and terrace are where Dalí threw many of his legendary parties in the 1970s, when international guests from Kirk Douglas to Luis Buñuel would drop in.

If you've got a couple of days to spare, you should definitely try to visit the region's other Dalí museums. The artist's greatest temple to eccentricity can be found at inland **Figueres** (35km/22 miles from Girona and 40 min. away by bus or car from Cadaqués), the rather dour capital of the Upper Ampurdán region. One of the most remarkable and idiosyncratic repositories of modern art on Earth, the **Teatre-Museu Dalí** ★★ (Plaza Gala-Salvador Dalí; ☎ 972-677-500; www.salvador-dali.org/museus; adults 11€ including Dalí-Jewels exhibition, free for children 8 and under; Nov–Feb 10:30am–6pm, Mar–June and Oct 9:30am–6pm, Jul–Sept 9am–8pm) dwarfs his Port Lligat home in size and content. The collection here is large and varied, from his early, more realistic works to a complete room created to look like the face of movie star Mae West. It was built by Dalí himself in 1974 in the former theater where his first exhibition was held.

A third Dalí museum, **Castell de Pubol** (Plaça Gala Dalí, Pubol-la-Pera; ☎ 972-488-655; 7€ adults; mid–Mar to mid–June and mid–Sept to Nov 1 10am–6pm, Nov 2–Dec 31 10am–5pm, extended hours mid–June to mid–Sept 10am–8pm, closed Dec 25, Jan 1, and every Mon from mid–Sept to mid–June), lies farther south in the tiny village of Pubol near Parlava. Dalí bought this 12th-century house for his Russian-born wife-muse Gala (otherwise known as Elena Ivanovna Diakonova), but relations between them were so bitter at that stage that she would only see him by appointment (and not always then). He did live here for several years before seriously injuring himself in a mysterious on-site fire in 1984. He was scheduled to be buried here in a tomb next to hers but changed his mind, and the tomb lies empty. You won't find many paintings here, but you will tour an impressive Gothic Romanesque building whose surrealistic furnishings and decor still reflect the artist's unique tastes. Exhibits of Gala's possessions abound, from haute couture gowns to a photo album of her alongside top Hollywood stars like Gregory Peck. Most treasured of all is her vintage black Sedan de Ville Cadillac, still kept in mint condition in the castle's garage.

Getting There

Hourly **trains** from Barcelona and Girona stop at **Figueres,** and there's a regular **Sarfa** bus service (☎ 902-302-025) from both cities. If you're coming by **car,** take the north-south A-7 highway and turn off at the EXIT 4 FIGUERES SUD sign. Seven buses a day run between **Figueres** and **Cadaqués** (1 hr. 5 min.; 4.50€). There are also two buses per day to Cadaqués from Barcelona (20€); in spite of the distance, because of a superb highway north, the trip takes just 2¼ hours. The service is again operated by **Sarfa** (☎ 972-25-87-13). For information, check out the **Tourist Office** (Cotxe 2; ☎ 972-25-83-15; Mon–Sat 10:30am–1pm and 4:30–7:30pm).

Where to Stay & Dine

€–€€ I have always found Cadaqués totally irresistible atmospherically, geographically, and—perhaps stretching this adulation to its limit—even spiritually. And I think it's fair to assume that you'll share some of those sentiments with me.

If you do, and you decide you simply have to stay the night, it's worth checking out the unpretentious **Hostal Ubaldo** ✦ (Carrer Unió 13; ☎ 972-25-81-25; www. hotelubaldo.com; cash only), which compensates for its lack of finesse by being most warm and welcoming. The compact rooms here have bare white walls, with rather stark lighting, plain wood furnishings, a wicker chair, a writing table, and a small satellite TV. Depending on the season, the rates range from 55€ to 80€ for a double—all with en suite bathrooms. Book at least six months ahead if you're thinking of visiting in the summer, as the prices and friendly service make the Ubaldo quite popular. The hotel stands in a narrow, picturesque street in the Old Town just below the Santa María Church and barely a stone's throw from one of the town's intimate little pebbly beaches.

€   Though Cadaqués is a far-from-cheap place to be when you're feeling peckish, you can get away with spending no more than 7€ or 8€ for an enticing single dish of falafel or *tajine* curry at the Lebanese-oriented **Gato Azul** (calle Curós 10; ☎ 972-258-844; daily 1–4pm and 8–11:30pm; V), tucked away in a quiet corner of the Old Town. Run by a friendly and charming couple, it's small, intimate, and relaxing. For a little extra (10€), you can enjoy the set two courses and wine menu.

€€–€€€   Seafood restaurants are, again, not the most economical place to head to at nosh time, but if you can't resist the fish in a place where the sea seems to greet you at every turn, then try **Es Trull** ✦✦ (Port Ditxos s/n; ☎ 972-25-81-96; www.resetrull.restaurantesok.com; Fri–Wed 12:30–4pm and 7–11pm; closed Nov–Easter; AE, DC, MC, V). This waterside favorite is named after the ancient olive press you'll see inside, and its highly reliable fixed-price lunch menu (18€–20€) may include *mejillones* (mussels), *merluza* (hake), or *paella negre* (paella cooked in octopus ink). The Trull's splendid *zarzuela* (seafood casserole) and *parrillada* (mixed grill of fish) are only served a la carte and are correspondingly dearer (you're looking at 25€–30€ a head) but worth it if you feel like splashing out. Book ahead if you want to eat here in high season.

LLEIDA

Least known and least visited of the Catalán capitals, agricultural **Lleida** (formerly known as Lérida) rises on a hillock above the River Segre surrounded by a fertile plain. It's more rough hewn and "authentically" regional than its counterparts Tarragona and Girona, with fewer surviving Roman and Gothic monuments, but a more genuine, less tourist-influenced atmosphere, and correspondingly lower prices in hotel and restaurants. Nearby, in lieu of beaches, it offers a multitude of outdoor activities in countryside settings. You can go walking or horseback riding in farmland areas around rural towns like Balaguer, or head up north to the Lleidan Pyrenees to climb the mountain paths of the Aigüestortes National Park, or explore the tiny Romanesque churches of the Vall del Boí, declared a UNESCO World Heritage Site in 2000. (See "Get Out of Town," below.)

A BRIEF HISTORY OF LLEIDA

Originally named *Ilerda* by early Iberian settlers and a subsequent hot spot during a Civil War between conflicting Roman rulers Pompey and Caesar, the town was captured and rebuilt by the Moors in the 8th century and conquered by Ramón Berenguer IV 400 years later. Further destructive sieges followed, from John II of Aragón's attack in 1466 right up to General Suchet's assault in 1820, and during the Civil War many religious buildings were burnt. Small wonder the surviving monuments only reflect a fraction of its past heritage, though a serpentine array of atmospheric medieval lanes still crisscross the old quarter. Today it's a quietly expanding agricultural town with an earthy rural character that's given a jet-age buzz by its vibrant student population.

LAY OF THE LAND

Inland Lleida's landscape and climate are totally different from those of its Mediterranean neighbors Tarragona and Girona. Though set in a fertile plain that produces an abundance of grapes, olives, and citrus fruits, it's surrounded by less-hospitable terrains, with the arid badlands of Aragón to the west and the wild gullies and canyons of the Pallars regions to the north. Its summers are very hot—untempered by sea breezes—and its winters can be bitterly cold. This exhilaratingly varied "continental" climate has more in common with central Castile than the rest of Catalonia.

GETTING TO & AROUND LLEIDA

For general information, contact the **Lleida Tourist Office** (Av. Madrid 36; ☎ 973-27-09-97; www.turismedelleida.com).

Trains and **buses** run regularly into Lleida south and southeast from Tarragona and Barcelona, and west from Zaragoza and Madrid. From Lleida railway station, FGC trains depart regularly for Pyrenean destinations, including Tremp (1½ hr.; 5.15€), La Pobla de Segur (1¾ hr.; 5.15€), and El Pont de Suert (the closest town to the Aigüestortes National Park). Buses (5.50€–6€ one-way) cover the same routes. For departure times, call ☎ 973-268-500 (9am–1pm).

This is an area that can be particularly rewarding if you have a **car** to get around. A reliable rental company is **ATESA** (Av. Garrigues 40; ☎ 977-212-428; www.atesa.es); its prices start at around 130€ per week for a small car such as a Ford Fiesta.

ACCOMMODATIONS, BOTH STANDARD & NOT

Lleida and its province have a rich variety of rooms and are wonderful places to try the basic but scenic and extremely cheap *refugis i albergs* (mountain refuges and hostels) predominantly in the peaceful and totally unspoiled rural areas north and northwest of Lleida up near the Pyrenees (see the "Refuge in the Pyrenees" box, below).

€   In town itself, the budgeters choice is the **Goya** (Alcalde Costa 9; ☎ 973-266-788; MC, V). Yes, the owner may be a bit dour, but her hotel, which lies at the western edge in an extension of the main traffic-free Eix shopping area, is a positive *ganga* (bargain) at just 40€ to 45€ a night for a double. It costs even less (30€–35€) if you're prepared to accept a room with shared bathroom amenities. From the outside, the building is blandly modern, but inside it's a different story: The whole place has been most impressively renovated, from the spotless reception area and corridors to the rooms themselves, which are all good sized with dark wood furnishings, comfortable beds, gleaming white walls, TVs, and pristine en suite bathrooms.

€ Right in the very heart of town, you'll find the traditional, if nowadays endearingly well-worn, **Hotel Principal** (Plaça de la Paeria 7; ☎ 973-23-08-00; MC, V), a genuine Lleidan institution that stands beside a central colonnaded and pedestrianized square where singers regularly croon *habaneras* (nostalgic Cuban songs introduced to Spain by returning emigrants) in the evenings. Rooms are fair-sized with tiled floors, comfy beds, aging wooden blinds, a pine writing desk, and good cupboard space, and each has its own bath/shower. Principal's quiet, too, with only the local church clock chiming every hour—and briefly on the quarter-hour—to disturb you. Included in the doubles standard price (55€–60€) is a hearty buffet breakfast taken in the ground-floor lounge beside a bar where you'll see the odd local pop in for a morning pick-me-up of anis. The multilingual staff could not be more friendly and obliging.

DINING FOR ALL TASTES

Lleida has its own Catalán culinary tradition. Its range of local dishes from *trucha as fines èrbes* (trout in fine herbs) to *òlha aronesa* (a cocido-like stew of beans, rice, celery leeks, and lamb, originating from the Vall d'Aran) have long been a source of admiration among resident and passing foodies. Snails (*caracoles* in Spanish and *cargols* in Catalán) are a particular passion with the Lleidans, and special tastings take place during the *Aplec del Cargol* ("Snail Fair") in May, when stalls set up on the south side of the River Segre serve seemingly endless plates of local snails cooked in an infinite variety of ways.

€–€€ You may initially feel there's a perverse conspiracy to put you off eating at the **Casa Tiell** ✸ (calle María Savet; ☎ 973-223-003; Mon–Sat 1:30–4pm; cash only). For a start, it's hard to find, as there's no name or street number above the entrance. And when you do manage to track it down, just a short walk south of the railway station, the bilious green exterior—its only real identifying factor—is hardly encouraging to the appetite. But step inside and you'll find this is all a coy sham. The family who own it, and the regulars who frequent it, just want to keep to themselves the fact that this is the best-value luncheon spot in town. (No evening meals are served.) There are two excellent fixed-price menus—one for vegetarians—at just 9€, the other at around 12€. Most of the grub—from *champiñones* to *croquetas*—is standard Catalán fare, but the portions and quality are superb. The local table wine that accompanies it is good, too.

€–€€ Really a tapas bar par excellence, the rustic **El Portón** ✸ (Sant Martí 53; ☎ 973-224-304; Mon–Sat 1:30–3:30pm and 8pm–midnight; cash only) is hidden away at the back of town just behind the great Seu cathedral. It serves such a tastily affordable variety of mini-dishes that you can gorge yourself without unduly bending the wallet. Fill yourself up on standards such as *tortilla* (omelet), *jamón serrano* (mountain ham), and *calamares* (squid), for about 8€ to 10€, including a couple of glasses of local wine. Expect to pay at least double that if you have a full restaurant meal.

WHY YOU'RE HERE: THE TOP SIGHTS & ATTRACTIONS

Though the past orgy of sieges (see "A Brief History of Lleida," above) left relatively few surviving monuments of real interest, a notable exception is the huge **Seu Vella (Old Cathedral)** ✚ (☎ 972-230-653; 2.50€, free Tues; summer Tues–Sun 10am–1:30pm and 4–7:30pm, winter 3–5:30pm) located entirely within the walls of the former (now ruined) La Suda fortress. Begun in the 13th century and finished a hundred years later, it's a superb meeting point of Romanesque and Gothic styles, with the occasional exotic Mozarabic traces. The most impressive feature is its great Gothic cloister, its multifaceted arcades skillfully woven together with the most intricate stonework. Its lanky, almost disproportionately tall tower is equipped with seven individually named bells (2 of them made in the 15th century) and can be seen from far off. You can get up to the Seu by walking briskly uphill for about 15 minutes from the city center or taking the aging elevator from behind the Plaça de Sant Joan (operating Tues–Sat 10am–2pm and 3–6pm; in winter 3–5pm only) for .50€.

Behind the cathedral in the stylish 16th-century Hospital de Santa María you'll come across a rarely patronized oddity, the **Museo Arqueológic** (☎ 972-271-500; free admission; Tues–Fri noon–2pm and 6–9pm, Sat 11am–2pm and 7–9pm, Sun 11am–2pm). This admittedly modest collection of Roman finds and artifacts might not be worth the trouble of a visit if it weren't for its hidden patio, which is a great place for relaxing on a sunny day with a book should those exhibits fail to set you on fire.

ACTIVE LLEIDA

Lleida province, with its sparsely populated and richly varied countryside, is one of Spain's leading areas for adventure sports, from canoeing and rafting to paragliding and skiing. (See "Get Out of Town," below.) Other less high-powered activities include playing golf and taking country walks.

For **golfers,** the nearest course is the 18-hole **Raimat Golf** (calle Afores, Raimat, 10km/6½ miles from Lleida; ☎ 973-73-75-40; www.raimatgolf.com; summer 9am–9pm, winter 9am–6pm). Greens fees are 45€ on weekdays, 70€ weekends. Designed by a highly respected local architect, Pepín Rivero, it's among the most prestigious courses in Catalonia, and its 6th hole—where the terrain drops 50m (164 ft.) from tee-off point to the green—is seen as a particularly stimulating challenge by serious players. Set in a fertile valley surrounded by oaks, pines, and vineyards, it's quite the lushest-looking course in the whole province and a delight to play on, whatever your level of proficiency.

Walkers, meanwhile, can follow several easy, well-marked itineraries along the Canal d'Urgell and in the Segre Valley close to Lleida capital. Pop into the **Patronat de Turisme de les Terres de Lleida** (Rambla Ferran 18—3°; ☎ 973-900-900; www.lleidatur.com; Mon–Fri 9am–2pm and 4:30–8pm, Sat 9am–2pm) to collect a map of this gentle lowland area, known as the "Holland of Lleida" because of its predominance of decades-old canals, which serve to irrigate the region. As long as you avoid the very hot months of July and August, a stroll alongside the canals—or River Segre itself—past orchards, olive groves, and vineyards is a relaxing pleasure. There's also a wide variety of local and migrant bird life here for ornithologists—amateur or otherwise—to observe en route.

ATTENTION, SHOPPERS!

Lleidans take their shopping very seriously and, as a result, have evolved what they claim to be the biggest shopping complex in Spain, namely **Eix** (www.eixcomercial lleida.com). This is not a standard modern commercial center or mall but an existing area of the Old City just below the Seu, which—while still preserving the original local architecture—has been converted into a pedestrianized area extending over 3km (2 miles) between Carrer Carme and Carrer Sant Antoni. Within its confines, over 400 shops cater to an estimated 15,000 shoppers a day, selling everything you'll ever need from books and sports items to jewelry to leatherwear—and all at understandably competitive prices. The best place to buy leather goods, by the way, is **Rodamilans** (Carrer Sant Antoni 46; ☎ 973-271-585; www.rodamilans-botigues.com).

NIGHTLIFE

Thanks to its large student population, Lleida is not as quiet after sunset as you might think. The streets around **Avinguda Prat de la Ribera**—at the northern end of town—are especially lively with bars and cafes open till the early hours. A popular late-night weekend rendezvous spot near the lower end of this avenue is **l'Antic** (Comptes d'Urgell 55; no phone; Thurs–Sat 10pm–5am; 10€ cover), which has two vibrant and very noisy salons catering to a variety of musical tastes. One specializes in Latin and Salsa, while the other is more into house club sounds.

A more mellow alternative to this ear bashing locale is the centrally located Irish-pub-styled **Antares** (Ballesteros 15; ☎ 619-855-043; daily 7pm–2am; cover 10€–12€), where you can enjoy nightly music with live jazz artists performing on Fridays.

During the gray unseasonable month of November, the city is livened up by its annual **Folk and Jazz Festival,** which claims to be international but is essentially a Hispanic celebration in which top Spanish and Catalán performers such as Joaquín Sabina and Joan Manuel Serrat perform in **Antares** (above) as well as in more low-key establishments such as the moderniste **Café Teatre del Excorxador** (Lluis Companys s/n; ☎ 973-279-356).

GET OUT OF TOWN

Vineyards, Mountains & Valleys

This area of Spain produces some excellent wines that are still barely known outside the country, so if you have a taste for the grape, schedule some time to tipple at the local bodegas. You can get a comprehensive list of top bodegas from Rosa Sánchez Muñoz at the **Costers del Segre office** (Complex de la Caparella 97; ☎ 973-26-45-83; www.costersdelsegre.es) in Lleida town, but you'll have to make contact with the bodega yourself, as well as making your own way there. Among the most highly renowned for the quality of its hearty red Oda Negre and Gotim Bru vintages is **Castell del Remei** (Finca Castell del Remei; ☎ 973-58-02-00; www.castelldelremei.com; Mon–Fri 9am–1pm and 3–6pm, Sat 4–7pm, Sun 10am–1pm) 40km (25 miles) west of Lleida off the A3 road to Balaguer and Tarrega, close to the village of Bellcaire. The bodega is open to the public and no charge is made for the visit, which includes a tour around the cellars, old distillery, and barrel workshop—as well as an 18th-century olive press. Tastings can be had by prior arrangement. Occasional free classical concerts are held in the bodega, so if you plan it right you could combine a little culture and hedonism.

A regional highlight is the famed **Raimat Grape Harvest** held at the village of that name during the first fortnight in October, where attractions also include theatrical shows and a communal lunch with (of course) plenty of wine. See www.lleidatur.com for a wealth of further details on wine and gastronomical events, including visits to the olive oil producing region of **Les Garrigues.**

Catalonia's only officially recognized National Park, the **Parc Nacional d'Aigüestortes i l'Estany de Maurici** ★★ (120km/80 miles north of Lleida) is one of just 10 that exist in the whole of Spain. It's a Pyrenean wonderland of meadows, forests, waterfalls, pristine lakes, and wild serrated mountain peaks such as the awesome **Les Encantats.** The main town is **Sort,** a high-summer tourist center that's packed with tourists in July and August, with shops selling equipment for a variety of river and mountain adventure sports. Just 5km (3 miles) north of Sort at the hamlet of Rialp is the **Port-Ainé Sports Center** (☎ 902-190-192) whose 44 kilometers (27 miles) of ski slopes are enclosed by wildly beautiful mountains. Ski lifts here charge 31€ a day for adults and 22€ for children (or 55€ and 39€, respectively, for a whole weekend), and added winter attractions include short trips on dog-drawn sledges. In summer, the center also arranges white-water rafting trips (from 13€ per person) and rock climbing outings (from 15€ per person).

The neighboring **Vall del Boí** and its emblematic **Sant Climent de Taüll church** ★, one of nine local Romanesque ecclesiastical gems that earned the whole valley a UNESCO Heritage Award in 2000, is a cultural beauty zone. The churches' original interior frescoes have long been moved to the MNAC in Barcelona (p. 292) to protect them from the severe Pyrenean winters; replicas now stand in their place. There are no fixed hours for visiting the church and no contact phone number. To gain access, you have to obtain the key from a local resident whose name and address the **Oficina de Turismo** (Plaza de Santa María 1; ☎ 973-69-40-00) in Taüll village will provide. The small town of **Boí** (1km/⅔ mile from Taüll) is popular and crowded in summer, providing sports like trekking, horseback riding, and mountain biking for those who feel the culture is not enough. It also houses the **Casa del Parc Nacional d'Aigüestortes i l'Estany de Maurici Information Office** (Plaça del Treio 3; ☎ 973-69-61-89); the entrance to the park is only 3km (2 miles) away. The area abounds with lakes, reservoirs, and rivers. Two small local agencies providing local aquatic activities are the **Centro NauticoAlta Ribagorça Aventura** at the nearby Pantano de Escales (☎ 608-63-56-59), which arranges rafting and canoeing trips, and the **Escuela de Pesca Efemera** on the Carretera Vall de Boi Km 0.5 (☎ 973-69-05-02 or 639-00-88-72), which provides fishing courses.

Completing the trio of Shangri-La valleys that fill this favored northwestern corner of Catalonia is the evergreen, butterfly-filled **Vall d'Aran** bordering the French Aquitaine. More like its Gallic neighbor than Spain, it even has its own French-influenced language: Aranese. The tiny capital is **Vielha,** with its central 12th-century church of Sant Miquèu and slate-topped, wooden-balconied stone buildings. Nearby, close to the tiny town of Salardú, is Spain's largest and most

Refuge in the Pyrenees

Mountains, woods, wildflowers . . . but without camping out. Here are some of the best of the Pyrenean Mountains refuges and *casas rurales,* for those who prefer alpine vistas to crowded beaches:

€ **La Bruna** 🧒 (Pla de Codina 2-20; ☎ 973-510-876; www.albergla bruna.com; cash only), located in the picturesque Pyrenean town of Bellver de Cerdanya, used to be an army barracks. Don't be put off! It's been thoroughly renovated and is well-equipped with all mod cons, even down to free Wi-Fi. The basic but clean rooms accommodate two to eight people, and all are equipped with bunk beds and en suite full bathrooms. Room-only prices range from just 25€ to 28€ per person per night, rising to 43€ to 42€ if you decide to take full board. (Otherwise, the set 3-course menu for lunch or dinner is 9.50€.) Other amenities include a lounge, music bar with games tables, and a swimming pool. The surrounding wooded countryside is ideal for leisurely walks.

€ **Refugi Gedar** (☎ 973-250-170; www.refugigerdar.com; cash only; closed Oct 16–Dec) is set inside the Aiguestortes and Sant Mauricio National Park close to the largest fir-tree forests in Spain. A large, traditional triangular-roofed mountain house, run by a friendly couple called Kiko and Jezabel, it has been converted into a modest *pensione.* Parties of four to eight people are accommodated in simple, clean rooms with bunk beds (you need to bring your own sleeping bag) and private bathrooms. Price per person here is 20€ including breakfast, though after the first night you have to take half-board at 32€ per person. If you like hearty traditional cooking you'll be in your element here as the restaurant provides dishes like *carne a la brasa* (wood-fire barbecued veal cutlets or

prestigious ski resort, **Bacqueira-Beret** (☎ 973-63-90-10; www.bacqueira.es), which was built in 1964 and named after two tiny villages in the scenic Pla de Beret valley. Here, in winter, you may see the King of Spain, a regular visitor, whizzing down the slopes or taking a more leisurely trip along the well-marked 7km (4⅓-mile) cross-country ski circuit. In summer, you can take exhilarating cable car rides (a brand-new model was installed in 2008) up to spectacular viewpoints (2 have restaurants) and go walking along mountain trails.

steaks). Nearby you can stroll in the forests, climb mountain slopes, and go rafting on the fast flowing rivers.

€   **Casa Font** (☎ 973-621-778), with six bedrooms (40€ per double), is a particularly tranquil family-run *casa rural*. Decor is homespun, with rustic pine-wood ceilings and bedsteads, very comfortable beds, and plenty of wardrobe space, though rooms share two full-size bathrooms. Communal facilities include a washing machine and a kitchen where you can prepare your own snacks. Casa Font itself is a fine, old, stone-built house with a traditional silver-hued slate roof located near a *font* (fountain) in the hamlet of Seuri in the Assua Valley 12km (8 miles) from the regional capital, Sort. The area is filled with lovely little Romanesque churches and offers idyllic walks along marked woodland and mountain trails.

€–€€   **Fonda Farré d'Avall** (calle Mayor 10; ☎ 973-694-029; www.farre daval.com; MC, V; closed Dec 25) is a majestic period house in the village of Barruera in the Alta Ribagorça region near the Boi Valley and close to the Pyrenees. This 14-room inn is also a working farm. All rooms have polished wood floors and ceilings, white walls, cozy beds, TV, Wi-Fi—should you decide to bring your own computer—and fully equipped bathrooms. They cost 65€ to 70€ a night including breakfast, and the superb lunch and dinner menus will set you back 17€ and are worth every centime.

Important note: It's essential to have at least a working knowledge of Spanish to book any of the above direct. Alternatively, you can make bookings though the following websites: www.lleidatur.com (the Lleida Tourist Board) and www.casa-fonda.com.

GETTING THERE

Alsa buses (www.alsa.es) run three times a day from Lleida bus station (calle Saracibar 2; ☎ 973-268-500) to Sort and Pont de Suert—each of which is located some 20km (12 miles) from the Aigüetortes park (southwest and southeast, respectively), and if you're the energetic outdoor type, long well-marked walking trails will lead you up into the park. **Alsa** buses also run three times a day from Lleida to Vielha (3 hr.) from where a local bus service operates to Salardú and Bacqueira-Beret. But for both these areas, a rental car is virtually essential if you're going to fully enjoy and explore them at leisure.

8 The Basque Country

Modern architecture, exquisite food, and an ancient and proud heritage make this one of Spain's most exciting regions

by Peter Stone

WHENEVER I GO INTO THE BASQUE COUNTRY I FEEL I'VE CROSSED NOT ONE but two borders and traveled a further 1,000 miles again north. Perhaps that has something to do with its mysteriously ancient language, which bears no resemblance to anything else spoken or written in these latitudes (see later box). Or maybe it's the countryside with its misty coastline, backed by an inland patchwork of Celtic-emerald grass-rich fields and valleys and high wooded mountains, which makes such a strong contrast to the parched terrain of the central Castilian *meseta* (plateau) and the garishly sun-drenched and overbuilt Mediterranean coast. The atmosphere is different: (comparatively) sedate and reserved, with the Alpine-like roofs of its inland country houses almost hinting at a Hispanic Switzerland. The weather is certainly different: often rainy and unsettled—while the vegetation consists less of palm trees and orange groves than of oaks and blackberry bushes, and the fields are full of cows. (Local chefs often make meals cooked in butter instead of olive oil.)

Its provincial capitals are also exhilaratingly different, not only from those of the rest of the country but also from each other. **Bilbao,** famed for decades as a dynamic but badly polluted industrial port, has ingeniously reinvented itself over the past decade as an ecologically aware, avant-garde architecture mecca. **San Sebastián** is the classiest coastal town in Spain, patronized by royals and multimillionaires and basking (no pun intended) in an unrivaled location beside a crescent bay framed by two headlands. The sandy, tide-washed beaches along its surrounding coast are also superb, and, as if that weren't enough, the restaurants have the best cuisine (and priciest menus) in the land. **Vitoria-Gasteiz,** the Basque's administrative capital, is the untrumpeted "secret achiever" of the three—a "green" city par excellence, winner of a UNESCO award for its clean-air policies, and regarded by many as having the best quality of life in Spain. Still largely unknown to most outside visitors, it lies way inland in wilder and slightly more arid country than its coastal counterparts, close to the rich wine lands of La Rioja.

The Basque country (or *País Vasco*), proud of all these differences and fiercely independent, barely regards itself as Spanish. Many Basques want nothing short of total self-rule, and their attitude is expressed in its most peaceful and civilized form by the autonomous Basque government *lehendaraki* (or leader) Juan José Ibarretxe, whose proposed new statute for independence has so far been rejected by Madrid, and in its most intransigent form by the ruthless minority terrorist

342

group ETA, who believe violence is the only way to achieve their goal and have, in recent years, declared and then broken several ceasefires as negotiations have—at least in their eyes—collapsed. (This is not to imply that visiting the area is dangerous, by the way. Politics rarely intrude on the holiday scene and the Basque people are exceptionally friendly and welcoming to outside visitors.)

DON'T LEAVE
THE BASQUE COUNTRY WITHOUT . . .

Seeing Bilbao's Guggenheim Museum.   Frank Gehry's titanium-sculpted masterpiece put Bilbao back on the map. See p. 351.

Strolling San Sebastián's La Concha Bay.   The loveliest city beach in Spain, it's a perfect sandy crescent of gently shelving sand enclosed by two headlands, backed by superb period buildings. See p. 364.

Admiring Vitoria-Gasteiz's Artium.   This white gleaming 21st-century cultural center is the Alavan capital's answer to Bilbao's Guggenheim. See p. 370.

Experiencing Pamplona's San Fermines Fiestas.   Whether you think it's crass, cruel, or simply crazy, there's no denying the energy of the whole frenzied July spectacle as mad-as-hell bulls charge down the narrow streets intent on getting their own back (see below).

LAY OF THE LAND

The three Spanish Basque provinces of Vizcaya (Biskaia), Guipúzcoa (Gipuzkoa), and inland Alava (Araba)—with their respective capitals Bilbao (Bilbo), San Sebastián (Donostia), and Vitoria-Gasteiz—occupy the high northeastern corner of Spain bordering France's own Basque region around Biarritz and Bayonne. Here the shoreline is an almost endless procession of inlets, long beaches, and wooded headlands behind which verdant valleys and forested hills spread from the eastern part of the Cantabrian peaks to the high ocean-straddling Pyrenean mountain range. It's a lushly fertile zone kept green by the omnipresent *txirimiri* (gentle drizzle) that typifies the local year-round mild climate. Farther south, toward La Rioja province, the countryside becomes drier, sunnier, more austerely Castilian-like with fewer trees, more exposed plains, brief hot summers, and often bitterly cold winters.

A BRIEF HISTORY OF THE BASQUE COUNTRY

That spirit of independence seems to have been there from the start. Successive Roman, Visigothic, and Moorish invaders failed to subdue the early Vascones, a Celtic tribe that held out in impregnable strongholds in the Pyrenees by fighting off, or making deals with, its would-be oppressors. In this way, the people managed to hang onto their traditions and language. They united under one ruler in the 9th century to form the Kingdom of Navarra and 300 years later formulated their laws in official *fueros* (municipal charters). These were respected even when they later became part of Castile, with centralist Madrid—their real ruler—recognizing their ancient rights and privileges until the 1876 Carlist Wars, when they

Who Are the Basques?

While it's largely acknowledged that they're probably the most ancient ethnic group in Europe, experts have puzzled for years over where the Basques actually came from in the first place. One theory is that they're descendents of the original Iberians who lived in Spain before the arrival of the Celts some 3,500 years ago. Successive invaders—Romans, Arabs, and Visigoths—probably drove them into the Pyrenean regions, where they stayed and evolved their own lifestyle, customs, and traditions, many of which are still practiced to this day. The Basque language (known as *Euskera*), with its tongue-twisting surfeit of *k*s, *t*s, and *x*s, bears no resemblance to any Latin-based language, unlike the at least partially recognizable and understandable Catalán spoken over on Spain's Pyrenean-Mediterranean side. Largely as a political gesture to show independence after the death of Franco and his brutally repressive treatment of the Basques (especially at Guernica—see below), their language is now taught in schools, spoken on TV stations in the region, and written on road signs (alongside Castilian Spanish) although it's still estimated that of the 2.5 million inhabitants of the region only 40% actually speak and understand the language.

were abolished—an action that led to the rebellious formation of the PNV (Basque Nationalist Party). The region suffered successive periods of repression, which ended after the death of General Franco in 1975.

Although the province has achieved quite substantial levels of autonomy since then and now has its own police force and parliament, ETA, the separatist movement seeking total independence from Spain (see introduction) is still actively simmering, and the unbending but increasingly-isolated militants returned to their now desperate policy of intimidation by murder in December 2005, when two Ecuadorians died in a Madrid airport bombing. They didn't stop there, in spite of national condemnation. In 2007, two policemen were assassinated in neighboring France and just before the Spanish General Elections in March 2008, a PSOE (socialist) candidate in a small Basque mountain town was murdered by an ETA gunman in an apparent attempt to deter people from voting. This in spite of various failed ceasefire agreements and reconciliation attempts—strongly criticized by the right wing PP (Conservative Partido Popular) party—on the part of the socialist Madrid-run government who, under José Luis Rodriguez Zapatero, were successfully reelected in March 2008.

BILBAO (BILBO)

Bilbao never claimed to be the most beautiful city in Spain. A few decades back, the Nervión River (like a sluggish brown snake) slithered between the sad gray buildings and chimneys belched fumes into the overcast skies. Traffic-ridden, gloomy, and drizzly, it was the sort of nightmare place visitors escaped as soon as

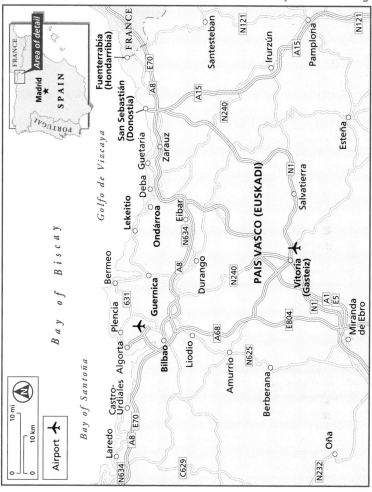

they could. Today, the weather's still the same—with sunny intervals, *naturelle-ment*—but practically everything else has changed for the better. The now sparklingly renovated riverfront has greatly helped erase that Bilbaino image of industrial smoke stacks and polluted waters. The Nervión, more attractively re-named the Ría de Bilbao, is cleaner. The Old Quarter is largely pedestrianized and its monuments, alleyways, and main colonnaded square are immaculate. And then—icing on the cake—there's Frank Gehry's giant rolled tinfoil masterpiece, the Guggenheim Museum, a name that instantly comes to everyone's mind when you mention Bilbao today. This winning move to culture and ecological con-sciousness seems a natural follow-up to the once flourishing—but now defunct—activities of shipbuilding, and steel-making that made the city great in the 19th century. And when it comes to exploring the city, it's so neatly divided into different zones—the Casco Antiguo, the new Ensanche, and the river and hillside areas—that it somehow seems smaller, more intimate, and more manageable than its half-million population suggests.

LAY OF THE LAND

Bilbao extends more than 8km (5 miles) down the serpentine valley of the River Nervión (or Ría de Bilbao) between green hills often shrouded by the area's gently swishing rain. Its name, incidentally, is said to have originated from two Basque words, *bi albo,* which mean "two sides," referring to the two banks of the river, which separates the old and new zones. To the north, along its Bay of Biscay coastline, a variety of attractive former fishing towns turned resorts with long sandy beaches and prominent headlands stretches in both directions. Inland lies a paradise of green valleys and wooded hilltops dotted with religious shrines, chapels, and hermitages, a delight for walkers, climbers, and lovers of historic monuments.

GETTING TO & AROUND BILBAO
Getting There

Bilbao's dazzling **airport** (Aeropuerto de Sordika, ☎ 902-222-265 and 944-533-340; www.aena.es)—innovatively designed by architect Santiago Calatrava who was responsible for Valencia's City of Science—is at Sondika just 10km (6½ miles) out of town. Flights arrive daily from Madrid, Barcelona, and a wide variety other Spanish destinations, as well as from major European cities such as Brussels, Frankfurt, Lisbon, London, Milan, Paris, and Zurich. Cheapest flights from the U.K. are by airline easyJet (www.easyjet.com; no phone) from London's Stansted airport and often work out around 100€ one-way, half the usual scheduled fares. **Iberia**'s main booking office is at the airport (☎ 902-400-500; daily 5am–10pm). A frequent bus service (every half-hour 6:15am–midnight) transports visitors in 40 minutes from the airport to Plaza Moyua in the new city center for 1.25€. Taxis into the town center cost around 20€.

There are also three railway stations in Bilbao, and traveling here by **train** usually costs around half the most economical scheduled flight fare. The busiest is the RENFE station, **Estación de Abando** (Plaza Circular 2, just off Plaza de España; ☎ 902-240-202; www.renfe.es), with trains arriving here from most parts of Spain: several a day from Madrid (4 hr. 45 min. on the Alvia, 45€ one-way; 6 hr. on the afternoon Talgo, 40€ one-way); two a day from Barcelona (9 hr., 40€ day train one-way; 10 hr., 51€ overnight train one-way); one train a day from Vigo in Galicia (11 hr.; 43€); and one overnight train a day from Málaga (14 hr.; 50€ one-way). Euskoktren trains also connect the city with nearby coastal and inland towns from here. Adjoining Abando is the **Estación de Santander,** which has regular connections with the Cantabrian capital situated 100km (62 miles) west (p. 414). It's a leisurely, economical, and very scenic ride if you're in no hurry. East of the Casco Viejo is the third station, **Estación Atxuri,** from which there are other rather slow but cheap rail connections with the two other Basque regional capitals: easterly coastal **San Sebastián** and inland **Vitoria-Gasteiz.**

If you happen to live in the U.K. or are combining a U.K. visit with one to Spain, you might consider arriving by **sea** (a useful entry point, though it can

Bilbao

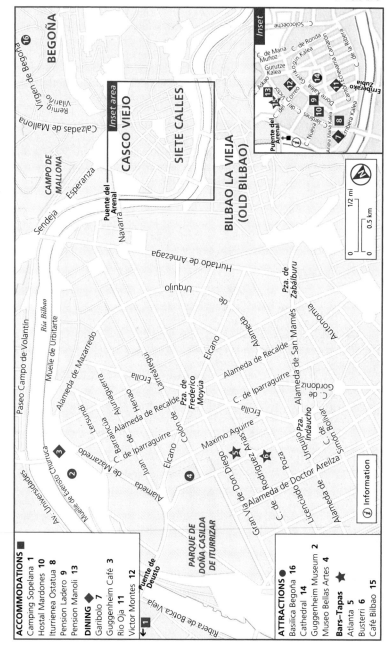

Inset

C. Solocoeche

C. de Maria Muñoz
C. de Ronda
Gojin Kalea
C. de la Ribera

Gurutze Kalea
13
Askao
1 C. del Victor
12 C. del Correo
14
Dorre Kalea
Camiño Etchevarria Camarón
Erribera zubia
Erriberako zubia
9
10
Andra Maria Kalea
Erribera Kalea
8
7
C. Nueva

Puente del Arenal

(i)

BEGOÑA
16
Remig. Virgen de Begoña
Remig. Vilariño

Calzadas de Mallona

CAMPO DE MALLONA

Esperanza

Sendeja

Navarra

Puente del Arenal

CASCO VIEJO

SIETE CALLES

BILBAO LA VIEJA (OLD BILBAO)

Hurtado de Amézaga

Urquijo

de

Pza. de Zabálburu

Autonomia

Ría Bilbao

Muelle de Ubitiarte

Paseo Campo de Volantín

Alameda de Mazarredo

Ercilla

Larreategui

Alameda de Recalde

Henao

C. Barraincua

Ajuriaguerra

Lersundi

C. de Iparraguirre

Juan de Mazarredo

Alameda de

Colón de Larreategui

Elcano

Pza. de Frederico Moyúa

Elcano

Alameda de Recalde

Alameda de San Mamés

C. de Iparraguirre

Ercilla

C. de Gordoniz

Máximo Aguirre
5

6

Pza. Indaucho

C. de Urquijo

poza

Alameda de Simón Bolívar

Gran Vía de Don Diego

C. de Rodríguez Arias

Alameda de Doctor Areilza

Licenciado Poza

Alameda de Doctor Areilza

Av. Universidades

Muelle de Enrico Churruca

3

2

4

PARQUE DE DOÑA CASILDA DE ITURRIZAR

Puente de Deusto
1

Ribera de Botica Vieja

1/2 mi
0.5 km

(i) Information

ACCOMMODATIONS ■
Camping Sopelana **1**
Hostal Mardones **10**
Iturrienea Ostatua **8**
Pension Ladero **9**
Pension Manoli **13**

DINING ◆
Garibolo **7**
Guggenheim Café **3**
Rio Oja **11**
Victor Montes **12**

ATTRACTIONS ●
Basilica Begoña **16**
Cathedral **14**
Guggenheim Museum **2**
Museo Bellas Artes **4**

Bars–Tapas ★
Atlanta **5**
Busterri **6**
Café Bilbao **15**

prove expensive). **P & O Ferries** (www.poferries.com.) operate a service on a large ship called the Pride of Bilbao (equipped with several restaurants, a movie house, a pool, and even a casino) across the English Channel and Bay of Biscay from **Portsmouth** to the U.K. docks at Santurtzi on the opposite shore of the Ría de Bilbao from Getxo. It's really a 2-night mini-cruise aimed at travelers who are taking a car; it can cost between 150€ and 200€ per person. Departures from Portsmouth are 8pm Tuesdays and Thursdays. Check www.poferries.com for the best rates.

PESA (☎ 902-10-12-10; www.pesa.net), at the **Estación de Buses de Garellano** (calle Gurtubay 1; ☎ 944-395-077; www.termibus.es), runs more than a dozen **buses** per day here from San Sebastián (1½ hours; 9.65€). Buses from Madrid's avenida de America station provide the cheapest option for traveling to Bilbao within Spain. **Continental Auto** has offices at the Bilbao bus station (☎ 944-274-200) and operates nine buses per day from the Spanish capital (5 hr.; 35€ one-way).

Finally, those with rental **cars** should know that Bilbao is right beside the A-8, linking the cities of Spain's northern Atlantic seacoast to western France. There is superhighway access from both Barcelona and Madrid.

Getting Around

In and around the metropolitan area are an interconnected web of **buses** (Biskaiabuses), **metro trains,** and **surface trams** (Euskotranes). The most practical and economical way to use these various forms of transport is to buy a **BilbaoCard** which costs 6€ for 1 day, 10€ for 2 days, and 12€ for 3 days. It also entitles you to use the **Artxanda Funicular,** which rises from the Paseo del Campo Volantín to Monte Artxanda (which has great panoramic city views). Alternatively, you can buy a collective **Creditrans fare pass** for 5€ to 15€ (available from tram stops and kiosks), which provides a discount on normal fare prices.

Buses within the city limits are red (1.10€ per trip); those that run to outer parts of the city (Biskaibuses) are colored blue and yellow and charge 1.25€ per trip. The stylish **Metro** (opened in 1995) was designed by Norman Foster and operates a very smooth and frequent (roughly every 4 min.) service from Extebarri in the south across the city center to Santurzi in the north. Single-journey tickets cost 1.20€. You enter these stations via slinky tubular steel-and-glass burrows known locally as *fosteritos.* The **Euskostrans** started operating in 2002 along a single line that connects the Guggenheim museum and Old Quarter with the San Mamés bus station. For general information, check with the **Oficina de Turismo** (Plaza Ensanche 11; ☎ 944-795-760; www.bilbao.net; Mon–Fri 9am–2pm and 4–7:30pm).

ACCOMMODATIONS, BOTH STANDARD & NOT

The high-tech, architectural razzmatazz of the city is eye-popping, but if you want to really understand the Basque soul, you need to get out into the countryside. Happily, the Basque government has made that a relatively risk-free and affordable proposition. In 1991, it created the **Nekazal Turismoa–Landa Turismoa** commission to encourage farm owners to take in guests and train inspectors to rate and accredit these new lodgings, which, by law, were to be affordable in their pricing. (The system they set up is based on Italy's wonderful and well-run *agriturismo* system.)

Today, when you visit www.nekatur.net (the government's site and the best place to research and book these accommodations), you'll find both full farmhouse rentals and guesthouses within farms, fully inspected, that sometimes drop down to as little as 30€ to 40€ per night for a double room; large groups can rent complete houses for half that amount per person (see below). And what's lovely about these places—and I've visited a number—is what they show about the personality of the folks who own them. These are not sterile vacation rentals; instead, you'll find real homes with knickknacks, family heirlooms, and photos of the cousins on the wall. All in all, Nekatur's choice is huge and spreads throughout the three sub-provinces.

The only two snags with this sort of lodging: July and August are inevitably more expensive, especially near the coast, and car rental may be an essential in some of the more isolated properties.

€ If renting a car is off-putting, but you're still looking for affordable rural digs, look at **Camping Sopelana** 🧒 (Playa Atxabiribil 30; ☎ 946-76-19-81; www.camping-sopelana.com; MC, V), which is right off the beach and within easy walking distance of the Metro stop in the town of Sopelana (from which you'll be able to zip quickly into the heart of Bilbao). Campsites are 6€ per person, but there are also cute (if frill-free) bungalows for rent here at just 24€ per night. Children will enjoy the playground and pool.

€ Also consider the slightly out-of-the-way **Pension Ladero** (calle Lotería 1; ☎ 944-150-932; www.pensionladero.es)—it's situated in the east riverside suburb of **Algorta,** a smooth half-hour's metro ride from the center and in easy reach of the city's main beaches. Here, a traditionally Basque room (pine furnishings and mellow corkwood floors give them a woodsy appeal) with shared bath cost 35€ year-round without any summer increases. The extremely helpful staff speak a limited amount of English.

Casco Viejo (Old Quarter)

€ A place that particularly attracted me in this atmospheric little district is the well-run **Pension Manoli** (Askatasuna 2; ☎ 944-155-636; MC, V), which occupies four floors (no lift) of an old building just off the Plaza Nueva right in the heart of *pintxo* land. It's a very friendly place and its genial owners have lived in this barrio for many years. Yes, rooms here are small, but they're spotless and you won't be tripping over your luggage. (There's plenty of wardrobe space.) A double with shared bath/shower costs 40€ a night.

€–€€ Close by and just off the same square, **Hostal Mardones** (calle Jardines, 4-2º-4ª; ☎ 944-153-105; www.hostalmardones.com; MC, V) is another very welcoming lodging that tries hard to please. Restored from a former town house that's retained the original oak beams, Mardones is in a prime Old Quarter location just a few steps from the river and the main covered market. Here you'll find warmly and intimately lit bedrooms with cream walls, polished parquet floors, light-wood bedsteads and dressers, and compact white-tiled en suite bathrooms. Room rates range from 40€ to 75€ per night depending on the season.

€–€€   My personal Casco Viejo favorite, a real pearl of a place, is, the **Iturrienea Ostatua** ✪✪ (calle Santa María 14; ☎ 944-161-500; www.iturrienea ostatua.com; DC, MC, V). Owned by two Basque sculptors, Jesus Chueca and Roberto Atance, the decor is informed by their artistic sensibilities—from the original art and curious on the walls to the pretty lighting fixtures. The house itself is also quite beautiful: a restored town house with wooden beams and 19th-century stone floors. It's stimulating, charismatic, and an excellent value for money (65€–75€ double). There's even a small cafe on-site and a garden. The one downside? The front rooms can be noisy, so ask for a room at the rear.

DINING FOR ALL TASTES

Bilbao can be one of the most expensive places in Spain to eat, on a par quality-wise with the best of Madrid and Barcelona. Some would say it's even better than either of them—with only San Sebastián (see below) as a serious rival. So if money is no object, you can have a culinary ball. If it is—and we're trying to give you value for money information here—there's not a total shortage of affordable spots as well.

€–€€   One such nosherie is the chic vegetarian **Garibolo** ✪✪ (calle Fernández del Campo 7; ☎ 944-273-255; daily 1:30–4pm and 8–11:30pm; MC, V), located in the heart of the Ensanche part of town west of the river and not far from the Indautxu Metro station. Using only natural ingredients, its kitchen turns out main-course specialties like *berenjenas rellanas* (stuffed eggplant, 8€) and *buñuelos de calabaza con piñones* (pumpkin fritters cooked in sunflower oil with pine cones, 9€), as well as a splendid fixed-price luncheon for just 10€. The mixed salads and fruit desserts are also delicious. The restaurant virtually doubles as an art gallery, regularly featuring local painters' work on its gleaming white walls, and the clientele tend to be young, theatrical, and vehemently green.

€–€€   If veggie food is not your scene, head for the northern end of the Casco Viejo, where you'll find the **Rio Oja** (calle Perro 4; ☎ 944-150-871; daily 1:30–4pm; AE, DC, MC). In addition to providing hearty standards like *guiso riojano* (a Riojan stew based on spicy *chorizo* sausage and potatoes, 10€) and *rodaballo a la plancha* (grilled turbot, 18€) this loud and boisterous eating spot, which winds around a busy U-shaped bar, also specializes in more adventurous dishes like *tortilla de bacalao con caracoles* (cod and snail omelets, 10€), which sounds weird but is great. The best value are the two workaday lunch menus (9€ and 12€).

€€   A perhaps surprising inclusion here is the **Guggenheim Museum Café** ✪ (☎ 944-239-333; Tues–Sun 9am–9pm; MC, V), which, despite being inside the classy Gehry monument (p. 351), manages to come up with a very reasonable 14€ weekday lunch menu. You're not likely to find it including top regional delights like *bacalao pil-pil* (that's around 20€ on the adjoining posher restaurant's menu—see below), but it offers two quality courses with wine and dessert and is usually packed with locals, which is a good sign. (The main restaurant, which specializes in Basque new cuisine of the Martin Berasategui school, is in a different—higher—price range altogether; unsurprisingly, since that particular prize-winning chef is rated by many gourmets as outclassing Catalunya's much vaunted Ferran Adrià.)

€–€€€   Of course, tapas—or *pintxos* to give them their Basque name—are such a marvelous treat here that you could forget all about conventional sit-down restaurants and just rely on them for meals. And there's no better spot for that than the inimitable **Víctor Montes** ★★ (Plaza Nueva 8; ☎ 944-157-067 or 944-155-603; www.victormontesbilbao.com; Mon–Thurs 1–4pm and 8:30–11pm, Fri–Sat 1–4pm and 8:30pm–midnight; MC, V), where you can dive into a monumental range of bar-top mini dishes priced from 2.50€ for *aceitunas rellenas* (olives stuffed with red peppers) to 4€ for *boquerones fritos* (oil-fried baby whitebait). Located right on the Plaza Nueva, with an outdoor terrace area that's packed in summer, this lavishly ornate grub emporium serves over 1,500 wines, so you won't be short of choice for your accompanying tipple. Traditional sip is the light, white, and slightly acidy *txacolí,* which comes from local vineyards. The joint has several sit-down restaurants, some upstairs, which are also pretty good value—10€ to 12€ for a *ración* of *calamares* (squid) or *bacalao* (cod)—but tend to get packed and frantic. Reservations are strongly recommended.

For a concentrated *pintxo* soirée **calles Pozas, Barrencalle,** or **Licenciado Poza** provide the liveliest selection of bars and *tascas* serving theses Basque tidbits. Look out in particular for excellent *jamón serrano* (cured ham) at the **Atlanta** (calle Rodríguez Arias 28; ☎ 944-415-067; Mon–Sat 1–4pm and 8pm–midnight; V) and plump grilled *anchoas* anchovies at **Busterri** (calle Licenciado Poza 43; ☎ 944-415-067; 8:30am–4pm and 8pm–12:30am; cash only). Best snack of all is the *bacalao al pil-pil* (salt cod with garlic emulsion) at the **Café Bar Bilbao** ★ (Plaza Nueva 6; ☎ 944-151-671; daily 9am–midnight; V). Richly decorated with *azulejos* (tiles), dark pillars, and white-painted ceiling beams, this has been one of the city's most popular meeting spots since 1911. The outside terrace right on the square is very popular in fine weather.

WHY YOU'RE HERE: THE TOP SIGHTS & ATTRACTIONS

One million people head to Bilbao every year, and they do so for one reason and one reason alone: to see the **Guggenheim Museum** ★★★ (calle Abandoibarra 2; ☎ 944-359-080; www.guggenheim-bilbao.es; 13€ adults, 7.50€ seniors and students, free for children 11 and under; Sept–June Tues–Sun 10am–8pm, July–Aug daily 10am–8pm, closed Jan 1 and Dec 25). Designed by the world's most famous architect, Frank Gehry, it's been called everything from the "greatest building of our time" (by critic Philip Johnson) to the "reincarnation of Marilyn Monroe" (by *The New York Times*). Whatever accolade you use, it's clear that this paradigm-shifting work of architecture has not only changed the way people look at museum spaces, but also the way they think about the Basque region.

Before 1997, when the museum debuted, Bilbao was known primarily for the bloody campaign the ETA separatists were waging. Though the city had started its regeneration, after years as a gray, industrial city, most visitors avoided it. (The museum itself sits on what had been an ugly, blighted warehouse district.) So the Bilbao city fathers chose a controversial course, courting the Guggenheim

Getting to the Sights

Most of the important monuments are a short distance from the **Gran Vía** in the heart of the main town. The narrow-alleyed Old Quarter, set inside a loop of the **Nervión** river with water protecting it on three sides, is ideal for relaxing strolls.

foundation by offering a whopping $100 million of taxpayer money for the museum's construction—over the vociferous objections of those who felt the money should go to local architects and artists or to schools or hospitals. To sweeten the deal even further, they pledged an additional $50 million to the museum to help it acquire more artworks. Their gambit paid off: The Guggenheim chose Bilbao, tourist revenues soared, but, more important, the city earned newfound respect. "What could be better than to channel the nationalist impulses into an art museum that would dazzle the world and blunt the harsh edges of ETA?" wrote Paul Goldberger in *The New Yorker* the year the museum debuted. "This great, living museum stands as a metaphor for Basque culture and the relationship it aspires to have with the world: a thing apart, yet entirely willing to make a connection on its own terms."

Whatever you think yourself of the use of public funding, the museum is an indisputably impressive sight, 105,000 sq. m (1,130,200 sq. ft.) in size, its curving, sculpted walls coated with titanium panels. (Gehry used computer simulations to create the shape of the building, thus performing engineering feats that likely would have been impossible for previous generations of architects.) Some have quibbled that what's housed inside—the permanent collection focuses on 20th- and 21st-century artists such as Picasso, Braque, Miró, and Kandinsky—has been less inspiring than the architecture, though recent temporary exhibitions have been well received. And Jeff Koonz's giant flower covered *Puppy* statue outside the museum's entrance is as much of an undisputed hit as the museum itself.

Be sure, after you shuffle through the museum's 20 galleries, to visit the riverside terrace for another perspective on the way the silver of the building (like a fish's scales) reflects and connects with the water below. And consider picking up an audioguide, which will give you more details on Gehry's inspiration, the way the lighting interplays with the architecture, and info on whatever temporary exhibit is taking center stage.

It's hard to imagine a greater contrast with the Guggenheim than the traditional **Museo a Euska/Museo Vasco** ★ (Plaza Miguel de Unamuno 4; ☎ 944-155-423; www.euskal-museoa.org; 3€ adults, 1.50€ students and children 10–16, free for all Thurs; Tues–Sat 11am–5pm, Sun 11am–2pm), which concentrates purely on Basque archaeology and ethnology and is housed in a beautiful old Jesuit cloister in the heart of the Old Quarter. If you want to know more about the city's past, it's the ideal place to have a browse around. Exhibits include a recreation of Basque commercial life during the 16th century through paintings and models of fishing boats, merchant ships, and reconstructions of rooms illustrating political and social life. Standout is the huge relief model of old Vizcaya on the top floor.

Back again in the world of art, we find a mingling of both past and present in the **Museo de Bellas Artes** ✦✦ (Plaza del Museo 2; ☎ 944-396-060; www. museobilbao.com; 5.50€ adults, 4€ seniors and students, free for children 11 and under, free for all Wed; Tues–Sat 10am–8pm, Sun 10am–2pm). Although you may be disappointed to find it in such a bland and functional building (no Guggenheim, this), it's widely considered to be one of the country's most important cultural museums, providing a truly comprehensive overview of Spanish artistic achievements through the ages from Velázquez and Goya to Picasso and Sorolla, and also including some prominent 20th-century Basque artists such as sculptor Eduardo Chillida, whose massive *Monument to Iron* dominates the modernist section. Other nationalities are represented in masterworks such as Van Dyck's *Lamentation Over Christ,* in which a memorably disconsolate Mary cradles the beautifully sculpted Rubens-like figure of her dead son; in its modern wing, you can see some lyrical paintings by lesser-known artists, such as the American Mary Cassatt.

Casco Viejo (Old Quarter) ✦

This compact, narrow-alleyed district, also known as the Siete calles, is a well-preserved reminder of how the city looked when it was officially founded in 1300, though the harmonious Plaza Nueva—enclosed by 64 graceful archways—is a more recent addition that wasn't completed till 1830. Declared a national landmark in its entirety, the district is connected to the modern town on the opposite bank by four bridges. If you're on the Gran Via, you can get here via the Puente del Arenal.

The most important religious building in the old town is the **Catedral de Santiago** ✦ (Plaza Santiago; ☎ 944-320-125; free admission; daily 11am–1pm and 4–6:30pm), built in the 14th century and restored after a fire 200 years later. Highlights of its high, stark interior include a wonderful, secluded cloister from its earlier period. Also worth a peek for its twin towers and baroque facade is the **Iglesia de San Nicolás de Bari** (calle Esperanza Ascao; ☎ 944-163-424; free admission; daily 10:30am–12:30pm and 4:30–8pm), behind which an elevator takes sightseers to the upper town. If you're feeling energetic, you can also get to the latter by climbing the 64 steps from the nearby Plaza Unamuno (named after the city's greatest literary figure—novelist, essayist, philosopher, and university lecturer, Miguel de Unamuno, who died, they say, of a broken heart shortly after the outbreak of the Civil War). From the top it's just a short walk to the 16th-century **Basílica de Begoña** (☎ 944-127-091; www.basilicadebegona.com; free admission; Mon–Sat 10:30am–1:30pm and 5:30–8:30pm, Sun during mass hours only [10am, noon, 1pm, 6pm, 8pm]), with its brightly illuminated depiction of the Virgin, the patroness of the province, and large sumptuous paintings by Luca Giordano, a passionate 17th-century disciple of Titian and Rubens.

ACTIVE BILBAO

Bilbao's nearest area for **beaches** and **watersports** is in and around the chic barrio of **Getxo** about 14km (9 miles) away from the center on the east bank of the Nervión, where it opens out into the sea. The main **swimming** beaches are located on the hotel-lined **Playa de Ereaga** with a beachside **Tourist Information** office (☎ 944-910-800; www.getxo.net; mid-June to mid-Sept daily 10am–8pm, mid-Sept to mid-June Mon–Fri 9:30am–2:30pm and 4–7pm, Sat–Sun and fiestas 10:30am–2:30pm and 4–8pm), which can arrange **half-** or **full-day sailing trips** (50€ and 80€ per person) around the estuary and along the coast.

Getxo itself is also fun to explore, a relaxed and prosperous resort of mansions, white cottages, narrow lanes, cozy (and expensive) restaurants, smart shops, and waterfront *paseos.* To get to the beach, take the Metro to the Larrabasterra, Sopelana, or Plentzia stops. Crossings by car or on foot cost 1.20€ or .30€, respectively, but using the bridge's high narrow walkway—a giddily memorable experience 50m (150 ft.) above the main bridge—will knock you back 4€.

Nearby **Mundaka** (45km/30 miles, 1¼ hours) is renowned for its fine **surfing** beach, which claims to have the longest left break in the world. (For the uninitiated, a *left break* is a wave that breaks from right to left as you look toward the beach). You can watch the surfers in action from a small square adjoining the church. A local school, **Mundaka Surf Eskola** (☎ 946-876-721), gives surfing lessons and rents surfboards (20€ per hour). A summer ferry from here (1.30€ per crossing) takes you to another white-sand beach on the opposite shore (Playa Laída). You can easily get to Mundaka on the train (p. 346).

THE OTHER BILBAO: JOIN THE BILBAO ART SET

Even before the groundbreaking Guggenheim Museum was a tiny glint in the eye of the local authorities, Bilbao had long been the Basque country's art mecca. Top-quality galleries fill its streets and avenues, and the sometimes-overlooked **Bellas Artes (Fine Arts) Museum** features one of the finest all-around collections in Spain. So if you're artistically inclined and enjoy learning more in the company of like-minded souls, it's a pretty good place to let some of the expertise rub off on you. An excellent place to do this is **Bilbao Arte** (calle Urazurrutia 32; ☎ 944-15-61-93, fax 944-15-61-93; www.bilbaoarte.org), run by the city's Fundación de Arte (Art Foundation), a highly regarded local institution providing a variety of year-round art courses in which motivated guests can participate. Each course is very intensive, usually lasting a week, with attendance hours from 10am to 7pm, at a total cost of between 60€ and 100€, depending on which artist is presenting it. Past hosts have included Valencian-born sculptor-painter Manolo Valdés, who commutes regularly between his New York studio and Spain; Bruce McLean, a Scottish surrealist who specializes in silkscreen work; and Peter Jones, a veteran Londoner who created semi-abstract impressionist landscapes right up to his death in 2008 at the age of 91. The courses—in which, after hearing the theory, you get to try to produce some masterpieces of your own—are usually held in Spanish, so a working knowledge of the language is needed. Sometimes, though, (such as in McLean's case), they're in English. As the courses are arranged at relatively short notice, it's a good idea to send an e-mail or consult the website (see above) to check the latest schedule beforehand. Participants are expected to have some specialist knowledge of the art field of the particular course they wish to attend and be able to provide proof of their prowess or interest—such as a letter from some cultural authority in their home town—before being allowed to enroll.

For complete laymen (with no formal prerequisites), there's also another—admittedly outside—possibility: You can try to get on one of the *talleres para todos* (workshops for everyone) year-round art courses covering, among other things, watercolor and oil painting techniques, which are organized by the **Bilbao Council.** The downside is that these extend over several months and tend to get fully booked up well ahead. They're a very good value (80€ for a whole course), even though, obviously, you'll only be able to attend a fraction of one, given the time you're likely to be there. You can check availability when you're here by contacting the **Bilbao Council (Ayuntamiento)** (Plaza Ernesto Erkoreka 1; ☎ 944-204-200; www.bilbao.net) and asking for the Sección Ciudadanos (Citizen's Center). Here, again, a sound working knowledge of Spanish is absolutely necessary.

ATTENTION, SHOPPERS!

To look like a true Basque, you need a *txapela,* the handsome, traditional beret still worn by many locals in countryside villages, though less in the city. The best selection is to be found at **Sombreros Gorostiaga** ✮ (calle Victor 9; ☎ 944-161-276), a family-owned business that has been operating since 1857, though berets and *makilas* (countryside walking staffs) are also sold at **Basandere** (calle Iparraguirre 4; ☎ 944-236-386), near the Guggenheim Museum. Basandere is also good hunting grounds for Basque books, paintings, sculptures, and **artisanal** and **gourmet** products. Local artists also have interesting exhibitions here every three months or so.

On a bigger scale—much bigger (it claims to be the largest market in Spain and has appeared in the *Guinness World Records*)—is the three-story **Riverside Market** (☎ 944-157-086; Mon–Thurs 8am–2pm [until 2:30pm in summer] and 4:30–7pm [until 7:30pm in summer], Sat 8:30am–2:30pm), which boasts 200 shops selling products of all types . It lies on the western edge of the Old Quarter beside the river. Originally built in 1929 by the Bermean architect Pedro de Izpizua y Susunaga, it was slightly modernized after serious floods 64 years later.

NIGHTLIFE IN BILBAO

As a prelude to a night out, do what the locals do and pop into one or two of the myriad bars in the Casco Viejo, and sip a small glass of wine *(chiquiteos)* with your *pintxo.* After that, you'll be ready to dance the night away in a top disco like **Pub Crystal** (calle Buenos Aires 5; no phone) or **El Palladium** (calle Iparraguirre 11; no phone), where leading DJs play a variety of wild sounds from house to techno and occasionally live Spanish groups perform. Both open from 10pm to around 4 am (5am on weekends) and charge 10€ entrance.

The main gay area here is on and around **calle Barrencalle,** and its most popular meeting place is the **Bar Consorcio** (calle Barrencalle 10; ☎ 944-169-904; www.consorciobilbao.com; Fri–Sat 11:30pm–5:30am, Sun matinees 10am–2pm; 10€–12€ including a drink), where deafening electro-house sounds add vibrancy to the very friendly and animated atmosphere.

An offbeat but highly popular nightspot, complete with bizarre decor of bottle cap–covered walls and 1920s jazz sounds, is the **Cotton Club** (calle Gregorio de la Revilla 25; ☎ 944-104-951; www.cottonclubbilbao.com; Mon–Thurs 4:30pm–3am, Sun 6:30pm–3am), optimistically named after New York's original Harlem joint. Beer begins at 3€, whisky at 5.50€, and there's no cover charge. Popular disc jockeys enliven the scene on the weekends, and live local performers like Loquillo and Greta y los Garbos—well known in Spain if nowhere else—make regular appearances.

If your tastes tend toward the **classical**—opera, symphonies, ballet, *zarzuelas* (comic operas)—Bilbao's most elegant cultural venue is the **Teatro Arriaga** ★ (Plaza Arriaga s/n; ☎ 944-310-310 for ticket purchases; www.teatroarriaga.com; AE, MC V), beside the Ría de Bilbao. Past performances included the Kremlin Ballet's *Romeo and Juliet* by Prokofiev. Comfortable seats are 30€ and up, but there are also stall-like pews for around 5€ if you're not so fussy and want to economize. Check for current programs and prices at the theater's **Information Office** (Mon–Tues and Fri 11am–2pm, Wed–Thurs 11am–2pm and 4–6pm). If you enjoy more popular commercial shows, the **Teatro Ayala** (calle Manuel Allende 18; ☎ 944-21-22-60) offers modern musicals such as their recent *Beatles—The Legend,* albeit with the Fab Four's hits sung in Spanish. Seats are between 15€ and 20€.

GET OUT OF TOWN: GUERNICA

On the afternoon of April 26, 1937, a defining tragedy struck the small city of **Guernica (Gernika).** Nazi airplanes, acting in support of Franco, bombarded the town in five successive sweeps, dropping powerful 50kg (110-pound) bombs that killed between 1,000 and 1,600 civilians (estimates vary). A full three-quarters of the city's buildings were turned to rubble and the ferocity of the attack, portrayed by Pablo Picasso in his most famous painting, brought international attention to the atrocities of the Spanish Civil War. That terrible day is brought to life at the **Fundación Museo de la Paz de Guernica (Guernica Peace Museum)** ★ (Foru Plaza 1; ☎ 946-270-213; www.museodelapaz.org; 4€ adults, 2€ seniors and students, free for children 10 and under; July–Aug Tues–Sat 10am–8pm, Sun 10am–3pm; Sept–June Tues–Sat 10am–2pm and 4–7pm, Sun 10am–2pm), which contains a permanent exhibition on the bombing as depicted in contemporary photos and wall text. A space has been reserved for Picasso's *Guernica* in the museum (it's currently exhibited in Madrid), to which locals have long been campaigning for it to be rightfully returned.

But Guernica's importance goes well beyond the Spanish Civil War. From the Middle Ages until 1876, the Basque parliament met here under the **Tree of Guernica** (today a young oak) making it the de facto heartland for the Basque people. That culture and history is celebrated at the **Euskal Herriko Museoa** (calle Allende Salazar; ☎ 946-25-54-51; free admission; June–Sept Tues–Sat, 10am–2pm and 4–7pm), a small museum of engravings, portraits, and documents of Basque culture.

The city is also a gateway to one of the loveliest areas in Vizcaya, the UNESCO-protected **Urdaibai National Biosphere Reserve.** A mix of oak forest and isle-dotted estuary, the 12km-wide (7½-mile) reserve has become a magnet for birders, kayakers, and folks who simply like to be out in pristine natural surroundings.

More information can be obtained from the **Guernica Tourist Office** (calle Artekalea 8; ☎ 946-255-892; summer Mon–Sat 10am–7pm, Sun 10am–2pm; winter Mon–Sat 10am–2pm and 4–7pm, Sun 10am–2pm). Guernica is located 35km (22 miles), or 55 minutes, from Bilbao; the easiest way to get here is aboard one of the 30 daily departures of the **Euskotren** (☎ 902-543-210; www. euskotren.es).

SAN SEBASTIÁN (DONOSTIA)

Once the chosen summer retreat of dictators, kings, and celebrities—Queen Isabella II spent the summer of 1845 here, the first of many such luminaries to do so—tiny Guipúzcoa's regional capital **San Sebastián (Donostia)** is the most elegant seaside town in Spain. Its waterfront and inland wooded hills are lined with Belle Epoque palaces and mansions and in what's now the city hall, built in 1887, a casino opened—Spain's first. (General Franco spent most of the summers here during his 40 year dictatorship.)

Beyond celeb-spotting, the city is famous for two major attributes: first, the beauty of its setting—a perfect crescent beach (**La Concha,** packed to capacity in summer) backed by a stylish promenade and bracketed by twin wooded headlands, and second (or first, depending on your point of view), for its gastronomy, generally acknowledged to be the best in Spain. Its modern district of elegant shops, wide boulevards, sidewalk cafes, and restaurants is complemented to perfection by the inimitable **La Parte Vieja (Old Quarter)** with its narrow streets, hidden plazas, medieval houses, and a countless selection of tempting *pintxo* bars offering an affordable alternative to the magnificent but expensive profusion of gourmet eating spots. In recent years, the city has also widened its cultural and ecology-friendly net, creating a number of innovative buildings such as the cube-shaped **Kursaal** cultural center (see "Why You're Here," below) and improving the urban landscape by pedestrianizing many streets and squares and creating bicycle trails alongside the city's **River Urumea.** If you enjoy coastal walks, you can follow a spectacular new pathway that leads you over the rocks at Monpas (beside the Kursaal) and along a beautiful cliff-top route as far as the easterly **Pasajes San Pedro (Pasai San Pedro)** lighthouse. You'll be equally captivated by the surrounding green and fertile countryside that rises to tree-cloaked hills and extends eastward along the coast past beaches, cliffs, and intermittent peninsulas toward the French border, and westward along a similar coast toward Bilbao. South beyond those nearby hills is a further inland wealth of fast-flowing rivers, village-dotted valleys, and high, perennially fuzzy mountains—an enticingly unspoiled natural paradise.

Summer Highlights

Summer is festival time in San Sebastián. The three biggest are:

* **Second half of July: Jazzaldia,** a noted Jazz fest
* **Mid-August: Aste Nagusia,** a riotous celebration of traditional Basque music and dance, accompanied by fireworks, cooking competitions, and sports events
* **September:** The more sedate San Sebastián **International Film Festival** ⭐ (www.sansebastianfestival.com), which usually takes place during the second half of the month, draws stars and celebrities from America and Europe.

Dates for all three events change slightly each year, so check with the tourist office (see below).

GETTING TO & AROUND SAN SEBASTIÁN

Three to six daily flights are available from Madrid and three daily flights from Barcelona via **Iberia Airlines** (☎ 902-400-500) to San Sebastián's airport at nearby Fuenterrabía/Hondarribia. They're not cheap from either airport: usually anywhere between 140€ and 350€ *one-way!* From the airport, buses make the 25-minute motorway run to San Sebastián city center every 20 minutes Monday through Saturday 6:45am to 9:15pm, and Sunday every 30 minutes 7:40am to 9:05pm. **Interbus tickets** (☎ 943-641-302; www.interbus.com) are 2€.

Much better value is the rail travel option with **RENFE** (☎ 902-240-202; www.renfe.es), which runs a 6½-hour Intercity train (38€ one-way) and two 5-hour Alvia trains (49€ to 57€ one-way) every day from Madrid to San Sebastián. RENFE also provides an 8-hour day train service (39€ one-way) from Barcelona to San Sebastián, plus a *preferente* (first-class) only 10-hour overnight service (51€ one-way)—both of which continue on to Bilbao.

Also good value is the bus service from Madrid's avenida de America bus station. **Continental Auto** (☎ 943-469-074; www.continental-auto.es) runs 11 daily buses taking 6½ hours and costing 35€ one-way. From Barcelona's Estació Nord, **Vibasa** (☎ 943-457-500 www.vibasa.es), operates two buses a day taking 5½ hours and costing just 29€ one-way. From Bilbao **Transportes Pesa** (Av. de Sancho el Sabio 33; ☎ 902-101-210 www.pesa.net), runs buses hourly from 6:30am to 10pm taking 1¼ hours (9.65€ one-way).

From Madrid by car, take the N-I toll road north to Burgos, and then follow A-1 to Miranda de Ebro, from where you continue on the A-68 north to Bilbao and then the A-8 east to San Sebastián.

For more information, visit the **Oficina de Turismo** (calle Reina Regente 3; ☎ 943-481-166; www.sansebastianturismo.com or www.donostia.org; June–Sept Mon–Sat 8am–8pm, Sun 10am–2pm, Oct–May Mon–Sat 9am–1:30pm and 3:30–7pm, Sun 10am–2pm).

ACCOMMODATIONS, BOTH STANDARD & NOT

While you'll pay more for an apartment in San Sebastián than you will in other towns along the coast, larger groups (ideally of 5 or more) can save by renting. If you fall into that category, or find the idea of having more space and cooking facilities appealing, surf to www.casaspain.com and check the Guipuzcoa section. A simple listing service for apartment owners who want to advertise, it doesn't offer the user any guarantees, but it does boast a good number of options. If you're willing to stay in the countryside, a better site is the Basque government's www.nekatur.net (p. 349). If you're visiting outside of peak season (July–Aug), it's possible to simply walk into a San Sebastián rental agency and obtain a property on the spot; bargain hard, as you'll be taking a property that otherwise would have stood empty.

In San Sebastián itself, you'll find the lowest-priced accommodations in the **Parte Vieja (Old Corner)** of town. Here are four worth considering:

€   **Hospedaje Kati** (calle Fermin Calbetón 21–5º; ☎ 943-430-487; www. hospedajekati.com; no credit cards) which provides five-to-a-room dormitory accommodations with shared amenities (bathroom down the hall) for 30€ to

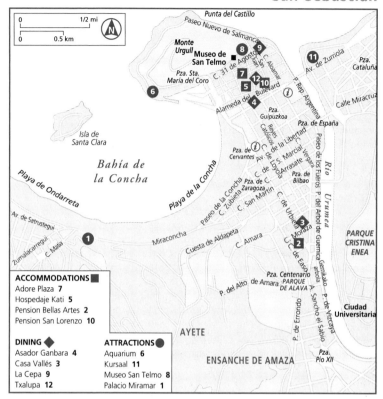

Map legend:

ACCOMMODATIONS ■
Adore Plaza **7**
Hospedaje Kati **5**
Pension Bellas Artes **2**
Pension San Lorenzo **10**

DINING ◆
Asador Ganbara **4**
Casa Vallés **3**
La Cepa **9**
Txalupa **12**

ATTRACTIONS ●
Aquarium **6**
Kursaal **11**
Museo San Telmo **8**
Palacio Miramar **1**

35€ a night. Groups of travelers willing to muck in will be in their element here; there are no age limits. In fact, the owners of Kati are a pair of friendly seniors who've been known to treat their guests to plates of paella on the terrace when the mood is right. The place is at the top of an old building (complete with elevator) and the dorms are reasonably clean, with comfortable beds, original bare floorboards, large windows that let in plenty of light, and adequate wardrobe space for your clothes. *One note:* The owners have a friendly dog that roams the hostel at will; if you're allergic or don't like canines, this may not be the place for you.

€   The small (5-room) **Pension San Lorenzo** (calle San Lorenzo 2–1°; ☎ 943-425-516; no credit cards) is another intimate find, this time offering just a teeny bit more than you'd expect for its modest 40€ a night. All rooms—though somewhat sparsely furnished and with bare-wood floors—have TV, fridge, and kettle, and some (45€) have private bathrooms. Guests also have access to the Internet and a self-catering kitchen. San Lorenzo's really popular, and since they don't accept reservations in advance, the best thing to do is phone before your arrival to see if they have a room free.

€   A little bit of everything is on offer at **Adore Plaza** ✸ 🅺 (Plaza de la Constitución 6; ☎ 943-422-270; www.adoreplaza.com; MC, V)—which places guests in doubles (40€–45€), triples (45€–55€), and quads (55€–65€). Prices for these rooms are *not* per person, so the more you bed down, the cheaper it works out per head (and you can fit more than the usual number in these rooms as they're quite good sized as well as being spotless and washed with sunlight). For true penny pinchers, there's also a dorm room on site (16€–25€). Well run and very friendly, the ambience is that of a large, fun-filled family house; a feeling enhanced by the fact that all rooms share bathrooms. The Zurriola and La Concha beaches are nearby.

€   Saving the best for last, if you can get in (and it's very, very popular, so book well in advance), **Pension Bellas Artes** ✸✸✸ (calle Urbieta, 64 1ºB; ☎ 943-474-905; www.pension-bellasartes.com; MC, V) is without a doubt one of the most charming hotels in the Basque region. That's not because of its decor, which is simple and pleasant (think wicker chairs, exposed stone walls, comfy beds wedged into smallish rooms) but nothing to write home about. No, the reason you stay here is to bask in the gracious hospitality of owner Leire and her mother, Marie Carmen. What does that consist of? Fresh flowers in your room, chocolates on your pillow, and the services of two astute foodies, who will book restaurants for you (always snagging the best table in the house) and give you a map, upon arrival, with their picks for the top tapas places clearly marked. Drop Leire's name and you're likely to get a plate or two of free tapas; she's that well-liked in this town. All rooms have private bathrooms and cost 59€ to 79€ double, 39€ to 59€ single; wheelchair-accessible rooms are available.

DINING FOR ALL TASTES

At first glance, it would seem to be easier for a rich man to pass through the eye of a needle than for the first-time visitor to find a cheap place to eat in San Sebastián. If anything, the place is even dearer than Bilbao, with a bewildering array of prize-winning restaurants (only Paris has as many Michelin 3-starred restaurants), especially around the privileged waterfront area where menu prices will make you think you need new glasses. The good news? There's a definite trickledown effect here, and even the more modest restaurants are creative in their offerings, using the highest-quality ingredients. In particular, the **Parte Vieja** is good for non-bankrupting nosh spots, whether you feel like sitting down for a full meal or standing up to munch exquisite *pintxos* and quaff white *txacolí* wine (fizzier here than in Bilbao and poured into your glass from a height as if it were cider).

€–€€   A place I've always enjoyed popping into when I'm feeling peckish and don't want to spend too much is the **Txalupa** ✸ (calle Fermín Calbetón 3; ☎ 943-429-875; 1:30–4pm and 8–11:30pm; MC, V), which serves up good, well-priced Basque fare (lunch menu 11€ weekdays, 14€ weekends) in a relaxed traditional setting with hanging hams over the bar and basic wooden tables and chairs in the adjoining eating area. Its exquisite *pintxos* of *tortilla* (omelet) are the best value at 5€ to 7€. More individual a la carte dishes include *codillo de jamón* (pig's trotters,

Pintxo Time

Having tapas anywhere in Spain is fun but in San Sebastián—where, Basque-style, they're known as *pintxos*—it enters another dimension of pleasure, even when the goodies laid out on the counter look deceptively simple. Some, like cheese cubes and *anchoas* (anchovies), you can pierce with the toothpicks you see poking out of tiny glasses. (The number of empty sticks afterward help the barman to tally up the bill.) Others—like *gambas* (prawns)—you eat with your fingers, while for slithery things like the costlier *anguilas* (baby eels), you'll need a small fork. All have one thing in common: They're absolutely delicious. Accompanying them traditionally is a cold, sharp white wine—usually the local *txacoli*, which is slightly fizzy in this town and served in a wide tumbler. (You can alternatively go for cider, regionally produced, though Asturias is really the place par excellence for that; see chapter 9.)

The most satisfyingly indulgent area for this enterprise is the **Parte Vieja** ✦, where you can pop into virtually any bar and have an economical blowout. In some, the range of choice is astounding rich. A couple of superior spots to seek out are the **Bar Asador Ganbara** ✦ (calle San Jerónimo 21; ☎ 943-422-575; Tues–Sun 11am–3:15pm and 6–11:45pm; V), which specializes in *calamares* (squid) and *chorizo* (spicy sausage); and **La Cepa,** (31 de Agosto 7–9; ☎ 943-431-973; Wed–Mon 11am–midnight; cash only), where the—admittedly not so cheap—*jamón jabugo* (a vintage ham from Huelva province) melts in your mouth. These places also have restaurants serving full meals, but it's the bar *pintxos* we're recommending and they average 2.50€ to 4.50€ per mini dish providing you stick to simple fare like *albóndigas* (meatballs) and *tortillas* (mini omelets), and lay off the *anguilas* and *jabugo*.

10€) and *rodaballo al horno* (oven-cooked turbot, 15€) all very good if you're in the mood to fork out more.

€–€€   You'll probably see a few more tourists in the **Casa Marita** (calle Euskal Erria 7; ☎ 943-430-443; 1:30–4pm and 8:30–11:30pm; MC, V) than in the Txalupa, but that doesn't mean you won't get good, honest Basque dishes—wallet-kind if you try meaty stuff like *estofado* or *salchichas de cerdo* (stew or pork sausages, 10€–12€), wallet bending if you go for fishy favorites *merluza* (hake) or *bacalao* (cod) as both are around 18€ to 20€. Casa Marita is silly fun to visit, too, with a mock baroque decor, which includes some ornate fresco work. Get there early if you want to be sure of a table.

€–€€   In a pedestrianized street near the cathedral, about a 10-minute stroll away from the outer fringe of the Parte Vieja, is **Casa Vallés** ✦ (Reyes Católicos 10; ☎ 943-452-210; www.barvalles.com; restaurant Thurs–Mon 1–3pm and

8:30–11pm, Tues 1–3pm; bar daily 8:30am–11pm; closed 2 weeks late May; DC, MC, V), a marvelously affordable bar-restaurant that serves great *pintxos* of *anchoas* (anchovies), *jamón* (ham), and *croquetas* (croquettes), among other things (only 2€–3.50€ each) as well as substantial and savory main courses like *ternera a la plancha* (grilled veal, 10€) or *merluza vasca* (Basque-style hake, 20€). Don't order *anguilas* (baby eels), though, unless you want to blow your week's allowance. (For more on *pintxo* bars, see box above).

WHY YOU'RE HERE: THE TOP SIGHTS & ATTRACTIONS

A chief delight of being in San Sebastián is simply strolling its streets, gazing at the eye-candy Belle Epoque mansions, the solid baroque and Gothic churches of the Parte Vieja, and the buff bodies on the beach, oiled to a high sheen with suntan lotion. A favorite walk is the virtual semicircle that goes along the **Paseo Nuevo (New Promenade)** from the jetty just below **Monte Urgull** all the way around the curving **La Concha** beach as far as Chillida's quirky waterside *Peine de Viento (Wind Comb)* sculpture at the foot of the verdant **Igueldo** promontory. You may want to pause en route for a swim or a paddle, depending on the season. (For more on Chillida see the "Get Out of Town" section.) From here, you can reach the top of **Monte Igueldo** ✸✸✸ and enjoy its panoramic vistas of the bay and Basque coastline by taking the **Funicular** (☎ 943-210-211; round-trip 2€ adults, 1.30€ children 7 and under; July–Oct Mon–Fri 10am–9pm, Sat–Sun 10am–10pm; Apr–June Mon–Fri 10am–8pm, Sat–Sun 10am–9pm, closed Dec 25, Jan 1, 2 weeks mid-Jan, and Tue Nov–Mar). Alternatively, you could get a single ticket and walk back down the winding coastal lane past the lighthouse (great views west). This stroll is particularly delightful in spring when the air is rich with the scent of honeysuckle.

The city also has a handful of notable sights. The place that most symbolizes San Sebastián's entry into the 21st century is the **Kursaal** ✸✸ (Av. de Zurriola 1; ☎ 943-003-000; www.kursaal.org; free admission; daily 11:30am–1pm and 5–9pm). It's been called San Sebastián's answer to the Guggenheim, and though it's not nearly as famous, extravagant, or eye-catching as that Bilbao icon, it does strongly project the contemporary cultural image of this beautiful seaside town. Unfortunately, it hasn't gone down so well with a fair number of traditionally minded locals who feel its spare unadorned cubic style—designed by the avantgarde architect Rafael Moneo—is totally at odds with the city's quintessential Belle Epoque architecture. Most visitors view it more favorably and the building has indubitably helped put the city on the world map, mainly for its increasingly prestigious **September International Film Festival** ✸ (see box) and additionally for its Quincena Musical (Musical Fortnight), open-air sessions of Jazzaldía and a wealth of other musical activities all shown in two state-of-the-art theaters separately accommodating 1,800 and 640 people. Inaugurated in August 1999, it revived the depressed Gros district that lies to the east of the Urgull headland and Urumea river, including its Zurriola promenade and surfer's beach—now also a favorite with nudists.

Halfway around the bay is the **Palacio de Miramar** (Paseo de la Concha s/n; ☎ 943-219-022), poised on its own little hill in between the two beaches. It was opened by Queen María Cristina in 1893, neglected in the troublesome 1930s and spruced up again four decades later when the city council undertook renovation work. Though you can still only admire the palace from outside, you can visit its lovely lawns and gardens any day from 8am to 9pm and feel suitably regal as you admire the splendid all-encompassing sea views.

Returning to the jetty below Monte Urgull is Basque country's number-one oceanographic center, the **Palacio del Mar Aquarium** ✦ kids (Plaza Carlos, Blasco de Imaz s/n; ☎ 943-440-099; www.aquariumss.com; 10€ adults, 8€ students, free for children 4 and under; Oct 1–Apr 2 Mon–Fri 10am–7pm, Sat–Sun 10am–8pm; Apr 3–June 30 and Sept Mon–Fri 10am–8pm, Sat–Sun 10am–9pm; Easter and July–Aug 10am–10pm). Its main attraction is a whiz-bang transparent underwater walkway that allows a 360-degree view of sharks, rays, and other fish as they swim around you. Upstairs is a maritime museum with a through-the-ages display of fishing gear, naval artifacts, and marine fossils, as well as the skeleton of the penultimate whale hauled in from the Bay of Biscay in 1878.

Located close to the only street in the Parte Vieja to escape the ravages of the great 19th-century fire (calle 31 de Agosto), the **Museu de San Telmo** ✦ (Plaza Zuloaga; ☎ 943-42-49-70; www.museodesantelmo.com; free admission; July–Aug Tues–Sat 10am–8:30pm, Sun 10:30am–2pm; Sept–June Tues–Sat 10:30am–1:30pm and 4–7:30pm, Sun 10:30am–2pm) provides an attractive exhibition of Basque art and ethnography within the confines of a former 16th-century Dominican convent, which features soulful portraits of Columbus and other historic luminaries by the eponymous artist Ignacio Zuloaga. The *capilla* (chapel) is decorated with colorful frescoes by the Catalán painter and muralist José Sert depicting scenes from local Basque life.

Now for something quite different (and slightly out of town). At the inland burg of Hernani, a 10-minute ride on the half-hourly no. 92 bus from calle Oquendo in San Sebastián, you'll find the extraordinary **Museo Chillida-Leku** ✦✦ (Caserío Zabalaga 66; ☎ 943-336-006; www.eduardo-chillida.com; 8€ adults, 6€ seniors and students, free for children 9 and under, guided visits 5€; July–Aug Mon–Sat 10:30am–8pm, Sun 10:30am–3pm; Sept–June Wed–Mon 10:30am–3pm; closed Dec 25 and Jan 1). It's a museum that's little known to outside visitors yet much revered by the Basques themselves, devoted to the artwork of local sculptor Eduardo Chillida, whose work appears in many of the world's museums. The surrounding woodlands of beech trees, oaks, and magnolias are studded with some 40 Chillida monoliths while the central 16th-century farmhouse, restored by the artist, displays hanging paper "gravitations," translucent alabaster sculpture, Mayan-style stone blocks, and "jigsaw" sculptures of metal and marble. Unusually for an artist, Chillida, who died in San Sebastián in 2002, was quite content for visitors to touch his works when he was in residence here, adding a tactile pleasure to their appreciation.

THE OTHER SAN SEBASTIÁN

The way to a Basque's heart is through his stomach, and this is especially true of San Sebastián, a place in which food is treated as devoutly as a religion. No, really: In and around the town are secretive places where they practice this religion diligently. These get-togethers are called *txokos,* and though they're, in effect, private clubs—originally founded back in the 19th century for members of different workers' guilds—it is possible to attend one if you can get a member to invite you. One method of doing this is to approach the helpful tourist board and delicately ask them if they can put you in touch with members. If you get lucky and are accepted into this clandestine fold, you'll find yourself in an out-of-the-way building, hunkered down in a large kitchen. You and other members will discuss the recipes and sauces to be used (you'll need a fair command of Spanish, if not Basque, here), and then together the members cook a hefty gourmet meal (though, perhaps, if you do manage to penetrate the secretive world of the *txoko,* it's best the first time just to watch). *A word to half our readers:* Unfortunately, these are male-only societies and women are barred from attending (though in typically sexist fashion, it's the wives, mothers, and girlfriends who usually come around afterward and clean up the mess the men have made).

Beyond cooking, **jai alai** is the major Basque obsession and nowhere will you see it performed better or more enthusiastically than in San Sebastián (apart from in Pamplona whose similar game of *pelota*—see later—is a close contestant). Here's how it's played: Two players with curved baskets tied to their hands scoop up the ball and slam it hard against a high wall, repeating the action on the rebound as the other player responds to his hit. The player who misses the ball loses the point. Spectators bet quite lavishly on the outcome of the game, so if the casino's not enough for you here's another good place to lose money. Both players and spectators can get highly animated during the course of the game, turned on both by the spectacle and the prospect of winning (cash or simply the match itself). As the excitement increases the participants are inspired to perform some astounding acrobatics in their attempts to return the ball. In comparison, tennis—and for that matter jai alai's tiny indoor cousin squash—is pretty tame fare. The nearest place to see it (10km/6¼ miles out of town) is the **Frontón de Galarreta** ✸ (Jauregi, Hernani; ☎ 943-551-023). The no. 93 bus runs here every half-hour.

ACTIVE SAN SEBASTIÁN

The unknown corners of San Sebastián are best explored by bike; there are cycle trails lining the rivers and surrounding countryside, making it a delight to pedal here. Pick up your set of wheels at **Bici Rent** (Av. de la Zurriola 22, right on Gros beach near the Kursaal; ☎ 943-279-260; 20€ per bike per day; daily 9am–9pm).

The finest surfing and watersports are available in nearby **Zarautz** 16km (11 miles) west of San Sebastián.

A long and golden-sanded beach with white-capped waves that sweep all the way in from the breezy Bay of Biscay, it's considered the province's top **surfing** area. Boards can be rented for around 20€ an hour at **Surf Esloka** (Mendilauta Kala 13; ☎ 943-132-647). Hop the Euskotren (p. 356) for the short trip here.

Those who don't want to ride the waves, but just stare at them, will enjoy **La Concha Beach and Promenade** ✸✸✸. As we said earlier, it's one of the loveliest strands in Spain (if not all of Europe), and it's visitor-friendly with free showers and *cabinas* that provide lockers and shade for a small fee. It also doesn't have the honky-tonk atmosphere of many European beaches, being largely free of ugly souvenir stands and fast food places.

ATTENTION, SHOPPERS!

Probably the coolest boutique in the whole Basque country **Parte Vieja** ✸✸ (calle Nagusia 3; ☎ 943-420-760) specializes in cutting-edge clothing and trendy adornments ranging from highly flexible "gladiator" shoes to Brazilian rubber

A Trip into the Wild

Most people who visit San Sebastián spend so much time wandering along La Concha *paseo* or exploring the intricate Parte Vieja that they don't realize one of the Basque country's most magnificent natural parks—the 6,000 hectare (14,826-acre) **Peñas de Aia** ★ (Aiako Harria in Basque)—is almost on their doorstep. As Pio Baroja wrote in 1900, "Here is Nature in all its forms: high mountains cloaked with oak woods, narrow valleys sheltering tiny villages surrounded by wheat fields, bare peaks rising up towards heaven, and joyful green meadows. . . ." He wasn't kidding. Rising high between the Urumea and Bidasoa rivers at the northern extremity of the Pyrenees, the park's filled with beech and oak woods, and the exotic wildlife on these fertile slopes even extends to mountain cats and wild boar. The **Herribus** bus service (☎ 943-491-801) lines H1, 2, and 3 from San Sebastián takes you just 12km (8 miles) east to the town of **Oiartzun** from where you can climb a marked footpath up to the park entrance. From there you can spend an exhilarating day out wandering the hills. Pack a picnic and take a bottle of wine with you. For more information, check with the **Oficina de Turismo de San Sebastián** (see above) or with the **Oficina de Turismo de Oiartzun** (☎ 943-490-142).

earrings in outrageous shapes and colors. If your tastes run more to quintessentially Basque items, head to the small, traditional **Txapela** (calle Puerto 8; ☎ 943-420-243), which sells *abarcas* (sandals) and the area's rough cotton shirts. For local berets and other regional headwear the choice should be the town's oldest hat manufacturer, **Ponsol** (calle Narrica 4; ☎ 943-420-876). And if you're more into window-shopping than actual shopping, simply stroll the Old Quarter, which has scores of vendors selling everything from T-shirts to cameras (old and new).

NIGHTLIFE IN SAN SEBASTIÁN

Though fairly restrained in its nightlife, San Sebastián has its modest share of music bars and discos. Coolest of them all—attracting a knowledgeable "in" crowd of variable age groups—is the **Altxerri Jazz Club** (Reina Regente 2; ☎ 943-424-046; Thurs and Sun 4pm–2am, Fri–Sat 4pm–3am). Its atmospheric cellar is a regular rendezvous for notable live jazz performers, and cover charges (8€–10€) are usually only applied when they're appearing. Another fashionable after-dark spot, located in a prime position overlooking the illuminated *paseo* that curves around La Concha beach, is the (literally) ship-shaped **Kabutzia** ★ (Paseo Muelle s/n; ☎ 943-429-785; www.lakabutzia.com; daily 8pm–3am), where nautical motifs proliferate, funky sounds by enthusiastic DJs fill the salons, and the cover and one drink cost 12€. Another beachside option is the **Rotonda** (Playa de la Concha 6; ☎ 943-429-095; cover 10€; weekends 10pm–dawn), which blends popular music with reggae and salsa. Farther back into the town is **Komplot** (calle Pedro Egaña 5; ☎ 943-472-109; cover 8€; 10pm–4am), a smaller and rather chic club, playing a slightly more adventurous mix of house music.

Probably the most beautiful gambling venue in Spain is the long established Belle Epoque **Casino** ★★ (calle Mayor 1; ☎ 943-429-214; 4€ after 10:30pm; passport or ID card with photo needed; jackets and ties for men not required; Sept 16–June 14 Sun–Fri 4pm–4am [until 5am Sat and fiestas], June 15–Sept 15 4pm–5am). Here you can step back beyond even a James Bond era to one where royals and *aristos* would come to have a dignified flutter. The minimum bets are 2€ to 50€ for roulette and 5€ for blackjack (only 2.50€ Sun).

VITORIA-GASTEIZ

Mention **Vitoria-Gasteiz** to first-time visitors to the Basque country and they'll probably give you a blank stare. It may be the capital of the sub-province of Alava (or Araba) and headquarters of the entire Basque region's autonomous government, but to most out-of-towners it's not simply an unknown quantity; it's simply unknown, period. It's neither as charismatically endowed as Bilbao and San Sebastián nor—like them—by the sea, which perhaps takes it off the main Basque tourist route. But it does hold some very pleasant surprises. Travelers who decide to drop in find themselves in an immaculate "green" town, with "a tree for every two inhabitants" and a larger overall area of parkland for its size than any other place in Spain. Pedestrianized thoroughfares and cycling trails abound, and both the almond-shaped Old Quarter—a kaleidoscope of winding narrow lanes, gray gold Renaissance mansions, and imposing Gothic churches—and the modern surrounding *ensanche* (city extension), which is crisscrossed in turn with wider tree-lined avenues, are models of preservation and building control, in which particularly careful attention has been paid to infrastructure, water supplies, and the trash recycling regulations. Small wonder that in 1998 UNESCO awarded it a prize for town planning (the first ever to be received by a Spanish city) and a recent poll voted it the location with the best quality of life in the country. In case this all sounds a bit too orderly, clinical, and downright perfect, it's also pretty raucous and lively at night, thanks to an abundance of hell-raising students, and has all the usual first-rate eating and drinking spots you come to expect in this corner of the country. So why not come and see this pristine wonder for yourself? (Be careful, though, not to drop any trash on the sidewalk.)

GETTING TO & AROUND VITORIA-GASTEIZ
Getting There

Vitoria-Gasteiz has its own airport, the **Aeropuerto Vitoria-Foronda** (☎ 902-404-704) which is 8km (5 miles) northwest of the city center. There are regular daily **flights** here from Madrid with **Iberia** (☎ 902-400-500; www.iberia.com), but these are invariably expensive (100€–200€ for a one-way flight) and, as before, compare very unfavorably price-wise with both train and bus transport.

Much more reasonable is **RENFE** (☎ 902-240-202; www.renfe.es), which runs five **trains** a day here from Madrid (one high-speed Alvia; 3¾ hr.; 43€ one-way) and four so-called "express" trains (4½–6 hr.; 31€–33€ one-way). Other services operate from Bilbao (5 a day; 1¼ hr.; 9€ one-way), San Sebastián (7 a day; 1½ hr.; 8€ one-way) and Barcelona (one fast Alvia train a day; 4½ hr.; 56€ one-way). The **Railway Station** is at Plaza Circular 2 (☎ 944-239-290) at the southern end of the pedestrianized calle Dato and just a 5-minute stroll from the Old Quarter.

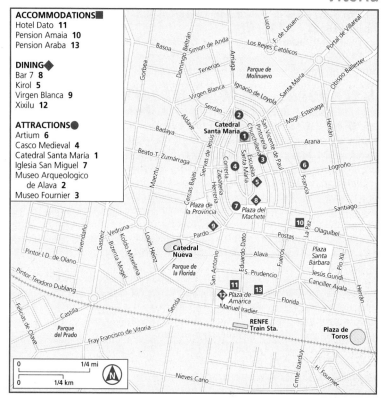

ACCOMMODATIONS ■
Hotel Dato **11**
Pension Amaia **10**
Pension Araba **13**

DINING ◆
Bar 7 **8**
Kirol **5**
Virgen Blanca **9**
Xixilu **12**

ATTRACTIONS ●
Artium **6**
Casco Medieval **4**
Catedral Santa María **1**
Iglesia San Miguel **7**
Museo Arqueologico
   de Alava **2**
Museo Fournier **3**

Buses are usually even cheaper than the train. They arrive and depart from the **bus station** (calle Los Herrán 50; ☎ 945-258-400), which is slightly to the east of the Old Quarter and just a few minutes' stroll from the center of this compact city. Main bus services are from **Madrid** via **Continental Auto** (www.continental-auto.es; 19 a day; 4½ hr.; 25€ one-way), **Bilbao** via **La Union** (www.labur undesa.es; 40 a day; 1 hr.; 9€), and **San Sebastián,** also via **La Union** (7 a day; 1½ hr.; 8€).

If you're **driving** in from Madrid, take the E-5 north to Burgos, until you see the clearly marked turnoff for Vitoria-Gasteiz. (On its more northerly stretches, this superhighway is identified as both E-5 and A-1.)

Getting Around

The local urban service runs **buses** (www.victoria-gasteiz.org) every 15 minutes on various routes round the city. On weekends, the service is reduced to a bus every 40 minutes. One-way trips cost .85€ one-way, 1.15€ round-trip.

Even better, a free **bicycle** lending service, arranged by the local town hall and unique in Spain, operates from June through November on a daily basis (total time allowed per day 4 hr.). There are 13 specified pickup points and several kilometers of bicycle trails in and around the city. The authority to contact for further details on this is the **Casa de Asociaciones Rogelia de Alvaro Elkarteen Etxea** (calle Panamá 14; ☎ 619-881-609).

For general **information,** visit the **Oficina de Turismo** (Plaza General Loma 1; ☎ 945-161-598; www.vitoria-gasteiz.org/turismo; Mon–Sat 10am–7pm and Sun 11am–2pm).

ACCOMMODATIONS, BOTH STANDARD & NOT

€   The homey—in every sense of the word—**Pension Araba** ✭ (calle Florida 25; ☎ 945-232-588; MC, V) is so pristine it looks as if it's recently been renovated, but its owner, the most genial lady of the house you'll meet in a while, swears no changes have been made and that it looks like new because of the serious cleaning she's been giving it every day in the 16 years she's been running it. (She does it alone, too, as the rest of the family, who all live in the house just across the hall, didn't want the hassle.) Its bright, fair-size rooms (35€–45€ per night) all have shiny polished wooden floors, ample wardrobes, and comfortable beds. See if you can get the one with its own secluded and surprisingly noise-free private terrace. (This has a private shower room, while the others have full bathrooms but no terrace.) The hotel is located close to the railway station.

€   Homespun, too—though this time the whole family lends a hand in running the place—the **Pension Amaia** (calle La Paz 15; ☎ 945-255-497; www.pension amaia.com; MC, V) is a long-established lodging, and the decor reflects that: Its quaint furnishings are stolidly old-fashioned with chintzy bedcovers, dark wood bed frames, and rather corny landscape copies on the walls. Ah well, the prices on the compact rooms will more than make up for any lapses in taste: Rooms cost between 35€ and 50€ (varying by whether or not they share bathrooms). One single room, three triple rooms, and four doubles are available. The Amaia is located in a converted old house with an eye-grabbing maroon facade and gleaming-white glassed-in window alcoves, adjoining a busy central road. (Don't worry—the noise inside is minimal.)

€   Nice though the above duo are, the place I head for when I'm in town is **Hotel Dato** ✭✭ (calle Eduardo Dato 28; ☎ 945-147-230; www.hoteldato.com; parking 10€; AE, DC, MC, V), which has the extraordinary aura of a private museum. Okay, it would be a kitschy and rather dinky museum, but that doesn't detract from its appeal. Owned by a former antiquarian, its crammed with original figures of cherubs and demure maidens, flamboyant Egyptian statues, elaborately tiled floors, vivid period portraits, maroon mauve pillars, and a disconcerting array of weathered mirrors. Your room, when you find it (after bumping into your reflection for the second or third time—darn those mirrors!), will be just as handsomely quirky with stained glass windows, ornate bedsteads, large dark-wood wardrobes, and even an alcove with a mini salon furnished with a small table and chairs adjoined by a brightly compact shower room. Some have views of Eduardo Dato Street; others, of the tranquil low-level townscape at the rear. Rates range from 44€ to 55€. Though no breakfast is served, there are plenty of cafes in the neighboring pedestrianized zone (such as the trendy Casablanca 2) where you can enjoy a morning *café con leche*.

DINING FOR ALL TASTES

As in Bilbao and San Sebastián, a popular midday and evening activity is hopping from *tasca* to *tasca,* knocking back small glasses *(chiquiteos)* of beer or wine. You'll understand the appeal when you visit such *pintxo* hot spots as the atmospheric **Kirol** ✪✪ (calle Cuchillería 31; no phone; daily 1:30–3pm and 7pm–2am; no credit cards), a noisy, old, wooden-beamed bodega that serves up mighty toothsome *raciones* (4€–8€; try the *oreja,* which is pig's ear!); and—on the same lively street—the student-patronized **Bar el 7** ✪ (calle Cuchillería 7; ☎ 945-272-298; daily 2–4pm and 7:30pm–2am; no credit cards), which is known for its generous *bocetas* (sandwiches) of *jamón serrano* (cured mountain ham) and *lomo montado* (pungent pork) at 3€ to 4€. A local specialty you should definitely try at one of these two is *perritxikos* (eggs cooked with mushrooms)—simple but delicious.

Vitoria-Gasteiz is quite pricey for sit-down meals, so you might consider doing what the locals do and taking the majority of your meals standing up, in a convivial *tasca* bar such as the ones described above. But if you do choose a bona fide restaurant, you can be sure of eating as well here as anywhere else in the Basque country.

€€ At times it seems that a few too many people are crushed into its small brick-walled dining room, but the Old Quarter's **Virgen Blanca** ✪ (Plaza de la Virgen Blanca 2; ☎ 945-225-040; daily 9am–2am; AE, MC, V) offers a mouthwatering fusion of traditional Basque and modern international dishes, ranging from *txangurro* (spider crab in a spicy sauce, 14€) to *chuletas de cordero* (lamb cutlets, 15€) that's too good to miss. Best value of all is the exceptional weekday 16€ 3-course menu, including wine. The main ground-floor restaurant enjoys great views of the picturesque plaza, and there's an overflow eating area down the steps in a compact low-ceilinged cellar, which is cozy for some but can prove slightly claustrophobic for others, so get there before the crowds if you want to eat in the popular top section.

€€ Over in the modern wide-avenued Ensanche part of town, the highly traditional **Xixilu** ✪ (Plaza Amarica 2; ☎ 945-230-068; daily 1–4pm and 9pm–midnight; AE, MC, V) is another winner, serving up good, honest Basque fare like *bacalao* (cod), *alubia rojas* (locally grown red kidney beans), and *litruelas* (grilled lamb) at between 12€ and 14€ per *cazuela.* (This is the standard local baked oven dish they're served up in.) It's an excellent value for the quality of the food, which is invariably purchased by the chef fresh from the city market. Decor plays second place here to the nosh, and customers sit on benches and eat from uncovered long tables. Service is rapid and spot on. As the place gets pretty busy, it's best to arrive early if you want to get your room on a bench.

WHY YOU'RE HERE: THE TOP SIGHTS & ATTRACTIONS

At the heart of Vitoria-Gasteiz is the lovingly preserved **Casco Medieval (Old Quarter)** ✪. The city was founded in 1181 by King Sancho of Navarre and soon after became an important, and rich, center for the wool and iron trades. Revenue from those industries built the handsome Romanesque and Gothic churches and buildings you'll see today; they're constructed on a series of steps and terraces in streets that weave in concentric ovals and are named after centuries-old artisan guilds. The compact district is bordered by the **Catedral de Santa María** (see below) to the north and **Iglesia de San Miguel** (see below) to the south. One of its most intriguing medieval streets is **calle Cuchillería** ✯, which is accessible via the courtyard of **Casa del Cordón** (no. 24) and was constructed in different stages from the 13th century over a total period of 300 years. Stop at no. 58 to view the lovely Gothic facade of the 15th-century **Bendana Palace** before popping inside for a gander at the fine ornate staircase that climbs up from its inner courtyard.

The city's monumental 14th-century Gothic **Catedral de Santa María** ✯ (calle Fray Zacaras; ☎ 945-255-135; www.catedralvitoria.com) is closed until 2010 for massive restoration work. You can, however, visit the cathedral by means of prebooked guided tours (Apr–Oct daily 10am–2pm and 5–8pm; 3€; ☎ 945-255-135 or contact the Oficina de Turismo). Tours start just off the Plaza de la Burullería on the northern side of the cathedral and take you—amid a forest of scaffolding—through the various stages of the monument's construction, starting in the 13th century, when the cathedral's high vantage point made it a key part of the city's defenses, and continuing through the Renaissance period, when the massive but now distinctly shaky-looking pillars were built. (They're a focal point of the reconstruction.) Standout art here—which the tour enables you to see from a higher level—are the marvelous carved array of saints' faces on the 14th-century western portal.

Just a short walk south of the medieval quarter is Vitoria-Gasteiz's fine **Plaza de la Virgen Blanca** ✯. (Its neoclassical balconies overlook a statue of the Duke of Wellington, erected in commemoration of his victory over Napoleon during the Peninsular War.) On the square is the impressive, 13th-century **Iglesia de San Miguel** ✯ (Plaza de la Virgen Blanca s/n; no phone; Mon–Fri 11am–3pm), notable for the late Gothic polychrome statue of the Virgen Blanca herself (the town's patron) adorning its portico and a 17th-century altarpiece carved by Gregorio Fernández, which is richly baroque in style yet remarkable natural in its expressiveness.

Vitoria-Gasteiz's contemporary pride and joy is the **Artium Culture Center** ✯✯ (calle Francia 24; ☎ 945-209-020; www.artium.org; 4€ adults, 1€ children; Tues–Fri 11am–8pm, Sat–Sun 10:30am–8pm). Designed by local lad José Luis Catón in a trapezoidal, semi-rectangular shape and built on the site of a former bus station, it's made a name for itself by mounting adventurous exhibits of largely unknown contemporary artists. (A recent audiovisual show explored "uncharted territories of expression in filmmaking" by five new young Basque directors.) That's not to say its permanent collection is anything to sneeze at (in fact, some think it outclasses the Guggenheim Bilbao's stash of art); on exhibit are modern creations by Basque painters and sculptors, plus classic works by Dalí, Picasso, and Saura. The main hall is dominated by Joan Miró's spectacular *mural cerámico* and a huge suspended glass sculpture created by artist Javier Perez and known as *un pedazo de cielo cristalizado*, or "a piece of crystallized heaven." (*Artium* means an "atrium with art," in case you wondered.)

Two final city museums are worth a gander: The **Museo de Arqueología de Alava** (calle de la Correría 116; ☎ 945-181-922; free admission; Tues–Fri 10am–2pm and 4–6:30pm, Sat 10am–2pm, and Sun 11am–2pm), behind whose

Sparkling Wine, a Flying Doll & the Trial of Judas

One of the craziest fiestas in the entire country is Vitoria-Gasteiz's 5-day knees-up celebrating the **Virgen Blanca (White Virgin)** ⚔ in the city's emblematic Plaza de la Virgen Blanca. The whole shebang starts on August 4, when a life-size doll—known as the Celedón—carrying an umbrella "flies" on a wire from the church tower over the plaza. The assembled crowds then proceed to spray each other with *cava* or Spanish bubbly (don't put on your best holiday gear if you're around then and decide to join in) and carry on partying till midnight on the last day (the 9th) when the Celedón is returned to his tower and the party is over.

Another bizarre fiesta takes place way out in a harsh corner of the Alava countryside—where birds of prey hover high above phantasmagorical rock formations. Here some 30km (20 miles) west of Vitoria-Gasteiz in the primitive salt-producing township of **Salinas de Añaña** ⚔—it's been extracting salt from local saline wells since Roman times—an effigy of **Judas** is burnt during Semana Santa to the jubilation of the attending crowds after having been tried and sentenced by a not exactly open-minded kangaroo court beforehand. (The verdict is always the same, of course.) It's a raw, vivid scene, almost pagan in its vitality, so if you're in Vitoria-Gasteiz then (Mar or Apr depending on the year) and want to preserve memories of one of the country's rarest happenings for posterity, load up your camera and catch one of the five buses a day that run here from Vitoria-Gasteiz. It's only a half-hour ride to get here.

half-timbered facade you can view Celto-Iberian and Roman pottery shards and statues unearthed from digs in the area (look out for the remarkably realistic tombstone carving of a Roman horseman known as the *Knight's Stele*); and the **Museo Fournier de Naipes** (calle Cuchillería 54; ☎ 945-181-820; free admission; Tues–Fri 10am–2pm and 4–6:30pm, Sat 10am–2pm, Sun noon–2pm), which traces the unique history of playing cards. As far as I know, Naipes is the only museum of its kind in the world, and it boasts a richly varied global selection of 15,000 decks through the ages.

Be sure to take the time to step outside and refresh yourself with an amble amid the green stuff. As we've already mentioned, the city is filled with beautiful **parks** and the largest of these is the sylvan **Juan de Arriago** ⚔, which boasts lush lawns, flower beds, and a cornucopia of trees ranging from stocky horse chestnuts to towering sequoias. The oldest park is the enchanting **La Florida,** which was first laid out in the 19th century, and the most exotic is the **Santa Catalina Botanical Garden** with its collection of plants from all over the world.

ACTIVE VITORIA-GASTEIZ

Several **golf** courses dot the Vitoria-Gasteiz area. Nearest is the **Club de Golf Larrabea** (Carretera Landa s/n; ☎ 945-465-485; www.larrabea.com), which has an 18-hole, par-72 course, as well as a swimming pool and restaurant. Greens fees are 45€ on weekdays, 75€ weekends. Children 17 and under pay 10€ and 20€, respectively, for these periods.

ATTENTION, SHOPPERS!

Two large shopping centers dominate the scene here, selling pretty well anything you're likely to be looking for. These are the **Centro Comercial** (Lakua Duque de Wellington 6), a spacious mall development with an infinite variety of *tiendas* and stores; and the newer and even bigger two-story **El Boulevard,** on the edge of the Casco Antiguo between calle Zaramaga and the Portal de Gamarra, with a total of 150 shops.

Leather, ceramic, and porcelain souvenirs are sold in a variety of shops around the **Plaza de España** and along the pedestrianized **calle Dato.** And if you're look-ing for that odd indeterminate bargain whose sheer incongruity or bizarreness will implant Vitoria-Gasteiz forever in your memory, check out **Segunda Mano (Second Hand)** (calle Prudencio María Verástegui; ☎ 945-270-007), which occu-pies hangar-size premises in the Old Town. It specializes, as its name suggests, in selling used antiques and other diverse artifacts of all shapes and sizes, from musi-cal instruments and sports gear (fancy a jai alai racket?) to—barely—roadworthy vehicles.

NIGHTLIFE

The center has a modest but lively choice of after-dark spots, many within easy walking distance of each other. In addition to those late night *pintxo* bars, which constitute an important part of Vitoria-Gasteiz's nocturnal fun scene, two popu-lar nightclubs are the gay-oriented **Studio 69** (calle Pintorería; no phone; cover 9€), which often features live local performers, and the **Cairo Stereo Club** (calle Aldalbe 9; no phone; cover 10€), where inventive DJs inspire the very mixed clientele with a deafening variety of electronic sounds and hold regular uninhib-ited "theme" parties. Both open mainly at weekends from 11pm to 5am.

One of the major jazz festivals in the north of Spain takes place here annually in mid-July. This is the weeklong **Festival de Jazz de Vitoria-Gasteiz** ★★ (☎ 945-141-919; www.jazzvitoria.com), which features big-name performers like Herbie Hancock and Chucho Valdéz. Tickets range from 10€ to 35€, depend-ing on who's appearing. Spontaneous entertainment also takes place on the street during this period, ostensibly free (although donations are always gratefully received).

GET OUT OF TOWN

What's the most famous and popular wine producing area in Spain? Any *vino* guz-zler worth his or her salt will be able to tell you straight away: **Rioja.** While many other zones of Spain produce quality wines that are highly regarded inside the country—such as Penedés (from Catalunya) and Ribera del Duero (from Castilla y Leon)—only Rioja has so far managed to capture international attention (almost to the same extent as Bordeaux in France, with which it has certain affini-ties). Its main wine-producing areas are in the adjoining province of La Rioja where they're principally concentrated in Logroño (Rioja Baja) and Haro (Rioja

Alta). Lesser known is the fact that Alava has its own little Rioja zone, centered around the captivating burg of **Laguardia** ⭐ which looms sentinel-style on a hilltop down near the border with La Rioja itself. This tiny treat of mainly pedestrianized narrow lanes and medieval buildings, highlighted by the 12th-century Gothic Santa María de los Reyes Church, would be interesting enough just for a historic visit. But its real attractions are the 300 wine *bodegas* (cellars) hidden in a honeycomb of tunnels underneath the town. The top place to visit and sample a couple of *copas* is the **Bodega El Fabulista** ⭐ (☎ 945-621-192; www.bodega elfabulista.com), located directly below the Palacio de los Sananiego and producing 32,000 liters (8,454 gallons) of quality wine a year using traditional methods. Just 2km (1¼ miles) out of town, the avant-garde **Bodega Ysios** (☎ 945-600-640; 3€; Mon–Fri 11am, 1pm, and 4pm; Sat–Sun 11am and 1pm) has a sinuously curving titanium roof—emulating the outline of the surrounding rugged mountains—designed by Bilbao airport architect Santiago Calatrava.

For general information on the town and its wine cellars, contact the **Oficina de Turismo** (Plaza San Juan in Palacio de los Sananiego; ☎ 945-600-845; www.laguardia-alava.com; Mon–Fri 10am–2pm and 4–7pm, Sat 10am–2pm and 5–7pm, Sun 10:45am–2pm). Here you can also get keys to visit the main church of **Santa María** de los Reyes, which is noted for its lavishly decorated Gothic portal. A good eating choice in the town is **La Muralla** (Paganos 42; daily 1–3pm), which does a sound inclusive 12€ lunch menu. **La Union bus service** (☎ 945-264-626; www.autobuseslaunion.com) runs four buses a day to Laguardia center from Vitoria-Gasteiz (1¾ hr.; 7€ one-way).

NAVARRE (NAVARRA)

Also strongly Basque in its heritage and temperament, the province of Navarre (Navarra in Spanish, Nafarroa in Basque), a proud semiautonomous area roughly the size of Massachusetts, extends below the Pyrenees just south of Alava and Guipuzcoa. The ubiquitous red beret, lively *jota* dance, and energetic game of *pelota*—that gutsier version of squash—are all emblematic expressions of its highly individual character. Occasionally, the vigorous determination that helped it trounce the retreating French at Roncevalles and defy centralist kings surfaces again in riotous form, never more so than during Pamplona's San Fermines bull-running and -fighting festivities.

A BRIEF HISTORY OF NAVARRE

Navarre has one of those resonant and suggestive names that reverberates with memories of an epic past filled with heroic exploits and stirring battles. Though the usual Romans, Christians, Muslims, and Jews all left their stamp here, it was for many years a totally independent region constantly embroiled in border skirmishes, fighting off invader after invader, until it united with Castille and Aragón under King Sancho III in the 11th century. Ferdinand of Aragón took the reins several centuries later and it became a fervent center of Carlism in the 19th century. Today it's a semiautonomous region, though the overriding majority wish for a full union with the Basque country's three provinces and the formation—with them—of a self-ruling state.

LAY OF THE LAND

Navarre is as scenically varied a province as any in the country, bordered by the Spanish and French Basque countries either side of the Pyrenees to the north, Aragón to the southeast, and La Rioja to the southwest. The landscape ranges from high mountains with lush wooded valleys and fast-running streams (as well as wide rivers such as the Ebro, which is the longest in Spain) to rich pasturelands producing some of Spain's best vegetables, and to the arid yellow plateau and dusty gray plains bordering Castile. Its architecture is equally diverse and reminders of constant past conflicts can be seen today in the lonely ruined castles and fortified walled towns that dominate its hilltops, while the Romanesque chapels, churches, and monasteries lining its green meadowlands were indirect results of the constant flow of medieval pilgrims on their way to Santiago de Compostela.

PAMPLONA (IRUÑA)

Pamplona (Iruña in Basque) today, outside of the riotous 9-day-long San Fermines fiestas, which have made it world famous (see below), is a prosperous, conservative, and surprisingly stolid township, low-key at least until sunset when, as in most Spanish cities, its bar life springs into action. For at least 50 weeks of the year, there's a lot more to do than run alongside stampeding bulls and avoid drunken daredevils weaned on the Hemingway ethos. Architectural delights abound for a start. As the city was the first big stop on the Camino de Santiago route across the Pyrenees from France it boasts a massive citadel (a remnant from its reign, from the 10th century on, as the capital of Navarre) and a wealth of churches and period mansions inside its colorful high-walled Old Quarter. Its parks too are a delight, especially the riverside Tejería and green fountain-filled La Taconera in the functional new Ensanche (Extension) zone where students from the University of Navarra come to study or simply have fun. And thanks to its location, it's also a great base for exploring the fascinating surrounding towns and countryside.

Lay of the Land

Apart from being interesting enough in its own right, Pamplona is conveniently located right at the entrance of the province, in easy reach of the Pyrenees, a host of verdant valleys with fast-flowing trout-filled streams, and a ubiquitous collection of the finest Romanesque and Gothic churches and monasteries in the country. Add to this some imposingly fortified hill towns, hidden mountain hamlets where you can really escape the hustle and bustle and wine-filled bodegas in areas of fine *crianza-* (vintage-) producing vineyards like southerly Olite, and you have a culturally and hedonistically rich environment.

Getting to Pamplona

The city is served by four to six daily **Iberia** flights from both Madrid and Barcelona, and fares from both those airports to Pamplona range between 150€ and 200€ one-way. Again, hardly the most economical option. Arrivals are at Aeropuerto de Noaín (☎ 902-404-704), 6.5km (4 miles) from the city center and accessible only by taxi for about 14€.

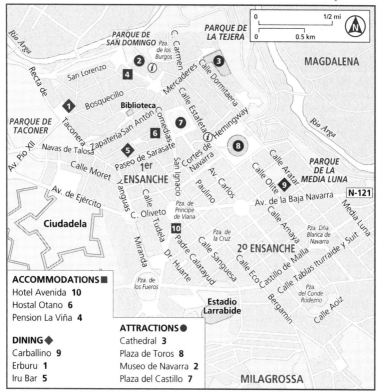

ACCOMMODATIONS ■
Hotel Avenida **10**
Hostal Otano **6**
Pension La Viña **4**

DINING ◆
Carballino **9**
Erburu **1**
Iru Bar **5**

ATTRACTIONS ●
Cathedral **3**
Plaza de Toros **8**
Museo de Navarra **2**
Plaza del Castillo **7**

Far better value is the RENFE service which operates four high-speed Alvia **trains** daily from Madrid (3¼ hours; 53€ one-way) and three a day from Barcelona: one fast Alvia train (3 hr. 40 min.; 53€ one-way); one regular-service day train (the cheapest): (6 hr.; 35€ one-way); and one overnight train with *preferente* (first-class) seats only (45€ one-way). For information, call ☎ 902-240-202, visit www.renfe.es, or stop by RENFE's office (calle Estella 8; ☎ 948-227-282; Mon–Fri 9am–1:30pm and 4:30–7:30pm, Sat 9:30am–1pm).

Most economical transportation is, as usual, by **bus.** Five daily Autobus Conda buses, with five more on Fridays and Sundays and one more Monday through Thursday and on Saturday, arrive from Madrid's avenida de America Station (5 hr.; 27€ one-way); and four daily Autobus Vibasa buses, with one more Friday and Saturday, arrive from Barcelona's Estacion Nord (5½ hr.; 25€ one-way). Check at the Pamplona's **Estación de Autobuses** (calle Conde Olivetto, corner of calles Yanguas and Miranda) or the **Oficina de Turismo** (see below) for time-tables.

If you're **driving,** the A-15 Navarra national highway begins on the outskirts of Pamplona and runs south to join A-68, midway between Zaragoza and Logroño. N-240 connects San Sebastián with Pamplona.

For general information, contact the **Oficina de Turismo** (calle Eslava 1; ☎ 848-420-420; www.navarra.es; Mon–Fri 10am–7pm, Sat 10am–2pm and 4–7pm, Sun 10am–2pm).

Accommodations, Both Standard & Not

As in the Basque region, you can enjoy the lovely Navarren countryside more fully by staying in a government-sponsored lodging or *casa rural*. These properties range from farmhouse or *pensione* rooms, averaging 60€ to 80€ per night for a double with en suite bathroom, to occasional fully equipped apartments which average out at 25€ per person per night for families or groups of four or more. Go to any of the local tourist offices, including the main one at Pamplona (see above) and get hold of a free brochure entitled ***Alojamientos de Turismo Rural*** for a fully documented list of lodgings currently available. Another excellent source is ***Navarra Selección*** (calle Larrabide 15 bajo; ☎ 948-291-327; www.navarraseleccion.com; Mon–Fri 9am–5pm), which provides a comprehensive choice of apartments in and around the city and *casas rurales* farther out in the countryside. Friendly, English-speaking staff man the phones on weekdays and are experts at finding reasonably priced accommodations. (An example: two-bedroom units in the University district of Pamplona, called Apartamentos Mirasierra, which run 28€–42€ per person per night; oddly the prices are lower on weekends.) For those who don't mind roughing it a bit, there's a fine campground 6km (3¾ miles) north of town on the N121 called **Ezcaba** (☎ 948-33-03-15; www.campingezcaba.com). On-site is a large pool and dining hall. Campers pay 5€ per person per night; those requiring bungalow accommodations (really a parked mobile home permanently moored) pay between 53€ and 86€ per night for up to six people, though the price drops if you stay more than one night. The campground is near a stop for a bus that heads into Pamplona four times a day.

Onto more standard accommodations. During Los San Fermines, prices for Pamplona hotels quoted below usually triple. So if you decide to book, do so well beforehand and be sure to confirm the correct price being charged. The best area in town for low-price accommodations is in the streets just off the Plaza del Castillo.

€   Whatever time of year you come—fiestas or not—you'll be hard pressed to find a cheaper place to stay (35€–40€ a night) than the very central **Pension la Viña**, (calle Jaurata 8-3º; ☎ 948-213-250; no credit cards). The good news is that the place is ultra-clean, the views of the old town are good from some rooms, and the staff is welcoming. The downside is that the rooms are austerely furnished and decorated, bath amenities are shared, and there's no lift to its third-floor location. (The graffiti on the walls outside is also a little off-putting too—best to just ignore it.)

€   Also recommended is the atmospheric **Hostal Otano** (calle San Nicolas 5; ☎ 948-227-036; MC, V), which is located in an old building in the traditional heart of town surrounded by shops and lively bars. The high-ceilinged rooms here (40€–50€ except during San Fermines) have large windows—some with tiny balconies overlooking the street—comfy beds with iron bedsteads, echoey wooden floors, large wardrobes, and good-size en suite bathrooms. Ostano's been run by the same chummy family for around 80 years, so you're pretty much guaranteed a warm welcome both at the hotel and at the downstairs bar and first-floor restaurant (which offer tasty *pintxos* and a solid 10€ weekday lunch menu, respectively).

€€–€€€ Fancy something a tad more stylish? Try **Hotel Avenida** ★ (Av. Zaragoza 5; ☎ 948-245-454; www.hotelavenida.biz; AE, DC, MC, V; Parking 11€), a centrally located inn with sleekly streamlined rooms in soothing shades of yellow and tan, satellite TV, free Wi-Fi, and en suite bathrooms with tub/shower combo. Some have small balconies. Prices are all over the map, but the website often features some terrific specials. For example, if you come for a Friday or Saturday night between January and June, a double could cost as little as 70€ a night. (Normally, it would be 140€, and during the July fiestas it would set you back 300€!)

Dining for All Tastes

As is the rule both here and in the main Basque country, *pintxo* nibbling in lively **tascas** is excitingly varied and extremely good value—even though the quantities are, of course, small. To enjoy the best of this world, explore three *casco antiguo* streets in particular: **calle San Nicolás, calle Estafeta,** and **calle de Jarauta.** Such is the unrelenting richness of choice here—many of the bars don't announce their name or even the fact that they *are* bars—that you won't know where to begin, so let me urge you to kick off at the **Iru Bar** ★ (calle San Nicolas 25; ☎ 948-211-094 or 942-23-428; daily 1–4pm and 8–11:30pm; V), where the *jamón serrano* in particular is out of this world, as is the range of suitably full-bodied Olite and Irache *vino tintos* (red wines) at 1.50€ or so a glass.

€–€€ Though it's miles inland, you can imagine yourself over in far west Galicia or even southerly Málaga from the delicious *pulpo gallego* (octopus, 10€) and *calamares a la romana* (oil-fried squid rings, 9€) served up at **Carballino** (calle Los Teobaldos 2; no phone; Mon–Sat 1:30–4pm and 8:30pm–midnight, Sun 1:30–4pm; no credit cards). Particularly good value is the 9€ set luncheon menu. So don't hold it against 'em that the setting's unadorned and rather echoey and service brusque: Here, they're putting their money into the food, not the ambiance.

€–€€€ The same could be said for my favorite local eatery, **Erburu** ★ (calle San Lorenzo 19; ☎ 948-225-169; daily 1:30–4pm and 8–11:30pm; Tues–Sun 9am–midnight, closed last week in July; AE, DC, MC, V; reservations recommended). Here veteran staff have been serving the clientele good old-fashioned regional grub for over 3 decades in a small dining room behind the busy bar. The totally traditional menu often includes dishes like *caracoles con ajo* (snails with garlic, 10€) and *merluza en salsa verde* (hake in a spicy green sauce, 15€). Other main courses range from 9€ to 21€ but the real bargain is the fixed-price lunch (11€). ***One warning:*** It's best to have some command of Spanish, as the waiters usually prefer to give diners an oral rundown on what's cooking out back rather than handing out menus.

"Europe's Biggest Party"—Los San Fermines ✫✫✫

For 9 riotous days beginning on July 6—when a rocket called "El Chupinazo" is fired—bulls are run through the streets of the very heart of Pamplona in a wild, semi-anarchic ceremony known the world over thanks to Ernest Hemingway. His incisive descriptions of this frenzied "*toro* fest" in his first novel, *The Sun Also Rises,* gave Pamplona an almost excessive dose of fame from which it's never really recovered, and each year the no-holds-barred fest attracts more and more visitors.

I'd guess very few know that they're hightailing it in honor of **San Fermín**, a 3rd-century Christian missionary who was born in Pamplona, declared bishop in Tortosa at the early age of 24, and executed 7 years later in Amiens, France, for what local religious authorities regarded as sacrilegious preachings. No matter, the crowds dash the length of the town to the Plaza de Toros, where revelers of all persuasions and conditions—from total sobriety to total drunkenness—sometimes pile on top of each other in a human barrier to try to stop them from entering the arena. But enter the bulls do, only to be made the centerpiece of a string of loudly cheered bullfights.

If you decide you want to get in on this unique shebang be sure you're up and about very early (or simply stay up all night), as things kick off at 8 every morning. In fact, the best procedure is to find yourself in a good spot for watching the proceedings about 2 hours earlier than that in the Paseo Estafeta, the high point of all the runs. Don't attempt to run, of course, if you're drunk or overtired or simply not fit. Occasionally, a college boy from Idaho gets gored in a doorway trying to dodge the charging beasts—the streets are narrow and the doorway space strictly limited—but by and large the blood count is far exceeded by the final *resaca* (hangover) toll.

Why You're Here: The Top Sights & Attractions

At the heart of Pamplona is the 19th-century **Plaza del Castillo (Castle Square),** which stands right on the southern edge of the old town, surrounded by narrow streets. During the San Fermines fests, its small fringe of lawn becomes a trash-strewn, unofficial campground, but it's all eventually cleared up with commendable efficiency by the valiant green-clad town cleaning workers at the end of the 9-day wine-and-bulls orgy. Before the nearby **Plaza de Toros**—alongside Paseo Hemingway (who, or what, else!)—was built in 1847, *corridas* (bullfights) actually used to be held in this now-paved-over, shady square. More enticing, though, for me is the long cobbled *tasca*- and shop-lined **Estafeta** *paseo* that runs parallel to the east—a main route for the bulls as they charge toward the bullring and a perennially vibrant spot frequented by fun-loving students in all weathers and seasons, fiestas or no.

As for the *corridas* (bullfights), you can—pending availability—buy tickets from 8pm the night before the *corrida* in question takes place, and if you want to economize, standing room only tickets can also be bought at around 4pm the same day as the event, usually from scalpers as travel agents will have long since sold out. Other fiesta events include brass-band performances, *peñas* (small clubs) celebrating their individual parties, processions, parades, fireworks, and live street performers. Bars and restaurants are open more or less round-the-clock. On the last day, at midnight, crowds chant *pobre de mi* ("poor me") in front of the town hall in Plaza del Castillo, mourning the end of all the fun (till next year).

Confirm any hotel booking *at least* 6 months in advance. There's a severe bed shortage in town over this period, and those that are available are exorbitantly expensive, which is why many younger members of the estimated half-million visitors sleep rough. If you decide to join them, the safest option is to sleep during the day in a group, and preferably on top of your belongings, keeping a clear eye out for petty thieves who regard this as a prime hunting season. The best place to wash up is at the calle Conde Oliveto bus station, where you can use the free (cold water) showers.

Many locals also rent rooms in their own homes—again at very high rates—and you may see posters to this effect in certain shop windows. Be wary of these though, as there is absolutely no guarantee of standards, and room conditions can vary from adequate to very basic, indeed.

Another economical option is to stay in one of the neighboring towns—like **Egüés** just 8km (5 miles) east—and catch the bus in.

To the east of here, calmly rising above the remains of a long disappeared Roman basilica—the town was named for Roman general Pompey Magnus who founded Pamplona in 75 B.C.—is the city's most impressive historical monument: the 14th-century **Catedral** ✪ (calles Curia/Dormitalería; ☎ 948-210-827; free admission to cathedral, museum 4.15€; Mon–Fri 10am–1:30pm and 4–7pm, Sat 10:30am–1:30pm). Don't be put off by the slightly daunting austerity of Ventura Rodríguez's neoclassical-baroque facade, but instead step inside and relish the delicious harmony of the magnificent 14th- and 15th-century Gothic cloisters. They're among the cathedral's greatest attractions, especially the east gallery chapel dedicated to the Bishop of Barbazana, which features some wonderfully delicate Gothic fan-vaulting work. At the center of the nave is the **alabaster tomb** ✪ of Charles III ("El Noble") and his spouse, Leonor of Castile, created by a highly gifted 15th-century Flemish sculptor from Tournai, Jean de Lome.

And before you leave, it's worth a peep at the atmospheric little **Museo Diocesano,** which houses gold and silver articles and Gothic reliquaries including the Holy Sepulcher in the cathedral's former refectory and kitchen.

Talking of museums, the city's top draw on that front is the **Museo de Navarra** ★★ (Cuesta de Santo Domingo 47; ☎ 948-426-492; 2€ adults, 1€ seniors and students, free for children 15 and under; Tues–Sat 10am–2pm and 5–7pm, Sun 11am–2pm), which, as the name suggests, explores the history of the province. You work your way up from Stone Age finds on the ground floor to modern local artworks at the top, en route taking in some impressive 2nd-century Roman mosaics, vivid 13th-century murals, and renaissance paintings. You'll learn, too, about Pamplona's most memorable military successes in 778 when furious local forces decimated Charlemagne's army in the Pyrenean mountain pass of Roncevalles after their retreating soldiery had sacked the city. (Most celebrated of the many Gallic victims on that occasion was the legendary knight Roland.) My favorite exhibit is the superb 1804 **Goya** portrait of the **Marqués de San Adrián,** whom the great Aragonese artist represents in a remarkably relaxed and realistic pose. It was painted at a time when Goya was suffering from a severe depression at having being turned down for the post of director general of the Spanish Academy of Art in Madrid because of his near total deafness. The *museo* is located just above the Arga River and small Rochapea Bridge in a former 16th-century hospital, Nuestra Señora de la Misericordia.

The Other Pamplona

Out of all the Spanish regions, you can only see Euskal Pelota here and in the neighboring Basque country. And watching a game of this hyped up, bigger-scale version of squash (which can be played either outdoors or indoors) may well be your best introduction to the Basque psyche. "It's a game . . . that brings out the character of the players and, although the Basques are reserved in most things, they show their feelings of rage, disgust, resentment, and shame when they fail in a stroke," wrote V. S. Pritchett in his book *The Spanish Temper* in 1954. And he added, "The audience does the same . . . ." Here's how it all works: Two players smash a ball against one or two high walls or *frontis,* each trying to score higher points than the other by not letting the ball fall to the floor. Sounds simple, but the drama (and betting) that ensues is mesmerizing.

If you want to see this uniquely regional activity performed at its best, just take a bus, taxi, or car trip 5km (3½ miles) out of town to the **Frontón Euskal–Jai Berri** ★ (avenida de Francia; ☎ 948-331-159; 15€), where real professionals let rip with an energy, enthusiasm, and competitive spirit that's exhausting just to watch. Games are usually limited to just four matches on Saturdays and start around 4pm. It's sometimes also played on Sundays and regional and national fiesta days. You can buy tickets any time during the sets.

You can bet on the outcome if you feel clued in enough (though this is probably best left to hard-core Navarren experts). It's by far the most popular Basque sport—either as a high-powered professional game or a friendly activity between enthusiasts who find it the most entertaining way to unwind.

Attention, Shoppers!

One thing you'll need if you're going to do full justice to the *fiestas*—or if you're not there then and are simply relaxing over a picnic in the countryside—is a typically Navarren *bota:* that bulbous leather wine skin from which you squirt wine into your mouth from as far away as your hand holding it will manage. (By the way, this requires a certain skill so make sure you're wearing old clothes when you first try it: The problem is not so much simply getting the stuff in your mouth, but swallowing it with your mouth still open as you continue squirting. If you don't swallow in time, your mouth just fills up and you're in trouble.) Buy this indispensable item at **Echeve** (calle Mercaderes 29; ☎ 948-224-215), which also sells *boinas* (berets), as well as more conventional tourist fare like ceramics and woodcarvings, or at **Las Tres ZZZ** (calle Comedias 7; ☎ 948-224-438; www.lastreszzz.com), which also stocks neckerchiefs and *gerrikos* (wide belts worn by the likes of weightlifters to strengthen their backs when they're lifting heavy things—not that we're recommending you go in for such hard-labor activities, but it's nice to look as if you could if you wanted to).

As well as wearing the right gear, you'll need to orient yourself, and an excellent bookshop, selling a variety of detailed maps on the city, is the **Librería Abarzuza** (calle Santo Domingo 29; ☎ 948-213-213). You may also run out of film during the fiestas—most people do—so you can replenish your stock at **Foto Auma** (Plaza del Castillo; ☎ 948-210-854), right in the old town center, where you can not only buy fresh film, but also pick up their prints of the highlights of that day's *corrida* for around 4.50€ a shot.

For more general shopping, you can here at last eschew the usually ubiquitous Corte Inglés in favor of Pamplona's very own grand department store, **Unzu** (calle Mercaderes 3; ☎ 948-209-100).

Nightlife in Pamplona

The western side of the Casco Viejo provides the liveliest late-night bar scene. Try the trendy internationally themed **Dunkalk** (calle Alhondiga 4; 10pm–2am) for its Mexican beers and Australian (yes!) tapas, which they claim are of kangaroo meat!

For later nightclub action head for the vast, cavernous **Marengo** (Av. Bayona 2; ☎ 948-265-542; Thurs–Sat 11pm–6am), which appeals mainly to elegant young things dancing to the very latest (recorded) sounds. Look your very best if you want to impress the seen-it-all-before doormen into letting you pass through its portals. Admission including a drink is 15€. Or you might prefer the most popular disco of all, **Reverendos** (Monasterio de Velate 5; ☎ 948-261-593; 11pm–5:30am), where 20s to 30s swingers also gyrate and imbibe till the birds start twittering. The cover charge of 5€ includes the price of a drink.

Get Out of Town

At the medieval Gothic town of **Olite** ✮44km (27 miles) south of Pamplona, in a rich agricultural belt of vineyards and cornfields, you not only have a chance to knock back some of the heartiest *vinos* this side of Rioja but also get to see a castle that, for sheer surrealistic beauty, rivals Segovia's great Disney-inspiring Alcazar in Castile. Topped by impossibly narrow turrets, from where you half-expect to see a veiled damsel awaiting the arrival of her number-one knight, the 15th-century **Palacio Real** ✮✮ (Plaza Carlos III; ☎ 948-740-035; www.palacioreal deolite.com; 3.10€ adults, 1.40€ seniors, students, and children; Apr–Sept daily 10am–7pm, July–Aug daily 10am–8pm, Oct–Mar daily 10am–6pm; closed Dec 25, Jan 1, and Jan 6) is a Gothic masterpiece and was a favorite residence of Navarran kings such as Charles III ("El Noble"), who made it the seat of the court during his reign.

If you decide to overnight it, stay at the highly hospitable **Merindad de Olite** (Rúa de la Judería 11; ☎ 948-740-735; MC, V), which has medieval decor and well-equipped rooms with en suite bathroom (65€–70€ a night). And you can have a true blowout of a meal at **Gambarte** ★ (Rúa del Seco 15; ☎ 948-740-197; daily 1:30–4pm and 8pm–midnight; MC). Its totally filling Navarren menu—complete with jug of splendid dark red Olite wine—is only 9€. No frills with the decor here—just a basic brightly lit salon and gruff but friendly service—but the food is primo.

For general information, contact the **Oficina de Turismo** (Plaza Teobaldos; ☎ 948-741-703; www.navarra.es; summer Mon–Sat 10am–2pm and 4–7pm, Sun 10am–2pm; winter Mon–Fri 10am–5pm, Sat–Sun 10am–2pm).

GETTING THERE

Four trains per day make the 40-minute trip from Pamplona. For rail information, call ☎ 942-240-202. Two bus companies, **Conda** (☎ 948-821-026) and **La Tafallesa** (☎ 948-222-886), run 7 to 12 buses a day from Pamplona, taking roughly the same time. If you're driving, take the A-15 expressway south from Pamplona.

9

Galicia, Asturias & Cantabria

Atlantic-washed beaches and lush green countryside form the unspoiled landscape of Spain's historic northwest provinces

by Peter Stone

THE THREE PROVINCES THAT EXTEND FROM THE WESTERN EDGE OF THE Basque country along the shores of the Bay of Biscay and then down the western Atlantic coast to Portugal have much in common geographically—fine sandy beaches, a verdant North European looking landscape, and lots of rain—but differ widely in character and atmosphere. Galicia is enigmatic, mysterious, something of an outcast, harried by the elements, and still the recent memories of a past poverty that forced many locals to emigrate across the wild Atlantic that pounds its shores to earn a living. Asturias, once a radical cradle of rebellion, is now comfortably sedate, home of apple orchards, cider, fat cows, and butter—a Spanish Maine, if you will. Cantabria is genteel, conformist, conservative—almost Anglophone in its history of regal visitors and recurring seaward links with the United Kingdom.

DON'T LEAVE GALICIA, ASTURIAS & CANTABRIA WITHOUT . . .

Exploring La Coruña's Old Town.   From the splendid María Pita Square, with its statue honoring the eponymous spear-clutching heroine, to its surrounding maze of pedestrianized, bar-filled lanes. See p. 384.

Paying homage to Santiago de Compostela's Cathedral.   The great Christian mecca for the Camino de Santiago pilgrims past and present. See p. 392.

Spelunking (well, sort of).   The Cave of Cavadongas is Asturias's treasured cradle of the Christian reconquest from which a small force led by the warrior Pelayo sallied forth to defeat a larger Muslim army in the 9th century. The Altamira Caves, by contrast, are the home of the oldest cave drawings in Spain, from well back in the Paleolithic Age. See p. 421.

Climbing in the Picos de Europa.   One of the most stunningly wild, natural, mountain parks in Spain. See p. 409.

Testing your libido against the romanesque architecture in Oviedo.   The beauty of this Golden Age town became an aphrodisiac in the Woody Allen film *Vicky Cristina Barcelona* (2008). See if it has the same effect on you.

GALICIA

Westerly Galicia is the antithesis of the popular conception of Spain: Instead of a blazing sun, a dazzlingly arid landscape, and the evocative sound of a flamenco guitar, it has cloudy skies, green countryside, and the mournful wail of bagpipes (known locally as *gaitas*). And in place of clichéd, lighthearted, nut-brown locals, we have a quiet, introspective, sometimes melancholy people (as typified by the beautiful but almost unbearably sad verses of its greatest poet Rosalia Castro), often with pale complexions, blue eyes, and red hair. It's a strange, mystical land where *meigas* (witches), exorcists, soothsayers, and fortune tellers still exist and superstitions prevail as they've done for centuries in the tiny isolated villages of the interior. Its aura is Celtic, not surprisingly: Its earliest visitors were the Celts, whose presence is still echoed by the dolmens and remains of hilltop forts *(castros)* that dot the countryside. But the relationship is more than just history: The land here actually *looks* like a portion of Ireland that's strayed 1,000 miles off-course. Two of Galicia's four provinces (La Coruña and Pontevedra) are indented by a nigh Scandinavian blend of fjord-like inlets, known as *rías*. Yet, culturally, Galicia doesn't look north. The people speak (in addition to Castilian Spanish) a language called Gallego that's closely linked to that of their Portuguese neighbors to the south. In the 1980s, it became a semiautonomous region, and, in many ways, its spiritual capital is Atlantic-facing Lisbon rather than landlocked Madrid.

LA CORUÑA (A CORUÑA)

Legend has it that the real founder of La Coruña was Hercules. The undisputed facts, however, are that Celts and Phoenicians were among the earliest visitors attracted by its magnificent natural harbor and that the Romans were the first to transform it into an important port, which they called Ardobicum Coronium. In the 16th century, it lived its finest hour (short-lived, alas) when Philip II's "Invincible Armada" sailed from here to do battle with the English fleet. Only half the ships made it back and, to add insult to injury, Sir Francis Drake and his ships later set fire to the port in reprisal for the ill-fated invasion. On that occasion, the inhabitants fought back, however, led by a young heroine called María Pita, and today the town's most picturesque square is named after her.

> ❝ *La ciudad donde nadie es forestero.* ❞ *(The city where no one is a stranger.)*
>
> —Anonymous paean to La Coruña

Unlike the agriculturally oriented interior of the province, La Coruña has rarely seen bad times and even flourished in its marine capacity during the troubled 19th and 20th centuries, when close trading links with England and Northern Europe kept the business wheels turning while other major Spanish ports were in decline. So, in this town, you can forget what I said earlier about the Galicians being melancholy. Prosperous and totally dominated by the sea in its lifestyle and thought processes, La Coruña and its inhabitants have tended to look outward rather than inward, and are open rather than closed to other influences. Many of them have already been to, and lived in, various other parts of the globe. Hence, the

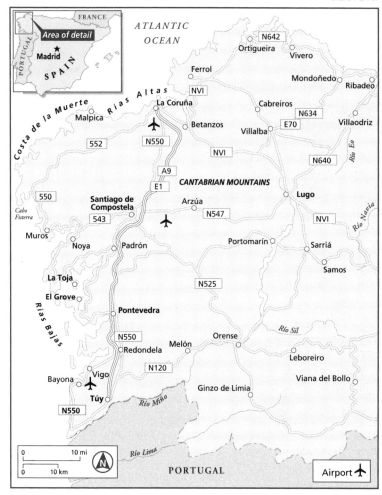

spontaneous readiness to welcome *forasteros* (foreigners) you'll encounter when you tour the bars of the old town, the focal and spiritual center of which, the colonnaded María Pita square, is ringed by smart cafes with outdoor tables packed to capacity the moment those perennial Atlantic clouds and showers decide to take a (pardon the pun) rain check. Its magnificent but surprisingly modern Riazor beachfront, dominated by high-rise apartments, is equally lively in summer.

Lay of the Land

Like Cádiz down south in Andalusia, La Coruña juts out into the Atlantic like a fist, surrounded by water on three sides. Stand and watch the waves crashing on the rocks near La Coruña's Torre de Hercules and you get the exhilarating sensation that you're on the edge of the world. The province extends northward along a rugged coast as far as neighboring Lugo province, and south past the long inlets of the Rías Bajas and great lighthouse-topped Cape of Finisterre to the gentler sub-province of Pontevedra. The wildest, rockiest, and most exposed section of the coast is known as the Costa da Morte (literally "Coast of Death") in Gallego because of the large number of shipwrecks that have occurred there.

Getting to & Around La Coruña

For **general information,** contact the **Oficina de Turismo** (Dársena de la Marina s/n; ☎ 981-22-18-22; www.turgalicia.es; Mon–Fri 10am–2pm and 4–7pm, Sat 11am–2pm and 5–7pm, Sun and fiestas 10am–2pm).

GETTING TO LA CORUÑA

There are seven Iberia **flights** a week from Madrid to La Coruña's **Aeropuerto de Alvedro** (☎ 981-18-72-00), which lies 10km (6 miles) from the heart of the city. The best bargains, though, are with easyJet (www.easyjet.com), which flies the same route from the Spanish capital at a far lower cost (except for July–Aug when fares rise dramatically). Buses run from the airport into La Coruña 10 times a day (journey time: 25 min.) and cost 0.95€ one-way. A taxi ride in will set you back 12€.

Because **RENFE rail services** (☎ 902-24-02-02; www.renfe.es) from Madrid still take a dawdling 8 to 9 hours and cost 48€ one way, hop aboard an **ALSA bus** (☎ 902-422-242; www.alsa.es) instead. (They're slightly faster and cheaper.) Seven buses a day trek from Madrid's Estación Sur (Mendez Alvaro) to La Coruña's bus station (calle Caballeros 21; ☎ 981-184-335) taking 6½ to 8½ hours and cost 30€ to 35€ one way.

If you're **driving** from Madrid, take the N-VI. If you're coming from San Sebastián or Bilbao, take the coastal highway, N-634, which runs virtually the whole length of northern Spain.

LOCAL & REGIONAL TRANSPORTATION

There is an efficient urban **bus service** (1€ one-way), which will take you to most corners of the city. The main terminus is the central Praza de María Pita. A **tourist tram** also runs between the Darsena de la Marina lighthouse, aquarium, and town beaches, every half hour in July and Aug from noon to 9pm (Sept–June and weekends hourly noon–7pm; 1€).

Monbus (☎ 982-292-900) runs buses between La Coruña and Santiago de Compostela every hour. The journey time varies between 50 minutes and 1½ hours and costs 6.15€.

The lowest rates for **rental cars** are at **Autos Brea** (calle Fernandez la Torre 110; ☎ 981-238-646; www.autosbrea.com), with compacts starting at 57€ including full insurance and 500km (311 miles) per day.

Accommodations, Both Standard & Not

€   I always enjoy staying at the **Hostal La Perla** (Rua Torreio 11–2º; ☎ 981-226-700; www.hostallaperla.es; MC, V). Sure it's not-even-art-on-the-walls simple in its decor, but the staff is sweet tempered and does its best to be helpful, the location is right in the old town, it's spotless, and the prices are right: 40€ to 50€ per night, and that's for a room adjoining a cream-tiled shower room.

Don't Pass on the Pass

Visitors staying longer than a couple of days will find it worthwhile to buy a **Coruña Card** at the tourist office (see above), which costs 7€ for one adult, 15€ for 2 adults and 2 children. This entitles them to free access to the lighthouse, archeological museum, and city tram, as well as discounts at many other attractions and 40% off car rental.

€–€€   Winter pricing (Oct–May) is only a tad higher at the modern **Hotel España** (Juana de Vega 7; ☎ 981-224-506; www.hotespa.com; AE, DC, MC, V; parking 10€), a good value at just 55€ a night for a standard double. (During the 4 summer months June–Sept it rises to 75€–95€). It may not have much regional character (or much character, period—think faceless but clean), but it's a great practical choice, as the hotel is handily located halfway between the port and Riazor beach, close to the Jardines de Méndez Núñez.

€–€€   Of course, you don't have to stay directly in La Coruña to enjoy its— and the region's—pleasures. A top choice among the *casas rurales* in the area is **Casa Outeiro** ★★ (San Sadurniño de Outeiro; ☎ 981-780-402; MC, V), a handsome country house of local stone walls, open fireplaces, and well-tended lawns and flower beds; there's even a tennis court and swimming pool on-site. In short, all you need to wallow in the bucolic (and beachy—the sands are just 10km/ 7 miles away) charms of the area. The nine rooms here come in a variety of styles: Some have polished dark-wood floors, bright cream and yellow walls, and wicker rocking chairs, while others boast original tiled flooring, rough brick walls, and pine bedsteads. Some (the cheaper ones: 55€–60€) are rather compact, others (at 75€–80€) are more generously spaced, and all have immaculate en suite tiled bathrooms. Continental breakfast is an extra 4€ and is served in the charming ground-floor dining room, which also provides Galician-grandma-style main meals (think empanadas or *lacon con grelos,* pork shoulder with turnip tops) for 12€ for three courses, with wine. While it's useful to rent a car, you can easily get here by bus as the La Coruña–based Arriva company (☎ 981-311-370) runs a regular service along the C-642 road, which stops near the house.

Dining for All Tastes

Seafood is—as you'd expect—*the* thing to go for in this town, and the favorite specialty is *pulpo* (octopus) served *a la vinegreta* (cold in vinaigrette sauce) or *gallego* (hot, sprinkled with paprika, and accompanied by boiled potatoes). It usually costs around 12€ to 16€ for a fair-size *ración,* depending on the bar or restaurant. Another exclusively Galician treat is *percebes* (goose barnacles), which look a bit like the inverted cloven hooves of microscopically small animals. For their size, they're the most expensive seafood item around (expect to pay 20€–25€ for a modest-size *ración*), so unless you're ready to splurge, just content yourself with watching other people trying to eat them and wincing when the juice from these weird little fellows squirts in their eyes. (The reason they're so expensive, by the way, is that they're lodged on the most inaccessible parts of rocks, and fishermen often risk their lives trying to pry them off in high seas.)

€–€€   The best place in town for *pulpo* (octopus) is—surprise, surprise—the **Mesón do Pulpo (Octopus Inn)** (calle de la Franja 11; daily 1:30–4pm and 8–11:30pm; V), a buzzy local bar in the heart of the Old Town where you get a good-size *ración* of the real McCoy, complete with spuds that have been appropriately boiled and smothered with olive oil and paprika as described above, for 14€. A glass or two of *albariño* white wine (from the province's top vineyards south of Pontevedra) go well with this chewy, bulbous, purple-tentacled cephalopod.

€€–€€€   Another traditional high spot for sampling Galician seafood is the **Adega O Bebedeiró** ✪ (calle Angel Rebollo 34; ☎ 981-21-06-09; Tues–Sun 1–4pm and 8pm–midnight; closed last 2 weeks in both June and July; AE, DC, MC, V) where you get a suitably congenial rustic atmosphere—enhanced by old stone walls, a cozy fireplace, hardwood floors, and pine tables—and more than a few frills with the excellent list of fare, which includes such delights as *dorada* (bream) stuffed with *mejillones* (clams) and baked in *hojaldre* (puff pastry) for 18€. Paellas are pretty good too (around 12€ per head), as are the local *setas* (mushrooms) in olive oil and *pimiento* (green pepper) sauce (8€).

Why You're Here: The Top Sights & Attractions

Pack your cushy-soled shoes, as La Coruña is a city where you'll want to wander. Start at the loveliest of the city's many squares—clearly dividing the Old Town and New Town—the stylishly arcaded **Plaza de María Pita** ✪. Its central statue honors La Coruña's young 16th-century heroine, a local housewife who fired a cannon to alert the citizens of an imminent invasion by Francis Drake. On a more intimate scale is the nearby cobbled **Plazuela de Santa Bárbara,** a tiny tree-shaded plaza flanked by old houses and the high walls of the Santa Bárbara convent.

Also good for a reflective stroll is the small but haunting 19th-century **Jardín de San Carlos,** laid out beside the Paseo del Parrote, on the site of an old fortress that once guarded the harbor. It contains the tomb of the British General Sir John Moore, who died heroically in a rear-guard action against Napoleon's forces, selflessly enabling 15,000 of his troops to escape by sea. Back in the very center of town, the charming **Jardines de Méndez Núñez,** between the harbor and Los Cantones (Cantón Grande and Cantón Pequeño), are great for a restful interlude during your sightseeing meanders.

Out on the Old City's headland, protected from the sea by a high wall, is the town's top Romanesque church, the 13th-century **Iglesia de Santa María del Campo** ✪ (calle de Santa María). Outside, look for the elaborately carved west-side door and the uniquely beautiful rose window above the entrance. Inside is a charming little religious art museum, which opens Tuesday through Friday 9am to 2pm and 5 to 7pm and Saturday 10am to 1pm. At the headland's extreme southeasterly tip—virtually surrounded by the Atlantic—the former Castillo de San Antón, built by Philip II in the 16th century, has been converted into the **Museo Arqueológico e Histórico** (☎ 981-18-98-50; 2€ adults, 1€ seniors and children 11 and under; July–Aug Tues–Sat 10am–9pm, Sun 10am–3pm; Sept–June Tues–Sat

10am–7:30pm, Sun 10am–2:30pm). Its main attractions are the dazzling collection of Celtic jewelry inside, and the superlative sea views from the rooftop. At the far northern end is the famed **Torre de Hercules lighthouse** (2.50€; Oct–Mar 10am–5:45pm; Apr–Sept Sun–Thurs 10am–8:45pm, Fri–Sat 10am–11:45pm). Considering its ancestry—the tower was originally built by the Romans in the 2nd century—what you see today seems disappointingly modern, since the building has been continuously renovated from the 18th century onward and evokes virtually no impression of its long past. Climb its 234 steps, though, and the knockout vistas of both city and coast that you get from the top more than compensate.

Close by, the next mini-headland along, the striking modern **Aquarium** (10€; July–Aug daily 10am–9pm; Sept–June Sun–Thurs 10am–8pm, Fri–Sat 10am–7pm) has an impressive assortment of fish from all over the world, plus kid-friendly interactive displays and a Nautilus tank, which takes you down to see what's going on in the Atlantic coast's submarine world. Finally, back on the main headland's west side overlooking Riazor Bay is another innovative building—the boat-shaped, Japanese-designed **Domus (Museum of Mankind)** (Rua de Santa Teresa 1; www.casaciencias.org; July–Aug daily 11am–9pm, Sept–June daily 10am–7pm). The 2€ combined ticket also includes entry to the **Casa de las Ciencias,** a science museum at Parque Santa Margarita. Both museums have highly detailed interactive displays on a variety of subjects, ranging from the analysis of "live" insects to studying the stars. The Domus's particular party piece is a fascinating instructional "journey" through the workings of the human body.

Active La Coruña

You can swim from a surprisingly clean, sheltered, and safe beach right in the city itself. This is the **Riazor,** which curves around a fine-sandy crescent bay, backed by a long line of high-rises on the west side of the town. On fine days in July and August, every inch of sand is covered by locals and visitors. Then it's better to head for the Santa Cristina beach, about 5km (3 miles) outside town. Buses regularly make the round-trip service there for 1€, but a more fun way to go there is by small steamer from the nearby Club Náutico (about 2€).

Or you could bike there (and around the area). The municipal bicycle shed on the Paseo de la Darsena, right alongside the leisure harbor, rents out bicycles for 22€ per day, or 7€ for 4 hours. The service is available from 9am to 9pm in the summer, and from 9am to 2pm and 4 to 9pm in winter.

Attention, Shoppers!

For Spaniards, the name **Adolfo Dominguez** (Av. Finisterre 3, ☎ 981-252-539; Juan de la Vega 6, ☎ 981-225-165; www.adolfo-dominguez.com) is a byword for urbane, highly wearable clothing. This Galician designer's eponymous stores exist in every major Iberian city, but the one on avenida Finisterre is the flagship, where you can buy a wide range of items from blouses to cocktail dresses for women to tailored jeans and well-cut suits for men. A hallmark is his use of natural fabrics in loose-fitting but still flattering garments. You'll also find a selection of downright adorable clothes for children.

On the foodie front, Galician **cakes** and **charcuterie** are the "gets," and you'll find them at the city's favorite delicatessen-cum-*pastelería* (pastry shop) **Colmado Blanco** (Juan Flórez 28) or the **covered market** at Plaza de San Agustín, which provides an exceptional daily display of fish freshly plucked from the Atlantic alongside all the colorful fruits and vegetables.

If you want to see what young Gallego artists are up to, check out **Arrancada** (calle Zapatería 4; no phone), which sells contemporary paintings at varying prices. If, on the other hand, your penchant is more for the written word, a first-rate bookshop to browse through is **Librería Xiada** (Av. de Finisterre 76-78; ☎ 981-276-950), which has a wide selection of the latest Spanish and international editions on subjects covering everything from travel to Greek tragedies.

Nightlife in La Coruña

La Coruña is packed with tiny hole-in-the-wall bars that seem hardly to have changed in 7 or so decades—ideal places to kick off the evenings with a few tapas and glasses of very reasonably priced Ribeiro white wine. One such spot, **A Roda** (Capitán Troncoso 8; ☎ 981-228-671; daily 1–4pm and 8pm–midnight), is admittedly dark, grungy, and unadorned but so packed with a raucous assortment of Gallegos and *extranjeros* (non-Spaniards) that it's usually a party. Most relish its plates of grilled sardines and steaming *pulpo a feira* (octopus in spicy sauce) at 6€ to 10€ a go.

If, after such indulgences, you feel the need to dance them off, head for the psychedelic and barn-size **Disco Playa Club** (Andén de Riazor; ☎ 981-277-514; www.playaclub.net; cover 10€; Thurs–Sat 11pm–5am). Having dominated the La Coruña night scene for more than half a century in one form or another, this legendary nightspot today features the latest sounds from funk and soul jazz to alternative pop and hip-hop. The setting couldn't be better—right beside the ocean and just a few steps away from the city's Riazor beach. Ideal on moonlit summer nights for a quick sobering dawn dip in the chilly Atlantic waters.

For a more regional mood, wander into the grungy, dimly-lit **A Cova Céltica** (Orzan 82; no phone; daily 10pm–4am), which is located on the buzzy central **Rúa**

The *Horreos,* the *Horreos!*

As you travel about the Galician countryside, you'll notice a proliferation of long, gray, granite or wooden rectangular constructions perched on stone columns, their tiny right-angled roofs topped by somber crosses or tiny stone pyramids, their sides covered sometimes by moss, their bases serrated by strange-looking vents. What are these miniature mystic-looking monuments? Churches for elves? Elongated cremation caskets? Avant-garde dog kennels? They are, in fact, *horreos* (small granaries used for storing wheat). The slits are to let in air and prevent the wheat from being ruined by humidity. The longest one, at Carnota near Cape Finisterre, is 35m (100 ft.) long. They originated in Roman times, and today there are still 35,000 of them in Galicia (the oldest survivor dating back to the 15th century). There are a further 18,000 in neighboring Asturias, where they're usually square shaped and known as *horrus*. In both provinces, these eye-catching symbols of northern Spain's traditional reliance on farming and agriculture are virtually a tourist attraction.

The Other Galicia: The Wild, Wild West

Probably one of the last things you'd expect to see in Spain is a rough-and-tumble rodeo, but if you're here in early July you stand a good chance of doing just that if you're in the right spot. Wild horses still roam the Galician countryside in fair numbers, and the beginning of the region's relatively short summer sees a sudden urge among local farmers to round some of them up (with vans rather than lassoes), put them in corrals, and brand them amid the raucous applause of the assembled crowds. They also give the horses a neat haircut in a ceremony called **A Rapa das Bestas** (The Shearing of the Beasts), which rivals The Death Coast (below) as the province's number-one would-be horror movie title. Then follows a lively phase of devil-may-care bareback riding by valiant *vaqueros* emboldened by liberal gulps of *orujo* (traditional firewater made, like the Italian *grappa,* from grape stalks and skins) amid a general party atmosphere. Two of the best places to see this crazy and chaotic spectacle are at **Candaosa** near Viveiro on the north coast and **Sabucedo** just above Pontevedra down south. The website www.rapadasbestas.es gives some colorful pictures and information on these events (but it tests your linguistic prowess by only printing it in Gallego).

do Orzan, one street back from the beach, and features boisterous evenings with live Gallego music (bagpipes and all!). Drinks are 4€ and up.

Get Out of Town: Rías Altas

A beautiful succession of coves, estuaries, and fjord-like fissures known as the **Rías Altas (Upper Inlets)** indents the northern Galician coast from La Coruña up and along the Bay of Biscay coast as far as the Ría de Ribadeo bordering Asturias. An ideal day's drive, the villages can also be seen (much less efficiently, unfortunately) by bus from La Coruña (p. 386).

The first town you come to on this route—directly west of the capital at the confluence of the Mendo and Mandeo rivers—is **Betanzos** ✹ (20km/14miles from La Coruña), a labyrinthine gem noted for its 12th-century churches, spacious main square, and an extraordinary park (O Pasatempo) that's filled with sculptures, murals, and a grotto with Gaudí-like columns. From here, turn north toward the long fingerlike **Cabo Ortegal**—Spain's most northerly point—and **Vicedo,** home to magnificent and swimmable **Xillo beach.** All along this route, just inland, lies unspoiled rural Galicia, where you can still see oxen plowing the cornfields.

Crossing into Lugo sub-province is the highlight of this coast, **Viveiro** ✹✹ (120km/80 miles from La Coruña) a blend of summer resort and historic town, complete with medieval walls, an old gateway (Puerta de Carlos V), and a number of churches, including the fine Gothic **Iglesia San Francisco.** It's a great area for coastal walks; the **Oficina de Turismo** (Av. Ramón Canosa s/n; ☎ 982-56-08-79; www.viveiro.es; July–Aug Mon–Sat 11am–2pm and 4:30–7:30pm, Sun noon–2pm; Sept–June Mon–Sat 11am–2pm and 4:30–7:30pm) can give you maps of trails. East of here is **Sargadelos,** a delightful little ceramic-producing town where you can see the full range of the famous Galician pottery at the **Fábrica de Ceramica de Sargadelos (Sargadelos Ceramic Factory)** (☎ 982-55-78-41; free admission; Mon–Fri 8:30am–12:30pm and 2:30–5:30pm). Best place to buy ceramics, however, at deeply discounted rates is not in Sargadelos itself but in the neighboring village of **Burela** (5km/3miles) at the **Victoria Naveira Vior retail shop** (Rua do Porto 1; ☎ 982-55-78-41).

SANTIAGO DE COMPOSTELA ✿✿✿

This pilgrimage city of warmly golden granite buildings—often seen gleaming under the effects of a gentle shower—has been the high point of any visit to Galicia ever since the medieval faithful of all persuasions, from princes to peasants, first came to honor the tomb of St. James, a disciple of Jesus who was beheaded in Jerusalem. Declared a UNESCO World Heritage Site in its entirety, it's a harmoniously integrated city whose maze of narrow and largely pedestrianized streets weaves past a veritable sea of churches, mansions, museums, and flagstoned squares. That perennial rain is an essential part of the atmosphere: Vegetation grows profusely out of clefts in cathedral's walls while its gargoyles regularly decant jets of water onto the heads of the passing crowds. (One of the most popular souvenirs is a small model of a priest carrying an umbrella.) Santiago always looks pristine and freshly washed because the weather never gives it enough time to collect dust or grime. (God's way of keeping it pure, say the locals.) It's actually quite small, and the 100,000-odd population is one-third students, accounting for a decidedly unholy liveliness at night in many bars. You can cross the whole center on foot in about 15 minutes and find yourself in open countryside before you know it, but you'd need at least that number of days if you ever really wanted to do the city's chockablock array of monuments full justice.

A Brief History of Santiago de Compostela

The history of Santiago is really the story of its great cathedral, the symbolic heart of the city. World attention was first drawn to the town by the early 9th-century discovery of the tomb of St. James inside the small church that used to stand on the site of the present cathedral. The story goes that a religious hermit followed a star (hence the name Compostela, which comes from the Latin *campus stellae,* or "field of the star") to the small church and somehow discovered that the remains of the saint had been transported there from the Holy Land many centuries previous. It's all a bit convoluted, but since then pilgrims have continuously followed the **Camino de Santiago** across the Pyrenees to pay homage to the saint—it's said a visit here guarantees a place in heaven—turning it into the most renowned religious route in Europe. In early days, robbers and cutthroats made the route dangerous. Then, with the decline of medieval culture, enthusiasm and interest waned and the number of travelers dwindled. During the Napoleonic Wars, the city was plundered by the French, but since then it has gradually risen in fame and prosperity and is now seat of the semiautonomous *xunta* (government) set up in 1982. Today, pilgrims arrive by every means imaginable from bikes to horses to wheelchairs, though, of course, the walking pilgrimage remains the standard.

Santiago de Compostela

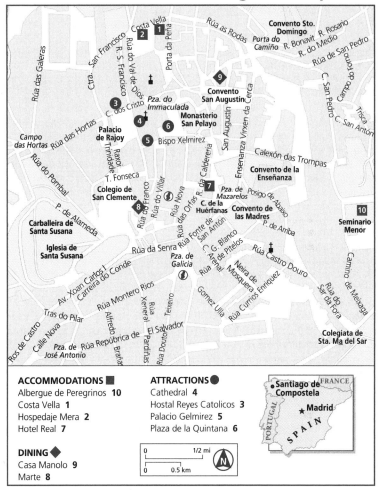

ACCOMMODATIONS ■
Albergue de Peregrinos **10**
Costa Vella **1**
Hospedaje Mera **2**
Hotel Real **7**

DINING ◆
Casa Manolo **9**
Marte **8**

ATTRACTIONS ●
Cathedral **4**
Hostal Reyes Catolicos **3**
Palacio Gelmirez **5**
Plaza de la Quintana **6**

Getting to & Around Santiago de Compostela

Iberia, Air Europa, Spanair, Ryannair, Air Berlin, and Veuling all offer **flights** to Santiago; shop around for the cheapest prices. (Try www.wegolo.com.) The city's airport is 11km (7 miles) northeast of the city. Buses run into the city every 35 to 40 minutes charging 2.50€ one-way. Taxis making the same trip charge 20€.

If you're coming from La Coruña, know that there are hourly **buses** between the two; contact **Monbus** (☎ 981-55-57-60; www.castromil.com).

You can also **ride the rails** here. From La Coruña, 20 trains make the 1-hour trip daily. Two trains also arrive daily from Madrid—an 8-hour journey. Contact the RENFE offices (☎ 902-240-202; www.renfe.es) for information.

If you're **driving,** take the express highway (A-9/E-50) south from La Coruña to reach Santiago. From Madrid, take the N-VI directly north to Galicia.

For general information, contact the **Oficina de Turismo** (Rua del Villar 43; ☎ 981-58-40-81; www.turgalicia.es; Mon–Fri 10am–8pm, Sat 11am–2pm and 5–7pm, Sun 11am–2pm).

Accommodations, Both Standard & Not

€   Short of pitching your own tent out in the woods, you won't find a cheaper place to stay in Santiago than the **Albergue de Peregrinos Seminario Menor La Asunción** (Rua de Belvis s/n; ☎ 981-589-200; www.albergueseminariomenor. com; cash only), which lies just a 10-minute walk east of the cathedral. Located in a huge, gray, stone building dating from 1829, this former priests' seminary provides basic hostel-type accommodations primarily aimed at *peregrinos* (pilgrims). Accommodations are in single beds in large dormitories sleeping up to 25 (12€ per person July 1–Sept 15, 10€ the rest of the year). There are communal bathrooms on each floor. Other facilities include a laundry, lounge with TV, and access to Internet services. This ain't the place for partiers: The hostel locks its doors at 11pm.

€   The white-walled **Hospedaje Mera** (Porta da Pena 15; ☎ 981-583-867; MC, V)—located high up in the laid-back northern corner of the Ciudad Vieja beside the Porta de la Peña (one of the 7 doors leading into the medieval sector of Santiago)—looks like just another 19th-century house but is in fact a chummy bargain-priced hotel. The pleasant lady owner lives downstairs and rents out airy, good-size double-bedded rooms, all with tiled floors and large windows letting in lots of light (50€ with private bathroom, 45€ without). If you don't mind not having your own bathroom, then plump for my favorite room, which has a huge north-facing terrace the size of the room itself and enjoys lovely views of a nearby church and the green countryside beyond.

€–€€   Right next door to the Mera is the traditional, glass-fronted **Hotel Costa Vella** ★ (calle Porta de Peña 17; ☎ 981-569-530; www.costavella.com; MC, V), which also enjoys lovely rooftop panoramas of the city. It's a step up in comfort from the Mera and its warmly atmospheric decor includes carved wooden head-boards, ceiling beams, and stone accents jutting out from the walls. All rooms have en suite bathrooms and are very reasonably priced at 65€ to 75€ per double (or 80€–90€ if you'd like your own small gallery or window-enclosed balcony). You can take breakfast (5€) in your room or out in the charming garden with its paved pathways, overhanging vines, and colorful flower beds.

€–€€   The one I like best, though, is the **Hotel Real** ★★ (Caldereria 49; ☎ 981-569-290; www.hotelreal.com; AE, MC, V), a former university lodging house that's metamorphosed into one of the most delightful and friendly guest-houses in town. The compact, tastefully converted rooms (65€–80€, including breakfast) are filled with natural light—brighter of course when the sun decides to come out—and furnished with dark-wood wardrobes; ornate iron bedsteads; and shuttered, double-glazed windows. (The latter are a blessing on the weekends when the seemingly inexhaustible student population cavorts till the early hours.) Walls are bedecked with darn nice original artworks from sketches of Old Town

On the Road to Santiago: A Superb Monastery Stay

For centuries, weary pilgrims have been stopping at **Samos Monastery** ✪✪ (☎ 982-546-046; www.abadiadesamos.com; cash only) on the way to Santiago, and likely dropping to their knees at the sight of this splendid, 12th-century (and later) complex, set up against a spectacular mountain backdrop. Samos still accepts visitors and two kinds of rooms are available. Those in the **Albergue (Inn)** are very bare and—dare I say it—monastic (simple white walls, a barracks-style bed, with the only decoration a cross), with communal bathroom facilities. Here only one night's stay is permitted, payment is left to the discretion of the visitor *(a voluntad)*, and guests of both sexes are welcome. The other accommodations are in the **Hospedería** (monastery guest quarters) and consists of similarly basic rooms, each with its own private bath, for 25€ a night. Stipulations here are that only men are allowed, stays must be for a minimum of 5 nights, and it's essential to phone beforehand to book. (You'll need to have at least a working knowledge of Spanish for that.) Still, if you're looking for a place to retreat in quiet contemplation, this is a spectacular choice. The monastery is a good 43km (29 miles) southeast of Lugo.

---

streets and buildings to colorful portraits. The one downside: no elevator, so guests must climb the winding wooden banistered stairway.

Dining for All Tastes

€   Opposite the police station and usually bustling with hungry cops, **Marte** ✪ (Av. Rodrigo de Padrón 11; ☎ 981-584-905; Mon–Sat 1:30–4pm and 8:30–11:30pm, Sun 1:30–4pm) is a popular family-run restaurant at the southern end of the Old Quarter. It's not mere proximity that keeps these officers coming back, but the two bargain lunch menus: one at 7.50€, which provides standard fare like *tortillas* (omelets) and *chuletas de cerdo* (pork chops), and another posher one at 12€ with dishes like *merluza* (hake) and *emperador* (swordfish), which you'd normally expect to be on the a la carte list. The atmosphere is loud and unstuffy; the food, solidly tasty; and the down-to-earth owners, very hospitable.

€   More bargain lunches are available in a century-old brick-house conversion up in the Casco Viejo. This is **Casa Manolo** ✪ (Plaza Cervantes s/n; ☎ 981-58-29-50; Mon–Sat 1–4pm and 8:30–11:30pm, Sun 1–4pm; MC, V), a family-run eating spot offering a marvelous two-course 10€ meat- and pasta-focused menu that usually includes the likes of grilled steaks, Milanese-style breaded veal cutlets, or cannelloni with ricotta cheese. Decor is bare and basic, but you're here—like the other assembled multitudes—for the generous portions (not the flaking walls).

Why You're Here: The Top Sights & Attractions

The iconic sight of Santiago, and arguably the most important church on the Iberian Peninsula, the **Museo Catedralicio de Santiago de Compostela** ✪✪✪ (Plaza del Obradoiro; ☎ 981-560-527; free admission; cathedral daily 7am–9pm, cloisters and the Palacio de Gelmírez [see below] June–Sept Mon–Sat 10am–2pm and 4–8pm and Sun 10am–2pm, Oct–May Mon–Sat 10am–1:30pm and 4–6:30pm and Sun 10am–1:30pm) is a supreme achievement of Spanish Romanesque architecture. Its incomparable **Pórtico de la Gloria** ✸✸✸, carved by Maestro Mateo in 1188, is the equal of the best of similar work done in Europe during that period—foreseeing the new Gothic realism with its unforced and humanized creations. Along the three portico archway is a line of biblical figures from the Last Judgment, with Christ in the middle, flanked by apostles and the 24 Elders of the Apocalypse, and below him a vivid depiction of St. James, crowning a carved column that includes a portrayal of Mateo himself at its base. Pilgrims through the ages have furrowed five ever-deepening indentations into the column as they line up to lean forward, place their hands on it, and touch foreheads with Mateo. The interior of the cathedral is classically designed with three cross-shaped naves and several chapels and cloisters, and the eye-catching altar is a stunning blend of Gothic austerity and baroque extravagance. Down in the crypt, a silver urn contains what are believed to be the remains of the Apostle St. James; in the cathedral museum, you can see tapestries and archaeological fragments. Adjoining the cathedral is the **Palacio de Gelmírez** ✸ (☎ 981-572-300), built during the 12th century for an archbishop, an outstanding example of Romanesque architecture (for visiting hours see above). Attending the noon pilgrims mass is a treat (other masses held at 9:30am and 7:30pm daily, 1:30pm and 6pm Sun). Consider also taking a **roof tour** (Pazo de Xelmírez; ☎ 981-55-29-85; 10€; Tues–Sun 10am–2pm on the hour), which traces the route taken by medieval pilgrims who would climb to the roof of the cathedral to burn their clothes under the so-called "Cross of Rags"—a symbolic gesture of rebirth. Views of the interior of the cathedral and the city itself are also spectacular from this vantage point.

Beside the cathedral, the magnificent Plaza del Obradoiro (also called the Plaza de España) is a repository of fine historic buildings. Right next door is what, for many, is the finest *parador* (government-run inn) in all Spain, the **Hostal de los Reyes Católicos** ✸. Previously a hospice, it was originally designed by Ferdinand and Isabella's favorite architect, Enrique de Egas, with the aim of accommodating royal guests, though by the 15th century its clientele had become a predominantly more humble mingling of pilgrims and passing traders. It's quite okay to stroll in and walk around this palatial, character-filled hostelry, even if you're not a guest. If you do, check out the highly evocative **Cloistered Courtyard** (☎ 981-582-200 for information; daily 10am–1pm and 4–7pm); its highlights are the lovely 16th- to 18th-century fountains and the main chapel. You'll need to show them the small, free cathedral guide, which they give you as you enter and which serves as a ticket to allow you access to the chapel.

You can get a breather from all this period grandeur in the student-frequented **Plaza de la Quintana,** which lies to the left of the cathedral's Goldsmith's Doorway and whose broad steps connect the back of the cathedral with the walls of a convent. Or, more relaxingly, take a peaceful stroll along the gardens of the **Paseo de la Herradura,** and enjoy the fine panoramic views of the old city.

Attention, Shoppers!

The town of Sargadelos in Lugo sub-province (see above) produces lots of "naïve-styled" porcelain, souvenirs that have become increasingly popular over the years with visitors. **Sargadelos** (Rúa Nueva 16; ☎ 981-581-905) sells a full range of this picturesque crockery. Cutest are those with small birdlike figures on top, known as the *Paxarica* style, while the simpler and more conventional versions are known as *Magdalena.* You'll learn about the history of the company at **Sargadelos Gallery** (Rua Nova 16; ☎ 981-581-905; www.sargadelos.com; free admission; Mon–Fri 10:30am–2pm and 4:30–9pm, Sat 10:30am–1:30pm and 5–9pm), though you can't buy anything there.

The **Amboa** (Rua Nueva 44; ☎ 981-583-359) also stocks ceramics but is far more popular for its mouthwatering regional delicacies such as *tarta Santiago* (a sweet pastry tart marked with an emblematic cross) and *queso de tetilla* (a local cheese saucily shaped like a breast). Continuing the gastronomic theme, many of the local **wines,** including assorted bottles of Ribeiro, Condado, and, most famous of all, Albariño—one of the very best *vino blancos* (white wines) in Spain—are sold untrumpeted in *colmados* (grocery stores) throughout Galicia. But for a really superior choice of Galician gourmet highlights—from quality *empanadas* (rich pies containing octopus, cod, or tuna) to *chorizo* (red, spicy local sausage)—check out Santiago's **Charcuterías Seco** (San Pedro Mezonzo; ☎ 981-591-267).

Nightlife

Believe it or not, ecclesiastical Santiago is outrageously lively at night. In particular, Rúa do Franco and its neighbor, Rúa da Raiña, boast scores of packed bars; wander along them and take your pick at random. My fave is **Beiro** (Rua da Raiña 3; ☎ 981-581-370), a connoisseur's wine bar, with vintages from across Spain and a very comprehensive selection from Galicia itself. Tasty *raciones* cost 5€ to 10€, and glasses of quaffable wine run from 1.30€ for a young sprightly Ribeiro to 3€ or more for a maturely ruminative Priorat.

The late-night scene is helmed by **Conga 8** (Rúa da Congo; ☎ 981-583-407; daily 10pm–5am; cover 10€), which is big on (recorded) salsa and meringue sounds. Toward dawn, strident *tunas* (student musical troupes) come on the scene and wake up everyone. Alternatively, you may prefer the techno, house, pop, and rock music of the luridly decorated **Retablo Café Concerto** (Rúa Nova 13; ☎ 981-564-851; summer daily 5pm–5am, winter daily 10:30pm–4am; cover 10€).

Costa Da Morte—The "Death Coast"

No, it's not the title of a seriously bad Sylvester Stallone movie. It's the name—none too popular with local tourist offices—that the Galicians have given the wildly beautiful and dangerous stretch of coast (the lower part of the Rias Altas coast mentioned above) that extends south of La Coruña between **Malpica** and **Cabo Fisterra** and has over 100 shipwrecks over the ages. A surprising number of them involved British ships en route from Liverpool or London on their way to America. The greatest tragedy of all occurred when a 19th-century training ship hit the rocks and a hundred teenage cadets perished. A plaque and memorial mark the fateful spot near Camariñas.

It's best to explore this area by car, though it can, in a pinch, be managed by public transport, as buses run five to seven times a day from La Coruña to Malpica (1½ hr.) and there are further intermittent bus services connecting it with the other towns. If you're driving from La Coruña, take the AG-55 highway to the no. 33 turnoff onto the AC-414, which runs northwest. Consider a stop at **Camariñas** (65km/42miles from La Coruña), a charming lace-making center located beside a crescent-shaped inlet, which is packed with vividly hued fishing boats and stylish yachts. Hidden away behind the cafe and apartment-lined waterfront, you'll still find traditional whitewashed blue shuttered houses with russet roof tiles and brick chimneys where the *palilleiras* (seamstresses) of yesteryear carried out their *encaje* (lace weaving) work. Today the town's main item of livelihood—fishing apart—is made in small modern workshops.

From Camariñas, a southbound secondary road leads around an increasingly rugged coast of wild headlands, windy wide-open bays, and tranquil sheltered *rías* (inlets) past the tiny town of Corcubión to **Cabo Fisterra (Cape Finisterre)** ✲ the most westerly point in Europe. Here, beside the weathered lighthouse, you can enjoy some of the most sensational sunsets anywhere (unpredictable Atlantic weather permitting).

ASTURIAS

I'll never forget my first view of Asturias. After driving across the dusty, sun-blinding landscape of its southerly neighbor Leon, I entered the long tunnel that passes under the mountain range at the Pasaje de Pajares and emerged on the other side into a different world: unbelievably green fields, apple orchards, fast-flowing streams, dinky (from a distance) alpine-looking houses, and herds of fat grazing cows, all bathed in a subdued grayish light filtering through the totally overcast sky. The change was so absolute it was hardly believable. Like traveling from the Mediterranean to central Scotland in the time it takes to drink a couple of coffees. Of course, if I'd arrived from Galicia or Cantabria to the west and east, respectively, I'd hardly have noticed any geographic—or climatic—difference. That mountain barrier between north and south made the change more abrupt and instantaneous. Combined with the Asturians' natural penchant for spirited resistance it helped explain why this remote and at one time virtually inaccessible province was the only part of Spain in which the Moors failed to secure the remotest foothold. It's still one of Spain's most proudly self-reliant regions, and the only province officially declared a principality thanks to its early role as the "cradle of Christianity." Today, King Juan Carlos's son Felipe bears the title of Prince of Asturias.

Asturias's wealth of prehistoric cave paintings testifies to a resident population dating from the Stone Age. The instinctive rebellious nature that's been in evidence since early Celtic tribes first resisted the Romans was most famously and successfully deployed several centuries later when the Christian chieftain Pelayo led his small army out to defeat invading Moors at Battle of Covadonga in 722. This, locals will proudly tell you, marked the very beginning of the Reconquista (Reconquest), though it took a further 700 years before the Moors were finally ousted as rulers of most of the country. The province's Golden Age came during the 9th century, when three successive kings—Alfonso II, Ramiro I, and Alfonso III—ruled the peninsula's most powerful state, creating an austere pre-Romanesque style of architecture that is unique in the country today.

Asturians continued their fight for independence in 1934 when miners rose up to declare a socialist republic only to be ruthlessly crushed by the future dictator

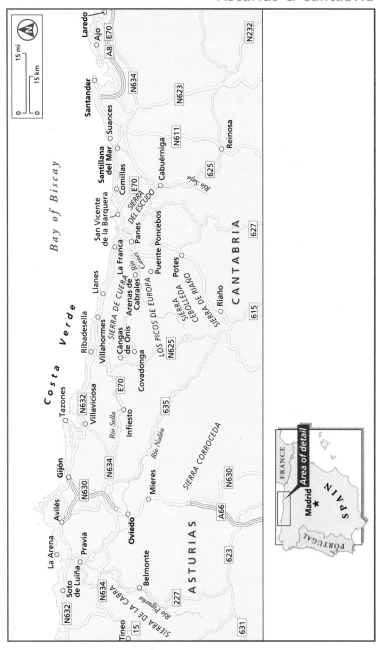

Franco—then an ambitious young general—who returned with his Nationalist forces a couple of years later to pulverize various cities—Gijón in particular—for their continuing fierce resistance during the Spanish Civil War. Today things are quieter and the province is more comfortably serene, enjoying its role as a principality and at ease with itself.

Both on and away from the sea, the Asturian countryside is mighty impressive. Its long shoreline, indented with narrow inlets and lined with fishing ports, rocky headlands, and long fine beaches, runs 300km (200 miles) west from Ribadeo, on the Galician border via Gijón all the way to San Vicente de la Barquera on the edge of tiny Cantabria. Inland, its green valleys, fishing villages, and woodlands are dominated by the high, perennially snow-tipped **Picos de Europa,** Spain's very first Spanish national park and a paradise for trekkers and climbers.

OVIEDO

The 20th century was not kind to Oviedo (see a "Brief History of Oviedo," below), but today it's a peaceful, comfortably bourgeois city whose largely pedestrianized center and superbly restored mansions, churches, and monuments have put it high on Spain's list of places with the best quality of life. If you want to catch a glimpse of the city before you arrive, rent Woody Allen's *Vicky Cristina Barcelona;* the erotic and lushly scenic weekend jaunt that the movie hinges on takes place in Oviedo.

A Brief History of Oviedo

Oviedo first came into being as an 8th-century monastery called Ovetao but developed into a powerful town when King Alfonso I moved his court here in 808. Its subsequent brief period of brilliance evaporated when the court moved to Leon a century later but flourished again in the Middle Ages when pilgrims on their way to Santiago made it one of their key stops. During the Middle Ages, the magnificent cathedral was constructed around the original 8th-century Holy Chamber (see "Why You're Here," below) and in 1600 a university was built. The discovery of coal made Oviedo a lucrative mining center and it flourished during the 19th-century Industrial Revolution. A union and socialist stronghold of some power once more, it revolted against the army's national forces in 1934 and suffered terribly both then and during the subsequent Civil War. Miraculously, some of its finer buildings managed to survive the overall destruction (neighboring Gijón fared far worse) and today the new revitalized city has been tastefully reinvented around its earlier architectural glories.

Getting to & Around Oviedo

GETTING TO OVIEDO

Oviedo's nearest **airport** is the **Aeropuerto de Asturias** at Ranón, 47km (30 miles) northwest of the city near the sea between Cudillero and Avilés. Iberia operates regular scheduled flights here from Madrid, as does the charter company easyJet (www.easyjet.com.) which offers seasonally variable, but generally much lower, fares. Contact ☎ 985-127-500 (www.aena.es) for information. An express bus service operates from the airport to Oviedo's bus station every 40 minutes from 7am to midnight and costs 6€ one-way. Beware of catching a taxi, as a

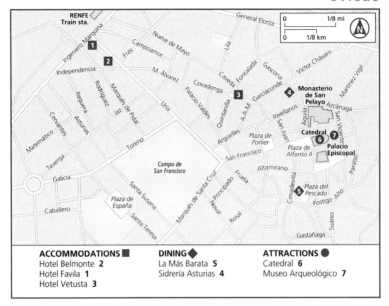

ACCOMMODATIONS ■
Hotel Belmonte **2**
Hotel Favila **1**
Hotel Vetusta **3**

DINING ◆
La Más Barata **5**
Sidrería Asturias **4**

ATTRACTIONS ●
Catedral **6**
Museo Arqueológico **7**

one-way trip to Oviedo city center costs 45€. (To neighboring Gijón, it costs 40€.)

The **train** journey takes 4½ hours and costs 45€ one-way. Contact RENFE for info (☎ 902-24-02-02; www.renfe.es). ALSA (☎ 902-499-949; www.alsa.es) operates 20 buses a day from the Spanish capital's Estación Sur (Mendez Alvaro). The standard one-way trip takes 5 hours and costs 35€. The Oviedo bus station (Estación de Autobuses de Oviedo) is at calle Pepe Cosmen (☎ 985-969-696), just north of the old quarter.

If you're **driving** yourself, coming from the south, take the N-630 or A-66 after León. If you're arriving from the east or west, take N-634 across the northern Spanish coast.

LOCAL & REGIONAL TRANSPORTATION
The blue local **buses** frequently cover a dozen routes throughout the city. Standard one-way fare is .90€, and routes begin and end at the main bus station (see above). Local FEVE **trains** (www.feve.es) run regularly to Gijón 30 minutes away.

For general information, contact the **Oficina de Turismo** (calle Cimadevilla 4; ☎ 985-213-385; daily 10:30am–2pm and 4:30–7:30pm).

Accommodations, Both Standard & Not

€   As in many cities, the area around the bus or train station is often jammed with low-cost lodgings, meant to lure weary travelers right as they alight. Problem is, because these lodgings have such a constant source of customers, they often fall behind less conveniently located hotels when it comes to upkeep. Not so with the

The Luarcan Rises

Asturias, like the rest of the Celtic-Nordic world, is prone to fanciful yarns. Like that of the Kraken, a terrifying beast which—legend has it—would rise from the deep to terrify mariners and landlubbers alike, and which has provided literary fodder for writers from John Wyndham (*The Kraken Wakes*) to Tennyson ("The Kraken").

The original Scandinavian version of the Kraken myth was of a horned monster up to 2.4km (1½ miles) long, which broke up into little islands as ships approached it. A more palatable present-day version is of a big (though not that big) sea creature with tentacles and the ability to discharge ink. Such a beast—albeit dead—can be found in the fishing port of **Luarca** 40km (27 miles) west of Oviedo. The pueblo resembles many other scenic backwaters along that stretch of coast. Except for one thing: It's home to the largest stuffed squid in Spain.

You'll find this salty Godzilla in the waterfront **Aula del Mar** (daily 11am–1pm and 4–9pm). The prize exhibit, some 5m (16 ft.) long, belongs to a family that can grow a length—tentacles included—of 20m (66 ft.), and whose natural habitat is 1,000m (3,281 ft.) below sea level in a permanently dark world where the pressure is up to 10 times that near the surface. For company down there it has a weird array of spindly misshapen fish that create their own light and look like the creations that wouldn't seem out of place in a science-fiction film. In some parts of the world, the giant squid has been known to claim human victims. In the Philippines, a few years back, a fisherman was killed by an outsize cephalopod, while spear-hunting deep down off some rocks. And during World War II, at least one U.S. sailor shipwrecked in the Pacific is said to have been eaten by one.

So beware when swimming off the Asturian coast. Instead of you eating *calamares en su tinta,* it could be one of them tucking into human sushi. (Please don't take this too seriously.) It is a fact, though, that a mere 30km (19 miles) out, in an area known as the Carlacci Deep, the Bay of Biscay suddenly plunges to a depth of 3,000m (9,843 ft.), and it's down here, just a short sailing trip from ports like Luarca, that the super-squid lives out its existence. On the rare occasions it finds itself near the surface, it's been known to blunder into the nets of surprised fishermen.

Six busses a day run from Oviedo (a 2-hr. ride) making a stop en route to Ribadeo on the Galician border.

Belmonte (calle Uría 31-2° derecha; ☎ 985-241-020; MC, V), an unpretentious second-floor *hostal* (complete with elevator service) right near the bus station. It's a spiffy place with whitewashed walls, shiny wood floors, and good-quality mattresses. The en suite bathrooms are on the small side, but at 40€ to 45€ for a double, they offer overall good value for money. Traffic can make the rooms at the front at bit noisy, as can your fellow guests occasionally on the weekends, so try to get one at the back—and bring some earplugs to be on the safe side. The owner is very obliging but speaks little English so it's a good place to practice your Spanish. (Be sure to negotiate a good standard discount—up to 20%—if you happen to be a student.)

€ Just 3 blocks away from the Belmonte, the **Hotel Favila** (calle Uría 37; ☎ 985-259-455) is essentially a business hotel, but a family-run one, giving it a homier vibe than usual for these sorts of places. (The staff deserves kudos for their helpfulness.) Rooms are comfy if a bit bland looking (45€–55€ double) but have plenty of wardrobe space, tiled private bathrooms, and a few extras including cable TV. Avoid front rooms if you want some peace and quiet at night. A real bonus is the downstairs restaurant, which provides a highly filling lunch menu for only 9€.

€–€€ My personal Oviedo favorite located on the northern edge of the old quarter, is the small and very welcoming **Hotel Vetusta** ★★ (calle Covadonga 2; ☎ 985-222-229; www.hotelvetusta.com; AE, DC, MC, V; nearby parking 10€). A pleasant yin and yang of contrasts, it's set in a handsome, old, wood and brick building, with traditional glassed-in double wooden balconies. Inside the style is ultra-contemporary, with lots of steel and wood fittings with enough cushioning to keep the ambience cozy. Rooms (65€–90€) are compact but come with fully equipped bathrooms containing tub/shower combos plus hydromassage in the pricier digs. All are exterior, and some also have private balconies.

€€ Or you may decide to visit Oviedo (or one of the other entrancing cities of Asturias) but bunk in the countryside. Like many other regions of Spain, Asturias is well stocked with *casas rurales,* and there's a wide choice of both houses and apartments—especially in the regions between the coast and the mountains. A typical example: **Casa de Aldea Picao** (☎ 608-392-785), a delightfully rustic, pink, two-story house in open countryside near the tiny village of **Santianes de Ola** (between **Llanés** and **Ribadasella**). Rent this house (70€–110€ a night, depending on season) and you'll have command of a comfy lounge with fireplace, a fully equipped kitchen, and three cute double bedrooms (wood-beamed ceilings, countrified furnishings). The only snag is that a rental car is essential if you stay here.

For more *casas rurales* like this (plus some chicer, pricier properties), a good resource is www.asturnor.com. Though the site is simply a clearinghouse for local properties, all homes that register to be rented in Asturias must obtain a Certificado de Calidad Turistica Española approved by the ICTE (Instituto de Calidad Turistica Española; www.icte.es). And this agency does, in fact, send out inspectors to make sure everything is up to code. (Look for a plaque with a white Q symbol on a dark blue background to confirm that a property has been approved.) Really, the only barrier to renting one of these properties is, well, a language barrier. More often than not, in Asturias, owners will not speak English, so you'll need to enlist the services of the tourist board (see above) or a Spanish-speaking friend to assist when making all the arrangements if you aren't fluent.

Dining for All Tastes

€   Cheap, chummy, and awash with fermented apple-beverage fumes, the **Sidrería Asturias** (calle Gascona 7; ☎ 985-211-952; Mon–Sat noon–4pm and 8pm–midnight; Sun noon–3:30pm; cash only) is located on a street sometimes called "Cider Boulevard" due to the number of *sidra*-oriented establishments that line it. It serves up solid, standard fare—*empanadas de pulpo* (octopus pie), *choriza en sidra* (sausage cooked in cider), and *fabada asturiana* (a rich bean and pork stew that's a whole meal in itself)—which is nonetheless exceptional for its portion-price ratio (5€–8€ per *ración*). And the high-decibel chatter is all part of the fun. Natural and still ciders, both sold in liter bottles which you can conveniently share between two, cost 2€. Wine is also available but generally frowned on as an effete softies' drink in such a staunchly traditional place.

€€   Not quite on the same level price-wise, in spite of its enticing name (which means, literally, "The Cheapest"), **La Más Barata** ✫ (calle Cimadevilla 2; ☎ 985-213-606; Mon–Sat noon–midnight; MC, V) is a more chic and refined establishment right in the heart of the Old Town center between the town hall and cathedral. The main attraction here is the amazingly varied range of tapas and rice-based *raciones* from yummy *morcillas* (blood sausage molded with rice) to seafood paellas, some of which are *negra,* or black—either naturally or from an infusion of squid's ink (genuine, of course). The texture of the rice varies from stickily risotto-ish to drier basmati style so check with the waiters—most of whom understand sufficient English for this—to find out which dish has what. Between 15€ and 20€ a head should see you happily filled, including cider or, for this occasion, a couple of *cañas* (small glasses) of local beer. It's very spacious, with none of that skimping of room between tables, and the large windows give you a panoramic view of the street scenes outside. (Incidentally, the name of the restaurant originally referred to a haberdashery that stood on this same spot and was renowned for the low prices it charged.)

Why You're Here: The Top Sights & Attractions

Topped by a high, deftly picturesque spire, the most important central city monument is the vast, bright, almost white-stoned Gothic-Romanesque **Catedral de San Salvador** ✫✫ (Plaza de Alfonso II el Casto; ☎ 985-221-033; July–Sept Mon–Fri 10am–8pm, Sat 10am–6pm; Oct–Jun Mon–Fri 10am–1pm and 4–7pm, Sat 4–6pm) which—begun in the 14th century—took no less than 300 years to complete. Once inside, head straight to the 9th-century **Camara Santa (Holy Chamber)** ✫✫✫ (3€ adults, 1€ children 10–15, free for children 9 and under, including the museum and cloister). Its inner cloister contains the finest examples of Asturian art in all Spain: the three splendid bejeweled Crosses of Don Pelayo, Victoria, and Los Angeles, which were originally presented to the church as gifts by kings Alfonso II and III. The latter, known in English as the Cross of the Angels, is the official emblem of the city, while the Victoria—or Victory—Cross represents the entire province and can be seen on the walls of many old houses in the form of a coat of arms. Behind the chamber, enclosed by glass, is a silver ark brought back from the Holy Land in the 7th century and said to have originally

Jurassic Park . . . The Museum

Beloved by kiddies of all ages (and Steven Spielberg fans) is the most comprehensive dinosaur museums in the world, **Museu del Jurásico del Asturias** ✹✹ (San Juan de Duz at Colunga; ☎ 902-306-600; www.museojurasicoasturias.com; 5.30€ adults, 3.20€ seniors 66 and over and children 4–11; July 15–Sept 15 daily 10:30am–2:30pm and 4–8pm; Sept 16–July 14 Mon 10:30am–2:30pm, Wed–Sun 10:30am–2:30pm and 4–6pm). It lies beside the sea 40km (25 miles) northeast of Oviedo, filled with exhibits gleaned from the long sandy beaches and towering cliffs of the so-called "Dinosaur Coast" on which many thousands of life-size bones and remains have been discovered over the years. A total of 800 fossils, of dinosaurs who roamed the planet up to 300 million years ago, are on show in three big exhibition areas. A nice touch is the way the museum itself is built in the shape of a big hoof print.

Several buses run daily from Oviedo to Colunga. Check for times with the Oviedo bus station (see above).

contained relics, including a piece of the cross and some bread from the Last Supper. At the back of the cathedral in a former 15th-century convent is the **Museo Arqueológico** (calle San Vicente 5; ☎ 985-215-405; free admission; Tues–Sat 10am–1:30pm and 4–6pm, Sun 11am–1pm), which boasts a display of prehistoric relics, pre-Romanesque sculptures, and old musical instruments that provides charismatic insight into Asturias's ancient past.

A lovely and not too strenuous 40-minute walk up into the wooded hills around the city brings you to **Monte Naranco,** where you can see two incomparable examples of great Asturian pre-Romanesque architecture. The first of these, enjoying unparalleled vistas of both the city below and the inland snowcapped Picos de Europa, is the **Santa María del Naranco** ✹✹ (☎ 985-295-685; 2.20€ including San Miguel de Lillo [see below], free Sun–Mon 10am–1pm; Apr–Sept Sun–Mon 9:30am–1:30pm, Tues–Sat 9:30am–1:30pm and 3:30–7:30pm; Oct–Mar Sun–Mon 10am–1pm, Tues–Sat 10am–1pm and 3–5pm), a former 9th-century palace that was also Ramiro I's hunting lodge. Though a church was built on the site of its original baths and apartments, you can still admire the barrel-vaulted archways, the innovative (for their time) open porticoes, and the complex and realistic stonework depictions of hunting scenes. Also built by Ramiro I, a mere 91m (100 yd.) away, is the second gem: another royal chapel in the Asturian pre-Romanesque style, the **San Miguel de Lillo** ✹ (Monte Naranco s/n, ☎ 985-295-685; 2€, free Mon; Tues–Sat 10am–1pm and 3–5pm, Sun–Mon 10am–1pm). This was largely ruined by overzealous medieval architectural changes after a landslide destroyed half of the 9th-century original, but the surviving stone carvings are, again, extraordinarily real and vivid. Most of the early sculptures have been transferred to the archaeological museum in town.

The Other Oviedo

Nosing around the traditional and delightfully aromatic **markets** of Spain are a wonderful way to get the pulse of daily life, and there's a top-notch one at **El Fontán** to explore, just behind the Plaza Mayor. Locally produced foods are the big sellers here, like cider from Villaviciosa, beans for making the top regional dish *fabada,* and tangy blue Cabrales cheese from Arenales de Cabrales on the northern foothills on the Picos de Europa. You'll find all these mouthwatering regional goodies and more in the array of specialty shops that stand alongside *sidrerías* under the graceful colonnaded arcades of Oviedo's most picturesque square, **Plaza del Fontán,** which has literary and theatrical connections that go back to the 17th century. (The now extinct Casa de Comedias [Comedy Theater] was located here, and you can still see and visit the Biblioteca de Asturias [Asturian Library].) In the same bustling little square, topped by old houses whose balconies overlook the lively scene, a *rastro* (flea market) is held on Thursdays, Saturdays, and Sundays selling a tacky mishmash of clothes, knickknacks, and regional souvenirs from 10:30am to 2pm. Weekends are when this area is at its most colorful, so bring your camera, watch your wallet, and come along then. Even if you don't buy anything, it's quite an experience.

Attention, Shoppers!

Oviedo is justly renowned among the serious shopping fraternity for being the home of some of Spain's best outlets for **handbags** and **shoes.** It's also famed for its fine **designer boutiques** such as Massimo Dutti and Purificación García, and the place to look for all these is at the junction of **calles Uria** and **Gil de Jaz** where you'll find several shops selling the same merchandise you'd find in major cities such as Madrid and Barcelona but costing 10% to 25% less. **Asturian ceramic ware** is also a good buy in this zone.

The new "in" place to shop is the **Espacio Buenavista** complex in calle Arturo Alvarez Buylla s/n, which boasts a grand total of 146 shops and stores. Located on the site of the Real Oviedo football stadium and opened in March 2008 to much fanfare, it's part of a vast, futuristic-looking, Santiago Calatrava–designed business and leisure center in which—characteristically for this avant-garde architect—21 metallic ribs hold up a ramp with a glass ceiling that enhances the passage of natural light throughout the entire building. The center's 40,000-sq.-m (430,550-sq.-ft.) area also houses a congress center for international business meetings and a Palacio de Exposiciones where the annual Principe de Asturias prizes will be handed out. The street-level and youth-oriented first floor is devoted entirely to fashion; shops here range from a large **C & A** store to more personal homegrown boutiques like **Zara** and **Bimba y Lola,** where discounts are also possible if you ask.

The best place to get a good up-to-date English-language guidebook to the city and surrounding province (or the latest Dan Brown novel for that matter) is **La Palma Libros** (calle Rua 6; ☎ 985-214-782), right in the center. You'll also find esoteric editions on the unique local patois (though hardly a language) called Bable, if you're really into linguistic investigations. (A preponderance of words ending in *u* is one of its more engaging features, such as the earlier mentioned *horru,* which replaces the Gallego *horreo.*)

Nightlife

Most after-dark activity in Oviedo takes place in the triangle formed by the Postigo Alto, San José, and Mon streets just to the east of El Fontán market. **Calle Jovellanos** is particularly busy with those **Irish pubs** that seem to have swept the country, and nearby you can actually hear Irish fiddles wailing, between other live performances by visiting pop groups, at the **Antigua Estación** (calle Martínez Vigil 9; no phone; cover 6€; Fri–Sat 9:30pm–2am). Pop in and join them in a jig.

Calle Mon is the heart of Oviedo's disco scene. The favorite nocturnal hot spot there is **El Duende** (calle Mon 27; ☎ 985-220-385; 6€ cover; Mon–Sat 10pm–4am), with tropical temperatures, deafening house sounds, and a small bar and dance-floor area that are totally packed on the weekends. (Next door's **Maná** is much the same but mainly frequented by teeny-boppers so don't go there if you're an old fogy of 30 or over.) Also very popular is the larger **Tribeca** (Plaza de Riego; 6€ cover; nightly 10pm–5am), where house sounds also rule and gays and heteros alike congregate nightly. Live artists give regular performances here, and it was the scenario for the last celebrated Oviedo City Rock Concert.

For clubbers who really enjoy their round-the-clock action, the only place to go is the weekends-only **La Real** (Calle Cervantes 19; ☎ 985-24-38-93; www.lareal.org; cover 6€; Fri–Sat 6pm–2pm), which features house sounds and leading DJs imported from the U.K. and Northern Europe. Its after-hours Saturday night through Sunday morning bashes start at 1am and finish around 9am. The rather high 18€ cover includes a drink.

GIJÓN

Grittier and more proletariat in character than Oviedo, the province's main port and most populated city, Gijón, lies 29km (18 miles) north of the Asturian capital beside a yacht- and fishing-boat-filled harbor and a truly magnificent Atlantic beach—the 4km-long (2½-mile) **Playa San Lorenzo**—one of the best on the entire northern Spanish coastline. It's a combined summer resort and industrial center which, like Oviedo, flourished under the three Asturian kings in the 8th century and later during the Industrial Revolution, only to suffer terribly during the Civil War, when nearly all its medieval and Renaissance buildings were destroyed as a reprisal against a violent 1936 revolt by miners who dynamited the Nationalist forces' barracks. The city slowly recovered and, in recent years, has made impressive efforts to turn some of its few remaining older buildings of note into small museums and centers of "cultural interest."

Getting to & Around Gijón

Regional **FEVE trains** run from Oviedo every half-hour to Gijón during the day arriving at the regional rail station (Plaza el Humedal; ☎ 902-422-242). The trip takes 35 minutes and a one-way ticket costs 2.50€. Long-distance **RENFE trains** also operate direct from Madrid, taking 6 to 7 hours to arrive at the main station (Av. de Juan Carlos 1; ☎ 902-240-202).

Buses also run every hour from Oviedo arriving at the stunning Art Deco bus station located between calle Ribadasella and calle Llanes. The one-way trip takes an hour and costs 2€. Two long-distance buses per day also arrive from Madrid, taking 5½ hours.

For **general information** on Gijón, contact the **Oficina de Turismo** (Puerto Deportivo; ☎ 985-341-771; www.gijon.info; July–Aug daily 10am–8pm, Sept–June daily 10am–2pm and 4–6pm).

Accommodations & Dining

Among the many low-cost hotels in Cimadevilla, I recommend the character-filled **Pension Gonzalez** (calle San Bernardo 30; ☎ 985-355-863; V), which has spacious, airy rooms with high ceilings in an old mansion close to San Lorenzo beach. Bathrooms are mainly shared, and doubles cost from 45€ to 50€ (add 50% or more July–Aug, bringing the total then to 75€–80€). Quaint hall decorations such as ancient prints of the bay and a generous number of porcelain dogs of the Lladró variety all give the vague impression that you're staying in the home of a genial old aunt. Ultra-gracious service adds to the unforced charm of the place.

The lowest price for a meal you could possibly expect to pay here—or virtually anywhere—is the 6€ three-course inclusive menu at the **Sol Naciente Chinese Restaurant** (calle Rufo Renduetes 4; ☎ 985-341-731; daily 1:30–4pm and 8pm–midnight; MC, V). Don't expect anything fancy—just an amalgam of solid Spanish and Chinese dishes ranging from *chuletas de cerdo* (pork chops) to *arroz con calamares* (rice with squid). You even get a glass of basic wine from Extremadura (not so good) included. If you want somewhere more typically Asturian, try **La Marina** 🗡 (calle Trinidad 9; ☎ 985-346-246; daily 1–3:30pm and 8:30pm–midnight; MC, V), an old-style, high-ceilinged joint serving up prodigious *fabadas* (bean and pork stews) and fresh grilled sardines with your cider for around 8€ all in. There's also a wide choice of tapas set out on wooden boards for you to choose from and priced from 2.50€ to 4€ apiece.

Why You're Here: The Top Sights & Attractions

Most rewarding of Gijón's new cultural sites is the **Museo-Casa Natal de Jovellanos** 🗡 (Plaza de Jovellano; ☎ 985-346-313; www.jovellanos.net; free admission; July–Aug Tues–Sat 11am–1:30pm and 5–9pm, Sun 11am–2pm; Sept–June Tues–Sat 10am–1pm and 5–8pm, Sun 11am–2pm), which was the birthplace of a multitalented 18th-century luminary, Gaspar Melchor de Jovellanos (1744–1811), an essayist, agrarian reformer, and far-seeing economist all in one, who paid for what the authorities regarded as his excessively liberal beliefs with a 7-year prison sentence in Mallorca's Bellver Castle. The charming old mansion is filled with Jovellanos's personal memorabilia, but the surprising eye-catcher is a vast, intricately detailed model reconstruction of the town's old fish market by the 20th-century artist Sebastian Miranda.

The real buzzy part of town today is the narrow-laned **Cimadevilla** quarter, formerly a Roman walled city, which straddles the narrow entrance to the green bulbous-shaped Santa Catalina headland that juts into the Bay of Biscay, dividing main beach and port; its far end is topped by a large iron sculpture by Eduardo Chillida called *Elogio del Horizonte*, which has become the town's symbol. Nearby, opening on to San Lorenzo beach, are the fully excavated **Termas Romanas (Roman Baths)** (Campos Valdés; ☎ 985-345-147; 2.40€ adults, free for children 15 and under; July–Aug Tues–Sat 11am–1:30pm and 5–9pm, Sun 11am–2pm and

Fiesta Note

Summers are the liveliest time to be in town and if you're there on the first Sunday in August, you'll be able to join in with the locals celebrating **Asturias Day,** a riot of processions, folk dancing, and music when locals patronize the *chigres* (cider taverns), eat grilled sardines, and indulge in singalongs in portside *tascas.*

5–8pm; Sept–June Tues–Sat 10am–1pm and 5–8pm, Sun 11am–2pm and 5–7pm), which were discovered in 1903 and are now a museum recording the city's Roman past. A rare 18th-century architectural gem in the center of Cimadevilla is the neo-baroque-cum-Renaissance **Palacio de Revillagigedo** (Plaza del Marqués s/n; ☎ 985-34-69-21; free admission; July–Aug Tues–Sat 11am–1:30pm and 4–9pm, Sun noon–2:30pm; Sept–June Tues–Sat 10:30am–1:30pm and 4–8pm, Sun noon–2:30pm), which hosts musical, theatrical, and other cultural events and has a permanent gallery of 20th-century artworks. The whole quarter is also packed with bars, cafes, and nightspots (see below) and has a robust bohemian—some say grungy—aura unlike anywhere else in the city.

At the other end of Playa San Lorenzo, you get a chance to see the only **bagpipe** museum in Spain: the **Museo de la Gaita,** which is part of the **Museo del Pueblo de Asturias** (Paseo Dr. Flemyng s/n; ☎ 985-332-244; free admission; Tues–Sat 10am–1pm and 5–8pm [until 9pm in summer]). *Gaitas* (bagpipes) have at least as long a past as in Scotland and Ireland and the tone of the Asturian version is piercingly shrill—an acquired taste for some. They come in various shapes and forms, the most luxurious on display being made of kid's skin (baby goat's, not small child's), adorned with jet trinkets and lined with velvet.

Nightlife

Most after-dark fun here centers round the Cimadevilla district, where a surfeit of boisterous bars is spearheaded by **El Lavaderu** (Plaza Periodista Arturo Arias 1; no phone; Mon–Sat 1–4pm and 8pm–2am), a highly traditional *sidrería* just a stone's throw from the beach, with alternate granite and brick-covered walls and cider-stained dark-wood tables and benches. Those still going end up, depending on the mood, at a top club-disco like **Otto's** (Jardines de Nautico s/n; ☎ 981-35-56-99; daily 9pm–3am; cover 10€), where you can dance to salsa, bolero, or even tango sounds right beside the sea. Pick your own route from the many, and enjoy!

INLAND ASTURIAS: PICOS DE EUROPA NATIONAL PARK, POTES & CANGAS DE ONÍS

Picos de Europa National Park

The **Picos de Europa** national park (www.picosdeeuropa.com) forms part of the long **Cordillera Cantábrica** mountain range, a mass of glacier-formed limestone cliffs, green valleys, and gleaming lakes that run parallel to the northern coastline of Spain. Most of it is in Asturias, though the southeastern section is in neighboring Cantabria (see "Potes & the Liébena Valley" at the end of this section). The highest of its three main summits rises to more than 2,590m (8,500 ft.), and the whole region is a mecca for rock climbers from all over the world. The park is geologically and botanically different from anything else in the country and contains some of the rarest wildlife remaining in Europe. Endangered species still run wild in this wild landscape, from the tubby little Astorcón ponies to the ever-decreasing numbers of Iberian brown bear. (At last count, it was calculated there were only 30 bears still left in existence.) In the jasmine-covered gorges, you can sometimes see lithe footed chamois goats leaping from one impossibly small rock to another while buzzards and golden eagles are among the (government-protected) birdlife that wheels high overhead.

Well-marked paths and trails throughout the park make it a great area for long-distance trekkers. Best to come prepared, though. Novice walkers should wear solidly treaded boots, keep to the well-marked routes, and avoid the often loose shale slopes that fall away beside them. A hat and a good supply of water are essential in summer; though the weather is often unsettled—with thunderous downpours appearing without warning—when the sun is out, it can get very hot and humid. (The ultraviolet rays are particularly strong at this altitude, so be sure to bring suntan lotion as well.) Winter is even more unsettled and far less sunny. Midwinter is out of the question, as snow covers most of the park then.

Guided walks are available at the park's main information office in Cangas de Onís (below). Lasting between 3 and 6 hours, they can offer a wonderful, highly professional introduction to the park (though few are offered in English).

Cangas de Onís

If you're approaching the Park from the northwest, the lively market town of Cangas de Onís, just inland from Llanes, will likely be your base in the region. One of the earliest homes for the Asturian-Visigothic kings, its most famed landmark is an ivy-covered **Roman bridge** spanning the Sella River, which has been rebuilt numerous times over the centuries and is distinguished by the large cross hanging from its apex. The town is charming and relaxing off-season but best avoided in summer when it becomes packed with people and traffic, many of them en route to the mountains. The rivers around here abound with fish, including the plumpest salmon in Spain if you decide to get hold of a rod (see p. 411 for more on that). Just outside the town across the River Güena, you can visit the 8th-century **Capilla de Santa Cruz** (no phone; free admission; Mon–Fri 10am–2pm and 4–7pm, Sat 10am–2pm and 4–7:30pm), which was originally built over a Celtic dolmen and rebuilt in the 15th century. For more information, head to the **Oficina de Turismo** in the main square (☎ 985-848-005; daily 10am–2pm and 4–7 pm).

Pico de Europa's main information center is also here at **Casa Dago** (avenida de Covadonga; ☎ 985-84-86-14; Easter to mid-Oct Mon–Sat 9am–2pm and 5–6:30pm, Sun 9am–3pm; mid-Oct to Easter Mon–Sat 9am–2pm and 4–6:30pm).

Just beyond the city, a potently symbolic road trip beckons to **Covadonga**. Revered as the birthplace of Christian Spain, the tiny town just 9.5km (6 miles)

Salmon Galore

The cold waters of Asturias's fast-flowing streams and rivers are the ideal habitat for salmon and even the most inexperienced fishermen will be hard pressed *not* to catch one or more of the sleek, silvery skinned *pescados* here. In Asturias, they even outnumber their close cousin the *trucha* (trout), which is far more abundant practically everywhere else in Spain. A signpost I once saw beside the river that runs through Arriondas just north of Cangas de Onís stated PESCAR PROHIBIDO EXCEPTO PARA SALMON (NO FISHING EXCEPT FOR SALMON). So there you are. Or rather there *they* are, just waiting for you to reel them in.

But before you try your hand, you need to do two things. First and foremost, obtain a tourist fishing license. You can do this by applying in writing after printing out an application from www.asturias.es and posting it to the address provided. (It's available in English as well as Spanish, and all you have to do is look for the "River Fishing Licence for salmon, trout and sea trout preserves" section.) Or call the Fisheries Bureau Office in Oviedo at calle Coronel Aranda 2, ground floor (☎ 985-105-348, fax 985-105-577), to collect and fill in the form there. (Alternatively, again, you can call the Servicio de Atención del Ciudadano [SAC] ☎ at 985-27-91-00, though this could be more of a hassle, because you'll need to speak some Spanish here.) The price for a license is a modest 12€ and covers a whole year; those 65 and over pay nothing.

With the official business out of the way, the second thing you'll likely need is to rent a rod (*caña de pesca* in Spanish). In Cangas de Onís, contact **Casa el Gordo** (☎ 985-848-042), a well-known centrally located shop that both sells and rents out the whole gamut of fishing equipment, with rods of all shapes and sizes a specialty.

on from Cangas is reached by four to nine buses a day (depending on the time of year). Here, a fairly modest skirmish in A.D. 718 between a bold band of Visigoths led by a chieftain named Pelayo and a small force of Muslims (though history has painted it as something grander) resulted in a victory that sowed the seeds for an eventual Christian kingdom in the largely Moorish-dominated peninsula. Pilgrims' objective here is the peaceful and diminutive **La Santa Cueva (The Holy Cave)**, which contains Pelayo's sarcophagus and where the Virgin is said to have appeared to the warriors. In contrast, the brash, 20th-century, neo-Romanesque basilica in the village's main square is packed in summer with coach-trip visitors commemorating the Christianization of Spain. To get here from Oviedo, there are 10 to 14 buses daily to Cangas de Onís taking 1 to 1½ hours for the trip.

An elegant yet still economical spot to spend the night, **Hotel Puente Romano** ✪ (Puente Romano 8; ☎ 985-84-93-39; MC, V) is a lovely russet-ocher-hued villa of rooms (all with bath en suite) featuring sloping ceilings with original beams and comfy beds. Most have direct views of the eponymous triangular-shaped bridge. Rates are usually 50€ per double, though prices rise 30% or more in July and August. A great *sidrería* with—coincidentally—the same name, **Mesón Puente Romano** (Av. Covadonga s/n; ☎ 985-84-81-10; www.mesonpuentermano. com; Mon–Sat 1:30–4pm and 8:30–11:45pm, Sun 1:30–4pm; DC, MC, V), is located right next to the bridge and has a large tree-shaded outdoor eating area. Specialty here as with most Cangas eating spots is river fish—above all freshly caught salmon at 9€. *Fabada* is also very good and the set lunch at 10€ is terrific value.

Potes

Still inside the **Picos de Europa** national park on its far southeastern side—though just "across the border" in Cantabria province (below)—is **Potes,** a lovely town of bridges, cobbled lanes, and marvelously preserved buildings dominated by the 15th-century Infanta Tower. Perched on a wooded slope above the River Deva at the confluence of four picturesque valleys, it was for many centuries a meeting point for cattle herders and even today a bimonthly livestock market is held here. The easiest way in is by bus from the Cantabrian capital of Santander (p. 414), passing by the equally scenic Liebana Valley. Potes's **Oficina de Turismo** (calle Independencia 30; ☎ 942-730-787; daily 10:30am–2pm and 4–7pm) provides walking routes up into the mountains, while the **Picos Aventura** office, next to the town's oldest bridge, also arranges mountain-bike hires, paragliding, and canyoning trips.

A highly recommended summer day trip from Potes, is along the twisting and turning mountain road to the hamlet of **Fuente-Dé,** from which you take the third-largest *teleférico* (cable car) system in the world (☎ 942-736-610; 7€ one-way, 14€ round-trip; July–Aug daily 9am–8pm, Sept–June daily 10am–6pm) up 800m (2,624 ft.) to an observation platform above a towering wind-scoured rock face. Eye-popping views are the payoff; it's a truly delightful way to spend an afternoon.

If you're hiking in the Picos, you'll be able to stay in ultra-cheap supervised alpine *refugios* **(basic hostels)** with shared amenities. The best contact is the **Federación Asturiana de Montaña** (calle Melquiades Alvarez 16, Oviedo; ☎ 985-25-23-62; www.fempa.net; Mon–Thurs 5–8pm), which gives general climbing and trekking advice and information as well as listing six well-run *refugios,* each of which has its own supervisor. These are just 10€ per night for bunk-bed accommodations in small shared dormitories. Sleeping bags can be rented for an additional 2€, and communal facilities in each of them include showers, toilets, and a dining room serving breakfast (5€) and hearty main meals (14€). A typical example of one such refuge—located 2,000m (6,562 ft.) up near Sotres in the lovely Vega of Urriellu—is the stone-built **Refugio Urriellu** (☎ 985-925-200), which has 96 beds in small, basic, pine-walled dormitories and is open year-round.

For details of all these and for information on walking routes (including free guided tours), weather conditions, and so on, call or visit the National Park headquarters at **Casa Dago** in Cangas de Onís (☎ 985-848-614), just a few steps away from the Oficina de Turismo (see above).

If you're not a hostel type, or you're too cranky for camping, the **Pension Picos de Europa** ✦ (calle San Roque 6; ☎ 942-730-005; www.hotelpicosdeeuropa.net; MC, V) is a nice affordable alternative. A stay here is a mellow experience, thanks to the graciousness of the staff and the level of comfort afforded by the rooms: Mattresses are solid quality, rooms are crisp with a cream color scheme, and bathrooms are fully equipped. Rates range from 45€ to 60€ per double per night and communal amenities include a charmingly over-decorated little lounge complete with TV, aging fireplace, and plenty of wall ceramics, and a warmly welcoming dining room. There's also private parking available. At mealtimes, you can enjoy the hotel's sound 12€ menu or try out one of the more economical bars along the **calle de la Cantabra,** such as the riverside **Café Llorente** (☎ 942-73-81-65; noon–3:30pm and 8–11pm; cash only) whose *raciones* include *tortilla* (omelet), *jamón serrano* (mountain ham), and *calamares romana* (squid covered with flour and cooked in oil) for 6€ to 10€.

Even more adorable and highly, highly recommended, **Casa Cayo** ✦✦✦ (Cantabra 6; ☎ 942-740-150; www.casacayo.com/hotel-i.htm; MC, V) is marked by small touches that set this affordable little inn (50€ a night) above the rest. Guests are greeted almost as if they were coming to a cocktail party, and offered nuts, tasty olives, and water as they check in. Rooms are larger than usual and pretty in a quaint sort of way, with handmade quilts on the beds, overstuffed furniture, and animal-skin rugs. And the bathrooms in some of the rooms are downright luxurious, with massage jets in the bathtubs. As with Picos de Europa, there's a solid (and not too pricey) restaurant on-site; most guests end up spending a good amount of time in the sociable bar area.

A final area lodging that's worth mentioning is not in Potes itself but in **Fuente-Dé,** actually up at the end of the cable-car ride (see above; you'll need to go an additional 5km/3 miles along a footpath to get there). So, **Refugio de Aliva** (☎ 942-730-999; June–Sept 15; MC, V) is remote, but oh so scenic. Don't let the name fool you, by the way. This is not a dormitory-sharing rustic mountain refuge like the above-mentioned Refugio Urriellu, but a comfortable and well-equipped hotel where doubles cost 75€. Clients booked in here are provided with free Land Rover service to and from the cable-car stop. If you opt for a meal (15€) or snack (4€–8€) at the hotel's restaurant, remember to allow enough time to return to the *teleférico* under your own steam before its last trip down (which, in turn, connects with the last bus back to Potes).

CANTABRIA

Adjoining Asturias to the east and sharing a great portion of the Picos de Europa national park is Spain's tiniest province Cantabria, another lush green region, which differs from its more radical and independently minded neighbors in having a staunchly conservative character. Its cities are among the few left in Spain where streets are still named after the former dictator Francisco Franco (referred to, alternatively, as El Caudillo or Generalisimo), who departed this world more than 3 decades back and is barely missed, let alone lamented, elsewhere. Inland, it's a timelessly traditional region where some of the country's most important cave drawings have been found (the Altamira Caves, which are plastered with

18,000-year-old paintings) and whose tiny valleys house a wealth of villages where rural life continues almost as it's done for centuries. The look of many of its towns and cities also harkens back numerous centuries; commerce flourished in the Middle Ages here, particularly after the discovery of the New World across the Atlantic, and many Romanesque buildings in the province date from that period. Its health-giving spas are renowned for aiding illnesses ranging from arthritis to kidney troubles, and the most famous of these, nationally at least, is Solares, which produces one of Spain's most prestigious mineral waters. Elegant capital **Santander** (see below) is one of Spain's major ports, enjoying long-standing communication links with Northern Europe as well as being one of the country's more fashionable summer resorts, especially popular with well-heeled Madrileños.

The province is sandwiched between the Basque country to the east and Asturias to the west, and its shoreline of long sandy bays, towering cliffs, and wooded promontories combine with theirs to form Spain's renowned Costa Verde (Green Coast). The huge northern Cordillera Cantábrica mountain range runs across it, rising abruptly to high 2,438m (8,000-ft.) peaks that are snow tipped most of the year—their closeness to the sea giving them an almost Wagnerian grandeur—while the valleys and plains below are filled with farming pueblos, surrounded by rich wheat fields and orchards.

SANTANDER

Opinions are divided about Santander. While San Sebastián—its chief competitor as Spain's most sophisticated seaside town—usually receives unqualified praise, the Cantabrian capital gets enthusiastic and lukewarm reactions in equal measure. Some see it as stylish; others, as colorless and bland. One reason for the latter view could be that its Casco Antiguo quarter was destroyed by a devastating 20th-century fire that left little of real historic interest. Its harbor has also suffered great damage: In 1893, a freighter exploded in the harbor killing more than 500 people and severely damaging many waterfront buildings. Yet its elongated modern center of immaculate wide boulevards and pedestrianized lanes and its lively waterfront promenade array of cafes and bars combine to form a nigh pristine city and seaport that I personally like very much. Long associated with Northern Europe thanks to its close ferry communications with England, it exudes a faintly international aura and the classy neighboring Sardinero district with its casino, white Regency-style hotels, and magnificent trio of consecutive beaches—Playa de Castaneda, Playa del Sardinero, and Playa de la Concha—in my opinion rivals Biarritz or Monte Carlo for style. The city was, in fact, a royal residence from 1913 to 1930, after city officials presented an English-style Magdalena Palace to Alfonso XIII and his queen, Victoria Eugenia. Today its floods of summer visitors are almost exclusively middle-class Spanish, providing a strong contrast with the international blue-collar hordes who frequent its showy rival resorts on the sunnier Mediterranean coast.

Lay of the Land

Santander's main cafe-lined waterfront is built alongside a long-protected south-facing inlet and connected by regular small ferry services to a number of quieter beach resorts on the other shore. The city's own main beaches—centered round

ACCOMMODATIONS ■
Hotel Celuisma Alisos **2**
Pension La Corza **9**
Hostal La Mexicana **5**

DINING ◆
Bodega El Riojano **7**
El Conveniente **8**
La Gaviota **1**

ATTRACTIONS ●
Biblioteca Menendez
  Pelayo **4**
Catedral **6**
Magdalena Palace **11**
Museo Bellas Artes **3**
Museo de Prehistoria
  y Arqueologica **10**

the magnificent Sardinero—are tucked away around its eastern side, enclosed by twin headlands. From here, the coast, lined with superb walking paths, extends up to the cliff-top lighthouse of Cabo Menor, beyond which a wild, less protected coast of exhilaratingly rocky promontories continues northward into the open Bay of Biscay.

Getting to & Around Santander

Iberia and Ryanair both offer **flights** into **Aeropuerto de Santander** (☎ 942-022-100), a little more than 6.5km (4 miles) from the town center. Ryanair (www.ryanair.com) is usually the price champ from Madrid with some flights as low as 50€ one-way and 70€ round-trip. (It also flies from other gateways; see its website.) Buses run into the town center from the airport every 30 minutes between 6:15am and 10:45pm and cost 1.50€ one-way. Taxis charge about 15€ for the same trip.

In addition, there's relatively frequent **rail and bus service** into the city. Three trains arrive (☎ 902-240-202; www.renfe.es) daily from Madrid (5½–9 hr.). Buses arrive at the Santander Bus Station (calle Navas de Tolosa; ☎ 942-211-995). Six to nine buses a day arrive from Madrid (4½–5½ hr.).

For general information, contact the **Oficina de Turismo** (Jardines de Pereda; ☎ 942-203-000; www.ayto-santander.es; Sept–June Mon–Fri 9:30am–1:30pm and 4–7pm, Sat 9am–1pm; July–Aug Mon–Sat 9am–9pm).

LOCAL TRANSPORTATION
The city has a frequent and efficient local bus and trolley service covering all corners of Santander, including El Sardinero's beaches both day and night. Single fares are 1€.

Accommodations, Both Standard & Not

€   The cheapest and chirpiest place to bed down in acceptable comfort is the **Pension La Corza** (calle Hernan Cortez; ☎ 942-212-950). Its pleasingly sunny modern rooms—all with en suite bathrooms—belie the amazing 40€ a night rate for a double. Its location is pretty good, too: right next to the Plaza Pombo in the heart of town and just a block away from the waterside.

€   My regular favorite watching-the-euros spot, though, is the excellent **Hostal La Mexicana** ✹✹ (calle Juan de Herrera 3; ☎ 942-222-350; www.hostallamexicana. com; MC, V), which is unpromisingly built on two floors of an outwardly characterless Franco-era 1950s building but has a family aura thanks to the quietly genial lady who's been running the place since the beginning. (Its reception area looks like a well-worn room in a much-lived-in home.) Rooms (50€ double) are long, some are rather narrow and the walls could be thicker. (You may hear more of your neighbors than you'd like.) But they have comfortable beds, TVs, and spotless white-tile shower rooms en suite. And you could hardly be more centrally located. Other bonuses include an on-the-spot laundry service and a diminutive restaurant that serves (continental) breakfasts and provides tasty home-cooked main meals for around 12€ a head.

€   Close to the railway station and just a short stroll from the main waterfront, the two-story **Hotel Celuisma Alisos** (calle Nicolas Salmerón 3; ☎ 942-222-750; MC, AE, V) initially seems a rather functional and unexciting choice, but it really delivers in the practical aspects. The rooms, all with en suite bathrooms, are furnished with good-quality beds, parquet floors, large windows, writing desks, and white-tile bathrooms, in a style that mimics hotels of a higher price range. (These are just 65€ double, providing you don't come in July–Aug when they rise about 30%.) Some of the ground-floor rooms are slightly worn and in need of updating, so your best bet is to ask for digs on an upper floor (which were more recently renovated). Also, avoid rooms at the front; they face a busy street and tend to get noisy. The round-the-clock staff here is very friendly and helpful.

Dining for All Tastes

€–€€   A great barn of a wine cellar unchanged since its 19th-century inauguration with huge barrels and ceilings as high as a small cathedral's, **El Conveniente** (calle Gómez Oreña 19; daily 8pm–midnight; MC, V) conjures up past days of Rabelaisean drinkfests when seas of wine bottles emptied like wildfire. Come to think of it, that's still pretty much the scene on a normal boisterous weekend. It's more a place to go for drinking and enjoying the atmosphere than for a full meal. But you can get delicious *raciones* of sardines, squid, and octopus for around 10€ to 15€ a plate to help absorb all that Rioja wine (10€–15€ a bottle).

€–€€   Another even older wine cellar, dating from the 1500s and complete with hoary old ceiling beams and bare-wood tables, is the **Bodega del Riojano** (Río de la Pila 5; ☎ 942-216-750; Tues–Sat 1:30–4pm and 8:30pm–midnight, Sun 1:30–4pm; DC, MC, V; reservations recommended). Known as the Round Museum (Museo Redondo), because of the corny but colorful paintings displayed on its old wine barrels, it positively oozes character and has been a favorite local tavern since 1940. (It escaped the ravages of the great fire—p. 414—the year after its inauguration.) Dishes change daily and often according to the seasons. Grilled *emperador* (swordfish) and *chuletas de cerdo* (pork chops) and *pimientos rellenos con carne picada* (sweet red peppers stuffed with ground meat) are all regular favorites, and the yummy *postres* (desserts) are homemade daily. Expect to pay between 8€ and 15€ per course.

€€–€€€   On the earthy **west** side of town, a 10-minute walk from the center, you'll find the **Puerto Pesquero.** (Despite the name, the crumbling buildings have no view of the sea, as they're blocked by dock-encompassing high fences.) I'm not going to sugarcoat it: This is a rough, gritty part of town, but its saving grace and unique attraction is the handful of genuine traditional *marisquerias* (seafood restaurants) such as the prized **La Gaviota** ✦✦✦ (calle Marques de Ensenada s/n; ☎ 942-221-132; Tues–Sat 1:30–4pm and 8:30pm–midnight, Sun 1:30–4pm; DC, MC, V), which serves up fish so fresh it's almost still wiggling on the plate. You don't have to spend a lot here; its three-course lunch menu is a terrific deal at just 12€ on weekdays The paella is excellent as well, though a splurge at 20€ per person—it's loaded with shellfish. Service is ultra-speedy and most accompany the meal with excellent cold draft beer in a jug or a smooth chilled Albariño from Galicia. As for ambience, the three noisy dining rooms have the happy-go-lucky vibe of a beachside haunt (which they nearly are).

Why You're Here: The Top Sights & Attractions

Although the city has only a few genuinely historic sites, there are plenty of cultural attractions for the discerning traveler.

Tops among the former is the fortress-like **Catedral** (Plaza José Equino Trecu, Somorrostro s/n; ☎ 942-22-60-24; free admission; daily 10am–1pm and 4–7:30pm; closed during Mass 11–11:30am and 6:30–7pm), which was severely damaged in the 1941 fire but still has one surviving medieval corner: the original, haunting and almost claustrophobically low-built, 12th-century **Crypt** ✦, which you enter through the south portico. In the main cathedral, you'll find the tomb of historian/writer Marcelino Menéndez y Pelayo (1856–1912), Santander's most illustrious man of letters.

An entire library dedicated to the same man, the **Biblioteca Menéndez y Pelayo** (calle Rubio 6; ☎ 942-234-534; free admission; guided tours available; Mon–Sat 9am–1:30pm and 4:30–9pm), is located in the Municipal Museum and contains a 50,000-volume collection amassed by him and bequeathed to the city on his death in 1912. His small study, preserved in the nearby Casa Museo (House Museum), shows just how simply the brilliant author lived and worked.

Classic paintings by fine masters are the draw at **Museo Municipal de Bellas Artes** ✪ (calle Rubio 6; ☎ 942-239-485; free admission; June 16–Sept 14 Mon–Fri 10:30am–1pm and 5:30–9pm, Sat 10am–1pm; Sept 15–June 15 Mon–Fri 10am–1pm and 5–8pm, Sat 10am–1pm), where, among the Zurburáns and Flemish and Italians works, a collection of **Goya** portraits is headed by his lightly mocking portrayal of a distinctly crafty-looking Ferdinand VII. The seamier side of the artist is revealed in his small etchings, which range from the horrifying no-holds-barred Disasters of War series to the only slightly less disturbing *Caprichos* (Whims) in which the artist is, at one stage, seen as being besieged by bats in his nightmares!

The best place to learn more about the real history of this ancient region, apart from visiting the marvelous (though now replica) Cuevas de Altamira (p. 421) is the superb **Museo Regional de Prehistoria y Arqueología de Cantabria (Regional Cantabrian Museum of Prehistory and Archeology)** ✪✪ (calle Casimiro Sáinz 4; ☎ 942-207-109; free admission; June 16–Sept 16 Tues–Sat 10am–1pm and 4–7pm, Sun 11am–2pm, Sept 17–June 15 Tues–Sat 9am–1pm and 4–7pm, Sun 11am–2pm). Exhibits here range from 15,000-year-old Paleolithic and Neolithic flint axes, bone harpoons, and bronze steles recovered from wall-painted caves all over the province to later collections of Roman ceramics and mosaics.

Out into the open now for some fresh air. On a wooded headland at the southern end of Sardinero Beach, you'll find the strangely un-Spanish-looking **Magdalena Palace.** Reputedly modeled on Osborne House in England's Isle of Wight, where Queen Victoria died, it was the summer residence of King Alfonso XIII and Queen Eugenia (Victoria's English-born great-granddaughter). From October through June only, it's open to the public; call ☎ 942-298-807 in advance for a tour. On the same headland are a sea lion– and penguin-inhabited zoo set in rocks on the sea's edge (come at noon to see the tiny *pingüinos* being fed) and the open-air **Museo del Hombre y el Mar** (all hours; free admission), with its replicas (built in 1977 by Vital Alsar) of the three galleons in which Orellana first discovered the Amazon and a further replica of a large raft used centuries ago. A tiny train—which travels on a narrow lane, not on rails—takes children of all ages around the headland to its tip, where you can see the rocky offshore islet of Mouro topped by a white lighthouse.

Attention, Shoppers!

A shop with true Cantabrian spirit, **La Muralla** ✪✪ (calle Arrabal; ☎ 942-661-420; Mon–Fri 9:30am–1:15pm and 4–8:30pm, Sat 9:30am–1:15pm), offers a retail-price selection of locally made goodies from dishes and bowls to clay masks. Especially popular are their grotesque but fun figurines of Celtic mythological creatures (ranging from the squat hairy "evil" Ojanco to the lithe "sweet and gentle" Anjana), which cost from 5€ to 10€.

If **leather** goods made by top brand names such as Vaporetto and Eleanora Silvestri are more to your taste, head for the small and trendy **Ares** (calle Hernan Cortés; ☎ 942-219-713), where you can also browse through a wide range of bags made of everything from chamois to snakeskin. You'll also find a good choice of bags at the nearby **Arrika** (calle San Francisco 23; ☎ 942-227-912), which also sells individually styled women's sweaters, shawls, and scarves. The staff here is extremely helpful and one of the owners speaks excellent English.

One of the biggest stores in town, selling everything from beauty products to household accessories, is the huge refurbished **Perez de Molino** in calle Juan de Herrera, which provides an interesting local alternative to the usual (excellent) Corte Inglés. On-site amenities also include a movie theater and a selection of smaller shops selling—among other things—shoes, cameras, and clothing.

The Other Santander

It's somehow reassuring to know that at least one old part of the city survived the 1941 conflagration that destroyed so much of old Santander (p. 414). In particular, it's loads of fun to wander around one of Spain's genuine, vintage, covered food markets, and Santander's pride and joy in this field is the hyper-lively **Mercado de Esperanza (Market of Hope)** (☎ 942-22-05-29), which was built in 1897 and has been carefully restored. It's a classical Industrial Revolution structure (compared by one writer to a 19th-century French railway station), dominated by a huge curved glass and metal ceiling. Unlike some of Spain's more recently "renovated" markets, which have retained the essential architecture but somehow lost their original atmosphere, Esperanza has not succumbed to the mammoth boutique syndrome where everything is just a bit too immaculate, too pristine, and—hey—where are all those evocative smells? Here there's still some sawdust and discarded bits of food you can crush underfoot as you stroll around, plus a positive orgy of nostalgia-invoking odors, colors, and sounds—nowhere more so than among the ground-floor fishmongers, whose fresh catches are sold daily to enthusiastic local shoppers amid piercing shouts and laughter.

Right behind the Mercado in the Plaza de Esperanza is another slice of old Santander: a smaller traditional open market selling fruit, flowers, and clothes old and new on weekdays from 8am to 2pm and 5 to 7:30pm and Saturdays from 8am to 2pm, its stalls run by a vociferous combination of locals and gypsies. (In fact, it's nicknamed the "Gypsy Market.") You may not see anything that you particularly want to buy here, but it's sure great on atmosphere.

Active Santander

Just 2km (1¼ miles) east of the center, overlooked by the casino and bordered by a pergola- and bench-lined promenade, is a dandy, long, tide-washed crescent of sand divided into three sections: **Playa del Camello, Playa de la Concha,** and **Playa de El Sardinero.** When the area becomes congested in high season, take a 15-minute boat ride to **El Puntal,** a beautiful neighboring beach that's rarely overcrowded, even in August.

At the northern end of El Sardinero Beach is the prestigious 9-hole **Mataleñas golf course** (avenida del Faro; ☎ 942-390-247) owned by resident Santanderiño Severiano "Seve" Ballesteros, who was one of Spain's former top golfers. Though smaller, it's said to be Spain's answer to Scotland's famous St Andrews, both in its classiness and in its fabulous panoramic coastal location. It's not necessary to be a *socio* (member) to play, and greens fees are 17€ for the 9 holes, or 30€ if you want to go around twice and make it 18 holes.

Nightlife

The best place to hear cool **jazz** sounds in the city is **Blues** (Plaza Cañadio; Thurs–Sat 10pm–5am; 10€ cover includes 1 drink) where you can dance on one of two floors or simply relax over a cocktail in the quieter bar zone. For die-hard disco fans, meanwhile, **Pacha** (General Mola 45; ☎ 942-310-067; daily 9pm–5am; cover 8€), located in the waterfront zone of Puerto Chico, is by far the biggest dance club in town. Its two levels of dance floors are packed on weekends.

While you're here, it would be a crime not to pop out to **Gran Casino del Sardinero** (Plaza de Italia; ☎ 942-276-054; daily 5pm–4am; bring your passport to get in; cover 3€) and try your luck on the roulette table. In the grand Belle Epoque tradition of its friendly Basque rival San Sebastián, this is one of the most elegant places in Spain to have a flutter. To celebrate your winnings or try to forget what you've lost, you might drop into the neighboring **Lisboa Bar** (☎ 942-272-020; daily 9am–2am, except Mon in winter), which serves fair-priced grub well into the early hours but tends to get packed in summer.

SANTILLANA DEL MAR ✯✯✩

When a town has been constantly praised by all in and sundry, including existentialist icons like Jean Paul Sartre who (in his novel *La Nausée*) called it "the prettiest village in Spain," you tend to approach it somewhat warily. I mean, is it really that good? The short answer is yes. It achieves the near miracle of being a national showpiece that has somehow escaped looking like a miniature theme park.

This is no contrived *Pueblo Español* of Barcelona and Palma de Mallorca fame, but the real thing: a perfectly preserved medieval village of churches, mansions, towers, and tiny squares that still functions as a farming community as well. Walk around the back of town, and you'll see sheep and cows grazing in the green bordering fields and may even have to avoid cackling geese as they waddle down the cobbled lanes past you. The name Santillana del Mar is a contraction of "Santa Juliana," but locals like to say it's the town of *dos mentiras* (two lies): It's not *llana* (flat), and it's definitely not beside the *mar* (sea), which is several kilometers away. (Some claim it's three lies, as Juliana was no saint and reputedly consorted with the devil on numerous occasions!) The top sight is the 800-year-old cathedral, **Colegiata de Santa Juliana** ✯✩ (calle Santo Domingo; ☎ 942-81-80-04; Tues–Sun 10am–1:30pm and 4–7:30pm [until 6:30pm in winter]), which houses a marvelously evocative cloister, site of the discreetly dignified tomb of Juliana herself and some 12th-century pillars delightfully embossed with the original medieval figurines. The cathedral's 3€ admission fee also includes the **Convento de Regina Coeli (Convent of the Poor Clares)** (Museo Diocesano; ☎ 942-81-80-04; Tues–Sun 10am–1:30pm and 4–8pm [until 6:30pm in winter]) at the other end of the main street near the entrance to the village. Here you can stroll around another picturesque ivy-covered cloister and view an eclectic art collection of portraits and painted wooden religious figures.

Back to the Paleolithic Era

Known in some circles as the "Sistine Chapel of Prehistoric Art," the **Cuevas de Altamira (Altamira Caves)** ★★★ (☎ 942-81-80-05; 2.40€ adults, 1.20€ students, free seniors 66 and over and children 17 and under, free Sat–Sun after 2:30pm; June–Sept Tues–Sat 9:30am–8pm, Sun 9:30am–5pm; Oct–May Tues–Sat 9:30am–6pm, Sun 9:30am–3pm; closed Jan 1, Jan 6, May 5, Dec 24, Dec 25, and Dec 31) are, without argument, one of the most important Paleolithic sites in all of Europe. Here visitors can gaze upon some of the greatest cave paintings ever discovered . . . or at least their replicas. To protect the originals from the damaging carbon dioxide emitted by the thousands of tourists who visit the place, the paintings have been isolated since 2001 from the part of the cave in which they were first discovered. They're now in the adjoining **Museum de Altamira.** The fakes have been created by computerized digital-transfer technology in an exact replica "neocave" that contains every crack and indentation of the original. (Though they're done miraculously well, you may feel you miss the experience of actually seeing the genuine 14,000-year-old Ice Age article.) The top spot is the array of 21 red bison in the Polychrome Chamber. As there is no bus service, be prepared for a short (about 2.5km/1½-mile) but enjoyable countryside walk from Santillana del Mar unless you've rented a car.

If replicas are not enough, and you want to see the real thing in its natural state, head south for the beautiful little mountain town of **Puente Viesgo** where you can visit **El Castillo** ★★ (☎ 942-598-425; 3.50€ adults, 1.50€ children 4–12; Apr–Oct Tues–Sun 9am–1pm and 3–7:30pm, Nov–Mar Wed–Sun 9am–2pm), another 15,000-year-old cave, here burrowed under a 3,350m (1,150-ft.) peak. Colorfully executed bison, deer, and horses dating from the Achelense Period—as far back as the Bronze Age (3,000 B.C.)—are on display in both El Castillo (discovered in 1903) and its neighboring Las Monedas cave. Though they seem at first similar in clarity and detail to the Altamira's Ice Age works (see above), they're, in fact, several thousand years younger. You can also see some highly spectacular stalactites and stalagmites during your walk though these caverns; both are included in your visit. The number of visitors is strictly limited, so you need to book at least 24 hours ahead to be sure of getting in. Continental Auto buses from Santander regularly cover the 28km (18-mile), 40-minute trip along the N-623 road to Burgos.

For information, visit the **Oficina de Turismo** (Av. Escultor Jesús Otero 20; ☎ 942-81-88-12; daily 9:30am–1:30pm and 4–7pm).

Getting to Santillana del Mar

La Cantábrica (☎ 942 720 822) operates four to seven buses a day from Santander (reduced to 4 Sept–June). Trip time is 45 minutes and one-way fare is 2.90€.

Accommodations & Dining

You'll find top-value accommodations on the northern edge of town, at **Casa La Solana** (calle de los Hornos 12; ☎ 942-818-106), a stately, stone-built house that looks as if it should be high up in the mountains instead of just 100m (328 ft.) from the central Colegiata de Santa Juliana (above). It's divided into several highly atmospheric rooms in which original features such as floor tiles, ceiling beams, and pinewood shuttered windows have been tastefully retained. The graciousness of the staff adds to the overall *encanto* (charm) of the place. A double with bath here costs just 60€ to 70€ a night from September through June (add on about 20% in summer).

Woodsy and romantic (the lighting's great!), **Café Concana** (calle de los Hornos 5, near the Plaza Mayor; ☎ 942-84-01-61; www.cafecoccana.com; daily 1:30–4pm and 8:30–11:30pm; V), a traditional cafe, specializes in—you guessed it—a wide range of coffees, but it also offers cocktails, mixed salads, and *tortillas españolas* (Spanish omelets) at 7€ to 8€. It has a charming outside terrace where you can lunch on fine days.

One of Santillana's best eating bargains, though, can be found just 15 minutes from the center at the **Hotel Restaurant Zabala** ✦ 🄺 (Barrio Vispieres 46; ☎ 942-83-87-41; Mon–Sat 1–4pm and 8:30–11:30pm; V), which offers a fine three-course lunch for 10€ (plus kids' menus for 7€–8€) in a spacious, long tabled, brightly lit dining room where the service is very attentive. (It also provides comfortable, warmly carpeted double bedrooms with TV for 70€–90€ per night.)

Another wonderful value eating spot, just 8km (5 miles) away in a country house that's set in its own gardens and surrounded by lush green Cantabrian fields, is the **Bar Restaurante La Torre** ✦ (Barrio Medivia 8, Ubiarco; ☎ 942-84-00-15; Mon–Sat 1:30–4pm and 8–11:30pm; MC, V). Here you can get a first-rate 10€ lunch (3 courses including Rioja wine) on weekdays (rising to 15€ on weekends) in a rustic-style dining room.

LAREDO

This seaside town with a Wild West name is, in fact, the coast's biggest summer resort, and its 5km (3 miles) of sandy beaches—overlooked by the 330m (1,000-ft.) Monte Ganzo—are backed by hundreds of apartments and villas. It's the nearest you'll get to an Atlantic Torremolinos or Benidorm, but without the mass charter-flight clientele from northern Europe. (Practically all the holidaymakers here are Spanish.) It also has a lot of traditional character: The **Puebla Vieja** was walled by Alfonso VIII of Castile to protect the place from pirate raids and is dominated by the imposing 13th-century **Iglesia de la Asunción,** which overlooks the port.

Cantabria's Moderniste Masterpieces

Tiny Comillas, a beachside town of quiet cobbled lanes and bobbing fishing boats, is home to not one, but two notable buildings. **El Capricho de Gaudí** ✦ (Barrio de Sobrellano; ☎ 942-720-365) was once the summer residence of Antoni Gaudí, the fabled Catalán architect who created the Sagrada Familia and several other eccentric monuments in Barcelona. Today, it's an expensive restaurant, but you can still view his signature gingerbread windows and Muslim-style curling turrets for free. Right next door is fellow Catalan and *moderniste* architect Juan Martorell's flamboyantly neo-Gothic **Palacio de Sobrellano** ✦ (guided tours only 3€; June–Aug daily 10am–9pm, Sept 10:30am–2pm and 4–7:30pm, Oct–May 10:30am–2pm and 4–7pm); its perpendicular English-style pantheon chapel, filled with marble sculptures, gives it the look of a small cathedral. Pop by to see the two, and perhaps take a swim at the town's serene beach.

Five buses a day run from Santander (journey time: 45 min.). Four buses a day also arrive from Santillana (journey time: 35 min.).

For more information on Laredo, visit the **Oficina de Turismo** (Alameda de Miramar s/n; ☎ 942-61-10-96; www.ayuntamientolaredo.com; July 1–Sept 15 daily 9am–9pm, Sept 16–June 30 daily 9am–2pm and 5–7pm).

There are 31 **buses** per day to Laredo from Santander (traveling time: 30 min.).

Accommodations

Don't remotely consider coming to Laredo in July and August when it's both busy and expensive. Spring and fall can be fine, though.

A good choice is the basic but clean central **Pension Cantabria** (calle Menendez Pelayo 7; ☎ 942-605-073; MC, V). Double rooms here are 45€ to 50€ for rooms with comfy beds and spotless private bathrooms.

Or you could treat yourself to my favorite place in town, the **Hotel Risco** ✦ (Boulevard Arenosa 2; ☎ 942-60-50-30; www.hotelrisco.com; MC, V), which stands on a small ridge 800m (875 yd.) from the center looking out at the ever restless Bay of Biscay waters. The sunny rooms, which go for 80€ to 100€, have a dignified but colorful decor (think plaids, prints, and plenty of dark-wood furniture) and windows offering great vistas of Santander's long sandy beach. Another plus: the hotel restaurant's first-rate 12€ set lunch.

Dining

Down in the town the **Mesón Casa Mariana** ✦ (calle Vargas 23; ☎ 942-23-00-24; Mon–Sat 1:30–4pm and 8:30–11:45pm, Sun 1:30–4pm; V) provides an even better value inclusive 9€ menu. But that's not the only reason it's popular. I think it's also because the place is so social, with patrons sitting side by side on long benches in the narrow dining room, or elbow to elbow on stools in the bar. Choose the dining room, and you'll get such Cantabrian delights as *cazuelitas* (mini casseroles served in earthenware pots), *embutidos* (spicy sausages), and *callos* (tripe), all served with a chummy briskness. Those who choose to nosh at the bar are offered a range of toothsome tapas such as garlicky olives, smoky mountain ham, or pungent *cabrales* cheese. In summer, terrace tables are opened up, allowing you to dine under a red canopy in the quiet *alameda* (boulevard). As I already said, it's popular, so be prepared for lines unless you get there early.

10 Majorca, Minorca & Ibiza

The tempting Balearic Islands

by Peter Stone

THE SURPRISING THING ABOUT SPAIN'S BEAUTIFUL MEDITERRANEAN archipelago is that, though all the islands are close to each other and linked by a common culture and language (variants on Catalán and standard Castilian Spanish), they're as different as chalk and cheese.

All-purpose, year-round **Majorca (Mallorca),** the largest, busiest, and most popular of them, offers something to all age groups, from wild night spots to unexpectedly serene backwaters. At its scenic best, in the center and northwest, it's a paradise of almond-tree-filled plains, rock-enclosed bays, and wild pine-cloaked mountains; at its worst, in the south and east, it's an endless rash of grossly overdeveloped beachside areas. Capital **Palma,** one of the most attractive small towns in Spain, has miraculously hung onto its old way of life, and its central Gothic-influenced quarter, unfazed by the mayhem all around it, appeals greatly to lovers of traditional Spain.

Sedate **Minorca (Menorca),** favored by a summer-only clientele of families with children, is restrained and low-key, with coastal urbanizations of white low-level buildings in the traditional style, superb beaches—for some, the best in the Balearics—and a slightly bleaker terrain that's windswept in winter. Its main towns, Moorish-influenced **Ciudadela (Ciutadella)** and Georgian-style **Mahòn (Maò)**—once occupied by the British—are architectural delights treasured by amateur historians.

Formerly bohemian **Ibiza (Eivissa),** with its golden-sand bays, gentle olive-grove-dotted hills and white pueblos, is, in contrast, a young person's fun island, though now it's largely traded in the 1960s image of an independent wild child gyrating under the stars on a balmy open-air Mediterranean dance floor for one of a zombie blowing his or her mind in a frenzied hangar-size climate-controlled disco that could be anywhere from Iceland to Indonesia. (Many youngsters who come these days think Ibiza *is* a disco.) Capital **Ibiza Town's** old quarter, rising like the prow of a ship above the harbor, saves the day for nostalgic 60-something hippies, with its warren of boutiques and trendy bars; some of the more isolated coves still retain something of that former serenity.

DON'T LEAVE THE BALEARIC ISLANDS WITHOUT . . .

Visiting Chopin's cell at Valldemossa Monastery. Okay, so the consumptive young Polish composer didn't exactly enjoy his stay on Majorca, but he did write some of his most memorable piano pieces in his "cell"—an immaculately spartan monk's bedroom—and the whole monastery is still hauntingly atmospheric, in spite of the constant flurry of visitors. See p. 444.

Exploring the Caves of Drach.   These huge east coast Majorca "Dragon's Caverns" are always packed, but that won't detract from the marvel and beauty of an eerily surrealistic haven complete with hallucinatory stalactite and stalagmite forests and a magical boat ride across what's said to be the world's largest underground lake. All this and fluty background themes from Chopin! See p. 449.

Taking the tiny mountain train from Palma to Soller.   An endlessly twisting and turning trip in a beautifully preserved 1920s wooden train up across the steep olive-wooded Serra de Tramuntana and down the other side to the orange-growing town of Soller—this is, by far, the most spectacular outing on Majorca, and one you'll never forget. See p. 449.

Checking out the "Taulas" and "Talaiots."   Time-trip into prehistory on Minorca with a gander at these haunting 4,000-year-old monuments that are dotted in abundance around the interior. See p. 463.

Scuba diving in the crystal-clear waters off S'algar.   That's where the best diving school is, but anywhere on the south coast of Minorca will amaze you with the clarity of its waters. (Don't believe all you hear about the murky and polluted Med, and bring a snorkel to economize.) See p. 461.

Boating around Vedra Rock.   Jutting 305m (1,000 feet) out of the sea just off Ibiza's port bow, this conical mini mountain, with its sheer cliffs and permanent frenzied swirl of marine bird life, is an awesome sight. See p. 464.

Watching the sun set on Sant Antoni Bay.   Join Ibiza's disco set over a drink in a beach bar and watch the orange orb merge with the pellucid waters of Sant Antoni de Portmany's still lovely inlet before yet another wild night begins.

MAJORCA (MALLORCA)

The famed Parisian socialite and avant-garde novelist George Sand wrote that Majorca was a "green Helvetia under a Calabrian sky, blessed with the calm and serenity of the Orient." She visited this largest of the Balearic Islands, accompanied by her lover, Frederic Chopin, in 1838, just before unusually severe winter weather set in. A few years later, the Catalán writer and moderniste-artist Santiago Rusiñol echoed her sentiments in a book on Majorca entitled *La Isla de la Calma (The Island of Calm).*

Today, *calm* and *serenity* are words rarely bandied about in high summer when the island seems about to burst at the seams. In 2007, Majorca (pop. 800,000) attracted 7 million visitors, most of whom arrived by air. You would think from such a figure that the island was in serious danger of sinking. Somehow, though, even in August, the island manages to absorb them all: Some are shunted off—or shunt themselves off—to still quiet hill retreats; the majority are dispatched in convoys to noisy overblown resorts throughout the island.

The Balearic Islands

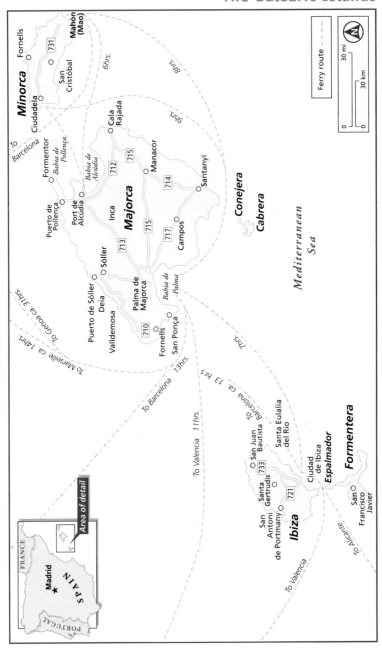

Ferry route

30 mi

30 km

Minorca
Fornells
731
Mahón (Mao)
San Cristóbal
Ciudadela
6 hrs.
8 hrs.
To Barcelona

Majorca
Formentor
Bahía de Pollença
Puerto de Pollença
Port de Alcúdia
Bahía de Alcúdia
Cala Rajada
712
715
Manacor
714
Santanyi
Inca
715
717
Campos
713
Sóller
Puerto de Sóller
Deia
Valldemosa
Palma de Majorca
Bahía de Palma
710
Fornells
San Ponça

Conejera
Cabrera

Mediterranean Sea

To Genoa ca. 31 hrs.
To Marseille ca. 14 hrs.
To Barcelona 13 hrs.
To Valencia 11 hrs.

Ibiza
San Juan Bautista
733
Santa Eulalia del Rio
Santa Gertrudis
San Antoni de Portmany
721
Ciudad de Ibiza
Espalmador
Formentera
San Francisco Javier
To Barcelona ca. 13 hrs
7 hrs.
To Alicante
To Valencia

FRANCE
PORTUGAL
SPAIN
Madrid
Area of detail

After 4 decades of hosting increasing hordes of tourists, the Majorcans have become adroit in juggling, transporting, and placing their loyal punters where they're most suited. At first, money and numbers were the main objectives for this hardworking but impoverished isle, badly battered as everywhere in Spain in the aftermath of the Civil War. Building was uncontrolled, standards were poor, and rock-bottom-priced charter holidays encouraged the arrival of British lager louts and German yobbos (or vice versa).

Now the people of the island are seeking to change its cheapo image and encourage a classier kind of visitor. They're already succeeding in many areas, especially in now chic hill villages like Estellenchs, Fornalutx, and Lluch Alcari, whose elegant hideaway guesthouses are light-years away atmospherically (and price-wise) from the multi-room hotels in sprawling pop resorts like Arenal and Magaluf—and now even these zones are seeing notable improvements in the form of better hotel service, meals, and accommodations; more planting of communal gardens; new palm lined *paseos;* and swish coastal cycle lanes.

Nowhere in Spain relies more on tourism for its livelihood. Nowhere else has gone to such ends to crudely set it up and—at long last—more objectively appraise it. Aware of their past hasty errors they're finally starting to patch the hole in the dyke to keep out the floods that might have swept it all away.

A BRIEF HISTORY OF MAJORCA

The island had the usual early Greek, Phoenician, and Roman visitors, followed by the Moors, who stayed 400 years and made the most lasting impact till King Jaime I of Catalonia and Aragón landed at Santa Ponsa Bay in 1229 and conquered the island for Christianity. Around this time Majorca's first figure of international stature, the philosopher Ramón Llull, emerged, founding Palma's first school of Oriental languages and eventually getting himself martyred at the age of 80 by a mob in Algeria while attempting to convert them to Christianity. (There are other versions of how he died, but that's the most dramatic.) Three hundred years later another visionary traveler, Fray Junípero Serra, a priest from the sleepy inland village of Petra, crossed the pond to America and founded California, erecting a mission where Hollywood now stands.

In the 15th century, Majorcans enjoyed a brief Golden Age of maritime exploration, and for a while were the finest cartographers in the world. In the following centuries, Barbary pirates consistently plagued both Majorca and the other islands with their raids, causing many towns to be rebuilt inland from their original ports (such as Andratx, Soller, and Pollensa). More peace-abiding foreign visitors eventually arrived. The most welcome of these newcomers was an eccentric Austrian aristocrat called Lluis Salvador (Ludwig), who lived 40 years on the northwest coast at Son Marroig. He made the island's beauties known to the world for the first time with a series of books called *Die Balearen,* which specifically detailed the island's landscape, flora, and fauna. Undoubtedly the least welcome of these visitors was the Parisian writer George Sand (*nom de plume* of the Baroness de Dudevant) who, together with her lover, the composer Chopin, spent an uncomfortable 2 months in the monastery at Valldemossa and lambasted the place and its inhabitants in print afterward.

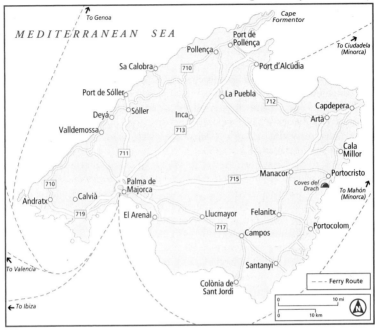

Majorca (Mallorca)

Such visitors were still relatively few, though, until the first tourist "invasion" began in the early 1920s. Then Palma, like Naples and Nice, became famous as a winter resort, and well-heeled foreigners began to settle in residential suburbs such as Terreny (now, alas, dismally run-down). The island's most famous expatriate literary figure, classical novelist and historian Robert Graves, arrived and set up home in the mountain village of Deyá in 1929. Though the next 2 troubled decades saw a corresponding drop in visitors, small-scale travel operators began to set up business in the 1950s, and the subsequent phenomenon of charter flights and block-booked hotels snowballed to its present monster proportions.

LAY OF THE LAND

Majorca lies some 209km (130 miles) from Barcelona and 145km (90 miles) from València. The island's 500km-long (311-mile) coastline could hardly be more richly varied and its image on a map always reminds me disconcertingly of a donkey's head. (I see this as a rural metaphor rather than any reflection on the nature of its astute and hospitable inhabitants, let me hasten to add.) To the south, capital Palma and its magnificent bay are flanked by heavily overbuilt beach areas—long expanses of golden sand spreading east past C'an Pastilla and Arenal to Cala Blanca, and smaller bays and coves extending west past Santa Ponsa and Paguera (the donkey's "mouth") as far as Andratx (the donkey's "nose"). Turn north from there up the coast to Puerto Pollença (one of the donkey's "ears" with the other one at neighboring Alcudia just around the bay) and the contrast is total. Now you're traveling along a picturesque 70km-long (44-mile) mountain range—a protected national park—overlooking a deep blue sea landscape of rocky headlands, pine-cloaked cliffs, and ancient olive groves that resembles a scene from Greek mythology. You almost expect to see fauns cavorting and satyrs ogling vestal virgins in white as they dance among silvery green woodlands.

The island's prettiest villages, Estellenchs, Banyalbufar, Deia, Lluc-Alcari, and Fornalutx, built from local golden-ochre stone, rest on its steep slopes or in neighboring valleys surrounded by almond, fig, and carob trees. Artists, writers, and celebrities by the score have made their homes in this area over the years; today's most famous regular is actor Michael Douglas (who owns Archduke Lluis Salvador's cliff-top mansion; p. 447).

Provençal-like Soller, surrounded by orange groves at the center of this coast (the donkey's "eye," if you'll forgive my stretching this burro-obsessed metaphor to its limit), is connected to its port by ancient tram—only one on the island—and narrow-gauge train to Palma, a zigzag cross-mountain route of just 45km (28 miles) that makes you feel you've traveled much farther.

The rest of the island is scenically less dramatic. The flat center—El Pla (the Plain)—is quiet agricultural country filled with old farmhouses and dour townships, and dotted with 10 million almond trees that blossom in February in a sea of pink and white cotton wool, while the east coast is a blend of long beaches and tiny inlets, overbuilt with hotels or seemingly endless bungalow and villa *urbanizaciones* in places like Costa del los Pinos and Cala d'Or.

Palma de Majorca

Palma comes as a pleasant surprise to most visitors. They don't expect a town that's ringed by German-dominated enclaves to the east and British expat–filled developments to the west—not to mention explored daily by tourists in the thousands—to be so resolutely Spanish (or, to be more precise, Mallorquin). Sip a coffee amid the columns of the aging Café Lirico, shop in the Avenida Rossello's long straggling open market, or wander the narrow medieval streets of the Sa Calatrava Quarter, and you'll almost forget that the other polyglot tourist-saturated world exists. With a current population of more than half that of the islands, Palma's a self-contained mini-metropolis in its own right. And it has smartly utilized revenue gained from tourism in restoration programs and new traffic-free areas. Its handsome streets are lined with boutiques, art galleries, bookshops, and trendy eating spots. Around the curving promenade that hugs the bay, the prominent La Seu cathedral and woodland-surrounded Bellver castle look down on an ever-active port and yacht harbor that positively teem with color and life.

GETTING TO & AROUND MAJORCA

Majorca is the only island of the four to accommodate year-round tourism. Visiting here between fall and spring can be both economical and relaxing (providing you don't get the freak stormy weather Chopin got during his Nov stay in 1838; p. 445). But avoid July and August like the plague: Even if you manage to get to the congested and overheated isle, you'll have a hell of a job getting off again if you don't have a round-trip ticket.

ATTRACTIONS ●
Banys Arabs **8**
Bellver Castle **14**
Can Oleza **6**
Convento Santa Clara **7**
Joan March Museu **5**
La Seu Cathedral **9**
Llotja (Lonja) **11**
Palau l'Almudaina **10**
Poble Espanyol **15**

ACCOMMODATIONS ■
Brondo **3**
Costa Azul **13**
Regina **2**

DINING ◆
El Gallego **4**
La Bóveda **12**
Sa Premsa **1**

Contact the **National Tourist Office** (Plaça Reina 2 Palma; ☎ 971-71-22-16;
Mon–Fri 9am–8pm, Sat 10am–2pm) or the **OIT** (Oficines d'Informació Turista
de Majorca, Parc de les Estacions next to Plaça España; ☎ 902-102-365) for
more information on the area.

Getting to Majorca

BY AIR

Iberia (☎ 902-40-05-00; www.iberia.com) and **Spanair** (☎ 902-92-91-91;
www.spanair.com) fly from Barcelona seven times daily and sometimes more frequently in summer. Better prices often come from British **easyJet** (www.easyjet.
com), which has a constantly changing program of flights to Palma from Madrid;
the best air values are off-season (Oct–May, excluding Easter). **Air Europa**
(☎ 902-40-15-01; www.aireuropa.com) also has regular, daily flights to Palma as
does budget airline **Vueling** (☎ 933-78-78-78; www.vueling.com), though the
latter is only from June through October, but you can get its flights for as low as
60€. Most foreign visitors to the island come from England or Germany, and
both of those countries have cheap flights throughout the summer from a wide

number of smaller towns as well as London and Berlin. (For a search of all the options, try www.wegolo.com.) July and August are the most expensive months to fly and tend to be riddled with problems; delays of 24 hours or more are common due to the sheer congestion of air traffic.

BY SEA

The only company that runs ferry services from the Spanish mainland is **Trasmediterránea** (Moll Sant Bertran 1–3; ☎ 902-45-46-45 for schedules and reservations). Depending on the time of year, one to three **ferries** a day leave from **Barcelona.** The 8-hour crossing costs from 60€ one-way; buy your ticket in the Trasmediterránea office (see above). The 4-hour sea trip from **València** costs from 50€ each way; ticket sales are at the Terminal Trasmediterránea Estación Marítima office in the port (☎ 963-76-10-62). Spanish travel agents can also make your reservation. Schedules are subject to change, so be sure to double-check.

Getting Around Majorca

BY BUS

The most important bus company covering the whole island is **TIB (Transport de les Illes Balears)** (☎ 971-177-777; http://tib.caib.es). Its comprehensive services from the d'Eusebi Estada station just above the Plaça España include major towns like Pollença, Alcudia, Cala Ratjada, Cala'Or, Valldemossa, and Soller, as well as a variety of smaller spots like the Caves of Drach and Colonia Sant Jordi. Similar services are provided by **TransunionMajorca S. L.** (☎ 971-900-209; www.transunion.info). For Palma city routes, see below.

BY TRAIN

See "Getting into & Around Palma & Palma Bay," below.

RENTING A CAR

This is probably a better value here than anywhere else in Europe, including the Spanish mainland. The cheapest outfit is **Car Jet** (☎ 902-120-009; www.carjet. com), which has an extremely helpful no-extras policy, which covers extra drivers and most damage to the vehicle. (Some companies require that a nominal amount of the damage repair work be paid for by the client.) Small cars start at 112€ per week in the low season and 139€ per week in the high season (July–Aug), including unlimited kilometers and local taxes. Drivers must be 21 or older with a minimum of 2 year's driving experience and possess an international driving license.

Getting into & Around Palma & Palma Bay

From Palma de Majorca–Son Sant Joan **airport,** bus no. 1 takes you to the center of Palma, leaving every 15 to 20 minutes, from 6:10am to 2:10am daily. The trip takes about 30 minutes and costs 2.50€. A metered cab costs 20€ for the 25-minute drive into the city center.

Buses throughout the center, up to neighboring suburbs like Genova, east around the bay to C'an Pastilla and S'Arenal, and west along the indented coast as far as Sant Agustí, are run by the very efficient **Emprese Municipal de Transportes (EMT)** (☎ 971-21-44-44). The main terminal is at Estació Central

D'Autobus, Plaça Espanya, and the standard one-way fare is 1.10€. If this is going to be your primary form of transportation, buy an 8€ booklet for 10 rides.

For stops west beyond Sant Agusti to Portals Nous, Magaluf, Santa Ponsa, Paguera, and Andratx the less frequent and more erratic **Transports de les Illes Balears** (**TIB**) service (calle Eusebi Estada 35; ☎ 971-177-777) averages one bus every half-hour at best; its standard one-way fare is 1.35€. In summer, buses on this service become impossibly crowded, so if you're staying in the nearest of those resorts it's only slightly more expensive, for groups of four to take a taxi into the center instead.

TIB also runs **train** services to Inca and Manacor and, in September 2007, launched Palma's first underground **Metro (subway)** service, covering eight stops between the center and the Universitat Illes Balears (UIB), or University City. Trains run every 13 minutes from 6:35am to 10:50pm. A one-way journey costs 1.10€. Still at the planning stage at press time are two further metro lines, planned to reach the inland northerly suburb of Cami dels Reis, the airport, and neighboring coastal Playa de Palma.

But you may decide to skip public transportation altogether. Palma has increased its number of pedestrianized areas in recent years and is a fairly easy city to simply stroll around in. The best areas for leisurely tours on foot are the pedestrianized calle Oms, which leads from the Plaça España to the Rambla, the Via Roma, and the Born. Most enjoyable are the seafront *paseos,* which extend to Portixol and Ciudat Jardí. The old quarter's lanes, while not traffic free, are usually quiet enough to make a stroll there both relaxing and fun.

ACCOMMODATIONS, BOTH STANDARD & NOT

Beyond the options listed below, keep in mind that home rentals (also known as *casas rurales*) are a key part of the lodging scene on the island and can offer groups good value. (They're often too pricey for couples.) Set in idyllic countryside locales or in seaside resorts, and almost always offering a full kitchen, they're a terrific choice for families (or anyone traveling with a picky eater). For the best mix of pricing and service, I recommend contacting such local agencies as **Rentals Pollensa** (www.rentalspollensa.com; ☎ 971-866-391) and **Terra Viva** (www. terraviva-majorca.com; ☎ 971-546-426), as they frequently inspect homes to maintain standards. For an even more affordable option, consider a monastery stay or government-sponsored *refuges* around the island (p. 434).

The best bargains to be found in the immediate vicinity of Palma de Majorca are right in the capital, which has the twin advantages of remaining steadfastly Spanish and being an ideal base for exploring the rest of the island. Hotels in beach resorts around Palma Bay, like C'an Pastilla and Magaluf, are usually block-booked with loud European charter holiday tourists and are impossible to get into, even if you wanted to, in high season.

€   You'll see what I mean about true Spanish ambience at **Hostal Brondo** ✿✿ (C'an Brondo 2; ☎ 971-71-90-43; www.hostalbrondo.net; cash only), a genuine old Majorcan house—the reception area is in an enclosed patio that dates back to the times of the Arabic occupation. Rooms are bright and high-ceilinged, featuring original roof beams and mahogany furniture aged enough to be called

Majorcan Monastery Stays

Majorca has a surprising number of guest-accepting monasteries for an island its size. A prime example, on the northern side of the island at Escorca—540 m (1,772 ft.) up a majestic mountain setting—is **Tossals Verds** (FODESMA, Consell de Majorca; ☎ 971-173-700; www.consellde Majorca.net; closed in Aug), which provides youth hostel–style accommodations in basic 8- or 12-bed dormitories (20€–25€ per person per night) with shared washroom amenities and a communal dining room serving hearty no-nonsense meals that are included in the price. Staff will give you full directions on how to reach other *refugis* on their books and provide you with bus or train schedules and walking routes. Book by calling between 9am and 2pm at least 5 days beforehand.

€   As basic, but a tad more, er, celestial are the digs at the **Santuari de Lluc** ✪ (☎ 971-871-525; www.lluc.net; cash only), near the tiny village of Escorca in a mountain valley on the road from Inca to the coastal gorge of La Calobra. The largest of Majorca's monastic sanctuary accommodations, this 18th-century building has 129 "cells" providing rooms for one to six visitors (25€ single, 32€ double, 40€ quadruple, and 50€ 6-bed room). All have writing tables, pictures of Jesus, and definitely no TV. There are also some self-contained two-bedroom apartments with bathroom and kitchen for 46€ to 50€ a night. Though this is no longer a working monastery, it does have a touch of the heavenly to it: A resident boys' choir known as Els Blauets, who have recorded various CDs and even sung in London's Westminster Abbey, sing the Salve every day in front of the monastery's statue of a Black Virgin (called La Moreneta like the one in mainland Montserrat Monastery [p. 306]). Lluc is also regularly visited by day-trippers who have lunch in one of the monastery's four restaurants. In the evenings (from 6pm onward), after most visitors have left, it's extraordinarily peaceful.

"antique" (though this is a budget property, so none of it is valuable, just character adding and comfy). Set right in the historic center of the city, off a pedestrian alleyway, the location is terrific—reasonably quiet at night, but close enough to the major sites to pop in and out if you forget something. The staff is a delight: genuinely caring and helpful. And did I mention the nightly rate? At 70€ for a double with private bathroom (or just 55€ if you're ready to share a communal bathroom) it's a superb value. A self-contained studio flat, complete with kitchen and accommodating up to three guests goes for a reasonable 90€ per night.

€   Another period outpost in the heart of the action is the 12-room **Hostal Regina** ✪ (Sant Miguel 77; ☎ 971-71-37-93; MC, V), which combines the friendly ambience of an English boardinghouse with genuine Majorcan character. From the quaint turquoise- and cream-hued reception area, you climb the stairs

€ At the top of the wooded Puig deMaría hill overlooking the town of Pollença you'll find more low-price (25€–30€) monastery accommodation in the **Santuari del Puig de María** (☎ 971-184-132; cash only). Though no longer inhabited by monks, this is one of the oldest religious centers on the island, located in a 14th-century stone building 333m (1,093 ft.) up with lovely views of the town. The 12 clean but, you guessed it, monastic-cell-like rooms have small writing desks and shared bathroom amenities, and there's a small bar providing snacks. Access is on foot in 40 minutes by winding path up through the pines, or in 5 minutes along an equally twisting road by car.

Along with these three, you may want to look into these other options (all between 30€ and 40€ per night, per double room). Rest assured, cleanliness truly is next to godliness at these places, so even though rooms will be quite simple, they should be immaculate:

- **Santuari de Sant Salvador** (Puig de Sant Salvador, Felanitx; ☎ 971-82-72-82; cash only)
- **Santuari de Cura** (Puig de Randa; ☎ 971-12-02-60; www.santuariodecura.com)
- **Ermita de Bonany** (at Petra; ☎ 971-826-568)
- **Santuari de Monti-Sion** (at Porreres between Llucmayor and Felanitx at the southern end of the central plain of El Pla; ☎ 971-647-185)
- **Castell de Alaró** (in between Alaró and Orient in the center of the Serra de Tramunta; ☎ 971-182-112)

(no elevator) to compact but equally gaily colored single (50€) and double or twin rooms (70€), each with private bathroom, TV, and air-conditioning. Avoid the noisy front rooms.

€€ Lovely views of the harbor yachts and twinkling bay are the strongest selling points at **Costa Azul** (Passeig Marítim 7; ☎ 971-73-19-40; AE, DC, MC, V)—though I also know travelers who return here just for its generous breakfast buffet. Another plus: a small pool on the third floor with a sun deck. As for the rooms, they're spacious and clean, if a tad faceless. (You'll forget what they look like the minute you close the door.) Ask the efficient (if sometimes distracted) staff for a room at the front so you'll be overlooking the waterfront promenade. Doubles are 90€ per night including breakfast, and all have private bathrooms.

DINING FOR ALL TASTES

During its periods of post–Civil War hardship, Majorca managed to create tasty dishes out of very little. Three such examples are *frito mallorquín* (a mixture of fried onions, potatoes, red peppers, diced lamb liver, lungs, and fennel); *sopa mallorquín* (local vegetables and bread cooked in olive oil, sometimes with garbanzos added); and *tumbet* (a baked dish of layered potatoes and sautéed eggplant). Today they still live on as cult—and correspondingly more expensive—items on the menu. (Top of the scale is *caldereta de langosta,* a delicious rich lobster broth, which is almost worth its heart-stopping price.) The most traditional meat creation on the island is *sobrasada,* a bright red minced pork pâté, which can be spread on bread and is still popular with some locals at breakfast. Another quintessential Majorcan creation that's a breakfast favorite is the *ensaimada,* a whirligig-shaped, lard-based, cholesterol-high pastry that makes croissants taste insipid. Larger versions in ornate circular boxes are taken off the islands by the thousands as souvenirs by tubby, irrevocably hooked tourists.

As for the local *vino,* Majorcan wines from Felanitx (Vins d'Or) and Binisalem (José Ferrer) have been making their mark and are well worth a sip or three.

€–€€   Just off La Rambla on a narrow lane is the classiest *económica* in town, **El Gallego** (Carrer de Carme 16; ☎ 971-710-313; Mon–Wed 1:30–4pm, Thurs–Sat 1:30–4pm and 8:30–11:30pm; AE, MC, V), a Galician-cum-Majorcan eating spot with roof beams, hanging hams, chummy waiters, and a highly affordable selection of seafood dishes. The *fritura de pescado* (fried fish selection) at 12€ will keep you filled for quite a while, as will the *calamares romana* (squid in batter) at 9.90€. The most popular time is at lunch on weekdays when the inventive and generous three-course set menu (9.90€) really draws them in.

€€   A traditional culinary haven, **Sa Premsa** ✮ (Plaça Bisbe Berenguer de Palou 8; ☎ 971-72-35-99; www.cellersapremsa.com; Mon–Sat noon–4pm and 7:30–11:30pm; AE, DC, MC, V) holds a special place in my heart—it was the first eating spot I visited in Palma many years ago. Founded in 1958, it's a huge, high-ceilinged barn of a place lined with wooden wine vats, bullfight posters, hanging garlic, and pics of old Palma. Here, the portions—from mixed salads to *bacalao Vizcaina* (Bilbao-style cod)—are so large that you'll need a stroll along the prom afterward to work it off. (Consider sharing to save a bit.) The a la carte specialty is the mouth-wateringly delicious *lechona* (roast suckling pig) at 14€. A generous set lunch menu is just 12€. Genial service by long-employed waiters adds to its *encanto* (charm). The restaurant is set on a leafy square about 5 minutes from the Gallego.

€€   You go to **La Bóveda** ✮✮ (Boteria 3; ☎ 971-71-48-63; Mon–Sat 1–4pm and 8:30pm–12:30am; closed Feb; AE, DC, MC, V)—a packed, noisy, and character-filled bodega bar with a flagstoned floor and ceiling fans—for the incomparable tapas. From *tortilla de espinacas* (spinach omelet) and *gambas pil pil* (prawns cooked in garlic) to *fabes con almejas* (fava beans with clams) and classic *jamón serrano* (mountain ham)—sliced wafer thin by an expert carver—they're all first rate, averaging between 8€ and 12€ for a good-size *ración*—none of your tiny

Andaluz portions here. For a brilliant example of how to make a lot out of a little, try the local *pa amb oli*—bread covered with olive oil, lightly sprinkled with salt, and rubbed with tomato—*delicioso*. Particularly good value is the house's Rioja wine at 10€ a bottle.

WHY YOU'RE HERE: THE TOP SIGHTS & ATTRACTIONS

The one historic building that stands head and shoulders above all the others in Palma—literally, it dominates the bay just as it's done for the past 4 centuries—is the great **Gothic Catedral (La Seu)** ✪✪ (Plaça Almoina 1, Almoyna; ☎ 971-72-31-30; www.catedraldemallorca.org; cathedral free, 3.75€ museum and treasury). Begun during the reign of Jaume II (1276–1311) and completed in 1601, it's another of Spain's remarkable generations-straddling monuments. Of its three great doors, the most dazzling is the sea-facing Portal del Mirador; intricate, Flemish-inspired Old Testament figures by Pere Morey and statues of saints Peter and Paul by Guillem Sagrera flank the doorway. Inside, the 43m-high (141-ft.) central vault, huge Royal Chapel, and wrought-iron *baldachin* (canopy) by Gaudí over the main altar are equally impressive—though for me, two of the most evocative sights nestle quietly in the pantheon-style Chapel of the Holy Trinity. These are the sepulcher containing the mummified remains of Jaime II and the Gothic-style tomb created by Frederic Mares in 1948 to hold the ashes of Jaime III, Majorca's second great medieval monarch (who had to wait 6 centuries to finally be deposited in this, his originally requested resting place). Cathedral hours change by the season (Apr 1–May 31 and Oct Mon–Fri 10am–5:15pm and Sat 10am–2:15pm, June–Sept Mon–Fri 10am–6:15pm and Sat 10am–2:15pm, Nov 2–Mar Mon–Fri 10am–3:15pm and Sat 10am–2:15pm).

Sharing the same superb Palma Bay location as the cathedral is its earlier constructed neighbor, the exotic **Palau de l'Almudaina** ✪ (Palau Reial s/n; ☎ 971-21-41-34; 3.40€ adults, 2.40€ children, free Wed; Apr–Sept Mon–Fri 10am–5:45pm, Oct–Mar Mon–Fri 10am–1:15pm and 4–5:15pm), a former Moorish fortress surrounded by scented gardens and twinkling fountains. When the Kings of Majorca enjoyed their brief medieval rule, it was converted into a royal Christian residence, and in recent years it's been transformed into a history museum displaying antiques, suits of armor, and Gobelin tapestries.

Just behind the cathedral and palace is a compact medieval world that's lightyears away from the garish modern excesses of Palma Bay. A smaller quieter version of Barcelona's Barri Gòtic, this narrow-laned quarter known as **Sa Calatrava** gives you the effortless impression you've stepped back a few hundred years. Hidden gems seem to appear out of nowhere, like the **Banys Arabs (Arab Baths)** (Can Serra 7; ☎ 971-72-15-49; 1.60€ adults, free for children 9 and under; Apr–Nov daily 9am–8pm, Dec–Mar daily 9am–7pm), a tiny but evocative reminder of how the city must have looked in the 10th century under Arab rule. It's the only Moorish building in the city to have survived fully intact, and its main room has striking archways and columns supporting a dome that is pierced with skylights to represent the stars.

Other worthwhile sights include the **Convento de Santa Clara** (calle Santa Clara s/n; no phone; free admission; daily 10am–2pm) a 13th-century Gothic convent in calle Santa Clara that still houses a few nuns (you can admire the wonderful Gothic facade but only enter the church); and an array of splendid 17th-century Renaissance mansions, all with traditional patios, external stairways, and Ionic columns. My favorite is **C'an Oleza** ⚔ (calle Morey 9; Mon–Sat 10am–2pm and 4pm–8pm); its grandiose facade, linteled archways, and serene courtyard earned it an Artistic-Monument award in 1973.

Farther up, in a less tranquil corner of the Old Town, a stimulating look at the modern-art scene is provided by the **Museu d'Art Espanyol Contemporani, Fundació Juan March (Juan March Foundation's Museum of Spanish Contemporary Art)** ⚔ (Sant Miquel 11; ☎ 971-71-35-15; www.march.es; free admission; Mon–Fri 10am–6:30pm, Sat 10:30am–2pm). Launched by the Majorcan financier and impresario Juan March, the foundation has been gleaning top works of art from all over the world since 1955. When March died 7 years later, it continued to expand, and today it has branches in all main Spanish cities. This particular museum features 70 works by such giants of Spanish modern art as Pablo Picasso, Joan Miró, Salvador Dalí, and Juan Gris, as well as contemporary pieces by up-and-coming Iberian talents. Among the many arresting works is Picasso's primitivistic (and frankly disturbing) *Tête de Femme (Head of a Woman)*, a highlight from his cycle of paintings known as *Les Demoiselles d'Avignon*. Rumor has it that the angry depiction of the women in these pieces may have to do with the artist contracting a venereal disease from the prostitutes he depicts in them.

Overlooking the harbor on the other side of the Born from the Almudaina Palace is the **Llotja** ⚔ (Plaza de la Llotja; ☎ 971-71-17-05; free admission; Tues–Sat 11am–2pm and 5–9pm, Sun 11am–2pm). The main interest of this 15th-century Gothic structure—a reminder of the island's wealthy seafaring Golden Age when it was an important mercantile exchange—is its wonderfully spacious and naturally lit interior: a masterpiece of huge windows, ribbed vaults, and intricately curving columns designed by the great Majorcan architect Guillem Sagrera. Today it only opens to host occasional art and cultural exhibitions: check local English-language newspapers like the *Majorca Daily Bulletin* to find what's on during your stay.

Like its big brother in Barcelona (p. 293) the **Poble Espanyol (Spanish Village)** 🧒 (Poble Espanyol 39; ☎ 971-73-70-70; 5.50€ adults, 4.50€ children; Apr–Nov daily 9am–6pm, Dec–Mar daily 9am–5pm) is an artificial Spain in miniature, designed by the distinguished writer-architect Fernando Chueca Goitia, opened in 1967, and featuring multifaceted styles of famous buildings from all over the country. Here you get Majorca's very own take on the Alhambra in Granada, the Torre de Oro in Seville, and El Greco's House in Toledo, among others. It's kitsch toy town, fun for the whole family, and not to be taken too seriously, as you'll gather from the ubiquitous piped background music and unseemly number of fast food spots around the central plaza.

The only completely circular castle in all of Spain, the **Castell de Bellver (Beautiful View Castle)** ⚔ (Camilo José Cela s/n; ☎ 971-73-06-57; 1.90€ adults, 1€ seniors, students, and children; Mon–Sat 8am–9pm [until 8pm Oct–Mar], Sun and bank holidays 10am–5pm) rises high in the woodlands above the Passeig Maritim. True to its name (beautiful view), it's famous today for its knockout vistas of Palma Bay and the east of the island that you get from its well-preserved ramparts. For most visitors who come here this is the star attraction.

Built in 1309 as a summer palace for King Jaime II, it had transformed by the 18th century—former glories long past—into a forbidding military prison. Still surrounded by its original double moat, the castle also houses a museum stacked with archaeological exhibits, old coins, and a small collection of sculpture. Buses take you from the center, west around the bay, to Carrer Camilo José Cela in the nearby suburb of Son Dureta, where it's a clearly marked 20-minute walk up through parklands and copses to the castle.

Marineland (kids) (Gracilaso de la Vega 9, Costa d'en Blanes s/n, Calviá; ☎ 971-67-51-25; www.marineland.es; 20€ adults, 18€ seniors, 14€ children 3–12; July–Aug daily 9:30am–6:45pm, Sept–June daily 9.30am–5:15pm; closed Dec 16–Jan 31) is a particular favorite with youngsters who like to see dolphins and sea lions going though their paces (and what kid doesn't?). Other attractions at the Balearics' greatest aquatic show include penguins, sharks (don't expect anything Jaws-size), and a Polynesian pearl-diving exhibition. There's also a small zoo and an aviary chockablock with multihued parrots. Buses marked MARINELAND leave the Eusebi Estada bus station roughly every half-hour to cover the 18km (11-mile) journey west of Palma that continues along the winding coastal route to Palma Nova and Paguera. Between shows, you can relax in the cafeteria or picnic area, let the kids have fun in the playground, or swim from the sheltered neighboring beach.

A word on guided tours: You don't need them. Yes, **Viajes Sidetours** (Passeig Marítim 19; ☎ 971-28-39-00) offers organized excursions to popular spots like Valldemossa, the Caves of Drach, and Pollensa, as well as to less accessible corners like Lluch monastery, La Calobra Gorge, and the Gardens of Raixa up in the hilly northwest of the island; prices for a day out range from 35€ to 50€. But if you're traveling with one or more people, simply renting a car and doing these sights on your own will be more cost-effective (and enjoyable, too, we think).

THE OTHER MAJORCA

You don't have to go far from the heart of Palma to find places that are little known by visitors, where locals go about their daily business just as they've done for decades, and where the eating spots are rarely patronized by tourists.

To get to the nearest such area, all you have to do is cross the—usually dry—Torrent de Sa Riera that follows the western course of the Old City walls and enter the district of **Santa Catalina,** which radiates around its long-established central market. Here you're definitely in foreign territory, but be careful: It's a thin line that separates unspoiled tradition and modern commercialization, and if you take one of the roads down from here toward the harbor, you'll find yourself on the far-from-unspoiled Passeig Maritim and back in tourist-land.

Santa Catalina comes even more sociably alive than normal on Saturdays, when the decades-old **Mercado de Abastos** (open food market) is held in the Plaza Navegació (Navigation Square) opposite the main covered market. Then throngs of locals and long-term stall holders maintain animated conversations amid stands of local peppers, cheeses, olives, sausages, and wines. Most have been living here and in the neighboring districts of Terreno and San Armadams since well before Franco died. You don't need to buy anything. Just wander and, without too much

Mass-Produced Pearls: A Fascinating Factory Tour

If there's one product that epitomizes the inventive energy of this island, it's the Majorca "faux" pearl. Probably the finest imitation gem in the world, this classy adornment is of such a high authentic-looking quality that even experts are hard pressed to distinguish it from the real McCoy. Originally the brain child of a German needle-producing magnate called Eduard Hugo Heusch who settled in Barcelona in 1890—and now in the hands of his adroit Majorca-based descendants—the pearls are the economical mainstay of the dreary, dun-colored inland town of Manacor, and a must on many island visitors' shopping lists.

To create this latent bestseller, Heusch picked up on a method first devised by a 17th-century Parisian rosary maker called Jaquin, who had used sticky material from fish scales to coat beads in order to give them an iridescent sheen indistinguishable from that of real pearls. The canny Teuton then perfected the production of this artificial essence so that it was resistant to heat, perfumes, skin moisture, and garment dyes, and evolved a complex production process in which the opaque nucleus of the "pearl" is made by melting the tip of a glass rod with a torch, which then flows onto a thin rotating copper wire, after which it's removed and dipped in the essence. The next stages of Heusch's process involved covering it with up to 30 more layers of essence, drying it, drilling it, and assembling it into the finished product (necklace, pendant, or whatever).

Today in his Manacor factory, trained workers produce the gems partly by hand and partly with the help of special machines. You can make your way from Palma to the factory either by public transport or by organized coach excursion and watch the process in all its intricate glory before buying your chosen earring, necklace, or even pearl-studded watch. They're not cheap, by the way: As quality products, they sell at quality prices. But just try to get your friends at home to tell whether these are real pearls off the ocean bed or not. If bona fide experts can't tell the difference, odds are they won't be able to, either.

The Majorca factory is in Carrer Pere Riche s/n, Manacor (☎ 971-550-900; www.majorica.com; free admission; Mon–Fri 9am–7pm, Sat–Sun 10am–1pm). The SFM (Serveis Ferroviaris de Majorca) runs a frequent daily train service via Inca to Manacor from the Estació Plaça Espanya in Palma (☎ 971-752-245). For a full timetable, contact TIB (Transports des Illes Balears) (☎ 971-177-777; http://tib.caib.es).

difficulty, imagine it during its beginnings in the 1930s when creaky trams scuttled up here from the center of town bringing shoppers eager to buy very much the same range of colorful goodies that are on display today.

Alternatively, you can walk east for about 20 minutes from the coastal area below the cathedral along the superb pedestrianized beachside *paseo*—or even pedal along the adjoining cycle trail if you decide to rent a bike—as far as **Portixol,** its tiny yacht-filled harbor resembling a miniature Piraeus or Marseilles, and then carry on to neighboring **Ciudad Jardi.** Here, though less numerously than in Santa Catalina, a variety of restaurants pop up unexpectedly among the rows of unadorned low-level houses and apartments, and rarely does a non-Spanish voice echo across the neighboring Med. This stretch of coast—a mere 4km or 5km (2½–3 miles) from the strongly Germanized zone that extends from C'an Pastilla farther east to S'Arenal—is where Spaniards live and traditionally take their holidays, and its lifestyle makes few concessions to that of other nationalities.

ACTIVE MAJORCA

West of **Palma** are the packed strands of **Magaluf** and **Palma Nova,** but you can do better. For peace and quiet, head to secluded **Cap de Cala Figuera,** where you can bathe in the nude, if you want (no one bothers anyone here). Palma Bay's best beach is the long, fine-grained **Playa de Palma,** which stretches between the hyper-popular resorts of **Ca'n Pastilla** and **El Arenal** east of the capital, while tiny **Cala Pi** farther on has a selection of tranquil coves wedged between rocky cliff tops.

Watersports

An abundance of sea life, from European barracuda to rainbow wrasse and goat fish, keeps the underwater sightseeing scene as lively as the one above ground. Though there are many outfits on the island, the most professional is **Planet Escuba** (Pont Adriano; ☎ 971-23-43-06 or 977-52-68-81; www.planetscuba.com), which has filled its staff with highly skilled dive masters. Along with the reef explorations, there are a few that will take you into cobalt blue caverns sheltering the odd octopus or moray eel if you're a qualified diver. Courses are also provided for beginners, starting at around 150€.

For general information on sailing as well as more underwater expeditions, contact the **Federacion Balear de Vela y de Actividades Subacuáticas y Puerto Deportivo Cala Nova** (calle Joan Miró 327; ☎ 971-708-785; www.fbdas.com).

Cycling

All of Majorca is popular with cyclists, who generally divide into two categories. An ambitious and energetic Lycra-clad minority tend to prefer the up-and-down challenges of the bendy northwest mountain roads around Deia and Soller (aware

Swimming Weather

You can swim comfortably from May through October, but it's usually too cold to swim in the other months unless you're of a particularly spartan, or masochistic, disposition. Spring and fall can be ideal weather-wise, and in summer the coastal areas are often pleasantly cooled by sea breezes.

A Drive to Remember

An area of stark, 200m (646-ft.) cliffs plunging into the deep blue sea far below makes the **Formentor Peninsula** ✪✪✪, quite simply the most scenic area of the island (and that says a lot on an isle as lovely as Majorca). Along the way, be sure to pop in for a coffee at the **Hotel Formentor** ✪, an elegant hideaway built in 1928 and once patronized by the likes of Winston Churchill and Grace Kelly. And if you need a break from driving (likely, as the road can get twisty), pack your bathing suit for a swim at the **Cal de Pi de la Posada,** a sweet little beach along the way. The drive along the peninsula is approximately 20km (13 miles), and the peninsula itself is on the northern side of the island.

of course that July and Aug, with their intense humid heat, are not the ideal months to do this). The more relaxed and easygoing majority, wearing simple shorts, sandals, and sun hats usually prefer the leisurely flat areas around northerly **Alcúdia Bay,** and across the central plain—known as **Es Pla.** Today a new third breed, unthinkable a few years back, is emerging: the urban cyclist! As the busy capital becomes more eco-conscious, cycle lanes in and around the city are increasing. One of the most attractive routes runs from the cathedral right along the eastern part of **Palma Bay** and will eventually link the town center with easterly **Playa de Palma** (which already has its own excellent 6km-long [3¾-mile] cycle lane that runs the length of the beach).

For rentals, try **Belori Bike** (Edificio Pilari, Marbella 22, Playa de Palma; ☎ 971-49-03-58). Daily rates are around 10€ depending on the model and its number of gears. You can get maps of half a dozen or more circular cycling routes from the **Federación Balear de Cioclismo** (calle Francesc I Fiol 2-1º.17ª, Palma; ☎ 971-75-67-628; www.fcib.org). Tourist Offices (p. 431) will also give you Guia del Ciclista maps.

Golf

Golf is not a cheap sport anywhere in Spain, and Majorca is certainly no exception. But if you feel an uncontrollable urge to swing that club in distinguished company, the best place to do it is at the **Son Vida Club de Golf** (☎ 971-78-71-00; greens fees 70€); you'll share its amenities with guests of the tip-top Son Vida and Arabella Golf hotels. The prized 18-hole course is about 13km (8 miles) east of Palma just off the Andratx highway.

Hiking

Majorca's richly varied countryside lends itself to a wide range of walking possibilities. Up in the northwest mountain range known as the Serra Muntana, you can wander through olive groves and gorges up to high peaks, while over on the lower cove-indented east coast there are cliff-top walks that allow you to break off for the occasional swim in the clear waters just below. Inland—the least spoiled area—marked trails guide you across El Pla's lush orchards and farmlands. To get the full picture, stop by the tourist office (p. 431) for a free booklet called *20 Hiking Excursions on the Island of Majorca.*

Horseback Riding

Bridle paths crisscross the central plain and lower slopes of the Serra Tramuntana, which are—as with hiking trails—the most popular areas. Two recommended schools where you can hire horses are **El Real Club Escola Equitació de Majorca (The Majorca Riding School)** (☎ 971-61-31-57) and the **Club Hipico de Son Molina** (☎ 971-61-37-39). Both are close to each other at Km12 on the Ma-11 Palma-Sóller road near the village of Bunyola, and both offer escorted rides into the lovely surrounding almond and pine groves at around 30€ an hour.

ATTENTION, SHOPPERS!

The greatest concentrations of shops is on **San Miguel, Sindicato, Jaume III**, and **Plateria streets,** plus the streets between the **Born** and **Plaça Cort,** where the city hall stands. Most of them close on Saturday afternoon and Sunday. The two island "bestsellers" are leather wear and artificial pearls. For the former you have a choice of at least three good shops. **Loewe** (Av. Jaume III no. 1; ☎ 971-71-52-75) offers fine leather, elegant accessories for men and women, luggage, and chic apparel for women, while **Pink** (Av. Jaume III no. 3; ☎ 971-72-23-33) has a funkier sensibility. **Passy** (Av. Jaume III no. 6; ☎ 971-71-33-38), meanwhile, sells high-quality, locally made shoes, handbags, and accessories for men and women, and has another branch, not as well stocked, at Carrer Tous y Ferrer 8 (☎ 971-71-73-38). But if you're looking for a bargain, they're all a much better value at inland Inca's outlet factories.

   Pearls come in a wide range of sizes and styles, and if baubles are your thing, you can pick up some good deals at **Perlas Majorica** (Av. Jaume III no. 11; ☎ 971-72-52-68), which is their authorized agency and offers a 10-year guarantee for their products. Again, it's better—and better value—to get out of town and see how they're made at the factory in Manacor on the east end of the island (p. 440).

   Two places you might pick up the odd bargain **souvenir** (ceramic, olive-wood decorations, and so on) are the **open market** held on Saturdays in Avenida Gabriel Alomar i Vilalonga and daily **crafts market** (Sat summer only) in the Plaça Mayor. Both start around 8am and finish around 2pm.

   Specialty shops—good but not particularly cheap—include **Casa Bonet** (Plaça Federico Chopin 2; ☎ 971-72-21-17), founded in 1860, which sells lovely and intricate needlework pieces including hand-embroidered tablecloths, napkins, and pillowcases. At **El Olivo** (calle Pescateria Vella 4; ☎ 971-72-70-25), you'll find olive-wood salad bowls, salt and pepper grinders, and even corkscrew handles.

   If you're a bookworm, wander around the area east of the Rambla and up as far as Carrer Om and you'll find a handful of shops—including **Dialog** (calle Carme 12; ☎ 971-22-81-29; www.dialog-parma.com)—that sell both new and secondhand volumes of English-language books (some quite cheap, for Spain).

NIGHTLIFE

The city's hottest after-dark mecca is **Tito's** (17 Passeig Maritim s/n; ☎ 971-73-00-17; www.titosmallorca.com; June–Sept daily 11pm–5am, Oct–May Thurs–Sun 11pm–5am; 16€ cover including the first drink), a huge nightclub that's cleverly changed its style with the times—it opened in 1923 as a traditional salon beside Plaça Gomila. Today its main entrance is 50m (164 ft.) lower in the Passeig Maritim, and international crowds and homegrown celebrities mingle in its six bars and on its terrace overlooking the Mediterranean, reached by glass elevators.

Older partiers tend to go for **Bar Barcelona** (Carrer Apuntadores 5; ☎ 971-71-35-57; nightly 11pm–3am), a more traditional club in the Old Town, which features live jazz, blues, and occasional flamenco.

A riotous disco to suit all tastes is the **Black Cat** (Av. Joan Miró 75; no phone; daily midnight–6am, closed Mon in winter; 8€ including drink), which attracts a mixed gay and straight crowd of young locals, as well as visitors from Spain and the rest of the world. Things don't usually get moving till 2am; there are nightly shows at 3:30am. Another gay favorite is **Baccus** (Carrer Lluis Fábregas 1; ☎ 971-45-77-89; daily 9pm–3am).

The biggest blast on the island for heterosexual youngsters who like Ibiza-style fun and action is **BCM** (Av. Olivera s/n, Magaluf; ☎ 971-13-15-46; www.bcm-planetdance.com; daily 11pm–4am; cover 16€ including first drink) a packed, strobe- and laser-lit three-story club with a variety of sound systems and musical styles located in the brash, brassy resort of Magaluf.

NORTHWEST TO VALLDEMOSSA, DEYÁ & SOLLER

The mountainous northwest corner of Majorca, with its pinewoods, ancient olive groves, and plunging coastal cliffs, is the most beautiful part of the island. You don't need to take an expensive organized tour to do it justice, either, as buses cover the route well and economically, and the evocative serpentine trans-mountain trip by 1920s train to Soller is worth the slightly extra outlay. Groups of four will also find that renting a car can work out less than taking the organized trip and allow you to seek out more offbeat spots.

Valldemossa

A stone-built pueblo of attractive houses surrounded by green valleys and towering pine-wooded slopes, **Valldemossa** (18km/11 miles from Palma) is quite simply one of the most attractive villages on the northwest coast. But the main reason to go there is to visit the Carthusian monastery, the **Cartuja Real (Cartoixa Reial)** ★ (Plaça de las Cartujas s/n; ☎ 971-61-21-06; 7.50€ adults, free for children 9 and under; Mon–Sat 9:30am–6pm [until 5pm in winter], Sun 10am–1pm), where Chopin and George Sand (a.k.a. Lucile Aurore Dupin, or Baronne Dudevant) once spent a far-from-comfortable winter in 1838 (see "Scandal in Valdemossa," below). Built in the 14th century and remodeled 400 years later, it's packed year-round with tourists eager to peer at the Polish composer's piano and into the separate spartan cells where they stayed. The monastery is interesting enough, but the downside to the town is that the coachloads of daily arrivals and departures have transformed it into a mass of souvenir shops and tourist-trap eating spots. The adjoining Moorish-built **Palau del Rei Sancho (King Sancho's Palace)** can also be visited on the same ticket; it features tours by guides in traditional dress.

Scandal in Valldemossa

A cross-dressing, cigar-chomping woman living in sin with her tubercular lover would raise few eyebrows today (well, she might raise a couple). But in 1838 when novelist George Sand arrived on Majorca with her lover, composer Frederic Chopin, and checked into a former monastery no less (the monks had moved out and Valldemossa was transformed into a very spartan hotel of sorts) . . . well, it was scandal par extraordinaire. They arrived in November of that year with the intention of spending the whole winter, having envisaged a peaceful Mediterranean idyll that would relax them both and ease the composer's tuberculosis. What followed was possibly the two most unseasonably cold and wet months that the island saw that century. And the chill in the weather was matched by the frigid reception the two were given (women who wore trousers and espoused a revolution in personal relations were not the sort of new neighbors this traditional community was seeking).

The unusual duo occupied cells 2 and 4, which are open to the public, but the only traces of their ill-fated visit that remain there today are a small painting and a French piano. The peasants burned everything else they found in the cells after the couple returned to the mainland, fearing they'd catch the composer's illness. Ironically, during his unexpectedly brief stay, Chopin composed some of his most imaginative pieces—including the seductively haunting Nocturnes 11 and 12—which evidently says something about the effect of adverse circumstances on the creative process. Even more ironically, Sand's vitriolic account of their stay, *Winter in Majorca*, in which she referred to the locals as "monkeys and savages" is a bestseller in local bookshops as a tourist souvenir.

Because of the touristy nature of the place, I only recommend it for a day trip and not an overnight visit. If you're looking for a solid meal while here, try **Hostal C'an Mario** (calle Uetam 1; ☎ 971-61-21-22; http://hostalcanmario.net; closed mid-Dec to mid-Jan; daily 1:30–4pm and 8:30–11:30pm; AE, DC, MC, V), one of the town's few remaining traditional restaurants. Its 10€ set lunch is an excellent deal.

GETTING THERE
Apart from an abundance of organized excursions arranged by local travel agents, there's an economical regular bus service daily between Palma and Valldemossa.

Deyá (Deià)
Idyllic Deyá (6km/4 miles from Valldemossa and 18km/12 miles from Palma) is a conglomeration of ocher sandstone houses tumbling down a hillside covered with olive, carob, and almond trees. Creeping bougainvillea fill the gardens and

Goodbye to All That

One of England's most illustrious classical writers lived several decades in Deyá and died here in 1985. He's buried in the local cemetery where his tomb bears the modest legend ROBERT GRAVES—POETA, though his vast output encompassed historical novels and biographies, Greek classical criticism, and an autobiography entitled *Goodbye to All That,* in which he unforgettably recounted his experiences as a young man in World War I prior to his moving—family and all—to Majorca in 1929. (This was coincidentally the same year the still operative Palma-Soller railway service was launched and Palma's moderniste bullring was built.) Apart from having to leave the island during and just after the Spanish Civil War, he spent practically all his creative life here, writing over 100 books and running daily down the steep path to rocky Cala Deià to swim.

Why did he stay? Read his work and you'll find that he believed that the moonlight in his village was stronger than anywhere else on Earth and that the magnetic field the area exuded gave him his creative energy. He also boasted that the island was bewitched, haunted, magical. His views on tourism were caustic, so God knows what he would have made of the Majorca today (though between the 1960s and '80s he, and we, got a pretty good idea).

It's largely thanks to Graves that the northwest coast has remained unspoiled. His clout as an international figure forced island authorities to listen to his entreaties not to let the place become ruinously overdeveloped. Tragically, his final years were marred by acrimonious disputes with family and friends and a descent into that most cruel of afflictions, Alzheimer's disease.

Paradise does not last forever. What lives on is his work, and the sight of his house amid the trees above the road out to Soller, where you can still imagine him at his desk, maybe contemplating another run down to the cove for a swim before lunch.

narrow paths wind past whispering streams. An Eden if ever there were one, as the rich and famous have discovered in recent years, creating a Brave New World of exclusive residences, pricey restaurants, and luxury hotels amid the greenery. The old Deyá, known by famed long-term resident Robert Graves (see "Goodbye to All That," above)—when few outsiders had appeared on the scene and the pleasures of life were simple and cheap—no longer exists. Still, the beauty of the place remains, mercifully unblemished by the tasteful architecture of its handful of new pricey establishments.

Most visitors to Deyá make a beeline for the **Son Marroig Museum** ✦ (☎ 971-63-91-58; 3.50€; Apr–Oct Mon–Sat 9:30am–2pm and 3–8pm, until 6pm in winter). Perched amid silvery olive groves high on the cliff top between Deyá and

Soller, it's located in one of the most beautiful and intriguing buildings on the entire northwest coast, a magnificent mansion, formerly owned by the eccentric German Archduke Lluis Salvador. He came and settled here with his young bride in 1870 and became so fascinated with the natural beauty around him that he wrote a multivolume work called *Die Balearen,* introducing the outside world to the island's charms. Faded photos, exquisite ceramics, and personal furnishings make up his personal collection, while the house gardens lead down to the cliff edge overlooking the Mediterranean and distant horizon. Immediately below is the distinctive Sa Foradada rock noted for its keyhole gap through the middle. Two of the Archduke's other imposing properties, the Moorish-style **S'Estaca** (now owned by actor Michael Douglas) and 13th-century **Miramar** (a one-time monastery and subsequent missionary's school) are close by.

WHERE TO STAY & DINE

€   Even though it's hard to find reasonably priced places to eat in this trendily transformed pueblo, a notable exception is the chic yet genial **Patricia's Bar** (calle Felipe Bauza 1; ☎ 971-63-91-99; Thurs–Tues 11am–11pm; cash only), where you can get snacks such as falafel and baguettes of *jamón* with a drink for under 10€. Hardly a full blowout, but you wouldn't want a stodgy *tortilla* (Spanish, not Mexican) or *frito mallorquín* in such a smart place, would you?

€–€€   The problem of finding affordable accommodations here is solved (if you can get a room; book far ahead!) by the presence of the charming **Hostal Villaverde** ★★☆ (Ramón Llull 19; ☎ 971-63-90-37; www.hostalvillaverde.com; MC, V). Tucked away in a peaceful lane just below the church, it offers gleaming white-walled bedrooms with the type of ornate, antique dark-wood headboards that family members come to blows over when a great aunt dies. A vase of fresh floors sits in each; ceiling beams, small balconies (in some), and cool tiled floors complete the ambience. Rates range from 70€ to 85€ for a double; along with the balconies, there's a lovely patio and tree-shrouded communal terrace overlooking the olive-grove-fringed coast.

Soller

Hemmed in by the massive Puig Mayor range in a basin filled with seemingly endless lemon and orange groves Soller (10km/6 miles from Deyá, 40km/28 miles from Palma) is one of the island's most spectacularly located towns. You get a great view of it as you come in by car, bus, or train (the latter even makes a special stop; see "On the Rails," below). The mountain barrier between Soller and the capital made traveling between the two towns an arduous day's venture in— and especially before—the 19th century, in spite of the short distance, and forced Soller to look across the sea to France for trade. The result is that many of the older residents speak French almost as well as Spanish, and the tree-lined streets and corner bars could be those of a small town in Provence. Year-round, in fine weather, the main square beside its main 17th-century church packs in so many cafe tables to accommodate the flow of visitors that it looks like a movie set.

Adding to the cinematic ambience mentioned above are the two vintage trams, said to have been modeled on those in San Francisco, that take visitors on down to the **Port of Soller** (5km/3 miles) through the orange groves every hour. Totally enclosed by wooded headlands, with a curving cafe-lined waterfront overlooking a tiny boat-filled bay fringed by a couple of beaches, the timeless port has a true island feel. Some hotels line the waterfront and rise up on the hills, but the place is mercifully not overdeveloped. It's from here that the orange-laden ships set out for Marseilles in the past.

For more information, head to the **Tourist Info booth** (Plaça España, Soller; ☎ 971-63-80-08; Mar–Oct Mon–Fri 10am–2pm and 3–5pm, Sat 10am–1pm; Nov–Feb Mon–Fri 9am–3pm, Sat 10am–1pm).

GETTING THERE & GETTING AROUND

Bus services run five times a day on weekdays and three times a day on weekends to Valldemossa, Deyá, and Soller from Palma's Eusebi Estada station. Call ☎ 971-75-06-22 or check www.emtpalma.es for the exact timetable. For train information, see "On the Rails," below.

WHERE TO STAY & DINE

€ You really get the essence of old Soller at the traditional, family-run seven-room **Pension Margarita Trias Vives** (calle Reial 3; ☎ 971-63-42-14; www.soller net.com/casamargarita; MC, V) tucked away in an almost claustrophobically narrow lane a few minutes from the station. The rooms here are surprisingly bright and sunny, though, with all white walls and ceilings (some retaining the original beams), pastel bedcovers, antique dark-wood wardrobes, and traditional touches such as a hanging lantern-style lamp and crosses on the walls. Some doubles include only a sink in the room and share the bathroom amenities, while others have their own en suite bathroom. One also has its own small private terrace. Rates vary from 30€ to 40€ a night.

€ One of the prime rendezvous spots on the town's perennially busy main square is **Café Soller** (Plaça de la Constitution 13; ☎ 971-63-00-10; daily 8am–midnight; AE, DC, V), which serves a variety of goodies from morning coffee and *ensaimadas* to generously portioned round-the-clock pastas and salads. The best value is the set 10€ lunch, which includes local wine and a dessert. You eat either outside on the terrace tables or in its roomy traditional interior, which is as bustling as its nonstop and seemingly inexhaustible waiters.

€–€€ Down at the port, consider a stay at the long established—and fairly recently renovated—**Hostal Miramar** (calle Miramar 12-14; ☎ 971-63-13-50; www.hotelmarinasoller.com; closed Nov–Jan; MC, V). Another sweetly welcoming, family-run operation, it stands right next to the harborside *paseo* overlooking the bay. The white-walled, terrazzo-floored doubles (40€–45€) enjoy either sea or inland hill views and all are neatly if undramatically furnished with standard wooden bedsteads, a small table, and a couple of wicker chairs. You can also self-cater in one of the hotel's new apartments (built in 2005), each of which has a twin bedroom, a small open-plan kitchenette, and a lounge-dining area with twin convertible sofa beds (60€–75€). There's also a restaurant serving good-value meals for around 10€ to 12€.

€ The immediate waterfront is packed with irresistible-looking seafood eating spots, but I'd advise budget-minded travelers to avoid these pricey joints and head uphill from the Carrer de la Marina to the genial and obliging **Es Racó** (Santa

On the Rails

It's one of the most eye-poppingly beautiful train trips in all of Spain. Setting off from Palma, you ride 27km (17 miles) across bridges and gulleys and though pine woods dotted with country houses. You emerge, after passing though half a dozen tunnels, on the other side of the Serra de Tramuntana. There, the view is so breathtaking, the train pauses for a full 10 minutes at the Mirador del Pujol d'en Banya so riders can take photos of the panoramic views of Soller nestling in a Shangri-La–like valley below.

Work started on the line back in 1907 and the first (steam-run) train, quaintly equipped with Belle Epoque banquette-type seats, brass fittings, and gaslights, was built 6 years later (incidentally on the very same day the *Titanic* sank!). In 1929, both the line and the train's lighting were electrified, another train was added, and a charming little moderniste-style station was built in Palma—the same one you still see today. The Soller station building at the other end is even older, dating back to the 17th century when it was one of the more grandiose town houses. From its busy neighboring square, a vintage windowless and wooden-seated *tranvía* (tram), built in 1913 and said to have been modeled on those that rattled up the hills of early San Francisco, takes you on a gentler, dream-like, 20-minute trip through the orange groves to the Port of Soller (see above).

In all, there are four trips a day on this narrow-gauge (916mm/36-in.) track lasting just over an hour and departing from **Ferrocarril de Sóller,** railway station Carrer Eusebi Estada 1 (☎ 971-75-20-51), just off Plaça Espanya. Train tickets from Palma to Soller cost 9€ one-way, 14€ round-trip. Trams between Soller and Port of Soller run from 7am to 8:30pm, coinciding with train arrivals and departures and charging 3€ for a one-way ticket (there's no discount here, by the way, so the round-trip costs 6€).

Caterina d'Alexandria 6; ☎ 971-63-36-39; Thurs–Tues noon–3:30pm and 6:30–11pm; closed Dec–Jan and 15 days in July; AE, DC, V), which boasts a charming little dining room where you can enjoy a sound paella for 10€ a head, or a more pricey *rape al estragón* (angler fish in tarragon sauce) at around 18€, served by some of the chummiest waiters in the port.

A DAY TRIP: EAST TO THE CAVES OF DRACH

The scenic highlight of the cove-dotted eastern coast of Majorca is actually underground. Near the overbuilt resort of **Porto Cristo,** situated next to a picturesque inlet 61km (38 miles) west of Palma, are the truly incredible **Cuevas del Drach (Caves of Drach)** ✪✪✪ 🄺🄸🄳🄢 (Carretar Cuevas s/n; ☎ 971-82-07-53; www.cuevas deldrach.com; 11€ adults, free for children 5 and under; Mar–Oct daily 10am–5pm; Nov–Feb guided tours 10:45am, noon, 2pm, 3pm), discovered in 1896 by the French speleologist E. A. Martel. Visitors are taken, partly, along the same path Martel first took, a kilometer-long walk along a narrow path that passes through three chambers: the Cueva Negra (Black Cave) and Cueva Blanca (White Cave)—named after the varied hues of the surrounding limestone rocks—and the Lluis Salvador Cave—named after the resident German aristocrat (p. 428) who first urged Martel to explore the caves. The path ends at a natural subterranean amphitheater whose "ceiling" is an illuminated upside-down fairy-tale forest of stalactites and stalagmites, under which you sit and listen to a concert of works by Chopin (who else?) as well as Offenbach and other famed composers. The classical strains are squeakily, cornily, yet somehow hauntingly performed—with the help of some amazing natural acoustics—by an enthusiastic group of boat-bound violinists who bob gently up and down on what's claimed to be the world's largest subterranean lake *(Lago Martel)*. When the concert's over, the audience gets into a small flotilla of boats and sails out of the cave in triumphant explorer style. Adults and kids of all ages love it.

Trains and buses run from Palma to **Porto Cristo.** For info, check the Palma tourist office (p. 431). From Porto Cristo to the Caves of Drach (4km/2½ miles) you must hire a taxi (around 12€). For more than two travelers, this can still work out cheaper than an organized trip from Palma, which costs at least 35€ a head.

MINORCA (MENORCA)

There's something decidedly un-Mediterranean-looking about Minorca. Frenchmen have compared it to Brittany; Scotsmen, to the Outer Hebrides islands; Englishmen, to Cornwall in the southwest of their country; and other travelers and writers, to Ireland, Wales, and the tiny Channel Islands that lie between England and France. They're referring mainly to its wild, windswept, almost treeless north coast, with its long unspoiled beaches, and to the flat green center with its strange ubiquitous *taulas* and *talayots*. Perhaps they sense an aura of Celtic mysticism in those areas, especially in winter.

The south, on the other hand, with its array of sandy, blue-watered coves enclosed by rock and pines, is something else: sunnier, less windy, more relaxingly southern, less bleak, more appropriate to its location. A slightly schizophrenic mix, if you will, crammed into an island less than 52km (32 miles) long and a mere 15km (9 miles) wide.

And that topography, plus its unique history, may be part of what has kept Minorca so different from the other Balearic Islands. Though the beaches here are among the very best in the archipelago, its tastefully controlled tourist developments have none of the wild excesses that have blighted certain corners of Ibiza and Majorca. This despite the fact that Minorca, with 70,000 permanent inhabitants, and another half-million visitors per year, is hardly a backwater. But it's laid back, and its low-key lifestyle is particularly enticing for families with young children. (Most visitors are happily tucked up in bed when youngsters in the more riotous neighboring islands are about to go out on the town.) Unique in the archipelago for its lack of total dependence on tourism, it has some industry, including leatherwork, costume-jewelry production, dairy farming, and even gin manufacturing. You'll also find plenty of interest in the worlds of history, archaeology, music, and art. The island's still unspoiled beauty has attracted many artists, who have frequent regular exhibitions in Ciudadela and Mahòn.

Minorca (Menorca)

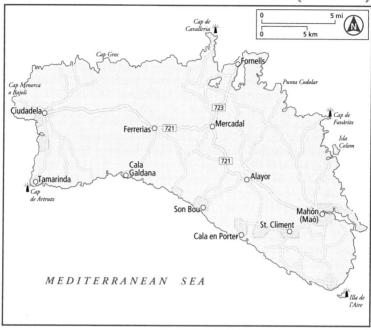

A BRIEF HISTORY OF MINORCA

Traces of the island's history go way back. Its 3,000- to 4,000-year-old primitive stone monuments (known as *taulas, talaiots,* and *navetas;* see "Megalithic Minorca," below) are superceded in the Mediterranean in quantity and age only by Sardinia's *nuraghi.* Over the centuries, Minorca was colonized by Arabs, conquered for Spain by King Jaume I, plundered by Turks and Barbary pirates, and briefly occupied by the British and French. The San Roque archway alone survives as a reminder of the fortifications built to protect the port in those violent days. During the Spanish Civil War, it was the only island to oppose Franco, and its consequent sufferings forced it to fend for itself, creating small local industries like shoes, gin, and jewelry, which still survive today.

LAY OF THE LAND

Minorca's capital city, Mahòn (pop. 22,000) stands on a rocky headland at the eastern end of the island overlooking a huge inlet 5.5km (3½ miles) long. Former capital, Ciudadela anchors the western side and a major highway connects the two. Its highest point, Monte Toro stands 358m (1,174 ft.) above sea level. Inland are gleaming white-walled market towns, removed from the tourist fuss on the coasts and carrying on a way of life that hasn't changed much in several centuries. The windier, open, long-beached **north coast**—centered around Fornells, a tiny white fishing town built around a series of defense fortresses and lined with upscale seafood restaurants—is also a peaceful haven. West is **Platja Binimella,** a handsome swoop of a beach (unofficially nudist) that's easily accessible by car. The best views on the island are from **Cap de Cavalleria;** its lighthouse at the northern tip of the island is reached by a meandering, often rough road. (*Note:* Some of the road is gated, but since all beaches in Spain are public, feel free to open the gate and drive on through; close it though, as it's there to keep cattle from roaming.) I urge you to visit these off-the-beaten-path parts of the island, but in this chapter, we'll be concentrating on popular Mahòn and Ciudadela.

Mahòn (Maò)

Mahòn's attributes as a sheltered port were fought over for centuries by the Turks, Barbary coast pirates, British, French, and Spanish. Called **Isla del Rey (Island of the King)** when the Christian king Alfonso II established a base in the harbor in 1287, it earned the nickname "Bloody Island" after the British built a hospital here to care for injured soldiers. Finally made island capital in 1722, after the seat of government was moved from Ciudadela, it feels pretty sober today by Spanish standards, perhaps because the British set the standards for how it still looks during their 18th-century period of rule. Both Mahòn and the neighboring former garrison town of Es Castell (formerly Villa Carlos and before that, during the British occupation, Georgetown) still feature Georgian facades on many buildings and include Chippendale reproductions among their furnishings. One of the finest mansions from this period, Golden Farm, overlooking the harbor, is where, in October 1799, Admiral Lord Nelson is said to have whiled away the time with his ladylove, Emma Hamilton (though the less romantic truth is that he was here alone working on *Sketches of My Life*).

Ciudadela (Ciutadella)

If Mahòn still has more than a touch of the straight-laced Brit about it, then sleepily exotic Ciudadela seems to have conspicuously turned its back on Europe. A white honeycomb of dazzling white houses, labyrinthine alleys, and souk-like boutiques, this pueblo could be somewhere in North Africa. It's by far my favorite tiny town in Spain.

GETTING TO & AROUND MINORCA

Getting to Minorca

Minorca International Airport (☎ 971-15-70-00) is 3km (2 miles) from capital Mahòn. In midsummer a flood of charter flights, mainly from northern European countries, especially Britain and Germany, fills it to capacity. Of the standard carriers **easyJet** (www.easyjet.com) tends to have the lowest fares from airports outside of Spain (but shop around at www.wegolo.com before booking). **Iberia** (☎ 971-36-90-15; www.iberia.com) runs regular domestic flights here from Madrid, Barcelona, and Palma de Majorca.

Buses run from the airport into Mahòn (4km/2½ miles) between May and October every half-hour from 6am to 10:30pm. Outside of those hours in summer and from November through April, unless you have a transfer organized, the only options are to rent a car or take a taxi into Mahòn. (It shouldn't cost more than 15€; a taxi to Ciudadela, however, will knock you back 45€.) The exception to this is at Easter, whenever that falls, as a mini summer timetable is briefly

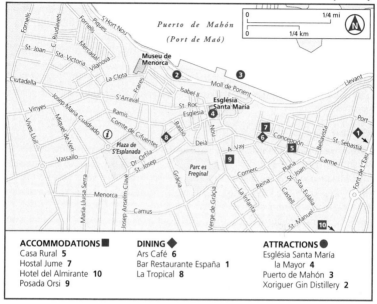

Puerto de Mahón
(Port de Maó)

ACCOMMODATIONS ■
Casa Rural **5**
Hostal Jume **7**
Hotel del Almirante **10**
Posada Orsi **9**

DINING ◆
Ars Café **6**
Bar Restaurante España **1**
La Tropical **8**

ATTRACTIONS ●
Església Santa María
 la Mayor **4**
Puerto de Mahón **3**
Xoriguer Gin Distillery **2**

resumed then. Best to come with hotel rooms, car rentals, and ferry or airplane tickets all booked ahead. In July and August, reservations are vital, because of the limited hotel and transportation facilities.

Regular summer **ferry services** connect the island with Barcelona, València, Palma de Majorca, and Ibiza. Ferries also run between Ciudadela and Alcudia on the north coast of Majorca. In winter a far more limited service operates. From Barcelona, the journey takes 9 hours aboard moderately luxurious lines. To economize, bunk in a four-person cabin, which costs virtually the same (46€ per person) as a single lounge chair (45€). The main ferry operator is **Trasmediterránea** (Estació Marítim, Moll Ponent, Mahón; ☎ 971-36-29-50; www.trasmediterranea .es; agency open Mon–Fri 8am–1pm and 5–7pm, Sat 7–10pm, Sun 2:30–5pm). You can also book a ticket with a travel agency in Madrid, Barcelona, València, Palma, and Ibiza.

Getting Around Minorca

There are two main **bus services** on the island. The Mahòn-based operator is **Transportes Menorca (TMSA)** (☎ 971-36-04-75), which runs a busy, year-round service between Mahòn and Ciudadela. (Most of its buses also stop in Alaior, Es Mercadal, and Ferreries.) It runs buses to Es Castell, Mitjorn, Cala'n Porter, and Sant Climent. The Mahòn tourist office can provide you with timetables. The Ciudadela-based company **Torres Allés Autocares SA** (calle Sastres 3; www.e-torres.net) mainly covers west-coast resorts.

Minorca, of all the islands, is a place where it would most useful to **hire a car,** as many interesting corners of the island are not served by public transport. Avoid pricey international companies like Avis and Hertz and choose a fair-priced local car-rental company such as **Morcamps** (Ramírez 29; ☎ 971-36-95-94), which charges from 40€ a day. They will deliver a vehicle either to the airport upon your arrival or to your hotel after you've checked in there—but you must specify in advance.

Call ☎ 971-36-12-83 for a local **taxi.** The main stop is at Plaça s'Esplanada in Mahòn. An average one-way fare from the capital to a beach like Cala'n Porter is around 15€.

Getting to & Around Mahòn

TMSA buses (see above) depart at least once an hour from the station in calle José Anselmo Clave in the heart of town. Around 20 buses per day run year-round to Ciudadela—some direct, most stopping at Alaior, Es Mercadal, and Ferrerias en route—and there are connections to other parts of the island. The tourist office (see below) distributes a list of schedules, and the list is published in the local newspaper, *Menorca Diario Insular.* Tickets cost 4€, and you pay for them once you're aboard. Make sure you carry some change, as drivers are reluctant to change notes larger than 10€.

Getting to & Around Ciudadela

A **taxi** from the airport to Ciudadela costs 45€ so it's cheaper to go into Mahòn by taxi or bus and catch the bus to Ciudadela from there. Around 20 **buses**—departing from Plaça s'Esplanada in Mahòn—go back and forth between the two towns every day (4€ one-way). If you're **driving,** follow the C-721 east-west road that connects the two towns.

Buses depart from Plaça d'Artrutx year-round for Mahón and summers only to beach locations either side of Ciudadela, including southerly white-sanded Cala Santandria (which is backed by rock caves inhabited in prehistoric times), and the sheltered clear-watered northwesterly coves of En Forcat, Blanes, and Brut.

For more information, contact the Ciudadela **tourist office** (Plaça Catedral 5; ☎ 971-38-26-93; June–Sept daily 9am–9pm, Oct–May Mon–Fri 9am–1pm and 5–7pm, Sat 9am–1pm).

ACCOMMODATIONS, BOTH STANDARD & NOT

Unlike Majorca, *agroturismos* and *casas rurales* (countryside houses and apartments) are still in their infancy here, and those that are available tend to be pricey. The pick of the bunch, economically, is **Son Triay Nou** ✪✪ (☎ 971-550-078; www.sontriay.com; closed Nov–Mar), a lovingly restored 19th-century neoclassical house dating from the era of the British occupation. It's a beaut, boasting a facade of russet walls and white-painted columns and arches set amid statues and formally styled gardens that surround a swimming pool and tennis courts. Six spacious double bedrooms are available and they, too, are lovely, with high windows, polished wooden floors, superb pinewood bedsteads, and tasteful wall etchings and paintings; nightly rates are 66€ to 120€. Breakfast—a delicious spread of homemade goodies—is taken in a charming rustic-style dining area, decorated with a range of ceramic and olive-wood knickknacks and a huge walk-in fireplace.

Ciutadella (Ciudadela)

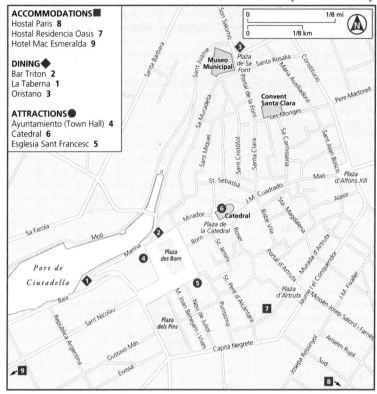

ACCOMMODATIONS ■
Hostal Paris **8**
Hostal Residencia Oasis **7**
Hotel Mac Esmeralda **9**

DINING ◆
Bar Triton **2**
La Taberna **1**
Oristano **3**

ATTRACTIONS ●
Ayuntamiento (Town Hall) **4**
Catedral **6**
Esglesia Sant Francesc **5**

The house is located at Km 3 on the road from **Ferrerías** to **Santa Galdana,** but bus transportation is available.

If you want to know more about other *agroturisme* properties available on the island, visit **www.menorca-rural.com**. Some twin-bedded rental beachside properties accommodating two persons in areas like Cala Santandria, Cala Blanca, and Binibeca are available for as little as 40€ to 60€ a night outside of July and August (when they can reach double that amount).

€   Halfway between **Alaior** and south-coast **Sant Jaume,** set in a lovely pine-wooded countryside, are some of the cheapest self-contained accommodations on the island. **Camping Son Bou** ★ (Carretera Sant Jaume Km 3.5; ☎ 971-372-605; www.campingsonbou.com) provides not only standard tent plots but also spacious water- and fire-proof "bungalow-tents" set in their own generous garden plots of 120 sq. m (1,292 sq. ft.), constructed from white plastic canvas and very simply equipped with two double beds, a table, chairs, gas cooking facilities, and a fridge. The only real hint you're roughing it a bit is the absence of running water in the bungalows. But immaculate communal bathrooms are close by, and there are also sinks you can use for washing clothes. Up to five people can be accommodated

"Citizen" Kane of Minorca

Even for an island as small as Minorca, it's unusual to see the "thumbprint" of a single man so clearly over 200 years after he died. But that's the case with the remarkable Sir Richard Kane, pioneer governor of the island for the first 2 decades of British 18th-century rule, who built the first road linking Maó and Ciudadela. Known as *el Cami de Kane* it followed the old Roman road, and parts of it can still be seen beside the modern highway.

Also a keen agriculturalist, Kane emulated the lush *huertas* of València (which had greatly impressed him during a mainland tour) by draining the cholera-inducing marshes and converting them into orchards and market gardens. (The apples from the trees he planted are known to this day as *pomes d'en Kane* after him.) He replenished the island's depleted livestock by bringing in sheep, pigs, horse, cattle, and poultry from North Africa, Sardinia, England, and France. Then, for good measure, he set about reducing crime by abolishing gambling dens, severely restricting ownership of weapons (among the locals), and imposing the supreme penalty on thieves—Minorcan and British alike. He also attracted foreign trade by developing infrastructure and building warehouses and piers.

Greatly respected by the islanders—in spite of the strictness with which some of the above methods were applied—he was a far more effective and compassionate ruler than most of his successors, who tended, by and large, to be a venal and colonially minded bunch.

Kane died at the age of 76 in 1736 and was buried in the Anglican Chapel in Maó's Fort Saint Philip (long since destroyed). On the outskirts of Maó, a memorial stands in his honor; in London's Westminster Abbey, a plaque bears a warm tribute to him in Latin.

for between 50€ a night off-season and 80€ in midsummer, and these rates include electricity costs and a weekly change of sheets. Families on a budget will find this a real money-saver, and kids especially love the back-to-nature setting. Communal facilities include a bar, restaurant, supermarket, and children's playground, and the nearest beach is 0.5km (⅓ mile) away. If you're renting a car, there's ample parking space, both private and communal.

Accommodations in Mahòn

€   The bright and breezy **Posada Orsi** ✹✹ (calle Infanta 19; ☎ 971-36-47-51; closed Jan; AE, DC, MC, V) is just about the best value right in the town of Mahòn. Its comfortable little doubles, vividly decorated in greens, reds, and blues, cost 35€ with shared bathroom and 50€ with private facilities. There's also a TV, salon, breakfast room, and large roof terrace where you get great views of the port. Close by is the colorful central market.

€ Run by an extremely friendly old couple, the gleaming-white 33-room **Hostal Jume** ✪ (calle Concepción 6; ☎ 971-36-32-66; closed Dec 16–Jan 8; MC, V) is a prime example of an old-style Minorca pension: Inside, it's cool, with traditional tiled floors and comforting touches such as antique furniture, decorative vases, and ceramic knickknacks. All these elements let you know you're in what was once a traditional island family home. The doubles, with their white walls, simple old-style window shutters, and comfortable beds—all with private bathroom—are 45€ to 55€ per night. Breakfast is served in a small salon, where you'll probably see a few mainland Spanish business visitors sipping their coffee alongside the summer tourists.

€ A definite third choice in the lowest-price category (I mention it in case the others are full), **Casa Rural** (La Isla calle Santa Caterina 4; ☎ 971-36-64-92; closed Dec; MC, V) is a no-nonsense *pensione* with airy, if somewhat spartan, rooms at 40€ to 50€ a night. Hospitable hosts and an equally good-value downstairs restaurant are among its pluses.

€–€€€ A genuine original, the 40-room maroon and white **Hotel del Almirante (Collingwood House)** ✪✪ (Carretera de Villacarlos s/n; ☎ 971-36-27-00; www.hoteldelalmirante.com; closed Nov–Apr; DC, MC, V) started life as home for Lord Nelson's chum, Admiral Collingwood. After subsequently serving as a convent, sculptor's house, and—until the end of World War II—German embassy, it was tastefully expanded into a hotel in 1964. Stay here if you can in May and October, when a double room is an absolute bargain at just 65€ a night including breakfast. (In midsummer, when the hotel is usually packed with British guests, the rate rises to 110€.) Decorated in a blend of Italianate, Georgian, and Minorcan styles, the building has retained its original 18th-century staircase along with vintage oil paintings, antiques, and sundry British memorabilia. The well-maintained rooms, all attractively and individually different from each other in styles and decor—have en suite bathrooms and are located either in the main building or neighboring bungalows. Insist on one with a terrace and view of Mahon Bay. Amenities include an outdoor pool and tennis court. Free parking.

Accommodations in Ciudadela

€ Conveniently tucked away in the heart of Ciudadela's old center, the **Hostal Residencia Oasis** (Sant Isidre 33; ☎ 971-38-21-97; closed mid-Oct to Mar; MC, V) is one of the best summer offers you'll find. Its nine compact, low-ceilinged bedrooms (30€–60€)—all with traditional cool tiled floors, ample wardrobe space, comfortable beds, and en suite bathrooms—are grouped around a tranquil flower-filled patio that's ideal for pondering the meaning of the universe . . . or just browsing through a book before you trot you out to one of the enticing nearby sandy coves. A continental breakfast of coffee or tea and toast (included in the price July–Aug) is served alfresco on the patio, and there's a wide choice of bars and restaurants just 5 minutes away.

€   Half the accommodations in the nearby Basque-run **Hostal Paris** (calle Santandria 4; ☎ 971-38-16-22; www.hostalparis.net; closed Oct–Apr; AE, MC, V) consists of singles (20€–35€), so it's a good budget choice for solo travelers as well as value-seeking couples, for whom doubles cost 25€ to 60€ (the highest rates being reserved for Aug). In fact, if you're traveling alone, you're sure to make friends here, as this is quite a friendly little place. Rooms have comfortable beds with basic wooden headboards and small bedside tables and—like the cozy ground-floor dining room—are decorated in relaxing pastel shades that match the hostel's cotton-candy pink Hansel and Gretel–like exterior. Only two rooms— both doubles (costing 30€–75€)—have private bathrooms. Those facing west have terraces. There's some traffic noise from rear-facing units, so ask for the front if you're a light sleeper.

€–€€   Out on the rocky Castell de Sant Nicolau headland, at the entrance to Ciudadela port, is something quite different. Big, modern, touristy, impossibly busy in July and August (when it's packed with fun-seeking northern European charter-booked holiday-makers) but terrific value either side of those months, the **Hotel Mac Esmeralda** ✪ (Av. Sant Nicolau 171; ☎ 971-30-02-50; www.mac-hotels.com; closed Nov–Apr; AE, MC, V) gives you a chance to enjoy stunning Mediterranean vistas at a highly affordable price: Doubles with bathrooms are 40€–55€ with an extra charge of around 10€ if you specify a sea-view room. It's also located right next to a sheltered sandy cove and is only a 10-minute stroll from the town center.

DINING FOR ALL TASTES

Fish dishes—especially lobsters—are the great Minorcan passion. Unfortunately they're very expensive. The king of them all, *caldereta de langosta*—pieces of lobster blended with onion, tomato, pepper, and garlic, and flavored with an herb liqueur—could set you back 60€ or more a head. Unsurprisingly, this is the favorite dish of Rey (King) Juan Carlos when he visits Minorca.

Somewhat less pricey is the ever popular **paella** (usually 10€–12€ a head), and sleuths in search of the bizarre should check out the shellfish known as *escupinas* ("warty Venus") and—strictly not for bird-lovers—*tordos con col* (thrushes with cabbage), though you're only likely to see the latter on menus in autumn. Simplest and cheapest of all is the ubiquitous pre-main-meal *pa amb oli*—bread flavored with salt and olive oil and rubbed with fresh tomato.

Wine comes from mainland Spain or neighboring Majorca, but gin is made on the island from local junipers and is another legacy of the British occupation. You can drink the gin by itself or mix it with lemon and ice. For the latter, ask the bartender for *palloza* (pah-*yoh*-thah). Gin mixed with soda or lemonade is called a *pomada*. The French contribution to Minorcan cuisine is mayonnaise, said to have been invented by the Duke de Richlieu's chef during the brief Gallic occupation of the island.

Dining in Mahòn

€   They never seem to rest at the old-style **Ars Cafe** (Plaça del Princep 121B; ☎ 971-36-80-41; Mon–Sat 8:30am–midnight, closed Aug; AE, DC, MC, V), a small traditional spot where the genial waiters bustle round-the-clock to provide their numerous customers with everything from *café con leche* and an *ensaimada* at breakfast to a full-blown meal at the end of the day. The reason for all this activity may be the low prices, most especially the superb 9€ fixed lunch menu consisting of three generous courses plus wine.

€   Even longer are the opening hours of **La Tropical** (Carrer Sa Lluna 36; ☎ 971-36-05-56; Thurs–Tues 7:30am–midnight, closed mid-Feb to mid-Mar; AE, DC, MC, V), a down-home cafe-cum-restaurant where you tuck into a simple, tasty snack like *pa amb oli* or *empanada* (fish or meat pie), or indulge in yet another hearty, flavor-packed, and low-price lunch. (Weekday 3-course set menu plus wine, like the Ars, comes to just 9€.)

€€–€€€   A couple of rungs up the ladder, price- and quality-wise, is the long-standing (since 1938) cosmopolitan **Bar Restaurant España** ✯ (Carrer Victori 48–50; ☎ 971-36-32-99; daily 1–3:30pm and 7:30–11pm; closed Dec 23–Feb 4; MC, V). The food is in a more-gourmet realm altogether, and its seafood in particular is among the best you'll find on the island. It still won't break the bank if you sample its 12€ set lunch, but be prepared to (justifiably) fork out for a la carte delights such as *merluza vasca* (Basque-style hake) or *dorada al horno* (baked bream), either of which can knock you back 18€ to 20€ a plate. The generous portions (you may want to share) are served with authentic Minorcan flair, and since English is widely spoken by the friendly staff, a lot of northern Europeans are among the regular clientele.

Dining in Ciudadela

If you want to eat well in Ciudadela, head for the port. The selection of nosh spots from dear to—as below—inexpensive is unrivaled on the island.

€   Instead of traditional Minorcan dishes, at **Oristano** ✯ (Borja Moll 1; ☎ 971-38-41-97; Thurs–Sun 6pm–1am; closed Dec–Mar; MC, V) you get pizzas: slender, crisply oven-cooked, and terrific value (6€–8€). The place is fairly bland atmospherically, and the other dishes are nothing special, but those yummy pizzas make it the best bargain in the port. As this is virtually a weekends-only place, the later you get there, the busier it becomes; if you want to eat in relative peace, arrive early.

€–€€   Another portside original, **La Taberna** (Port de Ciudadela; no phone; 1pm to early hours; cash only) is a nautically themed former boathouse turned highly popular eating spot that serves up fresh and affordable piscatorial delights (for example, *dorada*—gilthead—at 12€, and *calamares*—squid—for 10€). It even has a couple of fishing boats of its own that bring in a daily catch.

€–€€   Old port photos cover the walls and locals still play cards in the corner of the **Bar Triton** ✯✯ (Muelle Ciudadela 55; ☎ 971-38-00-02; Easter–Oct daily 4am–2am, Nov–Easter 4am–1am; MC, V), which is not only an unsullied survivor of old Minorca but also the top tapas bar for miles around. Sample their *pulpo* (octopus) or *escupiñas* (Minorcan clams) for 6€ to 12€ to see what I mean. It also serves up fine fishy *platos combinados* (combined dishes) that may range from fairly down-to-earth *merluza, patatas y ensalada* (fried hake, chips, and salad) to slightly more adventurous *mero con arroz i alioli* (oven-cooked grouper with saffron-flavored rice and rich garlic sauce) for around 10€ to 14€. As in earlier times, the place still opens at 4am, though the fishermen it used to cater for are now often replaced by worse-for-wear night owls, so be warned.

WHY YOU'RE HERE: THE TOP SIGHTS & ATTRACTIONS
Attractions in Mahòn

Apart from those Georgian facades mentioned earlier (p. 452), there is one monumental building in town worth a peek: the **Església Santa María la Major** (Plaça Constitució; ☎ 971-36-39-49; free admission; daily 8am–1pm and 6–8:30pm)— a much-altered edifice originally built in 1287 by the Christian conqueror Alfonso III, to celebrate the Reconquest and totally rebuilt in 1772. During the town's July and August music festival, the church's ornate Swiss 18th-century organ fills the cafe-lined square beside it with strains of Handel and Bach.

Most visitors get the greatest kick simply out of looking at Mahòn's magnificent boat-filled inlet, and there's no better way of taking a really close gander at it than by joining an hour-long **Catamaran tour** (12€ adults, 8€ children 10 and under). The vessel's below-the-waterline glass windows give you unique submarine-like views of the nonstop harbor activity. *One warning:* Departure times (May–Oct 9:30am hourly until 5:30pm) tend to be erratic, sometimes up to 30 minutes later than scheduled. You can buy tickets at the harborfront **Xoriguer Gin Distillery** (Moll de Ponent 91; ☎ 971-36-21-97), which also provides its own totally different kind of kick, a tour of giant copper vats simmering over wood-fed fires. After observing the process by which the famed Minorcan gin is made, you'll get to taste—only a wee sip of each, mind—up to a dozen brews. The distillery, and a store selling the products, is open Monday through Friday 8am to 7pm and Saturday 9am to 1pm.

The official Piccadilly or Times Square of this small metropolis is the Plaça de la Constitució; its 18th-century Town Hall was built in an English Palladian style. But the real heart of all the low-key action is the **Plaça S'Esplanada,** where you'll find the **Tourist Office** (Carrer Sa Rovellada de Dalt 24; ☎ 971-36-37-90; www.e-menorca.org; Mon–Fri 9am–1pm and 5–7pm, Sat 9am–1pm).

On Sunday, locals gather here to enjoy the best ice cream in the Balearics, and in summer, a twice-weekly market draws artisans from all over the island to sell their goodies. Mahón is not a beach town, but the waterside **Puerto de Mahón** compensates with a colorful choice of nautically influenced seafood restaurants.

Attractions in Ciudadela

It was known as Medina Minurka under the Muslims, which perhaps explains some of that African atmosphere. All the more surprising is how it's retained its character and beauty despite the devastating 1558 Turkish invasion and sacking of the city. An obelisk in memory of the city's futile defense against that invasion stands in the pigeon-filled Plaça d'es Born (Plaza del Born), the city's main square overlooking the port. Some 3,500 citizens died in that attack. Opposite it is the **Església de San Francisco** (calle Puríssima s/n; free admission; hours vary), a 14th-century Gothic church with splendid carved wood altars, and the very impressive 18th-century **Ayuntamiento (Town Hall).** The fort-like appearance of the Gothic **Cathedral** (Plaça de la Catedral; ☎ 971-380-739; free admission; daily 8:30am–1pm and 6–9pm), originally built by the conquering Alfonso III on the site of the former mosque, recalls the town's beleaguered past. A neoclassical facade was added in 1813, and the church was further restored after Spanish Civil War damage. More exotic is the Moorish influence that lingers on in the white-washed houses of **Ses Voltes,** off the Plaça S'Esplanada and the shop-filled arcaded **Carrer Quadrado,** but the town is at its most colorful down the long narrow **port,** where you'll find some impressive yachts in summer. The town's harbor is smaller than Mahòn's but far more romantic, twinkling at night with the lights of a score of waterside seafood restaurants. You'll also want to wander out to the Castell de Sant Nicolau (St. Nicholas's Castle) on the rocky headland that juts out from the town and view *señorial* 17th-century palaces that luxuriate indolently between the splendid Santa María cathedral and Borne Square.

The wildest event in this usually laid-back town is the **Sant Joan (San Juan) fiesta** in June when, after a colorful cavalcade, horsemen indulge in *jaleos* (mock battles) and try to ram passersby against the stucco walls as they thunder past, maddened by their unrestrained input of local gin. It starts around the 23rd so be warned if you come then that in addition to your life being in danger if you get too close to the proceedings, accommodations prices rise considerably.

ACTIVE MINORCA
Swimming & Beaches

This is where Minorca really comes into its own. There are said to be more beaches along its 217km (135-mile) coastline than on all the other islands put together. Which means a heckuva lot of beaches. Many of the northern ones—long, breezy, and dune backed—are still remarkably unspoiled, so if you do rent a car, you can discover some lovely peaceful picnic spots, even in summer, such as **Cala en Pilar,** between the busier Cala Morell and Fornells, and the islet of **Illa d'en Colom,** reached by boat from Es Grau, east of Fornells. Nude bathing is (unofficially) commonplace. South-coast beaches are more popular and built up, mainly because they're more sheltered and idyllically Mediterranean in appearance. Two of my favorites here are **Cala'n Porter,** a narrow estuary inlet protected by high promontories, and further west again and still delightful in spite of its proliferation of hotels, **Cala de Santa Galdana,** a picture-postcard bay with a backdrop of pines and rocks reached by an excellent wide road. Avoid both of them in July and August, when they're packed, and head for the quieter north.

Diving

The top dive shop on the isle is **S'Algar Diving** (Passeig Maritim; ☎ 971-15-06-01; www.salgardiving.com), which arranges up to eight dives a day. If you're proficient enough, you may get a chance to explore the fabulous 25m-deep (75-ft.) Cathedral Cavern. Its entrance is so large that the whole of its interior is illuminated in a mesmerizing pale turquoise haze, through which a statuesquely high rock at the end of the cave looms surrealistically. Though it may seem expensive at 55€ minimum per dive, this is the standard rate other diving schools charge on the island, and S'Algar is extremely well organized and efficient, with first-rate guides and instructors and optimum equipment.

Golf

The island's only course is **Urbanización Son Parc** (☎ 971-18-88-75; Urbanizacion Son Parc s/n, Carretara Mercadal-Mitjorn Gran Km 18, Mercadal; www.golfsonparc.com), a traditional 9-hole course that has added another 9 holes. Minimum greens fees: winter 120€, summer 160€ (175€ in Aug). No discounts are given for twilight or last-minute bookings.

Horseback Riding

Menorca's mainly flat terrain is ideal for leisurely trail rides, and one of the most helpful and well-run stables is **Picadero Alaior** (in Alaior; ☎ 608-323-566), which often arranges guided tours. You'll find their offices in front of the bridge by the beach. Beginners and advanced riders alike are catered for, and a 1-hour ride costs 20€. Another small and friendly outfit charging the same rates, offering similar services and run by local Spanish couple Toni and Catalina, is **Cavalls Son Angel** (just north of Ciudadela between the Torre de Quart tower and Son Angel pine copses; ☎ 609-833-902). For further general information on island horseback riding, contact the **Federació Hipica de les Illes Baleares** (Recinto Ferial d'Es Mercadal; ☎ 971-15-42-25; www.fhib.org).

Windsurfing & Sailing

The whole north coast is best for these two activities, especially at Fornells Bay, which is 1.6km (1 mile) wide and several miles long. There, **Windsurfing Fornells** (☎ 971-18-81-50; www.windfornells.com) offers some pretty comprehensive deals. Their windsurfing and dinghy sailing courses are personally tailored to individual needs and abilities at rates ranging from 114€ for two sessions to 252€ for six sessions, each of which lasts 2¼ hours in high season (June 23–Aug 31 9:45am–noon, 12:25–2:40pm or 4:25–6:40pm) and 2¾ hours low season (Apr 27–June 22 and Sept 1–Oct 29 10:15am–1pm or 3–5:45pm). Also available are slightly cheaper low-season, full-week courses, providing either four sessions for 184€ or six sessions for 234€.

ATTENTION, SHOPPERS!

Locally made shoes and leather goods are a top specialty in Mahòn, though they're not especially cheap. Two of the best shops are in Carrer de Ses Moreres. **Looky Boutique** (no. 43; ☎ 971-36-06-48) covers the whole gamut of leather wear, from shoes to handbags and clothes, made in the company's west-coast factory; it regularly arranges discounts of 15% to 20% off the usual prices. (Early summer is a particularly good time to look for these bargains.) **Jaime Mascaró** (no. 29; ☎ 971-36-05-68) sells classy but pricey shoes made at its Ferrerias factory. Not so wallet-busting are the peasant sandals *(abarcas)* sold at **S'Avarca de Menorca's old warehouse** (Carrer Angel 14; ☎ 971-36-63-41), which are ideal for slopping around in summer.

For shopping in Ciudadela (that may end up as much browsing as buying), troll the charming boutiques of the **Ses Voltes** area. As in Maó, leather wear is the thing, though if you don't want to spend too much, *abarcas*—sandals made from rubber tires (no kidding)—are far cheaper buys. Check out **Xoquins** (Baixada Capllonc 14; ☎ 971-38-00-97), which offers the widest leather and rubber selection (perhaps I should rephrase that!) in Ciudadela. Local cheeses and cured meat

Megalithic Minorca

Minorca is dotted with curious stone monuments that date back the better part of 4,000 years. They come in a variety of forms, from conical-shaped *talaiots* (mainly located on high ground and believed to have served as watchtowers) and T-shaped *taulas* (religiously oriented mounds enclosed by sanctuary walls) to the long rectangular *navetas,* which were ancient burial chambers.

The easiest site to visit, just 4km (2½ miles) from the capital off the Maó-Es Castell highway, is **Trepucó,** where you'll find both a 4m (13-ft.) *taula* (huge T-shaped stone structure) and a *talayot* (circular stone tower); while the same distance from Ciudadela is **Talatí de Dalt,** a *taula* with caves.

Big Daddy of this prehistoric world, though, is the restored **Naveta d'es Tudons** 5km (3 miles) east of Ciudadela, the best-preserved and most significant prehistoric collection of monuments on Minorca, and one of the oldest human-built monuments in Europe. Archaeologists have found the remains of many bodies at this site, along with a collection of prehistoric artifacts, including pottery, decorative jewelry, and weapons—but they have now been removed to museums.

A rare coastal addition is **La Cova d'en Xoroi,** ancient troglodyte habitations overlooking the sea from the upper part of the cliffs, which can also be visited (after dark it's converted into a disco!—see the "Nightlife" section). According to legend the neighboring caves of Calas Coves were once the refuge of a Moor called Xoroi, who had abducted a local maid and made his home here with her and their family.

Note: There are no fees to visit any of these sites.

are also first-rate at shops like **Ca na Riera** (Hospital Santa Magdalena 7; no phone) and **C'an Padet** (Plaça Francesc Netto; ☎ 971-38-00-91); and if you fancy taking back a bottle of local gin (it has the widest range of choices), try the quaint little **Ses Industries** (Santa Clara 4; ☎ 971-38-28-82).

NIGHTLIFE

For a town not known for its nightlife, Mahòn isn't doing too badly these days. Most of the after-dark action is down in the port area, where the string of late-night venues extending along the harborfront is headed by **Akelarre** (Moll de Ponent 41; ☎ 971-36-85-20; Jun–Sep 8am–4am, Oct–May 8pm–4am; 12€ including drink), a huge, cliffside barn of a place featuring everything from jazz and blues to stand-up comedy. The adjoining **Virtual** (12€ including drink), is a mecca for Caribbean salsa lovers and nos. 20 and 22 **Onda** and **Aura** (cover for both 10€) offer a more conventional groovy disco scene. All are at their liveliest between midnight and the official closing time of 4am. For something totally different—and far more romantic—head 8km (5 miles) south to Calan Porter's **Cova**

d'en Xoroi (☎ 971-37-72-36; 11pm–4am; 15€), a cliffside cave conglomeration of bars, terraces, disco floors, and intimate nooks and crannies, which enjoys incredible panoramic sea views. (During the day, this can also be visited as a historic troglodyte site; see "Megalithic Minorca.")

Though this is no Majorca or Ibiza, Ciudadela has a few lively spots where you can while away the after-dark hours. Top dog is generally considered to be the **Jazzbah** (Pla de Sant Joan 3; ☎ 971-48-29-53; June–Sept daily 11pm–6am, Oct–May Fri–Sat 11pm–6am), where you get to join the smart set, listen to quality jazz, and pay slightly over the average (10€ upwards) for a drink. The joint has several terraces where you can enjoy the balmy summer night air. Another popular jazz rendezvous is the tiny **Sa Clau** (Carrer Marina 93; ☎ 971-38-48-63; www.saclau.com; mid-May to mid-Sept 9pm–3am; cover 8€–12€); its cavern-like setting looks like something out of *Pirates of the Caribbean.* More quietly moody and laid back than either of these is the **Cactus** (Baixada Capllonc 15; ☎ 662-06-02-28; May–Sept 8pm–2am; drinks start at 4€), a stylish German-owned cocktail bar with a really big terrace.

IBIZA (EIVISSA)

Ibiza is often painted as one big Med disco. While there's a certain truth in this—the internationally famed "dance till dawn and then some" scene is uniquely inventive and high-powered, with top DJs and mind-bending sounds and lights filling these pleasure barns in the height of summer—there's an awful lot more going on as well.

For a start, the island—an effortlessly beautiful blend of white villages, almond and olive groves, and sandy coves lapped by crystal waters (to go a bit cliché)—has no fewer than 11 areas of protected natural beauty. (One of them, the 2,500-hectare/6,178-acre Cala d'Hort area between Cala Vadella and the imposing Vedra rock, for example, has been approved as an official Parc Natural.) And outside of the overbuilt mayhem of **Sant Antoni de Portmany,** notorious, alas, for its appeal to stoned and inebriated youth, and the hotel-packed coastline around **Figueretes** and **Santa Eulalia,** which attracts more mainstream charter holiday couples and families, much of the island is still remarkably unspoiled. Capital **Ibiza Town** is one of the most beautiful and trendy burgs in Spain, its unique white Moorish-cum–Greek island–style hulk rising ship-like above the ever busy harbor. Ibiza is also the best Balearic island for boat trips, whether out to the northern bays of Cala Bassa or Cala Conta, around Vedra Rock, or down south to the tiny, quiet, neighboring isle of Formentera. So it casts a pretty wide net.

A BRIEF HISTORY OF IBIZA

Carthaginians from Tyre were among the island's first occupants, and a surprising amount of their Punic relics can still be seen today in the museum on the Puig dels Molins of Ibiza Town. Next came the Greeks, who named it—along with neighboring Formentera—the Pitiusas (Pine-Clad) islands, followed by the empirical Romans, the ever-destructive Vandals, the creative and poetic Arabs, and the mainland Catalán Christians, who had the most lasting effect on today's culture. Since Franco's centralized, monolingual control of Spain ended in 1975, locals have given it back the original name of **Eivissa,** and **Eivissenc,** a dialectal

Ibiza (Eivissa)

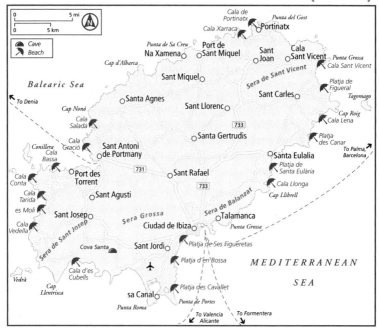

variation of Catalán, is widely spoken and written in preference to mainland Castilian (though both are understood and English is widely spoken).

LAY OF THE LAND

It may have been Pitiusa (Pine-Clad) to the Greeks, but though it's not quite so densely wooded as it must have been in their time, it does boast a charming patchwork of fig, almond, olive, and carob trees throughout its ocher-hued 528 sq. km (225 sq. miles) of gently hilly and, yes, pine-dotted countryside. Inland are whitehoused villages, and along its sometimes wild, sometimes gentle shoreline extends a delicious range of coves, bays, and long beaches, basking beside turquoise waters and the ever-reliable Mediterranean summer climate, its great combined gift to the world of tourism.

GETTING TO & AROUND IBIZA

First and foremost, try to avoid July and August. It's too hot, too busy, and too expensive. But if you must come then, be sure you have a round-trip ticket and a hotel reservation. The last thing you want is to get stranded in Ibiza in midsummer (an alarmingly frequent occurrence with the unprepared).

For more information, visit www.ibiza-spotlight.com or pop by the local **information office** (Ibiza town, Antonio Riquer 2, in the port; ☎ 971-30-19-00; June–Nov Mon–Fri 9am–9pm, Sat 9:30am–7:30pm; Dec–May Mon–Fri 8:30am–3pm, Sat 10:30am–1pm). There's also an office at the **airport** (☎ 971-80-91-18; May–Oct Mon–Sat 9am–2pm and 3–8pm, Sun 9am–2pm).

Getting to Ibiza

Low-price summer charter flights wing in not only from a wide variety of northern European towns to the island's **Es Codolar International Airport** (☎ 971-80-90-00), 5.5km (3½ miles) from Ibiza Town, but also—with **easyJet** and **Ryanair,** for example—from Madrid and Barcelona. (Outside the costly and heavily booked months of July and Aug, you can pick up some bargains.) **Air Europa** (☎ 902-40-15-01 in Ibiza) also offers competitively priced flights from Barcelona, Madrid, and Palma. For info on all low-cost air options, try the website www.wegolo.com. The main scheduled, and correspondingly more expensive, airline **Iberia** (☎ 902-40-05-00) has around seven daily flights from Palma de Majorca and three from Barcelona. The variable flight costs with all these operators are dependent on season, promotion, and availability.

An hourly **bus** service (7am–10pm) covers the 5.5km (3½-mile) ride from the airport into town. Sometimes **taxis** can be shared, especially outside these hours, which can be a real saving. In Ciudad de Ibiza, buses leave for the airport from Av. Isidor Macabich 24 (by the ticket kiosk).

Transmediterránea (Estación Marítim, Muelle Ibiza; ☎ 902-45-46-45; www.trasmediterranea.es) operates **ferry services** from Barcelona (4 per week; 70€ one-way), València (1 boat per day; 85€ one-way), and Palma (4 per week, Tues–Fri; 85€ one-way). You can buy tickets direct here or at local travel agents. Outside Minorca, check with travel agents in Barcelona, València, or Palma regarding ferry schedules and bookings.

Getting Around Ibiza

The two main **bus** terminals at Av. Isidor Macabich 20 and 42 (☎ 971-31-20-75) operate services to Sant Antoni, Santa Eulalia, Talamanca, and Figueretes, as well as to some smaller towns.

Once you get clear of Ibiza Town center, which has its own mini traffic problems, **mopeds** are a good, relaxing, low-cost option. **Casa Valentín** (corner of Av. B. V. Ramón 19; ☎ 971-31-08-22) rents them for 30€ to 35€ per day. Make sure the insurance covers theft and use a helmet.

Both Hertz and Avis have offices at the airport, if you'd like to rent a **car,** though a more economical option among the wide local range in San Antoni is **Betacar** (General Balanzat; ☎ 971-345-968; www.betacar.es). Its hire rates begin at around 38€ a day for a Ford Fiesta standard car.

ACCOMMODATIONS, BOTH STANDARD & NOT

Though there are **apartments** aplenty in the main resorts, these tend to be block-booked by northern European travel companies throughout the entire summer season from May through October and jacked up in price. Up behind the old part of **Ibiza Town** (the Dalt Vila), though, is an option that's both independent and affordable: **Apartamentos Rosselló** (calle General Juli Cirer i Vela s/n, Puig des Molins; ☎ 971-302-790; apartamentosrosselló@hotmail.com). These fully equipped units are located in a tiered, low-level, cream-colored block, on the south side of the headland below the Dalt Villa, just along the shore from Figueretes. Units are bland but well laid out, each with two convertible sofa beds, a small open-plan (American-style) kitchenette, and a double bedroom. Try to get

Ciudad de Ibiza

C. de Carlos V
C. de Bartomeu de Rosselló
Av. Andanes
Plaza de A. Riquer
Port de Ibiza
Calle de Vicente Cuervo
Calle de Aragón
Paseo de Vara de Rey
Pasco de Vera de Rey
Plaza del Parc
C. del Obispo Cardona
C. de Conde de Rosselló
C. del Mar
C. de Castelar
Barcelona-Ibiza
Palma de Mallorca-Ibiza
Ibiza-Formentera
Alicante-Ibiza
Valencia-Ibiza
Av. de les Andanes
C. de Cipriano Garijo
Plaza de sa Riba
Plaza de la Constitucion
C. de Antoni Palau
C. de Manel Sorá
C. del Passadizo
C. de la Mare de Déu
C. Alta
C. Fosc
Av. de Ignasi Wallis
C. del Jaime I
Ronda de Antoni Costa Ramón
Plaza de Vila
Plaza dels Desamparats
Baluarte de San Juan
Baluarte de Santa Lucia
Baluarte Puerta Nueva
C. de Sta Ana
C. de San José
C. de Joan Roman
C. Mayor
C. de la Carrossa
C. Pere Tur
Plaza dels Desamparats
D'ALT VILA
C. de Pere Tur
Plaza de España
Ronda del Fratin
C. de Sta. Maria
Plaza Catedral
Baluarte de San Jaime
Castillo
Baluarte de Santa Tecla
Mediterranean Sea
Ronda de la Almudaina
Baluarte de San Bernardo
Calle de Ramón Muntaner
C. del Calvario
Baluarte de San Jorge
C. del Calvari
Camino de Berenda
C. de Ramón Muntaner
ES SOTO

0   1/5 mi
0   0.2 km
N

ACCOMMODATIONS ■
Apartamentos Rosselló **8**
Hostal La Marina **4**
Hostal Montesol **2**
Hostal Residencias
  Juanito y Las Nieves **1**

DINING ◆
Bon Profit **3**
Los Pasajeros **5**

ATTRACTIONS ●
Cathedral **7**
Museo Arqueologico **6**

IBIZA
● Ciudad de Ibiza

467

an apartment with a terrace, as these have lovely sea views south toward Formentera. Though the building's not new, it's been constantly renovated over the decades, and rentals range from 60€ to 95€ per night (rising to 125€ in Aug)—a great saving for families or small groups who don't feel four's a crowd.

Agroturisme—tasteful, eco-conscious, inland farm accommodations—is a relatively new concept on the island and still functions primarily at a pricey upmarket level. That said, the best value is in self-contained studios for two to four people at the organic farm of **Can Marti** ✪ (Venda de Cas Ripolls 29, Sant Joan de Labritja; ☎ 971-333-500; www.canmarti.com; closed mid-Oct to end of March; AE, MC, V), set in tranquil seclusion in a valley near Sant Joan. It prides itself on having no swimming pool, no air-conditioning (thick traditional walls instead work as they have for centuries to keep out the summer heat), and no TV (though they *do* have individual Internet connection in each studio). Best of all, the apartments are set among 16 hectares of olive-, carob-, and pine-filled land where you can stroll at leisure; free bikes are provided if you want to explore further. Twins cost from 130€ to 160€ depending on the season. However, each includes a full kitchen (so you can save a bit by cooking) and has a theme to the decor—one studio has Mexican art on the walls and a South American vibe, another features a carved Indian staircase, and so on. Though this property is costlier than we usually recommend, it's a very special place and the savings from cooking your own meals in your kitchen do cut down on the overall costs.

Back down in Ibiza Town center, you'll find a handful of budget-priced, room-only lodgings on and near the harborfront.

€–€€ Among the most affordable of these are the **Hostal Residencias Juanito and Las Nieves** (Joan d'Austria 18; ☎ 971-190-319; MC, V), twin *hostales* located side by side in a mature but well-renovated town building close to the busy central Vara del Rey square. Jointly owned, and with the same genial reception staff, they both offer smart white-walled rooms with traditional cool tiled floors and plenty of wardrobe space. Some have a wash basin and shared bathroom amenities for 60€; others boast fully equipped en suite bathrooms for 75€. Come in May or October and you'll pay 20% less.

€–€€ The **Hostal La Marina** ✪ (Barcelona 7; ☎ 971-31-01-72; www.ibiza-spotlight.com/hostal-lamarina; AE, MC, V) goes one better. Located in a converted 19th-century *fonda* (inn), it's about as central as you can get, just one street back from the waterfront Passeig del Moll. All rooms have private bathroom, and, though small, are drenched in color, usually sunshiny yellow or maritime blue, giving them a cheery aspect. They're set in three adjoining buildings, all close to the Old Town's shops and restaurants. Doubles with window views are 62€ to 85€ depending on the season. Those with a tiny balcony are only fractionally higher (67€–91€). The hotel has a variety of alternative rooms of varying standards and prices (some starting at just 52€) in two other locations. ***One warning:*** Because of the central location, the hotel can be noisy. If you're a late sleeper, you'll probably want to face away from the ferry dock, to avoid the noise of revving engines. If you're an early-to-bed type, pick the ferry view, which will be quieter at night than the street.

A Word on San Antonio De Portmany

Though this spot has good bones—by which I mean its physical setting is lovely, and you can't beat it for a great sunset—it's become so overbuilt, so crowded by partying louts, that I can't in good conscience recommend spending much time here. You may want to make a quick detour for its night sports (see below) and because it offers charming boat trips to adjoining coves like **Cala Bassa, Cala Conta,** and **Es Torrent** (all 5€ one-way) and along Ibiza's most beautiful coast to the far northwest point of **Portinatx** (20€–25€ or so, negotiable). As well, north of the waterfront is **Sa Cova de Santa Agnès,** a tiny cave containing a national monument erected in gratitude—it's said—by a sailor who, after praying to Santa Agnès, survived a terrible storm and was saved. See it Monday (daytime) or Saturday (9am–noon). But other than these attractions, your time and money is better spent elsewhere.

€–€€   Also right on the waterfront, **Hostal Montesol** (Vara de Rey 2; 07800 Ibiza; ☎ 971-31-01-61; www.hotelmontesol.com; AE, MC, V) boasts panoramic views that (almost) make up for the prefab look of the rooms; they're perfectly comfortable, if a tad small, and motel generic. Double are 70€ to 75€ complete with en suite bath with tub/shower combos. (Avoid July–Aug when it rises to 110€.)

DINING FOR ALL TASTES

Authentic Ibizan cuisine is based on simple ingredients but difficult to find these days. (Most of the restaurants on the isle cater to more international tastes.) Two specialties to look out for among the sea of international dishes usually available are *sofrit pages* (a stew of pork, lamb, and chicken seasoned with pepper, cloves, cinnamon, and garlic and served with potatoes) and *bollit de peix* (a blend of *mero* [grouper] and *rape* [monkfish] served with rice). Another good seafood dish, expensive like all fish, is *borrida de rajada* (crayfish in an almond sauce). Some islanders feed figs to the local pigs to sweeten their meat, which is turned into such pungent cooked sausages as *sobrasadas* or *longanizas.* The most famous Ibizan dessert is *flaó,* a kind of cheesecake to which mint and anisette are added for flavoring. *Greixonera* is a spiced pudding, and *maccarrones de San Juan* is cinnamon-and-lemon-flavored milk baked with cheese.

Here are a couple of the town's remaining, authentic nosh spots:

€   A convenient location near the market ensures that the **Bon Profit** (Plaça des Parc 5; ☎ 971-393-403; daily 1–4pm and 8pm–midnight; cash only) gets the freshest local produce for its excellent-value 10€ menu. And that's a saving grace as there are no frills to the decor: It's just bare stone walls stuck with local photos. And you'll probably have to wait in line to get in—but that's always a good sign, right? By the way, the Ibicenco—and Catalán—word *profit* means "appetite" and has nothing to do with money.

€   A rather rough and ready cantina down in the lower part of Sa Penya, **Los Pasajeros** (Vicent Soler, 1st Floor; no phone; daily noon–4pm and 8pm–2am; cash only) not only dispenses low-price but mighty tasty rice, fish, and meat dishes—that include paella, *calamares romana* (squid in batter), and *chuletas de cerdo* (pork chops) (average 8€–10€)—but it also stays open until 2am to accommodate hungry clubbers. The later it is, the noisier it gets, as animated guests celebrate the approaching dawn with impromptu singalongs.

WHY YOU'RE HERE: THE TOP SIGHTS & ATTRACTIONS

Since the Carthaginians founded **Ibiza Town** 2,600 years ago, it's been continuously occupied, and such is its genuine historic value that in 1999 UNESCO declared it a World Heritage Site. If you enter the harbor by sea, you'll be knocked out by the steeply climbing array of dazzling white houses and fortified walls that tower above you. Those houses—many of them up to 500 years old with Gothic styling and spacious inner geranium- and bougainvillea-lined patios—form part of the **D'Alt Vila (Old Town)** ✗, and the enclosing walls dominate the harbor as majestically today as it did over the centuries when they repelled invader after invader. (Though today's partiers have—at least for the time being—breached its seemingly impregnable defenses.) The whole walled D'Alt Vila that rises above the town is a wondrous sight in itself, topped by the 13th-century Gothic **Catedral** (Carrer Mayor s/n; free admission; Jun–Sept Tues–Sun 9am–2pm, Oct–May Tues–Sun 10am–2pm). Its stunning exterior buttresses put the rather bleak white-walled interior in the shade. Inside, the tiny **Diocesean Museum** (1.50€), containing some interesting medieval Catalán art relics, is worth a peep. Outside, walk round the old city walls and stop to admire the panoramic views from its various *baluard* (bulwark) viewpoints.

Outside the walls the narrow-alleyed souk-like **Sa Penya** and **Marina** quarters—with their art galleries, dance clubs, bars, and boutiques—are fun to explore, while the main Vara de Rey boulevard and waterfront Passeig des Moll down below are favorite spots for an evening stroll.

By far the island's most impressive cultural and historical center **Museo Arqueològic de Ibiza y Formentera (Museum of Archaeology)** ✗ (Plaça de Catedral 3; ☎ 971-30-12-31; 2.50€ adults, 1.25€ students, free for children 17 and under; Oct–Mar Tues–Sat 9am–3pm, Sun 10am–2pm; Apr–Sept Tues–Sat 10am–2pm and 6–8pm, Sun 10am–2pm) houses the world's most important collection of Punic pottery and terra-cotta figurines from the 2nd to 7th centuries B.C. The museum is set in a former arsenal building on the **Puig del Molins (Hill of the Windmill).** Exhibits also include later Roman, Moorish, and Christian sculptures, artifacts, and ceramics.

ACTIVE IBIZA

Swimming & Beaches

Though sunbathing (often in the nude) is a prime pastime on Ibiza, some find the experience more akin to a subway ride, so packed together are the bodies on some beaches. So when I say that a beach is "popular," as I will with **Talamanca, Ses Figueretes, Playa d'en Bossa,** and **Playa San Antonio** (at rowdy **San**

Antonio de Portmany in the southwest), that's another way of saying "sardine-tin crowded." If you're more into serenity than beach blanket hopping, you may want to take a boat from the slightly quieter nudist beach **Playa Cavallet** in the southeast near Ibiza Town to **Cala Bassa, Port des Torrent, Cala Tarida,** and **Cala;** or better yet, rent a bike or moped and follow rough tracks to truly isolated coves like **Cala Mastella** or **Cala d'en Sella.**

Other options include the semi-crowded beach spots up the east coast at the rather boring **Santa Eularia des Ríu** (formerly Santa Eulalia del Rio), site of the third major tourist development in Ibiza, and better nearby beaches of **Cala Llonga** and **Playa d'es Caná,** both among the finest on Ibiza, and at the north-coast tourist developments of **Portinatx** and **Puerto de San Miguel,** north of the small town of San Miguel.

Horseback Riding

The **Centro Ecuestre Easy Rider** (Camí del Sol d'en Serra, Cala Llonga, outside Santa Eularia des Riu; ☎ 971-19-65-11 or 610-44-36-60) is a small outfit with only four horses, so it's ideal for families with two children or a quartet of friends who are looking for personalized attention. It's located just 400m (437 yd.) back from Calla Longa beach, offers two different trail rides, always accompanied by an experienced guide so that even the most inexperienced horseman is catered for. The shorter ride lasts 50 minutes and costs 22€; the longer ride lasts 1¾ hours and costs 44€. Both of these gentle scenic canters combine coastal routes with diversions into the inland countryside.

Tennis

You'll find several public tennis courts at the **Ibiza Club de Campo** (4km/2½ miles from Ibiza Town on the San José road; ☎ 971-30-00-88 or 971-30-00-88). It's open year-round from 9am to 10pm and only lightly supervised. Admission is 6€ per hour for nonmembers.

You can also play tennis at the secluded holiday development of **Port Sant Miguel** on the north side of the island 24km (16 miles) from Ibiza Town (periodic bus service). Courts there are at **Club San Miguel** (Carrer de Port San Miguel s/n; ☎ 971-334-530; daily 9am–10pm; 11€ per hr.). A sandy beach adjoins the property, so if you work up a lather in your game, you can easily run into the surf to cool off.

ATTENTION, SHOPPERS!

Ibiza Town is fairly costly for shoppers, with leather goods the prime seller. You can—at a price—get some mighty fine custom-made leather and silver goods at **Pedro's** (Carrer Aníbal 8; ☎ 971-31-30-26) and at the **Sandal Shop** (Plaça de Vila 2; ☎ 971-30-54-75), which—as you'd expect from its name—sells a range of quality sandals made by local artisans.

The best bargains are probably to be found out of town at the Saturday **flea market** at Las Dalias just beyond Sant Carles (San Carlos) on the road to Santa Eulalia. (You'll know where it is by all the cars parked along the road.) Open from about 10am until 8 or 9pm, it offers all kinds of clothing (both antique and new), accessories, crafts, and the usual odds and ends.

NIGHTLIFE

The choice of clubs, discos, and late-night bars around the island capital is mind-bogglingly varied. The top spot in this area, **El Divino Club** (Puerto Ibiza Nueva; ☎ 971-31-83-38; June–Sept daily midnight–6am) is, as its name suggests, aimed at the "beautiful people"—supermodels, celebs, and the like—so if you can afford it (cover charge 25€ up to 50€ in midsummer), then dress to kill and see if they let you in to mingle with the chic.

Now in its 40s is the veteran but still young-at-heart **Pachá** (Av. 8 de Agosto s/n; ☎ 971-31-36-00; Jun–Sept daily midnight–6am), a spacious split-level disco near the casino with three bar areas and dance floors, a swimming pool where you can cool off around dawn, deafening music, and painful covers of 20€ to 50€ depending on whether it's early or midsummer.

For lovers of the erotic, there's **The Blue Rose** (Carrer Navarra 27, Figueretes; ☎ 971-39-91-37; www.ibiza-online.com/bluerose; daily 11pm–6am), a high-class strip joint complete with fire pole and often described as the "Goddess Temple" due to the beauty of the performers who revolve around it in the most tastefully provocative manner (female except on Thurs when the lads perform for gay watchers). Cover is 35€ including first drink, then 10€ a tipple.

Blackjack and roulette junkies should head for the **Casino de Ibiza** (Passeig Juan Carlos I; ☎ 971-31-33-12; www.casinoibiza.com; daily 10pm–5am). A separate room for slot machines operates daily from 3pm to 8am. There's a nightclub next door whose corny live show (May–Oct from 11pm) features magicians, comedians, and pretty women in feathers and spangles and is popular with an older crowd. Casino entrance is 3€ and a passport is required.

Gay travelers will find plenty to keep them happy up in the Old Town, where dozens of bars are open from around 10pm to 3am. Liveliest and usually the busiest is the very loud haute electronic **Disco Anfora** (Carrer San Carlos 5; ☎ 971-30-28-93; June–Sept daily midnight–6am; cover 9€–12€, including the first drink). Other gay rendezvous include **Bar León** (calle de la Virgen; no phone), **Angelo's** (Carrer Alfonso XII no. 11; ☎ 971-31-09-68), and **Teatro** (Carrer de la Virgen 83; ☎ 971-31-32-25), which has an outdoor bar.

In Nearby San Antonio De Portmany

Two monolithic dance spots—the kind that made the island's name as a disco world mecca—loom on Carrer Salvador Espriu in this outlying town: **Es Paradis** (☎ 971-342-406; www.esparadis.com), which is topped by a huge glass pyramid, and the dazzlingly illuminated Moorish mosque–style **Eden** (☎ 971-803-240; www.edenibiza.com). Both feature top DJs—mainly from the U.K.—and are famous for their psychedelic lighting and mind-bending acoustics. They're open from around 11pm till dawn between mid-May and September only and will knock you back a budget-straining 25€ to 40€ including one drink.

On a relatively small scale back in the town are two so-called "sunset bars"—**Mambo** and **Cafe del Mar**, side by side in Vara del Rey—where you can listen to swinging sound played by another batch of proficient DJs in a less-frenzied atmosphere, as well as paying a lot less (around 5€ a drink).

The ABCs of the Balearic Islands

Consulates Key diplomatic contacts are the **U.S. Consulate** (calle Puerto Pi 8; ☎ 971-40-37-07; Mon–Fri 10:30am–1:30pm) and the **British Consulate** (Plaça Mayor 3; ☎ 971-71-24-45; Mon–Fri 9am–3pm).

Emergencies In case of an emergency, dial ☎ **112.** In case of illness, head for the **Centro Médico** (Av. Juan March Ordinas 8, Palma de Majorca; ☎ 971-21-22 00). (This is a private facility.)

Post Office For sending urgent mail, the central post office is at Carrer Paseo Bornet 10 (☎ 902-19-71-97; Mon–Fri 8:30am–8:30pm, Sat 9:30am–2pm). Otherwise, there are postboxes all over the city.

Holidays In addition to the usual Spanish holidays, Majorca also celebrates June 29, the **Fiesta de San Pedro (Feast of St. Peter)**, the patron saint of fishermen.

11 The Essentials of Planning

by Patricia Harris & David Lyon

THE BEST MOTTO FOR SUCCESSFUL TRAVEL IS "KNOW BEFORE YOU GO." We're all for spontaneity, but a little planning now will free you to improvise later. The rest of this guide is your essential tool for deciding what to do, where to go, where to stay, and where to eat. This chapter tells you everything else you need to know, from getting a good deal on travel to Spain to saving money on getting around.

WHEN TO VISIT

The best months to visit anywhere in Spain are May and October, when both weather and crowds are moderate. (You might run into rain on the Atlantic coast in Oct, but that's "Green Spain" for you.) September and April (after Easter) are also terrific. The worst month, hands down, is August. That's when the rest of Europe vacations in Spain, especially at the beaches, making it hard to even find a room. Moreover, the Spaniards also tend to go on vacation in August, which means that many restaurants and shops—and even some sights—are closed or have reduced hours. That said, if you can only go in August, still go—just be ready for some inconveniences.

Summer in Spain is hot—sometimes ferociously hot. Ecija, just east of Seville, has the dubious distinction of consistently reaching daytime highs above 110°F (43°C) in late July and August. There's even a folk saying about the weather in Castile: *Nueve meses de invierno y tres meses de infierno* (9 months of summer and 3 months of hell). The heat in Madrid and central Spain, however, is dry, and nights are generally much cooler. Barcelona gets nowhere near as warm, but the humidity guarantees steamy nights. By contrast, the Atlantic coast tends to bask in the temperate mid-70s F (low 20s C) as daytime summer highs.

Winter in Spain can be surprising. Most travelers flock to the Costa del Sol, west of Málaga, where daytime temperatures reach the 60s F (high teens C). Madrid has a reputation for cold winters, with nighttime temperatures sometimes dropping to freezing, but January and February often boast light-jacket weather with brilliantly blue skies. A significant advantage of winter travel is that hotel and airfare rates are at their lowest.

SPAIN'S CLIMATE AT A GLANCE

Except along the Atlantic coast, it's usually warmer (and drier) in Spain than in most of Europe. The average temperatures listed on this chart can be deceiving because temperatures drop substantially at night because of low humidity. Count on daytime highs in the mid- to upper-90s F (high 30s C) throughout the country (except in the north) during the summer. Coastal regions may not receive much actual precipitation, but they tend to remain humid all year. During the winter, southern coastal regions of Andalusia rarely fall much below the 50s F (10s C), even at night.

Barcelona's Average Daytime Temperatures & Rainfall

	Jan	Feb	Mar	Apr	May	June	July	Aug	Sept	Oct	Nov	Dec
Temp (°F)	48	49	52	55	61	68	73	73	70	63	55	50
Temp (°C)	9	9	11	13	16	20	23	23	21	17	13	10
Rainfall (in.)	1.7	1.4	1.9	2.0	2.2	1.5	0.9	1.6	3.1	3.7	2.9	2.0

San Sebastián's Average Daytime Temperatures & Rainfall

	Jan	Feb	Mar	Apr	May	June	July	Aug	Sept	Oct	Nov	Dec
Temp (°F)	45	48	51	52	55	65	67	67	61	52	52	48
Temp (°C)	7	9	11	11	13	18	19	19	16	12	11	9
Rainfall (in.)	0.9	0.8	0.9	1.3	1.5	1.2	0.6	0.7	1.0	1.2	1.4	0.8

Madrid's Average Daytime Temperatures & Rainfall

	Jan	Feb	Mar	Apr	May	June	July	Aug	Sept	Oct	Nov	Dec
Temp (°F)	42	45	49	53	60	69	76	75	69	58	48	43
Temp (°C)	6	7	9	12	16	21	24	24	21	14	9	6
Rainfall (in.)	1.6	1.8	1.2	1.8	1.5	1.0	0.3	0.4	1.1	1.5	2.3	1.7

Málaga's Average Daytime Temperatures & Rainfall

	Jan	Feb	Mar	Apr	May	June	July	Aug	Sept	Oct	Nov	Dec
Temp (°F)	54	54	64	70	73	81	84	86	81	73	68	63
Temp (°C)	12	12	18	21	23	27	29	30	27	23	20	17
Rainfall (in.)	2.4	2.0	2.4	1.8	1.0	0.2	0	0.1	1.1	2.5	2.5	2.4

Seville's Average Daytime Temperatures & Rainfall

	Jan	Feb	Mar	Apr	May	June	July	Aug	Sept	Oct	Nov	Dec
Temp (°F)	59	63	68	75	81	90	97	97	90	79	68	61
Temp (°C)	15	17	20	24	27	32	36	36	32	26	20	16
Rainfall (in.)	2.6	2.4	3.6	2.3	1.6	0.3	0	0.2	0.8	2.8	2.7	3.2

Spain's Major Annual Events

Spaniards rarely need an excuse to dance in the streets, set out huge feasts, and party from dawn to dawn. But sometimes they actually *plan* the festivities in advance. The following annual celebrations might help guide your visit—either because you want to enjoy the spectacle, or because you want to avoid the crowds and high hotel rates during festivities. If you plan to attend one of these events, be sure to make hotel reservations several months ahead and reserve tickets for concerts, plays, and other performing arts.

January

La Toma (☎ 958-247-128; www.turgranada.es): On Jan 1–2, Grenadinos celebrate the 1492 reconquest of Granada by Fernando and Isabel (Ferdinand and Isabella) with costumed processions and general merriment. Symbolic of the ouster of the Moors, the Alhambra's tallest tower, the Torre de la Vela (candlestick tower) is thrown open to the public.

Día de los Reyes: Epiphany, or Three Kings' Day, on Jan 6 is a bigger family event than Christmas, with parades across Spain and costumed kings dispensing sweets to youngsters. It's also a bank holiday.

Día de San Antonio: St. Anthony of Padua is the patron of cities and regions throughout Spain, including La Puebla on Mallorca. On Jan 17, the saint is honored with bonfires and torch-lit processions that usually involve revelers dressed as devils.

February

ARCO (☎ 915-881-636; www.ifema .es): Madrid's international contemporary art fair, held mid-month, showcases painting, sculpture, and graphic art from across Europe, the Americas, Australia, and Asia. Tickets are pricey (30€–60€), and the first 2 days of the fair are only open to art professionals, but the Feria Internacional de Arte Contemporáneo is one of the leading visual arts events of the year in Europe.

Carnaval de Cádiz (☎ 956-227-111; www.carnavaldecadiz.com): Every city in Spain celebrates the pre-Lent *carnaval* from the Saturday before Ash Wednesday right up until late Tuesday night. Cádiz does it with such panache and showmanship that its celebrations rank with those of Rio, Venice, and New Orleans. In addition to a giant parade with colorful floats, expect parties on every corner and characters in the streets in strange makeup and costumes. It's also considered the most gay-friendly *carnaval* in Spain.

March

Las Fallas, València (☎ 963-521-730; www.fallasfromvalencia.com): This mid-month fiesta in València marks the coming of spring by setting off fireworks and burning effigies of the demons of winter. The fiesta also launches València's bullfighting season.

April

Semana Santa: Spaniards stay away from church in droves for much of the year, but everyone gets religion the week before Easter. Processions of penitent brotherhoods bearing weighty images of saints through the streets are among the highlights, especially in Andalusia. Some of the most impressive processions take place in Cuenca, Seville, Jerez de la Frontera, and Málaga. Business grinds to a halt as almost everything closes, and hotel rooms are few and far between because Holy Week is prime season for family escapes or visiting relatives.

Feria de Seville (☎ 954-221-404; www.turismo.sevilla.org): Just 2 weeks after Semana Santa, Sevillanos pull out all the stops for their spring fair, with flamenco dancing, bullfights, and horseback and carriage processions. At the fairgrounds, local families and businesses throw invitation-only parties in *casetas* (canvas tent pavilions), and men and women alike dress in traditional costumes. Spaniards consider this the wildest party week in the country. Hotels book up a year in advance.

Moros y Cristianos (☎ 965-143-452; www.alicantecongresos.com): Guess who always wins in the reenactments of battles between the Christians and the Moors? The simulated fights are in good fun, and the pageantry is amusing. Alcoy, near Alicante, holds a reenactment in late April that is well set up for tourists, complete with the usual sideshow of concerts, fireworks, and food and drink booths.

May

Fiesta de San Isidro (☎ 913-665-477; www.turismomadrid.es): In the week leading up to the May 15 feast day of San Isidro, Madrileños cut loose with parades, music in the streets, dances, food fairs, and the launch of the bullfight season. Advance hotel reservations are essential.

Concurso de los Patios (☎ 957-201-774; www.amigosdelospatioscordobeses.es): Residents of the old quarter in Córdoba open their courtyard gardens over the first 2 weeks of May so visitors can admire their plants and decor. It's a prime chance to meet the locals and see how they live.

Feria del Caballo (☎ 956-331-150; www.turismojerez.com): It can be hard to tell if this mid-May fair, begun in 1284 as a livestock show, is about the famous horses of Jerez de la Frontera or the famous sherry. There's lots of prancing about on horseback in full regalia (men in tight pants, short jackets, and broad hats; ladies in ruffled flamenco dresses riding sidesaddle). Flamenco performances abound, and the sherry flows freely.

June

Corpus Christi: Large processions across Spain—especially in Toledo, Málaga, Seville, and Granada—mark this Christian holiday. The date varies depending on when Easter falls, but it's usually within the first 2 weeks of June.

Verbena de Sant Joan (St. John Carnival) (www.barcelonaturisme.com): This traditional late-June festival dedicated to St. John the Baptist also welcomes summer with bonfires, fireworks, and all-night dances in Barcelona. The festival climaxes with fireworks on Montjuïc.

Las Hogueras de San Juan (☎ 981-202-406; www.hoguerassanjuan.com): Alicante lights the St. John's bonfires as a traditional welcome of the summer solstice practiced here by Celts and Romans alike. All business ceases June 20–24 in favor of fireworks, parades, and public manifestations of enthusiastic eating and drinking.

Festival Internacional de Música y Danza de Granada (☎ 958-221-844; www.granadafestival.org): During the last week of June and first week of July, world-renowned artists perform at the Alhambra, Generalife, and other venues in Granada at one of Europe's most prestigious arts festivals. Hotel reservations are advised—as are ticket reservations. Many events sell out quickly.

July

Festival de Barcelona Grec (☎ 933-161-000; www.barcelonafestival.com): For a solid month, Barcelona overflows with theater, dance, and live music in venues all over the city. The festival, founded in 1976, is named for the open-air Greek Theater on Montjuïc, which was built for the 1929 Universal Exhibition. Much of the drama is staged only in Catalán.

Festival Internacional de Guitarra (☎ 957-480-644; www.guitarracordoba.com): Córdoba becomes guitar city for the first half of July, with two to three concerts daily of flamenco, jazz, fusion, and classical music, as well as guitar-building workshops, film screenings, and courses in flamenco dance and singing.

Fiesta de San Fermín (☎ 848-420-420; www.sanfermin.com): The running of the bulls in Pamplona gets all the press in this popular celebration, but the events over 9 days in early July also include extensive wine tastings, fireworks, and bullfights. Many Hemingway wannabes hitchhike into town and sleep outdoors. Book hotels very far in advance.

La Rapa das Bestas (☎ 981-546-351; www.galinor.es): The Capture of the Beasts in San Lorenzo de Sabucedo over the first weekend of July is one of several roundups of semi-wild horses from the Galician hills. Their manes and tails are cut, new foals are branded, and they're all checked out by veterinarians before being released. The spectacle attracts horse-lovers from across Europe.

Fiesta de Santiago (www.galinor.es): For 2 weeks leading up to the feast day of St. James the Apostle, Santiago de Compostela celebrates with street performances, concerts, and exhibitions. The July 24 fireworks are world-famous, while the religious rites on July 25 include the swinging of the *botafumeiro*, a gigantic incense burner.

Festival de Jazz de San Sebastián (☎ 943-440-034; www.jazzaldia.com): The oldest of the arts festivals in the Basque capital of San Sebastián (Donostia), the Jazz Festival in late July has been around since the 1960s. Indoor concerts are ticketed, but many performances are outdoors at Plaza de Trinidad.

August

Festival Internacional de Santander (☎ 942-223-434; www.festivalsantander.com): All month long, classical music, ballet, contemporary dance, chamber music, and solo musical and dance recitals are staged in Santander's custom-built Palacio de Festivales, a grand auditorium.

Feria de Málaga (☎ 952-135-000; www.andalucia.com): Starting the weekend before Aug 19, the 10-day Málaga Fair begins with a fireworks extravaganza.

Colorfully costumed riders and marchers parade up and down the city—the procession of highly decorated carriages pulled by proud Andalusian horses is one of the highlights.

Aste Nagusia, Bilbao (☎ 944-795-770; www.bilbao.net/bilbaoturismo): For 9 days toward the end of the month, Bilbao celebrates its Basque heritage with fireworks displays, the famous Strongman competitions, daily gastronomic contests, free performances in outdoor squares and churches, and a major concert that begins each night at midnight. Many shops close for fiesta week.

Misteri d'Elx (☎ 967-411-100; www.misteridelx.org): Performances Aug 11–15 of a medieval mystery play based on the Assumption draws thousands to this small town near Alicante. The sacred play is staged inside the Baroque Basilica de Santa María, and advance tickets are essential.

La Tomatina (☎ 962-500-151; www.bunyol.es): The world's largest tomato fight at 11am on last Wed in Aug concludes a weeklong celebration of Buñol's agricultural bounty. About 68,000kg (150,000 pounds) of tomatoes are mashed first, and then thrown. Public showers are provided for participants. Photographers are thicker than fruit flies.

September

Dia da Catalunya: Barcelona turns serious on Sept 11 with demonstrations and public events that offer a chance to show the *senyera*, the Catalán flag, on the anniversary of Catalonia's autonomy within Spain after decades of repression under Franco.

San Sebastián International Film Festival (☎ 943-481-212; www.sansebastianfestival.com): The Basque capital of San Sebastián (Donostia) hosts one of the top film festivals in Europe during the second week of Sept. Screenings are held at theaters all over town, prizes are given, film stars are photographed, wine is consumed.

Fiestas de la Merced (☎ 932-853-834; www.bcn.es): People dressed as lions, tigers, horses, and other animals parade through Barcelona to honor Nostra Senyora de la Merced, the city's patron saint (and the patron saint of animals). The mid-Sept event gives Barcelona another reason to party.

Bienal de Flamenco de Seville (www.bienal-flamenco.org): From mid-Sept to mid-Oct in even-numbered years, virtually every living flamenco star (dance and music) converges on Seville for performances in venues that range from small clubs to vast concert halls. It is, in effect, the world summit of flamenco.

October–November

Festival de Otoño (☎ 917-301-750; www.madrid.org): From late Oct through most of Nov, Madrid hosts artists from Spain and around the world to perform operas, ballets, dance recitals, concerts, and theatrical performances. The arts festival is so major that hotel reservations are tight, even in an otherwise slow tourism period. Performance tickets can be had for as little as 5€.

ENTRY REQUIREMENTS

Citizens of the United States, Canada, Australia, and New Zealand only need a passport valid for at least 6 months to enter Spain for tourist or business purposes for up to 90 days. (Citizens of Andorra, Liechtenstein, Monaco, Switzerland, and

Public Holidays

Every town or city (and each region) of Spain celebrates its own holiday, usually the feast day of a patron saint, in addition to the national bank holidays listed here. When a national bank holiday falls on a Tuesday or Thursday, you may encounter a *puente* (bridge) in which shops and attractions are also closed on Monday or Friday.

Año Nuevo (New Year's Day; Jan 1)

Día de los Reyes (Epiphany; Jan 6)

Jueves Santo (Good Thursday; Mar or Apr)

Viernes Santo (Good Friday; Mar or Apr)

Día de Pascua (Easter; Mar or Apr)

Día de Trabajo (Labor Day; May 1)

Asuncíon (Assumption; Aug 15)

Día de la Hispanidad (National Day; Oct 12)

Todos los Santos (All Saints' Day; Nov 1)

Día de la Constitucíon (Constitution Day; Dec 6)

Immaculada Concepcíon (Immaculate Conception; Dec 8)

Navidad (Christmas; Dec 25)

European Union countries, including Ireland and the U.K., need only present a national identification document.) You'll also need a return ticket to prove that you're leaving within 90 days. You're not allowed to work for a Spanish employer without a visa, but you can conduct your own business meetings. To obtain a long-stay visa for work, retirement, or school, contact the nearest Spanish consulate or embassy:

U.S.: Boston ☎ 617/536-2506; Chicago ☎ 312/782-4588; Houston ☎ 713/783-6200; Los Angeles ☎ 323/938-0158; Miami ☎ 305/446-5511; New Orleans ☎ 504/525-4951; New York City ☎ 212/355-4080; Puerto Rico ☎ 787/758-6090; San Francisco ☎ 415/922-2995; Washington, D.C. ☎ 202/728-2330

Canada: Halifax ☎ 902/422-0400; Montreal ☎ 514/935-5235; Ottawa ☎ 613/236-0409; Quebec ☎ 418/651-6548; St. John's, Newfoundland ☎ 709/722-6636; Toronto ☎ 416/977-1661; Winnipeg ☎ 204/896-4367

U.K.: London ☎ 020/7589 8989; Manchester ☎ 016/1236-1233

Ireland: Dublin ☎ 01-269-1640

Australia: Canberra ☎ 02-6273-3555; Melbourne ☎ 03-9347-1966; Sydney ☎ 02-9261-2433

New Zealand: Auckland ☎ 9-299-6019; Christchurch ☎ 3-366-0244

CUSTOMS REGULATIONS FOR INTERNATIONAL VISITORS

Spain is a member of the European Union and follows the same Customs regulations as other EU countries. You cannot bring *any* meat, meat products, milk, or dairy products into Spain except infant formula or other infant food sealed in its original package. Exceptions can be made for special diet foods, but you'll need a well-documented medical explanation to convince the Customs official to let them pass. You can bring up to a kilogram (2.2 lb.) of any other food. You're allowed to bring items for personal or family use, as well as gifts—if, in the judgment of Customs officials, they are not considered commercial merchandise. Anyone older than 18 years of age may carry a maximum of 200 cigarettes, 100 small cigars, 50 cigars, or 250 grams (about a half-pound) of cut tobacco. You're also allowed 1 liter (33.8 oz.) of spirits, and 2 liters (67.6 oz.) of wine or beer. Fragrances are limited to 50 ml (1.7 oz.) of perfume, and 250 ml (8.5 oz.) of *eau de toilette*. If you're carrying more than the equivalent of 6,000€ in cash, you'll have to declare it at Customs.

GETTING TO SPAIN

The dates that you fly to Spain influence the cost of airfare more than your choice of airline. **Low season** on most flights between North America and Spain is from mid-November through March, while **shoulder season** is March through April and September through mid-November. **High season** runs May through August. You can sometimes get lower rates from North America by booking flights on U.S. carriers through their European code-share partners, which have different seasonal pricing rules. When comparing airfares, make sure that you're including the add-ons for taxes, departure fees, fuel surcharges, checked luggage, and so on.

FROM NORTH AMERICA

Fares to Spain are constantly changing, as carriers raise prices and boost fuel charges (and reduce luggage allowances) to cope with spiraling energy costs. Expect to pay somewhere in the range of $750 to $1,800 for a direct round-trip ticket between New York, Boston, or Miami and Madrid in economy class. Los Angeles fares will vary from $975 to $1,800; Chicago fares, $800 to $1,800.

Flying time to Madrid from the East Coast is now 7 to 8 hours, and sometimes longer, as most carriers have switched to more fuel-efficient jets flying slower than the old fuel-guzzling wide-body jets. The slightly narrower configuration, however, means fewer seats in a row, which makes getting up and walking around slightly easier. Figure on 9 to 10 hours in the air with a Chicago departure, 11 to 14 hours flying from Los Angeles.

Spain's national carrier, **Iberia Airlines** (☎ 800/772-4642; www.iberia.com), has aggressively beefed up its direct flights between the U.S. and Spain, with service from Boston, New York, Washington (D.C.), Miami, and Los Angeles to Terminal 4 at Madrid Barajas and service from New York to Barcelona. Seat prices fluctuate daily, and can be the least expensive of all airlines on certain dates. Iberia's fly/drive packages also sometimes offer significant savings of up to $150 off the price of airfare and a one-week car rental purchased separately. Iberia offers the best connections from Madrid to other Spanish cities.

If you don't find the least expensive flight on Iberia, it will probably be on Iberia's scrappiest Spanish competitors, **Air Europa** (☎ 888/238-7672; www.air-europa.com) and **Spanair** (☎ 888/545-5757; www.spanair.com). Alas, Air Europa only flies from Newark, Spanair only from New York's La Guardia. But both offer good connections in Madrid to the rest of Spain. Spanair, in particular, often has excellent prices for flights to Palma de Mallorca.

U.S.-based carriers continue to maintain some service to Spain. **American Airlines** (☎ 800/433-7300; www.aa.com) offers daily nonstop service to Madrid from its Miami hub (as well as code shares on Iberia flights from New York). At this writing, **Delta** (☎ 800/221-1212; www.delta.com) has been operating daily nonstop service from Atlanta and New York's JFK to both Madrid and Barcelona. **Continental Airlines** (☎ 800/231-0856; www.continental.com) flies nonstop from Newark to Madrid from spring to fall. **US Airways** (☎ 800/428-4322; www.usairways.com) has also been offering daily nonstop service between Philadelphia and Madrid. Flights on US Airways and other carriers connect with the Philadelphia hub, but those connecting flights can be more expensive than similar flights to New York airports.

Air Canada (☎ 888/247-2262; www.aircanada.ca) flies nonstop between Toronto and Madrid, but Canadian travelers will generally find it less expensive to fly U.S. Airways, with a plane change in Philadelphia.

In many cases, North American travelers can score their cheapest fares to Spain by changing planes in Europe. We've had particularly good luck flying **Air France** (☎ 800/237-2747; www.airfrance.com), with a change in Paris. (The other advantage is that with Air France's tight scheduling, there's always a chance of missing your return flight and having the airline put you up overnight. The hotels are grim . . . but it *is* a free night in Paris.) **Northwest Airlines** (☎ 800/225-2525; www.nwa.com) often has good prices with a change to its partner, KLM, in Amsterdam.

FROM THE UNITED KINGDOM

Spain is a popular destination for British travelers, and airfares fluctuate wildly in the cutthroat competitive market. Expect to pay anywhere from £70 to £190 round-trip between Madrid and Liverpool, Manchester, or London.

Both **British Airways** (☎ 0870/850-9850; www.britishairways.com) and **Iberia** (☎ 0870/609-0500; www.iberia.com) fly several times a day to Madrid and Barcelona—and less frequently to Málaga—from London's Heathrow and Gatwick airports. The two carriers also fly to Madrid and Barcelona from Manchester and Birmingham. Some of the least expensive flights are from Luton or non-London airports on discount carriers **Ryanair** (www.ryanair.com), **easyJet** (www.easyjet.com), and **Air Europa** (www.aireuropa.com).

Check British newspapers for classified ads touting "slashed" fares to Spain (really just bulk-purchased seats), and pay special attention to the charter flights advertised in Sunday editions. Many charter flights leave from regional airports in Britain and go straight to Málaga to serve the Costa del Sol trade. One charter company with good Spanish packages is **Trailfinders** (☎ 0845/058-5858; www.trailfinders.com). The bucket shops around London's Victoria Station and Earls Court also offer cheap fares, but caveat emptor: Many restrictions may apply and cancellation penalties can be high.

SEEKING THE BEST AIRFARE DEALS

It's likely that 140 passengers in a given airplane cabin probably paid nearly 100 different fares for their seats. Without making yourself crazy trying to get the absolutely cheapest seat, there are several ways to make it probable that you paid less than the guy in the adjoining row.

Travel in the off-season. Sometimes this can be as simple as adjusting your flights by a few days to leave home on March 31, say, instead of April 1 and saving $200 or more. A Madrid flight in July can cost twice as much as one in January.

Fly midweek. Partly due to rate structures that encourage people to fly early or late in the week, it's usually cheapest to fly from North America to Spain on a Tuesday, Wednesday, or Thursday. There are also usually more open seats—which might even give you a chance to stretch out to sleep.

Work the Internet. For travel to and from Spain, the best fare-tracking site is Barcelona-based **eDreams** (www.edreams.com). Unlike U.S.-based programs such as **Expedia** (www.expedia.com), **Orbitz** (www.orbitz.com), **Travelocity** (www.travelocity.com), and **Lowestfare.com** (www.lowestfare.com), eDreams also searches for and will book fares on the discount airlines. Not every possible airline combination is shown, however; the system favors direct or one-stop flights but can be cajoled into showing two-stop itineraries (where the best bargains often lie). eDreams only deals in e-tickets, which can be a shortcoming if paper tickets give you more peace of mind. Fares are quoted (and charged to your credit card) in euros, not dollars, which can trigger a surcharge of 2% to 5% from your credit card company for a foreign currency transaction, if you're American. But you don't have to join the euro economy—use the search engine to find cheap flights, and then book directly with the airline.

Combine with other travel. North Americans who have reason to visit the U.K. or elsewhere in Europe—a business trip, an academic conference, a wedding—can find cheap fares to Spain from European cities. Best fares to Spain are usually from London, Amsterdam, Paris, and Milan, in that order.

Consider a consolidator. In the U.K., they're called bucket shops and they keep prices low by buying whole blocks of tickets, often on charter flights, to popular destinations. In the U.S., they advertise in the travel sections of *The New York Times, Los Angeles Times,* and *The Miami Herald.* You will find many of them listed in flight choices on CheapestFlights.com.

Subscribe to airline e-mail newsletters. When you join an airline's frequent-flier program, you'll get a periodic newsletter alerting you to special deals, discounted fares, and promotional packages. Joining the programs is free, and when you sign up, most airlines also give you the option of e-mail updates on last-minute fares. (For some reason, these notices are usually opt-in, presumably because most people can't drop everything to jet across the world the following day.) If you already belong to a program, check your settings to make sure that you get these last-minute notices.

Go along for the ride. You'll have to spend a lot of time researching, be ready to go at the drop of a hat, and pay $45 for an annual membership, but the **International Association of Air Travel Couriers (IAATC)** (www.courier.org in North America, www.aircourier.co.uk in Europe) does pair up casual couriers with freight companies. Once upon a time you could fly free by taking freight shipments as your "luggage," but nowadays the shippers charge couriers drastically reduced airfares instead (usually 50%–75%). Moreover, you'll probably have to give up you baggage allowance and fly with carry-on only.

PACKAGE DEALS

If you're reading this book, you're probably not planning to ride around Spain on a bus with 40 other people on an all-inclusive package tour. But two other kinds of packages *are* worth considering: the **fly-drive package** that generally includes just airfare and car rental, and the **air/hotel package** that includes airfare, transfers, and lodging. When advertised in English, this third option is usually to the Costa del Sol, and you'll find a discussion of such package tours in the Andalusia chapter (p. 180). Two outstanding providers of Barcelona and Madrid air/hotel packages are **Go-Today** (www.gotoday.com) and **Gate 1 Travel** (www.gate1travel. com). Off-season rates can go as low as $700 per person (double occupancy) for 6 nights. Airlines offering fly-drive packages usually partner with Hertz or Avis. Do some research to see if they really are less expensive than booking airfare and car rental separately. Iberia sometimes offers promotional fly/drive deals that are real bargains. The best fly/drive packages to Spain that we have found are through **1-800-FLY-EUROPE** (www.1800flyeurope.com), where, ironically, airfare alone is sometimes more expensive than airfare with car rental. Off-season packages of flights from the U.S. plus car for two people start around $700 per person.

TRAVEL INSURANCE—DO YOU NEED IT?

In a word, yes. Do you need to buy it? That depends.

If you've purchased a big-ticket travel item such as a guided tour or a cruise, you run the risk of losing all your money if unforeseen circumstances cause you to cancel or interrupt a trip. **Trip-cancellation insurance** helps you recover your

Untours—the UnPackage

Although the Spanish destinations are limited (Barcelona, a small city south of Córdoba, and sometimes Madrid), **Untours** (www.untours.com) is a great alternative to consider. The company bundles airfare, apartment rental, and in-country transportation with Untours's own local orientation program—and then leaves you free to fend for yourself, knowing you can always contact the local guide for help. A few group activities are usually thrown in, but otherwise you don't have to deal with the conflicting needs and interests of a travel group. Price per person drops as you add more people to a lodging, making Untours especially attractive for families or couples who really like each other. The strength of Untours, in our experience, is that the company shows you how to *live* in a place, not just to visit it. Rates for their Spanish packages are very competitive with lining up your own apartment from a local agent. Barcelona prices, for example, range from $3,119 to $3,329 double occupancy per person for 2 weeks, including airfare from the U.S. The comparable Andalusia package is $2,489 to $2,719.

investment if you have to back out of the trip due to illness or accident, natural disasters, or political turmoil at your destination. It also protects you in case the trip organizer goes bankrupt—so never buy insurance from the same company who is selling you the trip; always use a third party. Depending on your age and health and the cost of your excursion, such insurance usually costs 5% to 8% of the cost of the trip—and it's rarely worth it for a self-guided vacation in Spain. Moreover, many credit cards provide automatic cancellation insurance for trips charged entirely to the card—ask your issuer or check the fine print in your card agreement. Those planning apartment stays are well advised to buy travel insurance, as usually the required deposit is nonrefundable (unlike hotel stays where you can cancel within 24 hr. of arrival without penalty).

Medical insurance is a trickier matter. Spain's national health system has reciprocal agreements with other European countries—but not with American insurers. Note that most American health plans, including Medicare and Medicaid, don't cover you while you're overseas except for emergency treatment. Even then, you'll have to pay the Spanish healthcare provider up front and fill out a lot of paperwork both in Spain and with your health plan to request reimbursement when you get home. Before you leave home, it's worth finding out exactly what your own health insurance will and will not cover, especially in regard to medical evacuation. While most travelers will not be exposing themselves to the kind of risks requiring medical evacuation, do consider special insurance if you're going into the backcountry. If you're hiking in a remote area, and break your leg, you may have to be flown out by helicopter to the nearest hospital—a hefty bill ($5,000 and up) to put on your credit card. Moreover, if you're going to participate in what insurers describe as high-risk activities (skiing, water-skiing, bungee-jumping, diving, hang-gliding, and the like), even policies that normally cover medical evacuation won't pay the tab. (Our insurance, for example, covers the casual hiking scenario, and yours may too. But it doesn't cover hang-gliding.) You'll need special medical and **evacuation insurance** for high-risk activities. If you're ever hospitalized more than 150 miles from home, **MedjetAssist** (☎ 800/527-7478; www.medjetassistance.com) will pick you up and fly you to the hospital of your choice in a medically equipped and staffed aircraft 24 hours a day, 7 days a week. Annual memberships are $225 individual, $350 family; you can also purchase short-term memberships starting at $85. Non-daredevils can probably skip this option.

Canadians should check with their provincial health-plan offices or call **Health Canada** (☎ 866/225-0709; www.hc-sc.gc.ca) to find out the extent of their coverage and what documentation and receipts they must take home in case they are treated overseas. Citizens of the U.K. need a **European Health Insurance Card (EHIC)**, the replacement for the E111 form, to receive free or reduced-cost health benefits during a visit to Spain. For advice, ask at your local post office or see **www.dh.gov.uk/travellers**.

We're not big advocates of traveling with expensive property or clothing, but if you cart your most precious belongings with you, you might want to purchase **property insurance** or at least **lost-luggage insurance.** Americans usually find that homeowner's coverage will pay for lost, stolen, or damaged cameras or camcorders, but check with your agent to see if you need a special rider for an expensive piece of equipment. Homeowner's policies also usually protect you in case of theft from your hotel room. Be smart: Don't pack jewelry, cameras, or other obviously valuable items in checked luggage.

Airline liability for lost luggage on international flights is limited to about $1,500 (up to $2,500 on U.S. flights) and that doesn't cover all items. Again, you may find that the credit card you used for the airline ticket covers you for anything over that, but **lost-luggage insurance** can be a good hedge, as long as you don't buy the overpriced insurance available at airport kiosks. In truth, only about 2% of lost luggage stays lost; the more likely event is that it doesn't catch up with you until you're home, in which case you'll have to battle with the airline for compensation for the inconvenience. Most airlines will assure you that you'll be reimbursed for some minimal clothing and toiletries (usually less than $250). *Keep every single receipt until you've been paid.*

If you find your homeowner's insurance, credit cards, and health plan don't give you enough coverage to travel with peace of mind, visit **InsureMyTrip.com** to compare coverage and policies from several industry leaders in travel insurance. Or contact one of the following reputable companies directly:

Access America (☎ 866/807-3982; www.accessamerica.com)
CSA Travel Protection (☎ 800/873-9844; www.csatravelprotection.com)
MEDEX Assistance (☎ 800/732-5309; www.medexassist.com)
Travel Guard International (☎ 800/807-3982;www.travelguard.com)
Travelex (☎ 800/228 9792; www.travelex-insurance.com)

GETTING AROUND SPAIN

Non-European visitors are often surprised to discover that Spain is a lot bigger than it looks on many maps. While there's a lot to be said for concentrating a visit on one small area, chances are you'll want to see two or three regions in a 2-week vacation.

BY AIR

Domestic flights in Spain are cheap by European standards, and flying is a fast way to chew up the kilometers. **Iberia** (☎ 800/772-4642; www.iberia.com) has the most complete network of routes in Spain, but **Air Europa** (☎ 888/238-7672; www.air-europa.com) and **Spanair** (☎ 888/545-5757; www.spanair.com) may have cheaper fares. If you're planning to cover a lot of ground, Iberia's "Visit Spain" Air Pass might work for you. It's sold only in conjunction with an intercontinental ticket and allows you to buy additional flights in continental Spain and the Canary and Balearic islands. The trick is, you're not allowed to land at the same airport twice and can buy a maximum of four segments, priced by mileage. At press time, flights up to 450 miles were 65€, 450 to 950 miles were 85€, and flights over 951 miles were 115€. Fares for children 2 to 11 are half the adult fare; fares for children under 2 are 10% of the adult fare. You'll need to talk directly with Iberia to work out all the details.

BY TRAIN

While Americans were building more highways, the Spanish were building new rail lines. You can get around the country very nicely on the train, although we recommend using the fast TALGO trains for intercity travel—unless an even faster high-speed AVE line is available. And we do mean high speed: the AVE hurtles between Madrid and Barcelona, for example, in less than 3 hours with 20 trains a day in each direction. Fares ranges from 75€ to 190€, depending on date, time of day, and class of service. The Spanish national rail network, **RENFE** (www.renfe.es), has complete schedules online. You can also purchase tickets and reserve seats on the high-speed trains from the comfort of your own computer.

If your itinerary calls for a number of long-distance rail trips and you're willing to forgo the high-speed trains, you may find that a **Eurail Spain Pass** works for you. It's valid for unlimited travel for 3 days within a 2-month period, and you can buy extra travel days up to a maximum of 10 days. Prices start at $296 for first class, plus $45 for each additional day. Second class (a better value and hardly a hardship; in fact, that's what we always take!) starts at $231 with additional days costing $37. (Children 4–11 pay half-fare on any of these discount passes.) The pass is not good on hotel trains or high-speed trains, although it does provide a discount when purchasing tickets for these trains. To buy a Eurail Spain Pass, contact **Rail Europe** (☎ 877/272-RAIL; www.raileurope.com).

BY BUS

There's nothing wrong with Spanish bus service—in fact, it's better than bus service in most of North America. But rarely do the buses offer significant saving over trains, and they're always less comfortable and usually slower. Buses, however, are a fine way to do some local sightseeing from urban centers, or to connect between rural villages, where the "station" is likely to be the bar nearest the crossroad. Regional bus lines tend to dominate bus service. You'll find information on using the local and regional buses in each of the chapters in this guide.

RENTAL CARS

Spain is one of the last places in Europe where you need an **International Driving Permit** if your own driver's license isn't issued by an EU country. These are available from AAA (www.aaa.com/vacation/idpf.html), even if you're not a member. Bring your valid license, $15, and two original passport-type photos to any AAA office. Many car agencies will not rent to you unless you have an IDP, and police can fine you up to 400€ if you're stopped and cannot produce it. In effect, it's simply a folder that translates your driver's license information into several languages.

The major car-rental agencies in Spain are **Avis** (www.avis-europe.com), **Hertz** (www.hertz.es), **Europcar** (www.europcar.com), and **National Atesa** (www.atesa. es), and their rates differ by very little. Sometimes, but not always, **AutoEurope** (888/223-5555; www.autoeurope.com) gives a better deal. Check with them first. The best way to get a discount is to look for a fly/drive package from your airline (see above).

Take the smallest car in which you feel comfortable. Not only are they less expensive, but they're more economical. (Fuel in Spain costs roughly double what it costs in the U.S.) They're also easier to maneuver on narrow streets and in even narrower underground parking garages. Unless your credit card company covers damages to the vehicle, we strongly suggest paying extra for the collision damage waiver, as it's only too easy to crumple a fender and end up paying a 500€ fee to have it repaired. Manual transmission vehicles are usually less expensive than automatics. In any case, make sure your vehicle has air-conditioning; you'll need it. We're also big believers in vehicles with a closed trunk to keep your luggage out of sight; in practice, this usually means renting a vehicle one or two classes above the minimum.

SAVING ON ACCOMMODATIONS

Alternative accommodations recommended throughout this book—apartments, small family-run hotels, and hostels—are usually the best way to trim sleeping costs to the bone while immersing yourself in the Spanish way of life. You'll also find that many of the lodging recommendations listed here are small operations that are not plugged into the international booking systems.

But for those that are, a little Web research may turn up some treasures. Barcelona-based **eDreams** (www.edreams.com) outperforms the Big Three of online booking engines—**Expedia** (www.expedia.com), **Travelocity** (www.travel ocity.com), and **Orbitz** (www.orbitz.com)—for hotels and other accommodations in Spain because it includes a lot of smaller properties geared to the local market. (Despite the anemic dollar, some hoteliers still think of Americans as rich, but they cut their countrymen a break.) We have, for example, found small local hotels for 40€ to 50€ in areas where the Big Three can't find anything under 75€.

Use the discounters like **Hotels.com** and **Quikbook.com** to find last-second deals on rooms that remain unsold. When we've changed plans and needed a hotel room that night, we've had very good luck getting a 250€ room for as little as 60€ from Hotels.com; they don't always catch the smaller, locally oriented hotels, but they can offer deep discounts on chains, business, conference, and airport hotels. The British site **LateRooms.com** is also good on last-minute deals, especially in hotel-intensive areas like the Costa del Sol and Costa Brava.

Fit for a King—at a Bargain

Back in the 1920s, the Spanish government decided to take over a slew of old palaces, monasteries, castles, and other historic buildings and turn them into hotels to encourage tourism. In places where there were no colorful derelicts to appropriate (like Cádiz), the state built new resort hotels. Eventually the network grew into today's system of 86 *paradores* around the country. Most feature classic Spanish architecture and antique furnishings—along with modern baths, air-conditioning, and steam heat. Most also have pretty good restaurants that highlight the cuisine of their regions.

While the *paradores* tend to fall into the highest price category of this book, you can get some amazing bargains under certain conditions. For one thing, they almost never charge the official rack rate, and room rates can be quite modest on weeknights for walk-in guests. (Spaniards use them extensively for weekend getaways.) For another, if one member of your party is between ages 20 and 30, you can get a double room (with the ample breakfast buffet) for 111€ per night including taxes. This is a "youth rate" designed to build a future clientele for *paradores,* which have an image in Spain of being hotels for retirees. If one member of the party is 60 or over, you get 30% off the rate of the day (usually lower than the official rack rate). The best deal of all is the 5-night card for 514€, including taxes, that can be used at most *paradores* on most dates. The card is available for people of all ages. There are a few catches—some of the most exclusive and expensive *paradores* don't participate in the promotions, and they're not valid during Holy Week and some local festivals.

The central office for *paradores* is **Paradores de España** (Requeña 3, 28013 Madrid; ☎ 902-547-979; www.parador.es). The U.S. representative is **Marketing Ahead** (381 Park Ave. S., New York, NY 10016; ☎ 800/223-1356 or 212/686-9213; www.marketingahead.com). Travel agents can arrange reservations, but you'll need to go to the website to get the youth discounts or the 5-night card.

The opaque websites (those that don't tell you what you're getting until you've paid for it) like **Priceline** (www.priceline.com) and **Hotwire** (www.hotwire.com) let you choose a star rating and town or general urban neighborhood. The deals are often good, but not always budget. The knock on both systems is that they do a lot better finding five-star hotels at three-star prices than finding three-star hotels at one-star prices.

If you're going to be touring around in a rental car at the end of your trip, look into an airport hotel for your last night. As a general rule, they're less expensive than city hotels, usually have the amenities to get a good night's rest, and save you on airport transportation fees. Get up, have a leisurely breakfast, and then drive to the airport to drop your car and catch your flight! It definitely eases reentry after a vacation to go home refreshed.

MONEY MATTERS

Back in the days when the country was still on the peseta, Spain was a bargain for vacationers. The Franco government's mismanagement of the economy kept Spaniards poor and prices low. With democracy, Spain's economy blossomed. The transition to the euro economy in 1999 may have brought drastic inflation (prices almost doubled overnight), but it was eventually followed by widespread prosperity. Even so, the cost of living remains slightly lower in Spain than in England, Italy, Germany, and France, and meals and hotels cost a little less than in those countries. If the dollar and the euro were equal, Spain would be something of a bargain. The $15 steak in the U.S. (outside New York, of course) might only cost 12€ in Spain. But when you get home and receive your credit card statement, that bargain beef has become more like $20. That's why the restaurants in this book concentrate on getting you the best combination of quality and value.

CASH & ATMS

When we go to Spain we always bring enough euros in small bills and coins to take care of our first day's needs (a taxi, coffee, pastry, more coffee). We also have a small stash of traveler's checks for emergencies only. Otherwise, we count on getting cash from an ATM for everything that we can't put on a credit card.

In fact, the cheapest way to get euros is to withdraw them from your home bank account by using an ATM card. You'll get a far better exchange rate from your bank than from a money changer in Spain. Every traveler to Spain should have a working ATM card, preferably with a four-digit PIN (some machines only accept 4 digits), and enough cash in the primary checking account at home to cover all expenses. (Some Spanish bank systems don't ask which account you want to tap, and they automatically bleed your primary checking.)

The **Cirrus** (☎ 800/424-7787; www.mastercard.com) and **PLUS** (☎ 800/843-7587; www.visa.com) networks span the globe. Go to your bank card's website to find ATM locations at your destination. Be sure you know your daily withdrawal limit before you depart. Most banks charge a flat fee (1€–2€) for cash withdrawals, and your home bank will likely hit you as well with a foreign currency transaction fee. An exception to this rule are credit unions and certain banks well known for their policies of returning ATM fees to their customers, such as Commerce Bank (in the northeastern U.S. only). Note that **Global ATM Alliance** member banks charge no transaction fees for cash withdrawals at other Alliance member ATMs. Look for a Deutsche Bank in Spain if your ATM card is issued by Bank of America, Scotiabank (Canada), or Barclays (U.K.).

Before you leave home, alert your bank that you'll be traveling in Spain and making withdrawals. Otherwise, a diligent bank officer might put a stop on your account. Make sure that you know your PIN in numbers, as few Spanish machines have letters on the keypads.

Retrieve your card quickly when using Spanish ATMs, as many machines eat the card within 10 to 15 seconds for "security." You'll have to get it back when the machine is opened for servicing, which will inevitably be a huge waste of time.

CREDIT CARDS

Visa and MasterCard are widely accepted in Spain, although some merchants accept one but not the other. Ideally, carry one of each. American Express is less popular

A Few Words on Tipping

Leave a little something for people in service jobs, but don't overdo it. All restaurant and hotel bills have service charges of 15% already built in. Porters and doormen who help with luggage should get 0.75€ per bag, maids 1€ per day. Give cab drivers about 10% more than the meter shows—or round up to the next full euro. Do tip at restaurants and bars, but keep it around 5% to 10%. The standard tip for a tour guide when you're in a group is 2€ to 3€ per person.

and you may have to pay a surcharge that reflects the extra fees that Amex charges merchants. A few hotels and restaurants accept Diners Club, but it's usually a warning signal of high prices. You might as well leave your Discover Card at home, since we've never seen an establishment that accepts it. As with your ATM card, warn your issuer that you'll be making charges in Spain to avoid having the account deactivated by an overzealous employee or an automated computer program.

Most credit card companies now levy transaction fees of a few percentage points every time you make a charge abroad. Sometimes the fee is buried in the exchange rate. Even so, the international transaction fee is rarely as high as the premium you would pay by exchanging dollars for euros. The last major card issuer without an international fee, Capital One, joined the crowd of fee-chargers in August 2008.

Unless it's an emergency, don't withdraw cash on a credit card. You'll pay a currency exchange fee, and worse, you'll be charged interest from the instant you accept the transaction. If your credit card allows for online bill paying through links with your bank account, set up that capability before you leave—at the very least, you can pay off your withdrawals within hours, cutting your losses.

TRAVELER'S CHECKS & TRAVELER'S CARDS

With ATMs both common and convenient, old-fashioned traveler's checks seem downright quaint. They would be more enticing if you didn't pay a fee to buy them and take a hit on the exchange rate when you redeem them. But some travelers feel comfortable using them, and they do offer a bit of security, since stolen checks can be quickly replaced. Be sure to keep a record of the serial numbers separate from your checks in the event that they are stolen or lost. You'll get a refund faster if you know the numbers. American Express, Visa, and Thomas Cook traveler's checks are widely accepted in Spanish hotels, upscale restaurants, and by banks.

Several creditors have come up with **traveler's check cards,** also called **prepaid cards,** which are essentially debit cards encoded with the amount of money you elect to put on them. They're not linked to your personal bank accounts, they work in ATMs, and if you lose one, you can get your cash back in a matter of hours. If you spend all the money on them, you can call a number and reload the card using your bank account information. For use in Spain, the best of the bunch is **Visa TravelMoney** (www.visa.com), sold through AAA offices in the United States (☎ 866/339-3378), which works anywhere that accepts the Visa credit card. The card costs $10 and skims a bit more than 1% of the money you load onto it in addition to international transaction fees. That makes it about the same price as traveler's checks.

MONEY EXCHANGES

Like carrying traveler's checks, changing money from one currency to another is a disappearing practice. It's the surest way to lose money, thanks to ridiculous spreads between the price of buying and selling a given currency. Because ATM withdrawals are much better deals, old-fashioned *cambios* are few and far between these days. Nonetheless, you'll find a few at airports and in tourist-centric areas like Puerta del Sol and Plaza Mayor in Madrid or along Les Rambles in Barcelona. If you must change money, take advantage of the better rates offered by banks during regular banking hours (9am–2pm weekdays, 9am–1pm Sat). The worst exchange rates of all are usually in hotels.

HEALTH & SAFETY

Guarding your health while traveling in Spain comes down to two solid bits of advice: Limit your exposure to the sun, and watch what you eat and drink. Summer travel, especially in southern Spain, demands liberal applications of sunscreen, preferably with a protection level of SPF 30 or higher. Remember that children need even more protection than adults. People with extremely fair skin may want to wait until they arrive in Spain to purchase sunblock, as formulations of SPF 60 and SPF 90 are easier to find there than in the U.S. or Canada.

There has been a lot of nonsense written about dietary concerns in Spain. Tap water is safe throughout the country (but don't drink mountain stream water, no matter how clear) and is usually better for your digestive system and your blood pressure than bottled water laden with mineral salts. If you want to cut costs and help the environment at the same time, buy one bottle per person on the day you arrive and keep refilling it from the tap. Think of the energy you'll save that would have gone into bottle manufacturing and trucking the water around.

Drinking & Smoking

The legal drinking age in Spain is 18. You can buy wine, beer, and spirits in almost any market. Places that serve alcohol usually start doing so when they open—it's not uncommon to see people having a shot of brandy with their morning coffee. The establishments keep serving alcohol until they close, which is usually 1:30am or later.

Spain is a smoking country. Now that smoking has been banned in the workplace, stores, cultural venues, public transportation, and public areas in hotels (in accordance with EU health and safety regulations), Spaniards make up for it by smoking more everywhere else. While some restaurants do have designated nonsmoking areas, they usually share the same ventilation system as the larger smoking section. Nonsmoking rooms in hotels are uncommon.

Spanish cuisine can be heavy on garlic and olive oil, and the wine is so tempting and refreshing, you could easily overdo. Curb your enthusiasms—or if that doesn't work, tote around some anti-diarrhea medicine. There have been some alarming reports of pollution in the waters of the Mediterranean, but it's generally safe to eat fish in Spain. Most of the fish in the Spanish diet are either small fish low on the food chain (and hence unlikely to pick up pollution) or big fish like yellowfin tuna caught in deep waters of the Mediterranean or on the Atlantic coast off Cádiz. Shellfish are increasingly farmed in clean water, and shrimp and other crustaceans eaten in Spain don't live long enough to absorb pollution. For non-fish eaters, Spanish mountain hams are legendary, the beef is very tasty, and southern Spain produces a large percentage of the fruits and vegetables for Europe.

Spanish medical facilities are world-class. If you have a medical emergency, your hotel staff can usually put you in touch with a reliable doctor. Medical and hospital services are not free, so be sure that you have appropriate insurance coverage before you travel (see above).

CRIME

According to the Spanish national government, the principal tourist areas where muggings, attacks, and thefts occur are in Madrid and Barcelona. But it makes sense to exercise caution wherever you are. The best way to avoid becoming a victim is not to look like one. As in any large city, know where you're going so you're not standing around studying a map. Walk purposefully with any bags well secured by a strap (but *not* hugged to your chest—that posture marks you as an easy target). Avoid isolated ATMs, dark alleys, and large crowds. When you go out, leave unneeded cash, credit cards, passports, and travel documents in the hotel safe.

Thieves often work in pairs, especially on subways and at crowded outdoor markets. One distracts you while the other picks your pocket, slashes your purse, or grabs your camera. Common distractions range from asking the time to waving a map and asking directions to spilling a drink on you or "accidentally" bumping into you. Be alert to such pairs and try to travel with your hands free. When driving around, never leave *anything* in plain view when you park and leave a car—not even maps.

If you lose your passport, report it immediately to the local police and the nearest embassy or consulate. Here are the Madrid addresses and hours: The **United States Embassy** (calle Serrano 75; ☎ 915-872-200; Metro: Núñez de Balboa) is open Monday through Friday 9am to 6pm. The **Canadian Embassy** (Núñez de Balboa 35; ☎ 914-233-250; Metro: Velázquez) is open Monday through Thursday 8:30am to 5:30pm and Friday 8:30am to 2:30pm. The **British Embassy** (calle Fernando el Santo 16; ☎ 917-008-200; Metro: Colón) is open Monday through Friday 9am to 1:30pm and 3 to 6pm. The embassy of the **Republic of Ireland** (Paseo Castellana 46; ☎ 914-364-093; Metro: Serrano) is open Monday through Friday 9am to 2pm. The **Australian Embassy** (Pl. Diego de Ordas 3, Edificio Santa Engracia 120; ☎ 913-536-600; Metro: Ríos Rosas) is open Monday though Thursday 8:30am to 5pm and Friday 8:30am to 2:15pm. The embassy of **New Zealand** (Plde. la Lealtad 2; ☎ 915-230-226; Metro: Banco de España) is open Monday through Friday 9am to 2pm and 3 to 5:30pm.

A Word on Terrorism in Spain

We hesitate to raise alarms about terrorism because you're so utterly unlikely to encounter it, but we must point out that Spain, like the United Kingdom, suffered a major terrorist attack publicly linked to its participation in military actions in Iraq and Afghanistan. Terrorists attacked the Spanish rail system in Madrid on March 11, 2004, setting off 10 bombs that killed 190 people and injured 1,500 more. The attack toppled the Spanish government, which did an abrupt about-face and withdrew its troops from the war effort.

Spain also has its homegrown insurgency, the Basque separatist group known as ETA. The group tends to target politicians, police, and military. In 2001, ETA said it would attack tourist sites to force the government into negotiations but never carried through with the threat. Periodic truces are declared between the central government and the ETA, but conflict occasionally flares up. The violence rarely spills over to the general public.

What can you do to protect yourself from terrorism in Spain? Not much, nor do you need to. Although you are in unfamiliar surroundings, use the same common sense you'd use at home and be a good-natured, friendly traveler who steers clear of discussions of politics, religion, and ethnicity. U.S. tourists might consider referring to the U.S. Department of State's current edition of its terrorism alert list, **Worldwide Caution** (http://travel.state. gov/travel/cis_pa_tw/pa/pa_1161.html). Remember that you're at least as safe in Spain as in London, New York, Toronto, or Iowa.

U.S. citizens may refer to the State Department's pamphlet *A Safe Trip Abroad* for tips on a more trouble-free journey. The pamphlet is available by mail from the Superintendent of Documents, U.S. Government Printing Office, Washington, DC 20402; on the Web at www.access.gpo.gov/su_docs; or on the Bureau of Consular Affairs home page at http://travel.state.gov.

WHAT TO PACK

We understand the urge to be comfortable, but we think it's about time to raise the image of English-speakers abroad. Dressing better will make you more confident and let you fit in. The first people to identify the badly dressed as tourists are the pickpockets. The Spanish aren't the most snappy dressers. Even Barcelona isn't Paris. But they are more formal than Americans and Brits, opting for "smart casual" when they leave the house. For men this translates as jeans or slacks topped by a shirt with a collar; add a jacket for fine dining in the evening. Except at the beach, closed-toe leather shoes are the norm. For women, slacks and a blouse, a skirt and a blouse, or a dress are in order. Good-fitting un-ripped jeans remain very fashionable in Spain for both men and women.

Except at the beach, both men and women will do well to avoid short shorts or tank tops. For women, it's respectful to cover bare arms and cleavage when visiting churches.

If you're visiting from June through September, plan for hot weather by packing light colors and airy fabrics. Woven shirts and blouses, for example, will be much cooler than knits. But don't forget a shawl (for women) or a light jacket, as even summer nights can get chilly in the drier regions. You may also want a hat to shield your eyes from the intense Iberian sun.

SPECIALIZED TRAVEL RESOURCES

Not all travelers are alike. If you're traveling with the kids or have special physical challenges, you'll need extra help with logistics. Students and seniors can take advantage of price breaks and special services. Gay and lesbian travelers should be aware of safety issues—and special social opportunities.

ADVICE FOR FAMILIES

Spain is a family-friendly country. Spaniards adore infants and cater to them at every turn. But once children are old enough to walk, they're treated as height-challenged adults and are expected to comport themselves accordingly. Perhaps one reason that Spanish children behave in public is that they go everywhere with their parents, including to dinner. This comes as something of a shock to North American travelers used to getting a babysitter so they can go out in the evening; alas, babysitters are in short supply, except at resorts and large chain hotels that cater to a primarily non-Spanish clientele.

Attractions in Spain do not go out of their way for children, although those ages 6 to 17 usually get reduced admission and children 5 and under often get in free. The savings, of course, still won't make little Johnny and Susie interested in the dozens of cases of glassware at the Museum of Decorative Arts. (By contrast, children are fascinated by the Prado, where entire galleries are often packed with schoolchildren on field trips.) Be sensible and mix up museum days with visits to parks; skip a few wine tastings in favor of a boat ride.

Several family-travel websites can help prepare you for traipsing through Spain with offspring. **Family Travel Forum** (www.familytravelforum.com) is a comprehensive site offering customized trip planning. **Family Travel Network** (www.familytravelnetwork.com) offers travel features, deals, and tips. You'll find sound advice on long-distance and international travel with children from **Traveling Internationally with Your Kids** (www.travelwithyourkids.com). **Family Travel Files** (www.thefamilytravelfiles.com) has an online magazine and a directory of off-the-beaten-path tours and tour operators for families.

ADVICE FOR SENIORS

Old age seems to get younger all the time—just as "seniors" are more fit than ever. But if you want a break on prices and you're over 50 (or even better, over 60), whip out your ID card and claim your discount. Seniors in Spain are usually anyone 60 and over, and they get reduced admissions to almost every attraction under the sun, usually paying the same price as children.

AARP (601 E Street NW, Washington, DC, 24009; ☎ 888/687-2277; www.aarp.org) might be worth joining for member discounts on hotels, airfares, and car rentals. Membership is open to anyone 50 or older, although you may have to be 60, 62, or 65 to qualify for some of the discount programs. Be sure, however, to crunch the numbers to make sure that the AARP discount is better than one you can get another way. Travelers 50 and older can also take advantage of the Spanish cultural travel programs of **Elderhostel** (☎ 877/426-8056; www.elderhostel.org). Don't think these are all for doddering old folks; among the programs is a 13-day walking/hiking program on the Camino de Santiago. For other senior travel resources and discounts, check out the quarterly magazine *Travel 50 & Beyond* (www.travel50andbeyond.com).

ADVICE FOR TRAVELERS WITH DISABILITIES

Spain is slowly starting to deal with accessibility issues, but there's hardly a village or neighborhood in the country that doesn't have endless flights of stairs (indoors and out) or steep hills. New hotels and upscale restaurants tend to be wheelchair-accessible, but the situation is less dependable at lower-priced establishments. If you don't want to do a lot of advance research on accessibility, consider taking an organized tour specifically designed to accommodate travelers with disabilities. Among the travel agencies offering customized tours and itineraries for travelers with disabilities are **Flying Wheels Travel** (☎ 507/451-5005; www.flyingwheelstravel.com) and **Accessible Journeys** (☎ 800/846-4537 or 610/521-0339; www.disabilitytravel.com).

Access-Able Travel Source (☎ 303/232-2979; www.access-able.com) offers a pretty thorough database of travel agents with experience in accessible travel, as well as access information for specific destinations. The website also links to resources such as service animals, equipment rentals, and access guides.

Flying with Disability (www.flying-with-disability.org) is a comprehensive information source on airplane travel. Although **Avis** (☎ 888/879-4273) does not make it easy to book special equipment for rental cars through its website, the company does have an Avis Access program that offers services for customers with special travel needs; these include specially outfitted vehicles with swivel seats, spinner knobs, and hand controls. Be sure to reserve well in advance.

For a good overview of accessible travel, check out **MossRehab** (☎ 800/225-5667; www.mossresourcenet.org). Additional resources are available from the **American Foundation for the Blind** (☎ 800/232-5463; www.afb.org) and **SATH (Society for Accessible Travel & Hospitality)** (☎ 212/447-7284; www.sath.org). **AirAmbulanceCard.com** is now partnered with SATH and allows you to preselect top-notch hospitals in case of an emergency.

British travelers should contact **Holiday Care** (☎ 0845/124-9971; www.holidaycare.org.uk) for a wide range of information on travel for people with disabilities, including the elderly.

ADVICE FOR GAY & LESBIAN TRAVELERS

Although gay-bashing still occurs, Spain is among Europe's more open societies. The country legalized homosexual relations between consenting adults in 1978, and in 1995 the parliament banned discrimination based on sexual orientation. The final legal hurdle was passed in 2005, when the country legalized same-sex marriage with strong support of the general public. Widespread acceptance of gays and lesbians means that even areas with many openly gay residents have few strictly gay bars or clubs. The major centers of gay life in Spain are Madrid, Barcelona, Granada, and Cádiz. Among the most popular resort towns for gay travelers are Sitges (outside Barcelona), Torremolinos on the Costa del Sol, and the island of Ibiza.

The **International Gay and Lesbian Travel Association (IGLTA)** (☎ 800/448-8550 or 954/776-2626; www.iglta.org) is the trade association for the gay and lesbian travel industry, and offers an online directory of gay- and lesbian-friendly travel businesses and tour operators.

Many agencies offer tours and travel itineraries specifically for gay and lesbian travelers.

ADVICE FOR STUDENTS

Be sure you have an **International Student Identity Card (ISIC)** to get substantial savings on rail passes, air travel, and entrance fees. It also provides basic health and life insurance and a 24-hour help line. The card is available from **STA Travel** (☎ 800/781-4040 in North America; www.sta.com or www.statravel.com). If you're no longer a student but still under 26, you can get an **International Youth Travel Card (IYTC)** from the same source to get some of the discounts (but not reduced museum admissions). **Travel CUTS** (☎ 800/667-2887 or 416/614-2887; www.travelcuts.com) offers similar services for both Canadian and U.S. residents. Irish students should check out **USIT** (☎ 01-602-1600; www.usitnow.ie) for their student, youth, and independent travel programs.

STAYING WIRED WHILE YOU'RE AWAY

Spain took a while to get onto the information superhighway, but once on the road, the country has revved up quickly. Most Spaniards under 40 (and many over 40) have broadband Internet access, usually at home or work through a DSL connection. (Super-high-speed access is still rare.) Hotels, restaurants, and museums have embraced the Web, and most have at least a rudimentary website. Ironically, the cheapest, most ubiquitous Wi-Fi access is at the least expensive lodgings. You're more likely to find free Wi-Fi in a 10-room *hostal* than in a three-star business hotel. In fact, the business hotels often charge exorbitant fees (25€ and up per day) to connect to their systems. The idea of free Wi-Fi in cafes hasn't really caught on yet in Spain, so you may be reduced to visiting a cybercafe. Fortunately, there's usually one in even the smallest villages. Expect to pay from 1€ an hour to 5€ per day. If you have your own laptop, ask if you can connect directly. (Using a Spanish keyboard will have you gnashing your teeth in no time.)

RECOMMENDED BOOKS & FILMS

Spain looms large in the European (and American) imagination. While this guide should give you a lot of texture and practical information, you'll enjoy your visit even more by tapping into the rich trove of history, fiction, and film where Spain is as much a character as a subject. Here are some recommendations to get you started.

HISTORY & NONFICTION

A pair of histories in English capture Spain through the ages: *Spanish Labyrinth*, by Gerald Brenan, is one of the better histories of the country up to the Civil War, while ***The Spaniards,*** by John Hooper, is a clearly written and often insightful modern history of Spain.

The English writer Laurie Lee wandered through Europe with little more than his notebook, sheaf of poems, and a violin, and he happened to be in Spain at a turning point in history. His three lyrical volumes of memoirs—***As I Walked Out On Midsummer's Morning, A Moment of War,*** and ***A Rose for Winter***— recount journeys just before, during, and 20 years after the Spanish Civil War. Decide for yourself if he really participated in the combat, as he later claimed. George Orwell was there, too, living in Barcelona when the war broke out. ***Homage to Catalonia*** is classic Orwell—carefully observed and unapologetic in its polemics. But Orwell didn't just talk the talk: He also fought against the Falangists in Aragón.

Read ***Spain,*** by Jan Morris, for her sweeping, gorgeous style and careful observation of the small facts of Spanish life. At the same time, take her grand generalizations with a grain of salt. After all, she was writing about Spain circa 1965. For an overload of facts (along with a lot of admittedly turgid prose), the classic book on Spain is James Michener's ***Iberia.*** For additional amusing and revealing tales of travel in Spain, pick up a copy of ***Travelers' Tales: Spain,*** edited by Lucy McCauley. If you're partial to the I-gave-up-everything-for-a-house-in-the-south-of-X genre of memoirs, ***Driving Over Lemons: An Optimist in Andalusia,*** by Chris Stewart, is an entertaining, informative, and self-deprecating look at rural life in the hill towns south of Granada.

Sometimes narrowing the focus sheds more light on the whole. That's the case with ***The Basque History of the World,*** by Mark Kurlansky. The former *New York Times* correspondent treats the Basques as a separate people and, de facto, a separate nation. In the process he illuminates much of ancient and modern Spanish history, including ongoing hostilities between the central government in Madrid and the Basque separatists. In a similar vein, Robert Hughes recounts the whole history from ancient past to present in ***Barcelona,*** but he reserves the best of his colorful prose style for the city's architecture.

FICTION & POETRY

The classic historical epic of medieval Spain is ***The Lay of El Cid,*** the story of 11th-century Castilian nobleman Rodrigo Díaz de Vivar, one of Alfonso VI's chief generals in the battle against the Moors. The tales have been retold innumerable times in both poetry and prose. Of course, the one piece of Spanish fiction most people know is ***Don Quixote,*** by Miguel de Cervantes. The sometimes comic knight tilting at windmills remains a touchstone of Spanish identity—and Cervantes's prose (along with Lope de Vega's), the foundation of modern Spanish.

No less fanciful, though hardly as well written, Washington Irving's ***Tales of the Alhambra*** makes amusing reading while in Granada. Irving actually knew Spain well, but he couldn't stop himself from romanticizing the past.

Of course, Spain for Americans often means the novels of Ernest Hemingway. The best of the lot as literature is certainly ***The Sun Also Rises,*** and its depictions of running the bulls in Pamplona and drinking oneself to oblivion in Madrid do have a timeless quality. ***Death in the Afternoon*** may be the best book yet written by an American about the bullfight, while ***For Whom the Bell Tolls*** contains a

Spain Books for Children

The children's classic of Spain is **Platero y Yo,** by Juan Ramón Jiménez, available in English translation as **Platero and I.** Highly evocative of small-town life in southern Spain in the early 20th century, the narrator's donkey, Platero, is the star. It's good for middle-school children—or for learning to read Spanish. For small children, look for the illustrated book, **The Story of Ferdinand,** by Munro Leaf, illustrated by Richard Lawson. The protagonist is a little bull who likes to sniff the flowers in the meadow but is mistakenly sent to a bullfight in Madrid. Don't worry—it has a happy ending.

chilling account of the role that the gorge in Ronda played in the struggle between sides in the Spanish Civil War.

Set in post–Civil War Barcelona, the bestselling **The Shadow of the Wind,** by Carlos Ruiz Zafón, captures the claustrophobic terror of life under Franco. Fans of the intellectual thriller should seek out the Spain-based novels of Arturo Pérez-Reverte, including **The Club Dumas** (a Spanish book detective seeking to authen-ticate a manuscript fragment from *The Three Musketeers*), **The Flanders Panel** (a young Madrid art restorer stumbles into 500 years of repeating murders), and **Seville Communion** (investigating a hacker's breach of Vatican computers).

FILM

Ever since Pedro Almodóvar broke into the art-house circuit with his 1988 **Women on the Verge of a Nervous Breakdown**—a wild comedy about Spanish women and their man problems—the director has been the flag-bearer of contemporary cinema in Spain. Hallmarks of his films include neurotic but oversexed characters, unsettling mother-son relationships, and the leitmotifs of the death dance of the bullfight and the exuberant emotion of flamenco. His work is seen by critics (and many filmgoers) as defining modern Spanish sensibilities. As Almodóvar himself observed, "I was born at a bad time for Spain, but a really good one for cinema." Other essential Almodóvar films include **Tie Me Up! Tie Me Down!** (1990), **Kika** (1993), **All about my Mother** (1999), and **Volver** (2006).

Filmmaker Carlos Sauros, while expounding a more conventional style, is probably the other major figure in modern Spanish cinema. His flamenco tril-ogy—adaptations of Lorca's **Bodas de Sangre (Blood Wedding),** Bizet's **Carmen,** and Manuel de Falla's **El Amor Brujo (A Love Bewitched)**—represent a highly charged picture of modern Spain seen through three classic tales of love triangles.

The ABCs of Spain

Tourist information Apart from this book, the most comprehensive source for information about Spanish travel is the Tourist Office of Spain (www.okspain. org). To request brochures and travel guides, contact one of the following offices:

U.S.: 666 Fifth Ave., 35th Floor, New York, NY 10103 (☎ 212/265-8822); 845 N. Michigan Ave., Suite 915E, Chicago, IL

60611 (☎ 312/642-1992); 8383 Wilshire Blvd., Suite 956, Beverly Hills, CA 90211 (☎ 323/658-7188); 1395 Brickell Ave., Suite 1130, Miami, FL 33131 (☎ 305/358-1992)

Canada: 2 Bloor St. W., Suite 3402, Toronto, ON M4W 3E2 (☎ 416/961-3131)

UK: 79 New Cavendish St., 2nd Floor, London W1W 6XB (☎ 020-7486-8077)

We've also had good luck getting more on-the-ground detail from the individual tourist offices listed in each of the chapters. To augment the boosterish official views of the tourist offices, we're partial to the commercial websites of SoftGuides (www.softguide-spain.com) and AllaboutSpain (www.red2000.com). Just bear in mind that they make their money by booking lodging, so take the hotel information with a grain of salt.

Business hours Major stores are open Monday through Saturday 9:30am to 8pm, but smaller shops often take a siesta and are open 9:30am to 1:30pm and 4:30 to 8pm. Most offices are open Monday through Friday 9am to 5 or 5:30pm. In restaurants, lunch is usually from 1 to 4pm and dinner from 9 to 11:30pm or midnight. Bars, taverns, and cafeterias have no fixed opening hours. Many are ready for business at 8am, others at noon. Most stay open until 1:30am or later.

Electricity Spain uses 220–240 volts AC (50 cycles), which is standard in Europe, Australia, and New Zealand. Travelers from North America, where 110–120 volts (60 cycles) is standard, will need plug adapters for computers and other small appliances with universal transformers and voltage converters for other appliances.

Embassies All embassies are located in Madrid. For additional information on regional consular offices, check www.spain.info. **Australia:** Pl. del Descubridor Diego de Ordás 3; ☎ 913-536-600; www.spain.embassy.gov.au. **Canada:** Núñez de Balboa 35; ☎ 914-233-250; www.canada-es.org. **Ireland:** Paseo de la Castellana 46, 4th Floor,

Ireland House; ☎ 914-364-093. **New Zealand:** Pl. de la Lealtad 2, 3rd Floor; ☎ 915-230-226; www.nzembassy.com/home.cfm?c=27. **United Kingdom:** Fernando El Santo 16; ☎ 917-008-200; www.ukinspain.com. **United States:** Serrano 75; ☎ 915-872-303; www.embusa.es.

Emergencies For any emergency in Spain, call 112.

Language What the rest of the world calls Spanish, Spaniards call Castellano (that is, the language of Castile). It is the official national language and is spoken throughout the country, though other local languages (and hard-to-decipher Spanish dialects) may dominate casual conversation. Other languages coexist with Spanish: Catalán in Catalonia, Galician in Galicia, Euskera/Basque in the Basque country, Valencian in the València region, and a particular variety of Catalán spoken on the Balearic Islands. In most parts of Spain, the most useful second language is English, followed by French. English is almost universally spoken by people in the tourist industries.

Mail The Spanish postal system is Los Correos, and you'll have to go to the post office to mail almost anything beyond a letter or postcard. Most hotel front desks will sell you stamps and take care of dispatching your notes home. Stores with the big brown-and-yellow TABACO signs (which, indeed, sell tobacco products) are estancos, which sell stamps for the same price as the post office does.

Pharmacies Pharmacies are usually open from 9:30am to 1:30pm and 4:30 to 8pm, though in the larger cities a certain number remain open 24 hours. There is a listing displayed outside pharmacies and published in the daily press indicating which pharmacy is covering night or weekend service on a given date.

Restrooms Public toilets are generally available in restaurants, museums, and municipal buildings throughout Spain.

Public beaches also usually have free restrooms and changing rooms. Do not, however, expect public restrooms, even for patrons, at bars and cafes.

Taxes The value-added tax (IVA) rate in Spain is 16% for most goods and services. Nonresidents of the European Union can claim a tax refund on purchases, as long as they exceed 90€. *You must ask for a tax-free receipt at the point of sale and show proof of non-EU residence. Also ask for the forms for a company authorized to handle rebates.* When leaving Spain, show your purchases and have Customs stamp the tax-free receipts. Claim the amount due from the company processing the claim. They all have IVA reimbursement points at the main Spanish airports and borders, for payment in cash.

Telephone To call Spain, first dial the international access code: 011 from the U.S.; 00 from the U.K., Ireland, or New Zealand; or 0011 from Australia. Then dial the country code, 34, followed by the nine-digit number, which includes the city code. To make international calls from Spain, dial 00 and then the country code (U.S. or Canada 1, U.K. 44, Ireland 353, Australia 61, New Zealand 64). Next dial the area code and number. For directory assistance, dial ☎ 1003 in Spain. If you need operator assistance in making an international call, dial ☎ 025. Numbers beginning with 900 in Spain are toll-free, but calling an 800 number in the States from Spain is not toll-free. When calling within Spain, be sure to use the full nine-digit number. Note that many small Spanish establishments (bars, discos, tiny attractions) do not have phones. For more information on the Spanish phone system check the Telefónica website: www. telefonica.es.

Time The time zone on the Spanish mainland and the Balearic Islands is Greenwich Mean Time (GMT) plus 1 hour in winter and plus 2 hours in summer. Spain changes its time between summer and winter for daylight saving time. On the last weekend in October, clocks go back 1 hour; the last weekend in March, they go forward 1 hour.

12 The Art & Culture of Spain

by Patricia Harris & David Lyon

CUISINE & DINING IN SPAIN

THE RHYTHM OF LIFE IN SPAIN IS THE RHYTHM OF MEALTIMES. IF YOU WANT to understand the culture from the inside out, try eating like a Spaniard—or at least on a Spanish schedule. As you probably already know, Spaniards usually eat lunch between 2pm and 4pm, and it's easier to adjust to this afternoon hiatus than you might think. (If you get hungry in the late morning, join the Spaniards in a cafe for a quick coffee and pastry.) You'll soon discover that the late lunch provides a good break from the summer heat and that many shops and museums are closed anyway. In fact, you'll probably be eating with the shopkeepers and museum staff who are taking advantage of the *menu del dia,* a three-course meal with wine and coffee at a low fixed price. Whether you choose a top restaurant or a little neighborhood spot, these bargain menus are a great way to sample unfamiliar dishes and save money at the same time. When you get up from the table, you'll be ready to continue your day and probably enjoy it more.

Visitors often find it more difficult to adapt to the Spanish habit of eating dinner at 10pm or later. But tapas fill the gap—and can even make a fine meal if you really can't wait. Tapas time (usually 7–9pm) is an institution of peripatetic socializing—entertainment and sustenance rolled into one. Stand at the bar to sample a small plate of the house specialty along with a glass of beer or wine, rub elbows with locals, and then move on to the next place. Just be careful: The cost of a long evening of tapas and drinks can add up.

MENU NOTES

Served in humble truck stops and elegant restaurants, the ***tortilla española*** is truly Spain's national dish. Although there are as many variations as there are cooks, it usually consists of fried onions and potatoes mixed with eggs and then cooked until set. The typical round tortilla is about 2 inches thick and is cut into wedges. You'll find it served hot, cold, and at room temperature on breakfast, lunch, and dinner menus and as a tapa. It's both reasonably priced and filling.

But it's boring to live on eggs and potatoes alone when there are so many great Spanish dishes. Apart from the versatile tortilla, most Spanish cooking is regional, reflecting local products and historical influences. Here's a short guide to some of the principal ingredients and preparation styles of Spanish cuisine.

Fish *(Pescados)*

Spain has Europe's longest coastline and some of its richest fisheries, so Spaniards eat a lot of fish. The closest thing to a national fish is ***bacalao,*** which is dried, salted Atlantic cod that has been soaked to flush out the salt and rehydrate the flesh. The Basques grew rich as cod fishermen, so it's no surprise that there are dozens of traditional *bacalao* recipes in the Basque country. But *bacalao* is also the principal fish on the menu in inland Spain. If you're unfamiliar with salt cod, try it first in a diluted form as fried *bacalao*-potato croquettes or *bacalao*-stuffed roasted red peppers.

Spaniards also consume prodigious quantities of **yellowfin tuna** *(atún),* much of it landed from day boats at Barbate, south of Cádiz on the Atlantic coast. The tuna is usually sushi grade and is often served raw *(cruda).* It's a perfect counterpoint to a dry sherry. Some of the best yellowfin tuna is reserved for making *mojama,* a salt-cured, air-dried tuna jerky that's been a specialty of the Cádiz coast since the Phoenician era. Order a small plate (it can be expensive) to enjoy with beer. Chefs all over Spain use yellowfin tuna canned in olive oil—a richly flavored product vastly different from, say, white albacore tuna canned in water. Look for it crumbled on top of a salad or stuffed into roasted red peppers.

Wonderful wild-caught **trout** graces the menus in La Rioja, the Basque country, Navarre, and parts of Catalonia and Andalusia. One of the classic preparations *(trucha a la Navarra)* features roasted trout stuffed with bacon and topped with a little melted cheese. If you're in the Basque country during the winter eel season, don't miss trying *angulas a la Bilbaína,* which are baby eels "as tiny as bean sprouts" (as Hemingway wrote) quickly fried with lots of garlic.

Shellfish *(Mariscos)*

Spain's north coast along the Bay of Biscay yields a wealth of cold-water shellfish, from the big **spider crabs** of Basque country to the rich **scallops** of Galicia. The scallop shell is the symbol of St. James, or Santiago, and one of the most famous preparations is called *vieras de Santiago.* The scallops are sautéed with mushrooms, chili pepper, and herbs; doused with a little brandy; returned to their shells; and baked under a light tomato sauce. The perfect complement is a dry white Albariño wine from Galicia's Rías Baixas region. The **goose barnacle,** or *percebe,* another cold-water crustacean from Galicia, is highly prized in gourmet restaurants across Spain. It looks like a fat straw with a tiny hoof sticking out. You eat a *percebe* by pinching at the top near the "hoof," prying off the skin, and biting the fleshy stalk, which tastes much like crab. When you find them in Madrid, they're usually served with a dip of *aioli* (garlicky mayonnaise) on the side.

The warm oceans of southern Spain, on the other hand, yield the country's finest crustaceans. The tidal estuaries of the Atlantic coast in Cádiz and Huelva provinces are the ideal breeding grounds for nearly a dozen species of **shrimp** and **prawns,** and they're among the finest flavored in the world. When the season begins around Easter, Spaniards from across the country make the pilgrimage to Cádiz and its surrounding towns to eat huge plates of shrimp steamed or quickly grilled with garlic and olive oil. Fortunately, the crustaceans also travel well and are shipped live to Madrid and Barcelona all summer, where diners consume plate after plate of them in taverns and outdoor cafes. For a rundown on what to call some of the different shellfish, see "Crustacean Confusion" (p. 200).

Meat *(Carnes)*

Beef-eaters often find Spain disappointing because only isolated pockets of the country are suited for grazing beef cattle. If you're craving **beef,** your best bet is a rich casserole of braised beef called *rabo de toro,* served almost everywhere. Most cafes also serve small, tough, fried *bistec,* usually with fried eggs and a salad. One pocket of central Spain, however, serves meat with flavor and texture that rivals Argentine beef: In and around Avila, look for *chuletón de Ávila,* a T-bone steak to satisfy the most discriminating carnivore.

Pork is the most common meat in Spain. Whenever a menu specifies the cut (like a chop or steak) but not the meat, it's pork. It will invariably be cooked just slightly too much because Spaniards *like* their meat overcooked and heavily salted.

Keep this in mind when you indulge in the fantastic **lamb** of central Spain. If it's noted as *lechal* on the menu, it's so young that it hasn't started grazing for itself. To preserve the tenderness, ask your waiter to have the chef go easy on the salt and grill those tiny chops only until they're pink in the middle.

Both **milk-fed lamb** and **milk-fed piglet** are specialties of many restaurants in central Spain as well as in La Rioja and the Basque country. In central Spain, they're roasted in special wood-fired brick ovens that produce a searing heat. In the north, they're often spit-roasted over open charcoal. If four to six people order the dish, you'll get a whole pig or lamb served at the table—which some diners find thrilling and others off-putting. Most restaurants will also provide single servings.

Hams & Sausages

While the Spanish do put sweet, juicy slices of **baked ham** *(jamón York)* on sandwiches, they reserve a special passion for the air-dried, salt-cured mountain hams called *jamón serrano.* Most bars and cafes have a whole leg sitting on the counter and several more hanging overhead. Paper-thin slices are a popular but expensive tapa. Hams known as *jamón ibérico* must be made from the black-footed Iberian pig, which has spent its life in a semi-feral state dining primarily on acorns. A plate of *ibérico* will cost two to three times a plate of *serrano.* To an aficionado, it's worth the splurge.

Spain has as many sausages as it has villages, but you'll often find three main types: Served in slices as a tapa or chunked into stews and casseroles, *chorizo* contains ground and sliced meats with a great deal of garlic and sweet paprika. (Unlike Latin American chorizo, it's rarely hot.) *Morcilla,* often a hot tapa or crumbled with eggs, is a blood sausage. *Butifarra* is a Catalán white sausage typically spiced with cinnamon, nutmeg, and cloves.

Rice

Real **paella** originated in València, where the local short-grained rice is an essential ingredient. The modern *paella a la Valenciana* is a dish of saffron-infused rice studded with cooked chicken, chorizo sausage, cockles, mussels, clams, shrimp, and even lobster. You will find it all over Spain. (The traditional Valencian version, a delicacy that is rare outside València province, features rabbit, green beans, and snails.) Done properly with short-grained Valencian rice and generous quantities of La Mancha saffron, and cooked to produce a thick golden crust *(soccarat)* on the bottom, modern *paella a la Valenciana* is a transporting dish. Alas, it's rarely prepared properly outside of València, Murcia, and coastal Catalonia.

The Cataláns have their own repertoire of rice dishes, many of them made the same way as paella—in an uncovered shallow iron pan to keep the rice from steaming. The classic *arroz a la catalana* is made like a paella but also incorporates *butifarra* sausage, rabbit, and pork ribs. ***Arroz negro,*** or "black rice," is yet another paella-style dish, which uses squid ink and fish broth. The squid itself is served in rings and pieces atop the rice. It is a dish of surprisingly subtle flavors, even when topped with the traditional sauce of raw garlic pureed in olive oil.

Soups, Stews & Casseroles

Seafood stews are close relatives to paella. Along the Bay of Biscay, the Basque ***marmitako*** is a stew of bonito tuna, tomato, roasted red peppers, onions, and potato traditionally served aboard Basque fishing vessels but now a staple of restaurants. The stew known as ***zarzuela*** (literally a musical comedy) is a Catalán invention of mixed seafood in a tomato base, now served all over Spain. These seafood stews can be thought of as the country cousins of Provençal bouillabaisse, and are just as filling.

Northern Spain is famed for its hearty bean dishes, which are considered a whole meal. ***Fabada,*** also known as *fabas asturianas,* is a salty white bean stew with ham and sausage. ***Caldo Gallego,*** a Galician soup of white beans, potatoes, chorizo, and shredded greens in beef stock, is a proven body-warmer during cold, raw winters. The most famous of the hearty casseroles, however, is ***cocido,*** especially *cocido Madrileño.* Beans sometimes fill out this hearty stew of sausages and mixed cuts of meat, usually including tripe and other organ meats.

Cheese

Virtually every village where someone milks cows, goats, or sheep has its own style of cheese, but surprisingly few Spanish cheeses get national distribution. The best-known and most widely consumed is ***queso Manchego,*** the nutty sheep's milk cheese from the plains of La Mancha. Most Manchegos served in thin triangular slices as tapas are *semi-curados,* meaning that they've been aged for 6 months. Aficionados favor the much more expensive ***curados,*** aged more than a year to develop a sharper, more intense flavor. In the north, the similar ***Roncal*** cheese, a blend of cow's and sheep's milk from the Pyrenees, often fills the same role as Manchego. The distinctive ***Idiázabel,*** often offered on cheese plates and sometimes melted on savory dishes, is a smoked sheep's milk cheese from Basque country. Cabrales is Spain's contribution to the great blue cheeses of the world. Made from cow's milk in Asturias, it is typically stronger but smoother (and less bitter) than a French Roquefort. It appears on cheese plates and is sometimes smeared on toast as a tapa.

A PRIMER OF SPANISH ARTS & CULTURE

Like Spanish cuisine, Spanish arts belong strongly to the European tradition—but with a substantial seasoning from the cultures of North Africa, and, in the case of Spanish music, from the Near East and South Asia.

ARCHITECTURE

Most Spanish architecture differs little from the rest of Europe. **Romanesque** churches abound in Catalonia and along the northern pilgrim route to Santiago. **Gothic** churches and castles, especially in the north, are close cousins to their French counterparts. The **neoclassicism** of the 18th and 19th centuries infected

Spain along with the rest of Europe. But certain Spanish architectural styles are unique:

Moorish architecture evolved in Spain from a basically Middle Eastern and Arabic style that featured lavish surface decoration in abstract patterns based on calligraphy, geometry, and leafy vines. But Moorish architecture also borrowed from indigenous Spanish styles, adopting the horseshoe arch from the Visigoths. The first of the ornate Moorish styles reached its zenith in the 10th-century Umayyad dynasty, with the construction of **La Mezquita in Córdoba.** Later Moorish styles, such as the 12th- and 13th-century Almohad style evident in parts of the **Alcázar in Seville,** are far less decorative, in keeping with the fundamentalist austerity of the Berber kingdoms. Decoration and dazzling visual sophistication came back into style with the 13th- to 15th-century Nasrid dynasty in Granada, resulting in one of the visual wonders of Spain, the palaces of the **Alhambra** and **Generalife.**

Mudéjar architecture and surface decoration is perhaps the greatest synthesis of the various cultures of Spain. It is essentially a reinterpretation of European late Gothic and Renaissance styles through Islamic and Jewish eyes. Characterized by the extensive use of painted tiles, carved plaster, and stone surfaces, and carved and sometimes painted wooden-coffered ceilings, Mudéjar architecture was largely created by Moriscos—Muslims who remained in Spain after the Reconquista. The Mudéjar style dates from the 12th century up to the expulsion of the Moriscos in 1609–10. It is so much a part of the identity of Spain, however, that it enjoyed a brief revival in the 1890s, and even modern buildings sometimes reference Mudéjar decoration.

Spanish baroque differs from Italian or French in its extremity and its longevity. In many parts of Spain, architecture went straight from late Gothic to baroque as early as the late 16th century, and Spanish baroque churches were still being constructed into the mid-19th century. Exuberant sculpture and twisting, vine-like columns characterize the most extreme form, known as Churriguesque after the Churriguera family of architects from Salamanca (p. 124). Seville is practically an open-air museum of Spanish baroque.

Modernisme was a largely Catalán phenomenon contemporary with late 19th-century Art Nouveau but far more structural and less simply decorative than its French cousin. The principal examples of this organic style that introduced the parabolic curve to modern architecture are the masterpieces in Barcelona by Lluís Domènech í Montaner (1850–1923) and Antoni Gaudí (1852–1926).

VISUAL ART

Judging by the Cantabrian caves of **Altamira** (14,500–12,000 B.C.; p. 421), Spanish painting started early. From about 2000 B.C. until 500 B.C., pockets of artistic expression popped up around the country, usually mimicking styles from elsewhere in the Mediterranean basin. From 500 B.C. onward, Spanish art adopted the classical Greek and Roman styles of its colonizers and rulers. A distinctive Spanish style did not appear until about A.D. 1000 in Catalonia. By A.D. 1200, Catalán artists had already begun to make limited use of vanishing-point perspective and shadowing—innovations that would not appear more widely in European art for centuries to come. The surviving examples can be found in Barcelona's **Museu Nacional d'Art de Catalunya.**

Spain was so slow to adopt the Renaissance (most Renaissance painting was imported from Italy and the Low Countries), that the first great Spanish painter was Doménicos Theotokópoulos, born in Crete and known as **El Greco** (1540–1614). His work is scattered around Spain, but the largest concentrations are found at the Museo del Prado in Madrid and throughout Toledo.

The 17th century was Spain's first artistic Golden Age. **Diego Velázquez** (1599–1660) became Felipe IV's court painter as a young man and produced his greatest works—almost all portraiture—in the royal employ. The paintings were later deposited in the Prado, where several galleries are devoted exclusively to Velázquez. His masterpiece *Las Meninas* (1654) remains one of the most influential paintings in the history of European art.

Velázquez had three prolific contemporaries whose work you'll find not only in museums, but also in churches and some convents. **José de Ribera** (1591–1652) excelled in earthy depictions of religious scenes and seems to have made a specialty of somber crucifixions and renderings of the hermit saint, San Jerónimo. The dim lighting and deep shadows make his work instantly identifiable, even at a great distance. Similarly somber, **Francisco de Zurbarán** (1598–1664) painted with greater sensuality, often lighting the figures in his paintings with candlelight. Many of his greatest series were painted for monasteries where he was said to have used the monks as models for portraits of saints and martyrs. While many works are still found in religious buildings, his major works are in the Prado in Madrid and in the Museo de Bellas Artes in Seville. It has been said that Zurbarán painted for abbots, while his Seville contemporary and competitor **Bartolomé Esteban Murillo** painted for bishops. Murillo's style is brighter, softer, and often downright sweet, and his palette is full of pastels. While his paintings seem ubiquitous in Seville, some of the best are in the Museo de Bellas Artes.

Francisco de Goya (1746–1828) stands with Velázquez and Picasso in the triumvirate of Spain's greatest artists. His early work—especially his bucolic scenes created for tapestries—is frothy and decorative, but his style matured into unflinching realism. The Spanish struggle against French invaders in the early 19th century spurred Goya to paint some of the most harrowing and emotionally charged paintings seen in Europe to that time. The best of Goya's work is found in Madrid at the Prado, as well as in the small museum of the Real Academia de Bellas Artes de San Fernando.

The tragic political history of Spain in the 20th century meant that the country's greatest artists did most of their work outside the country. The colossus among giants was **Pablo Picasso** (1881–1973), who, simply said, changed everything. He was so prolific and worked in so many styles that one phase or another of his art is a touchstone for every modern artist. Many of his early works are housed in Barcelona's Museu Picasso, while an abbreviated survey of his life's work can be found in the Museo Picasso Málaga. The Centro de Arte Reina Sofía in Madrid also has a number of his works, most notably the iconic *Guernica,* his polemical 1937 painting protesting Franco's destruction of a small Basque town.

Juan Gris (1887–1927) co-founded Cubism with his countryman Picasso and the Frenchman Georges Braque. Perhaps owing to his work drawing political satire for magazines, Gris employed both a brighter palette and a wittier approach than either of his fellow painters. Although he died young, Gris is credited with infusing cubism with an emotional charge that lay the groundwork for surrealism.

Although he was shunned by most of the Surrealist movement for his reactionary politics, the showman **Salvador Dalí** ultimately became the most famous surrealist of all, employing a hyper-realist painting style to explore a world of fantasy and nightmare. While many of his works can be found in the Perrot-Moore Museum in Cadaqués and the Centro de Arte Reina Sofía in Madrid, fans of the artist must visit Figueres in Catalonia to see the grandly conceptual museum of his ego, the Teatro Dalí.

Nominally a surrealist (he signed the Surrealist Manifesto of 1924), **Joan Miró** (1893–1983) was more a poet of color than a dream-weaver. His sense of form owes more to the cave paintings of Neolithic Spain than to any of his contemporaries, and his lyric celebration of color is unmatched in modern abstract art. His vision is all the more powerful taken in large doses. The perfect spot is the Fundació Joan Miró in Barcelona, a one-man museum designed by his friend and fellow Catalán, the great moderniste architect Josep Lluis Sert.

Spanish art after World War II embraced Abstract Impressionism, with **Antoni Tàpies** (1923–) emerging as the most famous Spanish painter. His Fundació Tàpies in Barcelona offers a good overview of his work, which remains influential with contemporary Spanish painters.

FLAMENCO

The flowing skirts, ringing guitars, and staccato dance steps of flamenco are so utterly Spanish that any TV commercial striving to evoke Iberia invariably opens with them. Ironically, the roots of this "Spanish" music and dance stretch back thousands of years and as far away as the Arabian Peninsula and northern India. Flamenco as we know it finally coalesced in Andalusia in the early 19th century from several folk traditions. Aside from adding a few extra rhythms (like the rumba from Cuba), it has been passed down intact through teaching by example.

As the music of left-leaning Andalusia, flamenco was discouraged under Franco's dictatorship from the 1930s into the 1970s, and many flamenco artists went underground or abroad. Flamenco survived inside Spain as tourist dinner shows and in informal gatherings in private clubs. But the art was reborn after Franco's death in 1975. The emergence of guitar maestro Paco de Lucía and Gypsy singer Camerón de la Isla in the early 1980s galvanized the scene, and their styles remain the benchmark of the flamenco revival.

Flamenco's stock has risen so far that festivals with concert-hall performances have become common. But it is also a staple of evening entertainment in Madrid and throughout Andalusia. There are several ways you can experience flamenco. *Tablaos* are nightclubs that produce scripted revues geared to a tourist clientele. They're a good way to see a variety of dancers and musicians, and while aficionados scoff at the lack of spontaneity, many fans (us included) were first hooked on the art by one of these tourist shows. Most try to sell you an overpriced dinner before the show. Skip the meal and pay a much lower admission charge (25€–35€), which usually includes a drink, for the performance alone.

If you're extremely lucky, you may encounter an authentic *peña,* a club of flamenco aficionados dedicated to promoting the art form and discovering young performers. Most *peñas* are restricted to their members, but some have an occasional night for the general public (5€–15€). Public flamenco nightclubs like Madrid's famous Casa Patas (p. 72) are the next best alternative to a *peña.* They present a changing roster of performers, with well-known recording artists on the weekends and performers still making a name for themselves on weeknights. The admission charge (20€–35€) is justified by the high quality of the acts. The least expensive (free to 10€) and most informal flamenco takes place in smoky bars and taverns, where a small troupe performs around midnight. (See the "Nightlife" sections in this book for recommendations.)

Flamenco is unusual in combining the four elements of song, music, dance, and percussion. And while every advertisement for flamenco features a woman in a ruffled skirt striking a dramatic pose, traditionally the most important performer is the singer. (You'll easily grasp the mood of the music if not the actual lyrics.) The other essential performer is the guitarist, who historically strummed chords but today is more likely to play complex solos. Dancers are also important in most styles, though some forms of flamenco, like the *malagueña,* are never danced. All members of the company supply rhythm with *compas* (hand-clapping), and most groups also have a percussionist who sits on and plays the *cajón,* a wooden drum.

Each region of Andalusia has its signature style, but there are three traditional *palos* (forms) that you'll experience in most performances. The *soleá* is a slow, mournful style with haunting vocals, spare and stylized guitar, and very restrained but emotive dancing. The *alegría,* as the name "joy" suggests, is brighter, and is characterized by complex guitar solos, shifting rhythms, and intricate dancing. Most flamenco performances end with a *bulería,* a double-time exuberant style native to Jerez. If there are several dancers, the *bulería* will showcase each one in turn and usually ends with all dancers performing simultaneously with thunderous footwork.

13 Useful Terms & Phrases

MOST SPANIARDS ARE VERY PATIENT WITH FOREIGNERS WHO TRY TO SPEAK their language. Although you might encounter several regional languages and dialects in Spain, Castilian Spanish (*castellano* or simply *español*) is understood everywhere. In Catalonia, they speak *catalán* (the most widely spoken non-national language in Europe); in the Basque country, they speak *euskera;* in Galicia, you'll hear *gallego*. Still, a few words in Castilian will usually get your message across with no problem.

Basic Words and Phrases

ENGLISH	SPANISH	PRONUNCIATION
Hello.	**Hola.**	*oh*-lah
Goodbye	**Adiós**	ah-*dyohs*
Good morning.	**Buenos días.**	*bweh*-nohs *dee*-ahs
Good evening.	**Buenas noches.**	*bweh*-nahs *noh*-chehs
Good afternoon.	**Buenas tardes.**	*bweh*-nahs *tahr*-dehs
Good night.	**Buenas noches.**	*bweh*-nahs *noh*-chehs
How are you?	**¿Cómo está?**	*koh*-moh ehs-*tah*
I'm fine, thanks.	**Estoy bien, gracias**	ehs-*toy byehn*, *grah*-syahs
My name is ____.	**Me llamo ____.**	meh *yah*-mo
And yours?	**¿Y usted?**	ee oos-*tehd*
Please.	**Por favor.**	pohr fah-*vohr*
Excuse me	**Perdóneme**	pehr-*doh*-neh-meh
Thank you.	**Gracias.**	*grah*-syahs
You're welcome	**De nada**	deh *nah*-dah
Yes.	**Sí.**	*see*
No.	**No.**	*noh*
Good	**Bueno**	*bweh*-noh
Bad	**Malo**	*mah*-loh
Better (Best)	**(Lo) Mejor**	(loh) meh-*hor*
More	**Más**	mahs
Less	**Menos**	*meh*-nohs
I'm sorry, I don't understand	**Lo siento, no entiendo.**	loh *syehn*-toh no ehn-*tyehn*-doh
Would you speak slower please?	**¿Puede hablar un poco más lento?**	*pweh*-deh ah-*blahr* oon *poh*koh mahs *lehn*-to
Would you please repeat that?	**¿Puede repetir, por favor?**	*pweh*-deh rreh-peh-*teer* pohr fah-*vohr*
Do you speak English?	**¿Usted habla inglés?**	oos-*tehd* ah-blah eeng-*glehs*

509

Key Questions

With the right hand gestures, you can get a lot of mileage from the following list of single-word questions and answers.

ENGLISH	SPANISH	PRONUNCIATION
Who?	¿Quién? ¿Quiénes?	*kyehn? kyeh*-nehs?
What?	¿Qué?	*keh*
When?	¿Cuándo?	*kwahn*-doh
Where?	¿Dónde?	*dohn*-deh
How do I get to ___?	¿Cómo llego a ___?	*koh*-moh *yeh*-goh ah
Why?	¿Por qué?	pohr-*keh*
How?	¿Cómo?	*koh*-moh
Which?	¿Cuál?	*kwahl*
How much is it?	¿Cuánto cuesta?	*kwahn*-toh *kwehs*-tah
What time is it?	¿Qué hora es?	keh *oh*-rah es

Useful Phrases for Transportation & Directions

ENGLISH	SPANISH	PRONUNCIATION
To the right	A la derecha	ah lah deh-*reh*-chah
To the left	A la izquierda	ah lah ees-*kyehr*-dah
Straight ahead	Derecho	deh-*reh*-choh
Go straight.	Siga directo.	*see*-gah dee-*rehk*-toh
Next to	al lado de	ahl *lah*-doh deh
Down	abajo	ah-*bah*-hoh
Up	arriba	ah-*rre*-bah
Behind	detras de	deh-*trahs* deh
I am looking for ___	Estoy buscando ___	ehs-*toy* boos-*kahn*-doh
the check-in counter.	el mostrador de registro.	ehl mohs-trah-*dohr* deh reh-*hees*-troh
the ticket counter.	el mostrador de ventas de boletos.	ehl mohs-trah-*dohr* deh *vehn*tahs deh boh-*leh*-tohs
the men's restroom.	el baño para caballeros.	ehl *bah*-nyoh *pah*-rah kah-bah-*yeh*-rohs
the women's restroom.	el baño para damas.	ehl *bah*-nyoh *pah*-rah *dah*-mahs
the police station.	la estación de policías.	lah ehs-tah-*syohn* deh pohlee-*see*-ahs
the post office	el correo	ehl koh-*rreh*-oh
an ATM.	un cajero automático.	oon kah-*heh*-roh ow-toh-*mah*tee-koh
Can you show me on the map?	¿Puede mostrarme en el mapa?	*pweh*-deh mohs-*trahr*-meh ehn ehl *mah*-pah
How far is it from here?	¿Cuán lejos está de aquí?	kwahn *leh*-hohs ehs-*tah* deh ah-*kee*

ENGLISH	SPANISH	PRONUNCIATION
Am I close enough to walk?	¿Estoy suficiente-mente cerca como para caminar?	ehs-*toy* soo-fee-syehn-teh-*mehn*teh *sehr*-kah koh-moh pah rah kah-mee-*nahr*
Is this the right road for___?	¿Es ésta la carretera correcta para ____?	ehs *ehs*-tah lah kah-rreh-*teh*-rah koh-*rrehk*-tah *pah*-rah
How do I get to___?	¿Cómo llego a___	*koh*-moh yeh-goh ah
the train station	la estación del tren?	lah ehs-tah-*syohn* dehl trehn
the bus station	la estación de autobuses	lah ehs-tah-*syohn* deh ow-toh-*boo*-sehs
the subway station	la estación de metro	ehs-*tah* lah ehs-tah-
When is the next train?	¿Cuándo sale el próximo tren?	*kwahn*-doh *sah*-leh ehl *prohk*see- moh trehn
Do you have a schedule/timetable	¿Tiene un itinerario?	*tyeh*-neh oon ee-tee-neh-*rah*-ryoh
Do I have to change trains?	¿Tengo que cambiar trenes?	*tehng*-goh keh kahm-*byahr treh*-nehs
a one-way ticket	un boleto de ida	oon boh-*leh*-toh deh *ee*-dah
a round-trip ticket	un boleto de ida y vuelta	oon boh-*leh*-toh deh *ee*-dah ee *vwehl*-tah
Which platform does it leave from?	¿De cuál plataforma sale?	deh kwahl plah-tah-*fohr*-mah *sah*-leh
Is this seat taken?	¿Este asiento está ocupado?	*ehs*-teh ah-*syehn*-toh ehs-*tah* oh-koo-*pah*-doh

Lodgings Phrases

ENGLISH	SPANISH	PRONUNCIATION
I would like ____	Quisiera ____	kee-*syeh*-rah
a king-sized bed.	una cama king.	*oo*-nah *kah*-mah keeng
a double bed.	una cama doble.	*oo*-nah *kah*-mah *doh*-bleh
twin beds.	dos camas individuales.	dohs *kah*-mahs een-dee-vee-*dwahl*-ehs
adjoining rooms.	habitaciones adjuntas.	ah-bee-tah-*syoh*-nehs ad-*hoon*-tahs
a smoking room.	una habitación de fumar.	*oo*-nah ah-bee-tah-*syohn* deh foo-*mahr*
a non-smoking room.	una habitación de no fumar.	*oo*-nah ah-bee-tah-*syohn* deh noh foo-*mahr*
a private bathroom.	un baño privado.	oon *bah*-nyoh pree-*vah*-doh
air conditioning.	aire acondicionado.	*aye*-reh ah-cohn-dee-syoh-*nah*-doh
Internet access.	acceso al Internet.	ahk-*seh*-soh ahl een-tehr-*neht*
a beach view.	vista a la playa.	*vees*-tah ah lah *plah*-yah
a kitchenette.	una cocina pequeña.	*oo*-nah koh-*see*-nah peh-*keh*-nyah
Do you have a crib?	¿Tiene una cuna?	Tyen-eh *oo*-nah *koo*-nah

ENGLISH	SPANISH	PRONUNCIATION
Do you have a foldout bed?	**Tiene una cama desplegable?**	tyen-eh oo-nah kah-mah dehs-pleh-gah-bleh
Do you have room service?	**¿Tienen servicio de habitaciones?**	tyeh-nehn sehr-vee-syoh deh ah-bee-tah-syoh-nehs
When is breakfast served?	**¿Cuándo se servirá el desayuno?**	kwahn-doh seh sehr-vee-rah ehl deh-sah-yoo-noh
I have a reservation.	**Tengo una reservación.**	tehng-goh oo-nah reh-sehr-vah-syohn
When is checkout time?	**¿Cuál es la hora de salida?**	kwahl ehs lah oh-rah deh sah-lee-dah
May I see a room?	**¿Puedo ver una habitación?**	pweh-doh vehr oo-nah ah-beetah-syohn
I'd like a different room.	**Quisiera una habitación diferente.**	kee-syeh-rah oo-nah ah-bee-tah-syohn dee-feh-rehn-teh
Do you have a bigger room?	**¿Tiene una habitación más grande?**	tyeh-neh oo-nah ah-bee-tah-syohn mahs grahn-deh
I'd like a wake up call.	**Quisiera una llamada para despertar.**	kee-syeh-rah oo-nah yah-mahdah pah-rah dehs-pehr-tahr
We are staying here only one night/ one week	**Nos quedamos aquí solamente una noche/ una semana**	nohs keh-dah-mohs ah-kee soh-lah-mehn-the oo-nah noh-cheh/ oo-nah seh-mah-nah
Is there a Laundromat near here?	**¿Hay una lavandería cerca de aquí?**	eye oo-nah lah-vahn-deh-ree-ah sehr-kah deh ah-kee

Dining Phrases

ENGLISH	SPANISH	PRONUNCIATION
Is there a late-night restaurant nearby?	**¿Hay un restaurante cercano abierto hasta tarde en la noche?**	aye oon reh-stoh-rahn-teh sehrkah-noh ah-byehr-toh ahs-tah tahr-deh ehn lah noh-cheh
Is there a restaurant that serves breakfast nearby?	**¿Hay un restaurante cercano que sirva desayuno?**	aye oon reh-stoh-rahn-teh sehrka-noh keh seer-vah deh-sah-yoo-noh
Is it very expensive?	**¿Es muy caro?**	ehs moo-ee kah-roh
Do I need a reservation?	**¿Necesito una reservación?**	neh-seh-see-toh oo-nah reh-sehrvah-syohn
Are you still serving?	**¿Todavía están sirviendo?**	toh-dah-vee-ah ehs-tahn seer-vyehn-doh
How long is the wait?	**¿Cuán larga es la espera?**	kwahn lahr-gah ehs lah ehs-peh-rah
Do you have a no-smoking section?	**¿Tienen una sección de no fumar?**	tyeh-nehn oo-nah sehk-syohn deh noh foo-mahr

77

ENGLISH	SPANISH	PRONUNCIATION
A table for ____, please.	Una mesa para ____, por favor.	oo-nah meh-sah pah-rah ____, pohr fah-vohr
May we sit outside/inside please?	¿Podemos sentarnos afuera/adentro por favor?	poh-deh-mohs sehn-tahr-nohs ah-fweh-rah/ah-dehn-troh pohr fah-vohr
A menu please?	¿Un menú por favor?	oon meh-noo pohr fah-vohr
What do you recommend?	¿Qué recomienda usted?	keh reh-koh-myehn-dah oos-tehd
On the side, please.	Al lado, por favor.	ahl lah-doh pohr fah-vohr
May I make a substitution?	¿Puedo hacer una sustitución?	pweh-doh ah-sehr oo-nah soostee-too-syohn
I'd like to try that.	Me gustaría probar eso.	meh goos-tah-ree-ah proh-bahr eh-soh
I'm sorry, I don't think this is what I ordered	Lo siento, no creo que esto sea lo que ordené.	loh syehn-toh noh kreh-oh keh ehs-toh seh-ah loh kehohr-deh-neh
Is the tip included?	¿La propina está incluida?	lah proh-pee-nah ehs-tah een-kloo-ee-dah
The meal is good.	Me gusta la comida.	meh goo-stah lah koh-mee-dah
Check, please.	El cheque, por favor.	ehl cheh-keh pohr fah-vohr

Money Matters

ENGLISH	SPANISH	PRONUNCIATION
Is there a service charge?	¿Hay un cargo por servicio?	ay oon kahr-goh pohr sehr-vees-yoh
Is there tax?	¿Hay un impuesto?	aye oon eem-pwehs-toh
Will you accept a credit card?	¿Aceptarían una tarjeta de crédito?	ah-sehp-tah-ree-ahn oo-nah tahr-heh-tah deh kreh-dee-toh
Can you make change?	¿Puede hacer cambio?	pweh-deh ah-sehr kahm-byoh
A receipt, please.	Un recibo, por favor.	oon reh-see-boh pohr fah-vohr
Do I get a discount if I pay in cash?	¿Me da un descuento si pago en efectivo?	meh dah oon desh-kwehn-toh see pah-goh ehn eh-fehk-tee-voh
Do you have a less expensive one?	¿Tiene uno -a menos caro -a?	tyeh-neh oon/oo-nah mehnohs kah-roh/kah-rah
May I have the VAT forms?	¿Me puede dar los formularios IVA?	meh pweh-deh dahr lohs fohrmoo-lahr-yohs ee-veh-ah

When Things Go Wrong

ENGLISH	SPANISH	PRONUNCIATION
That's not the correct change	Ese no es el cambio correcto.	eh-seh noh ehs ehl kam-byoh koh-rehk-toh
I think this charge is a mistake	Creo que este cargo es un error.	kreh-oh keh ehs-teh kahr-goh ehs oon eh-rrohr
I've lost my way.	Estoy perdido -a.	ehs-toy pehr-dee-doh –dah
I'd like to speak with the manager	Quisiera hablar con el gerente.	kee-syeh-rah ah-blahr kohn ehl heh-rehn-the

ENGLISH	SPANISH	PRONUNCIATION
I locked myself out of my room.	**Me quedé fuera de mi habitación.**	meh keh-*deh fweh*-rah deh mee ah-bee-tah-*syohn*
I have an emergency.	**Tengo una emergencia.**	*tehng*-goh oo-nah eh-mehr-*hehn*-syah
I need an emergency prescription refill	**Necesito un reabastecimiento de emergencia de mi receta.**	neh-seh-*see*-toh oon rreh-ah-bahsteh-see-*myehn*-toh deh eh-mehr-*hehn*-syah deh mee rreh-*seh*-tah
Please call a doctor.	**Por favor llame a un doctor.**	pohr fah-*vohr yah*-meh ah oon dohk-*tohr*
I need an ambulance.	**Necesito una ambulancia.**	neh-seh-*see*-toh oo-nah ahmboo-*lahn*-syah
I was robbed.	**Me robaron.**	meh rroh-*bah*-rohn
Somebody broke into my room.	**Alguien entró en mi habitación.**	*ahlg*-yehn ehn-*troh* ehn mee ah-bee-tahs-*yohn*
Someone stole my purse/wallet	**Alguien robó mi bolso / cartera.**	*ahlg*-yehn rroh-*boh* mee *bohl*soh/ kahr-*teh*-rah

Days of the Week

ENGLISH	SPANISH	PRONUNCIATION
Sunday	**el Domingo**	ehl doh-*meeng*-go
Monday	**el Lunes**	ehl *loo*-nehs
Tuesday	**el Martes**	ehl *mahr*-tehs
Wednesday	**el Miércoles**	ehl *myehr*-koh-lehs
Thursday	**el Jueves**	ehl *hweh*-vehs
Friday	**el Viernes**	ehl *vyehr*-nehs
Saturday	**el Sábado**	ehl *sah*-bah-doh
Today	**hoy**	oy
Tomorrow	**mañana**	mah-*nyah*-nah
Yesterday	**ayer**	ah-*yehr*
one week	**una semana**	oo-nah seh-*mah*-nah
next week	**la próxima semana**	lah *prohk*-see-mah seh-*mah*-nah
last week	**la semana pasada**	lah seh-*mah*-nah pah-*sah*-dah

Months of the Year & Seasons

ENGLISH	SPANISH	PRONUNCIATION
January	**enero**	eh-*neh*-roh
February	**febrero**	feh-*breh*-roh
March	**marzo**	*mahr*-soh
April	**abril**	ah-*breel*
May	**mayo**	*mah*-yoh
June	**junio**	*hoo*-nee-oh
July	**Julio**	*hoo*-lee-oh
August	**agosto**	ah-*gohs*-toh
September	**septiembre**	sehp-*tyehm*-breh

ENGLISH	SPANISH	PRONUNCIATION
October	octubre	ohk-*too*-breh
November	noviembre	noh-*vyehm*-breh
December	diciembre	dee-*syehm*-breh
Spring	la primavera	lah pree-mah-*veh*-rah
Summer	el verano	ehl veh-*rah*-noh
Autumn	el otoño	ehl oh-*toh*-nyoh
Winter	el invierno	ehl een-*vyehr*-noh
next month	el mes entrante	ehl *mehs* ehn-*trahn*-teh
	el próximo mes	ehl *prohk*-see-moh *mehs*
last month	el mes pasado	ehl *mehs* pah-*sah*-doh

Numbers

1 **uno** (*oo*-noh)
2 **dos** (dohs)
3 **tres** (trehs)
4 **cuatro** (*kwah*-troh)
5 **cinco** (*seen*-koh)
6 **seis** (says)
7 **siete** (*syeh*-teh)
8 **ocho** (*oh*-choh)
9 **nueve** (*nweh*-beh)
10 **diez** (dyehs)
11 **once** (*ohn*-seh)
12 **doce** (*doh*-seh)
13 **trece** (*treh*-seh)
14 **catorce** (kah-*tohr*-seh)
15 **quince** (*keen*-seh)
16 **dieciséis** (dyeh-see-*says*)

17 **diecisiete** (dyeh-see-*syeh*-teh)
18 **dieciocho** (dyeh-see-*oh*-choh)
19 **diecinueve** (dyeh-see-*nweh*-beh)
20 **veinte** (*bayn*-teh)
30 **treinta** (*trayn*-tah)
40 **cuarenta** (kwah-*rehn*-tah)
50 **cincuenta** (seen-*kwehn*-tah)
60 **sesenta** (seh-*sehn*-tah)
70 **setenta** (seh-*tehn*-tah)
80 **ochenta** (oh-*chehn*-tah)
90 **noventa** (noh-*behn*-tah)
100 **cien** (*syehn*)
200 **doscientos** (doh-*syehn*-tohs)
500 **quinientos** (kee-*nyehn*-tos)
1,000 **mil** (meel)

Index

See also Accommodations index, below.

GENERAL INDEX

Abanicos Carbonell
  (València), 224
Abreu Tours, 179–180
Academia Hispánica
  Córdoba, 153
Accommodations. *See also*
  Accommodations Index;
  Apartment rentals and
  apartment hotels
    saving on, 487–488
Accommodation València, 215
Aceitunas San Miguel
  (Madrid), 68
A Cova Céltica (La Coruña),
  390–391
Adeva (Talavera), 93
Adolfo Dominguez (La
  Coruña), 389
Adrián Navarro (Cuenca), 104
Agua de València, 228
Air Canada, 481
Air Europa, 481, 486
Air France, 481
Air travel, 480–486
Akuarela Playa (València), 224
Alameda Marqués de Comillas
  (Cádiz), 205
Albaicín (Granada), 163
Alcalá de Henares, 76–77
Alcazaba (Granada), 162
Alcazaba de Málaga, 173
Alcázar
    Córdoba (Alcázar de los
      Reyes Cristianos), 151
    Jerez, 195
    Segovia, 110, 112
    Seville, 139–140
    Toledo, 88
Alcazar, Segovia, 3
Alcoy, 240
Alcúdia Bay, 442
Algarabia Outlet (Madrid), 69
Alhambra (Granada), 3, 160–162

Alicante, 229–241
  accommodations, 232–233
  getting to and around,
    230–232
  history of, 230
  lay of the land, 230
  nightlife, 236–237
  restaurants, 233–234
  shopping, 236
  side trips from, 237–241
  sports, 235–236
Alicianet Academy (Barcelona),
  297
Alminar (Córdoba), 153
Al Pie de la Vela (Granada), 166
Altamira Caves, 421
Altxerri Jazz Club (San
  Sebastián), 365
Amboa (Santiago de
  Compostela), 397
American Airlines, 481
American Express, Madrid, 77
Amfiteatre Romà (Tarragona),
  316
Andalusia, 127–209
  history of, 128–129
  lay of the land, 129–131
  top experiences, 127–128
Angel Batlle (Barcelona), 300
Antares (Lleida), 338
Antigua Casa de Guardia
  (Málaga), 170
Antigua "Casa Talavera"
  (Madrid), 72
Antiques
  Barcelona, 300
  Madrid, 68
  Tarragona, 317
Antique Theatro (Seville), 144
Aparcamiento San Pedro
  (Cuenca), 99–100
Apartment rentals and
  apartment hotels
    Barcelona, 250–251,
      254–255, 260
    Cuenca, 100
    Granada, 156
    Ibiza, 466

Madrid, 16–20
  Salamanca, 118
  Segovia, 106
  Seville, 134
Aquarium (La Coruña), 389
Aquarium de Barcelona, 294
Arab Baths, 164
  Girona, 326
  Palma de Majorca, 437
  Ronda, 189
A Rapa das Bestas, 391, 478
Archeological museum,
  Sagunto, 227
Architecture, 504–505. *See also*
  Gaudí, Antoni
Arco de Cuchilleros (Madrid), 60
Armory (Madrid), 53
A Roda (La Coruña), 390
Arrancada (La Coruña), 390
Art, 505–507. *See also specific
  artists*
Artesana i Coses (Barcelona),
  302
Artesanía de Santa Cruz
  (Cuenca), 104
Artesanía Morales (Toledo), 91
Artesanía Talaverana
  (Talavera), 94
Artesanía Textil (Seville), 144
Art Escudellers (Barcelona), 302
Artium Culture Center (Vitoria-
  Gasteiz), 370
Aste Nagusia (San Sebastián),
  357
Asturias, 383, 398–413
Asturias Day, 409
ATMs (automated teller
  machines), 489
Aula del Mar (Luarca), 402
Avila, 113–117
Ayuntamiento (Madrid), 62

Balearic Islands, 425–473.
  See also Ibiza; Majorca;
  Minorca
Banks, Madrid, 77
Baños Arabes. *See* Arab baths

Baños de Elvira Spa (Granada), 156

Banys Arabs (Arab Baths), 164
  Girona, 326
  Palma de Majorca, 437
  Ronda, 189

Barcas (València), 224

Barcelona, 242–310
  accommodations, 250–262
  hotels and B&B's, 255–260
  self catering apartments, 250–251, 254–255, 260
  average daytime temperatures and rainfall, 475
  getting around, 247–250
  history of, 243–245
  lay of the land, 245–246
  nightlife, 303–305
  outdoor activities, 298–299
  restaurants, 262–270
  shopping, 299–303
  sights and attractions, 271–296
    Barri Gòtic, 275–280
    Ciutat Vella, 274
    El Raval, 280–282
    Gràcia and Parc Güell, 289–290
    La Ribera and El Born, 282–283
    Port Vell and Barceloneta, 293–294
    suggested itineraries, 271, 274
    Upper Barcelona, 294–296
  taxis, 249–250
  top experiences, 243
  traveling to, 246–247

Barcelona Card, 248

Barceloneta, accommodations, 254, 261

Bar Consorcio (Bilbao), 355

Barrats outlet (Madrid), 70

Barri Gòtic (Barcelona), 300
  sights and attractions, 275–280

Barrio de las Letras (Madrid), 56

Barrio de Santa Cruz (Alicante), 234

Bar Zulema (Grazalema), 191

Basílica de Begoña (Bilbao), 353

Basílica de Nuestra Señora de la Macarena (Seville), 142–143

Basílica de Nuestra Señora de los Desamparados (València), 219

Basílica de Nuestra Señora del Prado (Talavera), 92–93

Basílica de San Francisco el Grande (Madrid), 61

Basílica de Santa María la Mayor (Morella), 229

Basílica de San Vicente (Avila), 116

Basílica Menor de Santa María (Elche), 237

The Basque country, 342–382
  history of, 343–344
  lay of the land, 343
  top experiences, 343

Basque people and language, 344

BCM (Palma de Majorca), 444

BD Ediciones de Diseño (Barcelona), 301

Beaches, 4
  Barcelona area, 304–305
  Bilbao, 353–354
  Cádiz, 207
  Costa del Sol, 177, 181
  Ibiza, 470–471
  Majorca, 441
  Minorca, 451–452, 461
  Santander, 419
  Tarragona area (Costa Dorada), 318
  València, 222

Beiro (Santiago de Compostela), 397

Benedictine monastery of Montserrat, 306

Benidorm, 238

Betanzos, 391

Biar, 235

Biblioteca Menéndez y Pelayo (Santander), 417–418

Biking
  Barcelona, 247
  Majorca, 441–442
  Parque Natural del Delta del Ebro, 320
  San Sebastián, 364
  Seville, 143
  València, 223
  Vitoria-Gasteiz, 367–368

Bikini (Barcelona), 304

Bilbao, 344–356
  accommodations, 348–350
  getting to and around, 346, 348
  lay of the land, 346
  nightlife, 355–356
  outdoor activities, 353–354
  restaurants, 350–351
  shopping, 355
  sights and attractions, 351–355

Bioparc València Zoo, 220

Bird-watching
  La Albufera, 225–226
  Sanlúcar, 201

Bizet, Georges, 141

Blanes, 328

Blasco Ibañez, Vicente, Casa Museo (València), 220

The Blue Rose (Ibiza), 472

Blues (Santander), 420

Boat tours and cruises
  Barcelona, 279
  Estartit, 331
  Minorca, 460
  Sanlúcar, 201

Bodega Casa del Pinar (Utiel), 228

Bodega de Mora (El Puerto de Santa María), 209

Bodega El Fabulista (Laguardia), 373

Bodega Mustiguillo (Utiel), 228

Bodegas. See Wines and vineyards

Bodegas Dionisos (Valdepeñas), 96–97

Bodegas Pedro Romero (Sanlúcar), 200–201

Bodegas Real (Valdepeñas), 97

Bodegas Tradición (Jerez), 197

Boí, 339

Books, recommended, 496–498

Bookstores, Barcelona, 300

Botanical Garden (València), 220

British Airways, 482

Buffet y Ambigú (Barcelona), 300

Bullfights
  Madrid, 66
  Mijas, 176
  Ronda, 189–190

518   Index

Buñol, 226
Burela, 392
Business hours, 499
Bus travel, 486

Cabo Fisterra, 398
Cacao Sampaka (València), 224
Cadaqués, 330–334
Cádiz, 201–211
    accommodations, 202, 204
    getting to and around, 201
    nightlife, 207–208
    restaurants, 204–205
    shopping, 207
    side trips from, 208–209
    sights and attractions,
        205–207
Cafe Moderno (Salamanca), 126
Café Novelty (Salamanca), 121
Café Royale (Barcelona), 304
Café Teatro Pay-Pay (Cádiz),
    207–208
Cafetería-Restaurante El Jardin
    (Málaga), 175
CaixaForum (Barcelona), 291
Calafell, 318
Cal de Pi de la Posada
    (Majorca), 442
Calderería Vieja and Calderería
    Nueva (Granada), 163–164
Calella de Palafrugell, 329–330
Callejón Pub (Alicante), 237
Camariñas, 398
Cambrils, 318
Camino de Santiago, 392
Camper Shoes (Madrid), 70
Camping
    Bilbao, 349
    Minorca, 455–456
Campo de Moro (Madrid), 54
Candaosa, 391
Cangas de Onís, 410–412
Caníbal Pub (Alicante), 237
C'an Oleza (Palma de Majorca),
    438
Cantabria, 383, 413–424
Capas Seseña (Madrid), 69
Cap de Cala Figuera (Majorca),
    441
Cap de Cavalleria, 452
Capilla de Santa Cruz (Cangas de
    Onís), 410
Capilla de Villaviciosa
    (Córdoba), 151

Capilla Real
    Córdoba, 151
    Granada, 163
Cardamomo Tablao Flamenco
    (Madrid), 73
Carlos III, 11, 48–50, 53, 54,
    56, 57, 59
Carmen (opera), 141
Carnaval (Sitges), 308
Car rentals, 487
Cartuja Real (Cartoixa Reial;
    Valldemossa), 444
Casa Amatller (Barcelona), 288
Casa Andalusí (Córdoba), 152
Casa Anselma (Seville), 145
Casa Batlló (Barcelona),
    288–289
Casa Carmen Arte Flamenco
    (Seville), 145
Casa Cuartero (Toledo), 87
Casa de Correos (Madrid), 56
Casa de la Ciutat (Barcelona),
    279
Casa de la Memoria
    (Seville), 145
Casa de las Ciencias
    (La Coruña), 389
Casa del Llibre (Barcelona), 300
Casa de Lope de Vega (Madrid),
    55–56
Casa de Pilatos (Seville), 142
Casa de Sefarad (Córdoba), 152
Casa Hernanz (Madrid), 70
Casa Lleo Morera (Barcelona),
    289
Casa Marita, 361
    Casa Vallés (San Sebastián),
        361–362
Casa Milà (La Pedrera;
    Barcelona), 288
Casa-Museo Antonio Machado
    (Segovia), 110–111
Casa Museo Ayuntamiento de
    Mijas, 176
Casa-Museo de Unamuno
    (Salamanca), 123
Casa-Museu Salvador Dalí
    Portlligat (Port Lligat),
        332–333
Casa Natal de Picasso (Málaga),
    171
Casa Palacio del Gigante
    (Ronda), 189
Casa Patas (Madrid), 72

Casas (Barcelona), 302
Casas colgadas (Cuenca), 103
Casas Rurales Tarragona, 314
Casa Vicens (Barcelona), 289
Casco Antiguo (Alicante), 236
Casco Medieval (Vitoria-
    Gasteiz), 369
Casinos
    Ibiza, 472
    San Sebastián, 366
    Santander, 420
Castalla, 235
Castell de Bellver (Palma de
    Majorca), 438–439
Castell del Remei, 338–339
Castell de Pubol, 333
Castell de Santa Bárbara
    (Alicante), 234
Castillo (Morella), 229
Castillo de Gibralfaro
    (Málaga), 173
Castillo de la Muela
    (Consuegra), 94
Castillo de Liria, 228
Castillo de San Marcos (El
    Puerto de Santa María),
        208–209
Castillo de Santa Catalina
    (Cádiz), 205
Catalán History Museum
    (Barcelona), 294
Catalán language courses,
    Barcelona, 298
Catalonia, 311–341. *See also*
    Barcelona
Catedral (Cathedral)
    Avila, 115
    Barcelona (La Catedral de la
        Santa Creu i Santa
        Eulàlia), 275–277
    Bilbao (Catedral de
        Santiago), 353
    Cádiz (Catédral Nueva), 205
    Ciudadela, 461
    Córdoba (Catédral Coro),
        151
    Cuenca, 103
    Girona, 325
    Granada, 162–163
    Ibiza, 470
    Jerez (Catédral de San
        Salvador), 195
    Lleida (Seu Vella), 337

Madrid (Catedral de Santa María de la Almudena), 54
Málaga, 172
Oviedo (Catedral de San Salvador), 404–405
Palma de Majorca (Gothic Catedral), 437
Pamplona, 379
Salamanca
  Catedral Nueva, 123–124
  Catedral Vieja, 124
Santander, 417
Segovia, 110
Seville, 140
Tarragona, 316
Toledo, 88–89
València (Seu), 218–219
Vitoria-Gasteiz (Catedral de Santa María), 370
Cathedral. *See* Catedral
Cava Baja (Madrid), 61
Cave paintings, 229, 398, 421, 507
Celestial (Alicante), 236
Cellers Scala Dei (Tarragona), 317
Central Cafe (Madrid), 74
Central Market (València), 223
Central Spain, 79–126
Centre Bonastruc Ca Porta (Girona), 326
Centre de Cultura Contemporània (CCCB; Barcelona), 280–281
Centre Municipal Tennis Vall d'Hebron (Barcelona), 299
Centro Andaluz de Flamenco (Jerez), 195–196
Centro Cultural Conde Duque (Madrid), 60
Centro de Interpretación del Puente Nuevo (Ronda), 188
Cerámica Artística (Talavera), 93
Cerámica Santa Ana (Seville), 144
Cerámica Triana (Seville), 144
Ceramics and pottery, 224
  Alicante, 236
  Barcelona, 302
  Cuenca, 104
  Girona, 327
  Manises, 224

Museums of Decorative Arts and Ceramics (Barcelona), 295
Oviedo, 406
Sargadelos and Burela, 392, 396–397
Seville, 144
Talavera, 92–93
Cervantes, Miguel de, Museo Casa Natal de Cervantes (Alcalá de Henares), 77
Cervantes Escuela Internacional (Málaga), 174
Children, families with, 494
Chillida, Eduardo, 363
Churches and cathedrals, best, 4–5
Cielo de Salamanca, 123
Cienfuegos (Alicante), 237
Cine Capital (Madrid), 58
Cine Doré (Madrid), 75
Cine Ideal (Madrid), 75
Cinemas
  Madrid, 75
  València, 225
Círculo de Bellas Artes de Madrid, 58
City of Science (Valencia), 5
Ciudadela (Ciutadella), 452
  accommodations, 457–458
  attractions in, 460–461
  getting to and around, 454
  restaurants, 459–460
Ciutat de les Arts y de les Ciències (City of Arts and Sciences; València), 220–221
Clamores (Madrid), 74, 75
Clan (Madrid), 73–74
Climate, 474–475
Cloistered Courtyard (Santiago de Compostela), 396
ClubABC, 179
Club de Golf Vallromanes (Barcelona), 298
Club de Natació Atlètic Barceloneta (Barcelona), 299
Club de Natació Montjuïc (Barcelona), 299
Club Nasti (Madrid), 75
Codorníu winery (Sant Sadurni de Noia), 305
Colegiata de Santa Juliana (Santillana del Mar), 420

Colegio Arzobispo Fonseca (Salamanca), 125
Colmado Blanco (La Coruña), 389–390
Colonia Güell, 305
Colón Tourism Centre (Madrid), 78
Columbus, Christopher, 129, 140, 208
Come2 Bcn agency (Barcelona), 254
Concurso Popular de Patios Cordobeses (Córdoba), 153
Conde Hermanos (Madrid), 70
Conga 8 (Santiago de Compostela), 397
Conjunt Monumental de la Plaça del Rei, 277
Consuegra, 94–96
Continental Airlines, 481
Convento de Carmelitas Descalzas (Ronda), 190
Convento de las Dueñas (Salamanca), 124
Convento de los Padres Carmelitas Descalzos (Segovia), 111–112
Convento de Regina Coeli (Santillana del Mar), 420
Convento de San Estéban (Salamanca), 124
Convento de San José (Avila), 116–117
Convento de Santa Clara (Palma de Majorca), 437–438
Convento de Sant Francesco (Morella), 229
Convento de Santo Domingo El Antiguo (Toledo), 89–90
Cook and Taste (Barcelona), 296–297
Cooking classes
  Barcelona, 296–297
  Córdoba, 153
  València, 222
Cool (Madrid), 75
Córdoba, 128, 129, 145–153
  accommodations, 146–148
  getting to and around, 145
  restaurants, 148–150
  shopping, 153
  sights and attractions, 150–153

Córdoba Patio Festival, 153
Corral des Comedias de Principe (Madrid), 55
Coruña. See La Coruña
CosmoCaixa (Museu de la Ciència; Barcelona), 295–296
Costa Blanca, 237
Costa Brava, 328–334
Costa da Morte, 397–398
Costa del Azahar, 227–228
Costa del Sol, 177–185
    accommodations, 180–181
    attractions, 181–182
    nightlife, 182
    package deals to, 178–180
    restaurants, 181
Costa Dorada, 318–319
Cotton Club (Bilbao), 355
Covadonga, 410–411
Cova Negra, 227
Credit cards, 489–490
Crime, 492–493
C2 Barcelona, 298
Cuarto del Almirante (Seville), 139
Cuenca, 98–104
Cuevas de Altamira, 421
Cuevas del Drach (Caves of Drach), 449–450
Cuisine and dining, 501–504
Cullera (València), 222
Currency exchange, 491
Customs regulations, 480

Dalí, Salvador, 438, 507
    Casa-Museu Salvador Dalí Portlligat (Port Lligat), 332
    Castell de Pubol, 333
    Teatre-Museu Dalí (Figueres), 333
Damasquinados y Grabados (Toledo), 91
Delta Airlines, 481
Deltebre, 320
Desigbarcelona (Barcelona), 255
Deyá (Deià), 445–447
Didimos Cafe (Jerez), 198
Dining, 501–504
Diocesan Museum (Ibiza), 470
Disabilities, travelers with, 495
Disco Playa Club (La Coruña), 390

Disco-Teatro Joy Eslava (Madrid), 75
Dmclub (Cádiz), 208
Domus (Museum of Mankind; La Coruña), 389
Donna Donna (València), 225
Don Quijote (Spanish language school; Salamanca), 125

The Ebro Delta, 320
Echeve (Pamplona), 381
Eden (Ibiza), 472
Egües, 379
Eix (Lleida), 338
El Arco Artesania (Madrid), 72
El Bañuelo Baños Arabes (Granada), 163
El Cabanyal (València), 221
El Capricho de Gaudí (Comillas), 423
El Castillo (Puente Viesgo), 421
El Cau (Tarragona), 318
Elche (Elx), 237–240
El Corte Inglés
    Barcelona, 301
    Madrid, 71–72
El Divino Club (Ibiza), 472
El Duende (Oviedo), 407
Electricity, 499
El Escorial, 76
El Flamenco Vive (Madrid), 70
El Fontán (Oviedo), 406
El Greco, 48–49, 58, 64, 79, 81, 86, 89–90, 219, 309, 506
    "El Greco House" museum (Toledo), 90
El Lagá de Tío Parilla (Jerez), 198
El Lavaderu (Gijón), 409
El Maestrazgo, 228
El Palmar (La Albufera), 226
El Postigo (Seville), 144
El Potro (Cádiz), 207
El Puerto de Santa María, 208
El Puntal, 419
El Rastro (Madrid), 62, 68
El Rejoneo (Seville), 145
El Rincón de San Pedro (Granada), 166
El Saler (València), 223
El Tablao de Carmen (Barcelona), 303–304
El Torcal de Antequera (near Málaga), 175

Embassies, 499
Emergencies, 499
    Madrid, 78
Emporium BD (Girona), 327
Empúries, 331
Entry requirements, 479–480
Equity Point chain (Barcelona), 261
Ermita de la Virgen de la Peña (Mijas), 176
Escola Municipal d'Hípica La Foixarda (Barcelona), 299
Escuela de Buceo Casco Antigua València, 222
Escuela de Cocina Eneldo (València), 222
Escuela Montalbán (Granada), 165–166
Església de San Francisco (Ciudadela), 460
Església de Sant Feliu (Girona), 325
Església Santa María la Major (Mahòn), 460
Espacio Buenavista (Oviedo), 406
Espacio Flamenco (Madrid), 73
Espai Barroc (Barcelona), 303
Espannola (Salamanca), 125–126
Es Paradis (Ibiza), 472
Estadio Santiago Bernabéu (Madrid), 65
Estadio Vicente Calderón (Madrid), 65
Estartit, 331
Estepona, 184–185
Eureka Academia de Español (Madrid), 67
Euskal Herriko Museoa (Guernica), 356
Expedia, 180
Explanada d'Espanya (Alicante), 234

Fábrica de Hielo (Sanlúcar), 201
Families with children, 494
Farrutx (Madrid), 70
Fashion, Madrid, 68–69
Fashions (clothing), Barcelona, 301
Federación Asturiana de Montaña (Potes), 412

Federopticos Dorff (Madrid), 69
Fernando Amat's Vinçón
(Barcelona), 301
Ferrocarril de Sóller, 449
Festival de Jazz de Vitoria-
Gasteiz, 372
Festival d'Estiu (Tarragona), 318
Festivals and special events,
476–479
Figueres, 333
Filmoteca (València), 225
Films, recommended, 498
Finca La Prudenciana (near
Tembleque), 96
Fishing, Asturias, 411
Flamenco, 507–508
    Barcelona
        classes, 297
        nightlife, 303–304
    Cádiz, 208
    Centro Andaluz de Flamenco
    (Jerez), 195–196
    Jerez, 198
    Madrid, 72–74
    Málaga, 175
    Seville
        Museo del Baile
        Flamenco, 142
        Taller Flamenco,
        143–144
        venues, 144–145
Flamenka Vive (Málaga), 175
Folk and Jazz Festival
(Lleida), 338
Fondo Reservado (Granada), 166
Font del Gat (Barcelona), 290
Formentor Peninsula, 442
Forum (Sagunto), 227
Forvm Ferlandina (Barcelona),
301
Fran Holuba (Alicante), 236
Friendly Rentals (Seville), 134
Frontón de Galarreta (near San
Sebastián), 364
Frontón Euskal-Jai Berri (near
Pamplona), 380
Fuengirola Zoo, 182
Fuente-Dé, 412, 413
Fundació Fran Daural
(Barcelona), 293
Fundació Joan Miró (Barcelona),
291–292
Fundación Antonio Pérez
(Cuenca), 103–104

Fundación Antonio Saura
(Cuenca), 103
Fundación Museo de la Paz de
Guernica, 356
Fundación Real Escuela
Andaluza del Arte Ecuestre
(Jerez), 196

Galería el Populo (Cádiz), 207
Galería Olímpica (Barcelona),
293
Galerias Piquer (Madrid), 68
Galicia, 383, 384–398
Gandía (València), 222
Gate1 Travel, 179
Gaudí, Antoni, 246, 258, 271,
274, 281, 282, 284–290,
305, 505
    Casa-Museu Gaudí
    (Barcelona), 290
    Casa Vicens (Barcelona), 289
    Colonia Güell, 305
    El Capricho de Gaudí
    (Comillas), 423
    Parc Güell (Barcelona), 289
Gays and lesbians
    advice for, 495–496
    Alicante, 237
    Barcelona, 304
    Bilbao, 355
    Granada, 166–167
    Ibiza, 472
    Oviedo, 407
    Palma de Majorca, 444
    Sitges, 310
    València, 225
    Vitoria-Gasteiz, 372
Gaytan (Madrid), 70
Generalife (Granada), 162
General Optica (Madrid), 69
Getxo, 354
Giangrossi (Madrid), 44
Gijón, 407–409
Giralda (Seville), 140
Girona, 320–327
Golf
    Alicante, 236
    Barcelona, 298
    Lleida, 337
    Majorca, 442
    Minorca, 462
    Santander, 419–420
    València, 223
    Vitoria-Gasteiz, 371–372

Goya, Francisco de, 11, 49,
57–59, 64, 76, 190, 197,
219, 380, 506
Gracia Mazuelo del Hierro
(Madrid), 71
Granada, 154–167
    accommodations, 154–158
    getting to and around, 154
    nightlife, 166–167
    restaurants, 158–160
    shopping, 166
    sights and attractions,
    160–166
Grand Optical (Madrid), 69
Gran Teatre del Liceu
(Barcelona), 278, 303
Gran Téatro Falla (Cádiz), 208
Gran Vía (Madrid)
    accommodations on or near,
    23–24
    attractions on and
    around, 58
    restaurants on and near, 36
Graves, Robert, 446
Gris, Juan, 51, 438, 506
Groove (Tarragona), 318
Grutas de San José, 228–229
Guantes Luque (Madrid), 71
Guernica (Gernika), 356
Guernica (Picasso), 51, 356, 506
Guernica Peace Museum, 356
Guggenheim Museum (Bilbao),
4, 351–352
Gypsy Quarter (Granada),
164–165

Harlem Jazz Club (Barcelona),
304
Health insurance, 484–485
Health and safety, 491–493
Hemingway, Ernest, 73
Herederos Luis Ramírez
(Córdoba), 153
Herrera, Joaquín, 297
Hibernian Books (Barcelona),
300–301
Hiking, Majorca, 442–443
Holidays, 479
Holy Grotto (Santa Cova;
Montserrat), 306, 307
Homes for Travellers (Madrid),
17, 28
Horizon Grazalema, 191
Horreos, 390

522 Index

Horseback riding
  Barcelona, 299
  Ibiza, 471
  Majorca, 443
  Minorca, 462
  València, 223
Hospitals, Madrid, 78
Hotels and hostales, Madrid, 20–29
Hoyos, Cristina, 142
Huerta de San Vicente Casa-Museo Federico García Lorca (Granada), 162
Huerto del Cura (Elche), 238

Iberia Airlines, 481, 482, 486
Ibiza (Eivissa)
  accommodations, 466–469
  getting to and around, 465–466
  history of, 464–465
  lay of the land, 465
  nightlife, 472
  outdoor activities, 470–471
  restaurants, 469–470
  shopping, 471
  sights and attractions, 470
Iglesia de la Asunción (Laredo), 422
Iglesia de la Vera Cruz (Segovia), 111
Iglesia de San Luis de los Franceses (Seville), 142
Iglesia de San Miguel (Vitoria-Gasteiz), 370
Iglesia de San Nicolás de Bari (Bilbao), 353
Iglesia de Santa María del Campo (La Coruña), 388
Iglesia de Santiago (Málaga), 171
Iglesia San Francisco (Viveiro), 391
Illes Medes, 331
Immaculada Concepción (Mijas), 176–177
Instituto Picasso Málaga (Málaga), 174–175
International Film Festival (San Sebastián), 357, 362, 478
Internet access, 496
Isla del Rey (Mahòn), 452
IslahAbitada (Cádiz), 207

IVAM (Instituto Valenciano de Arte Moderno; València), 220

Jai alai, 364
Jamboree (Barcelona), 304
Jardí Botànic (Botanical Garden; Barcelona), 290
Jardí Botànic Marimurtra (Blanes), 328
Jardín Botànic (Botanical Garden; València), 220
Jardín de San Carlos (La Coruña), 388
Jardines de Méndez Núñez (La Coruña), 388
Jardines de Sabatini (Madrid), 54
Játiva Castle, 226–227
Jazzbah (Minorca), 464
Jerez de la Frontera, 191–201
  accommodations, 192–193
  getting to and around, 191–192
  nightlife, 198
  restaurants, 193–195
  side trips from, 198–201
  sights and attractions, 195–197
Jijona (Xixona), 235
José Ramirez Guitarreria (Madrid), 70
Joyero Artesano Baillo (Salamanca), 126
Juan de Arriago (Vitoria-Gasteiz), 371

Kabutzia (San Sebastián), 365
Kane, Sir Richard, 456
Kastoria (Barcelona), 302
The Kraken, 402
Kursaal (San Sebastián), 362

La Alacena del Gourmet (Madrid), 68
La Albufera, 225
La Bauma, 328
La Bóveda (Granada), 166
La Caleta (Cádiz), 207
La Casa de los Piononos (Pastelería Gravina; Madrid), 38
La Casa dels Músics (Barcelona), 303
La Cava Taberna Flamenca (Cádiz), 208

La Concha Beach and Promenade (San Sebastián), 357, 362, 364
La Coruña (A Coruña), 384–392
  accommodations, 386–387
  getting to and around, 386
  lay of the land, 385–386
  restaurants, 387–388
La Cova d'en Xoroi (Minorca), 463
La Cuca Fera (Tarragona), 316
La Ermita de San Antonio de La Florida (Madrid), 59
La Favorita (Madrid), 69
La Fiesta de la Rosa del Azafrán (Consuegra), 95–96
La Florida (Vitoria-Gasteiz), 371
Laguardia, 373
La Guerra (València), 225
La Hipica (València), 223
La Indiana (València), 224
La Mancha, 93
Lambda (València), 225
La Mercè (Barcelona), 278
La meseta, 93
La Mezquita (Córdoba), 151
La Moreneta (Montserrat), 306
La Muralla (Santander), 418
Language, 499. See also Spanish-language classes
L'Antic (Lleida), 338
L'Antiquari (Tarragona), 318
La Palma Libros (Oviedo), 406
La Pedrera (Casa Milà; Barcelona), 288
L'Aquarium de Barcelona, 294
La Rapa das Bestas, 391, 478
La Real (Oviedo), 407
Laredo, 422–424
La Roca Village complex (Barcelona), 301
La Sagrada Família (Barcelona), 3, 284–287
La Sal (Granada), 167
La Sala del Cel (Girona), 327
La Santa Cueva (Cangas de Onís), 411
Las Carboneras Tablao Flamenco (Madrid), 73
Las Golondrinas (Barcelona), 279
Las Tres ZZZ (Pamplona), 381
La Taberna Flamenca (Jerez), 198
L'Auditori (Barcelona), 303

Lavapiés (Madrid), attractions
in, 62
La Victoria (Cádiz), 207
La Vila Joiosa, 237, 240
Leather goods
Alicante, 236
Barcelona, 302
Córdoba, 153
Madrid, 70–71
Oviedo, 406
Santander, 418–419
L'Eixample (Barcelona), 283–289
Les Encantats, 339
Les Garrigues, 339
L'Hemispheric (València), 221
L'Hospital de la Santa Creu i
Sant Pau (Barcelona), 287
Librería Abarzuza (Pamplona),
381
Librería Xiada (La Coruña), 390
Limón y Menta (Segovia), 109
Lleida, 334–341
Lloret de Mar, 328
Llotja (Palma de Majorca), 438
Loewe
Barcelona, 302
Palma de Majorca, 443
Lonja (València), 219
Lonja de la Seda (València), 219
Lo Nuestro (Seville), 145
Lope de Vega, Félix, Casa de
Lope de Vega (Madrid), 55–56
Lorca, Federico García, 162
Los Arcos (Ronda), 190
Los Cuatro Postes (Avila), 116
Los Jardines del Prado
(Talavera), 93
Los Tarantos (Barcelona), 304
Lost-luggage insurance, 485
Luarca, 402
Lupo (Barcelona), 302
Luz de Gas (Barcelona), 304

MACBA (Museu d'Art
Contemporani de
Barcelona), 281
Machado, Antonio, Casa-Museo
(Segovia), 110–111
Madrid, 9–78
accommodations, 16–29
apartment rentals,
16–20
Chueca and Malasaña,
24–25

on or near Gran Vía,
23–24
Lavapiés, 26
near the museums,
27–28
around Opera and
Palacio Real, 22–23
Plaza Mayor and La
Latina, 25–26
Plaza Santa Ana, 26–27
around Puerta del Sol,
20–22
Salamanca, 28–29
banks, 77
driving in, 16
emergencies, 78
getting around, 13
getting to and from the
airport, 12–13
history of, 10–12
hospitals, 78
Internet access, 78
layout of, 12
markets, 67–68
nightlife, 72–75
police, 78
post office, 78
restaurants, 29–45
in Chueca and
Malasaña, 36–38
on and near Gran
Vía, 36
Lavapiés, 40–41
near the museums,
43–44
around Opera and
Palacio Real, 33–36
in Plaza Mayor and La
Latina, 38–40
in and near Plaza Santa
Ana, 41–43
Puerta del Sol, 29, 33
Salamanca, 44–45
shopping, 67–72
sights and attractions,
45–67
Chueca and Malasaña,
58–60
Gran Vía, 58
around the museums,
48–52
around Opera and
Palacio Real, 52–55

the "Other" Madrid,
64–68
passes, 52–53
around Puerta del Sol,
56–58
suggested itineraries,
45, 48
taxis, 16
top experiences, 9–10
transportation options,
13, 16
Madrid Card, 52–53
Madrid Tourism Centre, 78
Madrid Vision, 57
Magdalena Palace (Santander),
418
Mahòn (Maò)
accommodations, 456–457
getting to and around, 454
restaurants, 458–459
sights and attractions, 460
Mail, 499
Majorca (Mallorca), 425,
426–450. See also Palma de
Majorca
accommodations, 433–435
getting to and around,
430–432
history of, 428–429
lay of the land, 429–430
northwest, 444–450
restaurants, 436–437
Málaga, 167–177
accommodations, 167–169
average daytime tempera-
tures and rainfall, 475
getting to and around, 167
nightlife, 175
restaurants, 169–171
side trips from, 175–177
sights and attractions,
171–175
Malpica, 397
Malvarrossa (València), 222
Manglano (València), 223–224
Mango Outlet (Barcelona), 301
Manises, 224
Marbella, 182–183
Marengo (Pamplona), 381
Mar Gran, 328
Mariano Zamoraño Fábrica de
Espadas y Armas Blancas
(Toledo), 91
Marineland (Majorca), 439

524   Index

MARQ (Museu Arqueológico Provincial de Alicante), 234–235

Marzipan confections, Toledo, 89

Medical insurance, 484–485

Medievo (Salamanca), 126

Mediterráneo (Sitges), 310

Mercado Antón Martín (Madrid), 67

Mercado de Abastos (Palma de Majorca), 439–440

Mercado de Colón (València), 223

Mercado de Esperanza (Santander), 419

Mercado de la Cebada (Madrid), 67

Mercado de la Paz (Madrid), 67–68

Mercatus (Salamanca), 126

Merienda (afternoon coffee break), 32

Meryan (Córdoba), 153

Metro (Barcelona club), 304

Metropolis (Madrid), 58

Mezquita (Córdoba), 151

Miguelete Tower (València), 219

Mijas, 176–177

Minorca (Menorca), 450–464
accommodations, 454–458
getting to and around, 452–454
history of, 451
lay of the land, 451–452
nightlife, 463–464
outdoor activities, 461–462
restaurants, 458–460
shopping, 462–463
sights and attractions, 460–461

Mirador Barrio Nuevo (Toledo), 88

Mirador de Colom (Columbus Watchtower; Barcelona), 278–279

Mirador San Nicolas (Granada), 164

Miró, Joan, 370, 438, 507
Fundació (Barcelona), 291

Misteri d'Elx (Mystery of Elche), 237

Moderniste architecture, 5, 286, 505

Monasteri de Vallbona de les Monges (Montblanc), 319

Monasterio de la Encarnación (Avila), 117

Monasterio de Las Descalzas Reales (Madrid), 54, 55

Monasterio de San Antonio El Real (Segovia), 111

Monasterio de San Juan de los Reyes (Toledo), 90

Monastery of San Miguel y Los Reyes (València), 219

Monestir de Pedralbes (Barcelona), 295

Monestir de Santes Creus (Montblanc), 319

Money matters, 489–491

Montblanc, 319–320

Monte Igueldo, 362

Monte Naranco, 405

Montjuïc (Barcelona), 290–293

Montón de trigo montón de paja (Segovia), 112

Montserrat, 306–307

Moog (Barcelona), 304

Moors (Muslims; Arabs)
Andalusia, 127–129
architecture, 505
Avila, 116
Córdoba, 151–152
Granada, 154

"Moors and Christians" festivities, 240

Morella, 229

Morella la Vella, 229

Moros y Cristianos, 477

Morvedre, 228

Movies. *See also* Cinemas
recommended, 498

Mudéjar architecture, 505

Mundaka, 354

Muralla de Avila, 114–115

Murillo, Bartolomé Esteban, 140, 141, 206, 506

Museo a Euska/Museo Vasco (Bilbao), 352

Museo Arqueológic (Lleida), 337

Museo Arqueològic de Ibiza y Formentera, 470

Museo Arqueológico
Granada, 163
Oviedo, 405

Museo Arqueológico e Histórico (La Coruña), 388–389

Museo Arqueológico Nacional (Madrid), 64

Museo Arqueologico y de Historia de Elche, 238, 240

Museo Arte Público (Madrid), 63

Museo Casa Hermandad Nuestro Padre Jesús Cristo del San Sepulcro y Nuestra Señora de la Soledad (Málaga), 174

Museo Casa Natal de Cervantes (Alcalá de Henares), 77

Museo-Casa Natal de Jovellanos (Gijón), 408

Museo Catedralicio de Santiago de Compostela, 395–396

Museo Chillida-Leku (San Sebastián), 363

Museo Cuevas del Sacromonte (Granada), 165

Museo de América (Madrid), 59

Museo de Arqueología de Alava (Vitoria-Gasteiz), 370–371

Museo de Arte Abstracto Español (Cuenca), 103

Museo de Arte Contemporáneo (Madrid), 60

Museo de Arte Contemporáneo Esteban Vicente (Segovia), 111

Museo de Bellas Artes
Bilbao, 353
Granada, 161
Seville, 140–142
València, 219

Museo de Cádiz, 206

Museo de la Alhambra (Granada), 161–162

Museo de la Gaita (Gijón), 409

Museo de la Real Plaza de Toros (Seville), 141

Museo de las Ciencias=Principe Felipe (València), 221

Museo del Baile Flamenco (Seville), 142, 144–145

Museo del Bandolero (Ronda), 189

Museo del Grabado Español Contemporáneo (Marbella), 183

Museo del Hombre y el Mar (Santander), 418

Museo del Pueblo de Asturias (Gijón), 409

Museo del Traje (Madrid), 59

Museo del Viño (Valdepeñas), 98
Museo de Málaga, 172–173
Museo de Navarra (Pamplona), 380
Museo de Salamanca, 123
Museo de San Isidro (Madrid), 61
Museo de Santa Cruz (Toledo), 89
Museo de Santo Tomé (Toledo), 90
Museo Diocesano (Pamplona), 380
Museo Fournier de Naipes (Vitoria-Gasteiz), 371
Museo Lázaro Galdiano (Madrid), 64
Museo Municipal de Bellas Artes (Santander), 418
Museo Municipal de Madrid, 60
Museo Nacional Centro de Arte Reina Sofía (Madrid), 51–52
Museo Nacional de Artes Decorativas (Madrid), 50
Museo Nacional del Prado (Madrid), 48–50
Museo Naval (Madrid), 50
Museo Picasso Málaga (Málaga), 171–172
Museo Regional de Prehistoria y Arqueología de Cantabria (Santander), 418
Museo Romántico (Madrid), 60
Museo Romantico (Sitges), 309
Museo Ruiz de Luna (Talavera), 92
Museo Sefardí (Toledo), 90
Museo Sorolla (Madrid), 63
Museo Taurino (Ronda), 190
Museo Teresiano (Avila), 116
Museo Thyssen-Bornemisza (Madrid), 50–51
Museo Vittorio Macho (Toledo), 90
Museo Zuloaga (Segovia), 110
Museu Arqueològic (Girona), 327
Museu Arqueológico Provincial de Alicante (MARQ), 234–235
Museu Barbier-Mueller Art Precolombí (Barcelona), 283
Museu Cau Ferrat (Sitges), 309
Museu d'Arqueologia de Catalunya (Barcelona), 292

Museu d'Art (Girona), 326
Museu d'Art Contemporani de Barcelona (MACBA), 281
Museu d'Art Espanyol Contemporani, Fundació Juan March (Palma de Majorca), 438
Museu de Arte del Siglo XX Asegurada (Alicante), 234
Museu de Ciències Naturals de la Ciutadella (Barcelona), 285
Museu de Cinema (Girona), 327
Museu de Geologia (Barcelona), 285
Museu de la Ciència (Cosmo-Caixa; Barcelona), 295–296
Museu de les Arts Decoratives/Museu de Ceràmica (Barcelona), 295
Museu del Jurásico del Asturias (near Oviedo), 405
Museu de Montserrat, 307
Museu de Sant Telmo (San Sebastián), 363
Museu de Zoologia (Barcelona), 285
Museu d'Història de Catalunya (Barcelona), 294
Museu d'Historia de la Ciutat (Barcelona), 277–278
Museu d'Historia de la Ciutat (Girona), 326
Museu Frederic Marès (Barcelona), 277
Museu i Necròpolis Paleocristians (Tarragona), 316–317
Museu Maricel (Sitges), 309
Museu Marítim (Barcelona), 293
Museu Militar de Montjuïc (Barcelona), 290–291
Museum of Altamira, 421
Museum of Mankind (Domus; La Coruña), 389
Museums, best, 6
Museums of Decorative Arts and Ceramics (Barcelona), 295
Museu Nacional Arqueològic (Tarragona), 316
Museu Nacional d'Art de Catalunya (MNAC; Barcelona), 292
Museu Paleocristià (Tarragona), 317

Museu Picasso (Barcelona), 283
Museu Tèxtil i d' Indumentària (Barcelona), 283
Musical Opera (Madrid), 70
Music stores, Madrid, 70
Muxart (Barcelona), 303

Naranco, Monte, 405
Navarre (Navarra), 373–382
Navarro, Adrián (Cuenca), 104
Naveta d'es Tudons (near Ciudadela), 463
Northwest Airlines, 481
Nuevas Galerias (Madrid), 68

Objetos de Arte Toledano (Madrid), 72
Oceanogràfic (València), 221
Ocho y Medio (Madrid), 75
Oiartzun, 365
Olde Worlde L' Arca de l' Aviva (Barcelona), 300
Olite, 381
Oratorio de San Felipe Neri (Cádiz), 206
Oratorio de Santa Cueva (Cádiz), 206
Otto's (Gijón), 409
Otto Zutz (Barcelona), 304
Our Lady of Mercy (Barcelona), 278
Oviedo, 400–407

Pachá (Ibiza), 472
Pacha (Santander), 420
Package deals, 483
Packing tips, 493–494
Paella, 218
Palacio de Carlos V (Granada), 161
Palacio de Gelmírez (Santiago de Compostela), 396
Palacio del Mar Aquarium (San Sebastián), 363
Palacio de Miramar (San Sebastián), 362–363
Palacio de Mondragón (Ronda), 189
Palacio de Sobrellano (Comillas), 423
Palacio de Viana (Córdoba), 152
Palacio Gótico (Seville), 140
Palacio Mudéjar (Seville), 139

526 Index

Palacio Real
  Aranjuez, 5, 76
  El Pardo, 76
  Madrid, 5
  accommodations
    around, 22–23
  restaurants around,
    33–36
  sights and attractions,
    52–55
  Olite, 381
Palau de la Generalitat
  (Barcelona), 279–280
Palau de l'Almudaina (Palma de
  Majorca), 437
Palau de la Música (València),
  225
Palau de la Música Catalána
  (Barcelona), 282, 303
Palau de les Arts (València), 221
Palau del Rei Sancho
  (Valldemossa), 444
Palau Güell (Barcelona),
  281–282
Palau Reial (Royal Palace;
  Barcelona), 278
Palau Sant Jordi (Barcelona),
  303
Palma de Majorca, 430–444
  accommodations, 433–435
  getting to and around,
    432–433
  nightlife, 444
  restaurants, 436–437
  shopping, 443
Palmera del Cura (Elche), 238
Palm Forest (Elche), 238
Pamplona (Iruña), 374–382
Panadería Todo Sierra
  (Grazalema), 190
Panoramis mall (Alicante), 236
Paradores, 488
Parc Central (Tarragona), 317
Parc d'Atraccions Tibidabo
  (Barcelona), 296
Parc de la Ciutadella
  (Barcelona), 284
Parc Güell (Barcelona), 289
Parc Nacional d'Aigüestortes i
  l'Estany de Maurici
  (Aiguestortes and Sant
  Mauricio National Park),
  339–341

Parc Natural del Delta del Ebre
  (Tortosa), 320
Parc Zoològic (Barcelona),
  284–285
Parque de Grazalema (near
  Ronda), 190
Parque del Retiro (Madrid), 50
Parque de María Luisa (Seville),
  143
Parque Deportivo Monte Tossal
  (Alicante), 235–236
Parque Doñana (Sanlúcar), 201
Parque Genovés (Cádiz), 205
Parrot's Pub (Sitges), 310
Paseo del Arte pass (Madrid), 52
Paseo del Prado (Madrid), 48
Passeig Arqueològic (Tarragona),
  317
Passeig de Gràcia (Barcelona),
  299
Pastelería Gravina (La Casa de
  los Piononos; Madrid), 38
Patio de Escuelas Menores
  (Salamanca), 122
Patio de las Doncellas (Seville),
  139
Patio de las Muñecas (Seville),
  139
Patio del Cuarto Dorado
  (Granada), 160
Patio de los Arrayanes
  (Granada), 160
Patio de los Leones (Granada),
  161
Patricia's Bar (Deyá), 447
Patronat de Turisme de les
  Terres de Lleida, 337
Pearls, Majorca, 440, 443
Pedro Soriano (Alicante), 236
Peña Flamenca Juanito Villar
  (Cádiz), 208
Peña La Perla de Cádiz, 208
Peña La Platería (Granada), 166
Peñas de Aia, 365
Penedés area, 305
Peñíscola, 229
Perfil (Granada), 167
Perfumería Alvarez Gómez
  (Madrid), 72
Pharmacies, 499
Picasso, Pablo, 51, 309,
  438, 506
  Casa Natal de Picasso
    (Málaga), 171
  Guernica, 51, 356, 506

Museo Picasso Málaga
  (Málaga), 171–172
Museu Picasso (Barcelona),
  283
Picos de Europa National Park,
  400, 409–410
Pink Elefant (Segovia), 112
Pintxos, 361
Piscina Bernardo Picornell
  (Barcelona), 298
Plaça de la Seu (Barcelona),
  275
Plaça Sant Jaume (Barcelona),
  279
Platamundi (Barcelona), 302
Platja Binimella (Minorca),
  451–452
Playa de Aro, 329
Playa de Ereaga (Bilbao),
  353–354
Playa de Malvarrossa (València),
  224
Playa San Lorenzo (Gijón), 407
Plaza de Dos de Mayo
  (Madrid), 60
Plaza de la Estación
  (Cuenca), 99
Plaza de la Lealtad (Madrid), 50
Plaza de la Quintana (Santiago
  de Compostela), 396
Plaza de la Villa (Madrid), 62
Plaza de la Virgen Blanca
  (Vitoria-Gasteiz), 370
Plaza del Ayuntamiento
  (Toledo), 88
Plaza del Cabildo (Sanlúcar),
  199
Plaza del Castillo (Pamplona),
  378
Plaza del Fontán (Oviedo), 406
Plaza de María Pita (La Coruña),
  388
Plaza de Oriente (Madrid), 52
Plaza de Toros
  Mijas, 176
  Pamplona, 378
  Ronda, 189, 190
Plaza de Toros Monumental de
  Las Ventas (Madrid), 66
Plaza de Zocodover (Toledo), 88
Plaza Mayor
  Madrid, 60
    accommodations, 25–26
    restaurants, 38–40

Salamanca, 122, 125
Segovia, 110
Plaza Redonda (València), 223
Plaza Santa Ana (Madrid), 55
    accommodations, 26–27
    restaurants, 41–43
Plaza Solymar (Benalmádena
    Pueblo), 182
Poble Espanyol
    Barcelona, 293
    Palma de Majorca, 438
Poble Nou (Barcelona), 296
Ponche segoviano, 109
Ponsol (San Sebastián), 365
Port-Ainé Sports Center (Rialp),
    339
Port Aventura (near Tarragona),
    318
Pórtico de la Gloria (Santiago de
    Compostela), 396
Port Lligat, 332
Porto Cristo, 449–450
Potes, 412–413
Pottery and ceramics, 224
    Alicante, 236
    Barcelona, 302
    Cuenca, 104
    Girona, 327
    Manises, 224
    Museums of Decorative Arts
        and Ceramics (Barcelona),
        295
    Oviedo, 406
    Sargadelos and Burela, 392,
        396–397
    Seville, 144
    Talavera, 92–93
The Prado, 3, 48–50
Priorat wines, 317
Pubol, 333
Pub Vaya Vaya (Cuenca), 104
Puente San Pablo (Cuenca), 103
Puente Viesgo, 421
Puerta de Alcalá (Madrid), 50
Puerta del Sol (Madrid)
    accommodations, 20–22
    attractions around, 56–58
    restaurants, 29, 33
Puerto Pesquero (Santander),
    417
Puntera (Madrid), 71
The Pyrenees, accommodations
    in, 340–341

Racó de l'Olla (La Albufera),
    225–226
Rafael Moreno (Granada), 166
Raimat Golf (Lleida), 337
Raimat Grape Harvest, 339
Real Academia de Bellas Artes
    de San Fernando (Madrid), 57
Real Alcázar (Seville), 139–140
Real Club de Regatas (Alicante),
    236
Real Escuela Andaluza del Arte
    Ecuestre (Jerez), 196
Real Monasterio de la
    Encarnación (Madrid), 55
Real Monasterio de San Lorenzo
    El Escorial, 76
Real Monasterio de Santa Maria
    de El Parral (Segovia), 112
Reial Club de Golf El Prat
    (Barcelona), 298
Requena, 227, 228
Restrooms, 499–500
Reverendos (Pamplona), 381
Revillagigedo (Gijón), 409
Rías Altas, 391–392
Riazor (La Coruña), 389
Rioja, 372–373
Riverside Market (Bilbao), 355
Rodamilans (Lleida), 338
Roman Aqueduct (Segovia), 109
Roman Baths (Gijón), 408–409
Romans (ruins and antiquities)
    Andalusia, 128
    Avila, 114–115
    Cádiz, 206
    Cangas de Onís, 410
    Gijón, 408–409
    Málaga, 173
    Sagunto (Sagunt), 227
    Valdepeñas, 97
Romerijo (El Puerto de Santa
    María), 209
Ronda, 185–191
RoomMadrid, 17
Rotonda (San Sebastián), 365
Royal Regatta Club (Alicante),
    236

Sabucedo, 391
Sacromonte (Granada), 164–165
Saffron, 71, 87
    La Fiesta de la Rosa del
        Azafrán (Consuegra),
        95–96

Sagrada Família (Barcelona), 3,
    284–287
Sagunto (Sagunt), 227
Sailing
    Alicante, 236
    Bilbao, 354
    Minorca, 462
St. James' Square (Barcelona),
    279
Sala d'Art Artur Ramón
    (Barcelona), 300
Sala de Ball (Girona), 327
Sala de Justicia (Seville), 139
Sala Juglar (Madrid), 73
Salamanca (city), 6, 117–126
    accommodations, 117–120
    getting to and around, 117
    restaurants, 120–122
Salamanca district (Madrid)
    accommodations, 28–29
    attractions in, 63
    restaurants, 44–45
Sala Mogambo (València), 225
Salinas de Anaña 5, 371
Salón de Embajadores
    (Granada), 160–161
Salou, 318
Salvador Bachiller (Madrid), 71
Salvation (Barcelona), 304
San Antonio de Portmany,
    469, 472
San Fermines fests (Pamplona),
    378–379
San Francisco, Església de
    (Ciudadela), 460
San Francisco, Iglesia (Viveiro),
    391
San Juan del Hospital
    (València), 219
Sanlúcar de la Barrameda,
    198–201
San Miguel de Lillo (Oviedo),
    405
San Nicolás de Bari (Bilbao),
    353
San Pedro (Buñol), 226
San Salvador, Catédral de
    (Jerez), 195
San Salvador, Catedral de
    (Oviedo), 404–405
San Sebastián
    accommodations, 358–360
    restaurants, 360–362

528   Index

San Sebastián (Donostia), 357–366

Santa Catalina (Palma de Majorca), 439

Santa Catalina Botanical Garden (Vitoria-Gasteiz), 371

Santa Cova (Holy Grotto; Montserrat), 306, 307

Santa Creu i Santa Eulàlia, Catedral de la (Barcelona), 275–277

Santa María Church (València), 221–222

Santa María del Campo, Iglesia de (La Coruña), 388

Santa María del Naranco (Oviedo), 405

Santa María de los Reyes (Laguardia), 373

Santa Maria del Pi (Barcelona), 280

Santa María de Poblet (Montblanc), 319

Santa María la Major, Església (Mahòn), 460

Santander, 414–420

Sant Climent de Taüll church, 339

Sant Feliu Church (Girona), 325

Sant Feliu de Guíxols, 328–329

Santiago de Compostela, 392–398

Santillana del Mar, 420–422

Santísima Trinidad (Málaga), 175

Sant Joan (San Juan) fiesta (Ciudadela), 461

Santo Tomé Obrador de Mazapán (Toledo), 89

Sant Pau del Camp (Barcelona), 281

Sant Sadurní de Noia, 305

Sardana, 276

Sargadelos, 392, 396–397

Sax, 235

Scuba diving
   Costa Brava, 331
   Costa del Azahar, 227
   Majorca, 441
   Minorca, 461
   València, 222

Seasons, 474–475, 480

Segovia, 104–113
   accommodations, 106–108
   getting to and around, 104, 106
   nightlife, 112–113
   restaurants, 108–109
   shopping, 112
   sights and attractions, 109–112

Segunda Mano (Vitoria-Gasteiz), 372

Seniors, 494–495

Seu (Cathedral; València), 218–219

Seu Vella (Old Cathedral; Lleida), 337

Sevilla Flamenco Biennial (Seville), 144

Seville (Sevilla), 131–145
   accommodations, 132, 134–136
   average daytime temperatures and rainfall, 475
   getting to and around, 131–132
   nightlife, 144–145
   restaurants, 136–139
   shopping, 144
   sights and attractions, 139–144

Sherry, 209
   Jerez, 196–197
   Sanlúcar, 200–201

Shoes
   Barcelona, 302–303
   Madrid, 70–71

Siglo I/Gran Cafe Centera (Salamanca), 126

Silver (Benalmádena Pueblo), 182

Sinagoga (Córdoba), 152

Sitges, 307–310

Skiing, Bacqueira-Beret, 340

Smoking, 491

Soccer, Madrid, 65

Soller, 447–449

Son Marroig Museum (Deyá), 446–447

Sorolla, Joachín, Museo (Madrid), 63

Sort, 339

Spanair, 481, 486

Spanish-language classes
   Córdoba, 153
   Granada, 165–166
   Madrid, 67
   Málaga, 174–175
   Salamanca, 125

Special events and festivals, 476–479

Students, 496

Summum Disco (Segovia), 113

Surfing, 354, 364

Swimming
   Alicante, 235–236
   Barcelona, 298–299
   Ibiza, 470–471
   La Coruña, 389
   Minorca, 461
   València, 222

Taberna Jovi (Cuenca), 104

Talaiots (stone monuments; Minorca), 463

Talavera de la Reina, 92–94

Taller Flamenco (Seville), 143–144

Tapas al minuto, 135

Tapestry of the Creation (Girona), 325

Tàpies, Antoni, 507

Taquilla Ultimo Minuto (Madrid), 74

Tarragona, 311–320

Taüll, 339

Taxes, 500

Teatre-Museu Dalí (Figueres), 333

Teatro Arriaga (Bilbao), 356

Teatro Ayala (Bilbao), 356

Teatro Cervantes (Málaga), 175

Teatro de la Maestranza (Seville), 145

Teatro Español (Madrid), 55, 74

Teatro Juan Bravo (Segovia), 112–113

Teatro La Tía Norica (Cádiz), 206–207

Teatro Lírico National de Zarzuela (Madrid), 74

Teatro Monumental (Madrid), 74

Teatro Real (Madrid), 54–55, 74

Teatro Romano (Málaga), 173

Teatro Villamarta (Jerez), 198

Teléfonica building (Madrid), 58

Telephone, 500
Tennis
    Alicante, 236
    Barcelona, 299
    Ibiza, 471
Teresa of Avila, 116
Termas Romanas (Gijón),
    408–409
Terrorism, 493
Tertulias, Madrid, 44, 64
Textil i d'Indumentaria
    (Barcelona), 301
Thyssen-Bornemisza Museum
    (Madrid), 50–51
Tibidabo, 249
Time zone, 500
Tío Pepe (Jerez), 196–197
Tipping, 490
Tito's (Palma de Majorca), 444
Toledo, 83–98
    accommodations, 83–86
    restaurants, 86–88
    shopping, 91
    side trips from, 92–98
    sights and attractions,
        88–91
    traveling to, 83
    visitor information, 83
Torre de Hercules lighthouse (La
    Coruña), 389
Torre de la Calahorra (Córdoba),
    150–151
Torredembarra, 318
Torre de Poniente (Cádiz), 205
Torres del Quart (València), 219
Torres de Serrano (València), 219
Torre Tavira (Cádiz), 205–206
Tortosa, 320
Tossa de Mar, 328, 330
Tourist information, 498–499
Toys (Segovia), 113
Train travel, 486
Transportation, 485–487
Traveler's checks and traveler's
    cards, 490–491
Traveling to Spain, 480–485
Travel insurance, 483–485
Tree of Guernica, 356
Trepucó, 463
Tribeca (Oviedo), 407
Tupperware (Madrid), 75
Turrón Museum (Xixona), 235
Txapela (San Sebastián), 365

Umbracle (València), 221
Unamuno, Miguel de, Casa-
    Museo de (Salamanca), 123
Universidad (Salamanca),
    122–123
Untours, 484
Urdaibai National Biosphere
    Reserve, 356
US Airways, 481
Utiel, 227, 228

Valdepeñas, 96–98
València (city), 211–229
    accommodations, 215–216
    day trips from, 225–229
    getting to and around,
        212, 214
    history of, 211–212
    Las Añadas de España, 224
    lay of the land, 212
    nightlife, 224–225
    restaurants, 217–218
    shopping, 223
    sights and attractions,
        218–222
València (province), 210–241
    top experiences, 210–211
Vall d'Aran, 339
Vall del Boí, 339
Valldemossa, 444–445
Vall d'Uixò Caves, 228–229
Velázquez, Diego, 10, 49, 63,
    64, 219, 283, 506
Venta El Gallo (Granada),
    166
Vía Libre Cafe Bar (Salamanca),
    125
Vicente Blasco Ibañez' Casa
    Museo (València), 220
Vielha, 339
Villas Turísticas de Grazalema,
    191
Villa Vieja (Old Quarter;
    Alicante), 234
Virgen Blanca (Vitoria-Gasteiz),
    371
Virgen de los Navegantes
    (Seville), 139
Visitor information, 498–499
Vitoria-Gasteiz, 366–373
Viveiro, 391

Windmills, Consuegra, 94
Windsurfing, 227, 462
Wines and vineyards (bodegas)
    Jerez, 196–197
    Laguardia, 373
    Levante, 228
    Lleida area, 338–341
    Málaga, 170
    Penedés area, 305
    Sanlúcar, 200–201
    sherry, 209
        Jerez, 196–197
        Sanlúcar, 200–201
    Tarragona, 317
    Utiel and Requena, 227
    Valdepeñas, 96–98

Xàtiva Castle, 226–227
Xixona (Jijona), 235
Xoriguer Gin Distillery (Mahòn),
    460

Zambra de María La Canastera
    (Granada), 165
Zara (Madrid), 69
Zarautz, 364
Zero Kilometer marker
    (Madrid), 57
Zoco (Córdoba), 153
Zoco de Artesanía (Jerez),
    197–198
Zurbarán, Francisco de, 58, 142,
    206, 506

ACCOMMODATIONS

Abba Fonseca Hotel
    (Salamanca), 120
Adore Plaza (San Sebastián),
    360
Alberge Juvenil La Florida
    (Alicante), 233
Albergue de Peregrinos
    Seminario Menor La Asunción
    (Santiago de Compostela),
    394
Alma Andalusí Hospedería
    (Córdoba), 146–147
Apartahotel Toboso
    (Salamanca), 118
Apartamentos Centro Colón
    (Madrid), 20
Apartamentos Goya (Madrid), 20

Apartamentos Puerta Real (Granada), 156
Apartamentos San Juan de los Reyes (Granada), 156
Apartamentos Santa Ana (Granada), 156
Aparthotel La Jabega (Los Boliches), 180–181
Aparthotel Puerto Azul (Marbella), 182–183
Aparthotel Silver (Barcelona), 260
Arteaga Hostal (Granada), 156
Ateneo Hotel (Madrid), 21
Barbieri International Hostel (Madrid), 24
Bar Restaurante La Torre (Santillana del Mar), 422
Bauzá Hotel (Madrid), 29
Bcn Houses (Barcelona), 251
Bellmirall (Girona), 324
Belmonte (Oviedo), 402–403
Café Concana (Santillana del Mar), 422
Camping Son Bou (Minorca), 455–456
Camping Sopelana (Bilbao), 349
Can Marti (Ibiza), 468
Casa Cayo (Potes), 413
Casa de Aldea Picao (Santianes de Ola), 403
Casa del Capitel Nazarí (Granada), 156–158
Casa de les Lletres (Barcelona), 254
Casa Font (Seuri), 341
Casa La Solana (Santillana del Mar), 422
Casa Monell (Girona), 322–323
Casa Outeiro (La Coruña), 387
Casa Rural (Mahòn), 457
Casa San Nicolas (Alicante), 232
Casa Villena (Segovia), 106
Cigarral de Caravantes (Toledo), 86
Ciudadela Hotel (Barcelona), 258
Constanza (Barcelona), 259–260
Costa Azul (Palma de Majorca), 435
El Clos (Tarragona), 314
El Coloso (Jerez), 192
Ezcaba (Pamplona), 376
The 5 Rooms (Barcelona), 260

Fonda Farré d'Avall (Barruera), 341
Friendly Rentals (Barcelona), 251–254
Gat Raval (Barcelona), 256
Gat Xino (Barcelona), 256
González Hotel (Córdoba), 146
Goya (Lleida), 335–336
Guest House Alicante, 232
High-Tech Hoteles Petit Palace Italia (Madrid), 24
Hôme Backpacker hostels (València), 216
Hospedaje Kati (San Sebastián), 358–359
Hospedaje Mera (Santiago de Compostela), 394
Hostal Adriano (Madrid), 27
Hostal Antigua Morellana (València), 216
Hostal Atenas (Seville), 135
Hostal Bianco II (Madrid), 21
Hostal Brondo (Palma de Majorca), 433–434
Hostal Callejon del Agua (Seville), 136
Hostal Canalejas (Cádiz), 202
Hostal de los Reyes Católicos (Santiago de Compostela), 396
Hostal Dos Naciones (Madrid), 26
Hostal El Nogal (Málaga), 168
Hostal El Pilar (Estepona), 184
Hostal El Pilar (Madrid), 21
Hostal Enriqueta (Marbella), 183
Hostal Ginebra (Barcelona), 259
Hostal Girona (Barcelona), 259
Hostal Goya (Barcelona), 260
Hostal Gran Duque (Madrid), 22
Hostal Greco (Madrid), 25
Hostal Hospederia Las Cortes de Cádiz, 202
Hostal Jume (Mahòn), 457
Hostal La Macarena (Madrid), 26
Hostal La Marina (Ibiza), 468
Hostal La Mexicana (Santander), 416
Hostal La Muralla (Morella), 229
Hostal La Perla (La Coruña), 386
Hostal Las Palomas (Jerez), 192
Hostal les Monges (Alicante), 233
Hostal Mardones (Bilbao), 349

Hostal Mediterrani (Tarragona), 315
Hostal Miramar (Soller), 448
Hostal Montesol (Ibiza), 469
Hostal Opera (Barcelona), 255–256
Hostal Otano (Pamplona), 376–377
Hostal Paris (Ciudadela), 458
Hostal Persal (Madrid), 27
Hostal Posada Mijas, 176
Hostal Regina (Palma de Majorca), 434–435
Hostal Residencia Bisbal (València), 216
Hostal Residencia Candilejas (Elche), 240
Hostal Residencia Galicia (Madrid), 23
Hostal Residencia Oasis (Ciudadela), 457
Hostal Residencia Oliva (Barcelona), 259
Hostal Residencias Juanito and Las Nieves (Ibiza), 468
Hostal Restaurante El Hidalgo (Segovia), 106
Hostal Salamanca (Madrid), 29
Hostal San Francisco (Cádiz), 202
Hostal Sara (Salamanca), 118
Hostal Sil & Serranos (Madrid), 25
Hostal Tijcal II (Madrid), 21
Hostal Ubaldo (Cadaqués), 334
Hostal Villaverde (Deyá), 447
Hostel Centric Point (Barcelona), 262
Hostel Gothic Point (Barcelona), 262
Hostel Sea Point (Barcelona), 261
Hotel Albucasis (Córdoba), 146
Hotel Alcántara (Seville), 135
Hotel Altamarina (Estepona), 184
Hotel and Apartments Murillo (Seville), 135
Hotel Astari (Tarragona), 315
Hotel Avenida (Pamplona), 377
Hotel Beatriz Toledo, 85
Hotel Bellas Artes (Jerez), 192–193
Hotel Buenavista (Estepona), 184

Hotel Celuisma Alisos
(Santander), 416
Hotel Costa Vella (Santiago de
Compostela), 394
Hotel Dato (Vitoria-Gasteiz),
368
Hotel de Francia y Paris (Cádiz),
202
Hotel del Almirante
(Collingwood House; Mahòn),
457
Hotel Doña Blanca (Jerez), 192
Hotel Don Curro (Málaga), 168
Hotel El Cid (Sitges), 309–310
Hotel El Hidalgo
(Valdepeñas), 98
Hotel El Tajo (Ronda), 186
Hotel España (Barcelona),
256–257
Hotel España (La Coruña), 387
Hotel Eurico (Toledo), 85
Hotel Eurostars Plaza Acueducto
(Segovia), 107
Hotel Faro (Elche), 240
Hotel Favila (Oviedo), 403
Hotel Historic (Girona), 324
Hotel Isabel (Torremolinos), 181
Hotel Jardí (Barcelona),
257–258
Hotel Kris Tribuna
(Málaga), 168
Hotel Las Helechos (Sanlúcar),
199
Hotel las Murallas (Avila),
113–114
Hotel Lauria (Tarragona), 315
Hotel Leonor de Aquitania
(Cuenca), 101
Hotel Los Cigarrales
(Toledo), 86
Hotel Los Tilos (Granada), 156
Hotel Mac Esmeralda
(Ciudadela), 458
Hotel Marian (Seville), 135–136
Hotel Mediodía (Madrid), 28
Hotel Miau (Madrid), 27
Hotel Moderno (Madrid), 22
Hotel Mora (Madrid), 28
Hotel Negresco (Madrid), 24
Hotel Noucentista (Sitges), 310
Hotel Opera (Madrid), 23
Hotel Palacio de los Navas
(Granada), 158

Hotel Palacio de los Veladas
(Avila), 114
Hotel Palacio de Santa Inés
(Granada), 158
Hotel Peninsular (Barcelona),
257
Hotel Peninsular (Girona), 323
Hotel Pintor El Greco
(Toledo), 85
Hotel Plaza Mayor (Madrid), 26
Hotel Principal (Lleida), 336
Hotel Puente Romano (Cangas
de Onís), 411
Hotel Real (Santiago de
Compostela), 394–395
Hotel Reina Cristina (Granada),
158
Hotel Residencia Leuka
(Alicante), 233
Hotel Restaurante Don Javier
(Ronda), 186
Hotel Restaurante Don Miguel
(Ronda), 186
Hotel Restaurant Zabala
(Santillana del Mar), 422
Hotel Risco (Laredo), 423
Hotel Ronda, 186
Hotel San Gabriel (Ronda),
186–187
Hotel Santa Isabel (Toledo), 85
Hotel Santo Domingo
(Madrid), 23
Hotel Tierras de Jerez, 193
Hotel Venecia (València), 216
Hotel Vetusta (Oviedo), 403
Hoz de Huécar (Cuenca), 100
Husa Hotel Paseo del Arte
(Madrid), 28
International Youth Hostel
La Posada de Huertas
(Madrid), 27
Iturrienea Ostatua (Bilbao), 350
La Bruna (Bellver de Cerdanya),
340
La Hostería del Laurel (Seville),
136
La Hostería Natura (Segovia),
107
Las Cuevas El Abanico
(Granada), 154
La Vida de Antes (Consuegra),
94–95
Lola Hotel (Córdoba), 147–148

Luna de Cristal (Córdoba), 146
Málaga Centro Hotel (Málaga),
169
Mare Nostrum (Sitges), 310
Marina Folch (Barcelona), 261
Marina View B&B (Barcelona),
261
Mas Pereta (near Girona), 323
Merindad de Olite, 382
Microtel Placentinos
(Salamanca), 118–119
Palacio San Facundo Hotel
(Segovia), 107–108
Parador de Cuenca, 101
Parador de la Arruzafa
(Córdoba), 148
Parador Hotel Atlántico (Cádiz),
202, 204
Pensio Margarit (Girona), 323
Pension Amaia (Vitoria-Gasteiz),
368
Pension Araba (Vitoria-Gasteiz),
368
Pension Bellas Artes (San
Sebastián), 360
Pension Cantabria (Laredo), 423
Pension Gonzalez (Gijón), 408
Pension La Corza, 416
Pension Ladero (Bilbao), 349
Pension La Noria (Tarragona),
315
Pension la Viña (Pamplona),
376
Pension Manoli (Bilbao), 349
Pension Margarita Trias Vives
(Soller), 448
Pension Picos de Europa
(Potes), 413
Pension San Lorenzo (San
Sebastián), 359
Pension Universal (València),
215
Picasso's Corner (Málaga),
167–168
Posada de San José (Cuenca),
100–101
Posada Orsi (Mahòn), 456
Refugi Gedar, 340
Refugio de Aliva (Fuente-Dé),
413
Refugio Urriellu (Potes), 412
Room Mate Laura Hotel
(Madrid), 22–23

Room Mate Lola (Málaga),
    168–169
Room Mate Oscar Hotel
    (Madrid), 25
Room Mate Vega (Salamanca),
    119
Sagrada Família B&B
    (Barcelona), 258–259

Samos Monastery, 395
Santuari de Lluc (Majorca),
    434
Santuari del Puig de María
    (near Pollença), 435
7 Balconies (Barcelona), 257
Sevilla, 132

Soho Rooms (Barcelona), 251
Son Triay Nou (Minorca),
    454
Villas Turísticas de Grazalema,
    191
YH Giralda (Seville), 136

NOTES

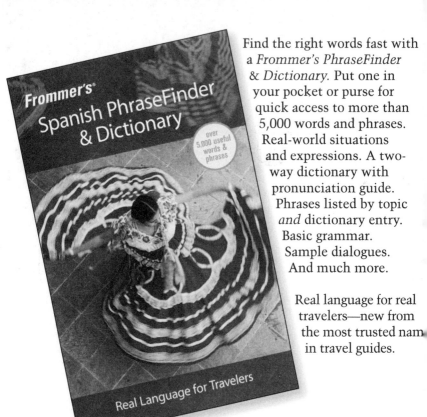